Columbian
Consequences

A Contribution from the Society for American Archaeology
in Recognition of the Columbian Quincentenary
1492–1992

Columbian Consequences

Volume 1

**Archaeological and Historical Perspectives
on the Spanish Borderlands West**

Edited by David Hurst Thomas

Smithsonian Institution Press, Washington and London

Copyright © 1989 by Smithsonian Institution
All rights reserved
Editor: Vicky Macintyre
Designer: Janice Wheeler

Library of Congress Cataloging-in-Publication Data
Archaeological and historical perspectives on the
   Spanish Borderlands West.
   (Columbian consequences; v. 1)
   "A contribution from the Society for American
Archaeology in recognition of the Columbian
quincentenary, 1492–1992."
   Bibliography: p.
   1. Spaniards—Southwest, New—History.
2. Southwest, New—History—To 1848.   3. Ethno-
archaeology—Southwest, New.   4. Indians of North
America—Southwest, New—First contact with Occidental
civilization.   5. Southwest, New—Antiquities.
I. Thomas, David Hurst.   II. Society for American
Archaeology.   III. Series.
F799.C66   vol. 1   979 s [979'.01]   88-29732
ISBN 0-87474-908-5

British Library Cataloguing-in-Publication Data available
Manufactured in the United States of America
10 9 8 7 6 5 4 3 2
98 97 96 95 94 93 92 91
∞ The paper used in this publication meets the
minimum requirements of the American National Standard
for Permanence of Paper for Printed Library Materials Z39.48-1984.

Contents ■

2 ■ TEXAS AND NORTHEASTERN MEXICO

3 ■ THE CALIFORNIAS

List of Illustrations ■

David Hurst Thomas

Columbian Consequences: The Spanish Borderlands in Cubist Perspective

Christopher Columbus certainly got around—the Italians bore him, the Portuguese educated him, the Spanish sponsored him, the Vikings preceded him, and the Native Americans greeted him. In the United States alone, there are 67 towns or cities named Columbus, 1 Columbus county, and 8 counties called Columbia; and 37 states officially celebrate Columbus Day. The upcoming Columbian Quincentenary likewise stretches across the Atlantic. The Christopher Columbus Quincentenary Jubilee Commission, appointed by President Ronald Reagan, has announced broad plans to encourage a host of activities from festivals, films, concerts, and exhibits to the re-creation of the voyages of the three ships from Spain and the establishment of a permanent museum dedicated to the Age of Discovery.

On the academic front, Quincentenary-related enterprises proliferate. The Smithsonian Institution has sponsored two symposia ("America before Columbus: Ice Age Origins" and "After Columbus: Encounters in North America") and Partners for Livable Places sponsored a conference ("Shaping America: Hispanic Heritage in the U.S. Environment"). The University of Wisconsin-Madison Arboretum plans to restore an island in the Caribbean to the way it was when Columbus arrived in the New World. To coincide with the Pan American Games in Indianapolis, Indiana and Purdue Universities convened a conference entitled "New World Dialogue" to explore related themes in literature, history, theology, and art. The Newberry Library sponsored "Transatlantic Encounters: A Comprehensive Institute Program for the Columbian Quincentennial," and Rutgers University sponsored a special seminar, "Christopher Columbus in Contemporary Literature. That is by no means the end of the list.

These public and scholarly undertakings have great potential, but it would be unfortunate if they advanced on parallel, nonintersecting tracks. A twofold challenge faces the academic community: to explore the range of contemporary thought about New World encounters and to provide an interested public with an accurate and factual assessment of what did—and what did not—happen as a result of the Columbian encounter.

In the *Columbian Consequences* seminars, we attempt to do both. In this scholarly exercise, we explore the social, demographic, ecological, ideological, and human repercussions of European–Native American encounters across the Spanish Borderlands. Although initiated and cosponsored by the Society of American Archaeology, this inquiry moves beyond the traditional scope of archaeological investigation, drawing together a multifarious assortment of perspectives. We have enlisted more than one hundred scholars to contribute to nine symposia, to be published in a three-volume series.

In this first installment, we address the European–Native American interface along the western Spanish Borderlands—from the Pacific Slope across the Southwestern heartland to East Texas, from Russian Fort Ross to southern Baja California. The contributors bring to the project a wide range of backgrounds, and they examine the Spanish Borderlands from numerous angles. Many are practicing archaeologists, and their essays treat the surviving material evidence relating to the sociopolitics, economics, iconography, and physical environment of the contact period in the Spanish Borderlands West. Other participants provide a critical balance from the disciplines of American history, art history, ethnohistory, physical anthropology, and geography. Two Native American scholars discuss the survival strategies employed by their ancestors in coping with the European newcomers.

The second volume of *Columbian Consequences* takes up a similar agenda in the context of the Spanish Borderlands East, concentrating on *La Florida* (modern Florida, Georgia, and South Carolina), the greater Southeast, and the Caribbean. The final volume will shed all geographic constraints, to seek an understanding of the processes behind the borderlands experience. In it, we will examine the Pan-American consequences of Hispanic–Native American interactions to the north, in Anglo-America, and southward, in what is now termed Latin America.

The format of *Columbian Consequences* is designed to bring the fruits of this inquiry both to the scholarly community and to the public at large. To render these specialized presentations palatable to a more general audience, several leading scholars in the field have prepared overviews designed to make the rest of the text comprehensible to nonspecialists. Each overview synthesizes current thinking about the specific geographical setting, the Native American context, a history of European involvement, and a history of scholarly research. Each overview also contains a concise chronological table of salient events and extensive suggestions for additional reading.

Why the Spanish Borderlands?

We arbitrarily circumscribe the scope of inquiry by resurrecting and refurbishing historian Herbert Bolton's classic definition of the Spanish Borderlands—as the regions between Florida and California over which Spain held supremacy for centuries (Bolton 1921). Although Bolton's borderlands were initially confined to territory that at present belongs to the United States, this artificial restriction apparently reflected only Bolton's need to shoehorn *The Spanish Borderlands* within "The Chronicles of America" series in which it was to be published (Weber 1987:342). In practice, Bolton and three generations of borderlands scholars maintained a loosely structured, pragmatic definition that stretches from San Francisco to St. Augustine and includes liberal portions of northern Mexico and the Caribbean, when appropriate.

Bolton perceived the borderlands as both a place and a process—a shifting frontier on the margins of the Spanish empire in North America. Decades of historical inquiry have demonstrated that, situated far from the nuclear centers of Spanish colonial civilization in the West Indies, Central America, Mexico, and Peru, this northern rim of New Spain prevailed as a distinctive historical entity for three centuries: the borderlands process beginning with European contact and lasting through the Mexican Revolution of 1821. Most of the contributors to *Columbian Consequences* concentrate on this interval, but we will often look toward prehistoric Native America for a meaningful context to the borderlands experience. Similarly, because the Spanish Borderlands today retain a certain distinctiveness, we must take note of the ways in which contemporary issues and attitudes color our perception of the past.

Parochialism in Traditional Borderlands Thinking

Bolton's Spanish Borderlands thus define our spatiotemporal framework. But the theoretical matrix surrounding traditional borderlands historiography is unacceptable for our purposes. When Bolton began his borderlands studies early in the twentieth century, American history was plagued by a persistent *leyenda negra*, a "Black Legend" that systematically overlooked and belittled Spanish achievements (Maltby 1971; Scardaville 1985). The Black Legend held that only the English initiated permanent colonies in the New World; and that Spain was motivated strictly by "glory, God, and gold," the implication being that something peculiar in the Spanish national character allowed bigotry, pride, and hypocrisy to color Spain's approach to the New World. Not only were the Spanish perceived as exceptionally cruel conquistadores of the Americas, but also as shirkers of manual labor, especially anything agricultural.

Anglo-American history portrayed the Hispanic colonization of the United

States as an insignificant footnote to later British developments: "St. Augustine is often the disreputable foil to the English colonies in Virginia and Massachusetts. The language, religion, law, and customs of the Spaniards are contrasted, always unfavorably, with those of the English" (Patrick 1964:xi; see also Scardaville 1985:184; Washburn 1985). The Black Legend held, in effect, that Spaniards were never true colonizers and that they contributed little, if anything, of lasting value to New World civilization.

One late nineteenth-century textbook, written by a leading American historian of the time, codified this succinct, if unwitting, caricature:

> The Spaniards were brave, and they could rule with severity. But they thirsted for adventure, conquest, and wealth, for which their appetite was early encouraged; their progress in Mexico, Peru, and the West Indies had been too rapid and brilliant for them to be satisfied with the dull life and patient development of an agricultural colony. . . . Their aims were sordid, their State was loosely knit, their commercial policy was rigidly exclusive, their morals were lax, and their treatment of the savages was cruel, despite the tendency of the colonists to amalgamate with the latter, thus to descend in the scale of civilization [Thwaites 1892:74].

In his borderlands-focused research program, Herbert Bolton set out to counterbalance this notion with the theme that American history consisted of more than merely the establishment and expansion of English settlements along the eastern seaboard of North America. Borderlands historians, while recognizing the conquistadores as explorers and adventurers, also emphasized their desire to colonize and transplant Spanish civilization: "Whoever fails to understand this, fails to understand the patriotic aim of the Spanish pioneers in America" (Bolton 1921:6).

Stating a problem rather than solving it, Bolton's seminal *The Spanish Borderlands* (1921) sketched the story of clashing frontiers between the northward-moving Spaniard and the southward-looking Anglo-American. The borderlands program at the University of California, started early in this century, has since turned out shelves of books, monographs, and edited volumes, and emerged as a new school of historical interpretation.

Bolton's attempt to refurbish the gloomy textbook image of Spaniards in North America defined a rewarding research direction, but the borderlands historians were not entirely successful in whitewashing the Black Legend. As documented recently by James Axtell, the textbook Spaniard has persevered. Even today, the story of Spain in the borderlands remains primarily "a 'tale of slaughter and conquest [with] no heroes.' 'Half-mad with greed,' *conquistadores* were 'unbelievably determined,' 'courageous,' 'fierce,' 'brutal,' and 'ruthless' . . . under the spell of the legend, truth gives way to fiction" (Axtell 1987a:625). Today's student of American history still encounters the Spanish empire only as a negative counterpoint to Protestant democracy ascending to the north.

Small wonder that many Hispanic people look toward the Columbian Quincentenary as a means of stamping out, once and for all, the ethnocentric patrimony of the Black Legend.

The Native American as "Borderland Irritant"

Eager to dislodge the Anglo-American interpretation of U.S. history, Bolton and his students were inextricably drawn toward more positive aspects of border-lands history (Weber 1987:336). They argued that Spanish colonial policy, "equalled in humanitarian principles by that of no other country, perhaps, looked to the preservation of the natives, and their elevation to at least a limited citizenship" (Bolton 1917:52).

However, while combating one simplistic textbook image, they inadvertently promulgated another. The most unfortunate byproduct of Spanish Borderlands research was the specious perception of the Native American. To Bolton, the mission system was an arm of the Spanish Crown reaching across the frontier to pacify and civilize an otherwise intractable population. This barefaced Hispanophilic bias simply lumped Native Americans (and other non-Hispanics) into John Francis Bannon's opprobrious catchall category of "Borderland Irritants" (1974: Chapter 8).

So defined, Native Americans became only peripheral participants in the borderlands experience, to be discredited and dismissed. Bolton viewed the Pima as little more than "children" and the Apaches as eternally "unsociable" (1921:200). Bolton approvingly described how Indians at Mission San Antonio (Texas), "once naked savages who lived on cactus apples and cotton-tail rabbits, had become . . . skilled and trustworthy." Mission farms and fields were tended by "erstwhile barbarians, civilized under the patient discipline of the missionaries, assisted by soldier guards and imported Indian teachers, not in our Southwest alone, but on nearly every frontier of Spanish America" (Bolton 1917:58). But to Bolton's mind, the California Indians were "the most barbarous . . . [and] while it is easy to pick flaws in the mission system of dealing with the [California] Indians, it is not so easy to point to any other system which has done better. The problem of civilizing a wild people has baffled others than the padres" (Bolton 1917:61; 1921:281–282).

Bolton's ardent student, John Francis Bannon, perpetuated such views into the modern era. Writing from a Jesuit perspective, Bannon glorified mission achievements in northern Mexico: "The tale of the Black Robes' first century on the Western Slope is a glorious one. Great names dot its pages" (1955:142). Like his mentor, Bannon dismissed Native American culture and explained resistance to Spanish encroachment as a character flaw. "Belligerent and marauding Apaches . . . and unruly Seris . . . were to retard for long years the normal civilian development of Sonora" (1955:139). Later in his career, when other historians began to comprehend the unsavory side of missionization, Bannon rejected their views as revisionist. "Bannon's own Christophilic, triumphalist bias had run in the opposite direction" (Weber 1987:338).

Bolton and his students are hardly unique in their misunderstanding and misrepresentation of the American Indian. When advancing his influential frontier thesis for understanding American civilization, Frederick Jackson Turner almost universally ignored all racial and ethnic minorities, elaborating instead the simplistic notion of frontier as a line between "savagery and civilization." Fr.

Zephrin Engelhardt, author of more than a dozen influential books on the California missions, wrote (apparently in all seriousness) that "all accounts agree in representing the natives of California as among the most stupid, brutish, filthy, lazy and improvident of all the aborigines of America" (1930:245). Another church historian, Francis Guest more recently echoed this sentiment, calling the California Indian lifeway "haphazard, irresponsible, brutish, benighted, and barbaric" (Guest 1966:206–207).

One would have hoped that such rash characterizations would have disappeared with the segregated water fountain. But recent surveys demonstrate that such inaccurate and unjust views of the Indian persist, on a somewhat watered-down scale, in even the most recent American history textbooks (for analyses of such textbook Indians, see Axtell 1987a, 1987b; Hoxie 1984; Josephy 1970; Vogel 1968).

Whereas textbook Spaniards lusted for God, gold, and glory, the textbook Indian is either a roguish hindrance to Anglo settlement or a pathetic chump and pushover. When it comes to Indians, the modern American history textbook almost uniformly sets out carping pronouncements about the lack of private property, the illogical nature of Native American governments, and especially the rudimentary or immoral condition of religion. Today's textbooks are still littered with quaint pejoratives like "war-whooping," "feathered foes," "painted allies," and "tawny-skinned pagan aborigines."

Echoing Hollywood's stereotyped attitude, today's textbook historian misreads Native American culture through a curious blend of racism, sexual imagery, and Victorian sentimentality. Texts still wax poetic about that "vast and lonely North American continent," a "virgin" land that, "like all virgins, inspired conflicting feelings in men's hearts." One historian writes how the New World "gracefully yielded her virginity" to the conquerors, and another was clearly relieved that this "vast and virgin continent . . . was so sparsely peopled by Indians that they could be eliminated or shouldered aside. Such a magnificent opportunity for a great democratic experiment may never come again" (cited in Axtell 1987a:624).

Against this background, it is hardly surprising that few American Indians are rushing forth to embrace a Quincentenary fiesta extolling Hispanic righteousness in the Americas.

Forging a Cubist Perspective

Given the surprising resilience of such scholarly and popular corruptions, the *Columbian Consequences* seminars look at the Spanish Borderlands from a rather different, more open-minded viewpoint, and I employ a cubist analogy to define more precisely the task at hand.[1]

The cubist movement in art began in early twentieth-century Paris as a reaction against then conventional European painting. Since the Renaissance, artists had labored to perfect their techniques for reducing three-dimensional visual reality to an artificial, two-dimensional medium. Traditionally schooled artists called upon various illusionary devices such as perspective, foreshortening, the use of color, and modeling to convince their viewers that reality could be comprehended by a spectator viewing a scene from a fixed position.

Rejecting this time-honored perspective, the cubists enlarged the spectator's vision to include multiple, simultaneous views of the subject—as if one could instantaneously move from point to point, up and down. In place of the familiar Renaissance vantage point, cubists substituted the radical notion that perspective can be shifted at will. In the cubist epistemology, heads, noses, and eyes could be depicted concurrently in profile and full-face view. Because the final statement still took place on a two-dimensional plane, cubists infused their subjects with an analytic form showing front, side, and even elements of the backside at once.

The cubist analogy suggests that a more thorough understanding of the Spanish Borderlands experience remains possible, and we implement this possibility in several ways.

Augmenting the Available Perspectives

Perhaps the most obvious way in which the *Columbian Consequences* seminars depart from traditional borderlands assessments is in their emphasis on fresh perspectives available from contemporary Americanist archaeology. For decades, historians, cultural anthropologists, and ethnohistorians have discounted the possibility of learning anything useful from archaeologists. And until recently, they were justified in this doleful assessment.

Prior to the mid-twentieth century, historical archaeology was restricted to a few selected sites, particularly houses of the rich and famous, Spanish missions, and military sites. Considerable control of this primitive historical archaeology resided in the hands of architectural historians, who paid precious little attention to the habitation middens and lesser structures. At this early stage, the archaeology of contact period sites focused on architectural minutiae and artifact typology—which were virtually irrelevant to an understanding of the Spanish Borderlands.

Within the past two decades, however, historical archaeology has taken a decidedly anthropological bent, turning away from what Noël Hume (1969:10) called a "Barnum and Bailey" infatuation with the "oldest," "largest," and "most historically significant" site. People recognized that historical archaeologists have access to the entire range of human behavior—spoken word, written word, preserved behavior, and observed behavior (Schuyler 1977)—neatly straddling the traditionally discrete fields of historical archaeology, ethnohistory, and anthropology.

Such "backyard archaeology" (after Fairbanks 1977) naturally led archaeologists working in the Spanish Borderlands to focus on historically disenfranchised groups within our own culture. Of particular note is Kathleen Deagan's research into the processes and results of Spanish–Indian intermarriage and descent in St. Augustine (Deagan 1973, 1983). That people of such mixed descent (mestizos) constitute nearly the entire population of Latin America, brought this issue to the forefront of anthropology and ethnohistory long ago. Similar processes took place in Spanish Florida, but the Hispanic occupation left no apparent mestizo population in *La Florida*—what Deagan calls "America's first melting pot."

Accordingly, Deagan has been digging on both sides of the archaeological fence—simultaneously doing the archaeology of both Hispanic and Native American communities in St. Augustine, and providing insights into virtually unknown early race relations in North America. Employing what has been termed the "archaeology of the inarticulate," dozens of archaeologists are now uncovering the archaeological roots of American black culture, Asian-American culture, Native Americans during the historic period, and Hispanic-American Creoles. One particularly effective thrust of such research has been the study of acculturation, emphasizing trading relations, religious conversion, and racial intermarriage.

As several chapters in this volume demonstrate, this recent revolution in historical archaeology is especially relevant for those grappling with America's borderlands experience, as it provides yet another independent perspective to our cubist vision. We now have new insights into the distinctive elements of various precontact Native American societies, notably the specific patterns of acceptance and rejection of Spanish material culture and life-styles and the demographic impact of European colonization, including the specific patterns of health and disease among Native American populations.

Such a diversified plan of action contrasts vividly with that of, say, Herbert Bolton, who, like the Renaissance masters, toiled to perfect and polish a particular, unified, unfluctuating point of view, which was perceived as reality. In their laudable attempt to demonstrate that "the importance of the Spanish period in American history has not yet been duly recognized" (Bannon 1964:25), the Boltonians unwittingly distorted and demeaned the roles of non-Hispanic players. Such distortions should not continue to take place because of the multiple perspectives currently available to the scholarly community.

The outlook employed in *Columbian Consequences* also differs from traditional approaches in anthropology and ethnohistory, which almost invariably adopted a pro-Indian/anti-Spanish perspective. Whereas the borderlands historians have tried "to set the record straight" about Spaniards and the Black Legend, anthropologists and ethnohistorians have conventionally felt a need to counterbalance the anti-Indian views fostered by borderlands and Anglo-American historians (and gobbled up by an already predisposed American public).

Like the early twentieth-century cubists, we think that more coherent depictions of reality can be obtained by looking for such fresh perspectives—provided we are willing to change such viewpoints frequently. Whereas few individuals can be expected to exercise an exhaustively cubist perspective, the *Columbian Consequences* seminars attempt to provide an overarching mechanism of balance, criticism, and synthesis.

Coping with an Artificial, Disjointed Past

Recognizing the self-delusion of seeking absolute truth, the cubist initiative viewed art as an imitation of the learning process, its basic assumption being that humans learn not from the single, all-encompassing glance, but rather from an infinite number of momentary glimpses, unified into a whole by the spectator's mind. Cubist paintings depict objects as one knows them to be, rather than as one sees them at any given point in time—from several angles at once. It becomes the duty of artists to select those angles that are primary and essential, perspectives capable of yielding a more complete representation of the subject. The selection process is dictated, of course, by the artist's temperament and sensitivity.

Just as Renaissance painters thought they were depicting reality, some borderlands scholars and special interest groups persist in pursuing their version of the "truth"—the way it *really* was. But the only truth is the artificiality of our perspective. To one degree or another, all views of the human past are created.

This point is neatly illustrated by Christopher Chippindale's recent (1983) analysis of changing perspectives on Stonehenge. Speaking both literally and figuratively, Jacquetta Hawkes (1967:174) once noted that "every age has the Stonehenge it deserves—or desires." During medieval times, the monoliths were explained in terms of patriotic British history, often directly involving the hand of King Arthur and/or Merlin the Magician. Then, during the seventeenth-century era of scholarship, people began to search for meaning in the enigmatic stones. Interpretations based on Druidic religion dominated the eighteenth-century imagination, whereas the best renderings of Stonehenge appeared in the early nineteenth century, the "Golden Age" of English landscape watercolors. During the hyperscientific 1960s, Stonehenge became a monumental Neolithic computer, constructed for eclipse prediction. In today's confused age, interpretations of Stonehenge hover between hard science (according to revamped astronomical interpretations) and antiscience (Stonehenge having been built in an idyllic ancient Britain peopled by gentle pastoralists in tune with their environment). As Chippindale (1983:6) has observed, "For centuries the people who have gone to see [Stonehenge] have found it a mirror which reflects back, more or less distorted, that view of the past which the on-looker takes there."

It is not uncommon for the past to be harnessed for social, political, and even nationalistic purposes. This is why the Native Sons of the Golden West donated money for fellowships to support Bolton's students as they revamped the image of the textbook Spaniard. This is why the Knights of Columbus donated $50,000 to the U.S. Quincentenary Jubilee Commission to ensure that, among other things, the Columbian Quincentenary would be a celebration of America's Roman Catholic heritage.

And this is why the issue of whether or not Junípero Serra—the "Father of the California Missions"—is a saint is being hotly contested for the 1992 Quincentenary. *The Catholic Encyclopedia* terms such canonization "the seal of approval" on a person's soul having actually arrived in heaven (Broderick 1976:92). Ultimately, the Pope will review the entire case for evidence that the candidate lived a life of "heroic" virtue, by practicing extraordinary faith, hope, charity, prudence, justice, and true sanctity.

The Cause of Father Serra hinges upon the efficacy and morality of the California mission system, and one's view of Serra's role depends heavily upon how such knowledge is to be employed in today's world. To members of the Franciscan order, such as Father Noel Francis Moholy, Serra embodies the best of establishment ethics: "Today, perhaps more than any time in history, our world needs to remember a hero who also had the qualities of a saint. Serra in our midst is a great consolation" (DeNevi and Moholy 1985:216). Presidential candidate John F. Kennedy celebrated a birthday by visiting Serra's crypt, crediting Serra's mission efforts with providing "the nucleus of what is now California." Although not himself Catholic, President Ronald Reagan saluted Serra as "one of the heroes of our land. His tireless work for the Indians of California . . . remains a shining page in our history. His missions stand as a monument to his powerful religious convictions" (cited in Morgado 1987:145). Curiously, this upbeat vision of Serra's achievements has spanned the political, social, and even religious agendas of both Kennedy and Reagan. As Jackson has noted, "Like most western European history, the cause for Fr. Serra becomes a justification of the social class structure of the time" (1987:101).

But Junípero Serra typifies something quite different to contemporary Native Americans. The Southern California Tribal Chairmen's Association, the Lone Pine Paiute-Shoshone tribe, the Manzanita and Viejas bands of Mission Indians, the Redding Ranchería, and the Chemehuevi Tribal Council (among others) signed petitions denouncing the canonization efforts for Fr. Serra. To many, Serra has become "a symbol of 18th century feudal forced labor and abuse to the Indians, and a symbol of the successful foreign domination to the establishment society" (Costo and Costo 1987:ix; see also Castillo, this volume).

Fr. Serra and the California missions clearly have not one, but multiple histories (e.g., Archibald 1978; Heizer 1978:125; Phillips 1974). Various special interest constituencies—sometimes complementary and overlapping, more commonly competing for primacy—have structured the past to aid and legitimize their contemporary activities. Although conventionally lumped together as the "Catholic" perspective, the Franciscan view of the California missions (e.g., Engelhardt 1930; Geiger 1969) tells a story rather different from the history of those same missions written by Jesuits (e.g., Bannon 1947, 1955; Polzer 1976, 1987). The history based on the analysis of California mission burial records (Cook 1976; Johnson, this volume) differs radically from both Native American oral history (e.g., Costo and Costo 1987) and from the history as interpreted by Guest (1979). Still another interpretation emerges from the human skeletal remains of mission residents (e.g., see Walker et al., this volume).

Previous interpretations of the Spanish Borderlands too often read like a collection of disconnected units (spanning dissimilar time periods, populations, and institutions). Although plenty of historical detail is available about each, we have had no way to fit these various individual histories together.

Strategies of the Past and for the Present

We seek articulation between these disparate and often conflicting histories in the *Columbian Consequences* seminars by accentuating the strategic diversity underlying the behaviors. It is the principal thesis of this endeavor—its justification, if you will—that meaning cannot be extracted from such diverse assessments unless they are viewed through the prism of the intricate lifeways that came into conflict along the Spanish Borderlands. Extraordinary demands were made on these life-styles by the actions and daily conduct of those involved. It was these lifeways that shaped the perceptions of each group for the other.

What were the primary Hispanic strategies for controlling the northern New World? What lessons had the Spanish learned from earlier experiences in Middle and South America? What specific tactics were employed at the assorted missions, presidios, and pueblos to implement the overall Hispanic strategies?

We break rank with traditional borderlands historians by insisting upon equal weight for the non-Hispanic, nonwritten records of the past. We seek to define the range of Native American counterstrategies for coping with the European intrusions. Why did some Native American groups retain their cultural identity while others disappeared virtually overnight? What was the role of disease and demographic collapse along the borderlands?

Numerous traps lie between the extremes of particularism and an emphasis on underlying dynamics. In line with the *cubist* analogy, our approach to the Spanish Borderlands strives to view events of the past from multiple directions simultaneously, thereby generating as much an overall understanding as a detailed reproduction. Too often, anthropologists and ethnohistorians have viewed Hispanic religious objectives as a monolith. We must distinguish between the Hispanic master plan for missionization and the way missions actually functioned throughout the borderlands. No longer can we proceed from Bolton's abstract notion of "mission as frontier institution" because multiple mission strategies were involved. The missions of California were different from those in Texas and New Mexico, and so were the life-styles of the Native American neophytes involved. The purposes of Jesuit missions in Baja California differed from those of the Franciscan missionaries to the north. Strategic and tactical differences engendered dissimilar Native American responses to the mission effort.

And yet, too intensive a handling of specific tribal groups, well-known skirmishes, individual missions and presidios—which constitute the primary data for the specialist—obscures the cubist view we intend to forge. However, excessive simplification for the sake of a general perception likewise defeats the purpose, by simmering the delightfully discrete historical tastes into a bland and even unrepresentative stew.

We follow a challenging recipe that has yet to be perfected. Like Picasso, we face the problem of creating a new system of understanding in which three-dimensional relationships are no longer dependent on the convention of an illusionistic, singular perspective.

Note

1. The cubist analogy is, alas, not originally mine. I am indebted to James L. Haley who raised the possibility, albeit only in passing, in his *Apaches: A History and Culture Portrait* (1981:xiii).

Acknowledgments

I am especially grateful to the officers (past and present) of the Society for American Archaeology (SAA) for their interest and support. The initial idea for its Columbian Quincentenary Symposia sprang up in conversation with then-President Don Fowler; Dena Dincauze and Jerry Sabloff continued the spirit of cooperation during their presidential terms. Sylvia Gaines, program chair for the 1988 Annual Meetings in Phoenix, assisted in a number of ways, and I also thank SAA Executive Committee members for their help and guidance, especially Kathleen Deagan and Bruce Smith.

The Advisory Board for this first volume deserves a special measure of thanks. Linda Cordell, Julia Costello, and Tom Hester worked closely with me in organizing the three symposia, and the final roster is largely a product of their expertise and awareness of the subject matter. Each chaired one symposium at the Phoenix meetings, and all graciously agreed to prepare the synthetic overview that begins each geographic subdivision.

I am likewise grateful to the staff of the Smithsonian Institution Press for taking on this ambitious project, and especially for adopting a streamlined schedule to mesh the timing of SAA symposia with book production. Daniel Goodwin's enthusiasm has kept the project on-line, and he is responsible for generating the necessary travel support to encourage Native American participation. I also thank Ruth Spiegel and Vicky Macintyre for working with us on a challenging schedule.

The proceeds from *Columbian Consequences* will be donated as scholarships to assist Native Americans seeking higher educational opportunities. The specifics of these scholarships are now being finalized, and all funding will be administered by the Executive Committee of the Society of American Archaeology.

Dennis O'Brien prepared the graphics throughout the volume, and I also thank my staff at the American Museum of Natural History—Margot Dembo, Laura Lundenberg, and Lorann S. A. Pendleton each helped out in dozens of ways.

References

Archibald, Robert
   1978 Indian Labor at the California Missions: Slavery or Salvation? *Journal of San Diego History* 24:172–182.
Axtell, James
   1987a Europeans, Indians, and the Age of Discovery in American Textbooks. *American Historical Review* 92:621–632.
   1987b Colonial America without the Indians: Counterfactual Reflections. *Journal of American History* 73(4):981–996.
Bannon, John Francis
   1947 Black Robe Frontiersman: Pedro Méndez, S.J. *Hispanic American Historical Review* 8:61–86.
   1955 *The Mission Frontier in Sonora, 1620–1687.* U.S. Catholic Society, New York.
   1964 *Bolton and the Spanish Borderlands.* University of Oklahoma Press, Norman.
   1974 *The Spanish Borderlands Frontier, 1513–1821.* University of New Mexico Press, Albuquerque.

Bolton, Herbert E.
    1917 The Mission as a Frontier Institution in the Spanish-American Colonies. *American Historical Review* 23:42–61.
    1921 *The Spanish Borderlands: A Chronicle of Old Florida and the Southwest.* Yale University Press, New Haven, Conn.
Broderick, Robert C.
    1976 *The Catholic Encyclopedia.* Thomas Nelson, Nashville.
Chippindale, Christopher
    1983 *Stonehenge Complete.* Cornell University Press, Ithaca, N.Y.
Cook, Sherburne F.
    1976 *The Conflict between the California Indian and White Civilization.* University of California Press, Berkeley.
Costo, Rupert, and Jeannette Henry Costo (editors)
    1987 *The Missions of California: A Legacy of Genocide.* Indian Historian Press, San Francisco.
Deagan, Kathleen
    1973 Mestizaje in Colonial St. Augustine. *Ethnohistory* 20(1):55–65.
    1983 *Spanish St. Augustine: The Archaeology of a Colonial Creole Community.* Academic Press, New York.
DeNevi, Don, and Noel Francis Moholy
    1985 *Junipero Serra: The Illustrated Story of the Franciscan Founder of California's Missions.* Harper and Row, San Francisco.
Engelhardt, Zephyrin
    1930 *The Missions and Missionaries of California,* 2nd ed., vol. 2, *Upper California,* pt. I. Published by the author, Old Mission, Santa Barbara.
Fairbanks, Charles H.
    1977 Backyard Archaeology as Research Strategy. *The Conference on Historic Site Archaeology Papers* 11:133–139.
Geiger, Maynard
    1969 *Franciscan Missionaries in Hispanic California, 1769–1848.* Huntington Library, San Marino.
Guest, Francis F.
    1966 The Indian Policy under Fermín Francisco de Lasuén, California's Second Father President. *California Historical Society Quarterly* 45:195–224.
    1979 An Examination of the Thesis of S. F. Cook on the Forced Conversion of Indians in the California Missions. *Southern California Quarterly* 61:1–77.
Haley, James L.
    1981 *Apaches: A History and Culture Portrait.* Doubleday, Garden City, N.Y.
Hawkes, Jacquetta
    1967 God in the Machine. *Antiquity* 61(163):174–180.
Heizer, Robert F.
    1978 Impact of Colonization on the Native California Societies. *Journal of San Diego History* 24:121–139.
Hoxie, Frederick E.
    1984 *The Indians versus the Textbooks: Is There Any Way Out?* Newberry Library, Chicago.
Jackson, Thomas L.
    1987 Father Serra Meets Coyote. In *The Missions of California: A Legacy of Genocide,* edited by Rupert Costo and Jeannette Henry Costo, pp. 99–110. Indian Historian Press, San Francisco.
Josephy, Alvin M., Jr.
    1970 Indians in History. *Atlantic* 22:67–72.
Maltby, William S.
    1971 *The Black Legend in England: The Development of Anti-Spanish Sentiment.* Duke University Press, Durham, N.C.

Morgado, Martin J.
1987 *Junípero Serra's Legacy*. Mount Carmel, Pacific Grove, Calif.
Noël Hume, Ivor
1969 *Historical Archaeology*. Alfred A. Knopf, New York.
Patrick, Rembert W.
1964 Editorial preface. In *Pedro Menéndez de Avilés: Memorial*, Gonzalo Solís de Merás, pp. xi–xii. University of Florida Press, Gainesville.
Phillips, George Harwood
1974 Indians and the Breakdown of the Spanish Mission System in California. *Ethnohistory* 21:291–301.
Polzer, Charles
1976 *Rules and Precepts of the Jesuit Missions of Northwestern New Spain*. University of Arizona Press, Tucson.
1987 Black, Gray, and White: The Founding and Fading of the California Missions. In *Early California Reflections*, edited by Nicholas M. Magalousis, pp. 6-1—6-24. Orange County Public Library, San Juan Capistrano.
Scardaville, Michael C.
1985 Approaches to the Study of the Southeastern Borderlands. In *Alabama and the Borderlands: From Prehistory to Statehood*, edited by R. Reid Badger and Lawrence A. Clayton, pp. 162–196. University of Alabama Press, University.
Schuyler, Robert
1977 The Written Word, the Spoken Word, Observed Behavior and Preserved Behavior: The Various Contexts Available to the Archaeologist. *The Conference on Historic Sites Archaeology Papers* 10(2):99–120.
Thwaites, Ruben Gold
1892 *The Colonies: 1492–1750*. Longmans, Green, New York.
Vogel, Virgil J.
1968 *The Indian in American History*. Integrated Educational Associates, Chicago.
Washburn, Wilcomb E.
1985 The Southeast in the Age of Conflict and Revolution. In *Alabama and the Borderlands: From Prehistory to Statehood*, edited by R. Reid Badger and Lawrence A. Clayton. pp. 143–153. University of Alabama Press, University.
Weber, David J. (editor)
1987 John Francis Bannon and the Historiography of the Spanish Borderlands. *Journal of the Southwest* 29(4):331–363.

Part 1 ■

The Southwestern Heartland

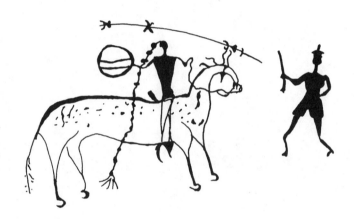

Chapter 1 ▓

Linda S. Cordell

Durango to Durango: An Overview of the Southwest Heartland

The Setting

The Southwest heartland includes those portions of the Spanish Borderlands that today form parts of Arizona and New Mexico in the United States, and Chihuahua and Sonora in Mexico. Aridity is the primary climatic feature uniting landscapes of topographic diversity, including rugged mountains, mesas, and broad valleys. The region encompasses the low basins of the Sonoran Desert, the higher and often wooded Colorado Plateaus, and the still higher wooded and forested mountain masses of central Arizona and New Mexico. Elevations range from near sea level in the basins to 4,265 m in the Southern Rocky Mountains. Ephemeral streams and internal drainage characterize much of the land surface. The Colorado, San Juan, Rio Grande, and Pecos are the major rivers.

Although the Southwest is not bounded by topographic barriers, it nevertheless formed a distinctive and cohesive culture area during the prehistoric, the protohistoric, and the Spanish Colonial periods. In prehistoric times, from about A.D. 1 until the mid-sixteenth century, Southwest peoples lived on cultivated corn, beans, and squash in addition to wild plant foods and game. Most groups were sedentary or semisedentary during the year and displayed the archaeological hallmarks of many sedentary peoples: permanent architecture, storage facilities, and ceramic containers for cooking and storage. At times, some groups may have developed sociocultural institutions that united several villages, but the complex, state-level institutions characteristic of Mesoamerican peoples to the south were not an indigenous feature. For the most part, Southwestern society seems to have been small in scale and organized along local kin lines.

The three cultural criteria used to identify peoples of the Southwest—the presence of agriculture, sedentism, and small-scale organization—should draw attention to the changing boundaries of the area as the limits of agricultural settlement expanded and contracted in response to changes in climate and regional population densities (Cordell and Gumerman in press; Dean et al. 1985). Its boundaries were also modified in response to the waxing and waning of Mesoamerican states, and the roles these states may have played in the formation of various aspects of Southwestern culture (see, e.g., Di Peso 1974; Mathien and McGuire 1986; Riley 1987). Of the three cultural criteria, the degree of sedentism is most difficult to establish because at times relatively nonsedentary populations interacted with their more sedentary neighbors in the region. Furthermore, in some areas, such as the low desert expanse between the Gila and San Pedro rivers, residential mobility was of necessity consistently high.

The essential unity of the Southwest during the protohistoric period (A.D. 1400 to 1700) is reflected in Riley's (1987) definition of the Greater Southwest as a single region or culture area comprised of seven provinces (Serrana, Desert, Colorado, Little Colorado, Rio Grande, La Junta, and Pecos; see Figure 1-1) that were united through "considerable sociopolitical, religious, and economic interaction" (1987:318). In his view, the weakest integrating mechanisms were political and the strongest were those of trade (see also McGuire and Villalpando Canchola this volume). In addition to various archaeological manifestations of trade and other forms of interaction, Riley notes that Spanish exploration of the area dramatically informs of its essential unity: "The Spaniards were operating within a closed universe which was delineated for them partly by natives and partly by their own observations and insights. One need only compare the neatly packaged expedition of Coronado with that aimless *wanderung* of the De Soto party" (Riley 1987:313).

Although Spanish administrative policy and modes of interacting with the indigenous population disrupted regional unity in certain respects, the Southwest as a whole was a distinct economic region among the Iberian colonies of the Americas. In 1793, with the redefinition of the Provencias Internas, the Southwest also became an administrative unit within the Spanish empire. In contrast to the lowland, littoral coasts of Brazil, Florida, Columbia, Ecuador, Peru, and the Caribbean islands, where plantation agriculture used African slave labor to produce sugar as a cash crop for export, the Southwest was one of the regions of Hispanic America devoted to extracting precious metals and to producing food for the mining enterprise (Wolf 1982:138–157). Like the Californias and Texas, however, the Southwest apparently lacked mineral wealth worthy of exploitation by the Spaniards. In these areas, souls became the currency of colonization, and missionaries led European settlement. Yet, in Texas and California

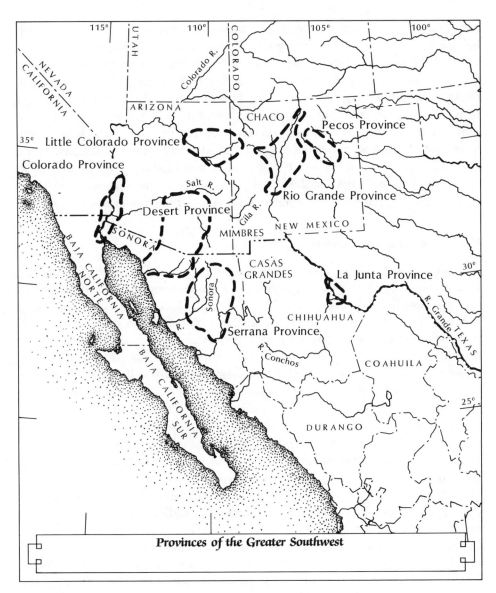

Figure 1-1. The dashed lines denote the provinces of the Greater Southwest as defined by Riley (1987:10).

the establishment of missions and colonial settlement was accomplished for defensive reasons. French military and commercial activities near Matagorda Bay and in Louisiana prompted the building of Spanish missions in Texas. The eventual founding of 21 Spanish missions in California was engendered by the threat of British and Russian intrusion from the Pacific. In neither Texas nor California was there a substantial number of Spanish colonists. By 1820, there were fewer than 2,500 people of European descent in Texas and only about 3,000 in California. Yet, in New Mexico and Arizona, there were approximately 28,000 people whose ancestors were Spanish Europeans, mestizos, or Hispanicized Indians

(Weber 1979:vii–xix). Even today, the Southwest maintains a tradition of Spanish language, law, and custom among its salient and unique features.

Of all the regions of the contiguous United States, the Southwest holds the largest number of American Indians who occupy their original homelands and retain their native languages, customs, and religious beliefs. In part, this is a result of isolation and the lack of development. Few Euro-Americans were drawn to the Southwest because it was far from European and American administrative and population centers in central Mexico and on the East Coast of the United States, and was so arid that environmental productivity was low. Lacking the gold of California and the "black gold" of Texas, the Southwest heartland was spared the frenetic development of other western frontier areas.

The Native American Context

The major native cultural traditions of the Southwest are those of the Pima and Papago of southern Arizona and Sonora and related peoples of northern Mexico (Lower Pima, Tarahumara, Yaqui, Mayo, and Tepehuan), the Yuman-speaking tribes of the Colorado River Valley and Baja California, the Pueblo Indians of Arizona and New Mexico, and the southern Athapaskan-speaking Apache and Navajo (Figure 1-2). At the time of the Spanish entradas, the horticultural Pueblo Indians were living in distinctive, multifamily dwellings along the Rio Grande and its tributaries, on the western margins of the Great Plains, and in an area extending westward from the Jemez Mountains to the Hopi Mesas. The horticultural Upper Pima, Papago, Sobaipuri, and related Sonoran groups were living in ranchería settlements, consisting of spatially separated dwellings for nuclear or extended family units, throughout northwest Mexico and north to the Gila and Salt River drainages. Yuman-speaking tribes lived along the Colorado River, where they practiced floodplain agriculture, and in the adjacent uplands, where they did some rainfall farming in addition to hunting and gathering. There is less agreement about the locations of the Navajo and Apache in the sixteenth century. The Navajo seem to have been west and north of the Pueblos, living in ranchería settlements and cultivating fields in addition to hunting and gathering (Brugge 1983). The more mobile, primarily hunting and gathering Apache bands are thought to have been dispersed and interdigitated among the more sedentary peoples throughout eastern Arizona, New Mexico, adjacent Mexico, Colorado, western Oklahoma, and the Texas Panhandle. Whether Apache bands also ranged through portions of present Kansas, Wyoming, Nebraska, Utah, and central and southern Chihuahua depends on interpretations of Spanish and French documentary records (Opler 1983).

The great diversity of Southwestern cultural traditions in historic and modern times has been described in terms of contrastive cultural types based on culture elements (traits) (Kroeber 1939; Jorgensen 1983), different histories of acculturation (Spicer 1962), adaptive strategies (Kirchhoff 1954), social organization (e.g., Dozier 1970; Eggan 1950; Fox 1972), language groups (see Hale and Harris 1979 for a detailed discussion), and provinces of internally coherent units (Riley 1987). Discussions of the Native American cultural context that existed at the

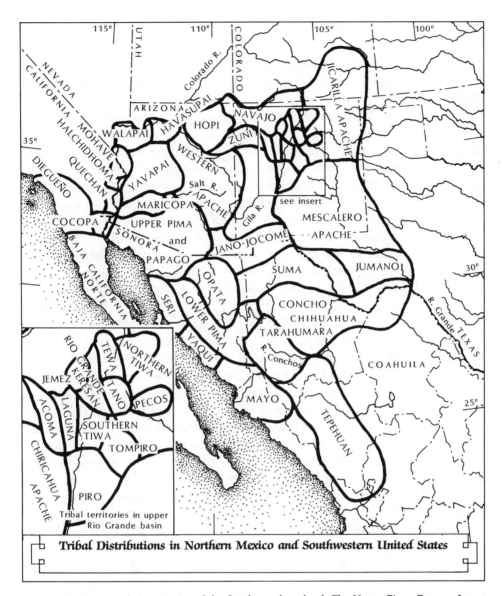

Figure 1-2. Historic tribal territories of the Southwest heartland. The Upper Pima, Papago, Lower Pima, Tarahumara, Yaqui, Mayo, and northern Tepehuan constitute the traditional southern, Uto-Aztecan-speaking peoples. The Maricopa, Cocopa, Quechan, Halchidhoma, Mohave, Yavapai, Walapai, and Havasupai speak Yuman languages of the Hokan language family and are tribes of the western tradition. The Rio Grande Pueblos and the Laguna, Acoma, Zuni, and Hopi are the traditional northern peoples; they speak diverse languages. The Apache and Navajo entered the Southwest late in prehistoric times and speak Athapaskan languages related to those of interior Canada. (After Cordell 1984:Figure 1.4)

time of the first Spanish exploratory expeditions are concerned with identifying particular tribal or ethnic groups, determining the levels of sociocultural integration represented by the native peoples, and estimating regional population densities. Although these subjects are discussed separately here, it should be kept in mind that they are closely interrelated.

Tribal Groups and Ethnicity

Particular Indian groups are easiest to identify in those cases where Spanish exploration was both relatively early and sustained over long periods of time, where ruined villages are well-preserved on the arid landscape, and where there is cultural and linguistic continuity from the sixteenth century to the modern period. The chronicles contain information on distances, days of march from one place to another, landscape features and places, and place names and thus have allowed translators to be quite confident of their identification. There is no hesitation in accepting the Zuni villages as the Cibola or Granada of Coronado's 1540 expedition, or Pecos as the pueblo of Cicuye to which "Bigotes" led Coronado and his men. The link between prehistoric and modern Pueblo Indians is clear, but questions remain about the identity of other archaeologically defined cultures and historically known tribes. For example, we do not know whether there is continuity from the prehistoric Hohokam to the historic Pima and Papago, nor do we know the nature of the continuity, if it exists, or the reasons for changes in burial practices and architecture (Di Peso 1956; Doyel, this volume; Ezell 1963; Haury 1976; Hayden 1970; McGuire and Villalpando Canchola, this volume). Another controversy is whether there is continuity between the archaeological Patayan branches and Yuman speakers (see Schwartz 1959, 1983).

Depending upon the recorder's interests and the period of time toward which observation is focused, the cultural map of the Southwest assumes different forms. Today, the Navajo constitute a tribal political entity within the United States and a linguistic unit that is most closely affiliated with the Apache. Yet, if the researcher focuses on subsistence economy as reflected in 182 cultural attributes, the Navajo most closely resemble the Yavepe Yavapai and the Walapai rather than the Apache (Jorgensen 1983). If the period of interest is the tenth century A.D., however, neither the Navajo tribe nor speakers of Southern Athapaskan languages are present in the Southwest, although groups with subsistence economies resembling the historically recorded Mescalero Apache may have been.

Establishing group identity and ethnicity in the historic period may be clouded by observer bias. The terms *Pima* and *Papago* are used by Euro-Americans to refer to people who recognize no such distinction but call themselves O'Odham, although in modern times the O'Odham distinguish between river and desert groups as well as dialects within their common language (Doyel, this volume; Fontana 1983a). Similarly, ethnic and tribal labels do not correspond in the case of the Maricopa tribe, which was formed during the historic period by the merging of the Halyikam, Kohuana, Halchidhoma, Opa, and Cocomaricopa (McGuire and Schiffer 1982). The events of the Spanish conquest and colonization also disrupted the correspondence between language and other cultural features. This disassociation occurred, for example, when the Tanoan-speaking Pueblo Indians moved from the Galisteo Basin of New Mexico to the Hopi First Mesa and established the Hopi-Tewa village of Hano. Despite their subsequent cultural "Hopification," they retained the Tanoan language (Dozier 1954; Lomawaima, this volume).

During the Colonial period, the Spaniards also created a new kind of land grant settlement and, in effect, a new ethnic group. *Genízaros* were detribalized Indians, former captives, and their descendants who were given land in communities surrounding centers of Hispanic population. The *genízaro* settlements were to function as living fortresses. Mixed communities of former Kiowa, Pawnee, Ute, Apache, Comanche, and other groups settled on the perimeter of densely inhabited areas. The *genízaros*, although genetically Indian and derived from many linguistic and tribal groups, were Hispanic in culture in that they were baptized and spoke Spanish. These communities eventually lost their distinctive legal status in the Mexican period, but most of them continue to acknowledge their origins today (see Horvath 1979).

Given the rich resources relating to ethnicity in the Southwest, it is disappointing to find that the topic has received so little attention from researchers. One reason for this oversight may be that ethnologists have only recently become interested in questions of ethnogenesis, and the fluidity of ethnic groups over time, as they undergo transformation, disappear, or become more prominent in response to changing resources (O'Brien 1986:898–899). Second, Southwestern archaeologists, who are in the best position to begin to evaluate long-term processes related to ethnicity, have, with few exceptions (and these include Snow 1984 and Upham 1982), assumed that modern peoples of the Southwest are appropriate analogs for most of the prehistoric and protohistoric periods, and that there is little to learn.

Levels of Sociocultural Integration

Twenty years ago, the consensus was that the native peoples of the Southwest were predominantly tribal and egalitarian. It had long been noted that there were hereditary offices at Zuni, yet the lack of economic stratification and the presence of consensual forms of decision making dominated interpretations of social organization (Upham 1982, 1986b, and the papers in Upham and Lightfoot 1988). The discussions of prehistoric complex societies in the Southwest seem to have arisen through archaeological demonstration of the size and scale of the eleventh- and twelfth-century systems centered in Chaco Canyon, New Mexico (e.g., Judge 1988; Mathien and McGuire 1986); descriptions of the Medio period "city" of Paquime at Casas Grandes, Chihuahua (Di Peso 1974); and interpretations of the scale of sites and trade and/or exchange networks among the fourteenth-century Western Pueblos (Upham 1982; Upham and Reed, this volume). Archival researchers (especially Riley 1987) have described small "statelets" among the Serrana of Northwest Mexico, but their existence has been questioned by McGuire and Villalpando Canchola (this volume).

Despite the diversity of referents and the sources of information used, the studies listed above argue that there were instances of supravillage organization in the prehistoric Southwest and that some of the social systems were inegalitarian. According to these works, most of the standard ethnographies produced in the 1930s and 1940s provide poor models of the prehistoric period because at the time they were written, Southwestern peoples had been decimated by European diseases and their social institutions altered by hundreds of years of subjugation by Europeans and Americans. Some argue that the ethnographers themselves were inadvertently biased in that they brought to their fieldwork and interpretation models of segmentary African systems that were then being taught at the major graduate institutions (see Lightfoot 1984; Upham 1986b; Upham and Lightfoot 1988). However, Spielmann (this volume) suggests that the development of social hierarchies among some Pueblo communities may have been a response to the Spaniards' demands for tribute during the Colonial period.

Population

Clearly, if there were prehistoric and protohistoric complex societies—whether midlevel societies (Feinman and Neitzel 1984), chiefdoms, big man-like systems (Grebinger 1978), or small states (Di Peso 1974; Riley 1987)—regional populations must have been considerably higher than accepted by Kroeber (1939) and by American ethnology in general ever since. Kroeber's estimates minimize the effects of the contact situation itself on aboriginal populations, a position that ethnohistorians or demographers find difficult to support. Much higher population estimates have been proposed by ethnohistorians and historical demographers. Ramenofsky (1987) provides an outstanding review of these issues, as well as the archaeological methods that might be used to resolve them.

In the Southwest, the controversy over numbers has also been fueled by acceptance of all or part of Dobyns's (1983) suggested rates of depopulation based on the notion that a smallpox pandemic in 1519–1526 spread through aboriginal social systems in the absence of European carriers and affected Native American populations from Chile to Canada. Upham (1982; 1986a) considers Dobyns's model, although not the specific pandemic, relevant for the U.S. Southwest. Riley (1987) accepts Dobyns's argument and population estimates for Serrana Province of Northwest Mexico, whereas others point out that there is no evidence of very early epidemics in the Southwest and that the great fluctuations in nineteenth-century records of population numbers among some groups must be understood in regional terms (Adams 1981, this volume; Palkovich 1985).

Although the population question probably cannot be resolved unless scholars work together using a variety of approaches, archaeologists are in a strong position to provide both the methods and critical analyses (Ramenofsky 1987) required to tackle this question and others about prehistoric social organization (Upham and Lightfoot 1988). The historical questions of ethnology cannot be resolved solely by recourse to traditional ethnographies. For example, the ethnographies have led Jorgensen (1982:688) to state that "the Eastern Pueblos did practically no dry farming," a conclusion that implies a causal relationship between irrigation agriculture and social organization and therefore suggests that strong status positions developed among the Eastern Pueblos in aboriginal times. Although this may have occurred, archaeological evidence accumulated over the past 15 years indicates that extensive dry farming was carried on in areas of Eastern Pueblo territory (Cordell, Earls, and Binford 1984) and supports

the ethnohistorically derived conclusion that dry farming was far more important among the Eastern Pueblo prehistorically than is normally assumed to be
the case (Ford 1972). Ethnographies generally minimize the long-term effects of
the events of the early contact period (see Lycett, this volume). Even long-term
ethnographic research is necessarily accomplished within a time frame that is
short by archaeological standards.

History of European Involvement

The Spaniards expanded into the Southwest from two directions, each at a different time (Figure 1-3). Initially, there was rapid exploration and colonization
from New Spain to the northeast into the Pueblo country of present New Mexico. The secular impetus for this thrust was greed for mineral wealth; the religious involved in this colonial effort were Franciscans. Nearly a century later,
the second wave of Spaniards moved into Arizona through Northwest Mexico,
after having incorporated tribal peoples along the way. This drive was also motivated by the desire for mineral wealth and for Indian labor for the mines and
haciendas, but its pace was slower, defense against hostile nomadic tribes had
a greater role from its inception, and during most of the period the missionary
effort was controlled by the Jesuits. Although both movements fed the corporeal
and spiritual aims of Spanish imperial expansion, they differed considerably in
terms of their contexts and events. That both efforts eventually failed may have
been a consequence of the remote location and the ineffectiveness of the logistic
structure against the increasing nomadic raids, which were themselves largely
a result of European expansion and disruption.

In 1528, Alvar Nuñez Cabeza de Vaca and three companions, survivors of the
ill-fated Navarez expedition to Florida, were shipwrecked on the Texas coast
south of present El Paso. They traveled west across the Sierra Madre Occidental
and in 1536 made contact with their fellow countrymen, possibly as far north
as the lower Yaqui Valley (Riley 1987:17). The party reported learning of wealthy
agricultural towns far north on the Rio Grande. Their story was instrumental
in leading to the entradas, first of Fray Marcos de Niza to Zuni in 1539 and then
to the large, well-organized Coronado expedition of 1540–1542 (Figure 1-3). De
Niza was accompanied by Indian servants and the Moorish slave Esteban de
Dorantes, who had been with Cabeza de Vaca. Esteban, traveling ahead of the
party, entered the Zuni village of Hawikuh, where he was killed by the Indians.
Fearing for his own safety, de Niza viewed the Zuni villages, which he called
Cíbola, from a distance, claimed the entire region for the king, and returned
to New Spain.

On February 23 of the following year, Francisco Vasquez de Coronado, governor of Nueva Galicia in western Mexico, left Compostela with 300 soldiers, 6
Franciscan friars, hundreds of Indian allies and retainers, 1,000 horses, and 600
pack animals. The Coronado expedition reached Hawikuh on July 7, 1540. The
Zuni resisted the Spaniards but were forcibly overtaken. Coronado and his men
were greatly disappointed by the lack of wealth among the Zuni Pueblos. Some
of the expeditionary forces, under Pedro de Tovar, went on to Tusayan (the Hopi

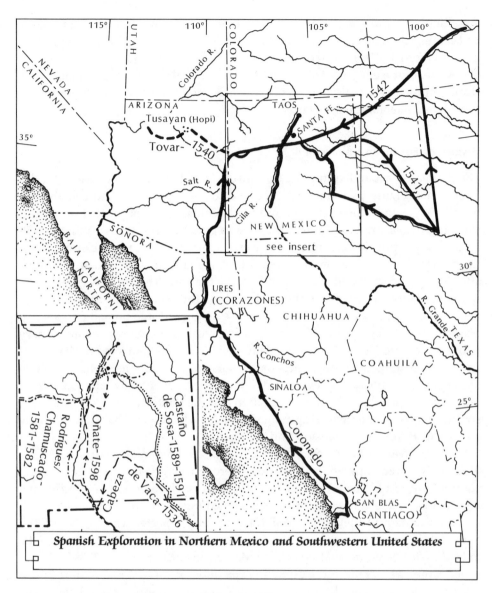

Figure 1-3. Routes of early European exploration in the Southwest heartland.

villages). Garcia Lopez de Cardeñas was sent west to the Grand Canyon of the Colorado. Coronado moved his army to the Tiguex pueblos, near present Bernalillo, New Mexico, where he spent the winter of 1540–1541. There relationships with the Tiguex deteriorated when the Spaniards made continual demands for food and blankets and molested Pueblo women. After the Indians resisted, the Spaniards attacked the pueblos of Arenal and Moho, killing their occupants in battle or later burning them at the stake. Many of the Tiguex fled their villages. Some of Coronado's men went on to Pecos and were led out onto the Great Plains in a fruitless search for the kingdom of Quivira. In 1541, Coronado returned to New Spain, leaving behind two friars, who were subsequently killed by the Indians. No formal expeditions returned to Pueblo country for 40 years. Francisco de Ibarra reached the edge of the Pueblo territory in Chihuahua, but he went no further. Interest in the west coast of Mexico declined: "The European-controlled areas of southern and central Sinaloa became Spanish settlement backwaters, and the regions still further north were left to their own devices" (Riley 1987:26)—at least for a time.

The 40-year hiatus in exploration is perhaps attributable to the discovery of silver deposits in Zacatecas. In any case, the pattern for future ventures was set, in part, by the conflicting interests engendered by the Royal Ordinances passed by Philip II in 1573, which mandated settlement for the purpose of missionization as well as the development of mineral wealth (Kessell 1979:32 and this volume; Spielmann, this volume). Thus, the 1581 expedition of Rodriguez and Chumascado, which was the first to follow the Rio Grande Valley into Pueblo territory, was both military and religious. Three friars of that expedition were slain by the Pueblos. The Espejo expedition was instigated ostensibly to rescue two friars left by Chumascado, but on learning that they had been killed, the party went west to Hopi and the Verde Valley in search of mineral deposits. The Castaño de Sosa expedition reached Pueblo country by ascending the Pecos Valley, fought a battle with the Pecos, and moved westward with the intention of founding a colony, but were arrested and returned to New Spain for launching a colonizing expedition without license.

In 1598, Juan de Oñate along with some 400 soldiers, colonists, friars, and Mexican Indians entered the Rio Grande Valley in order to found a colony and establish missions among the Pueblos. Oñate's expedition was privately financed and authorized under appropriate royal license. Oñate extracted pledges of loyalty from the Pueblos and, declaring New Mexico a missionary province of the Franciscan order, established the settlement of San Gabriel del Yunque across from San Juan Pueblo. Despite the missionary motive of the expedition, the colonists devoted themselves to mineral exploration, and the entire venture was supported by levies of food and goods extracted or stolen from the Pueblos. The almost immediate rebellion among the Acoma, Tewa, and Tompiro Pueblos is an indication of the hardship imposed by Spanish rule.

Oñate was removed from the governorship and replaced by Pedro de Peralta, who moved the settlers to Santa Fe, which he established as the colonial capital in 1610. Conditions over the subsequent years eventually led to the Pueblo Revolt of 1680 in which 21 missionaries and about 400 colonists were killed, Santa Fe was burned, and the Spaniards were driven from New Mexico for 12 years. In the seventeenth century, the missionary motive became the official focus of the colonial effort. Indian labor was conscripted and forced to build the governor's palace and other official buildings in Santa Fe, as well as mission churches and associated structures (*conventos*, priestly residences, etc.) at the pueblos. Eventually, about 40 mission churches were built in New Mexico, including Nuestra Señora de los Angeles de Porciuncula at Pecos, San Cristobal at Tano, San José at Jemez, La Purísima Concepción at Quarai, San Gregorio at Abo, San Buenaventura at Jumanas, San Estevan at Acoma, La Purísima Concepción at Hawikuh, San Bernardino at Awatovi, San Bartholome at Shongopavi, San Antonio de Padua at Senecu, and others (Hewett and Fisher 1943; see Figure 1-4). The scale of these endeavors and their cost in Indian labor and hardship have been described by twentieth-century archaeological excavators:

> Familiarity with colonial protestant religious structures in the East and with modern outlying protestant churches in the farming districts of the Mountain States led us to envisage a small church of thirty feet or so in length and a primitive outpost residence of a few rooms. We failed completely to realize two important factors in the problem we were about to tackle; the extent to which the Franciscan friars "kept their form," even in this farthest outpost of Spain; and the fact that from the very beginning the friars were building for the future and so erected an extensive establishment far beyond any possible needs of one or two fathers who were originally quartered on it [Montgomery et al. 1949:xix].

> We found a friary establishment of many rooms arranged in traditional fashion around a cloister garth or sacred garden; a group of offices and schoolrooms; the remains of three churches, two of them more than 100 feet in length; and a set of foundation walls best interpreted as the beginnings of barrack-stable for a military garrison [Montgomery et al. 1949:51].

Until the enactment of the Laws of the Indies of 1680, Indian submission to Spanish law and the church could be legally obtained by force (Simmons

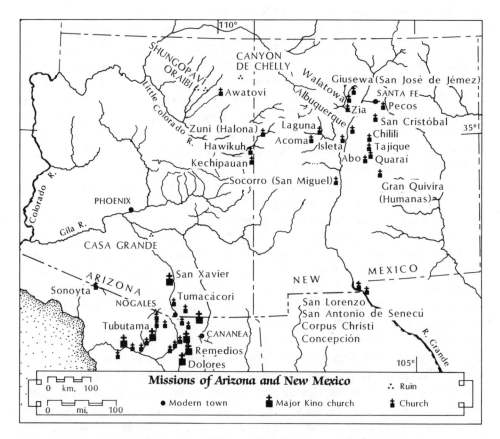

Figure 1-4. Selected Spanish missions of Arizona, New Mexico, and northern Mexico.

1979:181). (The 1680 laws, the *Recopilacion de Leyes de los Reynos de las Indias*, represented a detailed attempt to apply the spirit of Spanish law to the Indies.) Traditional Indian religious practices were prohibited. Dances were forbidden, sacred objects were destroyed, and individuals found committing acts of idolatry were killed. Indians were forced to provide labor to build the missions and churches, cultivate mission lands, and care for mission herds and flocks. In the missions and in the governor's palace, Indians worked in sweatshops, weaving, smithing, painting, and providing other services. The punishment for infractions was severe.

Under the repartimiento system, the Indians were forced to provide labor for Spanish farms, households, and mining activities. Although the Spaniards introduced new crops (wheat and fruit trees), livestock, and crafts such as smithing and silverworking, the benefits certainly seem to have been few. Under the encomienda, the Indians owed tribute in produce and goods. Indeed, a chief complaint of the Indians at the time of the 1680 Revolt "was that the Spaniards so burdened them with tasks that they had little time left to care for their own fields" (Simmons 1979:183).

Throughout the seventeenth century, when larger villages became more important for defense against nomadic tribes, the numbers of settled Indians declined as disease, crop failures, slaving, and raiding increased. Spanish policy and practice also disrupted relationships between Pueblos and Apache (see Spielmann, this volume). The trade relationships between Pueblo and Apache became more difficult to sustain because the Pueblos could not produce the surpluses they needed to trade for meat or the hides they were required to remit to the Spaniards by way of tribute. In addition, as the Apache acquired horses, they began raiding the Pueblos, who were prohibited from owning firearms. In 1673, the Apache raided Zuni Hawikuh, killing the priest and "200 Zunis, taking 1,000 captives and all livestock and burning the village" (Simmons 1979:184).

Finally, on August 10, 1680, the Pueblos carried out a carefully planned and coordinated rebellion, the details of which are given in several sources (e.g., Hackett and Shelby 1942; Sando 1979), and the result, as indicated above, was the removal of the Spaniards from New Mexico for 12 years (see Kessell, this volume). Although the Spaniards credited the San Juan Pueblo Indian Popé with organizing the revolt, in fact it was led by several "men who understood the Spanish mentality. . . . Thus, some of the mixed bloods and others who spoke Spanish entered the scene" (Sando 1979:195). From an anthropological perspective, then, the Pueblo Revolt, like other documented revitalization movements, was organized by somewhat or fairly acculturated individuals. In the process of destroying every vestige of the Spanish presence, the Indians burned all archival records so that census data and many descriptive details of the first 80 years of the Spanish colony in New Mexico were lost. This helps to explain why scholars have been surprised by the scale of the Franciscan building efforts and why archival research on the character of local and domestic life of the period has been hindered.

The events of the revolt dislocated some Pueblo populations and influenced the structure of subsequent inter-Pueblo interactions (see Kessell, this volume).

For example, the Piro Pueblos south of Socorro were not apprised of the revolt in time to participate. Thus, although some of the Piro fled and joined other villages, many retreated to El Paso with the Spaniards and never returned to their former homes. After the 1680 Revolt and during the reconquest, Pueblo groups established fortresses in inaccessible areas, such as the rugged areas of the Jemez Mountains. These refugee sites were occupied by people from various villages and included non-Puebloan peoples as well. Some Pueblo Indians joined Navajo and Apache communities for longer or shorter periods of time. Finally, disputes about whether to help the Spaniards return, or at least not to actively keep them out, caused inter-Pueblo hostilities that resulted in the destruction of some villages. Such was the case with Hopi Awatovi (Montgomery et al. 1949) and may also have been true of Pecos (Kidder 1958). In general, the early New Mexican experience with the Spanish empire was bitter and disruptive. In most of Pueblo New Mexico, Indian leaders became implacable foes of the Spaniards. The wall of secrecy built to protect Pueblo beliefs, religious practices, and political leadership remains in place today (Dozier 1970).

Following brief explorations of the Colorado River country associated with the Coronado expedition and the 1564–1565 failure of Francisco de Ibarra to find great riches in present Northwest Mexico, that area ceased to be of great interest to Spain until the 1590s. Then, just when Spain was about to abandon its efforts to colonize the area north of the Culiacan River, reports from Jesuit missionaries led the authorities to establish a Jesuit Missionary Province on the northwest coast of the Gulf of California: "Slowly, over the next forty years, the Blackrobes [*sic*] moved valley by valley into the heart of Sonora" (Riley 1987:29), establishing their mission outposts in the lower San Miguel and Upper Yaqui drainages by 1660. From 1687 until his death in 1711, Fray Eusebio Francisco Kino became the dominant figure of Jesuit expansion, pushing the missionary effort north to the Pima Alta and west to the Colorado River Yuma.

The Jesuit mission program differed from the earlier approaches to conversion. Better organized, educated, energetic and zealous, the Jesuits met with considerable success (Kessell 1970:12–15), founding more than two dozen missions between Dolores on the San Miguel River and San Xavier Del Bac, just south of Tucson (Figure 1-4). Although much of their success was due to their efficiency, zeal, and strength, it seems clear that by the time the Jesuits were active in the Southwest, the nomadic tribes had become such a menace that the more sedentary groups welcomed the new missionaries largely as protectors. The obverse was certainly true in that when "hostilities broke out between Spaniards and Apaches in the 1680s, . . . the Spaniards were only too happy to enlist Piman Indians as allies, especially the Sobaipuris and Pimas of riverine Sonora to serve as a buffer between themselves and Apache enemies" (Fontana 1983b:137). The missionary effort in Arizona and Sonora had a variable effect on the native peoples. Spanish settlement never penetrated into the heart of Papago territory, and the Areanos (Sand Papagos) "seem to have responded to European contact either by dying off or by becoming rapidly assimilated in Spanish mining camps" (Fontana 1983a:139). Despite the efforts of the Jesuits and after 1767, the Franciscans, "Arizona at the end of the Colonial period contained a minimal Spanish-Mexican population, centered in the Santa Cruz Valley. No Hispanic settlements lay north of the presidio of Tucson, founded in 1776, and much of the rugged plateau country north of the Gila River remained unexplored" (Weber 1979:ix). The lower Colorado remained peripheral until the last third of the eighteenth century, when the Spaniards established a route through Yuman territory to Upper California.

Despite the change in the Spaniards' approach (Kessell, this volume), the more peaceful reconquest of New Mexico claimed by de Vargas, the efforts of the Jesuits to allow the Indians "Christianity on their terms," and the promulgation of the Laws of the Indies of 1680, much of the eighteenth century was marked by rebellions, raiding by nonsettled tribes, and disease (see the chronology at the end of the chapter). In New Mexico, the Tompiro Pueblos south and east of the Sandia Mountains were finally abandoned, as were the Pueblos of the Galisteo Basin south of Santa Fe. In order to better administer and defend the distant provinces of northern New Spain, the Crown created the Provincias Internas (Nuevo Mexico, Nuevo Viscaya, Nuevo León, and Nuevo Santander), which were placed under the control of a commandant general. In 1793, the Texas Gulf Coast provinces of Nuevo León and Nuevo Santander were detached and placed again under the Viceroy of Nueva España. The authorities provided the Provincias Internas with further protection by allowing Pueblo Indians to bear arms; subsequently, many of them fought in the Spanish militias (Jones 1966). In the end, however, the Southwest was so remote from the population centers of Nuevo España and so nonproductive that if Mexico had not won independence in 1821, Spain would almost certainly have had to relinquish the Southwest as it simply could not afford to defend this area.

History of Research

In apparent contrast to other areas of the Spanish Borderlands, the Southwest has a long history of research, but only a few syntheses of this work are available (but see Fox 1984; Wilcox and Masse 1981a). Furthermore, the many studies that have been published contain few reports of the archaeological work. Most such reports remain in manuscript form or have been lost. Useful discussions about the history of archaeological research on the protohistoric and early periods of the Southwest are provided by Kessell (1979), Riley (1987), Wilcox and Masse (1981b), Marshall and Walt (1984), and Shenk (1976). These publications, as well as the two *Southwest* volumes of the Handbook of North American Indians (Ortiz 1979, 1983), contain extensive bibliographies that are essential beginning points for future research. The literature is so abundant that only a brief sketch of the research history can be given here.

The archaeological remains of the Southwest first gained widespread attention in the 1880s through the efforts of the Bureau of American Ethnology, the Hemenway Expedition, and the Archaeological Institute of America, all of which were influenced by the research program laid out by Lewis Henry Morgan (Cordell 1988; Wilcox and Masse 1981b; White 1940:Volume I). By and large, Morgan distrusted Spanish chronicles, which he considered exaggerations, and was concerned with the changes that had occurred in the social institutions of American Indians as a result of their contact with Europeans. His research program, which Bandelier and others carried out, entailed measuring and describing ancient monuments, and thereby providing an objective indication of the relative level of development achieved by ancient societies. Bandelier's (1890–1892) work provides the first descriptions of many of the monuments relevant to Spanish Borderlands research. However, his final conclusions carry little weight because he abandoned his own logic in order to support Morgan's notion that all American Indians—including the Aztec, Inca, and Pueblos—were organized along kin lines, in similar fashion to the Iroquois (White 1940:Volume I). Nevertheless, Bandelier's work would give a later generation of scholars an important guide to the ruins of the Southwest, particularly those with mission components (Figure 1-4).

During the early decades of the twentieth century, workers in the Southwest assumed the lead in developing chronological studies in archaeology, particularly those based on ceramic seriation and on the direct historical approach, which means working back from a known period. Nelson's (1916) work in the Galisteo Basin of New Mexico demonstrated the efficacy of these techniques by using the historic baseline provided by the seventeenth-century missions and associated Tanoan villages. Unfortunately, the complete results of Nelson's research were not published. Nonetheless, his strategy has had a tremendous influence:

> The admirable work of N.C. Nelson . . . had proved that stratigraphic excavation of refuse deposits, with analytical study of potsherds obtained, could yield information as to sequences of ceramic types, which in turn would permit recognition of contacts between, chronological ranking, and estimates of length of occupancy of all ruins at which these types appeared. . . . This immensely important contribution to Southwestern methodology set the pattern for all subsequent archeological research in the area [Kidder 1958:xii].

As Kidder (1924, 1958) suggests, he selected Pecos as his research focus because of the promised depth of occupation debris, diversity of ceramics, and known abandonment date. The decision of the Peabody Museum's Awatovi expedition to excavate Awatovi 25 years later (Montgomery et al. 1949) was made for many of the same reasons:

> At the time it was known that the site of Awatovi contained the remains of a 17-century Franciscan missionary establishment, and this knowledge was one of the deciding factors in the selection. For the presence of the mission made certain the continued existence of the native town well into historic times and indicated that we might find at Awatovi a longer time span than at any of the other larger pueblos along the Jeddito rim [Montgomery et al. 1949:xix].

Much of the archaeological work at early mission sites in New Mexico and Arizona was conducted in order to stabilize ruins and thereby promote tourism. Hewett's program for the seventeenth-century missions of New Mexico was designed to preserve rather than restore or rebuild, so that "they should be cherished as precious possessions of our state—possessions that will be cordially shared with millions from without our borders who will see them along the Mission to Mission Highway (a veritable Via Crucis) that New Mexico will build" (Hewett and Fisher 1943:17).

Similarly, Frank Pinkley's work at San Jose de Tumacacori from 1917 to 1921 was undertaken to stabilize and restore the church (Shenk 1976). In fact, a great deal of excavation was carried out, but little information was published about the results and little done with the bulk of collections amassed in the process. As Wilcox and Masse (1981b:6) so aptly state, "Great credit is due to those who have made at least some of these data generally available (Dutton 1963; Lambert 1954; Reiter 1938; Toulouse and Stephenson 1960; Vivian 1964)." To this list should be added Dutton (1981, 1985), B. Ellis (1957, 1976), F. Ellis (1987), Hayes (1974), Sinclair (1951), Snow (1975, 1976), and Stubbs (1959).

There are notable exceptions to research completed but not published, and there have been major changes as well in Park Service policy toward some kinds of research. Charles Di Peso's (1956, 1974) dedicated efforts provide superb information on the Upper Pima and on Casas Grandes. Recent cultural resource management efforts on the part of the Park Service, the Bureau of Land Management, and the Forest Service have provided funds and impetus for a series of overviews of the literature and the archaeological work on the lands of the Southwest. The Park Service overviews provide information primarily on specific monuments, many of which date back to the early historic period (see Shenk 1976; also Vivian 1964). The scope of the overviews of the other agencies is broader, and fortunately most of them have been written by a team consisting of a prehistorian and a historic site archaeologist (Tainter and Gillio 1980; Tainter and Levine 1987). The reports on the Mound 7 work at Gran Quivira (Hayes 1981; Hayes et al. 1981) also set a new precedent for comprehensive documentation by the Park Service. State Historic Preservation Officers have supported research and publication on the early historic period (e.g., Marshall and Walt 1984), as has the Bureau of Land Management with respect to one Piro site (Earls 1987). Unfortunately, little funding is available for such projects at present, so that the future of this kind work is very much in doubt.

Despite funding difficulties and the lack of an overall strategy of research, we are obtaining more information not only on stabilized mission walls, but also on the cultural context of the early historic period. For example, we have data on the Indian occupation of at least Gran Quivira (Hayes 1981; Spielmann, this volume) and on the economy and social relations involved in protohistoric Pueblo–Plains interaction (Spielmann, this volume). We have crucial information on the material culture of the contact period from the Hopi village of Walpi (Adams 1983, and this volume). Moreover, there is now a published description of the 1598 Spanish settlement at San Gabriel del Yunque (Ellis 1987). We also have new data on what appears to be the earliest Spanish camping place, at Bernalillo, New Mexico (Vierra 1977, 1988). This site consists of 15 shallow dugout shelters and associated artifacts and artifact scatters. Among the artifacts of predominantly local materials were a comal fragment of nonlocal sandstone, one obsidian item that may have originated in central Mexico, and a small number of metal objects. At present, the remains of this camp represent a site unique in the Southwest. With luck, renewed interest in the early historic period will lead to comparable discoveries and to new research endeavors at Hopi ancestral sites in Arizona, and at the Tanoan sites in New Mexico.

Chronology: Key Dates in the History of the Southwest Heartland

1539	Fray Marco de Niza expedition to Zuni. Esteban de Dorantes killed at Hawikuh.
1540–1542	Francisco Vasquez de Coronado expedition to Zuni, the Tiguex Pueblos, Pecos, Taos, and the Great Plains; Pedro de Tovar to the Hopi Pueblos.
1564–1565	Francisco de Ibarra reached ruins of Casas Grandes, Chihuahua.
1573	Royal ordinances of Philip II.
1581	Fray Augustin Rodriguez and Captain Francisco Chumascado expedition up the Rio Grande to the Pueblos of the Rio Grande, to Zuni, the Galisteo Basin, and the Plains.
1582	Antonio de Espejo expedition to Piro Pueblos, Acoma, Querecho.
1590	Gaspar Castaño de Sosa expedition to Pecos, Picuris, and Santo Domingo.
1598–1599	Juan de Oñate's conquest of New Mexico.
1598	First Spanish colony at San Gabriel del Yunque (near San Juan Pueblo); New Mexico declared a missionary province of the Franciscan order; and rebellion among the Tewa, Tompiro, and Acoma.
1610	Santa Fe founded; Pedro de Peralta named governor.
1626	Fray Alonso Benavides became custos (chief prelate) of the New Mexico missions.
1638	Fray Lorenzo de Cardeñas missionary effort in the Sonora Valley.
1639	Rebellion at Taos.
1640	First large-scale Apache attack on New Mexico.
1653–1670	Apache attacks on the Tompiros.
1673	Apache attack and burn the Zuni Pueblo of Hawikuh.
1680	Laws of the Indies.
	Pueblo Revolt (August 10); 21 missionaries and about 400 colonists killed. Spaniards driven from New Mexico.
1687	Fray Eusebio Kino to the Pimería Alta.
1692	De Vargas recaptures Santa Fe.
1695	Pima rebellion against Spaniards.
1696	De Vargas's reconquest complete. Northern Tiwa, Tewa, some Tano, and Keresans revolt, killing 5 missionaries and 21 settlers.
1751	Pima rebel.
1767	Society of Jesus expelled from New Spain by edict of the king.

1776	Formation of the Provincias Internas, Nuevo León and Nuevo Santander detached from Provincias Internas in 1793. Escalante and Domínguez expedition.
1786	De Anza establishes peace treaty with the Apache and Comanche.
1790	Galisteo Pueblo, the last Tano village in New Mexico, abandoned.
1821	Treaty of Cordova; Mexico becomes independent from Spain. Becknell opens Santa Fe Trail.
1829–1830	Spanish Trail (to California) opened.
1848	Treaty of Guadalupe Hidalgo.
1853	Gadsen Purchase.

References

Adams, E. Charles
    1981 The View from the Hopi Mesas. In *The Protohistoric Period in the North American Southwest, A.D. 1450–1700*, edited by David R. Wilcox and W. Bruce Masse, pp. 321–335 Anthropological Research Paper No. 24. Arizona State University, Tempe.

Bandelier, Adolph F.A.
    1890–1892 *Final Report of Investigations among the Indians of the Southwestern United States, Carried on Mainly in the Years from 1880 to 1885*. 2 vols. Papers of the Archaeological Institute of America, series 3 and 4. Cambridge, Mass.

Brugge, David M.
    1983 Navajo Prehistory and History to 1850. In *Southwest*, edited by Alfonso A. Ortiz, pp. 489–501. Handbook of North American Indians, vol. 10, William C. Sturtevant, general editor, Smithsonian Institution, Washington, D.C.

Cordell, Linda S.
    1984 *Prehistory of the Southwest*. Academic Press, Orlando, Fla.
    1988 History and Theory in Reconstructing Southwestern Sociopolitical Organization. In *The Sociopolitical Structure of Prehistoric Southwestern Societies*, edited by Steadman Upham and Kent Lightfoot. Westview Press, Palo Alto, in press.

Cordell, Linda, Amy C. Earls, and Martha R. Binford
    1984 Subsistence Systems in the Mountainous Settings of the Rio Grande Valley. In *Prehistoric Agricultural Strategies in the Southwest*, edited by Suzanne K. Fish and Paul R. Fish, pp. 233–243 Anthropological Research Paper No. 33. Arizona State University, Tempe.

Cordell, Linda S., and George J. Gumerman (editors)
    1988 *Dynamics of Southwest Prehistory*. Smithsonian Institution Press, Washington, D.C., in press.

Dean, Jeffrey S., Robert C. Euler, George J. Gumerman, Fred Plog, Richard H. Hevley, and Thor N.V. Karlstrom
    1985 Human Behavior, Demography, and Paleoenvironment on the Colorado Plateaus. *American Antiquity* 50:537–554.

Di Peso, Charles C.
    1956 *The Upper Pima of San Cayetano del Tumacacori: An Archaeo-historical Reconstruction of the Ootam of Pimeria Alta*. Amerind Foundation Publication No. 7, Dragoon, Ariz.
    1974 *Casas Grandes, A Fallen Trading Center of the Gran Chichimeca*, vols. 1–3. Amerind Foundation Publication No. 9, Dragoon, Ariz.

Dobyns, Henry F.
    1983 *Their Numbers Become Thinned*. University of Tennessee Press, Knoxville.

Dozier, Edward P.
1954 The Hopi-Tewa of Arizona. *University of California Publications in American Archaeology and Ethnology* 44(3):259–376, Berkeley.
1970 *The Pueblo Indians of North America*. Holt, Rinehart and Winston, New York.
Dutton, Bertha P.
1963 *Sun Father's Way; The Kiva Murals of Kuaua; a Pueblo Ruin, Coronado State Monument, New Mexico*. University of New Mexico Press, Albuquerque.
1981 Excavation Tests at the Pueblo Ruins of Abo (Part I). In *Collected Papers in Honor of Erik Kellerman Reed*, edited by Albert H. Schroeder, pp. 177–195. Paper No. 6. Archaeological Society of New Mexico, Albuquerque.
1985 Excavation Tests at the Pueblo Ruins of Abo, Part II. In *Prehistory and History in the Southwest, Collected Papers in Honor of Alden C. Hayes*, edited by Nancy Fox, pp. 91–104. Paper No. 11. Archaeological Society of New Mexico, Santa Fe.
Earls, Amy C.
1987 *An Archaeological Assessment of "Las Huertas," Socorro, New Mexico*. Maxwell Museum of Anthropology Paper No. 3. University of New Mexico, Albuquerque.
Eggan, Fred
1950 *Social Organization of the Western Pueblos*. University of Chicago Press, Chicago.
Ellis, Bruce T.
1957 Crossbow, Boltheads from Historic Pueblo Sites. *El Palacio* 64:209–214.
1976 Santa Fe's Seventeenth Century Plaza, Parish Church, and Convent Reconsidered. In *Collected Papers in Honor of Marjorie Ferguson Lambert*, edited by Albert H. Schroeder, pp. 183–198. Paper No. 3. Archaeological Society of New Mexico. Albuquerque.
Ellis, Florence Hawley
1987 The Long Lost "City" of San Gabriel del Yunque, Second Oldest European Settlement in the United States. In *When Cultures Meet, Remembering San Gabriel del Yunque Oweenge*, pp. 10–38. Sunstone Press, Santa Fe.
Ezell, Paul H.
1963 Is There a Hohokam-Pima Culture Continuum? *American Antiquity* 29:61–66.
Feinman, Gary, and Jill Neitzel
1984 Too Many Types: An Overview of Prestate Societies in the Americas. In *Advances in Archaeological Method and Theory*, vol. 7, edited by Michael B. Schiffer, pp. 39–102. Academic Press, Orlando, Fla.
Fontana, Bernard L.
1983a Pima and Papago: Introduction. In *Southwest*, edited by Alfonso A. Ortiz, pp. 125–136. Handbook of North American Indians, vol. 10, William C. Sturtevant, general editor. Smithsonian Institution, Washington, D.C.
1983b History of the Papago. In *Southwest*, edited by Alfonso A. Ortiz, pp. 137–148. Handbook of North American Indians, vol. 10, William C. Sturtevant, general editor. Smithsonian Institution, Washington, D.C.
Ford, Richard I.
1972 An Ecological Perspective on the Eastern Pueblos. In *New Perspectives on the Pueblos*, edited by Alfonso A. Ortiz, pp. 1–18. University of New Mexico Press, Albuquerque.
Fox, Nancy L.
1984 *Collected Papers in Honor of Harry L. Hadlock*. Paper No. 9. Archaeological Society of New Mexico, Santa Fe.
Fox, Robin
1972 Some Unresolved Problems of Pueblo Social Organization. In *New Perspectives on the Pueblos*, edited by Alfonso A. Ortiz, pp. 71–85. University of New Mexico Press, Albuquerque.
Grebinger, Paul
1978 Prehistoric Social Organization in Chaco Canyon, New Mexico: An Evolutionary

Perspective. In *Discovering Past Behavior: Experiments in the Archaeology of the American Southwest*, edited by Paul Grebinger, pp. 73–100. Gordon and Breach, New York.

Hackett, Charles W. (editor) and Charmion C. Shelby (translator)
1942 *Revolt of the Pueblo Indians of New Mexico and Otermin's Attempted Reconquest, 1680–1682.* 2 vols. University of New Mexico Press, Albuquerque.

Hale, Kenneth, and David Harris
1979 Historical Linguistics and Archeology. In *Southwest*, edited by Alfonso A. Ortiz, pp. 170–178. Handbook of North American Indians, vol. 9, William C. Sturtevant, general editor. Smithsonian Institution, Washington, D.C.

Haury, Emil W.
1976 *The Hohokam, Desert Farmers and Craftsmen, Excavations at Snaketown, 1964–1965.* University of Arizona Press, Tucson.

Hayden, Julian D.
1970 Of Hohokam Origins and Other Matters. *American Antiquity* 35:87–93.

Hayes, Alden C.
1974 *The Four Churches of Pecos.* University of New Mexico Press, Albuquerque.
1981 *Contributions to Gran Quivira Archeology: Gran Quivira National Monument, New Mexico.* Publications in Archeology No. 17. National Park Service, Washington, D.C.

Hayes, Alden C., Jon N. Young, and A. H. Warren
1981 *Excavations of Mound 7 Gran Quivira National Monument New Mexico.* Publications in Archeology No. 16. National Park Service, Washington, D.C.

Hewett, Edgar L., and Reginald G. Fisher
1943 *Mission Monuments of New Mexico.* Handbooks of Archaeological History, edited by Edgar L. Hewett. University of New Mexico Press, Albuquerque.

Horvath, Steven M.
1979 *The Social and Political Organization of the Genizaros of Plaza De Nuestra Senora De Belen, New Mexico 1740–1812*, Ph.D. dissertation, Brown University. University Microfilms, Ann Arbor.

Jorgensen, Joseph G.
1983 Comparative Traditional Economies and Ecological Adaptations. In *Southwest*, edited by Alfonso A. Ortiz, pp. 684–710. Handbook of North American Indians, vol. 10, William C. Sturtevant, general editor. Smithsonian Institution, Washington, D.C.

Jones, Okah I., Jr.
1966 *Pueblo Warriors and Spanish Conquest.* University of Oklahoma Press, Norman.

Judge, W. James
1988 Chaco-San Juan Basin. In *Dynamics of Southwest Prehistory*, edited by Linda S. Cordell and George J. Gumerman. Smithsonian Institution, Washington, D.C., in press.

Kessell, John L.
1970 *Mission of Sorrows, Jesuit Guevavi and the Pimas, 1691–1767.* University of Arizona Press, Tucson.
1979 *Kiva, Cross, and Crown, The Pecos Indians and New Mexico 1540–1840.* National Park Service, Washington, D.C.

Kidder, Alfred V.
1924 *An Introduction to the Study of Southwestern Archaeology, with a Preliminary Account of the Excavations at Pecos.* Papers of the Southwestern Expedition, No. 1. Phillips Academy, Yale University Press, New Haven, Conn. (reprinted in 1962).
1958 *Pecos, New Mexico: Archaeological Notes.* Papers of the Robert S. Peabody Foundation for Archaeology, vol. 5. Phillips Academy, Andover, Mass.

Kirchhoff, Paul
1954 Gatherers and Farmers in the Greater Southwest: A Problem in Classification. *American Anthropologist* 56:529–550.

Kroeber, Alfred L.
    1939 *Cultural and Natural Areas of Native North America*. Publications in American Archaeology and Ethnology No. 38. University of California, Berkeley.
Lambert, Marjorie F.
    1954 *Paa-ko, Archaeological Chronicle of an Indian Village in North Central New Mexico*. Monograph No. 19. School of American Research, Santa Fe.
Lightfoot, Kent
    1984 *Prehistoric Political Dynamics, A Case Study from the American Southwest*, Northern Illinois Press, Dekalb.
McGuire, Randall H., and Michael B. Schiffer (editors)
    1982 *Hohokam and Patayan, Prehistory of Southwestern Arizona*. Academic Press, New York.
Marshall, Michael P., and Henry J. Walt
    1984 *Rio Abajo, Prehistory and History of a Rio Grande Province*. New Mexico Historic Preservation Program, Historic Preservation Division, Santa Fe.
Mathien, F. Joan, and Randall H. McGuire (editors)
    1986 *Ripples in the Chichimec Sea, New Considerations of Southwestern-Mesoamerican Interactions*. Publications in Archaeology. Southern Illinois University Press, Carbondale and Edwardsville.
Montgomery, Ross Gordon, Watson Smith, and John Ottis Brew
    1949 *Franciscan Awatovi, The Excavation and Conjectural Reconstruction of a 17th-century Spanish Mission Establishment at a Hopi Indian Town in Northeastern Arizona*. Papers of the Peabody Museum of American Archaeology and Ethnology, Harvard University, vol. 36. Reports of the Awatovi Expedition. Peabody Museum, Harvard University, Report No. 3. Cambridge, Mass.
Nelson, Nels C.
    1916 Chronology of the Tano Ruins, New Mexico. *American Anthropologist* 18(2):159–180.
O'Brien, Jay
    1986 Toward a Reconstitution of Ethnicity: Capitalist Expansion and Cultural Dynamics in Sudan. *American Anthropologist* 88(4):898–907.
Opler, Morris E.
    1983 The Apachean Culture Pattern and Its Origins. In *Southwest*, edited by Alfonso A. Ortiz, pp. 368–392. Handbook of North American Indians, vol. 10, William C. Sturtevant, general editor. Smithsonian Institution, Washington, D.C.
Ortiz, Alfonso A. (editor)
    1979 *Southwest*. Handbook of North American Indians, vol. 9, William C. Sturtevant, general editor. Smithsonian Institution, Washington, D.C.
    1983 *Southwest*. Handbook of North American Indians, vol. 10, William C. Sturtevant, general editor. Smithsonian Institution, Washington, D.C.
Palkovich, Ann M.
    1985 Historic Population of the Eastern Pueblos: 1540–1910. *Journal of Anthropological Research* 41:401–426.
Ramenofsky, Ann F.
    1987 *Vectors of Death: The Archaeology of European Contact*. University of New Mexico Press, Albuquerque.
Reiter, Paul;
    1938 *The Jemez Pueblo of Unshagi, New Mexico with Notes on Earlier Excavations at "Amoxiumqua" and Guisewa*. Monograph No. 5–6. School of American Research, Santa Fe.
Riley, Carroll L.
    1987 *The Frontier People, The Greater Southwest in the Protohistoric Period*. Revised and expanded edition. University of New Mexico Press, Albuquerque.

Sando, Joe S.
  1979 The Pueblo Revolt. In *Southwest*, edited by Alfonso A. Ortiz, pp. 194–197. Handbook of North American Indians, vol. 9, William C. Sturtevant, general editor. Smithsonian Institution, Washington, D.C.

Schwartz, Douglas W.
  1959 Culture Area and Time Depth: The Four Worlds of the Havasupai. *American Anthropologist* 61:1060–1070.
  1983 Havasupai. In *Southwest*, edited by Alfonso A. Ortiz, pp. 13–24. Handbook of North American Indians, vol. 10, William C. Sturtevant, general editor, Smithsonian Institution, Washington, D.C.

Shenk, Lynette O.
  1976 *San Jose de Tumacacori, An Archaeological Synthesis and Research Design*. Arizona State Museum, Tucson.

Simmons, Marc
  1979 History of Pueblo-Spanish Relations to 1821. In *Southwest*, edited by Alfonso A. Ortiz, pp. 178–193. Handbook of North American Indians, vol. 9, William C. Sturtevant, general editor, Smithsonian Institution, Washington, D.C.

Sinclair, John L.
  1951 The Story of the Pueblo of Kuauau. *El Palacio* 58(7):3–11.

Snow, David H.
  1975 The Identification of Puaray Pueblo. In *Papers in Honor of Florence Hawley Ellis*, edited by Theodor Frisbie, pp. 433–480. Paper No. 1. Archaeological Society of New Mexico, Albuquerque.
  1976 Santiago to Guache: Notes for a Tale of Two (or More) Bernalillos. In *Papers in Honor of Marjorie Ferguson Lambert*, edited by Albert H. Schroeder, pp. 161–181. Paper No. 3. Archaeological Society of New Mexico, Albuquerque.
  1984 Spanish American Pottery Manufacture in New Mexico: A Critical Review. *Ethnohistory* 3(2):93–113.

Spicer, Edward H.
  1962 *Cycles of Conquest: The Impact of Spain, Mexico, and the United States on the Indians of the Southwest, 1533–1960*. University of Arizona Press, Tucson.

Stubbs, Stanley
  1959 "New" Old Churches Found at Quarai and Tabira (Pueblo Blanco). *El Palacio*, 66(5):162–169.

Tainter, Joseph, and David "A" Gillio
  1980 *Cultural Resources Overview: Mt. Taylor Area, New Mexico*. USDA Forest Service, Southwest Region, Albuquerque, and USDI, Bureau of Land Management, Santa Fe.

Tainter, Joseph A., and Frances Levine
  1987 *Cultural Resources Overview, Central New Mexico*. USDA Forest Service, Southwest Region, Albuquerque, and USDI, Bureau of Land Management, Santa Fe.

Toulouse, Joseph H., Jr., and Robert L. Stephenson
  1960 *Excavations at Pueblo Pardo*. Papers in Anthropology No. 2. Museum of New Mexico, Santa Fe.

Upham, Steadman
  1982 *Polities and Power: An Economic and Political History of the Western Pueblo*. Academic Press, New York.
  1986a Smallpox and Climate in the American Southwest. *American Anthropologist* 88:115–128.
  1986b The Tyranny of Ethnographic Analogy in Southwestern Archaeology. In *Coasts, Plains, and Deserts: Essays in Honor of Reynold J. Ruppé*, edited by Sylvia Gaines, pp. 265–281. Anthropological Research Paper No. 38. Arizona State University, Tempe.

Upham, Steadman, and Kent Lightfoot (editors)
  1988 *The Sociopolitical Structure of Prehistoric Southwest Societies*. Westview Press, Boulder, in press.
Vierra, Bradley J.
  1987 The Tiguex Province: A Tale of Two Cities. In *Secrets of a City: Papers on Albuquerque Area Archaeology in Honor of Richard A. Bice*, edited by Anne V. Poore and John Montgomery, pp. 70–86. Paper No. 13. Archaeological Society of New Mexico, Santa Fe.
  1988 A Sixteenth Century Spanish Campsite in the Tiguex Province. Paper presented at the 53rd Annual Meeting of the Society for American Archaeology, Phoenix.
Vivian, R. Gordon
  1964 *Excavations in a 17th Century Jumano Pueblo, Gran Quivira*. Archaeological Research Series 8. National Park Service, Washington, D.C.
Weber, David J.
  1979 Introduction. In *New Spain's Far Northern Frontier, Essays on Spain in the American West, 1540–1821*, edited by David J. Weber, pp. vii–xvii. University of New Mexico Press, Albuquerque.
White, Leslie A.
  1940 *Pioneers in American Anthropology, The Bandelier-Morgan Letters 1873–1883*. 2 vols. University of New Mexico Press, Albuquerque.
Wilcox, David R., and W. Bruce Masse (editors)
  1981a *The Protohistoric Period in the North American Southwest, A.D. 1450–1700*. Anthropological Research Paper No. 24. Arizona State University, Tempe.
  1981b A History of Protohistoric Studies in the North American Southwest. In *The Protohistoric Period in the North American Southwest, A.D. 1450–1700*. edited by David R. Wilcox and W. Bruce Masse, pp. 1–27. Anthropological Research Paper No. 24. Arizona State University, Tempe.
Wolf, Eric R.
  1982 *Europe and the People without History*. University of California Press, Berkeley.

Chapter 2 ■

Charles F. Merbs

Patterns of Health and Sickness in the Precontact Southwest

The health and sickness of human populations prior to 1492 can be thought of as consisting of two great patterns, similar in many respects, but also differing in dramatic ways. One of these patterns—that associated with Europe, Asia, and Africa, commonly referred to as the Old World—is reasonably well documented historically and is now being further elucidated by archaeology. The other pattern, that associated with North and South America, the so-called New World, is still poorly understood. Lacking a historical record, it must be painstakingly reconstructed from the archaeological record.

Following 1492, the two worlds became one as their patterns of health and sickness merged. Along with some scientific fact and considerable conjecture, a great myth has developed regarding this merging and the effects that it had on the health and very survival of the people concerned. This chapter examines various aspects of that myth in order to determine what health was probably like in the Southwest prior to contact with Europeans and why the European experience with disease appears to have differed so much from that of the American Indian. The primary theme of the myth, that the American Indian lived a basically healthy and happy existence largely devoid of illness, is eloquently expressed by a Yucatan Indian reflecting on life before the arrival of the European: "There was then no sickness; they had no aching bones; they had then no high fever; . . . no smallpox; . . . no burning chest; . . . no abdominal pain; . . . no consumption; . . . no headache. At that time the course of humanity was orderly. The foreigners made it otherwise when they arrived here" (Crosby 1972:36). According to this myth, the dentition of the American Indian was "strong and healthy" before the arrival of Europeans, who introduced the refined sugar and "junk food" that produced the extensive dental pathology seen in many Indians today.

The people of the Old World were pictured as being progressive, but warlike, and believed that nature existed solely for their own benefit, to be reshaped at will, whereas those of the New World were peace-loving, but culturally stagnant, and lived in harmony with nature as one of many coexisting forms of life. The filthy habits, poor diet, and frequent warfare of the Old World inhabitants gave rise to overall poor health. Although repeated epidemics ravaged the population, the survivors became extraordinarily tough and resistant to disease. In contrast, the New World inhabitants practiced better hygiene, ate a healthier, balanced diet, and did not have to fear epidemics. As a result, however, they were particularly vulnerable to the infectious diseases of the Old World once they arrived. The effect of one of these diseases on the Aztec capital, Tenochtitlán, has been described as follows:

> It [smallpox] spread over the people as great destruction. Some it covered [with pustules] on all parts—their faces, their heads, their breasts, etc. There was a great havoc. Very many died of it. They could not walk; they only lay in their resting places and beds. They could not move; they could not stir; they could not change position, nor lie on one side; nor face down, nor on their backs. And if they stirred, much did they cry out. Great was its destruction. Covered, mantled with pustules, very many people died of them [Crosby 1972:56].

Another epidemic, possibly influenza, had an equally devastating effect on the Cakchiquel Mayas of Guatemala in 1520 and 1521: "Great was the stench of the dead. After our fathers and grandfathers succumbed, half of the people fled to the fields. The dogs and vultures devoured the bodies. The mortality was terrible" (Crosby 1972:58). About the only New World disease carried back to the Old World, according to the myth, was venereal syphilis, which originated in the New World and produced a massive epidemic when carried back to the promiscuous population of the Old World.

How much of this myth is reality and how much is mere fantasy? In what ways did European contact really affect the health of the Southwest Indian? In order to answer these questions, we must first determine what American Indian health was like before contact and how the European experience with sickness differed from that of the American. The effects of European contact on the American Indian must then be evaluated in terms of immediate effects, later effects, and long-term or permanent effects. Obviously it would take more space than that allotted here to adequately deal with these questions, but at least some important points can be raised.

Reconstructing the Past

The precontact health profile of the Southwest Indian must be reconstructed from such diverse sources as present-day Indian health, historical documents, and the archaeological record, particularly the skeletal remains of the people who actually lived in this area before the Spanish arrived. Each of these sources has rather obvious limitations. The health of living Indians, for example, may exhibit some elements of the precontact pattern, but identifying those elements may prove very difficult. Although historical records bring the researcher closer to the time of contact, descriptions are often vague, sometimes intentionally exaggerated for political purposes, and usually open to more than one interpretation. Furthermore, of the vast quantities of Spanish records that have survived, only a small percentage have actually been studied in detail, and the results tend to focus on the dramatic and to leave out some of the more subtle, but nevertheless significant, aspects of the total picture. Although these records may have much to say about the health of Indians after contact, using them to reconstruct patterns that existed before contact may prove difficult and misleading. The study of human remains from the period before contact certainly provides the most direct evidence of what health was like at that time, but because such remains reflect only the conditions that directly or indirectly affected any given skeleton, archaeological studies also provide only a partial picture, and a biased one at that. However, the range of knowledge in this area of inquiry can be expanded somewhat through the study of mummified tissue and coprolites (ancient feces) when conditions of preservation allow their recovery.

The picture is further complicated by the diversity of groups living in the area at the time of contact, which may range from migratory hunter-gatherers to sedentary agriculturalists. Another problem is how to pinpoint precisely the time of origin so as to be certain that a particular skeletal series or event occurred before contact rather than afterward. The danger here is that one may confuse events that had nothing to do with European contact with those that did. A particularly difficult period to work on is the one immediately following the arrival of Europeans in the Americas, before any intensive contact took place in the Southwest. The earliest Spanish accounts of the Southwest may be describing a people already greatly changed by diseases that had spread rapidly from group to group after being introduced into the Americas.

Demographic Profile

The demographic profile of Southwest Indians prior to European contact can perhaps best be determined from data obtained from three quite different sites: (1) Arroyo Hondo, a large Anasazi pueblo ruin located 4 miles south of Santa Fe, New Mexico; (2) Grasshopper, a large Mogollon pueblo ruin 10 miles west of Cibecue, in east central Arizona; and (3) Sundown, a small Sinagua site 10 miles west of Prescott, in west central Arizona. Arroyo Hondo, excavated by the School of American Research in Santa Fe from 1970 through 1974, was occupied between A.D. 1300 and 1425 and had its largest population during its first three decades of existence (Palkovich 1980). Excavations at Grasshopper by the University of Arizona began in 1963 and are still continuing (Hinkes 1983). Grasshopper was occupied from A.D. 1275 to 1400 and experienced its maximum population between A.D. 1300 and 1350. The population of the pueblo at this time is estimated to have been approximately 600 people (Graves et al. 1982). Excavations at Sundown were carried out by the Yavapai (Prescott) Chapter of the Arizona Archaeological Society, primarily in 1981; it is thought to have been occupied around A.D. 1100–1200 (Merbs and Vestergaard 1985). Thus none of the three sites was occupied immediately before Spanish contact, but they are at least free of any possible early influence from European diseases. Skeletal preservation was relatively good at all three sites, so that age and sex could be determined with some certainty. Differential burial was practiced at Grasshopper, where infants were more often placed beneath room floors and adults in extramural areas (Hinkes 1983:13), and at Arroyo Hondo, where the trash middens contained fewer subadults than might be expected. All categories of areas were sampled extensively at both sites in order to avoid any systematic age bias in the resulting series. The high frequency of subadults found at both sites certainly supports this. No differentiation was noted at Sundown, where individuals of both sexes and all ages—with the possible exception of newborn infants—appeared to end up in the same burial area. The Grasshopper series consists of over 600 individuals, a large skeletal series by any standard, whereas that from Arroyo Hondo numbers just over 100, and that from Sundown only 26. Ordinarily, little attention would be paid to a series as small as that from Sundown, but it is included here because its composition is consistent with findings elsewhere, and also because more people probably lived in small communities such as this than in the large ones like Grasshopper and Arroyo Hondo.

The most impressive feature of the Grasshopper age profile is the high frequency of infants in the burials: 38.2 percent of the total series died before the age of 2 years. Of this group, 6.6 percent died during fetal development and another 9.9 percent around the time of birth (Hinkes 1983:16). Another 20.6 percent died between 2 and 8 years of age, and it was only after age 8 that the death rate dropped significantly. These results can also be considered in terms of an individual's chances of survival to any particular age. Once the skeleton had ossified to the point of becoming identifiable, the chance of surviving birth at Grasshopper was approximately 84 percent, that of reaching 1 year of age was 74.3 percent, of reaching 2 years of age 61.8 percent, and of reaching 8 years of age 58.7 percent. A similar situation existed at the other two sites: At Arroyo Hondo, nearly 27 percent of the recovered skeletons were those of infants less than 1 year old and 45 percent were those of children less than 10 years old (Palkovich 1980:32); at Sundown, 50 percent of the total series died before 6 years of age and close to 70 percent of these were infants 3 years of age or younger (Merbs and Vestergaard 1985:87).

The greatest hazards to continued survival appear to have existed in childhood, and thereafter the chances of living on to at least middle-aged adulthood were quite good at all three sites. Given the problems inherent in determining the age of older adult skeletons, the upper limits of the life span are difficult to establish, but 9.9 percent of the total Grasshopper series, or approximately 30 percent of those who had survived to age 20, lived on to at least 45 (Hinkes 1983:16). As with most present-day populations, the females at Grasshopper appear to have lived longer than the males; twice as many females as males are represented in the 45+ age category.

Cause of Death in Fetuses, Infants, and Children

The high level of infant mortality seen at Grasshopper, Sundown, and Arroyo Hondo was probably quite typical of the precontact Southwest, although the archaeological recovery of infant skeletons is seldom as ideal as it was at these sites. Of course, high infant mortality was by no means unique to this area in the centuries leading up to the contact period and is still seen today in some underdeveloped areas of the world. The high death rate among infants in the precontact Southwest was probably due to a combination of factors, including congenital malformation, trauma, malnutrition (including weaning stress), and infection. Some of the cases of fetal and neonate death could also represent difficulties (including death) experienced by the mother prior to or during birth. Although the skeleton frequently provides some general information on this question in the form of porotic hyperostosis (involving the external or internal surface of the cranium, the roof of the orbits, or the cortical surfaces of postcranial bones), linear enamel hypoplasia, growth arrest (Harris) lines in long bones, growth retardation, cortical bone loss in long bones, and congenital malformations (i.e., fused ribs and fused vertebrae), seldom can the actual cause of death be determined with reasonable certainty. Hinkes (1983:147) found all but 3 of the 100 fetal and neonatal skeletons from Grasshopper to show no obvious stress markers. She attributes this to "sickly or very young mothers" (p. 146), whose fetuses died either in an unhealthy uterine environment, at birth due to trauma, or after birth owing "to hypoxic or other stress due to immature organ systems and lack of medical intervention." "Infants who might have survived for a few months simply did not have enough time to register any stress on the skeleton and may have died from a single severe attack of diarrhea or upper respiratory infection" (p. 146). After birth, however, the frequency of stress markers in subadults from Grasshopper increases to 27 percent between 0 and 6 months of age and 70 percent between 6 and 12 months, and then drops to approximately 50 percent after 12 months. It remains steady at this rate through 18 years of age. Similarly, all of the Sundown juveniles between 3 months and 6 years of age showed evidence of anemia (porotic hyperostosis of the cranial vault) with the youngest individual (3 to 6 months of age) showing extensive postcranial periosteal reaction as well (Merbs and Vestergaard, 1985:89). Hinkes (1983:148) suggests that common infectious diseases of the respiratory and gastrointestinal systems were the primary killers of individuals in these age groups. This mortality can be thought of as a natural "weeding out" of the less fit, those less resistant to the biological stresses of life. It should be noted that this weeding process had essentially been completed by age 8.

Intestinal Parasites

The high frequency of anemia (porotic hyperostosis) observed in precontact Southwest Indian skeletons is frequently attributed to iron deficiency anemia (El-Najjar et al. 1976), but could instead, or at least in part, have been due to intestinal parasitization. This would be particularly true of Puebloan peoples living in close proximity to each other, their dogs, their food supply, and their own feces. It is probably no accident, for example, that one of the highest frequencies of porotic hyperostosis observed in any Southwest group was found among both Basketmaker and Pueblo peoples of Canyon de Chelly (El-Najjar 1976; Walker 1985), the same locality that produced evidence of an extraordinarily high rate of intestinal parasite infestation (Reinhard 1985).

The study of intestinal parasites in Southwest Indians began when pinworm (*Enterobius vermicularis*) eggs were found in feces from Mesa Verde (Samuels 1965). This ubiquitous human parasite is now known from several other sites in the precontact Southwest, including Inscription House, Canyon de Chelly (Antelope House), Danger Cave, Hogup Cave, Glen Canyon, Salmon Ruin, and Elden Pueblo (see Reinhard 1985). In addition, tapeworm eggs of the family Taeniidae have been recorded from Elden Pueblo, Hogup Cave, Danger Cave, and shelters in Glen Canyon, while those of the family Hymenolepidae are known from Elden Pueblo. Of the roundworms, *Ascaris lumbricoides* and *Trichuris trichiura* have been recovered from Elden Pueblo (Hevly et al. 1979), and a thorny-headed worm, *Moniliformes clarki*, from Glen Canyon, Danger Cave, and Hogup Cave.

Eggs from a tapeworm of the Hymenolepis type, probably of the genus *Railietina*, were also found at Antelope House. Genera of this type cycle between insects and small mammals, the mammals serving as the definitive hosts in which sexual reproduction and egg dissemination take place (Reinhard 1985). Entry of the worm into human hosts was most likely accomplished through the ingestion, intentional or accidental, of infected grain beetles (Reinhard 1985) whose presence at Anasazi sites has been verified (Graham 1965). It is doubtful that this tapeworm infection produced severe symptoms, but it probably contributed to the general debilitation of the population (Reinhard 1985).

The high rate of pinworm infection noted at Antelope House (Reinhard 1985) probably represents more than just itching, irritability, or nervousness. As Stiger (1977) points out,

> Few people have looked at the effects a massive infection might have on a person under stress. In such extremes a person may become anemic, and resultant death is recorded for untreated cases in wartime Europe. It is possible that in fact, the pinworm was more of a health hazard for the Anasazi than has previously been thought [Stiger 1977].

From the number of feces containing pinworm ova at Antelope House, Reinhard (1985:226) concluded that every person at this site "carried pinworm, and had worms to spare." It must be noted, however, that the rate of infestation seen at Antelope was not necessarily typical, being three to five times greater than that noted for other Southwest sites where similar information is available.

Found in much lower quantity in feces at Antelope House were the remains of *Strongyloides stercoralis*, a potentially more dangerous rhabditiform nematode. Present in dogs as well as humans, it was probably the dog that served as the reservoir for this parasite in Anasazi sites (Reinhard 1985). The worms gain entry to their hosts by burrowing into the skin and are then carried by the blood stream through the heart to the lungs, where embryological development is completed. From the lungs the worms wander up the trachea and are swallowed. After passing through the stomach, the worms take up residence in the intestine. Although damage is done to the host at each step in the life cycle, the most serious damage occurs in the intestine, where the worms plow through the mucosa and cause a loss of blood. One interesting feature of this parasite is that the host may be reinfected without again coming into contact with infested soil. Thus chronic infection may occur, with a loss of blood and reduced absorption by the intestine. Another feature is that infective strongyloides can be passed from an infected mother to a nursing infant through the milk. The finding of *Chenopodium* seed in just 1 of 140 feces from Antelope House (Reinhard 1985) indicates that this well-known antihelminthic agent was not used much at this site. Its presence in large quantity in the one feces with *Strongyloides*, however, suggests that it was used as a vermifuge (Reinhard 1985).

An infectious condition found today in the southern part of the Southwest that is quite clearly of New World origin is coccidioidomycosis caused by the fungus *Coccidioides immitis*. Airborne arthrospores of the fungus enter the lungs and, in serious cases, disseminate through the body, and cause the skeleton to deteriorate. Transmission from person to person is virtually unknown. Although it has generally been assumed that cocci was present in the precontact Southwest, convincing osteological examples from this area have yet to be identified. It is possible that the activities of the precontact Indians did not disturb the desert soils deeply or frequently enough to produce airborne arthrospores in sufficient quantity to cause a serious disease situation, or that *C. immitis* was introduced to the Southwest only recently, by migrant workers from Mexico.

Dental Health (Caries)

The illusion of good dental health in the precontact Southwest continues to survive in some quarters, despite evidence to the contrary reported nearly a hundred years ago (Matthews et al. 1893). Washington Matthews, director of the Hemenway expedition, was very impressed with the numerous carious dentitions he observed in the Salado (Hohokam) skeletons recovered in 1887 from Los Muertos and other sites near Phoenix, Arizona. Eighteen of the 35 skulls he judged to have been middle-aged adults or younger exhibited dental caries, which in some instances "resulted in almost complete destruction of the teeth" (Matthews et al. 1893:200). Another 7 showed evidence of tooth loss presumably from caries, even though the carious teeth were no longer present.

"Among those skulls beyond the middle period of life," according to Matthews et al. (1893:200), "fully 90 percent show caries and loss of teeth," and some, judging from the drawings included in his report, were completely edentulous. Matthews and his colleagues had little comparative data available at the time but noted that the Hohokam were far more carious than five other groups of New World aborigines ranging from Alaskan Indians (more likely Eskimos) to Peruvians. Matthews et al. (1893:171) also report that more than half of the Hohokam individuals they studied showed some degree of dental malpositioning or deformity of the dental arch.

A high incidence of dental caries has also been found in other Southwest agricultural groups, including those of Gran Quivira, New Mexico, where 17 percent of adult teeth were carious and 13 percent showed alveolar abscessing (Schmucker 1985). Occlusal caries were present in 31 percent of the individuals 15 years of age or older at Grasshopper (pre-Abandonment phase), in 38 percent at Point of Pines in east-central Arizona, and in 45 percent at the Houck site in northeastern Arizona (Berry 1985). Carious deciduous dentitions were also observed at the Grasshopper (Berry 1985) and Sundown (Merbs and Vestergaard 1985) sites. Schmucker noted a greater frequency of caries in New Mexico agriculturalists than in California hunter-gatherers, a difference that would likely hold true in the Southwest if comparable hunter-gatherer data were available from that area.

The high rate of caries seen in the Southwest has been attributed to a number of factors, including the possible inclusion of refined sugar derived from honey in the diet, but the two factors most commonly cited are the high carbohydrate diet associated with maize agriculture in the Southwest and the method of preparing the maize, which was ground into a fine flour on a metate and then formed into a tortilla-like bread that tended to stick to the teeth. Hypoplastic defects in dental enamel occurring as a result of malnutrition or disease in childhood can also serve as potential foci for caries in later life. This is not to say that dental pathology was worse in the Americas than in Europe at the time; the reverse was more likely the case.

Communicable Diseases

Tuberculosis, caused by the acid-fast bacillus *Mycobacterium tuberculosis*, was well known in the Old World prior to 1492 (Morse et al. 1964), but its presence in the New World was questioned for some time (Morse 1961). Although thought of primarily as a lung infection, tuberculosis can also affect the skeleton, and it was the tuberculosis-like skeletal lesions that could be mimicked by other diseases that made interpretation difficult. However, the finding of diseased pulmonary tissue along with acid-fast bacteria in three mummified individuals from Peru dating to the third and eighth centuries A.D. appears to have finally resolved this long-standing argument. Tuberculosis was indeed present in the Americas prior to European contact (Allison et al. 1981), and a number of convincing osteological cases from various parts of the Southwest indicate that it was also present in this area.

The earliest known case of tuberculosis for which the temporal factor is reasonably controlled comes from a small Kayenta Pueblo I (ca. A.D. 875–975) site (AZ-J-54-9) in northeastern Arizona (Sumner 1985). Affected are the last three lumbar vertebrae in a 16- to 18-year-old female. El-Najjar (1979) described a case involving vertebrae T11 through L2 in an 8- to 10-year-old child from Pueblo Bonito, New Mexico, dated somewhere between A.D. 828 and 1130. A still younger case involves a 4- to 5-year-old child from a Pueblo II–III period (ca. A.D. 900–1300) site near Tocito in northwestern New Mexico (Fink 1985). Along with tuberculous-like lesions involving vertebrae T2-4 and T12-L2, the cranium of the child also shows evidence of anemia. Four cases dated to A.D. 900–1100, all involving adults, have also been reported from the Sinagua site of Nuvakwewtaqa (Chavez Pass) near Winslow, Arizona (El-Najjar 1979). Affected vertebrae range from T4 through L4. In one of these, a male, the bodies of vertebrae T4-6 have collapsed and fused to produce a kyphosis (hunchback). An example of tuberculosis affecting the pelvis is found at Point of Pines, a site in east-central Arizona that dates to A.D. 1285–1450 (Micozzi and Kelley 1985). The individual in question, a young adult female, displays a perforating abscess and a shallow tracking channel on the right ilium and sacroiliac joint, along with destruction of the sacral ala. The X-ray appearance of this case is consistent with tuberculosis as seen in living patients.

These examples and others indicate that tuberculosis was indeed part of the disease pattern of the Southwest since at least the ninth or tenth centuries A.D., but its effect on the populations in question is difficult to determine. It seems certain, however, that those individuals showing skeletal involvement represent only a portion of the total involvement. Tuberculosis proved to be an especially serious problem for the American Indian during the nineteenth century, when one of every three deaths was attributed to this disease (El-Najjar 1979). Although this unusually high incidence of tuberculosis was interpreted by some as evidence that the disease was recently introduced among the Indians, a more likely explanation is that it was due to environmental factors, namely the cultural collapse, demoralization, crowding, and low levels of hygiene that Indians experienced during that period. It should be noted that the other well-known disease-causing mycobacterium, *M. leprae*, which produced so much misery in the form of leprosy in the Old World, appears to have been absent from the New World before 1492.

Another infectious disease of considerable interest to anthropologists because of its possible New World origin is venereal syphilis, one of four related infections caused by spirochetes of the genus *Treponema*, the other three being pinta, yaws, and endemic syphilis. Pinta, a mild condition spread through superficial contact, was certainly present in Mexico and parts of South America prior to contact, but its presence in the Southwest at that time seems unlikely. Yaws, another treponemal infection spread through skin contact, is now found in most of the world's tropical regions, including those of the Americas, but its presence in the New World prior to contact seems unlikely. Endemic syphilis, also spread through skin contact, prefers warm, arid climates such as those found in the Southwest, but its present distribution, which is limited to the Old World, argues against any precontact presence in the Americas.

The notion that venereal syphilis began in the Americas and was then transported back to Europe, popularly known as the "Columbian hypothesis" of syphilis, is based upon several lines of evidence, including the apparent newness of the condition in Europe and a syphilis epidemic that is said to have swept that continent at the end of the fifteenth century and into the early part of the sixteenth century (Crosby 1972). The skeletal evidence for venereal syphilis appears to favor the New World as the place of origin; examples from this area dating to before 1492 are quite numerous, whereas few have been found in the Old World and their temporal context is questionable. Hooton (1930) reported on two probable cases of syphilis from Pecos Pueblo, New Mexico, and additional likely specimens were found at the Arizona sites of Tuzigoot (Denninger 1938), Kinishba, and Vandal Cave (Cole et al. 1955), all clearly dating from the precontact period. More recently, El-Najjar (1979) described a Pueblo II period (ca. A.D. 900–1100) skeleton from Canyon de Chelly, Arizona, that appears to meet the criteria of syphilis. According to El-Najjar, the frontal and right parietal bones of this individual, a female between 20 and 25 years of age, "show strong evidence of gummatous destruction and bone necrosis" usually associated with syphilis. Although the various specimens cited here strongly indicate that venereal syphilis was present in the Southwest prior to 1492, its impact upon the populations of this area probably was not great.

Missing from the disease pattern of the Southwest, as from the Americas in general, were the great epidemic diseases of the Old World such as smallpox, diphtheria, measles, bubonic plague, typhus, cholera, and scarlet fever. Since the changes that these diseases produce cannot yet be read from the skeleton, their absence from the precontact Southwest is assumed from folklore, and, in particular, the disastrous effects they had on Indian populations following contact. The European experience with these great epidemic diseases differed dramatically from that of the Americas prior to contact for a number of reasons. The European experience cannot be viewed in isolation, but must be seen as part of the pattern that extended to Asia and Africa as well. In those terms, the affected land mass was much greater and included a much broader range of environments occupied by larger numbers of people than the Americas. Also, the area was occupied for a much longer period of time. Humans, after all, evolved in the Old World while their presence in the New World can be measured in mere thousands of years. When humans originally left the Old World for the New, they were at a hunting-gathering stage of subsistence, with the so-called crowd infections not yet evolved. The arctic or subarctic environment through which the early migrants passed served as a kind of filter, keeping some diseases such as malaria behind in the Old World.

Sharing the environment with humans in the Old World were their closest evolutionary relatives, the anthropoid apes and cercopithecoid monkeys. These animals are also close to humans in terms of their biochemistry and thus the internal environment they offer potential parasites. This can be seen, for example, in the forms of plasmodia and helminths shared by humans and chimpanzees (Dunn 1966). Also, smallpox appears to have evolved from monkeypox. Many more animal forms were present in the Old World than in the New, and the Old World had not only a longer tradition of animal domestication, but also a greater variety of domesticated animals. Since people of the Old World tended to live in close contact with these animals, it was relatively simple for them to contract various zoonoses.

Europe, thanks in large part to its proximity to Asia and Africa, which have warm climates conducive to the development of infectious diseases, had a long history of crowd infections, but in most cases achieved a kind of equilibrium with the disease agent in the form of immunity. That is not to say that this equilibrium was easily won or necessarily permanent. One has only to reflect on the Plague of Athens (430 B.C.) described by Thucydides, the Plague of Justinian (A.D. 542), the Black Death of the 1340s, and the "sweating sickness" of 1485, to name just a few, to see that Europeans paid dearly over the centuries for that immunity. In most cases, however, these diseases were not killers, but rather produced a relatively mild illness in childhood and thereby conferred lifelong immunity.

An Interpretation from the New World

The striking contrast between the Indian pattern of illness and that accompanying the European to the Southwest can be seen in the sickness theory of the Arizona Pimans (Bahr et al. 1974; Bahr 1983). The theory involves a basic distinction between two kinds of sickness, "staying sickness" (*ká-cim múmkidag*) and "wandering sickness" (*ʔóimeddam múmkidag*). The staying sicknesses, according to this theory, began among the Indians and will always be with them. Staying sicknesses are said to be like the ocean; they stay in one place and do not move about. They are never transmitted by contagion from one Piman to another, they never leave the Pimans to afflict other groups, and, although they may be cured when they afflict an individual, they can never be eradicated. Piman staying sicknesses such as horned toad sickness, enemy sickness, lightning sickness, and *wí-gida* (a ceremony) sickness (Bahr et al. 1974:26) defy recognition and understanding by modern scientific medicine, and their diagnosis and treatment lie entirely in the province of native medicine. An individual contracts a staying sickness by transgressing or violating the "way" (*hímdag*) of a dangerous object. The victim thus has some say in the matter, but the ways are complex and the transgression may be entirely inadvertent. Sometime after the transgression, the "strength" (*géwkadag*) of the dangerous object may enter the victim's body to produce the symptoms of the sickness. A shaman must then suck out the "strength" before it permeates the body (Bahr 1983:196).

Wandering sicknesses, on the other hand, are viewed as foreign entities, originating outside the Piman universe. They belong to Anglo-American medicine, and are to be diagnosed and treated by the methods of the modern medical laboratory. With wandering sickness, cause and effect are simple and direct, the sickness being caused by "germs" that are imperceptible to the usual senses, but nevertheless roam the world to invade bodies and cause disease. In contrast, wandering sicknesses are "here today and gone tomorrow," not only because epidemics move on, but also because new agents of disease evolve, spread throughout the world, and finally disappear (Bahr 1983:195). A classic example of wandering sickness is influenza (the "flu"), which is notoriously infectious. Each year's invasion is slightly different from those of previous years and has varying potential for sickness and death. Another wandering sickness still remembered for its virulence in the nineteenth century is smallpox.

The Indians were terrified of wandering sicknesses, and with good reason. These sicknesses were thought to be caused by malevolent agents whose sole function was to blow about the earth seeking any convenient victim. Russell (1908:267) reports that the Pimans regarded smallpox "as an evil spirit of which they did not dare show fear." "I like smallpox," they said, thinking the spirit would thus be placated. When Indian methods of curing proved ineffective against wandering sickness, non-Indian methods were also tried. Children were intentionally exposed to smallpox and measles, "that they may have the diseases in lighter form" (Russell 1908:267). In the case of smallpox, the Indians even attempted variolation, using persons who had experienced light attacks of the disease as the source of their inoculant, but the experiment only intensified the epidemic and in the process caused many deaths. As far as the Pimans were concerned, wandering sickness was indeed something from another world.

Summary

Although the precontact Indians of the American Southwest appear to have lacked most of the crowd infections that plagued Europe, their health was not as idyllic as often believed. Infant mortality was very high, and it was not until about the age of 8 that an individual's survival became reasonably certain. The high frequency of fetal and neonatal death suggests health problems involving the mothers, while evidence of anemia in infants and children points to dietary stress and infection from intestinal parasites as the primary killers of individuals in this age group. In some communities, at least, the parasite load appears to have been quite high, as is suggested by the pinworms, tapeworms, nematodes, and other forms identified in ancient feces.

Tuberculosis appears to have been present along with a treponemal infection, probably venereal syphilis, that left severe bone lesions. The search for coccidioidomycosis, a highly endemic fungus-caused condition found in the area today, has so far turned up negative evidence for the precontact period. Dental pathology, particularly caries, was prevalent among precontact agriculturalists in the Southwest to the extent that some individuals already had problems in childhood while others had become edentulous by middle age. The carious condition seen in these people is usually attributed to the high carbohydrate, maize-dominated diet of the region along with a method of preparation that left food adhering to the teeth. Missing from the inventory of diseases in the precontact Southwest, however, were the contagious crowd infections of the Old World. Lacking any immunity to these diseases, the Indians of the Southwest appear to have died in large numbers following contact. Sometimes these diseases spread more rapidly than the Europeans who initially introduced them, and thus may have had profound effects on the Southwest even before the area was first described by the Spanish. The epidemic diseases that accompanied the Europeans to the Southwest have been incorporated into the Piman theory of illness as "wandering sickness," a category of malevolent, germ-caused diseases that stands in sharp contrast to the native illnesses of the area, which the Pimans refer to as "staying sickness."

References

Allison, M. J., E. Gerzten, J. Munizaga, C. Santoro, and D. Mendoza
 1981 Tuberculosis in Pre-Columbian Andean Populations. In *Prehistoric Tuberculosis in the Americas*, edited by J.E. Buikstra, pp. 49–61. Northwestern University Archaeological Program, Evanston, Ill.

Bahr, D. M.
 1983 Pima and Papago Medicine and Philosophy. In *Southwest*, edited by A. Ortiz, pp. 193–201. Handbook of North American Indians, William C. Sturtevant, general editor. Smithsonian Institution, Washington, D.C.

Bahr, D. M., J. Gregorio, D. I. Lopez, and A. Alvarez
 1974 *Piman Shamanism and Staying Sickness (Ka'cim Mumkidag).* University of Arizona Press, Tucson.

Berry, D. R.
 1985 Dental Paleopathology of Grasshopper Pueblo, Arizona. In *Health and Disease in the Prehistoric Southwest*, edited by C. F. Merbs and R. J. Miller, pp. 253–274. Anthropological Research Paper No. 34. Arizona State University, Tempe.

Cole, H. N., J. C. Harkin, B. S. Kraus, and A. R. Moritz
 1955 Pre-Columbian Osseous Syphilis. *Archives of Dermatology* 71:231–238.

Crosby, A. W., Jr.
 1972 *The Columbian Exchange: Biological and Cultural Consequences of 1492.* Contributions in American Studies, No. 2. Greenwood Press, Westport, Conn.

Denninger, H. S.
 1938 Syphilis of Pueblo Skull before 1350. *Archives of Pathology* 26:724–727.

Dunn, F. L.
 1966 Patterns of Parasitism in Primates: Phylogenetic and Ecological Interpretations, with Particular Reference to the Hominoidea. *Folia Primatologica* 4:329–345.

El-Najjar, M. Y.
 1976 Maize, Malaria and the Anemias in the Pre-Columbian New World. *Yearbook of Physical Anthropology* 20:329–337.
 1979 Human Treponematosis and Tuberculosis: Evidence from the New World. *American Journal of Physical Anthropology* 51:599–618.

El-Najjar, M. Y., D. J. Ryan, C. G. Turner II, and B. Lozoff
 1976 The Etiology of Porotic Hyperostosis among the Prehistoric and Historic Anasazi Indians of the Southwestern United States. *American Journal of Physical Anthropology* 44:447–488.

Fink, T. M.
 1985 Tuberculosis and Anemia in a Pueblo III (ca. A.D. 900–1300) Anasazi Child from New Mexico. In *Health and Disease in the Prehistoric Southwest*, edited by C. F. Merbs and R. J. Miller, pp. 359–379. Anthropological Research Paper No. 34. Arizona State University, Tempe.

Graham, S. A.
 1965 Entomology: An Aid in Archaeological Studies. *American Antiquity* 32:167–174.

Graves, M. W., W. A. Longacre, and S. J. Holbrook
 1982 Aggregation and Abandonment at Grasshopper Pueblo, Arizona. *Journal of Field Archaeology* 9:193–206.

Hevly, R. H., R. E. Kelly, G. A. Anderson, and S. J. Olsen
 1979 Comparative Effects of Climate Change, Cultural Impact, and Volcanism in the

Paleoecology of Flagstaff, Arizona, A.D. 900–1300. In *Volcanic Activity and Human History*, edited by P. Sheets and D. Grayson, pp. 487–523. Academic Press, New York.

Hinkes, M. J.
1983 *Skeletal Evidence of Stress in Subadults: Trying to Come of Age at Grasshopper Pueblo*. Unpublished Ph.D. dissertation, Department of Anthropology, University of Arizona, Tucson.

Hooton, E. A.
1930 *The Indians of Pecos*. Yale University Press, New Haven.

Matthews, W., J. L. Wortman, and J. S. Billings
1893 *Human Bones of the Hemenway Collection in the United States Army Medical Museum*. Memoirs of the National Academy of Sciences, vol. 6, Memoir 7, pp. 141–286. Washington, D.C.

Merbs, C. F., and E. M. Vestergaard
1985 The Paleopathology of Sundown, a Prehistoric Site Near Prescott, Arizona. In *Health and Disease in the Prehistoric Southwest*, edited by C. F. Merbs and R. J. Miller, pp. 85–103. Anthropological Research Paper No. 34. Arizona State University, Tempe.

Micozzi, M. S., and M. A. Kelley
1985 Evidence for Pre-Columbian Tuberculosis at the Point of Pines Site, Arizona: Skeletal Pathology in the Sacro-Iliac Region. In *Health and Disease in the Prehistoric Southwest*, edited by C. F. Merbs and R. J. Miller, pp. 347–358. Anthropological Research Paper No. 34. Arizona State University, Tempe.

Morse, D.
1961 Prehistoric Tuberculosis in America. *American Review of Respiratory Diseases* 83:489–504.

Morse, D., D. R. Brothwell, and P. J. Ucko
1964 Tuberculosis in Ancient Egypt. *American Review of Respiratory Diseases* 90:524–541.

Palkovich, A. M.
1980 *The Arroyo Hondo Skeletal and Mortuary Remains*. Arroyo Hondo Archaeological Series, vol. 3. School of American Research Press, Santa Fe.

Reinhard, K. J.
1985 Parasitism at Antelope House, A Puebloan Village in Canyon de Chelly, Arizona. In *Health and Disease in the Prehistoric Southwest*, edited by C. F. Merbs and R. J. Miller, pp. 220–233. Anthropological Research Paper No. 34. Arizona State University, Tempe.

Russell, F.
1908 The Pima Indians. *Annual Report of the Bureau of American Ethnology* 26:3–389. Washington, D.C.

Samuels, R.
1965 Parasitological Study of Long-dried Fecal Samples. In *Contributions to the Wetherill Mesa Archeological Project*, edited by D. Osborne and B. S. Katz, pp. 175–179. Memoirs of the Society for American Archaeology, No. 19.

Schmucker, B. J.
1985 Dental Attrition: A Correlative Study of Dietary and Subsistence Patterns in California and New Mexico Indians. In *Health and Disease in the Prehistoric Southwest*, edited by C. F. Merbs and R. J. Miller, pp. 275–323. Anthropological Research Paper No. 34. Arizona State University, Tempe.

Stiger, M. A.
1977 *Anasazi Diet: The Coprolite Evidence*. M.A. thesis, Department of Anthropology, University of Colorado, Boulder.

Sumner, D. R.
1985 A Probable Case of Prehistoric Tuberculosis from Northeastern Arizona. In *Health*

and Disease in the Prehistoric Southwest, edited by C. F. Merbs and R. J. Miller, pp. 340–346. Anthropological Research Paper No. 34. Arizona State University, Tempe.

Walker, P. L.
    1985 Anemia among Prehistoric Indians of the American Southwest. In *Health and Disease in the Prehistoric Southwest*, edited by C. F. Merbs and R. J. Miller, pp. 139–164. Anthropological Research Paper No. 34. Arizona State University, Tempe.

Chapter 3 ▓

Steadman Upham and Lori Stephens Reed

Regional Systems in the Central and Northern Southwest: Demography, Economy, and Sociopolitics Preceding Contact

This chapter is about the late prehistoric and early contact period of regional settlement systems in the central and northern American Southwest. It is also about the social, political, and economic organizations that characterized these regional systems and about provinces and alliances, regionally organized systems of exchange, symbolic interaction, and sociopolitical complexity. Our treatment of these issues would not be complete without some consideration of the catastrophic consequences of European colonization, a process that brought about a social, political, economic, and demographic collapse of native regional settlement organization in the Southwest. We recognize that this is a substantial task for a short discussion. We therefore focus on a few key issues related to the formation of regional systems and regional interaction.

During the past decade, a few southwestern archaeologists have written books, monographs, and journal articles outlining a program designed to redress disparities in the interpretive record of the central and northern Southwest. This program seeks to align interpretation with archaeological, ethnographic, and historical records of contact and thereby to amend key elements of existing cultural history. The beginning point for such an endeavor lies in the sociopolitical, economic, and demographic changes wrought during 500 years of colonial domination, which render the ethnographic record of Pueblo groups, compiled only during the last 80 years, an inappropriate analog for archaeological interpretation (Lightfoot 1984; Upham 1980, 1982, 1987; Upham and Plog 1986; Wilcox 1981). Additional support for this interpretive program is found in four separate, but interrelated findings:

1. Catastrophic population loss during the first 75 years of Spanish contact, a process that has been poorly documented in the historical records of the northern Southwest, resulted from the introduction of acute European crowd infections (smallpox, measles, and influenza [Reff 1986; Upham 1980, 1982, 1986]). Moreover, initial epidemics appear to have spread within native interaction networks, and may have preceded face-to-face contact with the Spanish.

2. The loss of native population and the ensuing Spanish program of settlement reduction, missionization, and reeducation inexorably changed the sociopolitical and economic fabric of native society (Upham 1980, 1982, 1983; Wilcox 1981). This colonial onslaught, although experienced differentially by various native groups, resulted in community enclavement and compartmentalization and a breakdown of intercommunity ties, and led later historians and anthropologists to believe that the distinctions between southwestern native groups were more significant than similarities of economy, politics, and religion.

3. Late prehistoric and contact period populations in the central and northern Southwest were not uniformly sedentary, nor did they all reside in communities built in the characteristic pueblo style. They were, instead, an amalgam of both sedentary pueblo-dwellers *and* indigenous gatherer-hunters, a fact clearly reflected in contact period narratives written prior to A.D. 1600 (Upham 1982:35–51, 1984). This population structure has substantial implications for reconstructions that focus on regional interactive ties and the amity–enmity relationships that characterized different subregions of the central and northern Southwest prior to and during the years of initial Spanish contact.

4. Interdependent regional settlement systems were present during the late prehistoric period in the American Southwest and, although substantial organizational variability existed, hierarchical sociopolitical structures and managerial elite were present in more than a few of these systems (Lightfoot 1984; Upham 1982; Upham and Lightfoot 1988). Such organizational configurations facilitated high levels of interregional exchange (of various commodities). Exchange ties between communities and regions appear to have linked diverse populations in ways that transcended simple trading partner relationships.

The above interpretive position has met with some criticism. This is not surprising since many researchers continue to interpret the occupational history of very large pueblos as the seasonal refugia of small populations engaged in casual agriculture (Nichols and Powell 1987); or to apply directly the ethnographic Pueblo model (Reid 1985; Whittlesey 1978). In fact, the Southwest may be the only place in the New World where three archaeologists can look at exactly the same 2,000-room pueblo and conclude variously that it was (a) the seasonally occupied home of a highly mobile Puebloan population over a 250-year period, (b) a major population center whose affairs were managed by a hierarchically structured decision-making organization, or (c) a settlement exactly like Walpi.

This problem is beyond the scope of the present chapter, but it does bring to attention the existence of what we term historical imperialism in archaeological interpretation (see Upham 1988b).

In the remainder of the chapter, we treat each of the aforementioned points in the context of the late prehistoric and early contact periods. We focus on regional settlement structure and regional interaction during the two and one-half centuries preceding Spanish colonization, roughly from A.D. 1350 to 1600. The dramatic settlement changes that occurred in the central and northern Southwest during this time reflect not only the internal dynamics of Puebloan sociopolitical and economic systems, but also the catastrophic effects of initial Spanish contact.

Provinces, Alliances, and Settlement Clusters in Late Southwestern Prehistory

The central idea guiding the interpretive program alluded to above, in which larger, more heterogeneous organizational units are recognized, is that settlement organizations existed *at regional scales* in the Southwest during the late periods of prehistory. Moreover, these regional settlement systems are seen as coherent organizational units with formal interactive ties to other comparable units. Thus, the basic task of the new interpretive program is to identify regional settlement systems; all the specific details studied under the program will be examined with this end in mind, including restricted or differential access to certain classes of commodities, intensive agriculture, craft specialization, or any other organizational attribute one can identify. The reason for this approach is that we believe the *articulation* of large populations at regional scales gives rise to the distinctive characteristics anthropologists associate with increased organizational complexity (see Braun and Plog 1982). In this sense, restricted access to labor-intensive commodities, the intensification of agriculture, moves toward craft specialization, and other such processes may be considered epiphenomenal to the process of regional system formation. Consequently, we begin the chapter by (a) defining such systems, and (b) describing their extent during the late periods of prehistory in the central and northern Southwest.

A Notion of Regional Systems

The term *regional system* is now used by many Southwestern archaeologists to refer to both the spatial structure of settlements *and* the interactive ties that linked various settlements across a particular landscape. This conflation of settlement structure and interaction derives from one of the initial statements made concerning the method developed for regional analysis that was read widely by archaeologists (Smith 1976, 1978). Wilcox and Shenk (1977) adopt this combined usage in their description of the "Hohokam regional system," as do Judge and Schelberg (1984) in their discussion of a "Chacoan regional system." Operationally, such conflation may be heuristically useful, but for the purposes of this discussion we decouple settlement structure from interaction in describing regional southwestern systems. Thus, we use the terms *province* and *settlement cluster* to refer to aspects of settlement structure and the term *alliance* to refer to elements of interaction.

Provinces

Efforts to define spatial variation in the distribution of settlements at regional scales have a relatively long history in southwestern archaeology (Kidder 1924; McGregor 1965; Martin and Plog 1973; Willey 1953; Wormington 1947). Yet only within the last decade have archaeologists formalized this work in a fashion that now allows them to talk about discrete organizational units above the level of a single drainage or restricted geographic area (Cordell 1984; Hantman 1984; Lightfoot 1984; Plog 1979; Plog 1980; Riley 1987; Upham 1980, 1982; Wilcox 1981). Most explicit in this regard is Riley (1987:8), who uses the term *province* to describe "internally coherent units—tribal, town, or in at least one area, small statelets" during the sixteenth century in the Greater Southwest. Riley identifies seven large provinces in the area (see Figure 1-1), each of which encompasses between 30,000 and 50,000 km². His provinces are based on descriptions provided in contact period documents and thus probably come close to representing the Spanish view of native regional organization at the time of contact. Each province contains a number of "major centers" that were visited and described by the Spanish. Therefore Riley's provinces can serve as a historical baseline for comparing archaeological reconstructions.

Three of Riley's seven provinces are of direct relevance to the present discussion—Little Colorado, Rio Grande, and Pecos. Two of his conclusions are also germane to our argument: (1) Riley clearly demonstrates that at the time of first Spanish contact the Greater Southwest was an interaction sphere in which the major linkages between provinces were those created by trade, but which included other kinds of sociopolitical and religious contacts (1987:7); and (2) Riley recognizes that various hunting and gathering groups "filled the intersticies of the Greater Southwest," functioning as a "part of the larger polity to the extent that they were middlemen for [the] trade" network (1987:14).

The concept of *province* has also been used as an archaeological construct "to identify an area in which artifactual remains were sufficiently similar to suggest considerable exchange and interaction, but not a singular organizational entity such as a tribe" (Plog 1979:121 describing the work of Ruppé [1953]). Using this construct, Plog has identified 11 major archaeological provinces in the Western Anasazi zone of occupation, an area above the Mogollon Rim in Arizona that extends west into central-western New Mexico and north into southern Utah and Colorado (Figure 3-1). Plog's provinces range from 10,000 to 15,000 km², and are thus about one-third the size of Riley's sixteenth-century provinces. Much as Riley's formulation delimits the spatial structure of settlements at contact, Plog's analysis and reconstruction effectively bracket the spatial structure of the Western Anasazi region between A.D. 600 and 1300. The task that remains is to broaden the spatial coverage to include the Rio Grande and Pecos drain-

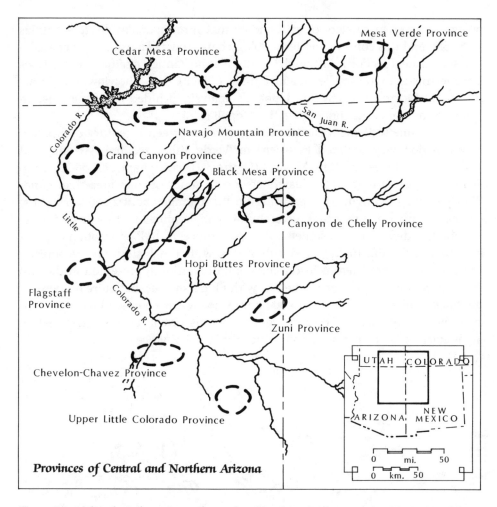

Figure 3-1. Archaeological provinces of central and northern Arizona as defined by Plog (1979:109).

ages, and to define regional settlement organization from roughly A.D. 1350 to contact.

Settlement Clusters

Efforts to define regional settlement organization during the fourteenth, fifteenth, and sixteenth centuries have been made by Kintigh (1985), Lightfoot (1984), and Upham (1982) for the Western Anasazi zone of occupation. In two of these studies, a key operational concept is that of *settlement cluster*, a quantitatively derived measure of spatial association whose terminological roots extend back to the work of Spicer (1962). Spicer used this term to refer to groups of proximate settlements (both pueblos and rancherías) that shared common threads of economy, religion, and politics and that were subject to the programs of enforced reduction employed by the Spanish. Upham adopted Spicer's terminology to refer to clusters of settlements that form spatially discrete entities (1982:58), and this concept and terminology have now been used in other analyses (see the next section). Although Lightfoot's and Kintigh's settlement analyses were restricted to the smaller spatial entities (Silver Creek–Showlow, and Zuni–Ramah–El Morro, respectively), Upham's analysis included all of the Western Anasazi zone of occupation above the Mogollon Rim.

Nine discrete settlement clusters representing fourteenth-century occupation in the region were defined between the Verde Valley (central Arizona) and Acoma (central-western New Mexico) (Figure 3-2; see Upham 1982:58-75). Map analysis suggests that these clusters covered a much smaller area than either Riley's or Plog's provinces, measuring on the average about 2,500 km². Thus, one can identify a conceptual hierarchy of spatial entities that begins with the quantitative definition of a settlement cluster, proceeds to Plog's notion of province (defined artifactually), and culminates with the historically recognized provinces of Riley. There is also a temporal dimension represented in the two different notions of province. It begins with Plog's smaller, but more numerous, provincial units (ca. 10,000 to 15,000 km²) prior to the fourteenth century and culminates with Riley's larger but less numerous provinces at contact. Settlement clusters are common to both conceptions of province.

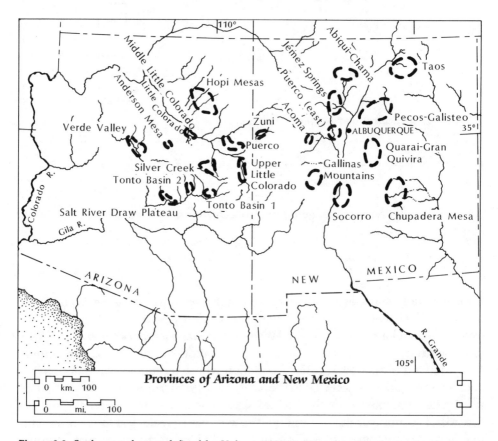

Figure 3-2. Settlement clusters defined by Upham (1982:58–75) and in this chapter for the central and northern Southwest.

During the three centuries before contact (and earlier), the overall pattern of settlement in the Western Anasazi region was one of settlement clusters. These clusters consisted of large pueblos (ca. 50 to 1,000 rooms) that were occupied for spans *averaging* 120 to 150 years (see Hantman 1984). Consequently, the configuration of settlement clusters during these three centuries changed considerably as various sites were built, occupied, and abandoned. However, our discussion of settlement clusters and provinces refers only to the latter part of this period, from A.D. 1350 to 1500. This 150-year period witnessed two notable developments: the formation of regional systems (especially at Zuni and in the northern Rio Grande and Pecos drainages) and, by A.D. 1500, their collapse in much of the Western Anasazi region.

One of the most interesting features of settlement organization across the plateau and montane Southwest during this time was that, despite the clustering of settlements, the distance between the clusters was strikingly regular (Upham 1982:117–119). Some archaeologists have complained that this conclusion regarding Southwestern spatial organization is based on an incomplete sample of settlements that fails to take into account the zone of occupation below the Mogollon Rim (McGuire 1983). However, a new analysis (Jewett 1988) utilizing the concept of settlement cluster covers a large area below the Mogollon Rim in Arizona that extends southeast into the Tonto Basin. Jewett defines three additional settlement clusters in this area (Salt River Draw Plateau and two in the Lower Tonto Basin). More important, however, she confirms that these newly defined settlement clusters encompass areas that rarely exceed 2,500 km² and that they are regularly spaced over the landscape at distances of 50 to 70 km. Moreover, Jewett correlates her findings with Upham's analysis of the Western Anasazi region, showing that settlement clusters both above and below the Mogollon Rim are, on the average, approximately 50 km from the nearest neighboring settlement cluster. She therefore concludes that "processes above and beyond the local level were operating to influence the location and distribution of large settlements across a wide region of the Southwest" (Jewett 1988:31).

Settlement Clusters in the Northern Rio Grande and Pecos Regions

Nearly all of the analyses of late fourteenth- and fifteenth-century regional settlement organization in the central and northern Southwest pertain to portions of the Colorado Plateaus in Arizona. Three notable exceptions are Kintigh's analysis of the Zuni region (1985), which revises substantially earlier ideas regarding Zuni settlement history (but see Upham 1988b), Earls's (1987) study of the Piro, and the work of Marshall and Wait (1984) in the Rio Abajo. However, significant archaeological research covers several key areas of central and northern New Mexico and thus makes it possible to evaluate the settlement cluster model in regions previously omitted from discussion. Predictions from Jewett's application of Upham's model of optimal settlement cluster spacing (i.e., 50 to 70 km to nearest neighboring settlement cluster), suggest that one can expect to find settlement clusters at regular intervals over central and northern New Mexico. Such predictions are, in fact, confirmed for a few regions. Using a model of equidistant spacing measured from Upham's Acoma settlement cluster (see Upham 1982:64-75), researchers have found similar clusters at 50 to 70 km intervals in the following areas: Jemez Springs (Elliot 1982), Abiquiu-Chama (Beal 1987), Albuquerque (Schroeder 1972, 1979), Taos (Schroeder 1972, 1979), and Pecos-Galisteo (Cordell 1984, 1986; Kidder and Shepard 1936; Nelson 1914). Additional settlement clusters occur south of Albuquerque, at Quarai-Gran Quivira east of the Rio Grande (Hayes 1981), and on the Rio Puerco (of the east) west of the Rio Grande (Hibben 1975). Another iteration of the model to the south reveals other settlement clusters located in the Gallinas Mountains (Cibola National Forest site files), at Socorro (Schroeder 1972, 1979), and on Chupadera Mesa (Beckett 1981; Wiseman 1986). These tentatively defined settlement clusters are shown in Figure 3-2.

Although it is clear that settlement clusters existed in these regions, little is yet known about their exact size and configuration, or their chronological position relative to other settlement clusters discussed in this chapter. However, existing information suggests late fourteenth- and fifteenth-century occupations for each of these areas.

Alliances

The notion that social factors operate to determine settlements is certainly not new. Social and economic geographers have been telling other social scientists this for the last several decades (e.g., Christaller 1966; Losch 1954; Zipf 1949), and some archaeologists have made significant discoveries using geographic models based on measures of social distance (e.g., Blanton 1975; Flannery 1976; Hammond 1974; Hodder and Orton 1976; Renfrew 1977; and others). Models based on social distance are derived from empirical studies that focus not only on the demands of market and transportation, but also on issues related to site catchment (see Vita-Finzi and Higgs 1970). Social distance models based on the latter concept are usually predicated on some notion of *minimum* distance between neighboring settlements and are driven by assumptions about the living space required to pursue subsistence needs without encountering undue competition. Social distance models based on the former concept, on the other hand, are usually predicated on notions of the *optimal* spacing required between settlements to facilitate the distribution of goods, services, and information. Each of these concepts of distance is founded on the notion that human interaction within and between neighboring populations must be managed. In this context, the spatial structure of precontact period populations in the central and northern Southwest, as reflected in a series of regularly spaced settlement clusters, assumes elementary meaning.

It is thus no coincidence that one of Riley's central concerns in his historical analysis of Southwestern provinces is to describe and explain the nature and extent of regional interaction, or that he amasses a considerable body of evidence to demonstrate the kinds of sociopolitical, economic, and religious ties that existed. The social character of the Southwest at contact, however, is not a proper analog to that of the previous century. Only Hopi, Zuni, and Acoma in the west and the Rio Grande and Pecos regions in the east were occupied during the period of initial Spanish exploration. Yet, as Riley shows, even after the consolidation of settlement, people all over the greater Southwest still "knew about each other" (1987:315) as a result of long-standing trading relationships and other forms of sociopolitical and economic interaction. Consequently, explaining the context of this interaction during the late fourteenth and fifteenth centuries becomes especially important as the central and northern Southwestwas, in a locational sense, "packed" with equidistantly spaced settlement clusters.

One of the most interesting, but controversial, attempts to contextualize the nature and extent of interaction during this period can be seen in the recent archaelogical studies concerned with the concept of *alliance* (Cordell and Plog 1979; Plog 1984; Upham 1980, 1982, 1987). Some of the controversy may stem from confusion over the anthropological baggage associated with this term, or from the way that it has been applied in interpretations of sociopolitical complexity in the Southwest. On the whole, however, the term *alliance* has been used in exactly the manner that formal alliance theorists have intended, and ideas that spring from the theory of alliance formation and generalized exchange (Levi Strauss 1969:233–310 passim) have been used by archaeologists to broaden discussions of regional system formation and connectivity between regions.

Levi-Strauss's ideas of generalized exchange include both the more conspicuous exchange of marriage partners and also, at a higher and more inclusive level, the exchange of all forms of material *and* information. In fact, his elucidation of alliance formation and generalized exchange is embedded in a conception of information theory that includes both material and nonmaterial (read symbolic) dimensions. Consequently, when a claim is made that an alliance of fourteenth-century settlement clusters "may have involved the establishment of affinal kin ties, the transmission of esoteric knowledge, and the exchange of . . . material" (Upham 1982:157), that claim rests on correlations in archaeological data used in conjunction with a structuralist definition of the alliance concept.

The alliance concept is used in a similar way by Plog, who describes an alliance in relation to the "mechanisms that unite inhabitants of social networks" (1984:218). For Plog, the essential mechanisms of integration "typically come to involve central sites, homogeneous architectural and ceramic styles, specialized production, evidence of trade and exchange, and, in some instances, evidence of ranking and stratification" (ibid.). Plog goes on to point out that both he and Upham have defined alliances in "the extreme circumstance of highly integrated social entities, in which local social networks cease to play a major function," although less complex alliance structures are also recognized. This latter point, for example, is illustrated by Upham, who argues that the fourteenth-century alliance system did not "provide a supraordinate political organization capable of integrating the entire Western Pueblo zone of occupation. Rather, the spatial and organizational data . . . suggest that each settlement cluster was a relatively autonomous political unit, and the political structure of each varied in complexity" (1982:157).

For archaeologists, the foundation of the alliance concept is the ability to demonstrate that persistent, high levels of exchange and interaction took place over a wide region, and that such exchange involved the transmission of specialized commodities that may not have been available to all members of a given population. The inference that mate exchange and the transmission of information took place in conjunction with the exchange of goods is based on (a) an incredibly large number of ethnographic case examples in which long-term, persistent material exchanges are accompanied by the exchange of marriage partners (see Levi-Strauss 1969), and (b) the fact that the exchange of information is embedded in overt and covert stylistic messages contained in the goods themselves (see Plog 1980; Wiessner 1983; Wobst 1974; 1977). Such stylistic messages are contained both in the design and form of commodities, and—as Wobst, Plog, and Wiessner have shown—can function as symbols to demarcate group identity. DeBoer (1984) has demonstrated the ease with which many such components of design travel, and has modeled boundary effects based on design varibility. Such boundaries have clear implications for the formation and maintenance of alliances.

The primary data upon which claims of alliance are made in the Southwest are ceramic in nature, and Upham (1982) has used a small sample of ceramics from a variety of fourteenth-century sites to describe one major alliance network, the Jeddito Alliance, which linked settlement clusters across the Colorado Plateaus from the Verde Valley to Acoma. This alliance was defined by the distribution of a highly distinctive ceramic style and technology, Jeddito Yellow Ware. Upham also postulated the existence of a Salado Alliance that encompassed populations residing in the Salt and Gila drainages and their major tributaries. This alliance was hypothesized on the basis of the widespread distribution of the Salado Polychromes, and Jewett's recent analysis defining three major settlement clusters in the region tends to support this notion.

Critics of the alliance-by-ceramic-distribution concept might argue that both Jeddito and Salado wares had multiple production loci, and may not have been as widely exchanged as once believed. The existence of multiple production loci has been demonstrated for ceramic types in each of these ware groups (Danson and Wallace 1956; Bishop et al. 1988). In the case of Jeddito Yellow, characterization of the paste of a large pottery assemblage from fourteenth- and fifteenth-century sites near the Hopi Mesas has revealed two highly distinctive chemical signatures that appear to be site specific. These signatures seem to identify production loci at Kawaika-a and Awatovi (Bishop et al. 1988). The same analytical techniques have been used to characterize pottery recovered from sites away from the Hopi Mesas. This preliminary analysis has shown that pottery with the distinctive Kawaika-a and Awatovi signatures is present in the ceramic assemblage from Pottery Mound, a major site in the Rio Puerco (of the east) settlement cluster (see Bishop et al. 1988). Widespread exchange, albeit at low levels, thus appears to link individual settlements, and possibly settlement clusters, over substantial distances. Other site-specific signatures appear to be present in the Hopi Mesa assemblage, and future work by Bishop and his colleagues is certain to provide additional information on the production/distribution sequences for this ware group.

More important than the verification of ceramic exchange, however, is the clear and unambiguous demonstration that information sharing occurred at a supraordinate level, and appears to have transcended the sphere of material exchange. Huse (1976) has undertaken a stylistic analysis of the Jeddito Yellow Ware assemblage from the site of Kawaika-a. A large subset of these vessels exhibit the distinctive Kawaika-a chemical signature. She found a series of unique exterior motifs that were specific to this Kawaika-a assemblage. Interestingly, an identical exterior motif has been identified on a Jeddito vessel from the site of Nuvakwewtaqa, a large pueblo located more than 100 km to the south in the Anderson Mesa settlement cluster. What makes this identification especially important is that *it occurs on a vessel that does not exhibit the distinctive Kawaika-a chemical signature.* In other words, the transmission of this stylistic (symbolic) information was fundamentally independent of direct exchange with Kawaika-a (see Bishop et al. 1988:28). Rather, the information content of the exterior motif circulated independently of ceramics made at Kawaika-a.

The transmission of the stylistic information that is independent of direct material exchange over a large area suggests that different spheres of exchange operated within and between settlements and settlement clusters. Emulation of design styles, as appears to be the case with the Kawaika-a exterior motif, would appear to signal information sharing and connectivity between groups, especially when one considers the potential spatial distribution of these materials across the Colorado Plateaus. Thus, given either multiple production centers with more restricted material exchange *or* specialized manufacture at a few locations and widespread exchange, alliances between groups occupying widely separated localities seem likely.

Exchange and Alliances in the Fifteenth-Century Northern Rio Grande

Given that settlement clusters can be defined over much of the central and northern Southwest and that widespread ceramic styles tie together and demarcate at least two broad stylistic regions of the Colorado Plateaus and Mogollon Rim country of Arizona, what evidence exists to suggest that other ceramic styles might demarcate similar entities in central and northern New Mexico?

Preliminary distributional analyses suggest that at least two major stylistic zones can be defined in the area encompassed by settlement clusters in the northern Rio Grande and Pecos regions. These stylistic zones are defined by Biscuit and Glaze ware ceramics, respectively. The distribution of these distinctive ceramics coincides approximately with different groups of settlement clusters, although some overlap is present. Biscuit ware pottery occurs primarily in the Abiquiú-Chama and Jemez Springs settlement clusters, whereas Rio Grande Glaze wares, especially Glazes A through C, are found in the assemblages of all the other settlement clusters, sometimes as the dominant bichrome or polychrome type. This distributional pattern was first recognized by A. V. Kidder (1915), who noted that Biscuit wares had a more northern distribution than Glaze wares. He noted further that Biscuit and Glaze wares were differentially distributed on large sites, the Biscuit wares being predominant on large sites of the Pajarito Plateau such as Otowi, Tsanankowi, and Tschirege, and Glaze wares being more common on large pueblos such as Puye, Tyounyi, and Yapashi. Kidder speculated about the origin of these broad stylistic zones, but concluded that more work was needed to resolve these complex distributional patterns. Unfortunately, such work has not yet been completed. However, previous physicochemical characterization of these wares (Honea 1973; Shepard 1942; Warren 1970, 1979) has suggested probable production loci and the extent of exchange during the fourteenth and fifteenth centuries. More recently, Reed (1988) has conducted additional source work on the Rio Grande Glaze wares using X-ray diffractometry. The following discussion builds on all of this work.

The ceramic tradition that developed in the Jemez Springs and Abiquiú-Chama settlement clusters during the fourteenth century mimicked the Glaze ware tradition in several important ways, but visually was a very different kind of pottery. The Biscuit wares—Abiquiú Black-on-gray (Biscuit A) and Bandelier Black-on-gray (Biscuit B)—consist of a thick, friable paste and a grayish slip with carbon paint decoration (Cordell 1979; Honea 1973). The Glaze wares, on the other hand, have a slip that varies from red to yellow (depending on the period of manufacture) and a lead-based paint or glaze. These latter ceramics were produced primarily in the Albuquerque and Pecos-Galisteo settlement clusters. Together, the distribution of these two distinctive wares appears to link sites and settlement clusters through exchange and information sharing.

The distinctive spatial distributions of these ware groups (the highest concentrations occur in core areas surrounding the zones of production) provide evidence of stylistic boundaries and interaction between populations occupying sites in the different production zones. Some Biscuit ware is found on sites in the Pecos, Galisteo Basin, and Albuquerque settlement clusters; and some Rio Grande Glaze ware occurs on sites in the Abiquiú-Chama and Jemez Springs settlement clusters. As in the Western Pueblo region, however, the sharing of stylistic elements appears more important than the exchange of ceramic items themselves. In this case, the two ceramic traditions obviously shared stylistic information. As Honea (1973) notes, "such an interaction was not without consequences, for some design elements, rim and even vessel forms came to be shared between the two areas." The kind of stylistic fusion described by Honea was not limited solely to the stylistic syncretism between Biscuit and Glaze wares. Strong stylistic continuity, for example, is apparent between the glaze traditions of the Little Colorado and Zuni areas and the Glaze wares of the Rio Grande (Cordell 1979, 1984; Honea 1973; Snow 1982; Wendorf and Reed 1955). In fact, researchers have suggested that the development of the Rio Grande Glaze ware tradition was stimulated by the appearance in the northern Rio Grande of trade wares like St. Johns Polychrome, Pinedale Glaze-on-Red, and Heshotauthla Polychrome. Honea (1973:80) argues further that Western-inspired design elements and layouts were frequently employed on early Rio Grande Glaze pottery. The Zuni and Little Colorado Glaze ware traditions offered a radical departure for Rio Grande potters: The pottery consisted of red-slipped wares fired in an oxidizing atmosphere, as opposed to the reduced firing atmosphere of black-on-white wares that were produced up to that time in the northern Rio Grande (Honea 1973).

One result of the interaction and trade with groups living to the west at Zuni and in the Little Colorado settlement clusters was that glaze-decorated ceramics began to be made in the Rio Grande region, and replaced black-on-white ceramics in many areas. However, this replacement was not uniform. Glaze pottery did not replace the Biscuit wares in the Jemez and Abiquiú-Chama settlement clusters (Cordell 1979; Honea 1973; Warren 1979). Moreover, between Zuni and the Rio Grande Valley, a new glaze type began to be produced. Mera (1935) has defined this pottery as Los Padillas ware. As Warren (1979:189) notes, "the Los Padillas ware is not well dated, but is found with Galisteo Black-on-white, Santa Fe Black-on-white, St. John's Polychrome, and Heshotauthla Polychrome, placing it within the early decades of the 14th century." Thus, from the Little Colorado settlement clusters to those of the Pecos-Galisteo, technological developments and stylistic innovation occurred on highly distinctive ceramic wares. Although more analyses need to be completed, it is also apparent that substantial stylistic fusion and syncretism occurred.

As we noted previously, the foundation of the alliance concept rests in the demonstration of high levels of interaction and trade, and in the differential distribution of specialized commodities that may not have been available to all members of a given population. Because our analyses are preliminary, we cannot demonstrate that the above conditions are satisfied for the Biscuit and Glaze wares. Although the work of Shepard (1942) and Warren (1970, 1979) has clearly established restricted zones of production and widespread exchange for the Rio Grande Glazes, we do not yet know enough about the distributional characteristics of this pottery at the intrasite level to offer a conclusion about the existence of alliance networks. One tentative conclusion that can be drawn from the ceramic stylistic and distributional data, however, is that style zones in the northern Rio Grande appear less pronounced than those defined by Jeddito Yellow Ware or the Salado Polychromes.

Part of the reason that these style zones are less clearly defined may be that the production of the Glaze wares shifted from one center to another. Glaze A-red, the earliest Rio Grande Glaze, appears to have been produced at such sites as Cochiti, San Felipe, Los Lunas, or Pottery Mound (Warren 1970), near the modern city of Albuquerque. This glaze type was traded to the Pecos-Galisteo, Jemez Springs, and Abiquiú-Chama settlement clusters, as well as to regions further south. For example, ceramic assemblages from sites in the Quarai–Gran Quivira, Gallinas Mountains, Socorro, and Chupadero Mesa settlement clusters contain predominantly Glaze A ceramics until the beginning of the sixteenth century (Snow 1982). Glaze A ceramics are also found in the Jornada Mogollon region of southern New Mexico, especially at Lincoln phase sites in the Sierra Blanca area (Kelly 1984), at sites near Socorro (Cordell and Earls 1984), and at El Paso phase sites near Las Cruces (Lehmer 1948).

By the mid-fifteenth century, however, the Pecos-Galisteo settlement cluster had become the primary producer of glaze pottery. In contrast to the Glaze

A-red pottery of the Albuquerque region, the pottery made in this settlement cluster had a highly distinctive yellow-slipped glaze. These are the types we refer to today as Glazes A-yellow, Glaze B, and Glaze C (Mera 1933, 1940). According to Warren (1970, 1979), San Marcos Pueblo in the Galisteo Basin was the major producer of the yellow-slipped wares. It is interesting to note that, during the height of yellow-slipped Glaze ware production in the Galisteo Basin, these types were not traded as extensively to sites immediately to the south as was Glaze A-red (Snow 1982). However, these yellow-slipped Glaze wares were traded to areas much farther afield in Mexico. Weigand (1976, 1979), for example, notes that sherds of Largo Glaze-on-yellow and Largo Glaze-polychrome were found in the citadel area of the Atitlan–Las Cuevas site in Jalisco, Mexico.

Conclusion

At the beginning of this chapter, we stated that we would discuss late prehistoric regional settlement systems in the central and northern American Southwest. To accomplish this task, we have expanded upon earlier analyses and have shown that settlement clusters existed over most of the study area during the fourteenth and fifteenth centuries. The distribution of these settlement clusters reveals a pattern of equidistant spacing at intervals between 50 and 70 km. Our interpretation of this pattern emphasizes sociopolitical and economic factors, especially as they relate to the management of human interaction.

We also said that our discussion would be about the social, political, and economic organizations that characterized these regional systems, about regionally organized systems of exchange, symbolic interaction, and sociopolitical complexity. We have approached these issues tangentially through the concept of *alliance*. Although such an abstract notion is difficult to pin to archaeological data, we believe that the expectations of the alliance concept are satisfied by the minimal distributional and stylistic data presently available in some areas. Our conclusions about alliances are stated more strongly for settlement clusters in the Western Pueblo region. Too little contemporary work has been done at large sites in the northern Rio Grande area to provide a sound basis for inference on this issue.

It is clear that systems of regional exchange operated at different intensities throughout the central and northern Southwest during the two and one-half centuries preceding contact. It is also clear that these systems were characterized by different spheres of exchange in which both material and information (and probably people) circulated. During the early fifteenth century, high levels of interregional commerce characterized the study area. In addition, the evidence of information sharing between widely separated groups is undeniable. Snow (1982:251), for example, has discussed a parallel developmental sequence for polychrome glaze pottery that links groups from the Mogollon Rim to the Rio Grande. We believe that equally broad connections between the yellow pottery traditions of the fourteenth and fifteenth centuries link populations from the Hopi Mesas to the Galisteo Basin. Such a linkage may, in part, explain why populations from the Galisteo fled to Hopi following the Pueblo Revolt in 1680. The ideological significance of the yellow ware tradition may be linked to points further south, to motifs of the *awanyu* (plumed serpent) and parrot that occur on many different fifteenth-century ceramic wares. That stirrup jars, rectangular bowls, and cylindrical jars—all Mesoamerican vessel forms—also appear with these motifs reinforces the inference about external connections.

A final point that we did not touch upon in this discussion, but that is implicit in our argument, has to do with the catastrophic consequences of European contact and colonization on the native system of interacting regional settlement clusters. The distribution of contemporaneous large sites during the fifteenth century suggests that sizable populations were present in the central and northern Southwest. In many of these regions, the prehistory of the 50 years immediately preceding and immediately following contact is unknown. In areas where archaeological investigations have taken place, like the Chama (Beal 1987) or Zuni (Kintigh 1985), an extremely turbulent settlement history is revealed for this 100-year period. The lesson learned from other New World areas where better textual and archaeological data exist is that the initial consequences of contact for aboriginal populations were catastrophic (see, for example, Gibson 1964; Ramenofsky 1987). Our data on settlement structure and regional interaction suggest that a comprehensive social, political, economic, and demographic collapse will be identified as more work is done on this critical time period in the Southwest, and will be linked directly or indirectly to the presence of Europeans.

References

Beal, John D.
   1987 *Foundations of the Rio Grande Classic: The Lower Chama River* A.D. *1300–1500*. Southwest Project No. 137. Southwest Archaeological Consultants, Inc.
Beckett, Patrick
   1981 *An Archaeological Survey and Assessment of Gran Quivira National Monument, New Mexico*. Report prepared for the National Park Service, Southwest Region. Cultural Resources Management Division, Department of Sociology/Anthropology, New Mexico State University, Las Cruces, N. Mex.
Bishop, Ronald L., Valetta Canouts, Suzanne P. De Atley, Alfred Qoyawayma, and C. W. Aikins
   1988 The Formation of Ceramic Analytical Groups: Hopi Pottery Production and Exchange, A.D. 1300–1600. Ms. in possession of the authors.
Blanton, Richard E.
   1975 The Cybernetic Analysis of Human Population Growth. *Memoirs of the Society for American Archaeology* 30:116–126.
Braun, David P., and Stephen Plog
   1982 Evolution of "Tribal" Social Networks: Theory and Prehistoric North American Evidence. *American Antiquity* 47(3):504–525.
Christaller, W.
   1966 *Central Places in Southern Germany*, translated by C. W. Baskin. Prentice-Hall, Englewood Cliffs, N.J.
Cordell, Linda S.
   1979 *A Cultural Resources Overview of the Middle Rio Grande Valley, New Mexico*. USDA Forest Service, Southwestern Region, Albuquerque, N. Mex.
   1984 *Prehistory of the Southwest*. Academic Press, New York.

1986 Rowe Archaeological Research Project Final Report. Submitted to the National Science Foundation, Washington, D.C.

Cordell, Linda S., and Amy C. Earls
1984 The Rio Grande Glaze "Sequence" and the Mogollon. In *Recent Research in Mogollon Archaeology*, edited by S. Upham, F. Plog, D. Batcho, and B. Kauffman, pp. 90–97. University Museum Occasional Paper No. 10. New Mexico State University, Las Cruces, N. Mex.

Cordell, Linda S., and Fred Plog
1979 Escaping the Confines of Normative Thought: A Reevaluation of Puebloan Prehistory. *American Antiquity* 44(3):405–429.

Danson, Edward B., and Robert S. Wallace
1956 A Petrographic Study of Gila Polychrome. *American Antiquity* 22(2):180–183.

DeBoer, Warren R.
1984 The Last Pottery Show: System and Sense in Ceramic Studies. In *The Many Dimensions of Pottery: Ceramics in Archaeology and Anthropology*, edited by S. E. Vander Leeuw, pp. 529–568. University of Amsterdam Press, Amsterdam.

Earls, A.
1987 *An Archaeological Assessment of Las Huertas, Socorro*. Papers of the Maxwell Museum No. 3. Albuquerque.

Elliot, Michael L.
1982 *Large Pueblo Sites near Jemez Springs, New Mexico*. Cultural Resources Report 3. Santa Fe National Forest, Santa Fe, N. Mex.

Flannery, Kent V.
1976 *The Early Mesoamerican Village*. Academic Press, New York.

Gibson, Charles
1964 *The Aztecs under Spanish Rule: A History of the Indians of the Valley of Mexico, 1519–1810*. Stanford University Press, Stanford, Calif.

Hammond, Norman
1974 The Distribution of Late Classic Maya Major Ceremonial Centers in the Central Area. In *Mesoamerican Archaeology: New Approaches*, edited by Norman Hammond, pp. 313–334. University of Texas Press, Austin.

Hantman, Jeffrey L.
1984 *Social Networks and Stylistic Distribution in the Prehistoric Plateau Southwest*. Ph.D dissertation, Arizona State University. University Microfilms, Ann Arbor.

Hayes, Alden C.
1981 *Contributions to Gran Quivira Archaeology, Gran Quivira Monument, New Mexico*. Publications in Archaeology 17. National Park Service, Washington, D.C.

Hibben, Frank C.
1975 *Kiva Art of the Anasazi at Pottery Mound*, K. C. Publications, Las Vegas, Nev.

Hodder, Ian, and Clive Orton
1976 *Spatial Analysis in Archaeology*. Cambridge University Press, Cambridge.

Honea, Kenneth
1973 The Technology of Eastern Pueblo Pottery on the Llano Estacado. *Plains Anthropologist* 18(59):73–88.

Huse, Hannah
1976 *Identification of the Individual in Archaeology: A Case Study from the Prehistoric Hopi Site of Kawaika-a*. Ph.D. dissertation, University of Colorado at Boulder. Ann Arbor: University Microfilms.

Jewett, Roberta
1988 Distance, Interaction, and Complexity: A Pan-Regional Comparison of the Spatial Organization of Fourteenth Century Settlement Clusters in the American Southwest. In *Sociopolitical Structure of Prehistoric Southwest Society*, edited by S. Upham and K. Lightfoot. Westview Press, Boulder, in press.

Judge, W. James, and John D. Schelberg (editors)
1984 *Recent Research on Chaco Prehistory.* Reports of the Chaco Center No. 8. Division of Cultural Resources, National Park Service, Albuquerque, N. Mex.

Kelley, Jane H.
1984 *The Archaeology of the Sierra Blanca Region of Southeastern New Mexico.* Anthropological Papers No. 74. Museum of Anthropology, University of Michigan, Ann Arbor.

Kidder, Alfred V.
1915 Pottery of the Pajarito Plateau and of Some Adjacent Regions in New Mexico. *Memoirs of the American Anthropological Association* 2(6):407–462.
1924 *An Introduction to the Study of Southwestern Archaeology, with a Preliminary Account of the Excavation at Pecos.* Papers of the Southwest Expedition 5. Yale University Press, New Haven, Conn.

Kidder, Alfred V., and Anna O. Shepard
1936 *The Pottery of Pecos, Volume 2.* Papers of Phillips Academy Southwest Expedition, No. 17, New Haven, Conn.

Kintigh, Keith W.
1985 *Settlement, Subsistence, and Society in Late Zuni Prehistory.* Anthropological Papers No. 44, University of Arizona Press, Tucson.

Lehmer, D. J.
1948 *The Jornada Branch of the Mogollon.* Social Science Bulletin 17. University of Arizona Bulletin 19(2), Tucson.

Levi-Strauss, Claude
1969 *The Elementary Structures of Kinship.* Beacon Press, Boston.

Lightfoot, Kent
1984 *Prehistoric Political Dynamics: A Case Study from the American Southwest.* Northern Illinois University Press, Dekalb, Ill.

Losch, A.
1954 *The Economics of Location,* translated by H. Stolpher. Yale University Press, New Haven, Conn.

McGregor, John C.
1965 *Southwestern Archaeology.* University of Illinois Press, Urbana.

McGuire, Randall H.
1983 Review of *Polities and Power: An Economic and Political History of the Western Pueblos,* by Steadman Upham. *American Antiquity* 48(3):651–652.

Marshall, M. P., and H. J. Wait
1984 *Rio Abajo: Prehistory and History of a Rio Grande Province.* New Mexico Historical Preservation Program, Santa Fe.

Martin, Paul Sidney, and Fred Plog
1973 *The Archaeology of Arizona.* Doubleday/Natural History Press, Garden City, N.Y.

Mera, H. P.
1933 *A Proposed Revision of the Rio Grande Glaze Paint Sequence.* Technical Series Bulletin No. 5. Laboratory of Anthropology, Santa Fe, N. Mex.
1935 *Ceramic Clues to the Prehistory of North Central New Mexico.* Technical Series Bulletin No. 8. Laboratory of Anthropology, Santa Fe, N. Mex.
1940 *Population Changes in the Rio Grande Glaze-paint Area.* Technical Series Bulletin No. 9. Laboratory of Anthropology, Santa Fe, N. Mex.

Nelson, Nels C.
1914 *Pueblo Ruins of the Galisteo Basin, New Mexico.* Anthropological Papers of the American Museum of Natural History, New York. 15(1).

Nichols, Deborah L., and Shirley Powell
1987 Demographic Reconstructions in the American Southwest: Alternative Behavioral Means to the Same Archaeological Ends. *The Kiva* 52(3):193–205.

Plog, Fred
  1979 Alternate Models of Prehistoric Change. In *Transformations, Mathematical Approaches to Culture Change*, edited by Colin Renfrew and Kenneth L. Cooke, pp. 221–236. Academic Press, New York.
  1984 Exchange, Tribes, and Alliances: The Northern Southwest. *American Archaeologist* 4(3):217–223.
Plog, Stephen
  1980 *Stylistic Variation in Prehistoric Ceramics: Design Analysis in the American Southwest*. Cambridge University Press, Cambridge.
Ramenofsky, Ann
  1987 *Vectors of Death: the Archaeology of European Contact*. University of New Mexico Press, Albuquerque.
Reed, Lori Stephens
  1988 X-ray Diffraction Analysis of Glaze Painted Ceramics from the Northern Rio Grande Region, New Mexico: Implications of Glazeware Production and Exchange. Master's Thesis Proposal submitted to the Department of Sociology/Anthropology, New Mexico State University, Las Cruces, N. Mex.
Reff, Daniel T.
  1986 *The Demographic and Cultural Consequences of Old World Disease in the Greater Southwest, 1520–1660*. University Microfilms, Ann Arbor.
Reid, J. J.
  1985 A Grasshopper Perspective on the Mountain Mogollon. Paper Presented at the Advanced Seminar, 1985. Society of American Archaeology.
Renfrew, Colin
  1977 Alternative Models for Exchange and Spatial Distribution. In *Exchange Systems in Prehistory*, edited by Timothy K. Earle and Jonathan E. Ericson, pp. 71–90. Academic Press, New York.
Riley, Carroll L.
  1987 *The Frontier People: The Greater Southwest in the Protohistoric Period*. University of New Mexico Press, Albuquerque.
Schroeder, Albert H.
  1972 Rio Grande Ethnohistory. In *New Perspectives on the Pueblos*, edited by Alfonso Ortiz, pp. 41–70. University of New Mexico Press, Albuquerque.
  1979 Pueblos Abandoned in Historic Times. In *Southwest*, edited by Alfonso Ortiz, pp. 236–254. Handbook of North American Indians, vol. 9, William C. Sturtevant, general editor. Smithsonian Institution, Washington, D.C.
Shepard, Anna O.
  1942 *Rio Grande Glaze Paint Ware: A Study Illustrating the Place of Ceramic Technological Analysis in Archaeological Research*. Contributions to American Anthropology and History, No. 39.
Smith, C. A.
  1976 *Regional Analysis in Archaeology*, vol. 1. Academic Press, New York.
  1978 *Regional Analysis in Archaeology*, vol. 2. Academic Press, New York.
Snow, David
  1982 The Rio Grande Glaze, Matte-paint, and Plainware Tradition. In *Southwestern Ceramics: A Comparative Review*, edited by A. H. Schroeder, pp. 235–278. A School of American Research Advanced Seminar. The Arizona Archaeologist, Arizona Archaeological Society.
Spicer, Edward H.
  1962 *Cycles of Conquest*. University of Arizona Press, Tucson.
Upham, Steadman
  1980 *Political Continuity and Change in the Plateau Southwest*. Ph.D. dissertation, Department of Anthropology, Arizona State University.

1982 *Polities and Power: An Economic and Political History of the Western Pueblo.* Academic Press, New York.

1983 Intensification and Exchange: An Evolutionary Model of Nonegalitarian Sociopolitical Organization for the Prehistoric Plateau Southwest. In *Ecological Models in Economic Prehistory*, edited by G. Bronitsky, pp. 219–245. Anthropological Research Paper No. 39, Arizona State University, Tempe.

1984 Adaptive Diversity and Southwestern Abandonment. *Journal of Anthropological Research.* 40(2):235–256.

1986 Smallpox and Climate in the American Southwest. *American Anthropologist* 88(1):115–127.

1987 The Tyranny of Ethnographic Analogy. In *Coasts, Deserts, and Plains: Papers in Honor of Reynold J. Ruppe*, edited by S. Gaines and G. A. Clark, pp. 265–280. Anthropological Research Paper No. 38. Arizona State University, Tempe.

1988a East Meets West: Hierarchy and Elites in Pueblo Society. In *The Sociopolitical Structure of Prehistoric Southwest Societies*, edited by S. Upham and K. G. Lightfoot. Westview Press, Boulder, Colorado, in press.

1988b Review of *Settlement, Subsistence, and Society in Late Zuni Prehistory*, by Keith W. Kintigh. *North American Archaeologist* 9(1):78–80.

Upham, Steadman, and Fred Plog
1986 The Interpretation of Prehistoric Political Complexity in the Central and Northern Southwest: Toward a Mending of the Models. *Journal of Field Archaeology* 13(2)223–238.

Upham, Steadman, and Kent Lightfoot
1988 *Sociopolitical Structure of Prehistoric Southwestern Society.* Westview Press, Boulder, Colorado, in press.

Vita-Finzi, C., and E. S. Higgs
1970 Prehistoric economy in the Mt. Carmel area of Palestine: Site catchment analysis. *Proceedings of the Prehistoric Society* 36:1–37.

Warren, Helene
1970 Notes on Manufacture and Trade of Rio Grande Glazes. *The Artifact* 8(4):1–7.

1979 The Glaze Paint Wares of the Upper Middle Rio Grande. In *Adaptive Change in the Northern Rio Grande Valley*, edited by J. V. Biella and R. C. Chapman, pp. 187–216. Archaeological Investigations in Cochiti Reservoir, New Mexico, vol. 4. Office of Contract Archaeology, Department of Anthropology, University of New Mexico.

Weigand, Phil C.
1976 Rio Grande Glaze Sherds in Western Mexico. *Pottery Southwest* 4(1)3–6.

1979 Largo Glaze Polychromes in Western Mexico. *Pottery Southwest* 6(4):2–3.

Wendorf, Fred, and Erik K. Reed
1955 An Alternative Reconstruction of Northern Rio Grande Prehistory. *El Palacio* 62:131–173.

Whittlesey, Stephanie M.
1978 *Status and Death at Grasshopper Pueblo: Experiments toward an Archaeological Theory of Correlates.* Ph.D. dissertation, Department of Anthropology, University of Arizona, Tucson.

Wiessner, Polly
1983 Style and Social Information in Kalahari San Projectile Points. *American Antiquity* 48:253–276.

Wilcox, David R.
1981 Changing Perspectives in the Protohistoric Pueblos, A.D. 1450–1700. In *The Protohistoric Periods in the North American Southwest, A.D. 1450–1700*, edited by David R. Wilcox and W. Bruce Masse, pp. 378–409. Research Paper No. 24. Arizona State University, Tempe.

Wilcox, David R., and Lynette O. Shenk
  1977 *The Architecture of the Casa Grande and Its Interpretation.* Archaeological Series No. 115. Arizona State Museum, University of Arizona, Tucson.
Willey, Gordon R.
  1953 *Prehistoric Settlement Patterns in the Viru Valley, Peru.* Bulletin of the Bureau of American Ethnology, No. 155, Washington, D.C.
Wiseman, Regge N.
  1986 *An Initial Study of the Origins of Chupadero Black-on-White.* Archaeological Society Technical Note No. 2, Albuquerque, New Mexico.
Wobst, H. M.
  1974 Boundary Conditions for Paleolithic Social Systems: A Simulation Approach. *American Antiquity* 39(2):145–178.
  1977 Stylistic Behavior and Information Exchange. In *Papers for the Director: Research Essays in Honor of James B. Griffin,* edited by C. E. Cleland, pp. 317–342. Anthropological Papers No. 61. Museum of Anthropology, University of Michigan, Ann Arbor.
Wormington, H. M.
  1947 *Prehistoric Indians of the Southwest.* Popular Series No. 7. Denver Museum of Natural History, Denver, Colo.
Zipf, G. K.
  1949 *Human Behavior and the Principle of Least Effort.* Harvard University Press, Cambridge, Mass.

Chapter 4 ■

E. Charles Adams

Passive Resistance: Hopi Responses to Spanish Contact and Conquest

The Hopi are the westernmost group of the Pueblo Indians. They speak a Uto-Aztecan language and inhabit the arid Colorado Plateau of northeastern Arizona in villages located about 120 km north of present-day Flagstaff. During the Spanish contact period, the Hopi occupied an area 65 km wide and 50 km long. They have lived in or near the same villages for 600 years or more, and their roots can be traced back at least another 1,200 years by archaeologists.

Today the Hopi are a homogeneous people. In the past, however, they frequently absorbed people of different backgrounds. The Hopi currently number about 10,000, and of this group about 8,000 live on the reservation in 12 villages (Figure 4-1). Since about 1300, the people have lived in multiple-story villages of square or rectangular rooms arranged in rows around plazas. These plazas are the foci for the day-to-day activities and for public ceremonies from April to November. The rooms are used for secular and ceremonial activities. As with all Pueblo groups, the kiva is the center of ritual. The seven traditional Hopi villages are Walpi, Sichomovi, and Hano on First Mesa; Shungopavi, Mishongnovi, and Shipaulovi on Second Mesa; and Oraibi on Third Mesa. All were built before 1700 except for Sichomovi, which dates to the early eighteenth century.

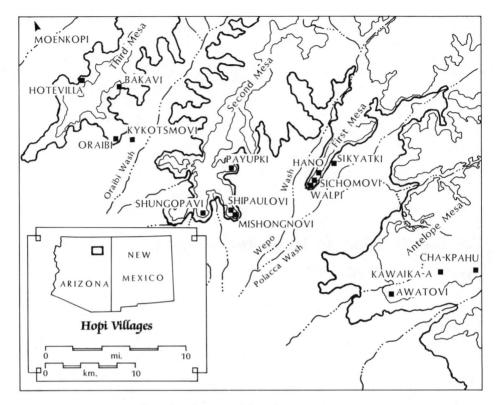

Figure 4-1. Major Hopi villages (northeastern Arizona).

The Hopi were never dominated by Spanish culture in their 280 years of contact. During the missionary period from 1629 to 1680, the Spaniards attempted to subjugate the Hopi people, but failed. After the Pueblo Revolt of 1680, the Spaniards never seriously attempted to subjugate the Hopi again and in fact treated the occupants of the Hopi Mesas as more or less an independent nation. How the Hopi were able to achieve and maintain this independence is the subject of this chapter.

Environment

Until 1700 the Hopi occupied four mesas that are actually southern spurs of Black Mesa (Figure 4-1). From west to east, the Hopi Mesas are called Third (West), Second (Middle), First (East), and Antelope Mesa. The area around the Hopi Mesas provides extensive and diverse resources—arable land; springs; plant, animal, and mineral resources—and physical isolation from competing cultural systems. Throughout the Spanish period, this area served as a natural buffer between the Hopi and nearby aggregated settlements, the nearest of which were the Zuni pueblos 150 km southeast. This isolation also played a significant role in blunting the Spanish program for the Hopi villages.

Documentary Evidence

Information on the relations between the Hopi and the Spaniards comes from three sources: Spanish documents, archaeological data, and Hopi oral history. Most Spanish visits to the Hopi country were chronicled. Many of these records have been located, translated, and published (Brew 1949b; Coues 1900; Hackett 1937; Scholes 1929; Spicer 1967; Thomas 1969), and the documented contacts have been listed chronologically (Dockstader 1954).

Archaeological data on Hopi villages of the Spanish period come from only two sources: the excavations at Awatovi and at Walpi. The Peabody Museum of Harvard University spent parts of five years, 1935–1939, excavating at Awatovi. The Spanish period, roughly 1629–1700 at Awatovi, is documented in *Franciscan Awatovi* (Montgomery et al. 1949). The excavation project at Walpi was conducted by the Museum of Northern Arizona in conjunction with the restoration of the village (Adams 1982). Walpi was moved to its present location about 1690 (Adams 1982; Ahlstrom et al. 1978). Therefore the Spanish period of occupation here ranges from 1690 to 1821.

The final data set consists of Hopi oral histories of the Spanish contacts. These are primarily personal accounts (Courlander 1971, 1982; Nequatewa 1936; Yava 1978).

Although the Hopi are an often-studied group and the broad course of their prehistoric development has been generally accepted, details of their development are still poorly understood. This fact is brought home when one attempts to outline the nature of Hopi society and even the approximate size, number, and population of villages occupied at contact in 1540.

Irrespective of these lacunae, general patterns of development over the 250 years prior to Spanish contact can be described and used to place Hopi society in context when Spanish contact was made. The following discussion offers primarily an archaeological and historical perspective of Hopi society from the thirteenth to nineteenth centuries. Hartman Lomawaima (this volume) discusses the course of Hopi history from a Hopi perspective. Table 4-1 separates the late

Table 4-1. Late Prehistoric and Historic Periods for the Hopi Mesas

Period	Time	Description
Aggregation and reorganization	1275–1400	Depopulation of much of the Colorado Plateau and development of large, aggregated pueblos
Consolidation	1400–1540	Consolidation of aggregated Pueblos into geographically restricted areas roughly coterminus with the historic villages
Contact	1540–1629	Exploratory period of Spaniards after contact and before establishment of missions at Hopi villages
Mission	1629–1680	Period of Spanish missions at Hopi villages
Postmission	1680–1821	Period after Pueblo Revolt up to end of Spanish rule, as marked by Mexican independence

prehistoric and historic periods into five divisions. The first two pertain to the late prehistoric period.

Aggregation and Reorganization

About A.D. 1275, many parts of the Colorado Plateau were abandoned. Although the factors involved in precipitating the abandonment are complex, the influence of a changing environmental regime is undeniable (Dean 1969; Dean et al. 1985; Euler et al. 1979). The net result was a consolidation of population into more restricted areas after 1275 and the aggregation of these populations into much larger villages. The aggregated fourteenth-century villages take on the size and layout of their historic counterparts throughout the Pueblo world.

Consolidation

Soon after 1400, aggregated settlements were abandoned along the Mogollon Rim and along the main course of the Little Colorado River and all tributaries, except those at the Hopi Mesas and along the Zuni River. No completely satisfactory explanation has yet been provided for the consolidation of the aggregated settlements into villages on the Hopi Mesas (including Antelope Mesa) and along the Zuni River (Upham 1982).

Whatever the cause, the results can be seen on the Hopi Mesas. Ten villages were present about 1400, some new and some of which had increased several-fold over the previous century. For example, Awatovi had perhaps 300 rooms during the fourteenth century, only half of which were probably occupied at any one time (Smith 1971:6); however, during the fifteenth through seventeenth centuries the village of Awatovi consisted of well over 1,000 rooms.

The 10 villages, each housing several hundred people, were occupied to about 1500 (Figure 4-1). Hopi oral histories describe intervillage conflict or withdrawal of villages, such as Kawaika-a, to the non-Hopi pueblos to the east (Ellis 1974; Courlander 1971; see also Lomawaima, this volume). At Spanish contact, five to seven villages were still occupied (Brew 1949b). Another plausible explanation of the reduction in the number of villages about 1500 could be European-introduced epidemics. Dobyns (1966) has argued for extensive, epidemic-induced population declines preceding Spanish entry into the Pueblo country of the northern Southwest. First exposure to smallpox by a population never before infected can result in 50 percent mortality. Early Spanish chroniclers do not mention epidemics, but several epidemics could have passed through Pueblo populations a decade or more before first contact and left little notable evidence to Spaniards after the populations had stabilized. This could explain the absence of demonstrable smallpox epidemics in the Pueblo Southwest until 1639.

Contact

If epidemics did occur, the Hopi first encountered by the Spaniards during the contact period could already have been radically affected by the first Europeans visiting the New World. Eggan (1967) documents a crisis in leadership in Walpi as a result of the extinction of the leadership clan, the Bear Clan, in the 1830s through 1850s. Epidemics struck Hopi several times in the early nineteenth century, and a severe epidemic struck First Mesa in particular in 1853 (Adams 1982). In societies such as Hopi, in which leadership is based on kinship affiliation, epidemics can have a serious impact on political, social, and religious institutions.

Whether the villages first encountered by the Spaniards in 1540 had already suffered these disruptions is not evident from the documents, but must be considered in historic reconstructions of Pueblo culture (Upham 1982). Nevertheless, a strong sense of Hopi culture in 1540 can be gained from Castañeda's account of Tovar's encounter with the Hopi as translated by Winship (1896:488).

> [Tovar] ordered his force to collect . . . and found a place to establish his headquarters near the village. They had dismounted here when the natives came peacefully, saying that they had come to give in the submission of the whole province, and to accept the presents which they gave him. This was some cotton cloth, dressed skins, corn meal, pine nuts, and birds of the country. Afterwards they presented some turquoise but not much. The people of the whole district came together that day and submitted themselves, and they allowed him to enter their villages freely, to visit, buy, sell, and barter with them.
>
> It is governed like Cibola, by an assembly of the oldest men.

The Hopi policy seems to have been one of appeasement, rather than confrontation. The Hopi almost surely knew of the conflict and loss of life that had taken place earlier at Zuni and may have wanted to avoid another such disaster. During the contact period, Spanish visits were always short and essentially non-confrontational, and were met with passive acquiescence on the part of the Hopi.

In general, the contact period allowed the Hopi to identify the Spaniards, sample minor aspects of Spanish culture, and, through contacts with eastern Pueblos, begin to understand the purpose of their presence. In 1598 Oñate established a seat of government for the northern frontier at San Juan Pueblo and began to colonize and missionize the region, dividing it into seven missionary districts each headed by a Spanish alcalde (Spicer 1967:56). Hopi was administered by an alcalde responsible for all of the western Pueblos (Hammond and Ray 1929). Oñate's visit to Hopi in 1598 served to crystallize the intent of Spanish policy. The Hopi people were expected to submit to the Spanish king (represented by the governor) in civil matters, and to the church (symbolized by Franciscan friars) in religious matters.

Although it is possible that minor elements of Spanish culture had affected Hopi culture prior to the establishment of missions among the Hopi in 1629, the effect is not recorded in Spanish documents, archaeological data, or Hopi oral history. The major effects were epidemics and the realization by the Hopi that the Spaniards were probably there to stay and had to be accommodated. Castano de Sosa's battle that ended with the defeat of Pecos in 1591 (Spicer 1967:155) and the Spanish battles with the Acoma people in 1598 and 1599 that resulted in the destruction of their village left little doubt as to the probable re-sults of a direct conflict with large forces of Spanish military. Nevertheless, the Hopi may already have begun to suspect that the infrequent visits by small and poorly equipped forces that came to Hopi were an indication of the logistical problems the Spaniards faced because the Hopi villages were so remote from Spanish seats of government.

Mission Period

The arrival on August 20, 1629, of Franciscan friars Porras, Gutierrez, and Concepción to establish a mission at Awatovi marks the beginning of the Mission period at Hopi. The Mission period ended just as abruptly with the killing of five missionaries in Hopi on August 10–13, 1680, in conjunction with the Pueblo Revolt (Brew 1949b).

The Spaniards' intent at Hopi, as elsewhere, was to convert the Pueblo vil-lages to economically self-sufficient units that would participate in a regionwide economic system administered from the new seat of government in Santa Fe. To promote economic self-sufficiency in each village, the Franciscans introduced domestic plants and animals and organized the people into work parties that were to build the mission and related buildings, plant and tend gardens, and generally transform each village so that it would be able to support a mission with no outside help.

The Peabody Museum's excavations at Awatovi indicate that the Spanish mis-sionaries introduced wheat, cantaloupe, watermelon, chili pepper, peach, apri-cot or plum, and probably other plants (Brew 1949a). These were found both in the firepits and the fill of historic structures and in the adobe bricks that the missionaries had the village people manufacture. Domesticated animal bones found at Awatovi included those of sheep, goat, cow, horse, burro, pig, cat, and Greyhound dog (Olsen 1978).

It is unclear whether the Spaniards were simply unable to effect the subsist-ence change in the Hopi economy that they desired in order to support the mis-sion program, or whether the local environment simply could not support the desired program. The Spanish mission program had proven effective only when two factors were present. First, the native population had to be dependent on domesticated plants, and thus would be sedentary settlements organized into villages or communities. Second, irrigation had to be available for agricultural fields. The history of Spanish settlement and missionization in the northern provinces of what was to become northern Mexico, southern Arizona, and into the Rio Grande River Valley hinged on the availability of water and the ability to use this water for irrigation (see Spicer 1967).

Successful establishment of settlements near the Eastern Pueblos was depen-dent on the location of the villages and the availability of irrigable land. At Hopi, the circumstances of agriculture could support missions, but not settlement by colonists. Only small gardens could be developed by terracing around springs at Hopi. Otherwise, 99 percent of the agriculture depended on floodwater farm-ing or dry farming (Page 1940). Spanish domesticates, especially wheat, fared poorly under these conditions. Therefore, the Spanish were never able to establish a satisfactory subsistence base for their program at Hopi.

Spanish civil and religious authorities also constantly bickered (Brew 1949b:15). Both sides were jealous of the other and the balance of power was in constant flux. Hearings at which either civil or church authorities were called upon to answer charges of improper conduct by the other side were frequent. The constant undermining of each other's authority also served to weaken the efforts to Christianize and civilize the natives.

Frequently, the missionaries were alone at the mission or left it with no one in charge when they were away on business (Scholes 1929:13–14). The extreme isolation of the missionizing effort at Hopi is underscored time and again in Spanish documents. Friars frequently traveled alone. Escorts could not be provided to the outer provinces, such as Zuni and Hopi. The local Hopi economy could not support garrisoned troops, and Spanish colonies usually needed them nearby for safety. Because the land could not support European settlers, the missionaries were basically on their own at Hopi, and this situation greatly diluted Spanish influence.

The second purpose of the mission program, of course, was to convert the natives from their idolatry to Christianity. At Awatovi, as elsewhere, this purpose was made manifest in the construction of the church over a kiva. This act symbolized the dominance of the Catholic doctrine over that of the native (Montgomery 1949:134–135). Each mission, given the local resources available, was to be modeled after missions built by Catholic missionaries throughout the New World. The Awatovi mission contained the church, friary, a garden area (garth), the friars' cells, offices, and schoolrooms (Montgomery 1949:127; Brew 1949a). At Awatovi, the church was fitted with a copper bell, an altar stone, a baptistry, and sacristies so that the friars could perform their basic duties, such as saying mass, performing baptisms, and hearing confessions (Brew 1949a:62, Figure 6). When the ideal items could not be imported, which was true of much of the remote northern frontier and particularly Hopi, local adjustments were made. An excellent example is the "painted tiles" in the Awatovi mission. When ceramic tiles could not be imported, painted replicas were depicted in the appropriate places within the church (Smith 1949:301–305).

Overall, the conversion program at Hopi during the mission period would have to be judged a failure. In 1700, after the reconquest of the Pueblo province by Don Diego de Vargas, a group of "Christianized" members of Awatovi visited the missionary at Zuni, Friar Juan de Garaicoechea, and requested that a church be reestablished. Garaicoechea visited Awatovi briefly and put the Christianized residents to work in reestablishing a mission. He was asked to return to Zuni, but before any missionary could return, Awatovi was destroyed by warriors from other Hopi villages (Courlander 1971). Many of the men were killed, and some of the women and children were taken and divided among the remaining villages. The sequence of events just described for Awatovi was documented in the excavations by the Peabody Museum (Brew 1949b:22–23). Hopi oral traditions and Spanish documents fill in the other two perspectives on the destruction of Awatovi (Brew 1949b; Courlander 1971). The oral history leaves no question that the Hopi intended to stamp out Christianity. Thus, from any perspective, the Spanish civil and missionary programs at Hopi, which ended in the destruction of Awatovi, could be deemed total failures.

Post-mission

Vargas's policy in his 1692 "reconquest" was to avoid conflict. He went from village to village absolving the members of wrongdoing and, where appropriate, asking them to return to their villages (Kessell, this volume). The Hopi, fearing retaliation, had already taken the precautions, prior to Vargas's visit, of moving their villages from the benches at the base of the mesas to the mesa tops (Adams 1982). The Hopi gladly accepted Vargas's peaceful action and Vargas, his men and horses exhausted, returned to El Paso. In 1693–1694 Vargas began the resettlement process by forcefully dislocating some villages in the Rio Grande area and waging war to regain Santa Fe. Revolts in 1693 and in 1696 were quelled with considerable bloodshed and the Tanoan and southern Tiwan rebels moved to Hopi, establishing the villages of Tewa (Tano) at First Mesa and Payupki at Second Mesa (Dozier 1970). In 1703, unrest at Zuni resulted in the deaths of three settlers. It is even possible that the unrest was encouraged by the Tanoans at Hopi. Subsequently, a small faction of Zuni, the Asa clan, according to Hopi oral tradition, settled at First Mesa, where they established Sichomovi (Espinosa 1942:347–349). Thus the ranks of the Hopi were increased considerably by what Brew (1949b:20) referred to as the apostates of the Pueblo world. These groups had rebelled before and had even fought the Spaniards.

Also about 1703, a group of Hopi led by an Oraibian, Espeleta, visited Santa Fe and asked Governor Cubero to treat the Hopi as equals, and to allow the Hopi people to be an independent nation with its own religion. Cubero turned a deaf ear to their requests, and the Hopi visitors left.

In 1701, a small contingent led by Cubero visited Hopi to punish them for the destruction of Awatovi. He briefly held 300 prisoners, but soon released them and returned to Santa Fe with only Hopi promises to obey. Cubero responded to the Zuni revolt in 1703 by abandoning the mission, then pulling out of Zuni altogether (Espinosa 1942:349–352). The clear signal this sent to the Zuni and the Hopi was that the Spaniards were either unable or unwilling to force missionization and colonization into these provinces. The isolation of the Hopi province, the expansion of their population by immigrants, and the weakness of the Spanish position in the northern provinces as a result of increased raiding by Navajo and Apache made the Hopi in reality, if not in the eyes of the Spanish government, the independent nation that they had asked to become.

Numerous missionaries and occasional military expeditions visited the Hopi villages up to 1780, but reconquest was never again attempted. Because of their isolation and the undesirability of the area for either resettlement or mineral exploration, the Hopi were only of interest to the missionaries. Without the support of the civil government, and in the face of the fighting that went on between Jesuit and Franciscan factions of the church in the early 1700s, the mission program was also doomed to failure.

The excavations at Walpi revealed a wealth of information about the indirect effect of Spanish contact and even about native attitudes toward the Spaniards. An example of the latter could be found in the ceramics from the mission and post-mission periods. The missionaries encouraged or forced several changes in native ceramics. They discouraged the use of pottery as burial offerings and encouraged the use of Spanish-inspired designs, such as flowers, the Maltese cross, and the eight-pointed star. Flat bottoms or rings added to bottoms became fashionable, as were new forms, such as candlesticks and the widely everted rims that came to characterize many of the serving bowls of the mission period (Wade and McChesney 1981:44).

The ceramic assemblage at post-missionary Walpi is quite different. Both the form and design of the bowls and jars were strongly influenced by Tanoan émigrés. All trappings of Spanish form and design were eliminated and ceramics once again attended burials. The manufacturers were reasserting traditions in ceramic production and use, which symbolized the "conquest" of the Spaniards and their material culture by Pueblo values and beliefs (Adams 1979:153, 1982:89–90).

The subsistence base of the Hopi also remained intact. The dominant subsistence item remained corn; however, domestic plants of secondary importance (i.e., varieties of beans and squash) were supplemented by Spanish introductions (Gasser 1981). Escalante's (Adams and Chavez 1956:135) account of Hopi commerce in 1776 listed sheep, cattle, corn, beans, chili, cotton, melon, watermelon, and peaches, all recorded from the Walpi assemblage. Perhaps the major impact on eighteenth-century Hopi economy was made by sheep (Czaplewski and Ruffner 1981). Native ungulates, such as deer and antelope, were replaced by sheep as food items. Wool replaced cotton as the most popular textile, both for everyday and religious dress (Kent 1979). Cow and sheep hide replaced deer hide in the manufacture of leather goods, especially moccasins (Adams 1982:100, 102; Adams 1980). Other borrowings from the Spaniards were knitting and blacksmithing, although the latter was not evident in the Walpi assemblage.

Spanish documents continue to offer insights into Hopi government and religion. Time after time during the eighteenth century, Franciscan friars or military leaders relate that contact was made with the religious leaders of each village. On at least two occasions (Velez's visit in 1775 and Garces's visit in 1776), these village leaders directly intervened when the friars began to preach to the people (Adams and Chavez 1956; Coues 1900).

Similarly, Bolton (1950:228) relates that the Hopi told Friars Domínguez and Escalante that they did not want to become Christians because the ancient ones had counseled them never to subject themselves to Spaniards. Clearly, the traditional Hopi religious leadership was in place and functioning during the eighteenth century. This leadership insulated the general populace from the Spanish missionaries and even occasionally debated or denounced the padres in public after the priest had spoken (Bancroft 1889:256).

The Hopi leaders promoted their own religion just as fervently and made sure that the general populace practiced it. Anza, visiting in 1780, noted that the Oraibi people were in a state of heathenism (Thomas 1969:234), and Croix reported in 1781 that "the chief priests were inexorable in their purpose of remaining heathen, preserving these customs, and remaining in their desolated pueblos" (Thomas 1969:109). Excavations at Walpi (Adams 1982:94, 100) from eighteenth-century deposits recovered a substantial assemblage of artifacts that were still in use in religious ceremonies historically (Stephen 1936) and give clearcut indications that the religious foundation of Hopi culture was little affected by Spanish missionizing efforts.

The documents and artifacts also reflect the extensive trade network of the Hopi. For instance, in 1713 a group of eight Hopi under the guise of emissaries to Santa Fe turned out to be traders rather than ambassadors (Bancroft 1889:233). In 1776, Garces met Zuni at Oraibi who were there to trade (Coues 1900). Padres identify nearby groups in contact with the Hopi as Ute, Navajo, Zuni, Paiute, Havasupai, and Apache. Garces (Coues 1900) also observed that groups in western and southern Arizona were using Hopi cotton blankets that had apparently been traded into the area. At Walpi, ceramics and basketry from Zuni, moccasins of Apache style, basketry from the Ute, Gulf of California shells that were probably obtained through the Havasupai, and turquoise, probably from mines controlled by the Pai tribes, were recovered from assemblages dating to the eighteenth century (Adams 1982:104).

The Spaniards commented on the extent and importance of Hopi trade and alliances in the 1770s. Don Juan Bautista de Anza was governor of New Mexico in 1780, and Don Teodoro de Croix was commandant general of the interior provinces of New Spain. Anza proposed a conquest of the Hopi, but Croix instead asked that they be bargained with, essentially as equals, to obtain their friendship so that they might open their trade with the Spanish settlements (Thomas 1969). The Spaniards also hoped that by establishing friendly relations they could convince the Hopi to at least remain neutral in the Spanish campaigns against the Apache. Anza also wished to go to Hopi because they were suffering through a horrendous drought and he believed they could be persuaded to abandon their villages and move to New Mexico. Although a few Hopi evidently did choose to return with a padre in advance of the Anza entourage in 1780, most chose to stay and face whatever consequences befell them (Thomas 1969:23–24). Anza did note that the Hopi were leaving their villages and uniting with other Indian groups.

The documents suggest that many of the Hopi had left their villages by the late 1770s, fleeing the drought and moving in with their Zuni neighbors and apparently with the Navajo in Canyon de Chelly. The sudden transformation of the unslipped Hopi decorated ware of the 1700s to white-slipped decorated ware after 1780 reflects the strong influence of Hopi refugees returning home from Zuni (Adams 1979:153).

The Spanish period ended in 1821 with Mexican independence. Although Mexican expeditions did make some thrusts into northern Arizona on one or two occasions, they did not directly involve the Hopi. Thus, for all intents and purposes, the Spanish period ended at Hopi in 1780 with Anza's departure.

Conclusions

The Hopi were affected in substantial ways by the presence of Spaniards in the New Mexican province. However, these effects were not so much a result of

Spanish policy as they were the repercussions of having a totally alien culture among the Pueblo peoples. All the same, the Spanish were unable to implement their program at Hopi: They not only failed in their effort to establish missions, but they never even attempted to start settlements there. Thus, true animosity between the respective governments never really had an opportunity to develop.

In the main, the legacy that the Spaniards left to the Hopi consisted of diseases and domestic plants and animals. Disease can be devastating. Initial reports by the Zuni to Coronado in 1540 cited seven Hopi villages. The chronicler of the Vargas expedition to Hopi fails to make clear whether Awatovi was the only town on Antelope Mesa (Brew 1949b). In any case, in view of the possibility that a smallpox epidemic preceded the Spanish contact with Hopi and the fact that several Hopi villages were abandoned around 1500, it may be that Hopi culture had already been severely affected by the arrival of the Spaniards in the New World. The precise effects on the social, political, and religious structure of Hopi villages, both individually and collectively, cannot be assessed without additional research. The serious impact of an epidemic on First Mesa social institutions in the mid-nineteenth century suggests that such disruptions may have been extensive.

The Spanish missionary program at Hopi can only be considered a failure. The Hopi attitudes toward the Christian influence were forcefully stated in the destruction of Awatovi. However, economic changes that the Spaniards introduced had a long-term positive effect on the Hopi. In particular, domestic animals provided the Hopi with a dependable source of meat with which to supplement their diet. The archaeological, documentary, and later ethnographic research all emphasize the primary importance of maize agriculture to the economic well-being of the Hopi people. The Spanish introductions complemented the existing subsistence scheme of the Hopi, but did not alter it or the overlying social and religious institutions.

Spanish missionaries of the 1770s remarked on the large herds of cattle and horses grazing well away from the villages and the flocks of sheep nearer the villages. Inasmuch as sheep herding was a male activity and sheep were gradually gaining ascendancy in the subsistence base of Hopi society, the structure of that society began to change. This change was in full effect by the early twentieth century, when new circumstances induced still further changes. The Hopi became surrounded by the male-dominated economic and bilateral descent social system of U.S. culture. This model, supplemented by a forced educational system, was responsible for a shift in the structure of twentieth-century Hopi social organization. No such model or dominant culture was present in the eighteenth century.

Rather, the Hopi had a stable subsistence base before, during, and after the Spanish mission period that permitted them to maintain the social institutions that are the hallmark of their culture. The consistent references in Spanish documents from 1540 to 1780 to a leadership comprised of a group of older men and to the people's continued belief in heathenistic rituals certainly imply that the political and religious system remained stable throughout the Spanish period.

Why were the Hopi able to withstand or deflect Spanish influence? A number of interrelated factors may have been involved, but there is no question that the society was successful in this regard because of the physical isolation of the Hopi villages and the nature of their subsistence base. The Hopi Mesas are 450 km in direct line from Santa Fe and 150 km from the nearest Pueblo group, the Zuni. Spanish settlement priorities lay in areas populated mainly by sedentary groups employing irrigation agriculture. The Hopi region offered neither of these attractions and thus never was given high priority on the agenda of Spanish policy-makers. Although the existence of a village people so distant from the Spanish resources concentrated in the Rio Grande River Valley was an ever-present nettlesome problem in the Spanish consciousness, other problems, such as revolts or nomadic raids, always took precedence over this one.

Another factor after 1700 was the increased strength of the Hopi position, which, according to Spanish documents, was bolstered by apostates from the eastern Pueblos and alliances with neighboring groups, in particular the Apache. In addition, constant bickering between church and state and indecisiveness in foreign policy on the part of the Spaniards bolstered Hopi confidence. What is perhaps more important, it was virtually impossible to wage war against this isolated group from the far-flung Spanish outposts in New Mexico, which in any case never had very many Spanish settlers.

The abuses of the natives of the New World by Spanish administrators and settlers did not go unnoticed in Spain and prompted the authorities to amend their policies of exploitation and Christianization. After the *Recopilacion de Leyes de los Reinos de las Indios*, published in 1681, the Spanish program gave the native people more rights and offered little support for the conquest and reduction of groups such as the Hopi.

The Hopi were also able to resist Spanish culture through their skillful use of diplomacy. The Hopi leadership always had advance warning of impending visits by Spaniards because Zuni and other villages served as intermediate stopping points on the trip to Hopi. This allowed Hopi leaders to give the visitors the appearance of a united front when they finally arrived. In some cases, Hopi were dispatched to Zuni or even to Santa Fe to intercept the Spanish visitors. Having seen or heard about the consequences of Pueblo defiance of the Spaniards, the Hopi leadership pretended to acquiesce to Spanish desires in order to avoid conflict. The Hopi told the Spaniards what they wanted to hear—that is, the Hopi people promised to obey and recognize the authority of the Spanish king and the church—but as soon as the Spaniards left, they went about life as before. The Spaniards, owing to the Hopi isolation, could not back up their threats of punishment if the Hopi failed to keep their promises. They did not even punish the Hopi for murdering five missionaries in the Pueblo Revolt. The Hopi learned quickly that there was little substance to the Spaniards' threats. All they had to do was promise obedience to the Spaniards in order to ensure their continued freedom.

In the final analysis, the Hopi were able to select the elements of Spanish culture that would improve their own situation, principally subsistence items, while resisting the more destructive elements of Spanish policy. The isolation of the Hopi villages together with the villagers' passive resistance enabled the

Hopi to preserve their culture virtually intact throughout the Spanish period and into the American period.

References

Adams, E. Charles
1979 *Native Ceramics from Walpi*. Walpi Archaeological Project, Phase II, vol. 3. Museum of Northern Arizona, Flagstaff and National Park Service, Western Region, San Francisco.
1982 *Walpi Archaeological Project: Synthesis and Interpretation*. Museum of Northern Arizona, Flagstaff.

Adams, Eleanor B., and Fray Angelico Chavez
1956 *The Missions of New Mexico, 1776; a Description by Fray Francisco Atansio Dominguez with other Contemporay Documents*. University of New Mexico Press, Albuquerque.

Adams, Jenny L.
1980 *Perishable Artifacts from Walpi*. Walpi Archaeological Project, Phase II, vol. 5. Museum of Northern Arizona, Flagstaff and National Park Service, Western Region, San Francisco.

Ahlstrom, Richard V. N., Jeffrey S. Dean, and William J. Robinson
1978 *Tree-ring Studies of Walpi Pueblo*. Laboratory of Tree-ring Research, University of Arizona, Tucson.

Bancroft, Hubert Howe
1889 *History of Arizona and New Mexico, 1530–1888*. History Co., San Francisco.

Bolton, Herbert E.
1950 *Pageant in the Wilderness; the Story of the Escalante Expedition to the Interior Basin, 1776, including the Diary and Itinerary of Father Escalante Translated and Annotated*. Utah State Historical Society, Salt Lake City.

Brew, John Otis
1949a Part 2: The Excavation of Franciscan Awatovi. In *Franciscan Awatovi: The Excavation and Conjectural Reconstruction of a 17th Century Spanish Mission Establishment at a Hopi Town in Northeastern Arizona*, by Ross G. Montgomery, Watson Smith, and J. O. Brew. Papers of the Peabody Museum of American Archaeology and Ethnology, Harvard University, vol. 36. Cambridge, Mass.
1949b Part 1: The History of Awatovi. In *Franciscan Awatovi: The Excavation and Conjectural Reconstruction of a 17th Century Spanish Mission Establishment at a Hopi Town in Northeastern Arizona*, by Ross G. Montgomery, Watson Smith, and J. O. Brew. Papers of the Peabody Museum of American Archaeology and Ethnology, Harvard University, vol. 36. Cambridge, Mass.

Coues, Elliot
1900 *On the Trail of a Spanish Pioneer. The Diary and Itinerary of Francisco Garces in His Travels through Sonora, Arizona, and California, 1775-1776*. 2 vols. Francis P. Harper, New York.

Courlander, Harold S.
1971 *The Fourth World of the Hopis*. Crown Publishers, New York.
1982 *Hopi Voices: Recollections, Traditions, and Narratives of the Hopi Indians*. University of New Mexico Press, Albuquerque.

Czaplewski, N. J., and George A. Ruffner
1981 *An Analysis of the Vertebrate Fauna of Walpi*. Walpi Archaeological Project, Phase II, vol. 8, part I. Museum of Northern Arizona, Flagstaff and National Park Service, Western Region, San Francisco.

Dean, Jeffrey S.
1969 *Chronological Analysis of Tsegi Phase Sites in Northeastern Arizona*. Papers of the Laboratory of Tree-ring Research, No. 3. University of Arizona Press, Tucson

Dean, Jeffrey S., Robert C. Euler, George J. Gumerman, Fred Plog, Richard H. Hevley, and Thor N. V. Karlstrom
  1985 Human Behavior, Demography, and Paleoenvironment. *American Antiquity* 50:537–554.
Dobyns, Henry F.
  1966 Estimating Aboriginal American Populations: An Appraisal of Techniques with a New Hemispheric Estimate. *Current Anthropology* 7:395–416.
Dockstader, Frederick J.
  1954 *The Kachina and the White Man; a Study of the Influence of White Culture on the Hopi Kachina Cult.* Cranbrook Institute of Science, Michigan.
Dozier, Edward P.
  1970 *The Pueblo Indians of North America.* Holt, Rinehart and Winston, New York.
Eggan, Fred
  1967 From History to Myth, A Hopi Example. In *Studies in Southwestern Ethnolinguistics; Meaning and History in the Languages of the American Southwest*, edited by Dell H. Hyme and W. E. Bittle, pp. 33–53. Mouton, The Hague.
Ellis, Florence H.
  1974 The Hopi: Their History and Use of Lands. In *Hopi Indians*, edited by David A. Horr, pp. 25–277. Garland, New York
Espinosa, Jose Manuel
  1942 *First Expedition of Vargas into New Mexico, 1692.* University of New Mexico Press, Albuquerque.
Euler, Robert C., George J. Gumerman, Thor N. V. Karlstrom, Jeffrey S. Dean, and Richard H. Hevley
  1979 The Colorado Plateaus: Cultural Dynamics and Paleoenvironment. *Science* 205:1089–1101.
Gasser, Robert E.
  1981 *The Plant Remains from Walpi.* Walpi Archaeological Project, Phase II, vol. 7, part I. Museum of Northern Arizona, Flagstaff and National Park Service, Western Region, San Francisco.
Hackett, Charles W.
  1937 *Historical Documents Relating to New Mexico, Nueva Vizcaya, and Approaches Thereto to 1773, Collected by Adolf F. A. Bandelier and Fanny R. Bandelier.* Carnegie Institution of Washington 330(3). Washington, D.C.
Hammond, George P., and Agapito Rey
  1929 *Expedition into New Mexico Made by Antonio de Espejo, 1582–1583, as Revealed in the Journal of Diego Perez de Luxan, a Member of the Party.* The Quivera Society Publications, Los Angeles.
Kent, Kate P.
  1979 *An Analysis of Textile Materials from Walpi Pueblo.* Walpi Archaeological Project, Phase II, vol. 6, part I. Museum of Northern Arizona, Flagstaff and National Park Service, Western Region, San Francisco.
Montgomery, Ross G.
  1949 Part III: San Bernardo de Aguatobi, an Analytical Restoration. In *Franciscan Awatovi: The Excavation and Conjectural Reconstruction of a 17th-Century Spanish Mission Establishment at a Hopi Indian Town in Northeastern Arizona*, by Ross G. Montgomery, Watson Smith, and J. O. Brew. Papers of the Peabody Museum of American Archaeology and Ethnology, Harvard University, vol. 36. Cambridge, Mass.
Montgomery, Ross G., Watson Smith, and John Otis Brew
  1949 *Franciscan Awatovi: The Excavation and Conjectural Reconstruction of a 17th-Century Spanish Mission Establishment at a Hopi Indian Town in Northeastern Arizona.* Papers of the Peabody Museum of American Archaeology and Ethnology, Harvard University, vol. 36. Cambridge, Mass.

Nequatewa, Edmund
  1936 *Truth of a Hopi: Stories Relating to the Origin, Myths, and Clan Histories of the Hopi.* Museum of Northern Arizona Bulletin No. 8. Flagstaff.
Olsen, Stanley
  1978 The Faunal Analysis. In *Bones from Awatovi*. Papers of the Peabody Museum of Archaeology and Ethnology, Harvard University, vol. 70, no. 1. Cambridge, Mass.
Page, Gordon B.
  1940 *Hopi Agricultural Notes*. Soil Conservation Service, Washington, D.C.
Scholes, Frances V.
  1929 Documents for the History of the New Mexican Missions in the Seventeenth Century. *New Mexico Historical Review* 4(1):45–48 and 4(2):195–201.
Smith, Watson
  1949 Part IV: Mural Decorations of San Bernardo de Aguatabi. In *Franciscan Awatovi: The Excavation and Conjectural Reconstruction of a 17th-Century Spanish Mission Establishment at a Hopi Indian Town in Northeastern Arizona*, by Ross G. Montgomery, Watson Smith, and J. O. Brew. Papers of the Peabody Museum of American Archaeology and Ethnology, Harvard University, vol. 36. Cambridge, Mass.
  1971 *Painted Ceramics of the Western Mound at Awatovi*. Papers of the Peabody Museum of Archaeology and Ethnology, Harvard University, vol. 38. Cambridge, Mass.
Spicer, Edward H.
  1967 *Cycles of Conquest*. 2nd printing. University of Arizona Press, Tucson.
Stephen, Alexander M.
  1936 *Hopi Journal*. 2 vols. Edited by Elsie Clews Parsons. Columbia University Contributions to Anthropology, No. 23, New York.
Thomas, Alfred B.
  1969 *Forgotten Frontiers: A Study of the Spanish Indian Policy of Don Juan Bautista de Anza, Governor of New Mexico, 1777–1787*. 2nd printing. University of Oklahoma Press, Norman.
Upham, Steadman
  1982 *Polities and Power: An Economic and Political History of the Western Pueblo*. Academic Press, New York.
Wade, Edwin L., and Lea S. McChesney
  1981 *Historic Hopi Ceramics: The Thomas V. Keam Collection of the Peabody Museum of Archaeology and Ethnology, Harvard University*. Peabody Museum Press, Cambridge, Mass.
Winship, George P.
  1896 The Coronado Expedition, 1540–1542. *Fourteenth Annual Report of the Bureau of American Ethnology*. Smithsonian Institution, Washington, D.C.
Yava, Albert
  1978 *Big Falling Snow: A Hopi-Tewa Indian's Life and Times and the History and Traditions of his People*. University of New Mexico Press, Albuquerque.

Chapter 5 ▪

Hartman H. Lomawaima

Hopification, a Strategy for Cultural Preservation

> [It's] about the eccentricity of a culture not understood by another culture. It's about acceptable mysticism in our time and it's about the decimation of a culture because of profit. When profit [or some other objective] comes in, perched ready to wipe out a tradition, what does the culture do about trying to hold [onto] itself? [Actor/director Robert Redford reflecting on his recent experience filming *The Milagro Beanfield War* in northern New Mexico]

Contacts among native populations in the prehistoric Southwest were legion. When the Spanish entered the area in the sixteenth century, it became abundantly clear to them that natives on the lower Colorado River were familiar with natives to the north (Pueblos) and the the east (Pimas). The Conquistador Coronado took full advantage of this familiarity. Guided by two Plains Indians, Coronado and his men ventured out of Pecos Pueblo to explore Quivira and other areas of the present state of Kansas. These guides, who had been held captive by the Pecos war chief, were knowledgeable about the Plains and its inhabitants and even about people from Mississippian cultures. One reason for this was commerce. To these people, commerce was a strategy for dealing with the problem of food shortages (for a prehistoric Southwestern example, see Minnis 1985).

The economies of nomadic and sedentary natives complemented each other. Although conflict may have occurred between populations from each region, the need for commerce prompted them to keep relations open.

Food, dyes, textiles, jewelry, and small pottery vessels figured largely in their trading circles. As there were no beasts of burden, goods had to be transported on the backs of traders and their helpers. The trading complex was wide in scope and personal contact was the standard of the day. When Fray Marcos de Niza ventured north from Mexico to Zuni in 1539, he encountered natives traveling southward to trade hides for the goods of Mexican Indians (Hodge 1945:230). In the present century, Spier (1928:244) has reported that the Walapai of northern Arizona killed deer and traded the hides to the Havasupai for woven goods procured from the Hopi. The Havasupai tanned the hides and traded them to the Hopi for woven goods and pottery. The Hopi fashioned the buckskin into shoes for their women or traded the shoes to the Zuni and Rio Grande Pueblos, receiving in return turquoise from Santo Domingo, Mexican indigo from Isleta, and buffalo skins from the Plains.

Commerce also helped people to keep abreast of conditions in the environment and to monitor the activities of their neighbors, near and far. The greater Southwest formed a distinct sphere of interaction, as exemplified by the fact that the Spaniards in the 1540s reached virtually every corner of it within a matter of a few months. But, apart from the Quivira expedition, they never went beyond it. The fact that the people of Pecos encouraged Coronado to explore the Great Plains was obviously a strategy aimed at ridding their lands of the Spanish. The Zuni made a similar effort by informing Coronado of the "warlike" people among the seven pueblos of Tusayan (Hopi area). In response, Coronado dispatched a complement of soldiers to Tusayan, but they found only "people of peace" living among the Hopi villages. The Spaniards were operating within a closed universe that was delineated for them in part by the natives and in part by their own observations (Riley 1987:313).

Not only did native people know about each other, but with the gradual shrinking of their world, the Pueblo world in particular, a Pueblo national character began to emerge. Schroeder (1972: 45) has argued that, as a result of population shifts, people became concentrated in smaller regions, and each move ted new cultural situations and experiences. This forced them to learn about new materials and techniques for producing food, clothing, and shelter and to adapt old practices to new situations. The Pueblo people developed their practices through centuries of physical hardship and almost incessant danger—ranging from warfare and drought to European encroachment. Collier (1949:71) has passionately argued that the Pueblo people met new situations creatively, employing their institutions and value systems to transmute danger and hardship into character, into social form and individual and social strength, and into the mystic splendors that flash forth from the Pueblo soul.

Let us now move on to some collective Hopi observations of the Pueblo world. At Hopi, the oral tradition is still the single most viable means of transmitting information to new generations. Religious and secular knowledge is held by individuals and collectives (clans and religious societies) and is transmitted according to a specific plan. Part of this information has been entered into the ethnographic record over the years since the arrival of the first European chroniclers and historians. More recently, individual Hopi have begun to record their memoirs in published testimonies and autobiographies. For students of Hopi culture, and for Hopi themselves, this is a significant development in the documentation of Hopi history. To illustrate how oral history and the archaeological record can mesh, portions of the published testimony of Albert Yava are included in this chapter. Mr. Yava's statements exemplify both individual and collective Hopi-Tewa observations. These observations represent an attempt to search for truths about a culture, a goal of all ethnologists, Hopi and others. To the question about Hopi origins, Yava (1978:36) replies that they came from almost every direction. The Snake and Horn clans came from *Tokonave*, an area in northern Arizona now bearing the name Navajo Mountain. Other clans, including the Sand, Water, and Tobacco clans, came from a place far to the south called *Palatkwa*. A number of clans traveled up and down the Colorado and Little Colorado rivers for several years before settling at Hopi. The Coyote clan, among others, migrated to the Hopi area from the east. Yava's point is that modern Hopi are descendants of numerous groups, including Plains Indians, who were attracted to the Hopi homeland. He is somewhat critical of archaeologists who state that all Hopi are descendants of basketmakers who lived in the San Juan Valley:

> We Hopis can't be explained so easily. Those migrating groups that came here spoke several different languages. For example, the Water Coyote group that came here from the north spoke Paiute or Chemehuevi or some other Shoshonean dialect. We had clans, even whole villages, coming here from the Eastern Pueblos, where various languages are spoken. We had Pimas coming in from the south. And there's an Apache strain too. Those clans that came here from *Palatkwa* brought Pimas and Apaches with them. My father's group, the Water clan, claims to be *Uche*—that is, Apache—in origin. It could be that the first people to settle these mesas were Shoshonean speakers from the San Juan Valley, but other people joined them and it was this mixture that came to make up what we now call *Hopitu*, the Hopi People [Yava 1978:36].

The Hopi place great emphasis on the extended family or clan. Today *Hopitu* consist of more than 30 clans. Matrilineal clans have a number of functions, not the least of which is to provide members with an identity, a place in society that transcends many boundaries. A Bear clan member, for example, is part of a family that extends across all communities at Hopi and elsewhere in the Pueblo world. When a Bear clan member visits another village, whether it be at Hopi, Zuni, or Jemez, he or she is comforted by the thought that somewhere in the village there are fellow clan members who will make the visitor feel at home. Most often it will be the occupants of the Clan House who will take in their extended kin. According to the oral history, the first Spanish contact with Hopi was made near Antelope Mesa, in present-day northeast Arizona. There were a number of villages on Antelope Mesa and along Jeddito Wash. The main village was called *Awatovi* (see Figure 4-1). The other villages of *Kawaiku* and *Chakpahu* were settled by *Kawaikas*, Laguna people who at present reside in northern New Mexico. There was also a settlement of Jemez people called *Akokavi*. *Awatovi* was originally a Hopi village, but it had taken in many *Kawaikas*, *Akokavis*, and other Pueblo people who now reside along or near the Rio Grande in New Mexico.

People were attracted to the Hopi area mainly because it was believed to be *Sichdukwi*, or Flower Mound—a promised land where they could follow good teachings and a good way of life. A prophecy held by many clans was that *Sichdukwi* would eventually be settled after centuries of migrations.

By the end of the sixteenth century, more Spanish had come to the greater Southwest, bringing with them many changes in the religious, economic, political, and social life of the native people. Missionization of the Pueblos became a high priority, second only to the ongoing quest for gold and other resources sought by the Spanish Crown. In 1629, missions were established at *Hawaiku* in the Zuni area and at *Awatovi* in the Hopi area. The following year another mission was built in the Hopi area, at the village of Oraibi. In an effort to supplant the ceremonial patterns and beliefs, missionaries baptized natives, forced them to attend Mass, and made instruction in Catholic doctrine compulsory. Spain also imposed a new political system. In 1620 it decreed that a governor should be placed in charge of the province, assisted by an alcalde and native officers elected by majority vote in each village. In practice, the traditional Pueblo religious leaders chose the slate of so-called Spanish officers, who conveniently attended to the temporal, external affairs of the village while the old theocracy carried on the vital functions of leadership in the ancient tradition (John 1975: 68). If anything, the system enabled the natives to preserve their beliefs and rites, and did not force them to serve the goals of the Spaniards. It served the villages and villagers handily through later occupations and well into the present century.

The Hopi, being on the perimeter of the area under Spanish domination, experienced fewer interruptions of their daily life than did their eastern brethren. However, their remoteness also made them vulnerable to increasing pressures from neighboring groups such as *Tasavum* (Navajo) and *Utem* (Utes). It has been argued that the Hopi were willing to risk oblivion at the hands of Navajos, Utes, and Apaches rather than allow Spanish institutions to destroy their way of life (John 1975:147).

In August 1680 the Pueblo Revolt brought a temporary halt to the Christian missionization of the Southwest. It has been said that this uprising ended in a loss for the Christian God and a win for the Kachinas (Montgomery et al. 1949:18). Spanish survivors in the Rio Grande area fled southward. At Hopi, there were no Spanish survivors. About a dozen years later, the Spanish attempted to regain their mission stronghold at the village of *Awatovi*. This led Hopi warriors from nearby villages to sack *Awatovi* in an effort to eliminate all vestiges of the religion that had been imposed on them and the people who had introduced it. However, several remnants of Hopi-Spanish contact were assimilated into native life. Plows and hoes replaced the old sticks used in farming. Melons, apples, peaches, and apricots remained part of the diet along with mutton and chicken. Craft traditions were enriched by the new techniques the people had been taught, which included methods of weaving in wool, metallurgy, and woodworking (Dozier 1961:137).

Popé, a member of San Juan Pueblo and leader of the Revolt, and his lieutenants urged the natives to discard all that the Spanish had taught them and to return to their former ways. Although many citizens probably understood the intent of this plea, few were willing to relinquish everything that had been introduced. Those innovations that appealed to their sense of economy and did not offend their sense of fitness became assimilated into their daily lives (John 1975:149). The fabric of Pueblo culture was and continues to be tough and flexible, giving wherever and whenever necessary, but scarcely tearing, much less shredding. The Pueblo allowed alien patterns to enter the weave, as they had for many centuries, but incorporated them into a truly Pueblo pattern (Riley 1987: 169). It has been argued that, in prehistoric times, outside influences may have come from the south (Mesoamerica), but that these influences were altered in detail by the Pueblo people and adapted to their culture. The Kachina cult, for example, may have originated in the south, but it was certainly modified to fit Pueblo ceremonialism (Brew 1943:243). These changes were not due so much to evolution as to incorporation of new elements by clans and adoption of new symbols from foreigners. However, the Pueblo themselves influenced others. For example, the meteorological and fertility symbols in the sandpaintings of the Navajo (relatively recent arrivals to the Southwest) were most certainly borrowed from the Hopi and fitted into a shamanistic curing ritual, with little effect, except that it invested the ceremony with vividness and picturesque interest (Kroeber 1928:385).

It is difficult to know precisely what foreign concepts entered Hopi life as a result of contact with other native populations or missionization. The Hopi concept of *Maski*, or Land of the Dead, has been misinterpreted as a kind of purgatory or hell (Courlander 1982:xxi), but *Maski* has no punitive connotation for Hopis: It refers to the destination of souls when they leave the present world. If *Maski* was derived from an introduced concept it has certainly been imbued with Hopi values so that its origin is difficult to ascertain. Making the correct interpretation is all the more difficult for the outsider because of the secretive nature of Hopi religious institutions, which to this day are treated as the private property of individuals and collectives.

The synthesizing process by which an idea or thing became imbued with Hopi values may be called "Hopification." This is a process by which Hopi view, test, analyze, and make decisions about the actions or impositions of alien cultures or elements. Hopification most often occurs at the clan level. It is the clan that decides how alien people and ideas that successfully survive this process will become integrated into the culture. Individuals who are accepted quickly learn about the system of obligations that tie Hopi families and their entire culture together. Such outsiders have included Hopi reared away from the Hopi homeland, non-Hopi spouses, orphans, and even an anthropologist or two! Foreign elements are viewed as opportunities to add certain elements to the Hopi cultural inventory. For example, formal education introduced during the past century was initially viewed in the same light as missionization, as a great imposition and threat to Hopi values. This precipitated resentment and hostility toward education and toward the Americans who proffered it. Hopi parents went to great lengths to demonstrate their feelings. For their actions they were punished or physically removed to distant penal institutions. Toward the end of the last century Hopi men were imprisoned as far away as Alcatraz Island in San Francisco Bay.

It became clear to the Hopi that compulsory education was not going to go away. Thus, a conscious decision was made to accept schooling, and the decision was supported by most Hopi. Not learning English was seen, in effect, as an unwitting way of giving the white man power over Hopi lives. The underlying rationale in learning the white man's ways was not to become more like him, but rather to take advantage of an opportunity to pick what was best from him and reject what might be harmful to the Hopi way of life. The result of this conscious decision is a well-educated population of Hopi who maintain a strong respect for traditional Hopi institutions, religious societies, and the like. The formal education, with its physical facilities and staff (many of whom are Hopi) is now an integral part of Hopi community life. Hopi students are encouraged to pursue a higher education and each finds ways to apply his or her acquired knowledge and skills toward maintaining the quality of Hopi life.

In this chapter, I have attempted to show what a culture does about maintaining itself in the wake of ongoing changes and outside influences. Hopi are often regarded as one of the few Native American ethnic groups that have successfully met some of the challenges intended to break down their institutions. In prehistoric, historic, and contemporary times, Hopis have indeed done remarkably well in managing change, although it has been painful at times. Few Hopi would deny the soul-searching that must have taken place during the Hopi destruction of *Awatovi*, when fellow clan members were forced into a combative situation in order to preserve their culture. The Kachinas won that one, too, but the costs were great. That civil war was perhaps an extreme case of Hopification. Other, more moderate forms of Hopification have served the people well. They have enabled the people to contend with forces that threaten their way of life and preserve the values of the ancients for posterity. As Albert Yava and other Hopis before him have said, "If you don't survive, you don't have anything, do you?"

References

Brew, John O.
    1943 On the Pueblo IV and on the Kachina-Tlaloc Relations. In *El norte de Mexico y el sur de Estados Unidos, tercera Reunion de Mesa Redonda sobre Problemas Anthropologicos de Mexico y Centro America*, D.F.: Sociedad Mexicana de Anthropologia, pp. 241–245.
Collier, John
    1949 *Patterns and Ceremonials of the Indians of the Southwest*. E.P. Dutton, New York.
Courlander, Harold
    1982 *Hopi Voices*. University of New Mexico Press, Albuquerque.
Dozier, Edward P.
    1961 Rio Grande Pueblos. In *Perspectives in American Indian Culture Change*, edited by Edward H. Spicer. University of Chicago Press, Chicago.

Hodge, Frederick W.

    1945 *Fray Alonso de Benavides' Revised Memorial of 1634*. University of New Mexico Press, Albuquerque.

John, Elizabeth A. H.

    1975 *Storms Brewed in Other Men's Worlds*. Texas A & M University Press, College Station.

Kroeber, Alfred L.

    1928 Native Culture in the Southwest, *University of California Publications in America Archaeology and Ethnology* 23(9): 375–398. Berkeley.

Minnis, Paul E.

    1985 *Social Adaptation to Food Stress*. University of Chicago Press, Chicago.

Montgomery, Ross G., Watson Smith, and John O. Brew

    1949 *Franciscan Awatovi: Report #3* of the Awatovi Expedition. Papers of the Peabody Museum of American Archaeology and Ethnology, vol. 36. Harvard University, Cambridge, Mass.

Redford, Robert (Interviewed by Jill Kearney)

    1988 No More Playing It Safe. In *Datebook*, a supplement to the *San Francisco Examiner*, March 24, pp. 19–21.

Riley, Carroll L.

    1987 *The Frontier People*. University of New Mexico Press, Albuquerque.

Schroeder, Albert H.

    1972 Rio Grande Ethnohistory. In *New Perspectives on the Pueblos*, edited by Alfonso A. Ortiz, pp. 41–70. University of New Mexico Press, Albuquerque.

Spier, Leslie

    1928 Havasupai Ethnography. *Anthropological Papers of the American Museum of Natural History*, vol. 39(3). New York.

Yava, Albert

    1978 *Big Falling Snow*, edited and annotated by Harold Courlander. University of New Mexico Press, Albuquerque.

Chapter 6 ◼

Katherine A. Spielmann

Colonists, Hunters, and Farmers: Plains–Pueblo Interaction in the Seventeenth Century

Prior to Spanish contact, Plains hunting populations and Pueblo farmers on the eastern border of the Greater Southwest had developed an ongoing exchange system in which corn and other Pueblo goods were traded annually for bison products. Spanish colonization of the Rio Grande Valley in 1598 profoundly affected this exchange system. In this chapter, I provide a brief overview of Plains–Pueblo interaction as it was observed at the time of contact in 1540, and place this exchange system in the context of the protohistoric Puebloan economy. The significance of Plains–Pueblo exchange cannot be understood without a broader picture of Puebloan economic activities. Next, I outline the Spanish activities of the seventeenth century that affected the Puebloan economy in general, and the Plains–Pueblo exchange system in particular. From these data, I infer resulting changes in Plains–Pueblo exchange and the strategies that eastern border pueblos may have developed to deal with them. Finally, I briefly discuss archaeological data that document change in economic activities at Gran Quivira (also known as the Pueblo of Las Humanas), an eastern border trading pueblo.

One point that will become clear from this discussion is that surviving seventeenth-century Spanish documents provide information on Spanish actions, but say next to nothing about the strategies that Native Americans used to cope with the intrusion of Spanish colonists. Consequently, further archaeological research is extremely important if we are to document and understand Puebloan behavior in the seventeenth century.

Protohistoric Pueblo Economic System

The protohistoric Pueblo economy was based on a combination of farming, hunting, gathering, craft production, and trading. Each of these components is discussed briefly to provide a baseline against which to measure the subsequent Spanish impact on the Pueblo economy (see Figure 6-1).

Archaeological data from two eastern border trading pueblos, Pecos and Gran Quivira (see Figure 3-2), document a heavy reliance on corn in the Pueblo diet. Bone chemistry data from Pecos burials suggest that approximately 80 percent of the diet consisted of corn (Spielmann et al. 1988). At Gran Quivira, 100 percent of the flotation samples contained corn, which also suggests a high reliance on corn (Raymer and Minnis 1987). Ethnobotanical data from Gran Quivira and other Rio Grande pueblos (e.g., Arroyo Hondo near Santa Fe) indicate that corn was supplemented with beans and squash as well as a variety of locally available wild plants such as chenopodium, cacti, and piñon (Raymer and Minnis 1987; Scott 1987; Wetterstrom 1986).

Early Spanish documents indicate that these pueblos were capable of producing enough corn to keep fairly large quantities in storage. In fact, a stated goal of many historic Pueblos was to have two years of corn in storage as a buffer against periodic poor yields (Slatter 1979). Although most surplus corn was probably stored, the eastern border Pueblos also traded some of their surplus to Plains nomads who came every fall to exchange bison products for grain. A

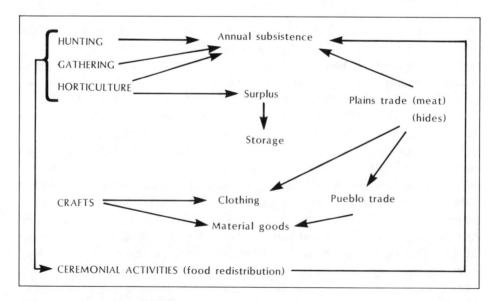

Figure 6-1. Eastern border Pueblo economic activities (pre-Spanish).

simulation I conducted of corn production at Pecos Pueblo suggests that this population could easily supply the nomads' caloric needs for several months and not risk depleting their stores beyond what would be needed as a buffer against a poor crop (Spielmann 1982).

Historically, corn production, consumption, and distribution appear to have been conducted at the household level. Men were involved in all aspects of crop production, from field preparation to harvest, while women also worked in fields and processed and stored the corn (Ford 1968; Snow 1981).

Corn and other plant foods were supplemented by hunting, which provided significant quantities of protein for the Puebloan diet. Again, bone chemistry data for Pecos suggest that about 45 percent of the pueblo's protein needs were met by meat (Spielmann et al. 1988; see also Wetterstrom 1986). Most of this meat would have come from large game such as mule deer. Historically, men generally hunted the large game, whereas women and children collected smaller game, such as rabbits and rodents, near the pueblo.

Given the centuries of occupation in protohistoric Rio Grande pueblos, and the fact that these pueblos tend to occur in clusters, it is highly likely that the large game in their vicinity were overhunted and that hunters were forced to travel further afield in search of game (Speth and Scott 1985; Spielmann 1988). Faunal data from Gran Quivira suggest that this was indeed the case by the sixteenth century. Bone elements of antelope, the primary large game species available near Gran Quivira, occur in much lower frequencies in midden levels dating to this period than in levels dating to the previous century. This decline in antelope bone suggests longer transport distances from kill sites to the pueblo (Binford 1978).

An alternative to long-distance hunting expeditions was available to the eastern border Pueblos, such as Pecos and Gran Quivira, which were well-situated to trade with Athapaskan groups on the Southern Plains in the protohistoric period. Coronado and other early Spanish explorers of New Mexico recorded that these nomads came every fall to trade bison meat, fat, and hides for corn, cotton blankets, and ceramics at these eastern pueblos. They often stayed several months before returning to the Plains (Hammond and Rey 1953, 1966; Spielmann 1982, 1983; Winship 1896).

The meat that these Plains groups exchanged could have made up as much as 20 percent of the annual Pecos or Gran Quiviran protein needs, thereby providing a significant supplement to deer and antelope (Spielmann 1982). Bison hides were important both for clothing in these pueblos, and for trade with other Pueblo groups farther to the west. Coronado, Oñate, and Benavides all reported that many Pueblo men, from Pecos to Hopi, were clothed in bison robes during the winter (Kessell 1979; Hammond and Rey 1953; Winship 1896).

Finally, trade *among* pueblos also provided access to important resources. Ford (1972a) and Snow (1981) have documented the lively trade that took place among Rio Grande pueblos during the protohistoric and historic periods. There was some specialization in pottery production, particularly in the glazewares, as well as trade in turquoise, obsidian, and cotton or cotton products. In addition, Ford points out the importance of exchange in ritual items such as feathers and pigments, as well as ritual knowledge among different pueblos. Although exchange of ritual items is often difficult to detect in the archaeological record, Snow suggests that Gran Quivira may have been a significant supplier of feathers to other pueblos, owing to the fact that migratory waterfowl and hawk bones are present in high frequencies in the Gran Quivira faunal assemblage. Rituals *within* pueblos formed an important adjunct to subsistence activities in that quantities of food were often accumulated and distributed in the context of pueblo-wide ceremonies (Ford 1972b).

When the Plains–Pueblo and inter-Pueblo exchange systems are examined together, it becomes clear that the eastern border pueblos represent loci of articulation between the Plains and Pueblo economic systems. Gran Quivira and Pecos imported and consumed both Plains and Pueblo products. These pueblos also served to transfer goods between these two areas. Bison hides moved from Gran Quivira and Pecos west to the Rio Grande and beyond in return for ceramics, turquoise, and obsidian. Some of these Rio Grande Pueblo goods were then exchanged at the eastern border pueblos to Plains trade partners.

Spanish Impact on the Pueblo Economy

In 1598, Don Juan de Oñate and several hundred followers colonized New Mexico. Initially they settled at San Gabriel del Yunque, across from San Juan Pueblo near the confluence of the Chama and the Rio Grande. In 1610, the colony was moved to Santa Fe by Oñate's successor, Peralta (Hammond and Rey 1953).

This initial period of colonization had a direct and profound impact on Puebloan subsistence. The Spaniards established a system of resource mobilization in which Pueblos were required to provide goods such as food, skins, and blankets in support of the Spanish colony. Colonists writing to Spanish authorities in Mexico City concerning Oñate's behavior documented that, if food and clothing were not freely given, they were taken by force (Hammond and Rey 1953). This pattern persisted throughout the seventeenth century.

In addition to supplying goods, the Pueblos were expected to provide labor to assist in cultivating Spanish fields and to act as servants in Spanish households. Often they received nothing in return for their services. As a result of these demands, New Mexico was in a state of famine by the early 1600s (Hammond and Rey 1953; Snow 1981). One important point to note is that, although these documentary data establish the nature and size of the burden placed on Pueblo groups, they give no indication of how individual households dealt with these demands.

Oñate's colonizing effort ended largely in failure, as many of the colonists returned to Mexico. Nonetheless, the authorities decided to maintain New Mexico as a missionary field at the expense of the Crown. With the subsequent establishment of Santa Fe as its capital and home to its civil authorities, and the assignment of 16 friars to various Puebloan and Apachean groups, the stage was set for further exploitation of the Pueblo populations. Numerous historians have eloquently documented the struggles between the civil and religious authorities in New Mexico for access to Pueblo goods and labor (e.g., Forbes 1960; Kessell

1979; Scholes 1936–1937, 1937–1941). The review that follows covers only those aspects of the struggle that had an impact on the Pueblo economic system (see Figure 6-2).

To begin with the civil authorities, New Mexico provided few resources for the economic advancement of its governors and their associates. Its primary products were natural resources such as hides, piñon nuts, and salt; locally produced goods such as cotton mantas and livestock; and human resources, which included captives from the Plains. The majority of New Mexico's seventeenth-century governors sought to make some profit in the export of these commodities to the mines in northern Mexico. The providers of these goods were the Pueblo populations (Scholes 1937–1941).

These products were mobilized through two channels: the encomienda tribute and direct tapping of Pueblo labor by New Mexican governors. Encomiendas were land grants that were supposed to be given to settlers as a reward for 5 to 10 years of service in the colony. However, because the grants were important sources of revenue, they were often given to particular allies of the governors (Benavides 1945; Scholes 1937–1941). These grants included access to the goods of a pueblo or part of a pueblo in the form of tribute. Encomenderos were al-

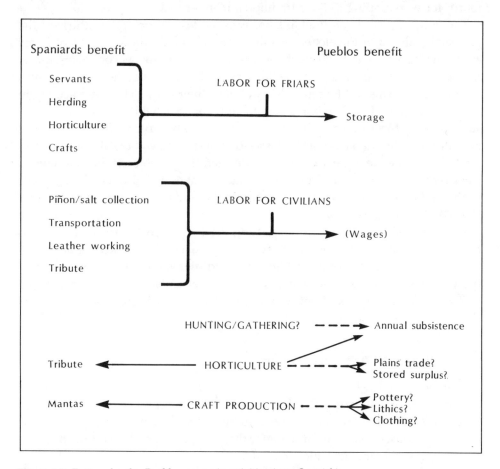

Figure 6-2. Eastern border Pueblo economic activities (post-Spanish).

lowed to collect tribute in food, cotton cloth, and hides twice a year. This tribute was generally one *manta*, or hide, and one *fanega* (1.6 bushels) of corn per household per year.

Although encomienda tribute payments were the only legal means by which Pueblo resources could be tapped without recompense, New Mexican governors managed to mobilize a fair amount of Pueblo labor for their own profit. Documents record that Pueblo groups, often those from the eastern border pueblos, were required to collect and transport piñon nuts, salt, and corn for various governors. In addition, Puebloans were required to wash and tan hides, weave cotton and woolen cloth, and build carts for the transport of these goods to Mexico. Dozens of Puebloans, often men, were employed in these tasks for weeks at a time, and thus were unable to carry out tasks at home. They were rarely paid for their efforts, although strict wage rates were in place for such activities (Scholes 1936–1937, 1937–1941).

Interestingly, the governors also sought to acquire goods from Puebloans by promising that they would be allowed to continue their religious ceremonies, which the friars were active in eradicating. For example, both governors Eulate and Rosas encouraged the inhabitants of Pecos to provide them with hides in return for worshipping in their traditional manner (Scholes 1936–1937).

The friars' demands on Pueblo labor were no less onerous than those of the governors, although Puebloans may have received a bit more in return. Friars employed approximately 20 Puebloans in their conventos as cooks, organists, translators, and bell ringers (Benavides 1945). Of more significance, they also required Puebloans to till their fields and herd their stock. The latter activity in particular drained Pueblo labor in that the missionaries held the majority of livestock in New Mexico. The importance of Pueblo labor to church enterprises is demonstrated by the fact that the losses of maize and head of cattle were enormous when one New Mexico governor decreed that Puebloans did not have to work for friars without pay. Periodically, Pueblo labor was also required to assist in the building of churches and to produce clothing for the friars' use (Scholes 1936–1937, 1937–1941).

The Pueblos gained little from assisting the friars. Most stock was exported to Mexico in order to pay for church furnishings. The friars did keep grain stores to be used to feed Puebloans in times of need. Benavides (1945) reported that the poor were fed from these stores, as were servants. In the famines of the 1660s, the food supplies of entire pueblos were supplemented for a time from the friars' grain (Scholes 1937–1941).

Spanish Impact on Plains–Pueblo Trade

As mentioned at the beginning of the chapter, Spanish documents provide data on the kinds of activities that affected the Puebloan economy, but not enough data to quantify that impact, or to determine specific Pueblo responses to these demands. Consequently, we must infer these responses and then test the inferences against the archaeological record.

The combined demands for goods and labor by friars and civil authorities had a profound effect on the traditional Pueblo economy. The burden of these demands is indicated by Puebloans who testified before Spanish authorities concerning the reasons for the Pueblo Revolt. They cited two causes: religious persecution and labor demands that did not leave them time to plant or do the other things they needed to do (Hackett and Shelby 1942).

Given that there was not enough time or labor to carry out necessary activities, certain choices must have been made within Pueblo families and villages as a whole concerning how to deal with shortfalls. First, with regard to farming, the demands on both male and female labor would have meant that fewer people were available to plant, weed, and harvest. This would have reduced Pueblo crop production to the point that there may have been no surplus, and possibly have left families without enough food for the coming year. Without a surplus villagers would have had no buffer against shortfalls in corn. The household would no longer have been able to provide its own buffer through storage. Instead, any surplus would have been produced in the friars' fields, and distribution to the Puebloans would have been controlled by them.

The friars also deprived the people of a second buffer, that of religious ceremonies, leaving Pueblo families even more vulnerable to crop fluctuations. The famine of the 1660s, which caused hundreds of deaths and ultimately led the survivors to abandon the Gran Quivira area, illustrates this vulnerability. This famine followed droughts that were not as severe as droughts in the sixteenth century that do not appear to have caused famine and abandonment. The devastating impact of the 1660s drought suggests that the buffers of the traditional economic system had broken down, and that the friars did not have the stores needed to meet the needs of entire Pueblo populations.

It is likely that Spanish labor demands also affected Puebloan acquisition of meat. Demands for male labor would have left much less time for hunting. The response to decreases in hunting in the eastern border pueblos might have been to increase trade for meat. However, given lower crop production, it is doubtful that the Pueblos had surplus corn to trade. The alternative would have been for women and children to increase the take of game, such as rabbit and rodents, which they traditionally hunted and collected near the pueblos.

This stress on Pueblo crop production and hunting must be taken into account in any explanation of seventeenth-century changes in Plains–Pueblo exchange. Clearly, individual families would have been hard-pressed to produce a surplus of grain for trade with the Plains. However, they were not in a position to cease trading, for several reasons. First, the Apache were acquiring horses through trade and raid of Spanish villages, making raid a viable option if the Pueblos were not willing to trade. Second, the Spanish demands for hides as tribute, coupled with the fact that Pueblo men had less time to hunt, would have made trade with Plains groups for hides of continuing importance to the eastern border Pueblos. This demand for hides probably resulted in a shift away from exchange for meat. Possible support for this shift can be found in statements referring to Plains–Pueblo trade in the 1660s, which report that Apaches came

Pueblos to trade *hides* (Kessell 1979). Meat is not mentioned at all, in stark contrast to documents from the mid-sixteenth to the early seventeenth century, which always listed meat and fat as Plains trade items (e.g., Hammond and Rey 1953, 1966; Winship 1896).

How the Pueblos coped with a need for trade but a lack of materials to trade is not dealt with in the Spanish documents. Three possibilities present themselves, but they have yet to be investigated with archaeological data. First, although they lacked "surplus" corn, Pueblo families may have been willing to trade any corn they had in return for hides. This would have led to acute nutritional stress if shortfalls of corn could not be compensated for with larger quantities of gathered wild foods. Second, an influx of Spanish material items, particularly knives, which governors and friars provided for the Pueblos, might have taken the place of traditional subsistence products. Third, it is possible that Plains–Pueblo trade became increasingly controlled by a few, well-placed individuals in the pueblos.

Spanish documents report that governors generally dealt only with the "caciques," or headmen, of the Pueblos. Occasionally they provided these caciques with goods to trade with Plains Apaches. For example, Governor Lopez gave a Salinas cacique, Don Esteban Clemente, goods to take with him on a trading expedition to the Seven Rivers Apache (Scholes 1937–1941). The increasing involvement in Plains trade of a few Puebloans who were well connected with Spanish authorities might explain why the caciques of Pecos and the Galisteo Pueblos were *not* interested in taking part in the Pueblo Revolt of 1680, although their followers were (Hackett and Shelby 1942). Also, at the time of the reconquest in the 1690s, the inhabitants of Pecos were particularly interested in assisting the Spaniards. They hoped that Spanish goods would reenter Plains–Pueblo trade, and shore up a system that apparently had atrophied in the 1680s (Kessell 1979).

The hypothesis that a few Puebloans could have risen in power through increasing interaction with Europeans and participation in long-distance trade finds support in socioeconomic changes that occurred among northern Plains groups in the eighteenth and nineteenth centuries. Among the Cheyenne, for example, white traders tended to work with individuals rather than whole tribes, and thus enhanced the prestige and wealth of those that traded with them (Jablow 1951). In addition, acquisition of the horse increased wealth differences within northern Plains tribes (Ewers 1955). This gave rise to horse-poor families that depended on loans of horses for access to bison hunting, and to wealthy families who maintained horse herds through trade and raid, and profited from their loans.

I suggest that, for the seventeenth-century Southwest, the fact that each family was required to provide hides as tribute payments possibly created a situation of indebtedness within pueblos. Hides could have flowed from more wealthy individuals, who could maintain active trading, to those who lacked the means to continue trade with Plains groups. Another interesting question is whether Spanish involvement in Plains–Pueblo trade was responsible for the status differences that evolved within Rio Grande pueblos, or whether they simply built upon existing, prehistoric status differences. However, this question is beyond the scope of this chapter.

Spanish Direct Involvement in Plains–Pueblo Trade

The foregoing discussion has focused primarily on indirect effects of Spanish activities on Plains–Pueblo trade. However, the Spaniards were *directly* involved with Apachean groups in a variety of cooperative and hostile ways. These involvements also would have affected change in the protohistoric interdependent system.

First, the Spanish governors attempted to trade directly with Plains Apaches. For example, Governors Romero, Rosas, and Lebaros traded directly with Apaches visiting at Pecos (Scholes 1937–1941). Their trade was welcome as it provided the Apaches with metal tools and horses. As early as 1622, friar Juarez at Pecos commented on how important the Plains–Pueblo trade was for Puebloans and Spaniards alike, in that it provided both populations with clothing and materials for sacks and tents (Kessell 1979).

Second, Spanish governors also sponsored expeditions onto the Plains to seek out Apachean traders. At least three trading expeditions are reported in the documents, two in the 1630s and one in the 1660s. In addition, several exploring expeditions were sent to the Plains by various governors in the 1630s–1650s (Kessell 1979; Scholes 1937–1941; Tyler and Taylor 1958). These also may have engaged in trade.

The impact of this attempt at coopting the Plains–Pueblo trade is unknown. Clearly, Spaniards were tapping a supply of goods that normally would have gone to Puebloans. However, it is also possible that Spanish trading activities bolstered Plains–Pueblo trade at a time when fewer Pueblo families had goods to exchange with their Plains trade partners. Again, the apparent lapse of trading at Pecos between the revolt and the reconquest suggests that, without Spanish participation in the trading system, exchange activity decreased sharply.

Spanish interaction with nomadic groups was not always in the form of amicable trade. Plains captives were as much in demand in northern Mexico as hides were, and the Apache were often the target of Spanish raids to procure such captives. The documents report several instances in which Apaches trading at Pecos, Taos, and Jemez were seized and enslaved. Spanish expeditions to the Plains also raided Apache bands for captives (Scholes 1937–1941).

Although Spanish hostilities are often said to have impeded Plains interaction with Puebloan groups, there is actually little indication that Plains–Pueblo interaction decreased (Forbes 1960; Kessell 1979). Instead, it took a more hostile turn. Apache raids were often made in retaliation, and the Apache began to deal in captives themselves. They often brought other Plains captives directly to Spaniards in return for horses, firearms, and knives (Scholes 1937–1941; Tyler and Taylor 1958). Perhaps it is a measure of the importance of Plains–Pueblo trade to Plains groups that this trade continued despite the risk of being captured at the trading Pueblos. The continuation of alliances between Puebloan and Apache groups throughout the seventeenth century also suggests that Plains–Pueblo interdependence was not severely affected by Spanish raiding.

Archaeological Data

Thus far, the data that have been used to discuss the impact of Spanish colonization on Plains–Pueblo trade have been documentary. Clearly the documents provide a wealth of data concerning Spanish activities. They do not, however, shed much light on Pueblo responses until the Pueblo Revolt of 1680. In the preceding discussion I have postulated several potential consequences of and responses to Spanish activities that might be testable with archaeological data. In this section, I outline what those data might be and provide illustrations from excavations at Gran Quivira Pueblo.

It appears that Spanish colonization severely restricted Pueblos from carrying out subsistence activities, both hunting and farming. The burden of labor appears to have been placed on males in particular, and I would therefore expect to find that male activities such as hunting had decreased substantially. Locally, small mammals would probably be taken by women and children around the pueblo. These changes should be reflected in the faunal material from eastern border pueblos.

It is also likely that less time would have been available to devote to the cultivation of crops as both males and females worked for the Spaniards. Therefore, each household would have had less to store and would have used fewer storage vessels.

Nutritionally, the pueblos would have been under stress as their corn intake and especially their meat intake would have been affected by (1) less time for hunting, (2) less to trade with Plains groups, and (3) more focus on trade for skins than for meat. Consequently, I would expect to find that nutritional health decreased dramatically in the seventeenth century. Archaeologically, bone chemistry analysis can provide data concerning dietary change, and osteological analyses will provide information on overall nutritional health (see also Walker et al., this volume).

Archaeological data from excavations at Gran Quivira Pueblo provide some information concerning protohistoric subsistence change. The faunal data indicate that small mammals, particularly cottontails and woodrats, do become much more frequent in the seventeenth-century deposits. At the same time, bison bone decreases in the middens, and antelope, the locally available larger game animal, does not increase. These patterns would reflect a situation in which local small mammal collection is substituted for both long-distance hunting of large game and trade for bison meat (Spielmann 1988).

With regard to nutritional health, Turner's analyses of the Gran Quivira skeletal material excavated by the Park Service in the 1960s indicate a decrease in life expectancy in the seventeenth century (Turner 1981). This decrease is the result of both higher infant mortality and a decrease in the proportion of old adults in the population, both of which indicate a population under stress.

Neither the documents nor the archaeological data indicate the strategies that households used to deal with Spanish demands for labor and goods. If these demands were unequally distributed among families at any given time, I would expect that increasing interhousehold cooperation among kin might provide a viable support network. However, if acute stress was experienced fairly uniformly throughout a pueblo, then greater atomization of households, such as that documented in many famine situations, might develop (e.g., Laughlin and Brady 1978; Dirks 1980). Measuring an increase or decrease in suprafamily connections within the seventeenth century will be difficult, however.

There is a possibility, as discussed above, that a small number of Pueblo leaders profited from their connections with Spanish governors and acted as middlemen for Spaniards in Plains–Pueblo trade. These wealthier Puebloans, who were in a better position to exchange with Plains groups, could have become sources of the hides needed for tribute by all Pueblo families. In addition, it is possible that these leaders also functioned to redistribute other goods within pueblos, especially in the absence of ceremonies that had previously functioned to distribute food among families. In essence, I am hypothesizing that Pueblo social structure may have responded to increasing stress through the evolution of a vertical hierarchy, as predicted by certain models for the evolution of ranked society (e.g., Johnson 1982; Peebles and Kus 1977).

Archaeologically, documenting the existence and activities of a higher-status segment within the eastern border pueblos will be extremely difficult. We do not know whether hypothesized differences in wealth and prestige would be reflected in differential burial practices, personal adornment, and/or household materials. It is likely that persons of higher status would enjoy better nutritional health, but a fairly large sample of seventeenth-century burials would be necessary to detect these individuals. In addition, the abandonment of many eastern border pueblos in the latter half of the seventeenth century complicates the documentation of status differences in this area.

Conclusions

It appears that Spanish economic demands on Pueblo populations, coupled with Spanish involvement in Plains–Pueblo trade, profoundly restructured the initially mutualistic Plains–Pueblo exchange system. Mutualism requires that the majority of members of each population have access to goods and services provided by the other (Keeler 1981). On the Pueblo side of the system, such access may have become increasingly restricted. It is unlikely that individual families could have kept up their trade partnership obligations in the face of lower crop production. On the Plains side of the system, demand appears to have shifted from Pueblo subsistence products to Spanish material goods, such as metal weapons and horses. In turn, corn appears to have been cultivated by these Plains groups, possibly to compensate for its decreasing availability through exchange (Spielmann 1982).

In sum, within a few decades of Spanish colonization, the prehistoric Plains–Pueblo exchange system evolved into an historic Plains–Spaniard exchange system. By 1680, many of the eastern border trading Pueblos had ceased to exist, and others, such as Pecos, were unable to maintain the tempo of trade when the Spaniards were driven south.

References

Benavides, Alonso de
  1945 *Fray Alonso de Benavides' Revised Memorial of 1634*. Edited by Frederick Hodge, George Hammond and Agapito Rey. University of New Mexico Press, Albuquerque.
Binford, Lewis R.
  1978 *Nunamiut Ethnoarchaeology*. Academic Press, New York.
Dirks, Robert
  1980 Social Responses during Severe Food Shortages and Famine. *Current Anthropology* 21(1):21–44.
Ewers, John C.
  1955 *The Horse in Blackfoot Indian Culture*. Bureau of American Ethnology Bulletin 159, Washington, D.C.
Forbes, Jack D.
  1960 *Apache, Navajo, and Spaniard*. University of Oklahoma Press, Norman.
Ford, Richard I.
  1968 *An Ecological Analysis Involving the Population of San Juan Pueblo*. Unpublished Ph.D. dissertation, University of Michigan, Ann Arbor.
  1972a Barter, Gift, or Violence: An Analysis of Tewa Intertribal Exchange. In *Anthropological Paper* 46, edited by Edwin Wilmsen, pp. 21–45. University of Michigan, Museum of Anthropology, Ann Arbor.
  1972b An Ecological Perspective on the Eastern Pueblos. In *New Perspectives on the Pueblos*, edited by Alfonso Ortiz, pp. 1–17. University of New Mexico Press, Albuquerque.
Hackett, Charles W., and Charmion Shelby
  1942 *Revolt of the Pueblo Indians of New Mexico and Otermin's Attempted Reconquest, 1680–1682*. University of New Mexico Press, Albuquerque.
Hammond, George P., and Agapito Rey
  1953 *Don Juan de Oñate, Colonizer of New Mexico*. Coronado Cuarto Centennial Publication, vols. 5 and 6, University of New Mexico Press, Albuquerque.
  1966 *The Rediscovery of New Mexico, 1580–1594*. University of New Mexico Press, Albuquerque.
Jablow, J.
  1951 *The Cheyenne in Plains Indian Trade Relations, 1795–1840*. American Ethnological Society Monograph 19:1–110.
Johnson, Gregory
  1982 Organizational Structure and Scalar Stress. In *Theory and Explanation in Archaeology*, edited by C. Renfrew, M. J. Rowlands, and B. A. Segraves, pp. 389–421. Academic Press, New York.
Keeler, Kathleen
  1981 A Model of Selection for Facultative Nonsymbiotic Mutualism. *American Naturalist* 118(4):83–109.
Kessell, John L.
  1979 *Kiva, Cross, and Crown*. National Park Service, Washington, D.C.
Laughlin, Charles, and Ivan Brady
  1978 *Extinction and Survival in Human Populations*. University of Columbia Press, New York.
Peebles, Christopher, and Susan Kus
  1977 Some Archaeological Correlates of Ranked Societies. *American Antiquity* 42:421–448.

Raymer, Leslie E., and Paul E. Minnis
  1987 Ethnobotanical Relationships at Gran Quivira (LA 120), New Mexico. Ms. in possession of the author.
Scholes, France V.
  1936–1937 Church and State in New Mexico, 1610–1650. *New Mexico Historical Review* 11(1):9–76, (2):145–178, (3):283–294, (4):297–349; 12(1):78–106.
  1937–1941 Troublous Times in New Mexico, 1659–1670. *New Mexico Historical Review* 12(2):134–174, (4):380–452; 13(1):63–84; 15(3):249–268, (4):369–417; 16(1):15–40, (2):184–205, (3):313–327.
Scott, Linda J.
  1987 Pollen Analysis of Stratigraphic Midden Deposits from Gran Quivira National Monument, New Mexico. Ms. possession of the author.
Slatter, Edwin D.
  1979 *Drought and Demographic Change in the Prehistoric Southwest U.S.: A Preliminary Quantitative Assessment*. Ph.D. dissertation, University of California. University Microfilms, Ann Arbor.
Snow, David H.
  1981 Prehistoric Rio Grande Pueblo Economics: A Review of Trends. In *The Protohistoric Period in the North American Southwest*, edited by D. R. Wilcox and W. Bruce Masse, pp. 354–377. Anthropological Research Paper 24. Arizona State University, Tempe.
Speth, John D., and Susan L. Scott
  1985 Horticulture and Large Mammal Hunting: The Role of Resource Depletion and the Constraints of Time and Labor. In *Farmers as Hunters: The Implications of Sedentism*, edited by Susan Kent. Cambridge University Press, Cambridge, in press.
Spielmann, Katherine A.
  1982 *Inter-Societal Food Acquisition among Egalitarian Societies: An Ecological Study of Plains/Pueblo Interaction in the American Southwest*. Ph.D. dissertation, University of Michigan. University Microfilms, Ann Arbor.
  1983 Late Prehistoric Exchange between the Southwest and Southern Plains. *Plains Anthropologist* 28(102):257–272.
  1988 Changing Faunal Resource Procurement at Gran Quivira Pueblo, New Mexico. Paper presented at the 53rd Annual Meeting of the Society for American Archaeology, Phoenix.
Spielmann, Katherine A., Margaret J. Schoeninger, and Katherine Moore
  1988 Human Diet at Pecos Pueblo, New Mexico. Manuscript in preparation.
Turner, Christy G.
  1981 The Arizona State University Study of Gran Quiviran Physical Anthropology. In *Contributions to Gran Quivira Archaeology*, edited by Alden Hayes, pp. 119–121. National Park Service Publications in Archaeology, vol. 17, Washington, D.C.
Tyler, S. Lyman, and H. Darrel Taylor (editors)
  1958 The Report of Fray Alonso de Posada in Relation to Quivira and Teguayo. *New Mexico Historical Review* 33:285–314.
Wetterstrom, Wilma
  1986 *Food, Diet, and Population at Prehistoric Arroyo Hondo Pueblo, New Mexico*. School of American Research Press, Santa Fe, N.Mex.
Winship, George P.
  1896 *The Coronado Expedition, 1540–1542*. Bureau of American Ethnology Annual Report 14, Part I. Washington, D.C.

Chapter 7 ▪

Mark T. Lycett

Spanish Contact and Pueblo Organization: Long-term Implications of European Colonial Expansion in the Rio Grande Valley, New Mexico

Spanish colonial expansion, which began to directly affect the the Rio Grande Pueblo at least as early as the Coronado entrada of A.D. 1540–1541, resulted in extensive disruption in the social and economic organization of aboriginal cultural systems of the northern Southwest. However, the ramifications of contact are not restricted to the impact of colonial strategies and institutions designed to exploit, displace, or effect change in native social, political, economic, and ceremonial organization (Spicer 1962). Among the most important factors to condition discontinuity during the contact period was the introduction of a number of infectious pathogens of Old World origin into the nonimmune populations of the North American Southwest (Lycett 1984; Upham 1986). The consequences of European-introduced disease include shifts in the magnitude and age structure of mortality, and this in turn produced transgenerational shifts in the size and stability of Pueblo populations.

Despite nearly a century of research, our understanding of the impact of European contact on the organization and operation of aboriginal cultural systems remains limited. Archaeologists working in the region have traditionally emphasized the persistence and cultural stability of Puebloan peoples (Cordell and Plog

1979). This focus on historical continuity has obscured the many discontinuities that characterize the contact period in the Rio Grande Valley (Cordell 1984). Future investigations of these issues must take into account both the patterns of behavioral organization that obtained prior to and during contact and the processes acting to condition change.

Patterns in the Archaeological Record

On the Eve of Conquest

The long history of archaeological research in the Rio Grande Valley and surrounding areas has provided a wealth of data on late prehistoric land use and settlement (Cordell 1979). General patterns in the spatial structure of the archaeological record that reflect the organization of settlement and economy on a regional scale are emphasized in this chapter (see Binford 1982, 1983). After A.D. 1300, large, multiroom habitation sites decrease in frequency, increase in size, and become concentrated at low elevations that have access to permanent water. At the same time, the number and variety of small nonhabitation sites increase. Among these small sites are a series of agricultural facilities designed to retard erosion, retain soil, and conserve rainfall (Cordell and Earls 1983). These facilities incude gridded and bordered gardens, waffle gardens, gravel-mulched fields, raised fields, check dams, and terrace systems. Small structural sites with relatively ephemeral architecture and limited material inventories appear as satellites of the large sites. A number of nonstructural sites that vary in extent, density, and artifact composition are also present. Such patterns have been documented throughout the region north of Albuquerque (Biella and Chapman 1977; Blevins and Joiner 1977; Buge 1984; Dickson 1979; Hill and Trierweiler 1986; Lang 1977; Woosley 1986).

These patterns reflect considerable diversity in the agricultural component of the economy, as well as a form of land use that is consistent with logistically organized procurement systems (see Earls 1985). Logistically organized systems address spatial incongruities in the distribution of resources through the allocation of labor to special task groups who move resources to consumers (Binford 1980). Such strategies would not be unexpected in an environment in which many critical resources, including rainfall and solar radiation, exhibit high spatial and temporal variability (Cordell 1979).

Subsistence agriculturalists may cope with potential instability in the distribution and availability of resources in part through the maintenance of diversity both in the number of components in the economic system and the mix of strategies within each component (Colson 1979). Late prehistoric Anasazi subsistence economies in the Rio Grande Valley were no exception to this pattern. These incorporated gathering, hunting, extensive and intensive agriculture, and the procurement of nonsubsistence resources (Cordell 1980). Sustained commitment to the maintenance of all components of such an economy would be expected to result in a highly scheduled and structured use of the landscape, especially during periods of peak labor demand (Cordell and Upham 1983).

The Morning After

With some important exceptions (Earls 1985; Hayes 1981; Lang 1977; Marshall and Walt 1984), most research pertaining to the archaeological record of the early Historic period was conducted in the first half of this century. This early work focused exclusively on large sites and concerned itself with issues of chronology and description (Cordell, this volume). Data on regional patterning were not regularly collected until relatively recently. In most cases, however, postcontact materials are incidental to the goals of this research and many of the areas surveyed may have been marginal to early historic Pueblo occupations. Nevertheless, in the first 150 years following contact, the frequency of all site types decreases, although there is a greater decline in the number of small sites and agricultural facilities than in the number of large habitation sites (Biella 1977; Blevins and Joiner 1977; Dickson 1979; Hill and Trierweiler 1986; Lang 1977). Many of the large habitation sites of the protohistoric continued to be occupied into the historic period, but the area occupied within each site was consideraly reduced (Kidder 1958; Lambert 1954; Marshall and Walt 1984; Nelson 1914).

Our knowledge of the changes in settlement during this period is based in large part on the historical record. However, determination of long-term demographic trends in Pueblo populations from this source of information is problematic. Early population figures suffer from uneven and haphazard coverage. Nevertheless, documentary sources indicate that significant depopulation occurred among the Rio Grande Pueblos following Spanish contact (Palkovitch 1985). Both the number of occupied settlements and average number of individuals per settlement declined between the seventeenth (Ayer 1916; Scholes 1929, 1944) and eighteenth (Adams and Chavez 1956; Hackett 1937) centuries. This decline was the result of both depopulation and outmigration of some groups following the Pueblo Revolt and Spanish reconquest. Migration of individuals and domestic groups between settlements appears to have been common throughout the colonial period.

Disease Ecology and Demographic Change

The Spanish contact had severe ecological consequences among the populations of the Southwest. The effect of the pathogens introduced by the Spanish cannot be fully understood without some knowledge of the dynamic relationships between parasites and their human hosts (Howell 1976).

Wherever parasites are common or endemic in the environment, infection is persistent, and there is little variation in prevelance. To some extent, newborn infants receive partial and temporary protection from disease from antibodies transferred from the mother before birth and afterward via breast milk. Both the type and number of antibodies that a child receives depend on the immunological experience of the mother. Any subsequent immunity that a child develops depends on exposure to pathogens present in the child's environment. Survival from infection confers some degree of immunity, which is reinforced by subsequent exposure. Consequently, by age three, most children have developed immunity to those pathogens that are common in their environment (Burnet and White 1972; Carpenter 1984). The age pattern of mortality under these conditions may be represented by a U-shaped curve to indicate that mortality from all causes is highest in the very young and the aged. Those age groups with the highest fertility rates are also among those with the lowest mortality (Howell 1976). Therefore, disease-related mortality does not alter the age structure of the population, but if prereproductive mortality is sufficiently high, it may regulate the size and growth rate of the population (Kunstader 1972).

The situation changes when an infection is newly introduced into an ecosystem: It may significantly disrupt the demographic parameters of human populations. Asexual infections, which may be introduced by a single source, multiply rapidly wherever they have not circulated previously or are rare (Dunn 1968). Under these conditions, epidemics may pass through virtually the entire population in a relatively short period of time, and then, in the absence of a nonhuman reservoir, disappear completely (Black 1975).

The level of mortality during such epidemics depends on a number of factors. When morbidity is widespread, care for the ill becomes difficult and infants and children may be neglected (Burnet and White 1972). Epidemics in nonimmune populations are often accompanied by simultaneous or sequential outbreaks of other diseases as well as increased mortality due to complications and secondary bacterial infections (Adels and Gajdusek 1963; Black et al. 1977). Although mortality rates from individual epidemics vary, exposure to pathogens such as measles, poliomyelitis, plague, smallpox, or influenza may result in death rates as high as 30 percent in nonimmune populations with no access to modern medical care (e.g., Corney 1913; Dixon 1962; Hollingsworth 1969; Nagler et al. 1949; Wells 1932). Mortality on this scale is, by itself, significant; nevertheless, the long-term effects of abnormal patterns of survivorship may be even more important.

In a population with no previous exposure to an infection, all age groups are at risk. However, mortality is neither independent with respect to age nor does it follow a normal, U-shaped, curve. Although death rates are elevated for all age groups, a third mode of age-specific mortality often occurs in the young adult segment of society (Burnet and White 1972). Many pathogens, including measles, mumps, poliomyelitis, and chickenpox produce significantly more severe reactions and have a greater probability of complications when contracted by adults (May 1984). Elevated levels of adult mortality have been documented following the introduction of poliomyelitis (Rosen and Thooris 1953), plague (Hollingsworth and Hollingsworth 1971), smallpox (Hansen 1980), influenza (Crosby 1977), cholera (Pierce 1984), viral hepatitis (Gust 1984), and measles (Corney 1913).

This shift in the age pattern of mortality has profound implications for the size, age structure, and stability of affected populations. For mortality to initiate a sustained decline in a stable population, it must be highly specific with respect to age. Uniform mortality throughout all age groups would preserve the age structure of the population, allowing fertility and mortality to return to their former levels within a few years (McArthur 1967). In contrast, elevated mortality among young adults, particularly among women in their childbearing years, results in the loss of both the current population and future reproductive potential. This diminished potential has repercussions on succeeding generations as depleted cohorts attain reproductive maturity. Thus, epidemics that concentrate mortality among the reproductive and prereproductive portions of a population initiate a decline in fertility and impair a population's capacity to replace itself, and thereby result in a transgenerational decline (Chagnon and Melancon 1983; Roberts and Mohan 1976).

A demographic decline will be maintained and exacerbated by recurrent or reintroduced epidemics, which preferentially affect cohorts born between epidemics, who thus have neither previous exposure nor immunity. Exposure to many pathogens—including measles, mumps, chickenpox, and smallpox—confers lifelong immunity. As a result of the long life span and relatively low reproductive rate of humans, a large population is required in order to ensure that susceptibles are continuously introduced into the population (Fenner and White 1976). Measles, for example, requires an annual input of 4,000 to 5,000 susceptibles in order to persist (Black 1966). A figure of 300,000 individuals is commonly cited as the population size required to perpetuate density-dependent asexual infections (May 1984). In addition to population size, the density of the host population affects the ability of parasites to perpetuate themselves (Anderson and May 1979). In the absence of new sources of infection, only those pathogens that can remain latent for long periods of time or that have nonhuman reservoirs can persist in small or highly dispersed human groups (Black et al. 1974).

In populations with insufficient growth rates to support the continuous perpetuation of a pathogen, such as the Rio Grande Pueblo, the frequency of recurrence is determined by reintroduction and is therefore dependent upon the frequency of contact with new sources of infection. Continued high prereproductive mortality from periodic epidemics diminishes reproductive potential as it impairs a population's ability to replace itself. Note that if the frequency of recurrence is low, epidemics may be fewer in number but more devastating in effect (Kunstader 1972).

High mortality, abnormal age-specific mortality, and recurrent epidemics have long-term effects on the size, stability, and age structure of nonimmune populations struck by epidemic disease. Renewed population growth is associated with a return to normal patterns of survivorship coupled with a decrease in overall rates of morbidity and mortality (Burnet and White 1972; Ikwueke 1984). These patterns are indicative of a transgenerational evolution between parasite and host. Although disease is still killing individuals, it is neither removing large numbers of people nor depressing reproductive potential.

Demographic Instability and Behavioral Organization

Given the long-term demographic implications of infections introduced by Europeans, it may be suggested that Spanish colonial expansion into the northern Southwest resulted in drastic, extensive, and fundamental changes in the land-use and adaptive systems of the Rio Grande Pueblos.

Instability in the size, age structure, and growth rate of local populations has important implications for the organization of labor in Pueblo economies of the contact period. It is vital to consider these implications at the level of the household, the most basic unit of production and economic organization (Snow 1981). The multicomponent land-use strategies of the protohistoric Anasazi depended on human labor to maintain the viability of both intensive and extensive agricultural strategies, as well as nonagricultural procurement systems. The processing and handling time associated with the storage and consumption of agricultural produce creates additional demands on the labor force (Gilman 1987). Productive units respond to these demands through scheduling, or the allocation of labor in response to the timing and sequence of required tasks (Wilk and Netting 1984). The demographic consequences of contact, then, include not only the loss of reproductive capacity, but also the loss of productive capacity and potential. This loss of available labor intensifies existing scheduling conflicts and results in increased dependency. To ensure that some procurement strategies are maintained, a group may have to abandon or modify some of its other strategies. Continued population decline exacerbates labor and scheduling stress, disrupting an individual household's ability to regularly procure a wide variety of resources. If the maintenance of economic diversity is an important buffering strategy among subsistence agriculturalists (Colson 1979), then one implication of European contact is a decrease in the economic stability of households.

If a declining population concentrates on the agricultural component of the economy, extensive procurement and productive systems will suffer significant reductions or drop out entirely. Thus, Pueblo communities would have used marginal fields and extensive agricultural systems, including upland agricultural facilities dependent on rainfall, with decreasing frequency, or abandoned them entirely in favor of relatively more productive locales. Resources that required logistical expeditions for their procurement, and any raw materials normally acquired during these expeditions, would have become increasingly difficult to obtain. As both the frequency and extent of trips into the environment decreased, resource monitoring and thus available environmental information would have been lost. These trends would both contribute to and be intensified by instability in productive organization. Over a period of several generations, the sustaining area of individual settlements would have been used with decreasing frequency and intensity, and the area from which most resources were obtained would have become increasingly localized. The end result would have been an economy focused on the immediate foraging radius and primary agricultural zone of the Pueblo settlements, a pattern evident in the ethnographic literature (See Cordell and Earls 1983).

In addition to changes in the scale and organization of land use, the legacy of contact includes a steep decline in the number of occupied settlements. Although these historic abandonments have been recognized, they have generally been seen as the result of a series of proximate causes (Schroeder 1979). However, these changes cannot be evaluated without reference to the role of individual settlements in a system of land use and social and economic organization. That is, pueblos are not independent of the technological organization, land-use, and mobility strategies of their occupants. The loss of villages reflects not only population decline, but the instability of settlements and their constituent households as units of production, reproduction, and social organization (Lycett 1984). Increases in both mortality and migration result in the loss of individuals necessary for ceremonial, social, political, and economic viability. At some point in this process, a community is no longer capable of supporting itself as an independent entity. Thus, in the first two centuries following initial contact with the Spaniards, the area occupied and utilized by the Pueblos was substantially reduced. Long-term patterns of population decline and demographic instability form an important background condition to this spatial contraction.

Discussion

Efforts to understand and explain the consequences of the contact period in the Rio Grande Valley must focus attention on the role of both Spanish strategies and institutions and the changes conditioned by the presence of the Europeans in an environment in which they had not previously been an element. The Spanish colonial empire, and its diverse subpopulations, affected virtually every aspect of the organization of Pueblo society, and was in turn affected by it. Although I have concentrated on the biological consequences of the contact, I do not wish to minimize the importance of colonial institutions and behavioral strategies. In coopting native labor and the products of that labor for colonial economic systems and encroaching into the sustaining areas of native settlements, the Spanish would have exacerbated the trends in labor organization and land use discussed above. In addition, the presence of the colonists, their domesticates, and technology changed the nature of available resources in the Pueblo environment.

Pathogens introduced by the Spaniards resulted in devastating epidemics characterized by abnormally high morbidity and mortality. The impact of contact-period epidemics, however, is not restricted to changes in population size, nor should the biological disruptions that occurred during this period be considered a series of events. Rather, changes in the health status and demographic parameters of aboriginal populations occurred within the context of a transgenerational process. Long-term shifts in patterns of morbidity and mortality resulting from newly introduced infections are best viewed in terms of an underlying pattern of demographic instability, which in turn produces selective pressure for changes in the organization of land use and settlement.

References

Adams, E. B., and A. Chavez (editors and translators)
  1956 *The Missions of New Mexico 1776: A Description by Fray Francisco Atanasio Dominguez with Other Contemporary Documents.* University of New Mexico Press, Albuquerque.
Adels, B. R., and D. C. Gajdusek
  1963 Survey of Measles Patterns in New Guinea, Micronesia, and Australia with a Report of New Virgin Soil Epidemics and the Demonstration of Susceptible Primitive Populations by Sereology. *American Journal of Hygiene* 77:317–343.

Anderson, R. M., and R. M. May
    1979 Population Biology of Infectious Diseases: Part I. *Nature* 280:361–367.
Ayer, Mrs. A. E. (translator).
    1916 *The Memorial of Fray Alonso De Benevides, 1630.* Privately Printed. Chicago.
Biella, J. V.
    1977 Previous Anthropological Research in the Cochiti Study Area. In *A Survey of Regional Variability*, edited by J. V. Biella and R. C. Chapman, pp. 105–149. Archaeological Investigations in Cochiti Reservoir, New Mexico, vol. 1. Office of Contract Archaeology, University of New Mexico, Albuquerque.
Biella, J. V., and R. C. Chapman
    1977 Survey of Cochiti Reservoir: Presentation of Data. In *A Survey of Regional Variability*, edited by J. V. Biella and R. C. Chapman, pp. 201–294. Archaeological Investigations in Cochiti Reservoir, New Mexico, vol. 1. Office of Contact Archaeology, University of New Mexico, Albuquerque.
Binford, L. R.
    1980 Willow Smoke and Dogs' Tails: Hunter-Gatherer Settlement Systems and Archaeological Site Formation. *American Antiquity* 45:4–20.
    1982 The Archaeology of Place. *Journal of Anthropological Archaeology* 1:5–31.
    1983 Long Term Land Use Patterning: Some Implications for Archaeology. In *Working at Archaeology*, pp. 379–386. Academic Press, New York.
Black, F. L.
    1966 Measles Endemicity in Insular Populations. *Journal of Theoretical Biology* 11(2):207–211.
    1975 Infectious Disease in Primitive Society. *Science* 187(4176):515–518.
Black, F. L., W. J. Hierholder, DeP. Pinheiro, A. S. Evans, J. P. Woodall, E. M. Opton, J. E. Emmons, B. S. West, G. Endsall, W. G. Downs, and G. D. Wallace
    1974 Evidence for Persistence of Infectious Agents in Isolated Human Populations. *American Journal of Epidemiology* 100:230–250.
Black, F. L., DeP. Pinheiro, W. J. Hierholder, and R. V. Lee
    1977 Epidemics of Infectious Disease: The Example of Measles. In *Health and Disease in Tribal Societies*, edited by P. Hugh-Jones, pp. 115–136. Excerpta Medica, Amsterdam.
Blevins, B. B., and C. Joiner
    1977 The Archaeological Survey of Tijeras Canyon. In *The 1976 Excavation of Tijeras Pueblo, Cibola National Forest, New Mexico*, edited by L. S. Cordell, pp. 126–152. Archaeological Report No. 18. USDA Forest Service, Southwest Region, Albuquerque.
Buge, D.
    1984 Prehistoric Subsistence Strategies in the Ojo Caliente Valley, New Mexico. In *Prehistoric Agricultural Strategies in the Southwest*, edited by S. K. Fish and P. R. Fish, pp. 27–34. Anthropological Research Paper No. 33. Arizona State University, Tempe.
Burnet, M., and D. O. White
    1972 *Natural History of Infectious Disease.* 4th ed. Cambridge University Press, Cambridge.
Carpenter, C. C. J.
    1984 Acute Diarrhea. In *Tropical and Geographical Medicine*, edited by K. S. Warren and A. A. F. Mahmoud, pp. 9–13. McGraw-Hill, New York
Chagnon, N., and T. F. Melancon
    1983 *Epidemics in a Tribal Population, The Impact of Contact: Two Yanamomo Case Studies.* Occasional Paper No. 11. Cultural Survival Incorporated, Cambridge, Mass.
Colson, E.
    1979 In Good Years and Bad: Food Strategies of Self-Reliant Societies. *Journal of Anthropological Research* 35:18–29.

Cordell, L. S.

1979 *Cultural Resources Overview of the Middle Rio Grande Valley, New Mexico*. USDA Forest Service and USDI Bureau of Land Management. U.S. Government Printing Office, Washington, D.C.

1980 Prehistoric Climate and Agriculture. In *Tijeras Canyon: Analyses of the Past*, edited by L. S. Cordell, pp. 60–70. University of New Mexico Press, Albuquerque.

1984 Rio Grande Prehistory: Prelude to Contact. *New Mexico Geological Society Guidebook* 35:287–289.

Cordell, L. S., and A. C. Earls

1983 Mountains and Rivers: Resource Use at Three Sites. Paper presented at the Second Anasazi Conference, Bloomfield, N. Mex.

Cordell, L. S., and F. Plog

1979 Escaping the Confines of Normative Thought. *American Antiquity* 44:405–429.

Cordell, L. S., and S. Upham

1983 Agriculture in the Southwest. In *Theory and Model Building: Refining Survey Strategies for Locating Prehistoric Heritage Resources*, edited by L. S. Cordell and D. F. Green, pp. 39–58. USDA Forrest Service Cultural Resources Document No. 3, Albuquerque.

Corney, B. G.

1913 A Note on An Epidemic of Measles at Rotuma, 1911. *Proceedings of the Royal Society of Medicine* 6(2): 138–143. London.

Crosby, A. W.

1977 The Influenza Pandemic of 1918. In *Influenza in America, 1918–1976*, edited by J. E. Osborn, pp. 5–14. Prodist, New York.

Dickson, B. D.

1979 *Prehistoric Pueblo Settlement Patterns: The Arroyo Hondo Site Survey*. Arroyo Hondo Archaeological Series, vol. 2. School of American Research Press, Santa Fe.

Dixon, C. W.

1962 *Smallpox*. J. and A. Churchill, London.

Dunn, F. L.

1968 Epidemiological Factors: Health and Disease in Hunter-Gatherers. In *Man the Hunter*, edited by R. B. Lee and I. DeVore, pp. 221–228. Aldine, Chicago.

Earls, A. C.

1985 *The Organization of Piro Subsistence, A.D. 1300–1680*. Unpublished Ph.D. dissertation, Department of Anthropology, University of New Mexico.

Fenner, F. L., and D. O. White

1976 *Medical Viriology*. Academic Press, New York.

Gilman, P. A.

1987 Architecture as Artifact: Pit Structures and Pueblos in the American Southwest. *American Antiquity* 52:538–564.

Gust, I. D.

1984 Viral Hepatitis. In *Tropical and Geographical Medicine*, edited by K. S. Warren and A. A. F. Mahmoud, pp. 572–585. McGraw-Hill, New York.

Hackett, C. W. (editor)

1937 *Historical Documents Relating to New Mexico, Nueva Viscaya, and Approaches Thereto, to 1773*. Collected by A. F. A. Bandelier and F. R. Bandelier. Vol. III. Publication No. 333. Carnegie Institution, Washington, D.C.

Hansen, H.

1980 Some Age Structural Consequences of Mortality Variations in Pre-Transitional Iceland and Sweden. In *The Great Mortalities: Methodological Studies of Demographic Crises in the Past*, edited by H. Charbonneau and A. Larose, pp. 113–132. International Union for the Scientific Study of Population. Ordina Editions, Liège.

Hayes, A. C.

1981 *Excavation of Mound 7, Gran Quivera National Monument, New Mexico*. Publications in Archaeology No. 16. National Park Service, Washington, D.C.

Hill, J. N., and W. N. Trierweiler
　1986 *Prehistoric Responses to Food Stress on the Pajarito Plateau, New Mexico: Technical Report and Results of the Pajarito Archaeological Research Project, 1977–1985*. Submitted to National Science Foundation.

Hollingsworth, T. H.
　1969 *Historical Demography*. Cornell University Press, Ithaca.

Hollingsworth, M., and T. H. Hollingsworth
　1971 Plague Mortality Rates by Age and Sex in the Parish of of St. Bartolph's Without, Bishopsgate, London, 1603. *Population Studies* 25(1):131–146.

Howell, 1976
　1976 Toward a Uniformitarian Theory of Human Paleodemography. *Journal of Human Evolution* 5:25–40.

Ikwueke, K.
　1984 The Changing Pattern of Infectious Disease. *British Medical Journal* 289(6455):1355–1358.

Kidder, A. V.
　1958 *Pecos, New Mexico: Archaeological Notes*. Papers of the Robert S. Peabody Foundation for Archaeology No. 5. Andover, Mass.

Kunstader, P.
　1972 Demography, Ecology, Social Structure, and Settlement Patterns. In *The Structure of Human Populations*, edited by G. A. Harrison and A. J. Boyce, pp. 313–551. Clarendon Press, Oxford.

Lambert, M. F.
　1954 *Paa-ko: Archaeological Chronicle of an Indian Village in North Central New Mexico*. Monograph No. 19. School of American Research, Santa Fe.

Lang, R. W.
　1977 *Archaeological Survey of the Upper San Cristobal Arroyo Drainage, Galisteo Basin, Santa Fe County, New Mexico*. Submitted to New Mexico State Planning Office. School of American Research Contract Office, Santa Fe.

Lycett, M. T.
　1984 Social and Economic Consequences of Aboriginal Population Decline from Introduced Disease. Paper presented at the 49th Annual Meeting of the Society for American Archaeology, April 11–14, Portland, Oreg.

McArthur, N.
　1967 *Island Populations of the Pacific*. Australia National University Press, Canberra.

Marshall, M. P., and H. J. Walt
　1984 *Rio Abajo: The Prehistory and History of a Rio Grande Province*. New Mexico Prehistoric Preservation Division, Santa Fe.

May, R. M.
　1984 Ecology and Population Biology. In *Tropical and Geographical Medicine*, edited by K. S. Warren and A. A. F. Mahmoud, pp. 152–166. McGraw-Hill, New York.

Nagler, F. P., C. E. VanRooyen, and J. H. Sturdy
　1949 An Influenza Virus Epidemic at Victoria Island, North West Territory, Canada. *Canadian Journal of Public Health* 40:457–465.

Nelson, N. C.
　1914 *Pueblo Ruins of the Galisteo Basin, New Mexico*. Anthropological Papers of the American Museum of Natural History 15(1). New York.

Palkovich, A. M.
　1985 Historic Population of the Eastern Pueblos: 1540–1910. *Journal of Anthropological Research* 41:401–426.

Pierce, N. F.
　1984 Cholera. In *Tropical and Georgraphical Medicine*, edited by K. S. Warren and A. A. F. Mahmoud, pp. 703–709. McGraw-Hill, New York.

Roberts, D. F., and M. Mohan
  1976 History, Demography, and Genetics: The Fiji Experience and Its Evolutionary Implications. *Journal of Human Evolution* 5:117–128.
Rosen, L., and G. Thooris
  1953 Poliomyelitis in French Oceania: Epidemiologic Observations on an Outbreak with Notes on the Incidence of Paralysis Following Intramuscular Injections. *American Journal of Hygiene* 57:237–252.
Scholes, F. V.
  1929 Documents for the History of the New Mexico Missions in the Sixteenth Century. *New Mexico Historical Review* 4:48–58, 195–201.
  1944 Correction. *New Mexico Historical Review* 19:243–246.
Schroeder, A. H.
  1979 Pueblos Abandoned in Historic Times. In *Southwest*, edited by A. Ortiz, pp. 236–254. Handbook of North American Indians, vol. 9, William C. Sturtevant, general editor. Smithsonian Institution, Washington, D.C.
Snow, D. H.
  1981 Protohistoric Rio Grande Pueblo Economics: Review of Trends. In *The Protohistoric Period in the Southwest: 1450–1700*, edited by D. R. Wilcox and W. B. Masse, pp. 354–377. Anthropological Research Paper No. 24. Arizona State University, Tempe.
Spicer. E. H.
  1962 *Cycles of Conquest*. University of Arizona Press, Tucson.
Upham, S.
  1986 Smallpox and Climate in the American Southwest. *American Anthropologist* 88:115–128.
Wells, M. W.
  1932 Epidemiology. In *Poliomyelitis*, pp. 306–478. The International Committee for the Study of Infantile Paralysis, Baltimore, Md.
Wilk, R. R., and R. McC. Netting
  1984 Households: Changing Forms and Functions. In *Households: Comparative and Historical Studies of the Domestic Group*, edited by R. McC. Netting, R. R. Wilk, and E. J. Arnould, pp. 1–28. University of California Press, Berkeley.
Woosley, A. I.
  1986 Puebloan Prehistory of the Northern Rio Grande: Settlement, Population, Subsistence. *The Kiva* 51:143–164.

Chapter 8 ■

John L. Kessell

Spaniards and Pueblos: From Crusading Intolerance to Pragmatic Accommodation

A Fundamental Shift in Strategy

In his anxious, millenarian *Memorial* of 1630 to the king of Spain, Fray Alonso de Benavides, who personified the age of spiritual conquest in New Mexico, described a land of Pueblo Indian communities once under the devil's sway, torn by bloody strife between warriors and sorcerers, subject to pagan rites, and dotted with dens of idolatry he called estufas (kivas). Yet now, in contrast, thanks to its gentle conversion by the Franciscans, the kingdom rejoiced in the true God, Christian missionary priests administered the sacraments in decent churches, and the natives greeted each other with "Praise be to the Most Holy Name of Jesus Christ" (Benavides 1916:30–36, 117–125).

A century and a half later, Franciscan missionaries still ministered to the Pueblo Indians, but a profound change had taken place. Reporting to his superiors in Mexico City, Fray Francisco Atanasio Domínguez in 1776 matter-of-factly described Pueblo ceremonials, which he judged "not essentially wicked," and estufas, which he described as their "chapter, or council, rooms." Although the missionaries vigorously opposed scalp dances, they had been unable to eradicate them because, according to Domínguez, someone always made the excuse that the Indians were only neophytes. "Under such pretexts," the friar lamented, "they will always be neophytes and minors with the result that our Holy Faith will not take root and their malice will increase" (Domínguez 1956:254–258).

From self-assured intolerance to despairing accommodation, the Franciscans had compromised. So had the Pueblos. The friars had come to disregard certain native practices that were more Pueblo than Christian—superstitions, they called them—just as the Pueblos had adopted, to whatever degree, certain sacramental behavior that was more Christian than Pueblo.

During the span of six generations that elapsed between Benavides and Domínguez, a momentous, shared event—the Pueblo-Spanish war—dramatically rent the history of colonial New Mexico into prewar and postwar periods. A war in three acts, it erupted with furious fighting in 1680; existed mostly in abeyance for a dozen years, with the contending parties widely separated; and was joined again in close quarters during the 1690s. The Pueblos, united momentarily, had stunned their Spanish exploiters in 1680 and sent the survivors fleeing down the Rio Grande to El Paso (Hackett and Shelby 1942). Beginning in 1692, however, don Diego de Vargas, taking full advantage of Pueblo disunity, led Spaniards back to Sante Fe, winning allies among the Pueblos, defeating others militarily, and reimposing Spanish rule in New Mexico (Espinosa 1942).

Christianization in Pre- and Postwar New Mexico

The colony's prewar history of intolerance can be further divided into subperiods based on changing Pueblo-Spanish relations. The short, unproductive proprietorship of don Juan de Oñate from 1598 to 1609, which saw the Pueblos defeated in battle and forced to acknowledge Spanish overlordship, gave way to a longer, more intense effort to conquer the Pueblos spiritually (Hammond and Rey 1953). In remote New Mexico, the Franciscans belatedly and passionately carried on in the tradition of the mendicant friars' massive, sixteenth-century apostolate in New Spain (Ricard 1966). Between 1610 and 1680, while the Spanish Crown subsidized the colony as a missionary vineyard and friars and colonists contended jealously for Pueblo produce, labor, and loyalty, the Pueblos stored up their grievances (Scholes 1937, 1942).

In an innovative, recent study, historian Ramón A. Gutiérrez offers a striking interpretation of cultural give-and-take in prewar New Mexico. Seeking entrance to both the earthy world of the Pueblos and the tense world of honor-bound Spanish conquerors and ascetic friars, he details "how the Spanish conquest weakened the native hierarchy of power and authority, allowing a group of charismatic Franciscans assisted by fierce soldiers to seize control of the native religio-political apparatus" (Gutiérrez 1988:2–111). The seemingly magical friars sought to usurp not only the role of the cacique, or inside chief, who controlled law and the sacred in Pueblo society, but also the functions of war and hunt chiefs, rain chiefs, and medicine men. The missionaries "could mobilize force, conjure rain, heal the sick and provide the community with meat through their powers over animals" (Gutiérrez 1988:2–54).

In time, as the friars-intent-on-becoming-Pueblo-chiefs showed their impotence against disease, drought, Apache raiders, and other Spaniards, rifts between "Christianized" Pueblo Indians and "traditionalists" widened. The latter, consoling themselves in a renewal of Pueblo ceremonialism, united in 1680 and had their day.

Unfortunately, we have no synthesis of the Pueblos' evolving postwar response to Christianity—to baptism, the sacrifice of the mass, Jesus Christ and the saints, Franciscan celibacy, and enforced monogamy—or, for that matter, of the Christian missionaries' avoidance of Pueblo caciques and non-Christian ritual and their less frequent resort to corporal punishment. We are left asking how disenchanted friars and Pueblos in the eighteenth century worked out their syncretistic compromises or spiritual compartmentalizations, yet knowing from hindsight that they did (Ortiz 1969; Spicer 1962).

Military, Economic, and Social Relations

In other areas, too—military affairs, economics, and social relations—Spanish and Pueblo interaction after the war contrasted notably with earlier designs. In the beginning, the Spaniards had demonstrated military superiority over the Pueblos in sieges and pitched battles—at Hawikuh, Arenal and Moho, Puaray, Pecos, and Acoma—and then dominated the natives for most of the seventeenth century. Still, from time to time, Pueblos and Spaniards found occasion to kill each other selectively. Pueblos "martyred" missionaries, and Spaniards executed "subversives." During the eighteenth century, in contrast, as both girded against common enemies, Pueblos and Hispanos fought side by side, with the former regularly outnumbering the latter on campaign (Simmons 1979a).

In the economic sphere, the most notable feature of prewar New Mexico that was not reinstated after the war was the encomienda, which demanded annual tribute in commodities from each Pueblo household (Gutiérrez 1988; Scholes 1935; Snow 1983). In theory, at least, the Pueblos were paying for their defense by the Spanish encomendero, a function subsequently assumed by government-salaried presidial soldiers. After the war, when a majority of the sedentary population found itself bound to a hard life of subsistence, increased barter between Hispanos and Pueblos, shared trade with non-Pueblo Indians, and competition for land and water, featuring local agreements and readier Pueblo access to Spanish law, came to characterize the colony (Cutter 1986; Domínguez 1956; Hall 1987; Jenkins 1966, 1972).

Another indication of postwar accommodation, very much related to expanding economic intercourse, was the evolution in social relations between Hispanos and Pueblos at the community level. Increasingly, at least along the Rio Grande and its tributaries, they joined in ritual coparenthood (*compadrazgo*) and lived in close proximity (*vecindad*), becoming *compadres* and *vecinos*. This era of relatively good feelings—which, of course, varied from place to place and from time to time—seems to have lasted down to the late nineteenth or early twentieth century, when the U.S. government, urged on by Anglo-American "friends" of the natives, discovered that the Pueblos were Indians after all and began redrawing the lines between them and non-Indians, especially with regard to land and water rights (Hall 1987; Simmons 1979b)

Diego de Vargas and Spanish Recolonization

It is tempting to see Vargas's vigorous recolonization during the 1690s, the tumultuous third act of the Pueblo-Spanish war, as the pivot between centuries of intolerance and accommodation, and, in a sense, it was. Bold in battle, confident in diplomacy, and forceful in restoration of Spanish civil and religious authority, Diego de Vargas was not an innovator. Still, he applied previously successful Spanish strategies with such vigor that they carried decisively into the new century.

More than one contemporary reporter called Vargas the second Hernán Cortés, and he loved it. No Spaniard, in fact, before or after Vargas, utilized Pueblo Indian auxiliaries more effectively. For him, to divide and conquer was not a matter of rallying native subjects against an oppressive ruling class, as Cortés had done, but instead of exploiting the traditional factionalism between and within Pueblo communities.

The earliest Spaniards to come among the Pueblos, members of don Francisco Vázquez de Coronado's medieval outfit of 1540, had commented on the enmity between certain native towns or groupings of towns (Hammond and Rey 1940). Nearly a century later, Father Benavides recalled conflict within Pueblo communities, which he reduced to the formula "warriors" versus "sorcerers." Whether this intramural dissension resulted from competing generational, occupational, or social factions, it evidently was endemic. At the pueblo of Pecos, for example, Vargas and other Spaniards were able to exploit (and A. V. Kidder cogently to infer) the tension between what may have been a "liberal," outward-looking, hunting, fighting, and trading faction and a comparatively "conservative," inward-looking, farming faction (Kessell 1979; Kidder 1958).

Vargas planned and carried out a two-stage reconquest: first, a fast-moving, military reconnaissance in 1692 to demand the Pueblos' allegiance, by force of arms if necessary. Through sheer bravado and the threat of a siege, the Spanish governor gained entrance to Santa Fe, where the low-slung, adobe governor's "palace" and nearby structures had been converted by their Pueblo tenants into a defensible, multistoried housing complex. Here, on September 14, 1692—an anniversary still commemorated in the Santa Fe Fiesta—Vargas, momentarily unopposed, presided over a ritual act of repossession, while Franciscan friars absolved the Pueblos of their apostasy and baptized the children born since 1680.

Intent on extending his symbolic reconquest to Pecos, some 25 miles southeast of Santa Fe, Vargas found the community temporarily deserted. Now he displayed his diplomatic skills and restraint. Instead of plundering Pecos, as his predecessors might have done, he left the houses and stores intact, released his few captives, and admonished the latter to inform the others that he expected them to be there when he returned in several weeks. And they were, in considerable numbers. As part of a ritual familiar before the war, Diego de Vargas swore in don Juan de Ye, the pro-Spanish Pecos leader, as governor of the native town (Espinosa 1940). Ye and his assistants would deal with the outside world, leaving the cacique, the community's principal inside chief, whatever spiritual sway he could command.

After Vargas had repeated the ceremonial repossession in most of the other Rio Grande and Western Pueblo communities, he returned to El Paso with his men and proclaimed that he had reconquered New Mexico without firing a shot. In 1693, however, when the reconqueror sought to implement the second stage of his program with a larger expedition to resettle colonists in New Mexico, he met determined resistance.

Had don Juan de Ye refused Vargas's urgent request to send Pecos fighting men late in December, when the Tano and Tewa occupants of Santa Fe defiantly objected to vacating their homes, the Spaniards might have frozen to death outside the walls. Instead, in a bloody, room-by-room assault, they and their Pueblo auxiliaries won back the Spanish capital. Then, in an act reminiscent of Oñate's terrible, deterrent punishment of Acoma prisoners in 1599, Vargas decreed that 70 of the defenders be executed and some 400 bound into servitude.

At the same time, the Spanish reconqueror honored Pueblo war leaders—men like don Bartolomé de Ojeda of Santa Ana and Juan de Ye—who had cast their lot with him, presenting them with horses, firearms, and Spanish military titles and dress. In return, it would seem, they expected the honors, a share of the spoils, trade advantages, and Spanish protection of their communities from Pueblo and non-Pueblo enemies.

In 1696, when most of the Tewas, Tanos, and Jemez rose a second time against Spanish rule, Vargas could count on Pueblo warriors. Expediently, the remnant survivors of two native towns that had been brutally assaulted and sacked by Vargas's predecessors (Santa Ana and Zia) sided with him for protection. At Pecos, don Felipe Chistoe, the new leader of the loyal faction, laid a trap, with Vargas's concurrence, inviting the anti-Spanish leaders to talks in a kiva, where he hanged them. This internecine act, a symptom of the heavy stress occasioned by the Pueblo-Spanish war, drove the Pecos community to the verge of disintegration (Espinosa 1942; Kessell 1979).

Precedents for the Eighteenth Century

Long after Vargas, with most of the Pueblos resigned to Spanish dominion, successive royal governors kept summoning Pueblo auxiliaries to campaign against common Apache, Comanche, Ute, or Navajo enemies, and, from time to time, European rivals, real or imagined. Hispanos continued honoring Pueblo war leaders and sharing the prospect of spoils. "Pueblo auxiliaries," reckons one historian, "served as the most consistently reliable element in the pacification of hostile tribes and the defense of New Mexico during the eighteenth century" (Jones 1966:178). Little wonder that the Franciscans at the time of Domínguez were frustrated in their desire to ban Pueblo scalp dances.

The willingness of Spanish civil and military authorities to support the friars in suppressing Pueblo religious and cultural practices seemed to depend, understandably enough, on how secure they felt. One such campaign, in which the Spanish governor ordered his district administrative officers to destroy Pueblo kivas, occurred in 1714, when the memory of the Pueblo-Spanish war had begun to fade and before the Comanches unleashed their fury on the colony (Kessell 1979). Another took place in 1793, after Gov. Juan Bautista de Anza (1778–1788) had achieved peace treaties with the Comanches and other former enemies (Gutiérrez 1988).

In the meantime, the evolving, eighteenth-century economic regimen seemed not so onerous as before. As far as the Pueblos were concerned, the encomienda did not survive the Pueblo-Spanish war. No Spaniard in postwar New Mexico came around every May and October to collect encomienda tribute from them as he had before. Although it may have seemed so to the natives, the encomienda's discontinuance in the colony was not necessarily a result of the war. In all Spanish America, largely for demographic and economic reasons, the institution was passing (Simpson 1950). Still, as a reward for his services, Diego de Vargas bid for and received a personal encomienda of 4,000 pesos annually to be collected from the Pueblo Indians he had reconquered. But he died before putting it into effect.

Later, agents for Vargas's heirs sought to have the encomienda imposed on the Pueblos, whereupon colonists and missionaries, under the thumb of Gov. Juan Ignacio Flores Mogollón (1712–1715), objected, pointing not only to the Pueblos' poverty but also to their participation in campaigns against the enemies of the colony at their own expense. Vargas's half-brother in Mexico City then suggested to the family in Spain that the grant be transferred to Indians in a more stable area of New Spain. Instead, the reconqueror's grandson, following a then familiar procedure, had it converted to a royal pension, and that was that (Bloom 1939; Kessell et al. 1989).

What Governor Flores Mogollón called poverty applied as much to most Hispanos in New Mexico as it did to the Pueblos. In some respects—occasional economic role reversals, for example—it blurred socioeconomic distinctions. Petitioning for lands on the Río Puerco in 1753, impoverished Alburquerque Hispanos admitted hiring themselves out to weed fields and haul firewood for the local Pueblo Indians (Simmons 1982:107). According to Gov. Pedro Fermín de Mendinueta (1767–1778), reporting 20 years later, Hispanos regularly repaired to Pueblo communities, which he called the storehouses of the colony, to purchase maize and other foodstuff (Mendinueta 1965:16).

As governor, Vargas had encouraged barter between Spanish colonists and Pueblos, at the same time forbidding the random sale of firearms or horses to Indians. He encouraged Hispanos to take part in renewed trade fairs at Pecos and granted them lands close to Pueblo communities, policies continued by later Spanish governors. The employment of Pueblo Indian laborers on public works was resumed in the eighteenth century, as levies of *semaneros*, or workers for a week, rotated in and out of Santa Fe, but, seemingly, the practice was less arbitrary and exploitative than it had been earlier.

Perhaps the clearest example Vargas gave to the colonists in their dealings with the Pueblos was his frequent and publicized spiritual coparenthood of Pueblo Indian children. Beginning on his reconnaissance in 1692, don Diego made it a point to stand as godfather at the baptism of sons and daughters of Pueblo Indians, especially the principal men. By this practice, he bound the leaders to him, in Roman Catholic terms, as his *compadres*.

How widespread this practice may have been in the prewar colony is not known, because the church registers for the period did not survive, and other documentation makes little mention of it. After Vargas, however, extant records testify that *compadrazgo* between Hispanos and Pueblos remained common. What this meant in terms of closer personal relations depended, of course, on how the godparents chose, or were invited, to socialize with the parents and to perform their spiritual duty toward the child.

Surely there are any number of other ways to gauge the degree to which Hispano farmers, herders, and wage laborers did or did not fraternize with their Pueblo counterparts in the postwar colony, and vice versa. This mixing had a greater effect, most certainly, on the Pueblos who lived along the Rio Grande and its tributaries in the vicinity of developing Hispano settlements than it did on the relatively isolated Western Pueblos.

One measure of such fraternizing is the exchange of material culture: architecture and furnishings; ceramics, crops, and tools; food and dress. Folkways and curing, and those practices Europeans called witchcraft, along with ritual paraphernalia, seemingly worked back and forth, influencing both groups. Pueblo Indians danced frequently at celebrations in the Santa Fe plaza, and a variety of Hispanic types, portrayed by Pueblo clowns and actors, turned up to cavort in native ceremonials (Tamarón 1954:50–53).

Inquisition cases from prewar New Mexico are replete with native "superstitions" employed by Spaniards, who often borrowed them from their domestic servants (Simmons 1974). And although the Inquisition in the eighteenth century concerned itself more with immorality, bigamy, and revolutionary literature, the interplay must have continued (Greenleaf 1985; Parmentier 1979).

Language, too, had a part in accommodation. When they conversed with Hispanos, the Pueblos, it would seem, generally spoke Spanish. It is difficult to say how many Hispanos knew one or more of the several Pueblo languages or dialects. Some did. Vargas relied heavily on half a dozen returning colonists to act as interpreters. A few Franciscans, both before and after the Pueblo-Spanish war, earned reputations as Pueblo linguists, but most did not, a constant complaint of their superiors (Tamarón 1954). But whose fault was that? The Pueblos, if not always consistently, have long guarded their languages to preserve the boundaries of their culture.

Spanish, on the other hand, became a sort of lingua franca or trading language for the Pueblos in colonial New Mexico. An undetermined number of Pueblo Indians in the prewar colony, trained by the friars, learned Spanish, and some were literate (Kessell 1980). Bishop Pedro Tamarón in 1760 and Father Domínguez in 1776 judged the Pueblos' understanding of Spanish, especially in the spiritual realm, imperfect at best. Most had to confess through interpreters. On the other hand, "in trade and temporal business where profit is involved," Tamarón observed, "the Indians and Spaniards of New Mexico understand one another completely" (Tamarón 1954:49; Domínguez 1956). Words and phrases must also have been traded along with chilies and beans.

Imperial and Demographic Considerations

Don Diego de Vargas, who set Pueblos and Hispanos on a course of accommodation in postwar New Mexico, was aided by larger forces. The end of the Pueblo-Spanish war in New Mexico coincided with the passing of the Spanish crown from the last of the Hapsburgs to the more modern, more secular Bourbons. Although the Spanish government would continue to subsidize the colony, its justification for doing so shifted from evangelization, which tended to be intolerant, to a more pragmatic defense of the empire.

Numbers, too, favored the trend toward accommodation. Demographically, prewar New Mexico, in which the Spaniards were always a small and nervous minority and the Pueblos an overwhelming but declining majority, contrasted with the postwar colony, where the steadily increasing Hispanic population by the mid-eighteenth century surpassed the more-or-less stabilized Pueblo population. Although Spain imposed its imperial monarchy at all levels of government in New Mexico throughout the colonial period, from royal governor and district administrative officers to elected Pueblo officials, those authorities acted very differently in 1600—when there were perhaps 50,000 to 60,000 Pueblos and 500 to 600 Spaniards—and in 1800—when the Pueblos numbered only 10,000 and the Hispanos double that number (Simmons 1979a; Tjarks 1978).

Because ethnic designations were not applied consistently in censuses or church records, it is impossible to know how many Pueblo Indians left their communities to live culturally among the Hispanos or how many married Hispanos. It seems evident from scattered references in the later colonial period that at least some of the so-called *genízaros* in postwar New Mexico, a rugged, servant class of Hispanicized Indians and their descendants, were former Pueblos (Chavez 1979).

Fray Angelico Chavez has called Vargas's reconquest "a new and distinct colonization of New Mexico" (Chavez 1954:x–xi). Few of the survivors of 1680 came back. Those who did found themselves greatly outnumbered by the new settlers, a few from Spain but mostly from in and around Mexico City and the northern mining districts. In recognition of the break, I have chosen to call the colonists of the prewar period Spaniards and those who came later Hispanos, the most neutral ethnic label used by the group today (Bustamante 1982). Like the Pueblos, their partners in accommodation, the Hispanos have endured. Most of the names on Vargas's muster rolls from the 1690s are present in New Mexico today.

Epilogue and Conclusion

Hispanos and Pueblos, campaigning together and sharing the spoils during the eighteenth and early nineteenth century, formed lasting bonds. These they renewed in 1837, against agents of the centralist regime in Mexico and, again in 1847, against the U.S. government of occupation (LeCompte 1985; Simmons 1979b). It was as if outsiders had for the moment replaced their traditional mutual enemies.

Eventually, the Anglos who came to rule and to stay, with their bias in favor of "thrifty" Pueblo Indians over "lazy" Mexicans (Hispanos), would break down the accommodation forged in the previous century. In the 1880s, even as Adolph F. Bandelier noted in his Southwestern journals how far accommodation had progressed in the vicinity of Cochiti, San Juan, and other pueblos, he betrayed his preference for the Pueblo people and publicized their uniqueness (Bandelier 1966–1984).

The U.S. government followed Bandelier's lead, particularly after New Mexico became a state in 1912. By 1923, writes legal historian G. Emlen Hall, "the war over Pueblo land and water had escalated to the point in New Mexico where racial status had become critical. United States law had divided long-time neighbors into mutually exclusive categories" (Hall 1987:116). But the process of unaccommodation, an equally complex and intimately related subject, is for another essay.

In 1980, as Pueblo Indians prepared to commemorate the Tricentennial of the Pueblo Revolt, they were disappointed to discover how little detail about their ancestors' stunning victory over the Spaniards in 1680 had been preserved and passed down in the tradition of their people (Joe S. Sando, personal communication 1988). The memory of the Pueblo-Spanish war had been all but lost in the generations of accommodation that followed.

If the overly buoyant Father Benavides and the meticulously observant Father Domínguez had been able to change places—the latter carried back in a time machine to the seventeenth century and the former beamed into the eighteenth—they would have been perplexed by the differences. But surely the two friars, even while debating the wording, would have agreed that the fundamental shift from crusading intolerance to pragmatic accommodation in colonial New Mexico was a theme worth pursuing.

References

Bandelier, Adolph F.
  1966–1984 *The Southwestern Journals of Adolph F. Bandelier*. 4 vols. *1880–1882* and *1883–1884*, edited by Charles H. Lange and Carroll L. Riley. *1885–1888* and *1889–1892*, edited by Charles H. Lange, Carroll L. Riley, and Elizabeth M. Lange. University of New Mexico Press, Albuquerque.

Benavides, Alonso de
  1916 *The Memorial of Fray Alonso de Benavides, 1630*. Translated by Mrs. Edward E. Ayer. Annotated by Frederick Webb Hodge and Charles Fletcher Lummis. Privately printed, Chicago.

Bloom, Lansing B.
  1939 The Vargas Encomienda. *New Mexico Historical Review* 14:366–417.

Bustamante, Adrian Herminio
  1982 *Los Hispanos: Ethnicity and Social Change in New Mexico*. Unpublished Ph.D. dissertation, Department of American Studies, University of New Mexico, Albuquerque.

Chavez, Fray Angelico
1954 *Origins of New Mexico Families in the Spanish Colonial Period*. Historical Society of New Mexico, Santa Fe.
1979 Genízaros. In *Southwest*, edited by Alfonso Ortiz, pp. 198–200. Handbook of North American Indians, vol. 9, William C. Sturtevant, general editor. Smithsonian Institution, Washington, D.C.

Cutter, Charles R.
1986 *The Protector de Indios in Colonial New Mexico, 1659–1821*. University of New Mexico Press, Albuquerque.

Domínguez, Francisco Atanasio
1956 *The Missions of New Mexico, 1776: A Description by Fray Francisco Atanasio Domínguez with Other Contemporary Documents*. Translated and edited by Eleanor B. Adams and Fray Angelico Chavez. University of New Mexico Press, Albuquerque.

Espinosa, J. Manuel
1942 *Crusaders of the Rio Grande: The Story of Don Diego de Vargas and the Reconquest and Refounding of New Mexico*. Institute of Jesuit History, Chicago.

Espinosa, J. Manuel (editor and translator)
1940 *First Expedition of Vargas into New Mexico, 1692*. Coronado Cuarto Centennial Publications, 1540–1940, vol. 10, George P. Hammond, general editor. University of New Mexico Press, Albuquerque.

Greenleaf, Richard E.
1985 The Inquisition in Eighteenth-Century New Mexico. *New Mexico Historical Review* 60:29–60.

Gutiérrez, Ramón A.
1988 *When Jesus Came, the Corn Mothers Went Away: Marriage, Conquest and Love in New Mexico, 1500–1846*. Stanford University Press, Palo Alto, Calif., in press.

Hackett, Charles Wilson (editor) and Charmion Clair Shelby (translator)
1942 *Revolt of the Pueblo Indians of New Mexico and Otermín's Attempted Reconquest, 1680–1682*. 2 vols. Coronado Cuarto Centennial Publications, 1540–1940, vols. 8–9, George P. Hammond, general editor. University of New Mexico Press, Albuquerque.

Hall, G. Emlen
1987 The Pueblo Grant Labyrinth. In *Land, Water, and Culture: New Perspectives on Hispanic Land Grants*, edited by Charles L. Briggs and John R. Van Ness, pp. 67–138. New Mexico Land Grant Series, John R. Van Ness, series editor. University of New Mexico Press, Albuquerque.

Hammond, George P., and Agapito Rey (editors and translators)
1940 *Narratives of the Coronado Expedition, 1540–1542*. Coronado Cuarto Centennial Publications, 1540–1940, vol. 2, George P. Hammond, general editor. University of New Mexico Press, Albuquerque.
1953 *Don Juan de Oñate, Colonizer of New Mexico, 1595–1628*. 2 vols. Coronado Cuarto Centennial Publications, 1540–1940, vols. 5–6, George P. Hammond, general editor. University of New Mexico Press, Albuquerque.

Jenkins, Myra Ellen
1966 Taos Pueblo and Its Neighbors, 1540–1847. *New Mexico Historical Review* 41:85–114.
1972 Spanish Land Grants in the Tewa Area. *New Mexico Historical Review* 47:113–134.

Jones, Oakah L., Jr.
1966 *Pueblo Warriors and Spanish Conquest*. University of Oklahoma Press, Norman.

Kessell, John L.
1979 *Kiva, Cross, and Crown: The Pecos Indians and New Mexico, 1540–1840*. National Park Service, Washington, D.C.
1980 Esteban Clemente, Precursor of the Pueblo Revolt. *El Palacio* 86(4):16–17.

Kessell, John L., Rick Hendricks, Meredith D. Dodge, Larry D. Miller, and Eleanor B. Adams (editors and translators)
1989 *Remote Beyond Compare: Letters of don Diego de Vargas to His Family from New Spain and New Mexico, 1675–1706*. University of New Mexico Press, Albuquerque, in press.
Kidder, Alfred Vincent
1958 *Pecos, New Mexico: Archaeological Notes*. Papers of the Robert S. Peabody Foundation for Archaeology, vol. 5. Phillips Academy, Andover, Mass.
Lecompte, Janet
1985 *Rebellion in Río Arriba, 1837*. University of New Mexico Press, Albuquerque.
Mendinueta, Fermín de,
1965 *Indian and Mission Affairs in New Mexico, 1773*. Translated and edited by Marc Simmons. Stagecoach Press, Santa Fe.
Ortiz, Alfonso
1969 *The Tewa World: Space, Time, Being, and Becoming in a Pueblo Society*. University of Chicago Press, Chicago.
Parmentier, Richard J.
1979 The Pueblo Mythological Triangle: Poseyemu, Montezuma, and Jesus in the Pueblos. In *Southwest*, edited by Alfonso Ortiz, pp. 609–622. Handbook of North American Indians, vol. 9, William C. Sturtevant, general editor. Smithsonian Institution, Washington, D.C.
Ricard, Robert
1966 *The Spiritual Conquest of Mexico: An Essay on the Apostolate and the Evangelizing Methods of the Mendicant Orders in New Spain, 1523–1572*. Translated by Lesley Byrd Simpson. University of California Press, Berkeley.
Scholes, Frances V.
1935 Civil Government and Society in New Mexico in the Seventeenth Century. *New Mexico Historical Review* 10:71–111.
1937 *Church and State in New Mexico, 1610–1650*. Historical Society of New Mexico, Albuquerque.
1942 *Troublous Times in New Mexico, 1659–1670*. Historical Society of New Mexico, Albuquerque.
Simmons, Marc
1974 *Witchcraft in the Southwest: Spanish and Indian Supernaturalism on the Rio Grande*. Northland Press, Flagstaff, Ariz.
1979a History of Pueblo-Spanish Relations to 1821. In *Southwest*, edited by Alfonso Ortiz, pp. 178–193. Handbook of North American Indians, vol. 9, William C. Sturtevant, general editor. Smithsonian Institution, Washington, D.C.
1979b History of the Pueblos Since 1821. In *Southwest*, edited by Alfonso Ortiz, pp. 206–223. Handbook of North American Indians, vol. 9, William C. Sturtevant, general editor. Smithsonian Institution, Washington, D.C.
1982 *Albuquerque: A Narrative History*. University of New Mexico Press, Albuquerque.
Simpson, Lesley Byrd
1950 *The Encomienda in New Spain, the Beginning of Spanish Mexico*. University of California Press, Berkeley.
Snow, David H.
1983 A Note on Encomienda Economics in Seventeenth-Century New Mexico. In *Hispanic Arts and Ethnohistory in the Southwest: New Papers Inspired by the Work of E. Boyd*, edited by Marta Weigle with Claudia Larcombe and Samuel Larcombe, pp. 347–357. Ancient City Press, Santa Fe.
Spicer, Edward H.
1962 *Cycles of Conquest: The Impact of Spain, Mexico, and the United States on the Indians of the Southwest, 1533–1960*. University of Arizona Press, Tucson.

Tamarón, Pedro
1954 *Bishop Tamarón's Visitation of New Mexico, 1760*. Edited by Eleanor B. Adams. Historical Society of New Mexico, Albuquerque.
Tjarks, Alicia Vidaurreta
1978 Demographic, Ethnic and Occupational Structure of New Mexico, 1790. *The Americas* 34:45–88.

Chapter 9 ■

David E. Doyel

The Transition to History in Northern Pimería Alta

Pimería Alta was the Spanish name given the area in northwest Mexico and southern Arizona that is bounded on the west by the Colorado River, on the north by the Salt and Gila river valleys, on the east by the San Pedro River, and on the south by the Spanish villages of Dolores and Caborca (Figure 9-1; Fontana 1983a:126). This vast territory, which covers in excess of 161,000 km^2, is characterized by rugged basin-and-range topography, low rainfall, and extreme temperatures; rainfall varies from 0 to 19 cm, generally increasing from west to east as elevation rises from 150 m to over 1,525 m above sea level. High temperatures in the central part of this arid region average 65° F in the winter and 107° F in the summer months (Gasser 1988). Most of the region lies in the Arizona uplands of the Sonoran Desert Province and is characterized by leguminous and deciduous trees, numerous cactus species, and a wide variety of bushy and annual plants (Nabhan 1985). Like the vegetation, animal life reflects great diversity; it includes deer, big horn sheep, antelope, bear, lion, fox, coyote, fish, migratory fowl, and numerous small mammals and reptiles.

At the time of the entrada, northern Pimería Alta was occupied by speakers of the Piman language, a member of the more inclusive Uto-Aztecan language

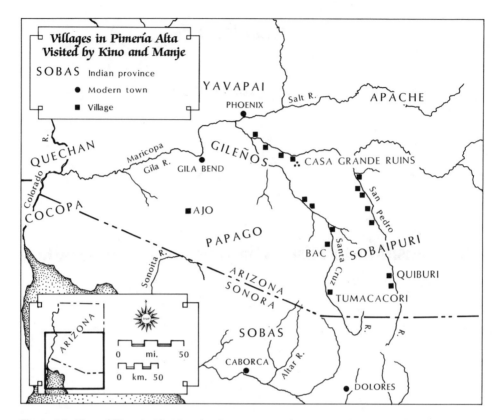

Figure 9-1. Map of Pimería Alta showing late seventeenth-century villages visited by Father Kino and Captain Manje. (Modified from Doelle 1981).

family (Miller 1983; see Figure 1-2). They were given various names by the Spanish, which were usually based upon geographic, life-style, and linguistic differences. Padre Eusebio Kino, the energetic Italian and driving force among the Jesuits in the northern frontier, initially referred to all the occupants of Pima Bajo and Pima Alta as "Pima," taken from the Piman word for "nothing" (Fontana 1983a:134), or "I don't know" (Underhill 1939:14). Subsequently, a variety of appellations were visited on these people, who themselves recognized far more similarities than differences (Ezell 1983; Fontana 1983b). The most northern Pima, the Sobaipuri (*Soba y Puris*), lived along the San Pedro and the middle and upper Santa Cruz river valleys, whereas the Gilenos lived along the Gila River. Papagos (Manje's "Papabotas" or "bean-eaters," 1954:102; see Fontana 1983a:134 for a discussion) were Pima who lived to the south and west of the major river valleys. The Sobaipuri disappeared by the early 1900s (Hoover 1935), whereas the Gila Pima and the Papago continue to occupy traditional lands in southern Arizona (Ezell 1983; Fontana 1983a).

These Upper Piman groups were further distinguished by their settlement and subsistence patterns, and more specifically by the degree to which they depended on agriculture. The Sand Papago or "No-Village People" were nomads who wandered throughout the extremely arid western part of Pimería Alta and subsisted on native plants, animals, and the precious water found in the *tinajas* (natural tanks or springs) in the region; they also traded salt, seashells, and ceremonies for food (Fontana 1983a:128). Papagos were "Two-Village People" who occupied central Pimería Alta (Papagueria) and maintained a settlement pattern that shifted between well (winter) and field (summer) villages (Underhill 1939). This pattern may have been a result of historic contacts due to better transportation. Relying on floodwater agriculture and hunting and gathering desert products such as mesquite, cactus, and rabbits, the Papago lived adjacent to, intermixed with, and often worked for the riverine-dwelling Pima, including the Gilenos and the Sobaipuri (Castetter and Bell 1942; Hackenberg 1983; Russell 1908). The Pima, or "one-villagers," used floodwater and irrigation for agriculture but also relied on the natural bounty of the desert for survival; they are known as the Akimel O'Odham (river people), in contrast to the Papago, who call themselves Tohono O'Odham (desert or country people).

By diversifying their subsistence pursuits, remaining flexible in their settlement behavior, and maintaining alliances with other groups, these desert people greatly enhanced their chances for survival, and to this extent the above typology cannot be considered overly rigid. Flexibility is illustrated by the Kohatk, who would have been classified as Pima in the winter and Papago in the summer on the basis of where they were living and how they were farming (Ezell 1983:145).

Several non-Piman groups also figured prominently in the prehistory and history of northern Pimería Alta. Yuman-speaking peoples occupied the Colorado River Valley and the lower reaches of the Gila River to the north and west of Papagueria. There is evidence that Yuman-Piman interaction in this area began in ancient times (Doelle and Wallace 1988; Ezell 1955). During the historic period, the Pima, Maricopa, Cocomaricopa, and Quechan peoples of this region were known for their endemic warfare, active trade, shifting alliances, and economic competition, all of which culminated in a major battle along the Gila in 1857 (Ezell 1983:140).

When Espejo and Farfan, leaders of mineral prospecting expeditions subsidized by the Spanish Crown, visited the middle Verde Valley between 1582 and 1598, they encountered the Yavapai, another Yuman-speaking group that may have moved in from the north and west (Pilles 1981; Schroeder 1974; Spicer 1962:265). It is said that the Yavapai and the Pima were enemies (Gladwin and Gladwin 1935:258) and this circumstance, along with the Apache threat, may have kept the Pima out of the Salt River Valley in the late seventeenth century; no Europeans actually entered the valley until much later (Doelle and Wallace 1988; Gifford 1936).

The Sobaipuri Pima in the San Pedro River Valley were fighting the Apache at the time of Spanish contact. Chronic warfare with the Apache and their compatriots—the Jacomes, Sumas, Janos, and other groups to the east and south—continued to be a major problem for the resident Pima until almost the end of the nineteenth century. It has been noted that the Pima were already involved in military alliances prior to the Spanish entrada around 1700 (Doelle 1984:206; Sheridan 1988:163). The numerous small-scale local polities present in the desert region may have sprung up after the disappearance of the highly integrated Hohokam regional system after 1450. The intrusion of mobile and warlike populations further increased the competition in a region already under stress owing to shifting climatic patterns and demographic shock caused by the introduction of European diseases after 1525 (Dobyns 1988; Ezell 1983). Alarcon is known to have visited Yumans along the lower Colorado River around 1540, during the Coronado expedition (Riley 1987:21; Spicer 1962:262). Carriers of European diseases were therefore near northern Pimería Alta from an early post-Columbian date. Suffice it to say that the regional cultural context of northern Pimería Alta at the time of the Spanish contact was not static and stable, but rather was characterized by competition among unrelated groups—including the Pima, Yuma, and Apache—that possessed different life-styles and adaptive patterns.

Continuity or Discontinuity?

When the Spanish first visited the region in the late seventeenth century, there were at least six Pima villages along the Gila River to the west of Casa Grande ruins; one additional village was located along the Santa Cruz River near Picacho Peak. The total population of these settlements was approximately 2,000–3,000 people, although both this estimate and the number of villages may be on the low side (Ezell 1983:152). Individual thatch or brush-covered houses were distributed throughout the villages in a ranchería pattern. Each village was self-sufficient, politically autonomous, and organized along the lines of patrilineal extended families. Each village had a civil leader and possibly a shaman. The Pima were agriculturalists who possessed a simple digging stick technology but may also have constructed dams, dikes, ditches, and perhaps irrigation canals; the construction of canals, however, remains a matter of dispute (Doelle 1981; Ezell 1961:36, 1983; Hackenberg 1983; Haury 1976). Corn, beans, and squash were cultivated along with cotton. Like their Papago neighbors, the Pima depended upon mesquite beans, cactus fruits, and other native products to supplement crop production; trade in food products was also common practice (Ezell 1983; Hackenberg 1983). Long-distance trading relationships were maintained with the Pueblos, the Maricopa, and other groups (Ayres 1970; Doelle 1984; Riley 1987).

Doelle (1981, 1984) has argued that greater complexity in sociopolitical and economic organization may have existed in the middle Santa Cruz River Valley among the Sobaipuri Pima at the time of historic contact. Several large villages were located near present-day Tucson, with the village of Bac containing 800 people, where irrigation agriculture was being practiced along the river floodplain. Kino and his followers were especially impressed with the Sobaipuri at Bac but reported few details from the Gila.

The above description appears discontinuous when compared with the prehistoric Hohokam occupation of the Salt-Gila and Tucson areas. Here, a 1,500-year sequence has been outlined (Doyel 1979, 1988; Haury 1976; Jacobs and Hartmann 1984; Wilcox and Sternberg 1983), which includes monumental architectural features in the form of ball courts and platform mounds, adobe architecture, extensive irrigation systems, a distinctive artistic tradition, a unique cremation burial complex, extensive exchange networks, site hierarchies, and highly integrated social systems.

Current information, however, suggests a return to less complex architectural, settlement, and presumably economic patterns between 1375 and 1450. Simple brush and mud-covered structures represent the latest architectural forms found at a number of prehistoric sites in the Phoenix Basin dating to the fifteenth century (Hayden 1957; Howard 1988; Mitchell 1988; Sires 1985). It now appears that the Classic period of Hohokam culture had ended by 1450, after a period of agricultural intensification and widespread interaction, and that the resident populations returned to a simpler way of life (Doyel 1981; Gladwin and Gladwin 1935:256–259; Sires 1985). Irrigation agriculture may not have been emphasized during this period. The historic Pima pattern of residential mobility, subsistence diversification, and apparent de-emphasis on stored crops may represent an adaptation related to a significant population decline at the end of or after the Hohokam Classic period. The characteristics of the Classic period—such as agricultural intensification, specialization, and ritual elaboration—probably depended on critical population levels and did not survive in unaltered form into the historic period in the desert region. Vestiges of greater social complexity may be present in the moeity organizations among the Pima, but little is known about their functions (Ezell 1983:156).

Recent archaeological investigations have shed additional light on what appears to be overlapping architectural traditions between the Hohokam and Pima. The Hohokam are now known to have constructed pithouses, surface rooms made of adobe, ramadas (Rice 1987), and a wide range of specialized house types (Cable and Doyel 1985). The overhanging porch typical of some historic Pima houses may have been identified at the fourteenth-century Escalante Ruin (Doyel 1974:115, 126; Russell 1908:Plate XXXV). Outdoor kitchens were used by the Pima and may also have existed among the Hohokam, since the small fire hearths usually found inside Hohokam houses would have been adequate for heating but not for food preparation. The Pima utilized the traditional *ki*, a brush structure built in a pit similar to Hohokam styles, until about 1900, at which time severe acculturative pressure gave rise to the sandwich adobe house, which, interestingly enough, is reminiscent of Hohokam above-ground adobe houses of the Classic period.

A number of factors may have contributed to the demise of the Classic period culture. Soil exhaustion and salinization (Hayden 1957), floods (Graybill et al. 1986), or general environmental deterioration (Doyel 1981; Ezell 1983:150) may have been involved. Shifts in the centers of power, warfare, or the desire to control interregional trade have also been suggested (Di Peso 1974; Riley 1987; Wilcox 1979). Regardless, it is probable that the Classic period did not survive beyond 1450 (Doelle and Wallace 1988; Doyel 1981; Haury 1945). There is no reliable archaeological evidence to support any post-1500 dates for the Classic period (Eighmy and McGuire 1988), which undermines the hypothesis that introduced European diseases caused a collapse of the Classic Hohokam (DiPeso

1956, 1974; Dobyns 1988; Reff 1988). The demise of the prehistoric Classic Hohokam culture must be viewed from a Southwest-wide perspective, wherein major population disruption, movement, and change were characteristic of the fifteenth century (Haury 1976:355).

Some material and behavioral parallels that link the historic Pima and Papago with the prehistoric Hohokam are the uses of village plazas and council houses; ball games; dancing on mounds; numerous subsistence practices; plain brown, polished red, and red-on-buff pottery; and the use of both inhumation and cremation burial—although the red-on-buff pottery and cremation burial may have come to the Pima from the Maricopa (Bahr 1983; Doyel 1981; Ezell 1963, 1983; Haury 1976). Recently, a series of inhumation burial chambers were uncovered at several late Classic Hohokam sites in Phoenix that reveal striking parallels to historic Pima and Papago burials (Howard 1988; Mitchell 1988). Similarities include seated burials, log cribs, clustered burial pits, open (not backfilled) pits, the use of hematite, the presence of food remains and personal possessions, and other highly specific traits known to occur historically (Brew and Huckell 1987; Densmore 1929; Ezell 1961; Pueblo Grande Museum files; Russell 1908:193–194; Underhill 1939). This documented continuity of specific mortuary ritual behavior reveals a shift away from cremation during the late prehistoric period while adding time depth to historic period practices. Although not conclusive, the evidence strongly suggests that the Pima are descendants of the prehistoric Hohokam. This does not, however, exclude the possibility of biological mixing between Hohokam and Pueblo (Turner and Irish 1988) or the adoption of some Puebloan ceremonial or other behavioral traits (Hayden 1987).

A key factor in the transition to history in northern Pimería Alta is that of population (Doelle 1981; Ezell 1983), but satisfactory population estimates are not yet available for the late prehistoric or early historic period. If Haury's (1976:356) estimate of 60,000 people is used for the late prehistoric period and if Ezell's (1983:152) estimate of 3,000 is used for the early historic period, the population decreased 20-fold. Perhaps the former estimate is too high (it could be as low as 30,000) and the latter too low, but that does not reduce the probability of a significant population loss. Whether this loss occurred during one or more episodes during the late prehistoric period—for example, after the demise of the Classic period but prior to the entrada as suggested herein (see Ezell 1983:150)—has not been established. Furthermore, the relative roles of warfare, disease (see Merbs, this volume), and population displacement in this decline have yet to be fully defined. Clearly, a change of the above magnitude within the same environmental setting would have a direct impact on the level and expression of cultural complexity within any single population.

The Spanish Occupation of Northern Pimería Alta: 1687–1821

The Pima were already well established in the deserts and river valleys when the Jesuit missionaries penetrated into northern Pimería Alta in 1687. It is also likely that the Gilenos and Sobaipuri had prior knowledge of these new people. One hundred and fifty years earlier, Cabeza de Vaca had ventured as far north as Fronteras on the east and Ures along the Rio Sonora on the west, and was thus within 200 km of the future site of the San Xavier del Bac Mission near Tucson (Sauer 1932:16). Spanish slave raiding had extended into Pima Bajo by the end of the sixteenth century. Spanish missions, mines, and ranches were well established in central Sonora and on the southern edge of Pimería Alta between 1650 and 1675 (Pennington 1980:74–75; Spicer 1962:118). News about Spanish activities probably traveled up the established trade routes (Riley 1987). Sheridan (1988:160) has suggested that the Pima in Arizona had obtained horses prior to the arrival of the Spanish.

By 1687, Kino and his associates had established mission centers at Dolores and elsewhere in northern Sonora (see Figure 1-4). Missionary activities along with the introduction of domesticated plants and animals initiated a new cycle of aggregation and agricultural intensification that would last for several generations. Among the crops introduced were garbanzos, lentils, cabbage, onions, garlic, mustard, peppers, melons, grapes, apples, peaches, plums, apricots, figs, and wheat. Herds of cattle, horses, mules, donkeys, sheep, and goats were introduced along with chickens and ducks. Kino's headquarters at Dolores rapidly developed from a ritual center into an economic and administrative headquarters from which missionary efforts could be expanded to the west and north (Sheridan 1988:157).

Two new items in particular had a rapid and dramatic impact on Piman culture: wheat and the horse. Unlike the native crops, wheat thrived in the winter climate of southern Arizona, and filled an empty ecological niche which required little cultural adjustment to deploy. It allowed the Pima to farm in the winter, which created surplus production, which supported larger villages and supplied a growing market in Spanish Sonora (Castetter and Bell 1942; Doelle 1981; Ezell 1983). Wheat was introduced at Caborca and Bac around 1694, and was well established in the Santa Cruz River Valley by 1750 (Sheridan 1988:157). Sedelmayr (Dunne 1955:24) reported that by 1744 the Gila Pima were growing wheat by means of an extensive system of canals and ditches. As Sheridan has summarized (1988:157), the introduction of wheat "triggered a chain reaction of developments that affected what the Pimans ate, where they lived and how they interacted with their neighbors, even among groups like the Gilenos who never became a part of the Spanish Empire."

The horse had an equally profound impact on native Piman culture. Apache raiding had become so severe that the Sobaipuri abandoned the northern San Pedro around 1730, and at least part of them joined the Gilenos (Spicer 1962:129). By the late 1740s, the mission at Dolores was abandoned owing to disease and continued Apache raids. During this period, the Gilenos developed enough of a livestock industry to trade horses to Yumans along the Colorado River (Sheridan 1988:160).

Wheat provided a frost-tolerant crop that enabled the Gila Pima to intensify agricultural production and to live in more concentrated settlements, and the horse provided mobility that allowed them to respond to the Apache threat. Nevertheless, by 1774, the traditional village territory of the Gilenos had shrunk from 83 to 29 km, while population density had increased from 42 to 154 people per square mile (Upham 1983:42–43). The Spanish eventually constructed presidios in the San Pedro and Santa Cruz valleys, such as Tubac in 1752 (Shenk and Teague 1975) and Tucson in 1776 (Barnes 1984; Williams 1988), but it was too little, too late. Debilitated by disease and war, the Sobaipuri left the southern San Pedro by 1762 (Ezell 1983:149; Nentvig 1980:73). The Spanish military position had been so weakened by warfare with the Seri and Pima to the south during this period that their northern garrisons were no match for the increasing Apache raids.

By the time the Jesuit order was expelled from New Spain in 1767, it had forever transformed the resident native cultures of northern Pimería Alta. Most areas had been affected by recurring epidemics. The mission at Bac was maintained only by attracting Papagos to replace the Sobaipuri lost to disease (Dobyns 1976; Doelle 1984:209; Jackson 1981; Sheridan 1988:161). Apache depredations further reduced local populations. Perhaps because they were never missionized and thus did not feel the full impact of Spanish control, the Gilenos were apparently undergoing a population *increase* during this period (Doelle 1981). It took less than 80 years for continued warfare to transform the Gila Pima settlement pattern from one of politically autonomous, dispersed villages into nucleated settlements functioning under a chief and council, with their subsistence system dependent upon communal work projects (Upham 1983:45).

The subsequent Franciscan period (1767–1842) was a time of decline in the mission communities; no new missions were established (Kessell 1976:3; Upham 1983:46). Frequent Pima revolts against the mission system between 1695 and 1756 further dissuaded the Spanish from investing more resources in northern Pimería Alta (Fontana 1983b:137; Spicer 1962). To the west, a revolt in 1781 among the Yuman Indians brought death and destruction to the mission communities along the Colorado River (Spicer 1962:264). In addition, Apache raiding intensified after 1820, in the absence of organized Spanish resistance.

The continued Apache pressures gave rise to a spirit of militarism among the Gila Pima, and by 1800, the Gilenos had a standing army of 1,000 men, many of whom were routinely away from the villages on punitive expeditions (Sheridan 1988:163). Also by this time, leadership may have become centralized under a single individual, and may have taken on hereditary associations (Ezell 1983:155; Kessell 1970:140). In general, agricultural production increased and trade was active during this period (Upham 1983:46). No missions were constructed among the Gila Pima, who, unlike their less fortunate relatives to the south and east, were able to be more selective about how they would accommodate the Spanish occupation—numerous subsistence and technology-related items were incorporated into Gileno culture but the native religion remained intact (Ezell 1983:153–155).

Themes of Spanish and Native American Adaptation in Northern Pimería Alta

Several themes can be identified here to emphasize the diversity of adaptive strategies and motives underlying the Spanish occupation. From the beginning, intense competition existed among different segments of the Spanish community in northern New Spain. As agents of the Spanish Crown, the missions represented the vanguard of colonial expansionism, which implied, in part, the wholesale economic and social reorganization of the resident native populations. The Spanish expected to use native labor in agricultural and construction projects, for example, and hoped to make the mission settlements as self-sufficient as possible, although a stipend was provided by the Crown for at least the Lower Pima missions (Pennington 1980:58). Large supplies of labor were also needed to work the mines and to service the growing Spanish colonies in Sonora. In sheltering the natives from the "corrupting influences" of secular life, the mission communities were also protecting their own economic interests (Nentvig 1980:55–56; Pennington 1980:73–74; Spicer 1962:120–314). The Spanish ranching communities resented what was regarded as unfair competition from the missions in the beef, hide, and produce markets that had grown up around the mines. Around 1700, Manje, then alcalde mayor of Sonora, petitioned to have the missions secularized in order to free up the native labor force and to reduce the competitive advantage of the mission system; in response, the Jesuits had him incarcerated (Spicer 1962:128). The original 10-year plan for secularization was increased by Kino to 20, but eventually lasted over 100 years (Kessell 1970).

Underlying the competition among the Spanish factions was a shared negative attitude toward the Native Americans. The Pima were regarded as savage, ignorant, ungrateful, inconsistent, and lazy people (Nentvig 1980:55; Spicer 1962:120). As Sheridan (1988:156) has pointed out, the Jesuits represented a religious order founded on obedience to authority, and, like Americans today, they placed great emphasis upon sedentary village life. This cultural bias persuaded the Spanish to interpret the fluidity of Piman society not as an ecologically and socially viable adaptation to an unpredictable environment but rather as pagan intransigence or ignorance. The aggregation of the natives into villages under the Spanish *reduccion* policy utimately contributed to the demise of the mission system.

The Native American community of northern Pimería Alta consisted of a series of unstable populations motivated by local needs and intergroup competition. Piman groups fought with other Piman groups (such as the northern and southern Sobaipuri) and also fought with Apaches, Yavapais, and other Yumans. However, they formed alliances when necessary for warfare and commerce. At the same time, factions arose among converted Christian and non-Christian groups. Local "big men" used the Spanish to promote their own political advantage or to bring attention to themselves, as the Pima Luis of Saric did when he incited the rebellion of 1751 (Nentvig 1980:55). In time, the Yumans to the west became jealous of the Pima because of the commercial advantages that the Spanish bestowed on them, and this led to further hostilities (Ezell 1983:149).

The situation was made even more complex by the attitudes of the various Spanish and Native American populations toward one another. The Spanish saw the Pima as important allies against the mutual enemy, the Apache. The Pima also provided them with labor and served as the objects of conversion for the mission community, which itself served the greater economic and political interests of the Spanish. The Pima, and especially the Gilenos, profited almost immediately from the relationship with the Spanish, as the introduction of horses and winter wheat may have saved them from extinction as eventually happened to the Sobaipuri Pima to the east.

Unfortunately, the Spanish also brought with them deadly microbes capable of causing rapid death. As a result, the Pima were strongly motivated to resist missionization and to avoid Europeans. According to traditional Pima beliefs, certain powerful individuals (shamans) were capable of causing death. Thus the Spanish were both feared and respected: Not only could they provide new tools and sources of food, but they also had the power to kill (Sheridan 1988:162–163).

There are few accounts of how the Pima felt about the events of the seventeenth century; the reports that we do have are from Europeans and should be recognized as such. It may be said, however, that basically the Pima mistrusted the Spanish for not keeping their promises. The Spanish built few missions, did not provide permanent missionaries until the 1730s, offered little protection against the Apache, and seldom kept mission supplies at an adequate level. Furthermore, they continued to punish the people, to appropriate their lands, and to introduce disease. All of this affected the morale of the people (Shenk 1976; Spicer 1962:124–126), and with no local Spanish institutions nearby, the Gilenos had no exposure to the shared values of the mission community (Bahr 1988; Sheridan 1988).

Although the success of the missionaries in converting the Pima to Christianity could be debated, it is clear that by the end of the Spanish period the economic systems of northern Pimería Alta had undergone basic structural changes (Ezell 1983:155). The new economics influenced exchange systems as well. Aboriginally, northern Pimería Alta was near the center of four major trade routes connecting northern Mexico with the Puebloan Southwest (Riley 1987:122); these routes may be an indication of the active exchange systems that existed among the prehistoric Hohokam (Doyel 1988). A wide variety of materials, including marine shells, feathers, turquoise, cotton products, hides, and exotic stone, were transported along these exchange corridors. Riley (1987:26) has suggested that the north–south exchange systems into Mexico were "beheaded" by the Spanish around 1600, and that considerable reorganization occurred as a result. Historically, the Pima traded agricultural produce, cotton blankets, baskets, horses, and captives, while the Papago traded horses, cotton, hides, mescal and desert foodstuffs, and other products (Ezell 1983:153; Russell 1908:97). Horse trading involved many complex transactions, especially once the horse became a status symbol (Ezell 1961:45). It is not clear whether trade in slaves was an aboriginal pattern, but it was encouraged by the Spanish (Spicer 1962:28) and conformed to the raiding and warfare system developed among the Gilenos, Yumans, and Apache. After taking part in complex exchange transactions with the Spanish and other groups, the Gila Pima were prepared to participate in the market system and cash economy in subsequent periods of their history.

The Mexican and American Periods: 1821–1910

Lingering suspicion and mistrust rekindled by the broken promises of the Spanish led the northern Pima to remain neutral in the Mexican War of Independence (Ezell 1983:156; Spicer 1962). In any case, the remote location of the northern territory combined with the political instability in Central Mexico left the Spanish Franciscans free to continue their missionary work until their resources ran out, in the 1840s (Fontana 1983b:139). The nascent Mexican government was unable to defend its northern territories from the Apache, who then increased their raiding, with the result that Tubac and Tumacacori were depopulated by 1848 (Shenk 1976). The repressive economic policies of the Spanish and Mexican governments forced northern frontier settlements such as Tucson to begin trading with the Americans coming in from the north and east and along the newly opened Santa Fe trail (Barnes 1984). Even the threat of Apaches could not stop the flow of Mexicans from the unstable south or the "forty-niners" rushing to California in the hope of striking it rich. Much of this traffic moved through the Santa Cruz and Gila river valleys.

The Gilenos had become a formidable economic and military force in the region and are said to have been the primary restraint against Apache raiding. By the 1840s they were participating in cash markets to supply beef and wheat to civilians and military personnel passing through the area (Ezell 1983:155–156). The rush of Mexicans into the Papagueria continued without regard to Papago traditional rights, and by 1840 hostilities broke out between the Indians and Mexican ranchers and miners in the Papagueria, which eventually ended with the acquiescence of the Papago (Fontana 1983b:137). At the same time, Anglo miners had begun to filter into the upper Santa Cruz River Valley and as far west as Ajo, although Ayres (1984:227) states that mining sites in the Santa Cruz area generally appeared after 1880 (but see Shenk and Teague 1975:11–13). Although the Spanish had been aware of the mineral wealth of Arizona since the late 1500s, the Spanish had been unable to expand their colonial system far enough north to fully exploit these resources. This opportunity was soon seized by the Americans, who were rapidly moving into the Southwest from the east and north.

The Mexican-American War and subsequent Gadsden Purchase resulted in the American takeover of the homelands of the northern Pima. Administrative reorganization was facilitated by previous economic ties with the Americans (Barnes 1984; Weber 1982). The 1850s were prosperous for the Gilenos and their allies the Maricopa, but by 1860 the Pima were growing suspicious of the Americans because of poor treatment. They were routinely denied access to tools and equipment and were becoming concerned about their water rights (Ezell 1983:156; Spicer 1962:147).

The end of the American Civil War proved costly for the Pima, as thousands of Anglos passed through or settled in southern Arizona. In 1870 Jack Swilling constructed the first Anglo canal for the new town of Phoenix, and the government set up military installations to the east and north to control the Apache (Cable and Doyel 1986; Spicer 1962; Zarbin 1978). Also by 1870, the water of the

Gila River, the lifeblood of the Gilenos, was being diverted by Anglo and Mexican farmers upriver from the newly established Pima reservation. In 1867, wheat production by the Pima-Maricopa was recorded at 3,000,000 tons, up from 100,000 tons in 1858 (Hackenberg 1983; Upham 1983:47). By the early 1870s, hundreds of Pima had been forced to move to the Salt River because of the lack of water on the Gila, and in 1879, a reservation was established there, but upstream diversion by the Mormons in Mesa soon created similar problems in this new habitat (Ezell 1983:158; Spicer 1962).

The Gila Pima refer to the period between 1870 and 1910 as the "years of famine" (Ezell 1983:158–159). With no irrigation water at their disposal, they were forced to disperse; the locus of political power returned to the village level. Disputes over water rights mounted until hostilities broke out at Santan, Casa Blanca, Blackwater, and elsewhere between 1878 and 1880 (Hackenberg 1983:171; Upham 1983:47–48). A prolonged drought in the region only made matters worse: By 1895, many Pima were on welfare and had developed "a culture of poverty" (Ezell 1983:159; Hackenberg 1983:173).

During this period the Pima were also heavily missionized by Protestants, who convinced many to give up their traditional beliefs. An empahsis on inequality and private wealth began to replace values centered in the family, security, and sharing (Hackenberg 1983). The American government was also placing severe acculturative pressures on the Pima, encouraging them to change their life-style, architecture, and economics. The Land Allotment Act of 1914 scattered families further as it increased their autonomy and encouraged them to abandon their villages. A sign of the mounting social pressure during this period is the increase in violent crime, including homicide and witch-killing, and in alcoholism (Ezell 1983:159); the social order was crumbling (Spicer 1962:408–409).

Instead of returning to the old ways of living, the Pima began to rely on other natural resources on their land in order to maintain their position in the cash economy. For example, they began harvesting mesquite wood and used the new railroad to transport it; by 1905, 12,000 cords of firewood from the reservation were being sold in Phoenix (Garrett and Russell 1983:149; Hackenberg 1983:173). For the first time in 2,000 years, the Gilenos were not raising their children within the framework of their agricultural traditions.

Spanish and American Colonial Strategies in Northern Pimería Alta: A Brief Comparison

It is instructive to compare the strategies utilized by the Spanish and later by the Americans as they expanded into the northern reaches of Pimería Alta. Neither group engaged the northern Pima in open warfare for sustained periods as they did the Apache, Navajo, and Pueblo Indians. Several of my Navajo friends suggest that the Pima simply acquiesced in the face of a foreign power, but this view does not take into account the relative geographic, economic, and strategic positions that different groups found themselves in at the time of the entrada. The Pima were sandwiched between the Apaches, who were moving in from the north and east, and the Spanish, who were coming in from the south. To cope with the situation, the Pima developed exchange networks and alliances with the Spanish on one hand, and stepped up their defense against the Apache on the other. The above strategies can be considered "successful," to the extent that the Gileno bloodline survives today whereas many other groups perished. Another point to note is that no non-Piman villages were constructed on Pima land along the Gila River until late in the historic period.

For both the Spanish and the Americans, the road to the riches of California ran through Gileno territory. Given the productivity of Gileno fields and the strength of their warriors, the Spanish and Americans were wise to forge economic ties with the Pima rather than to attempt military solutions. Early on, the Pima had recognized the value of the new subsistence products and advanced technology, and at the time of the entrada saw that the Spanish could be an important ally against the Apache. It was several decades into the American period before the Apache were subdued, and by then the Pima, Mexican, and American settlers had developed mutually beneficial economic relationships. It was only later that American occupation proved fatal to the specialized Gileno economic system by cutting off irrigation water upstream.

The Jesuit entry into northern Pimería Alta was subsidized by the Spanish Crown. Thus, the missionaries served as agents of change for the Spanish colonial empire. One of their objectives was to protect the land from encroachment by other nations and another was to save souls. In general, the mission system was seen as "an accepted step from barbarism to civilization" (Spicer 1962:332). The system expanded through the establishment of planned communities and the incorporation of native people, who were expected to become functional parts of the economic system; racial admixture was characteristic of the Spanish frontier in North America (Barnes 1984:214; Sheridan 1986:9). Indeed, under Spanish policy Native Americans were granted titles to land as a means of incorporating them into the commonwealth (Ezell 1983:153). The preferred policy was for Spaniards to live among the Natives to demonstrate the Christian way of life, but, by their own admission, the Spanish often provided some "extremely inferior specimens" (Spicer 1962:330).

In contrast, on the Anglo-American frontier, the general policy was to exclude Native Americans from development efforts (Barnes 1984:214). To the Anglos, missionization did not come first. Rather, it was the trappers, traders, and miners who represented the vanguard of American expansionism. Russell (1908:32) has remarked: "The Pima were visited by some of the vilest specimens of humanity that the white race had produced" during the early American period in southern Arizona. These entreprenuers brought with them the spirit of capitalism and frontier free-enterprise economics. The American strategy was to permanently separate the native from the non-native; this strategy was institutionalized in the reservation system, which was almost the opposite of the Spanish plan for incorporation.

Some Contemporary Issues

The study of Spanish colonial and early American history in northern Pimería Alta appears to be entering a dynamic period. The region is commanding greater attention as a result of many new study programs, grant-funded projects, and professional conferences. Also important are the numerous recent publications of vast quantities of information. These works provide the interested public and the scholarly community with more objective and more precise data than earlier histories (such as Bolton 1948), which tended to express a strong bias (see Burrus 1971; Kessell 1970, 1976; Polzer 1972, 1982; Sheridan 1986; Spicer 1962 and the bibliographies therein).

As Fontana (1983a:127) has observed, however, archaeology has been of little assistance in the research process thus far. The problem is not a lack of data, but a combination of historical factors and little commitment to research. When Emil Haury of the University of Arizona attempted to excavate a village known to have been visited by Kino in 1698, he was denied permission because the descendants of the village strongly objected (Haury 1975:21). Since many of the contact period sites available for study are located on Indian lands, a cooperative agreement would be necessary to conduct new field research.

At present, we have only vague outlines of Gileno and Sobaipuri culture at the Spanish entrada. Existing estimates of population and reconstructions of settlement patterns, as well as models of social organization, exchange systems, and subsistence, are based upon too little data and too much extrapolation. Whether the Pima and Papago are the descendants of the Hohokam has not yet been established. Information is also lacking on the structural and spatial relationships within post-1450 sites; we do not know, for instance, whether storage rooms were utilized by the Pima before wheat production increased (Ezell 1983; but see Doyel 1981:81).

We also know little about the treatment of Pima who died of disease and epidemic. Were they normally interred in cemeteries at mission sites (Jackson 1981) or were they cremated within their homes at non-mission sites (Ezell 1961; Haury 1975)? Were Apache raids *not* a leading cause of death among the Pima, as Jackson suspects (1981:247; but see Dobyns 1963)? Were warfare and slave raiding endemic among the precontact populations? Can various disease theories and tribal legends be evaluated archaeologically? Much historical information still needs to be verified (Polzer 1984:232–234). The suggestion that Gila Pima society developed into a highly integrated militaristic system complete with a paramount chief should be of considerable interest to archaeologists: A chiefdom level of social organization lacking monumental architecture? What are the implications of this for models of Hohokam social organization? Clearly, new archaeological field research is needed to advance our knowledge of issues related to the prehistory and history of northern Pimería Alta.

It is encouraging that archaeologists are expressing renewed interest in these archaeo-historic problems. Recent studies have addressed topics ranging from architecture and site structure (Doelle 1983; Rice 1983) to material culture (Doyel 1977; Masse 1981; Ravesloot 1987), to regional history and economy (Doelle 1981, 1984; Sheridan 1988; Upham 1983). Valuable survey data currently exist for the Gila River Valley but have yet to be analyzed in detail. Of almost 400 archaeological sites recorded during a partial survey of the Gila River Reservation, a minimum of 10 percent contain Piman components, some of which are thought to be protohistoric to early contact period in age (Wilcox 1979:94; Wood 1972:23). An assessment of these materials would no doubt help researchers to refine their plans for future fieldwork.

Interest in such issues should not be restricted to the academic community. There are numerous reasons why the modern-day Pima and Papago should be equally interested. If the Gilenos are to regain their legacy as superior farmers, they cannot do it without water. Claims of long-term occupancy and traditional rights to a region or a resource can be supported through archaeological research. Similarly, requests for consultation and/or repatriation rights to material collections are strengthened by arguments of affinity. And if the tribes wish to present their own history to their children or to tourists at their new museums, they would benefit immeasurably from partnerships with the professional community, which they could form either by developing their own programs or by supporting research into their history. Such research could best be conducted by Native Americans and archaeologists working together in a spirit of mutual trust, cooperation, and common interest. To borrow a phrase from Robert Hackenberg (1983:177), there is no proper end, but only another beginning; the Pima and Papago systems are still evolving.

Acknowledgments

I would like to thank Donald Bahr, Thomas Sheridan, and several anonymous reviewers for providing comments on the draft version of this chapter. Credit should also be given to William H. Doelle and W. Bruce Masse; their research has done much to rekindle interest among archaeologists in the protohistoric period in Pimería Alta. Thomas Hulen was helpful during the research phase, while Rebecca Young typed several drafts of the paper. The city of Phoenix provided administrative support.

References

Ayers, James E.
   1970 An Early Historic Burial from the Village of Bac. *The Kiva* 36:44–48.
   1984 The Anglo Period in Archaeological and Historical Perspective. *The Kiva* 49:225–232.
Bahr, Donald M.
   1983 Pima and Papago Social Organization. In *Southwest*, edited by Alfonso Ortiz, pp. 178–192. Handbook of North American Indians, vol. 10, William C. Sturtevant, general editor. Smithsonian Institution, Washington, D.C.
   1988 Pima-Papago Christianity. Ms. on file, Department of Anthropology, Arizona State University, Tempe.
Barnes, Mark R.
   1984 Hispanic Period Archaeology in the Tucson Basin: An Overview. *The Kiva* 49:213–224.
Bolton, Herbert E.
   1948 *Kino's Historical Memoir of Pimería Alta, 1683–1711.* University of California Press, Berkeley.

Brew, Susan A., and Bruce B. Huckell
  1987 A Protohistoric Piman Burial and a Consideration of Piman Burial Practices. *The Kiva* 52:163–191.
Burrus, Ernest J., S.J.
  1971 *Kino and Manje: Explorers of Sonora and Arizona*. Sources and Studies for the History of the Americas, vol. 10. Jesuit Historical Institute, Rome.
Cable, John S., and David E. Doyel
  1985 Hohokam Land-use Patterns along the Terraces of the Lower Salt River Valley: The Central Phoenix Project. In the *Proceedings of the 1983 Hohokam Symposium*, edited by A. E. Dittert and D. E. Dove, pp. 263–310. Occasional Paper No. 2, Arizona Archaeological Society, Phoenix.
  1986 The Archaeology of Swillings Ditch: Phoenix' First Historic Canal. Ms. on file, Pueblo Grande Museum, Phoenix.
Castetter, Edward F., and W. H. Bell
  1942 Pima and Papago Indian Agriculture. *Inter-Americana Studies I*. University of New Mexico Press, Albuquerque.
Densmore, Frances
  1929 *Papago Music*. Bureau of American Ethnology Bulletin 90. Government Printing Office, Washington, D.C.
Di Peso, Charles C.
  1956 *The Upper Pima of San Cayetano del Tumacacori: An Archaeohistorical Reconstruction of the Ootam of Pimeria Alta*. Amerind Foundation 7. Dragoon, Ariz.
  1974 *Casas Grandes: A Fallen Trading Center of the Gran Chichimeca*. Amerind Foundation 9. Dragoon, Ariz.
Dobyns, Henry F.
  1963 Indian Extinction in the Middle Santa Cruz River Valley, Arizona. *New Mexico Historical Review* 38:163–181.
  1976 *Spanish Colonial Tucson: A Demographic History*. University of Arizona Press, Tucson.
  1988 Comments on Prehistoric to Historic Transitions. Paper presented at the Southwest Symposium, Tempe.
Doelle, William H.
  1981 The Gila Pima in the Seventeenth Century. In *The Protohistoric Period in the North American Southwest, A.D. 1450–1700*, edited by D. R. Wilcox and W. B. Masse, pp. 57–70. Anthropological Research Paper No. 24. Arizona State University, Tempe.
  1983 *Archaeological and Historic Investigations at Nolic, Papago Indian Reservation, Arizona*. Anthropological Paper No. 2. Institute for American Research, Tucson.
  1984 The Tucson Basin during the Protohistoric Period. *The Kiva* 49:195–212.
Doelle, William H., and Henry Wallace
  1988 The Transition to History in Pimeria Alta. Paper presented at the Southwest Symposium, Tempe.
Doyel, David. E.
  1974 *Excavations in the Escalante Ruin Group, Southern Arizona*. Archaeological Series No. 37. Arizona State Museum, Tucson.
  1977 *Excavations in the Middle Santa Cruz River Valley, Southeastern Arizona*. Contribution to Highway Salvage Archaeology in Arizona No. 44. Arizona State Museum, Tucson.
  1979 The Prehistoric Hohokam of the Arizona Desert. *American Scientist* 67:544–554.
  1981 *Late Hohokam Prehistory in Southern Arizona*. Contributions to Archaeology No. 2. Scottsdale, Gila Press.
  1988 Hohokam Cultural Evolution in the Phoenix Basin. In *Changing Ideas on Hohokam Archaeology*, edited by G. J. Gumerman. University of New Mexico, Albuquerque, in press.

Dunne, Peter M.

1955 *Jacobo Sedelmayr: Missionary, Frontiersman, Explorer in Arizona and Sonora*. Arizona Historical Society, Tucson.

Eighmy, Jeffrey L., and R. H. McGuire

1988 *Archaeomagnetic Dates and the Hohokam Phase Sequence*. Technical Series No. 3. Colorado State University Archaeometric Lab, Fort Collins.

Ezell, Paul H.

1955 The Archaeological Delineation of a Cultural Boundary in Papagueria. *American Antiquity* 20:367–374.

1961 *The Hispanic Acculturation of the Gila River Pimas*. Memoir No. 90. American Anthropological Association, Menasha.

1963 Is There a Hohokam-Pima Culture Continuum? *American Antiquity* 29:61–66.

1983 History of the Pima. In *Southwest*, edited by Alfonso Ortiz, pp. 149–160. Handbook of North American Indians, vol. 10, William C. Sturtevant, general editor. Smithsonian Institution, Washington, D.C.

Fontana, Bernard L.

1983a Pima and Papago: Introduction. In *Southwest*, edited by Alfonso Ortiz, pp. 125–136. Handbook of North American Indians, vol. 10, William C. Sturtevant, general editor. Smithsonian Institution, Washington, D.C.

1983b History of the Papago. In *Southwest*, edited by Alfonso Ortiz, pp. 137–148. Handbook of North American Indians: vol. 10, William C. Sturtevant, general editor. Smithsonian Institution, Washington, D.C.

Garrett, Billy G., and Scott C. Russell

1983 A Model for the Household Complex of the Gila Pima: 1853–1920. In *Alicia: The History of a Piman Homestead*, edited by G. E. Rice, S. Upham, and L. Nicholas, pp. 11–36. Anthropological Field Studies No. 4. Office of Cultural Resource Management, Arizona State University, Tempe.

Gasser, Robert (editor)

1988 *The Prehistory and History of Ak Chin*. Soil Systems Publications in Archaeology. Phoenix, in press.

Gifford, Edward W.

1936 Northeastern and Western Yavapai. *University of California Publications in American Archaeology and Ethnology* 34:247–254.

Gladwin, Winifred, and Harold S. Gladwin

1935 *The Eastern Range of the Red-on-buff Culture*. Medallion Papers No. 16. Gila Pueblo, Globe.

Graybill, Donald A., Fred Nials, and David A. Gregory

1986 A stream-flow model for the Salt and Verde Rivers, A.D. 750–1380. In *The 1982–1984 Excavations at Las Colinas*. Archaeological Series. Arizona State Museum, Tucson, in press.

Hackenberg, Robert A.

1983 Pima and Papago Ecological Adaptations. In *Southwest*, edited by Alfonso Ortiz, pp. 161–177. Handbook of North American Indians, vol. 10. William C. Sturtevant, general editor. Smithsonian Institution, Washington, D.C.

Haury, Emil W.

1945 *The Excavation of Los Muertos and Neighboring Ruins in the Salt River Valley, Southern Arizona*. Papers of the Peabody Museum of Archaeology and Ethnology 24(1). Cambridge, Mass.

1975 *The Stratigraphy and Archaeology of Ventana Cave*. University of Arizona Press, Tucson.

1976 *The Hohokam: Desert Farmers and Craftsmen*. University of Arizona Press, Tucson.

Hayden, Julian D.
1957 *Excavations, 1940, University Indian Ruin, Tucson, Arizona*. Technical Series No. 5. Southwestern Monuments Association, Gila Pueblo, Globe.
1987 The Vikita Ceremony of the Papago. *Journal of the Southwest* 29:273–324.
Hoover, J. W.
1935 Generic Descent of the Papago Villages. *American Anthropologist* 37:257–265.
Howard, Jerry B. (editor)
1988 *Excavations at the Casa Buena Site, City of Phoenix*. Soil Systems Publications in Archaeology. Phoenix, in press.
Jackson, Robert H.
1981 The Last Jesuit Censuses of the Pimeria Alta Missions, 1761 and 1766. *The Kiva*: 242–272.
Jacobs, G. Michael, and Gayle H. Hartmann (editors)
1984 From Prehistory to History: The Archaeology of the Tucson Basin. *The Kiva* 49:131–241.
Kessell, John L.
1970 *Mission of Sorrows: Jesuit Guevavi and the Pimas*. University of Arizona Press, Tucson.
1976 *Friars, Soldiers, and Reformers: Hispanic Arizona and the Sonora Mission Frontiers, 1769–1856*. University of Arizona Press, Tucson.
Manje, Juan Mateo
1954 *Unknown Arizona and Sonora 1693–1721, from the Francisco Fernandez de Castillo Version of Luz de Tierra Incognita*, translated by Harry J. Karnes. Arizona Silhouettes, Tucson.
Masse, W. Bruce
1981 A Reappraisal of the Protohistoric Sobaipuri Indians of Southeastern Arizona. In *The Protohistoric Period in the North American Southwest, A.D. 1450–1700*, edited by D. R. Wilcox and W. B. Masse, pp. 28–56. Anthropological Research Paper No. 24. Arizona State University, Tempe.
Miller, Wick
1983 Uto-Aztecan Languages. In *Southwest*, edited by Alfonso Ortiz, pp. 113–124. Handbook of North American Indians, vol. 10, William C. Sturtevant, general editor. Smithsonian Institution, Washington, D.C.
Mitchell, Douglas R. (editor)
1988 *Archaeological Investigations at the Grand Canal Ruins: A Classic Period Site in Phoenix, Arizona*. Soil Systems Publications in Archaeology No. 12. Phoenix, in press.
Nabhan, Gary P.
1985 *Gathering the Desert*. University of Arizona Press, Tucson.
Nentvig, Juan
1980 *Rudo Ensayo: A Description of Sonora and Arizona in 1764*. Translated, clarified, and annotated by Alberto Francisco Pradeau and Robert Rasmussen. University of Arizona Press, Tucson.
Pennington, Campbell W.
1980 *The Pima Bajo of Central Sonora, Mexico*, vol. I. *Material Culture*. University of Utah Press, Salt Lake City.
Pilles, Peter J.
1981 A Review of Yavapai Archaeology. In *The Protohistoric Period in the North American Southwest*, edited by D. R. Wilcox and W. B. Masse, pp. 163–182. Anthropological Research Paper No. 24. Arizona State University, Tempe.
Polzer, Charles W.
1972 *Evaluation of the Jesuit Mission System, 1660–1767*. University of Arizona, Tucson.
1982 *Kino Guide II: His Missions—His Monuments*. Southwestern Mission Research Center, Tucson.
1984 Use and Promise in the Documentary Record. *The Kiva* 49:233–238.

Ravesloot, John (editor)
1987 *The Archaeology of the San Xavier Bridge Site*. Archaeological Series No. 171. Arizona State Museum, Tucson.
Reff, Dan
1988 Old World Diseases in the Protohistoric Period. Paper presented at the Southwest Symposium, Tempe.
Rice, Glen E. (editor)
1983 *Alicia: The History of a Piman Homestead*. Anthropological Field Studies No. 4. Office of Cultural Resource Management. Arizona State University, Tempe.
1987 *The Hohokam Community of La Ciudad*. Office of Cultural Resource Management Paper No. 69. Arizona State University, Tempe.
Riley, Carroll L.
1987 *The Frontier People: The Greater Southwest in the Protohistoric Period*. University of New Mexico Press, Albuquerque.
Russell, Frank
1908 The Pima Indians. *Twenty-sixth Annual Report of the Bureau of American Ethnology* 1904–1905:3–390. Smithsonian Institution, Washington, D.C. Reprinted 1975. University of Arizona Press, Tucson.
Sauer, Carl O.
1932 *The Road to Cibola*. Ibero-Americana 3. University of California Press, Berkeley.
Schroeder, A.
1974 *A Study of Yavapai History*. Garland, New York.
Shenk, Lynette O.
1976 *San Jose de Tumacacori: An Archaeological Synthesis and Research Design*. Archaeological Series No. 94. Arizona State Museum, Tucson.
Shenk, Lynette O., and George A. Teague
1975 *Excavations at Tubac Presidio*. Archaeological Series No. 85. Arizona State Museum, Tucson.
Sheridan, Thomas E.
1986 *Los Tucsonenses*. The University of Arizona Press, Tucson.
1988 Kino's Unforeseen Legacy: The Material Consequences of Missionization. *The Smoke Signal* 151–167. Tucson Corral of the Westerners, Tucson.
Sires, Earl W., Jr.
1985 Hohokam Architecture and Site Structure. In *Hohokam Archaeology along the Salt-Gila Aqueduct, Central Arizona Project*, edited by L. S. Teague and P. L. Crown, pp. 115–139. Archaeological Series No. 150(9). Arizona State Museum, Tucson.
Spicer, Edward H.
1962 *Cycles of Conquest*. The University of Arizona, Tucson.
Turner, Christy G., II, and Joel D. Irish
1988 Further Assessment of Hohokam Affinity: The Classic Period Population of the Grand Canal and Casa Buena Sites, Phoenix, Arizona. In *Archaeological Investigations at the Grand Canal Ruins: A Classic Period Site in Phoenix, Arizona*. Soil Systems Publications in Archaeology No. 12. Phoenix, in press.
Underhill, Ruth M.
1939 *Social Organization of the Papago Indians*. Columbia University Press, New York.
Upham, Steadman
1983 Aspects of Gila Pima Acculturation, In *Alicia: The History of a Piman Household*, edited by Glen E. Rice, pp. 39–59. Anthropological Field Studies No. 4. Office of Cultural Resource Management, Arizona State University, Tempe.
Weber, David J.
1982 *The Mexican Frontier, 1821–1846: The American Southwest under Mexico*. University of New Mexico Press, Albuquerque.
Wilcox, David R.
1979 The Hohokam Regional System. In *An Archaeological Test of Sites in the Gila Butte-*

Santan Region, south-central Arizona, edited by G. Rice, D. Wilcox, K. Rafferty, and J. Schoenwetter, pp. 77–116. Anthropological Research Paper No. 18. Arizona State University, Tempe.

Wilcox, David R., and Charles Sternberg
  1983 Hohokam Ball Courts and Their Interpretation. Archaeological Series No. 160. Arizona State Museum, Tucson.

Williams, Jack S.
  1988 Fortress Tucson: Architecture and the Art of War (1775–1856). In *The Smoke Signal*, pp. 168–183. Tucson Corral of the Westerners, Tucson.

Wood, Donald
  1972 *Archaeological Reconnaissance of the Gila River Indian Reservation: Second Action Year*. Archaeological Series No. 7. Arizona State Museum, Tucson.

Zarbin, Earl
  1978 *The Swilling Legacy*. Salt River Project, Phoenix.

Chapter 10 ■

Randall H. McGuire and María Elisa Villalpando

Prehistory and the Making of History in Sonora

In 1531 Nuño de Guzmán completed his subjugation of west México by establishing the Spanish settlement of Villa San Miguel de Culiacán in what is now Sinaloa. In the 10 years since Cortés's sacking of Tenochtitlán, the conquistadores had extended the frontiers of New Spain 1,100 km to the northern edge of Mesoamerica and destroyed two of the most powerful aboriginal empires in the New World, the Aztec and the Tarascan. In 1540 Coronado set forth from Culiacán to conquer the Northwest. His expedition returned two years later, a dismal failure. It would take nearly 250 years for Spanish settlement in Sonora to reach its northernmost extent at Tucson, 900 km north of Culiacán. The Spanish ultimately settled the southern half of the Northwest (northwest México, primarily Sonora and Chihuahua) and the Río Grande Valley in New Mexico but were unable to occupy most of modern Arizona and New Mexico. The Spanish colonization of the Northwest[1] was profoundly different from that of Mesoamerica, and the historical and cultural outcomes in each area were also quite different.

The unique character of the Spanish experience in the Northwest can be traced to the Native American cultures of the region. The world that the Spanish encountered was not of their own making, nor was it the same as the one that they had just conquered. The native peoples of the region had created it before the Spanish came, with no anticipation of the Spanish arrival. Furthermore, it was a dynamic world. The aboriginal cultures were not set and static but the result of centuries of development. The cultural variation that existed within this world made the conquest of New Mexico more like Mesoamerica than was the colonization of northwest México. To understand the European experience in the Northwest and why it differed from that in Mesoamerica, one must know something of the circumstances inherited from the aboriginal past.

Archaeology is extremely helpful in this respect.[2] Our examination of the prehistory of Sonora reveals the circumstances of the Native American past and gives us insight into the processes in the encounter between Spaniards and Native Americans that caused northwest México to differ from central México. The structure of northwestern Méxican aboriginal and Spanish cultures shaped this encounter even as their interaction changed both aboriginal and Spanish cultures. If the Spanish had entered northwest México 100 to 150 years earlier, in the late prehistoric period, they would have confronted a different aboriginal world, a world more similar to Mesoamerica and the Pueblo world of New Mexico than sixteenth-century northwest México. The consequences of this confrontation would have been profoundly different.

The Spanish Conquest of New Spain and the Northwest

In highland Mesoamerica, the Spanish encountered well-organized aboriginal city states and empires under centralized control. The hierarchy in these polities made it possible for the Spanish conquest to proceed rapidly. The Spanish were able to replace an indigenous ruling elite with Spaniards and their lackeys. Once in control of the Mesoamerican states, the Spanish modified institutions derived from the reconquista of Spain and the existing aboriginal social structure so that a few Spaniards could rule a great mass of Indians (Gibson 1964:167–168; MacLachlan and Rodriguez 1980:78).

Spanish forces consistently beat larger opposing armies by using Indian allies and superior military technology, and by making it a policy to kill or capture the opposing war leaders. Indian allies with 5 to 10 times the Spanish strength supported Spanish armies in the conquest of highland Mesoamerica (MacLachlan and Rodriguez 1980:70; Wolf 1959:154). In battles such as Otumba, the Spaniards found that killing the opposing war leader caused the hostile force to evaporate before them.

The Spanish attempt at ideological dominance consisted of a hybridized Catholicism that became the locus of Spanish control and the focus of Indian resistance. Representatives of the mendicant orders established themselves within existing Indian communities and fitted European organization to the aboriginal structure (Gibson 1964:102). The resident friars waged a constant campaign of preaching and whipping to try to stamp out aboriginal religious practices (LaFaye 1976:18–29; MacLachlan and Rodriguez 1980:86–87).

Individual Spaniards received grants of Indian labor called encomiendas (Gibson 1964:56–97; Zavala 1973). A native lord and his subjects were placed under the control of an encomiendero who had rights to Indian labor and tribute (Gerhard 1972:8). Labor drafts (repartimientos) supplemented these grants, usually for large-scale projects (Gibson 1964:27). The Spanish Crown outlawed the encomienda in 1670, but a tribute relationship between the Crown and Indian communities, the corregimiento, replaced it and survived until 1786 (Gibson 1964:84).

Through these mechanisms and practices, a small number of Spaniards quickly conquered and exploited the tens of thousands of Indians in Mesoamerica who were already subordinate to indigenous states. In a sense, it seems paradoxical that the most powerful polities in aboriginal North America were the least able to resist the Spanish conquista.

The society created by this process included a handful of Europeans and their descendants ruling over thousands of Indians and a growing *mestizo* population consisting of an admixture of Europeans and Indians. Even after the dramatic depopulation of the sixteenth century caused by European epidemics, Indians remained the most numerous segment of the population in México into the late nineteenth century. MacLachlan and Rodriguez (1980) argue that a true mestizo society emerged in New Spain, with clearly delineated castes of Spaniard, mestizos, mulattos, zambos, and chinos, among others.

The Northwest

The policies, institutions, and strategies that had so quickly reduced highland Mesoamerica could not serve as well in the north (Bannon 1970:29). The Indians of this region were not subservient to already existing states. Conquest in this case meant converting and subjugating the people on a village-by-village basis. The Spanish followed four basic strategies in their exploitation of the northern frontier, which were determined in part by the existing structure of the native societies: (1) the Nueva Galicia, (2) the Chichimeca, (3) the Nueva Viscaya, and (4) the Nueva México. Each of these strategies is named after the region or political administrative unit in which it was most common. All four strategies greatly affected the native populations of northwest México, and two were used in the Northwest, the Nueva Viscaya in northwest México and the Nueva México in New Mexico.

Nueva Galicia. Guzmán created Nueva Galicia after conquering the west coast of México and exploited the Indian population through a system of encomienda, which was a social way of covering slavery, a practice that had been officially abolished by that time. The northernmost limit of Nueva Galicia lay in Sinaloa. To expand the northern frontier, the Spanish had to depend on the large aboriginal populations for their labor force. Slavery, epidemic disease, and warfare quickly decimated the aboriginal populations of the west coast, and by the late 1530s Spanish raiders ranged into the Northwest to capture more slaves. We still do not fully understand how this slaving affected Northwest Indians before missions were established in the region.

Chichimeca. The Spanish called the mining frontier from Culiacán to Monterrey the Chichimeca, and here all-out war dominated their relations with the Indians. The Crown granted encomiendas in the region, but they failed as systems of tribute and instead became a form of slavery (Gerhard 1982:165). In this violent crucible, the Spaniards developed the institutions of the mission and presidio, later so prominent in northwest México. Spaniards occupied fortified towns and mines and established a system of presidios to secure the roads between the fortified settlements and protect the flow of silver to New Spain (Bannon 1970:30; Gerhard 1982:29; Naylor and Polzer 1986:20).

In converting the Indians in the north, the friars had to contend with problems they had not encountered in the south. The "New Laws" of 1542 and further reforms in 1573 made the mendicant orders responsible for the first contact with Indian groups (Hammond and Rey 1953:8). The friars, accompanied by military forces, entered new areas as advance agents. They sought to reduce and concentrate the Indian populations in missions where they could be Christianized and acculturated as a prelude to becoming Spanish citizens (Gerhard 1982:27–28). The Indians thus came under the control of missionaries, who were charged with producing the surplus needed to maintain the mission itself. At the same time, missionization opened up the countryside for Spanish settlement, which provided a market for mission products.

Nueva Viscaya. Most of the Northwest, modern Sonora, Chihuahua, and Arizona lay in the province of Nueva Viscaya. Exploitation of Indian labor here was based on the servicio personal system whereby Spaniards employed or enslaved individual Indians rather than whole villages. Under this system, Spanish towns were established close to sedentary Indian villages. An important first step in this strategy was to reduce scattered Indian groups around missions, and this led to conflict between secular and mission claims on Indian land and labor.

However, Indian labor was difficult to exploit. When faced with the repartimiento, whole villages might simply flee. The Spaniards enslaved Indians to obtain labor, but only a limited number of Indians were available, they fiercely resisted the slavers, and few survived enslavement for long. To build up a reliable work force, the Spanish had to import "civilized" Indians from the south, such as Tlaxcaltecas or Tarascos, or mestizos (Gerhard 1982:25). Many of the mestizos sought to pass into the Spanish community and succeeded in doing so (Gerhard 1982:27).

The new institutions that the Spanish employed to conquer northwest México—the mission and the presidio—have been romanticized by many U.S. and Mexican writers. The attention given these two institutions tends to obscure the important role settlers played in advancing the frontier in northwest México. European groups, families, and individuals established farms, ranches, mines, and towns, decimating the Indian population, forcing the remnants into smaller and smaller enclaves, and finally replacing them. Indians represented the minority in Spanish-controlled areas of northwest México by the late eighteenth century (Gerhard 1982:24–25).

Today northwest México holds itself apart from the rest of México, and a distinctive Norteño culture exists in the region (León-Portilla 1972). The people there also have different physical features from the population of central México. The Norteño is taller, has fairer skin, and looks more European than Mexicans from further south (León-Portilla 1972:111–112). The multitudinous racial distinctions of the south, the *castas*, disappeared in the north during the colonial period, and from the seventeenth century to today the principal ethnic distinction has been between the European-derived *gente de razón* and *los indios* (Gerhard 1982:27). Most Norteños reject the national ideology of *Indigenismo* and instead glorify Spanish origins as opposed to the Indian.

Nueva México. It was only among the pueblos of New Mexico that the institutions and mechanisms of the conquest had some, albeit limited, success. The Spanish strategy in early Nueva México was more like that of New Spain than anywhere else in the north. Although the Spanish did not encounter states, they did come upon a more concentrated settlement system than elsewhere north of New Spain, with large villages that may have contained up to two thousand people each (Kessell 1979:12). Here, as in New Spain, a small number of Spaniards were able to conquer a large aboriginal population, introduce the encomienda, convert the Indians, and carry out a speedy conquest.

In 1598, Oñate leap-frogged the Spanish frontier and established the New Mexico colony, an island of Spanish settlement 900 km from the northern border of New Spain (see Figure 1-3). As in Mesoamerica, a few hundred Spaniards supported by Indian allies conquered an indigenous population of 40,000 or more (Spicer 1962).

Oñate executed a centralized plan of colonization, a conquista, that sought submission and tribute from the Pueblo tribes. He attempted to attract new settlers by giving out grants of encomienda (Hammond and Ray 1953:10). The colony's survival in the period before the Pueblo Revolt of 1680 depended in large part on the tribute drawn from the Pueblo villages. The Franciscans who accompanied Oñate did not establish missions as integral units, but instead set up churches in the villages and, as in Mesoamerica, attempted to prohibit native beliefs and religious practices (Spicer 1962:298).

The strategy did not enjoy long-term success. Before the Pueblo revolution of 1680, the Spanish Crown maintained the colony as a moral obligation, because it was committed to furthering the conversion of the Indians. With the reconquest of New Mexico in 1692, the encomienda was abandoned and the area resettled by ranchers and farmers utilizing paid Indian labor. This strategy was more like the Nueva Viscaya typical in northwest México (Gerhard 1982:322).

Because the aboriginal groups of northwest México lacked the central organization and hierarchy of the aboriginal Mesoamerican states, they were better able to resist the Spanish conquest, slowing and eventually stopping the colonial advance. The form and nature of these aboriginal societies had differed in prehistory, and it appears that a period of greater hierarchy and integration preceded the Spanish entry into the region.

The Archaeology of Sonora

The Spanish first penetrated the Northwest in what is now northern Sinaloa and southern Sonora. The southern boundary of Sonora approximates the southern boundary of the Northwest cultural area and the eastern boundary follows the Sierra Madre, including a small portion of the Casas Grandes tradition of northwest Chihuahua (Figure 10-1). We also discuss the Tucson Basin in order to in-

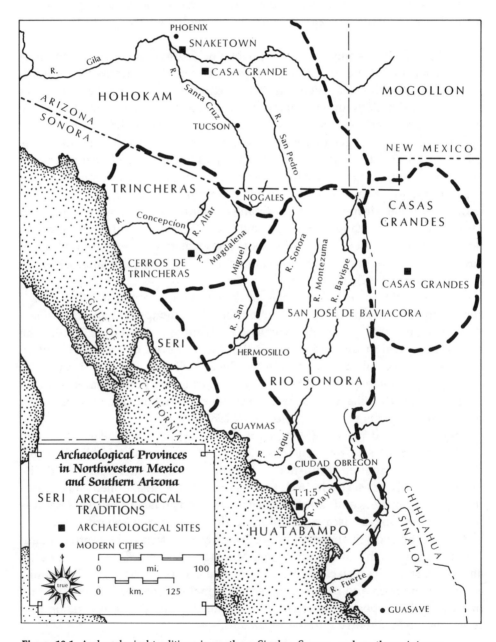

Figure 10-1. Archaeological traditions in northern Sinaloa, Sonora, and southern Arizona.

clude all of Spanish Sonora. This broad definition of Sonora allows us to discuss the best-known archaeological traditions in northern México.

The study of Sonoran archaeology could contribute greatly to our understanding of the transition from prehistory to history because the first Spanish in the Northwest discuss this region. Archaeologists in northwestern México have consistently discussed the transition and linked archaeology and history in their studies (Bowen 1976; Braniff 1985; Di Peso 1956; Doolittle 1988; Pailes 1980; Reff 1986; Sauer and Brand 1931; Villalpando 1984). The dearth of archaeological research in Sonora limits our ability to realize this potential. All of the archaeological traditions in the region are defined on the basis of a handful of surveys and excavations in only four or five sites. Over the past 20 years, fewer than a half dozen major projects have been completed in the region. We know as little about the region today as we knew about the rest of the Northwest in 1940.

Archaeologists have defined five major Formative archaeological traditions in Sonora (Figure 10-1): (1) the Huatabampo along the southern coast of the state, (2) the Seri in the central coast, (3) the Trincheras in the northwest, (4) the Casas Grandes primarily in northwest Chihuahua, and (5) the Río Sonora along the west flanks of the Sierra Madre Occidental (Alvarez 1985). These traditions do not cover the entire state, and the archaeological record along the coast from Guaymas to the Río Mayo remains virtually unknown. The Hohokam represent a sixth tradition in the far north of Sonora and there are several summaries available for it (Doyel this volume; Gumerman and Haury 1979; Haury 1976; McGuire and Schiffer 1982).

Huatabampo Tradition

The Huatabampo tradition is known from the work of Ekholm in the 1930s and the more recent work of Ana María Alvarez (1985). These researchers excavated at two sites, only one of which (Son.T:1:5 cr) produced chronometric dates. Huatabampo sites occur along the coast from the Río Fuerte to the Río Mayo.

Archaeologists have found large sites along lagoons, estuaries, and the major rivers. The inhabitants located villages so that they could maximize access to marine, riverine, and bajada resources. These people grew corn and beans, but fish and shellfish appear to have been more important to their economy. They constructed houses from perishable materials and possibly adobe. The villages consisted of scattered noncontiguous dwellings and included communal plazas, trash mounds, cemeteries, and offertories. Burial was by inhumation. Huatambambo potters made a distinctive redware but apparently did not make painted pottery. Excavation in village sites produces extensive evidence of shell jewelry manufacture.

Scholars have not yet worked out an adquate phase sequence for the tradition. Existing efforts are based on a handful of C-14 dates from a single site (Son. T:1:5cr). The tradition clearly existed by A.D. 700. There is evidence for shell trade at this time, and turquoise and obsidian appear to be among the items received in exchange for the shell. Alvarez (1985) has hypothesized that the people traded with groups in Sinaloa and in northwest Chihuahua, in the Casas

Grandes region. The tradition appears to end at around A.D. 1000, but the lack of information on subsequent prehistory may reflect nothing more than the paucity of research in the area.

In the mid-sixteenth century, the Spanish encountered Cahitan-speaking Mayos and Yaquis in the same region. At the present time we cannot link these people to the prehistory of the area through archaeology. This represents an important area for future research.

Seri Tradition

Thomas Bowen (1976) has defined a Seri archaeological tradition along the central coast from just north of Guaymas to Puerto Lobos. The tradition starts at or before A.D. 700 with the introduction of Tiburón plain pottery. This exceedingly thin and hard pottery persists to at least A.D. 1700. Bowen discusses the tradition as a Seri manifestation. This group did not change its marine-oriented hunting and gathering way of life for over a thousand years.

The central coast region is quite inhospitable. It has few sources of potable water and little or no potential for aboriginal irrigation agriculture. Without herd animals or mechanized agriculture, hunting and gathering would be the only adaptation possible in the region. The coast provides the richest resources, so that this adaptation should be heavily marine oriented. We expect, however, that further research will reveal variation in the form and nature of cultures in the region (Villalpando 1984).

Trincheras Tradition

The Trincheras culture of northern Sonora included an area stretching from around the international border on the north to Puerto Libertad on the south, and from the Río Sonoita on the west to the Río San Miguel on the east. Sites of this culture centered on the Magdalena-Altar-Concepción drainage.

Archaeological research in the region includes several extensive surveys (Bowen n.d.; Wasley 1968) and a variety of limited excavations (Johnson 1963; Robles 1973, n.d.). The most detailed survey to date is our own in the Altar Valley, and the most extensive excavations to date are those of Beatriz Braniff (1985) near Caborca and on the Río San Miguel.

Archaeologists cannot agree on whether the Trincheras should be considered a separate tradition or a regional variant of the Hohokam. Some archaeologists (e.g., Haury 1950:547; Johnson 1963:182–185) include the Trincheras in the Hohokam, but others (e.g., Di Peso 1979:158; Braniff 1985) regard it as a separate tradition. In early historic times O'odham (Piman) groups occupied the Trincheras area and the southern half of the Hohokam area.

The development of the Trincheras tradition broadly parallels that of the Hohokam. Initially this population occupied shallow pithouses much like the Hohokam structures and appears to have been heavily involved in the shell trade—as indicated by raw shell and waste at the site of La Playa on the Río Magdalena. Trincheras people produced shell bracelets using a different manu- facturing technique than the Hohokam but their Purple-on-red pottery exhibit numerous stylistic parallels to Hohokam wares.

In the fourteenth and fifteenth centuries they built massive *cerros de trincheras* along the major rivers. These sites are isolated hills covered with terraces, walls, and rooms. They cover up to 1/2 km² and may contain 40 to 50 terraces. Excava- tions in the Tucson Basin indicate that many of the terraces served as platforms for pithouses (Downum 1986; Fraps 1936), and some may have been used to grow agave (Fish et al. 1984). These sites appear to represent mountainside vil- lages whose occupants engaged in a wide range of activities of the type normally associated with habitation sites. They were located on steep isolated hills, often with curtin walls and walled entrances, most probably for defense purposes (Fontana et al. 1959); Wallace and Holmlund 1984:180; Wilcox 1979).

Our research in the Río Altar suggests that the Trincheras may be best consid- ered a separate tradition in its early stages and a part of a southern Arizona tradi- tion in the later prehistoric period. The earliest ceramic sites in the Altar are vil- lages with shallow pithouses and cremation burial, but other aspects of their material culture do not resemble Hohokam. The pottery includes reddish plainware and Trincheras Purple-on-red. Both these types often exhibit scraping marks on their interior that indicate a coil-and-scrape manufacture technique.[3] Trincheras sites of this period lack certain key Hohokam traits, including ball courts, censors, and palettes. They often contain non-Hohokam material items such as rectangular ground stone *mocajetes* (chili grinders), drop-ended manos, and narrow metates for drop-ended manos. This period can be subdivided to match Bowen's (n.d.) phases II and III. Trincheras Purple-on-red ceramics occur in Colonial and Sedentary period Hohokam sites, and they probably date from A.D. 700 to 1300.

Most sites in the Altar Valley date to the subsequent period that Hinton (1955) initially called the plainware period. The material culture of these sites greatly resembles late prehistoric assemblages from the Papaguería, Tucson Basin, and San Pedro River Valley in southern Arizona. The plainware is a polished, paddle-and-anvil brownware very similar to the plainware of southern Arizona. A polished redware similar to Sells Red accompanies this plainware. Altar Valley potters apparently did not produce painted pottery at this time. Village sites are still shallow pithouse villages, but the local population also built *cerros de trincheras*. Shell manufacture waste occurs on sites of this period and suggests a continued involvement in the shell trade. Burials include both urn cremations and inhumations (Robles n.d.). The intrusive pottery here—principally Salado Polychromes and Casas Grandes Polychromes—suggests that these sites date from A.D. 1300 to 1450.

The Altar Valley protohistoric assemblage was essentially the same as that from southern Arizona (Doelle and Wallace 1988; Masse 1981). The plainware was thin, finger impressed, and unpolished. It differs from San Pedro Valley Whetstone plain principally in color and nonplastic inclusions. Projectile points were small and triangular, with basal notches. Oval to square outlines of rock provide the only surface indication of protohistoric houses. The documented contact period sites in the Altar Valley yield this assemblage.

The Sopa O'odham were living in the valley when the Jesuits arrived in the seventeenth century, and modern villages exist at all but one of the valley's Jesuit missions. A continuum of occupation and material culture in the valley, as well as the Tucson Basin, San Pedro River Valley, and the Papaguería, suggests that the O'odham descended from the late prehistoric Hohokam population of these areas. The Tohano O'odham (Papago) moved into the valley during the late eighteenth century and lived there until the last decades of the nineteenth century.

Casas Grandes

The site of Casas Grandes is located in northwestern Chihuahua and should not be confused with the Hohokam site of Casa Grande south of Phoenix, Arizona. Casas Grandes is one of the largest and most elaborate sites in the Northwest and also one of the most Mesoamerican looking. At its height, the site included several large multistoried apartment blocks, an extensive irrigation and public water system, and a ceremonial complex with several mounds and two I-shaped ball courts. Charles Di Peso (1974, 1983) excavated the site in the 1960s and reported on the results of that excavation in the 1970s. He divided the sequence for the area into four periods: Viejo, Medio, Tardio, and Españoles. We draw our summary primarily from Di Peso (1974, 1983).

Considerable debate surrounds the dating of the Casas Grandes sequence. Estimates for the beginning of the Medio period have varied from A.D. 1050 (Di Peso 1974) to after A.D. 1300 (Ravesloot et al. 1986). The site did yield 53 tree-ring dates, but they were all noncutting dates from shaped or eroded beams. Ravesloot et al. (1986) recently reanalyzed 53 dates to estimate the cutting date for each sample. We use these revised dates in our summary.

In the earliest Viejo period (A.D. 700–1200), the Casa Grande region was an extension of the Mogollon tradition found in the mountains of Arizona and New Mexico. The local potters produced brownware decorated with surface texturing or red paint. The people lived first in round and then in square pithouses. The larger villages in the region had pit structures called great kivas that were several times bigger than normal domestic pithouses.

The town of Casas Grandes was established at the beginning of the Medio period (A.D. 1200–1490). It initially consisted of 20 single-storied, walled compound units. About A.D. 1300 a major planned construction episode created a central multistoried residential core with a ceremonial district along one side. The irrigation and public water system were also built at this time. The town probably had a peak population of over 2,000 people. Casas Grandes apparently controlled a hinterland that included all of northwest Chihuahua and may have extended into New Mexico and Sonora. At the end of the Medio period, the site was sacked and burned.

A distinctive polychrome pottery style with red and black paint on a cream slip characterized the Medio period. Casas Grandes potters excelled at making zoomorphic and anthromorphic effigy vessels. Gila polychrome and a locally made copy of Gila polychrome was common in the later levels of the site.

Particularly exciting were the large amounts of trade goods found at the site. These included thousands of pieces of shell, foreign pottery, birds, and a variety of minerals. The occupants of the site raised turkeys and macaws. The natural range for the macaws lay hundreds of miles to the south in lowland México. Artisans at the town produced bells and other objects of copper. Casas Grandes is the only site in the Northwest that has yielded evidence of macaw-raising or copper metallurgy.

Di Peso (1974, 1983) postulated that Mesoamerican merchants (*pochteca*) established the Medio period town as a trade outpost for the shipment of turquoise and other Northwestern items to Mesoamerica. Other researchers question both the Mesoamerican origin of the town's builders (McGuire 1980) and the town's status as a trade center (Minnis 1988). It appears that Casas Grandes developed from the local Mogollon tradition and was a major regional center that was the destination for trade goods and not a transhipment point. The Mesoamerican flavor of the site suggests that important direct or indirect connections must have existed between Casas Grandes and cultures in Mesoamerica.

In the Tardio period (A.D. 1490–1660), scattered nomadic-living peoples occupied the region. When Ibarra passed through the area in A.D. 1564–1565, he reported a ruined town that was probably Casas Grandes.

Río Sonora Tradition

Research by Richard Pailes and William Doolittle has produced most of the data for the Río Sonora culture. Pailes (1980, 1984) excavated the site of San José Baviácora, and during the same project Doolittle (1988) intensively surveyed the river valley near the site. The tradition occurs on the west flank of the Sierra Madre Occidental from the international border to Sinaloa, and west from the Río San Miguel to the Chihuahuan border.

Río Sonora resembles the Mogollon tradition and the Viejo period of Casas Grandes in Chihuahua (Di Peso 1974). Río Sonora potters produced a brownware with surface texturing; their only decorative technique. Shallow pithouses were used early in the sequence, but these were later replaced by surface rooms. Compounds exist, but late Mogollon-style pueblos are absent. Settlements concentrated linearly along the rivers with very little occupation between rivers.

Pailes (1980) has proposed a four-part phase sequence for the tradition. In Period 1 (A.D. 1080–1200), small pithouse villages exist with incised brownware pottery and Playas Red. In Period 2 (1200 to early 1300s), the number of sites increases and surface dwellings appear. The general trend through both periods seems to be toward more and bigger settlements.

This trend culminates in the third period, which probably dates to the fourteenth and fifteenth centuries. Multivillage communities appear with a central village and daughter settlements. The central villages have walled enclosures with attached platform-like strucures and unusually large houses in pits. The largest sites of this period cover up to 25 ha and have 100 to 200 or more structures (Doolittle 1984:19). Pailes found increased evidence of trade in the Casas Grandes trade pottery, shell, copper tinklers, and one possible pseudocloisonné item present. Radiocarbon dates for the phase range from A.D. 1310 to 1500.

Pailes (1980:35) has suggested that the third phase is a response to the breakup of Casas Grandes. The recent reanalysis of the tree-ring dates for the Medio period at Casas Grandes places this period in the fourteenth and fifteenth centuries (Ravesloot et al. 1986). Period 3 of the Río Sonora culture cannot result from the demise of Casas Grandes since it was contemporary with the height of Casas Grandes development.

Pailes's (1980) fourth phase is a continuation of the third phase. It dates from the late fifteenth century through contact. When the Spanish missionized this region in the seventeenth century, they encountered Opata speakers. Pailes would interpret these people as the descendants of the Río Sonora tradition.

Riley (1987) and Reff (1981) have proposed that a string of "statelets" existed in the Río Sonora region at the time of the Spanish entrada and that the end of the fourth Río Sonora phase is the archaeological manifestation of these statelets. They base their inference largely on early Spanish documentary accounts, especially secondhand descriptions, written by Las Casas in 1560, of Fray Marcos de Niza's account of the region from 1539–1540 and Obregón's chronicles of the Ibarra expedition in 1564–1565 (Riley 1987). According to these authors, the "statelets" had planned towns with as many as 800 to 3,000 houses, armies of 10,000 or more, forts on the high ground, and elaborately costumed leaders with large retinues.

These inferences have considerable bearing on the relationship between prehistory and history in Sonora because they connect the two directly. However, we are skeptical about these inferences because we believe that available archaeological data do not support them and their authors have been too uncritical in their use of documentary sources.

In proposing that a series of statelets existed in eastern Sonora, both Reff and Riley are less critical of early Spanish accounts then we would be. They accept as correct Spanish estimates of village size, military strength, social hierarchy, and other details. The earliest Spanish explorers were not social scientists and the accounts they left of northwest México are often conflicting and vague and always filtered through a European ethnocentrism. The documents they left behind were often written decades after the fact, and often the intent was to defame or defend some participant. Many of the documents of the Coronado expedition speak of eastern Sonora as being impoverished and underpopulated, whereas other documents give the accounts cited by Reff and Riley.

The interpretation of early Spanish documents is a complex problem that requires at least a brief comment here. Such documents clearly cannot be used without critical evaluation of their author's purpose and stylistic or ideological conventions. We should remember that Marcos de Niza reported seven cities of gold in New Mexico and that Las Casas emphasized the "civilized" aspects of New Spain's Indians because he was arguing for more humane treatment of these people. We also must be cautious about the Spanish use of terms such as *provincias*, *reynos*, and *naciones*, which imposed European political entities on very different forms of aboriginal organization (Naylor 1983). The documentary evidence for "statelets" in the Río Sonora is contradictory and subject to a wide range of interpretations.

Riley (1985:424) cites the archaeological data from the fourth period of the Rio Sonoran tradition, especially Doolittle's (1984, 1988) data and interpretations, as proof that the statelets existed. Doolittle (1988) ably reconstructs prehistoric settlement patterns and agricultural practices in the valley, and his data do suggest that prehistoric settlements and populations were larger than some early researchers thought (Amsden 1928; Brand 1935; Ekholm 1939). However, he seems to consistently overestimate the size and complexity of the archaeological remains in the area.

This inflation is apparent in inferences concerning population size and architectural complexity. Doolittle's (1988:52) assumption that all of the houses dating to a period of several hundred years are contemporary and occupied throughout that period fails to control for the uselife of the dwellings and is probably incorrect. The uselife for pithouses in the Sonoran desert probably ranges from 5 to 25 years and adobe structures 25 to 50 years (McGuire and Schiffer 1983:291). In either case, to assume that structures were used for a period of several hundred years exaggerates population estimates. The ruins of multistory structures in other parts of the Northwest usually consist of substantial rubble or adobe mounds and are far more impressive than the rectangular triple rows of rock that Doolittle (1988:26) found in the Río Sonora. The Río Sonora remains resemble the small jacal and adobe compounds of the Tanque Verde and Soho Phases in southern Arizona, not the large multistoried adobe buildings found in the Civano period in the Phoenix Basin and the Pueblo IV period in the Río Grande.

Even if we accept the archaeological interpretations, the remains in the Río Sonora are not particularly large, elaborate, or numerous when compared with other Northwestern sites. In the rest of the Northwest, archaeologists would not interpret villages of 25 ha with a few hundred structures, platform mounds, and compounds as evidence of "statelets" or of the type of society described by de Niza. None of these sites come close to the thousands of structures, temples, and tombs described by Las Casas. Furthermore, when compared to the truly large sites of the Northwest such as Snaketown, Casas Grandes, Pueblo Bonito, and the other town sites in Chaco Canyon, Puye, Sapawe, Cerros de Trincheras, or any of a dozen others, the Río Sonora sites are of middling size and organizational complexity.

The archaeological remains of the Río Sonora do suggest larger, more permanent villages than the Jesuits report for eighteenth-century Opatas in the same region, but the prehistoric remains do not support the presence of "statelets" or chiefdom-like polities in the area. They demonstrate that the Las Casas and Obregón descriptions of the Serrana do suffer from hyperbole.

From Prehistory to History

We can make a tentative summary of the general trends in the development of Sonoran prehistory and the relationship of that prehistory to the historic period. Such a summary must reach outside the boundaries of Sonora, especially to the

Hohokam of southern Arizona and Casas Grandes in Chihuahua to be complete. By the fourteenth century, if not before, the Trincheras and Río Sonora cultures of northern Sonora were part of a much larger system of cultural integration and exchange that centered on the Classic period Hohokam and Medio period Casas Grandes. This system appears to have collapsed in the century preceding the Spanish entrada. The early Spanish explorers, such as the chroniclers of the Coronado expedition (Hammond and Rey 1940), speak of large despoblados or deserted areas. Many of these same regions supported large sedentary, agricultural populations in the fifteenth century.

It is clear that by A.D. 700 a number of agricultural and ceramic-producing societies existed in what is now Sonora. Such societies almost certainly existed before this date, but we lack sufficient data to say much before this time. The period between A.D. 700 and 1100 seems to be a time of economic consolidation during which the major traditions took form. Evidence for extensive exchange, especially in shell, appears at this time, and the peoples of Sonora probably established trade relationships with the Hohokam on the north and Casas Grandes on the northeast (Alvarez 1985:255; Braniff 1988).

From A.D. 1100 to 1300, these trends continued in the north but not the south. The Huatabampo tradition was interrupted and the cultures of northern Sinaloa became increasingly Mesoamerican in character. In the north, both the Trincheras and Río Sonora traditions continued to grow, with more and larger sites.

In the late prehistoric (A.D. 1300 to 1500) the Trincheras and Río Sonoran traditions were probably linked by trade with the developments of the Classic period Hohokam in southern Arizona and the Medio period Casas Grandes. Both these pan-regional centers of development flourished during the fourteenth and the fifteenth centuries. Late prehistoric Trincheras and Río Sonora sites yield more evidence of trade, foreign ceramics, shell, and other items than do earlier periods. Sonoran sites frequently contain Gila Polychrome and Casas Grandes Polychromes, Classic period Hohokam and Medio period Casas Grandes types, respectively. The largest prehistoric settlements—such as San José Baviácora on the Río Sonora and Cerros de Las Trincheras on the Magdalena River—occur in this period. There is increased evidence of a defensive posture with *cerros de trincheras* visually linked in a network throughout the Concepción-Altar-Magdalena drainage and walled settlements and signaling sites in the Río Sonora.

We suggest that the demise of this system of polities and exchange is linked to the collapse of the Classic period Hohokam and of Casas Grandes in the fifteenth century. The latest tree-ring date from Medio period contexts at Casas Grandes is 1493 (Ravesloot et al. 1986), and Dean's (1988) recent evaluation of Hohokam chronometric information indicates the Hohokam Classic period terminated between A.D. 1450 and 1500. In southern Arizona and the Trincheras area, there is a marked decline in the number and size of sites in the late fifteenth century (Doelle and Wallace 1988).

Reff (1986, 1988) claims that archaeologists have subscribed to a "civilization-savagery" myth that led them to discount the complexity of aboriginal societies in the Northwest and to postulate a collapse before the Spanish arrival and a gap in the archaeological record in the protohistoric period. He argues that the Medio period at Casas Grandes and the Hohokam Classic period lasted into the early sixteenth century, at which time these peoples were decimated by European disease, and that no gap in fact exists.

Reff's arguments ignore recent findings concerning Northwest prehistory. Major reinterpretations of prehistory published over the past decade have argued that the prehistory of the Northwest was far more complex and that small, economically simple communities can by no means be assumed. In southern Arizona, archaeologists have filled in the protohistoric "gap" and now recognize a ceramic, lithic, and architectural assemblage that characterizes the smaller and more limited number of sites in this time period (Doelle and Wallace 1988; Masse 1981). Furthermore, recent analyses of tree-ring dates, archaeomagnetic dates, and C-14 dates indicate that the Classic and Medio periods ended in the fifteenth century (Dean 1988; Eighmy and McGuire 1988; Ravesloot et al. 1986).

The evidence for continued occupation into the historic period is much better in northern Sonora than in Arizona or Chihuahua. In the Altar Valley, Hinton (1955) reported a continuation of sites and ceramic types connecting the earlier Trincheras sites with known mission sites and Papago villages through time. Our recently completed survey in the Altar supports Hinton's interpretation. However, we recognize that the number and size of sites in the protohistoric (late fifteenth and early sixteenth centuries) and early historic periods is markedly less than in the late prehistoric (fourteenth and early fifteenth centuries). We also have no evidence of public architecture at the protohistoric sites and little or no evidence of exchange. The seventeenth-century cultural pattern that Manje and Kino reported in the Altar Valley originated before the Spanish entrada of the sixteenth century.

The world that the Spanish invaded in 1540 was less integrated, less nucleated, less populated, and possibly less militaristic than it had been 100 years before (Villalpando 1985:285). Paradoxically, the lack of integration and nucleation hindered, slowed, and eventually stopped the Spanish colonial advance. If the Spanish had arrived 100 to 150 years earlier, the settlement of northwest México might have been more like that of Mesoamerica, or at least the New Mexico colony. In addition to finding the settled villages of the Pueblos, the Spanish would have encountered concentrated populations in southern Arizona, northern Sonora, and at Casas Grandes, Chihuahua. These groups were probably more centralized than the New Mexico Pueblos and would have been equally or more susceptible to the Spanish program of conquest than the Pueblos were. Instead of being an isolated outpost, the New Mexico colony could have been linked through these areas to Sonora and New Spain. Earlier and greater settlement of the Northwest could have limited or restrained the later colonial advance of the United States into the area.

In 1531 Guzmán stood at the southern edge of a world in transition. The Spanish intrusion guaranteed that the aboriginal peoples of northwest México would not be able to remake their world on their own terms. The world they had created, however, transformed the Spanish advance and forced the Spanish to remake their colonial effort even as that world passed away. The study of Sonoran prehistory helps us to understand the circumstances of the aboriginal past that structured one side of the encounter.

Notes

1. The aboriginal cultural area presently incorporated in the modern states of Sonora, Chihuahua, Arizona, New Mexico, southwest Colorado, southeast Utah, and trans-Pecos Texas was for 300 years the Northwest, first of New Spain and later México. Most U.S. authors refer to this cultural area as the Southwest.

2. Many Native Americans use their religion, myths, and legends as the primary means of knowing this past. This leads to a spiritual understanding of prehistory very different from the inferences of archaeologists.

3. The scraping marks on the interior of Trincheras pottery have often been misinterpreted as "brushing." Scraping the wet clay vessel with a straight-edged tool would produce these marks as the tool dug up and dragged bits of temper along the surface.

Acknowledgments

A number of people assisted us in the preparation of this paper. William Doolittle and Carroll Riley reviewed earlier drafts of the paper and provided valuable comments. Russell Weisman pointed out that the so-called brushing in Trincheras pottery was in fact scraping marks. Lon Bulgrin kindly proofread the final draft. Our work in the Altar Valley was supported by NSF grant BNS-8703515.

References

Alvarez, Ana Maria
  1985 Sociedades Agrícolas. In *Historia General de Sonora*, vol. 1, edited by J. C. Montané, pp. 225–262. Gobierno del Estado de Sonora, Hermosillo.
Amsden, Monroe
  1928 *Archaeological Reconnaissance in Sonora*. Paper No. 1. Southwest Museum, Los Angeles.
Bannon, John Francis
  1970 *The Spanish Borderlands Frontier 1513–1821*. Holt, Rinehart and Winston, New York.
Bowen, Thomas
  n.d. A Survey and Re-evaluation of the Trincheras Culture, Mexico. Ms. on file, Arizona State Museum, Tucson.
  1976 *Seri Prehistory; The Archaeology of the Centeral Coast of Sonora, Mexico*. Anthropological Papers No. 27. University of Arizona, Tucson.
Brand, Donald D.
  1935 The Distribution of Pottery Types in Northwest Mexico. *American Anthropologist* 37(2):287–305.
Braniff, Beatriz
  1985 *La Frontera Protohistorica Pima-Opata en Sonora, Mexico*. Universidad Nacional Autonomía de México.
  1988 Observations on the Elites of the Pimeria and Opateria in Prehispanic Times. Paper presented at the Southwest Symposium, Tempe.

Dean, Jeffrey S.
  1988 Thoughts on Hohokam Chronology. Paper presented at the Changing Views on Hohokam Archaeology Seminar, Amerind Foundation, Dragoon, Ariz.
Di Peso, Charles C.
  1956 *The Upper Pima of San Cayetano del Tumacacori*. Amerind Foundation Publication No. 7. Dragoon, Ariz.
  1974 *Casas Grandes: A Fallen Trading Center of the Gran Chichimeca*. Amerind Foundation Publication No. 9. Dragoon, Ariz.
  1979 Prehistory: Southern Periphery. In *Southwest*, edited by Alfonso Ortiz, pp. 152–161. Handbook of North American Indians, vol. 9, William C. Sturtevant, general editor. Smithsonian Institution, Washington D.C.
  1983 The Northern Sector of the Mesoamerican World System. In *Forgotten Places and Things*, edited by A. E. Ward, pp. 11–22, Center for Archaeological Studies, Albuquerque.
Doelle, William H., and Henry D. Wallace
  1988 Spatial Variation in the Hohokam Regional System. Paper presented at the Changing Views on Hohokam Archaeology Seminar, Amerind Foundation, Dragoon, Ariz.
Doolittle, William E.
  1984 Settlements and the Development of "Statelets" in Sonora, Mexico. *Journal of Field Archaeology* 11:13–24.
  1988 *Pre-Hispanic Occupance in the Valley of Sonora Mexico*. Anthropological Papers No. 48. University of Arizona, Tucson.
Downum, Christian E.
  1986 The Occupational Use of Hill Space in the Tucson Basin: Evidence from The Linda Vista Hill. *The Kiva* 51(4):219–232.
Eighmy, Jeffrey L., and Randall H. McGuire
  1988 *Archaeomagnetic Dates and the Hohokam Phase Sequence*. Technical Series No. 3. Colorado State University Archaeometric Lab, Ft. Collins.
Ekholm, Gordon
  1939 Results of an Archaeological Survey of Sonora and Northern Sinaloa. *Revista Mexicana de Estudios Antropologicos* 3:7–10.
Fish, Suzanne K., Paul R. Fish, and Christian Downum
  1984 Hohokam Terraces and Agricultural Production in the Tucson Basin. In *Prehistoric Agricultural Strategies in the Southwest*, edited by P. R. Fish and S. K. Fish, pp. 55–71. Anthropological Research Paper No. 33. Arizona State University, Tempe.
Fontana, Bernard L., J. Cameron Greenleaf, and Donnely D. Cassidy
  1959 A Fortified Arizona Mountain. *The Kiva* 25(4):41–52.
Fraps, Clara Lee
  1936 Blackstone Ruin. *The Kiva* 2(3):9–12.
Gerhard, Peter
  1982 *The Northern Frontier of New Spain*. Princeton University Press, Princeton, N.J.
Gibson, Charles
  1964 *The Aztecs under Spanish Rule*. Stanford University Press, Stanford, Calif.
Gumerman, George C., and Emil W. Haury
  1979 Prehistory: Hohokam. In *Southwest*, edited by Alfonso Ortiz, pp. 75–90. Handbook of North American Indians, vol. 9, William C. Sturtevant, general editor. Smithsonian Institution, Washington D.C.
Hammond, George P., and Agapito Rey
  1940 *Narratives of the Coronado Expedition, 1540–1542*. University of New Mexico Press, Albuquerque.
  1953 *Don Juan de Oñate, Colonizer of New Mexico 1595–1628*. University of New Mexico Press, Albuquerque.

Haury, Emil W.

1950 *The Archaeology and Stratigraphy of Ventana Cave*. University of Arizona Press, Tucson.

1976 *The Hohokam:Desert Farmers and Craftsmen*. University of Arizona Press, Tucson.

Hinton, Thomas B.

1955 A Survey of Archaeological Sites in the Altar Valley, Sonora. *The Kiva* 21(3–4):1–12.

Johnson, Alfred E.

1963 The Trincheras Culture of Northwestern Sonora. *American Antiquity* 29(4):174–186.

Kessell, John L.

1979 *Kiva Cross and Crown*. National Park Service, Washington D.C.

Lafaye, Jacques

1976 *Quetzalcóatl and Guadalupe*. University of Chicago Press, Chicago.

León-Portilla, Miguel

1972 The Nortaño Variety of Mexican Culture: An Ethnohistorical Approach. In *Plural Society in the Southwest*, edited by E. H. Spicer and R. H. Thompson, pp. 77–114. Weatherhead Foundation, Santa Fe.

McGuire, Randall H.

1980 The Mesoamerican Connection in the Southwest. *The Kiva* 46(1–2):3–38.

McGuire, Randall H., and Michael B. Schiffer

1982 *Hohokam and Patayan: The Archaeology of Southwestern Arizona*. Academic Press, New York.

1983 A Theory of Architectural Design. *Journal of Anthropological Archaeology* 2(3):277–303.

MacLachlan, Colin M., and Jaime E. Rodriguez

1980 *The Forging of the Cosmic Race*. University of California Press, Berkeley.

Masse, C. Bruce

1981 A Reappraisal of the Protohistoric Sobaipuri Indians of Southeastern Arizona. In *The Protohistoric Period in the North American Southwest*, A.D. 1450–1700, edited by D. R. Wilcox and W. B. Masse, pp. 28–56. Anthropological Research Paper No. 24. Arizona State University, Tempe.

Minnis, Paul E.

1988 Four Examples of Specialized Production at Casas Grandes, Northwestern Chihuahua. *The Kiva* 53(2):181–194.

Naylor, Thomas

1983 Review of Riley: The Frontier People. *The Kiva* 49(1–2):119–121.

Naylor, Thomas H., and Charles W. Polzer

1986 *The Presidio and Militia on the Northern Frontier of New Spain* 1570–1700. University of Arizona Press, Tucson.

Pailes, Richard

1980 The Upper Río Sonora Valley in Prehistoric Trade. *Transactions of the Illinois State Academy of Science* 72(4):20–39.

1984 Agricultural Development and Trade in the Río Sonora. In *Prehistoric Agricultural Strategies in the Southwest*, edited by S. K. Fish and Paul Fish, pp. 309–325. Anthropological Research Paper No. 33. Arizona State University, Tempe.

Ravesloot, John C., Jeffrey S. Dean, and Michael S. Foster

1986 A New Perspective on the Casas Grandes Tree-Ring Dates. Paper presented at the Fourth Mogollon Conference, Tucson.

Reff, Daniel T.

1981 The Location of Corazones and Senora: Archaeological Evidence from the Rio Sonora Valley, Mexico. In *The Protohistoric Period in the North American Southwest*, A.D. 1450–1700, edited by D. R. Wilcox and W. B. Masse, pp. 94–112. Anthropological Research Paper No. 24. Arizona State University, Tempe.

1986 *The Demographic and Cultural Consequences of Old World Diseases in the Greater Southwest, 1519–1660*. Ph.D. dissertation, University of Oklahoma. University Microfilms, Ann Arbor.

1988 Old World Diseases and the Protohistoric Period in the Greater Southwest. Paper presented at the Southwest Symposium, Tempe.

Riley, Carroll L.

1985 Spanish Contact and the Collapse of the Sonoran Statelets. In *The Archaeology of West and Northwest México*, edited by M. S. Foster and P. C. Weigand, pp. 419–430. Westview Press, Boulder, Colo.

Robles, Manuel

n.d. Un Sitio de la Cultura Trincheras en el Valle del Río Altar. Ms. on file, Centro Regional de Noroeste de INHA, Hermosillo.

1973 El Arroyo Bacoachi y el Trafico de Concha Trincheras. Ms. on file Centro Regional de Noroeste de INHA, Hermosillo.

Sauer, Carl O., and Donald D. Brand

1931 Prehistoric Settlements of Sonora with Special Reference to *Cerros de Trincheras*. *University of California Publications in Geography* 5(3):67–148.

Spicer, Edward H.

1962 *Cycles of Conquest*. University of Arizona Press, Tucson.

Villalpando, María Elisa

1984 Correlación Arqueológico-Etnográfica en Isla San Esteban, Sonora México. Thesis. Escuela Nacional de Antoplogiá, México.

1985 Cazadores—Recolectores y Agricultores del Contacto. In *Historia General de Sonora*, vol. 1, edited by J. C. Montané, pp. 225–262. Gobierno del Estado de Sonora, Hermosillo.

Wallace, Henry D., and James P. Holmlund

1984 The Classic Period in the Tucson Basin. *The Kiva* 49(3–4):167–194.

Wasley, William

1968 Archaeological Survey in Sonora, Mexico. Paper presented at the annual meetings of the Society for American Archaeology, Santa Fe.

Wilcox, David R.

1979 Implications of Dry Laid Masonry Walls on Tumamoc Hill. *The Kiva* 45(1–2):15–38.

Wolf, Eric R.

1959 *Sons of the Shaking Earth*. University of Chicago Press, Chicago.

Zavala, Silvio A.

1973 *La Encomienda Indiana*. Editorial Porrúa S.A., México.

Chapter 11 ■

Charles W. Polzer, S.J.

The Spanish Colonial Southwest: New Technologies for Old Documents

The convergence of the disciplines of history and anthropology for purposes of research, especially archaeological research in the American Southwest, has created serious methodological problems because of the presumptive definitions those disciplines have employed. It has taken me half a professional lifetime to learn not to use the term *borderlands*, and I am still struggling to limit my use of *Southwest*. The reason for my discomfiture is that these labels imply definitional concepts that create climates of generalization that are often misleading, although these same concepts are compatible with the established vocabulary of their individual disciplines. The "Spanish Colonial Southwest" is a fictional region conjured up by academes of the Atlantic seaboard, embraced by mid-Westerners, and written into the descriptive academic catalogs of California. The term has created enormous difficulties because anthropologists and archaeologists have utilized the findings of historians of the Southwest whose work has evolved in near isolation.

Consider the connotation of *borderlands*. The term implies multiple areas that are contiguous to some definitor—geographic or political. The region borders the Gulf of Mexico, or the area extends along the international border. Aren't the states along the Canadian border as much a borderland as those along the Mexican border? Isn't Florida as much a borderland as California? But a more incisive criticism of the term is that most anthropologists and historians are concerned with the period of contact, when major cultural changes occurred—and when there was no border! Furthermore, the borderland mentality cloaks a north–south bias, whereas the factors affecting culture exchange moved from the south to the north. The major cultural complex was Mesoamerican, and its influence simply must be given its proper place in the study of southwestern cultures.

Here again, in the term *southwest* the problem of cultural bias lies gently hidden. Southwest of what? If one considers the culture of Pueblo Indians to be southwestern, why not include Yaquis, who are even farther southwest? Moreover, the momentum of the southwest idea must perforce come from somewhere in the northeast, again reinforcing the hidden bias.

Both terms cleverly avoid the need to invest time and energy in understanding the vast stretches of "arid America" and their role in the culture of the entire region. Nor do they require mastery of the Spanish language, the language of record for the region. No one need cross the border physically or intellectually. And it would be very dangerous to do so because established academia has already drawn the line that is never to be crossed—American (a misnomer for U.S.) history stops at the border; Latin American studies begin at the border, but anyone who does not drench himself or herself in South America is not a Latin Americanist. The borderlands are an academic no-man's-land crying for recognition beyond the ready-made labels in use (Garreau 1981).

The whole problem began innocently enough toward the end of the nineteenth century when universities on the Atlantic seaboard introduced a battery of new courses that reflected fresh interest in the Americas—not unassociated with their own concerns about celebrating the four hundredth anniversary of the discovery of the Americas. An example is Frank Blackmar's study of Spanish institutions (Blackmar 1891). Pick up almost any book on American history that mentions the Spaniards and you will find that the *California* missions are taken as the prototype of the Spanish mission system. In reality, they corresponded to a total shift in Spain's cultural policy in the Americas that sounded the death knell of the "mission" era; California's missions are post-typical, not prototypical. The study of the Spanish military system has been equally distorted. Late eighteenth-century military dominance along the northern perimeter of New Spain is taken as the archetype of Spanish military presence along the frontier for more than a century and a half. Yet the studies of the defensive posture of Spain's crumbling empire in the late 1700s corresponds more to early twentieth-century social science paradigms than seventeenth-century and early eighteenth-century realities. Max L. Moorhead, for example, devoted only 17 percent of his book on the presidio to the Spanish military before 1772 and focused the balance of the study on only 12 percent of the total period of Spanish presence in the north (Moorhead 1975)! Please understand, I am not finding fault with either of these useful works. Their authors, like most, had to work with the documentary sources that were available. I merely insist that vast amounts of basic archival work and careful comparative analysis remain before us; we cannot rest easy about any research. And we must adjust our ideas to conform to a cultural reality larger than a borderland.

Institutional History

It has been extremely popular and convenient for historians to treat Spanish colonial phenomena according to the themes of institutional history—the mission, the presidio, the hacienda, and the real de minas (Bolton 1917; Brinckerhoff and Faulk 1965; Chevalier 1963; West 1949). In many ways this covered the frontier, so to speak, and has set up a convenient fiction for archaeological work—dig up a mission, a presidio, a hacienda, and a real de minas, and, voilà, one has exposed the Spanish colonial frontier in the Southwest! The intense institutional dependence on social systems in the interior of New Spain and the long centuries of development and change, like the trade and social networks that once existed between the north and Mesoamerica, have been largely overlooked because the data base farther south, whether historical or archaeological, has never been adequately studied (Di Peso 1973).

The Documentary Relations of the Southwest

When the Documentary Relations of the Southwest (DRSW) project was begun at the Arizona State Museum in 1974, we were aware of these disciplinary discrepancies, but we did not understand the gravity of their deficiencies. The project title (DRSW) has persisted largely to satisfy political prejudice rather than scientific or historical fact. DRSW was laboriously derived from the "Jesuit Relations of North America" that some anthropologists recognize as having been seminal in the creation of the discipline (Barnes et al. 1981). There were enough Jesuit documents on the Southwest to publish more than 10 times what Reuben Thwaites had produced for the Northeast (Thwaites 1896–1901)—plus the relatively untouched Franciscan documents and the civil-military documents. So we abandoned any adjective except *documentary* for the relations we intended to publish. Knowing that we had to face federal and state agencies for funding, we retained the descriptor *Southwest* because politics, not truth, rules the realities of research. We are just now tidying up the compilation of documents for an ethnohistory of the Seri Indians of northwestern Mexico. To the academic purist, these people lie outside the borderlands (and therefore are not genuinely American) and are not Puebloan enough to be southwestern. Yet the Seri Indians were one of the chief reasons for stalling the Spanish advance to the northwest. Not to understand them and their influence would constitute a major error in presenting the history of the region, including their links to the western Apache in the eighteenth century. But can you imagine a panel of traditional academics recognizing the radical validity of such a study?

Certainly, Paul Kirchhoff's "Arid America" and Charles Di Peso's "Gran Chichimeca" offered alternatives to our politically motivated use of *Southwest*, but can you imagine Senator William Proxmire descending on the Gran

Chichimeca like a Union general (Di Peso 1974; Kirchhoff 1954)? Now, Carroll Riley has brought the field back to Ralph Beals's "Greater Southwest" (Beals 1932; Riley 1987)—all represent attempts to label the reality of the region with which we are so familiar, but whose history is far more extensive and complex than can be suggested by the title "Spanish Borderlands"—with all due apologies to Herbert E. Bolton, whose effort to expand the horizons of American history has unwittingly led to its confinement by men of lesser vision (Bolton 1921).

There is hardly a historian or anthropologist who is not well versed in the outpouring of Spanish colonial documentary literature sponsored by the Quivira Society. Beyond the society's dozen editions, Herbert Eugene Bolton, Fray Angelico Chávez, Charles Wilson Hackett, George P. Hammond, Lawrence Kinnaird, Agapito Rey, Alfred Barnaby Thomas, Ralph Twitchell, and George Parker Winship flesh out a litany of documentary editors who seem to many to be the final word on sources for Southwestern research. But the truth is that tens of thousands of pages of documents remain—rarely seen and more rarely used. These documents are not always the rich relations of an expedition or a reconquest; more commonly they are the scattered diaries of military operations, the routine correspondence of an isolated missionary, the waybills of merchants and freight haulers. But they tell an intricate story of people struggling to survive, to regain lost territory, to conquer, to develop, to gain respect and wealth; they are the paper traces of history that sought to overlay the unwritten evidences of lost civilizations.

The choice pieces of historical evidence have, for the most part, been discovered and published. They form the skeletal frame of our understanding of the Spanish occupation of North America. But once the muscles are again attached to these bare bones of history, the gaunt and shadowy specter changes its shape and form. This is a process that was unthinkable a score of years ago. The vast quantities of information were so scattered that even a genius endowed with a photographic memory would have been hard pressed to relate the facts at his or her disposal. The era of the mindless computer, however, with its vast memory capacity and processing speed has brought a new power of relational organization to bear on the unmanageable plethora of available information (Barnes et al. 1981).

Rewriting, Not Revising, History

In the opinion of some, this commentator being one of them, the whole history of Spanish presence in North America, or anywhere else for that matter, can and must be rewritten, not because it is wrong, but becasue it is incomplete. Furthermore, the powerful presence of these Europeans brought change swiftly into the lives of Native Americans. Whatever thin record that remains is still hiding in the pages of Spanish contact. Unfortunately, we spend our energies lamenting the tragic spread of disease, counting the dead, estimating the living, and fixing blame on men who never knew they were carrying death in the same breath by which they preached life. If we could turn our efforts to a careful combing of the extant record, we would find delicate bits of information that would cast light on archaeological as well as historical investigations. The protohistoric should then emerge as a bridge, albeit shaky, to the prehistoric—if we do our work with the precision required.

Perhaps Southwestern researchers can learn a lesson from the Southeasterners. Today the tedium of Eugene Lyon's leafing through thousands of pages in the Archivo General de Indias in Sevilla has interwoven with the tedium of Kathleen Deagan's scientific "rummaging" through unromantic Spanish ruins in Florida and the Caribbean (Deagan 1987; Lyon 1986). The world now stands in awe as a story of conquest and expansion based on their work has graced the pages of the *National Geographic* Magazine. Spanish names lie next to familiar features of the topography of the Atlantic seaboard, for example, *Cabo de Trafalgar* instead of Cape Hatteras, *La Bahía de la Madre de Dios* instead of Chesapeake Bay, *Santa Elena* instead of Charlesfort—names that were given and forgotten decades before their orphaning to the English (Sauer 1971).

For none of us, as historians and anthropologists, is this a case of one-upmanship—"We were here first." This is a case of looking objectively at the record because change, immediate change, was introduced with the presence of European peoples and their technologies. The Spanish record is quintessential in understanding the prehistory, protohistory, and the history of our continent.

Importance of the Quincentenary

If I may interject at this point, this is precisely why the celebration of the Columbian Quincentenary is so vitally important. We may be momentarily distracted by the Landfall dispute, which is, in essence, rather unimportant, because the fact of the discovery—really the encounter of two worlds—is what emerges as significant. And even as we attempt to mount an objective, meaningful celebration, we have come to realize our information base is hardly known, poorly organized, and inadequate to the task. We cannot build the caravels because we do not know how they really looked or how they were actually built. Conjecture tempered with fragments from marine archaeology has helped, but not definitively. This is not to say that there is no information; it is only to say that we are not in control of the evidence at hand—and much, much of this resides in Spanish archives the world over.

The Computer Era

Fortunately for archivists, the computer era has dawned. The power of binary logic will command the field of information storage and exchange. But, unfortunately for this generation, the time lag between application and availability promises to be a long one.

Let me paint the current picture in broad strokes. Only five years ago most archivists and researchers knew little about the power of digital storage and presentation; those who knew realized that graphic presentation of documents required horrendous amounts of computer memory. The great potential of computer technology dampened the early flush of interest when researchers learned that it would be many years before optical character recognition would be capable of turning manuscripts into ASCII codes—a transferral process that would solve the mass storage problem. Unknown to the computer expert was the archivist's inherent aversion to losing the character of the original in "electronic typescripts." But technology surged rapidly ahead in those same five years, and mass memory storage has become so vast and affordable, especially through the development of optical digital disk storage, that the entire problem is being rethought.

In April 1988, at a joint meeting of the U.S. and Spanish Quincentennial Commissions, I listened to the *illuminati* in Sevilla describing the current work of IBM at the Archivo General de Indias. They were aglow with pride that IBM was "microfilming" some of the more important and most used *legajos*. So that you will not make that same mistake, let me describe briefly the process that is coming on line for archives.

Microfilming versus Digital Imaging

The old method of preserving and disseminating documents was photographic. Documents were filmed under strong light that itself aided in deteriorating the written images on paper. Under the most enlightened archival management, the resultant negatives were safeguarded and positive copies were sent on request to the researcher. Under less, and usually more pragmatic, management, this reproduction process was repeated time after time. The recurrent handling, flattening, and lighting continued to take their toll of the documents' integrity. And every time a new-generation film was made from negative or positive, a deterioration in quality was witnessed in the copy.

The new method is to scan a document with a laser beam that generates a long string of binary codes, which record intensities and colors. The image of the document is thus broken into thousands of pixels (picture elements), which are recorded as binary values in the computer's memory. The density of the pixels is controlled by the scanner. For example, IBM of Spain announced 200 dots per inch (dpi) as its standard for the AGI project in Sevilla. Advanced Projects International, whose personnel digitized the manuscript archive of Werner von Braun while they were still a team at the National Air and Space Museum, uses between 300 and 900 dpi. A standard of 300 dpi will render an image of approximately the same resolution and quality as microfilm; 900 to 1200 dpi exceeds even the fine resolution of microfilm!

The document image, thus digitized, is held in memory and its projection on the computer screen is checked for clarity and enhancement if necessary. Unlike microfilming, the computer process can filter out stains, lift out faded letters—in general, it can renew the original within acceptable limits. After the document has passed inspection, the magnetic file is compressed (noninformational areas—i.e., "white areas"—are extracted) and written onto an optical disk by laser beam. The document exists on the disk in an irremovable, uncorrectable fashion—a feature very much favored by archivists. It is not written as an analog (or video) record, but as a digital record that permits much finer resolution and accuracy. This whole scanning and writing process takes about fifteen seconds, or somewhat longer if the document is particularly "dirty." And a single 2-gigabyte optical disk can contain upward of 40,000 pages. The entire collection at the Archivo General de Indias consists of 80,000,000 documents that take up an entire city block. Once digitized, the entire archive can be placed on 2,000 optical disks, which can be placed in a single room.

The optical digital disk has the advantage of random access as opposed to serial access on microfilm. Access is almost instantaneous on a mounted disk. "Juke box access" would, of course, be required for an entire archive, but this presents no technical problem, only a minor slowdown in reaching the information. Entire disks can be easily, accurately, and inexpensively duplicated; subsets can be created for segments of an archive and placed on smaller optical digital disks; and the entire holdings can be transmitted by telecommunications!

Furthermore, current search programs scan be used to identify patterns, which in this case are words or signatures. Eventually, when the marvel of artificial intelligence is mastered, it will be possible to read and translate the digitized documents into ASCII codes to permit direct printing of document transcriptions.

Frankly, it is immaterial whether the computer world ever reaches the nearly miraculous state of optical character recognition in the case of manuscript writing—it has already done marvels with the printed page. Digital preservation of the unique documents of history is in itself a sufficient reason to launch an immediate, urgent campaign. I work in a building surrounded by millions of pot sherds whose commonality defies classification; each one is labeled, boxed, shelved, and placed under maximum security. When I go to an archive, most documents are not even labeled. They are tied in bundles of loose papers, shelved, and casually guarded—yet each piece of paper contains unique information. The loss of a sherd will probably not upset the conclusion of archaeology; the loss of a single document often changes history—with due apologies to Admiral Poindexter and Colonel North.

Imaging and Integrated Finding Aids

Once an archive is digitized, the archivist's task of preservation is materially advanced because we the user-researchers can rummage through the images on the disks without having to consult the original, except to ferret out a palimpsest or forgery. The availability of digitized archives should finally make it possible for consortia of academic or professional researchers to compile standardized finding aids that can interact with the digital images. For example, Advanced Projects International (API) and our DRSW demonstrated a fully integrated system last September in conjunction with the Hispanic Archival Conference at the Library of Congress. Documents were integrated with the full DRSW Master Indexes, BIOFILE (a biographical dictionary for northern New Spain), and GEOFILE (a geographical locating system for northern New Spain). And the complete API system, dubbed DARS for Digital Archival Retrieval System, is currently capable of integrating information data bases, document images, maps, illustrations, and material culture inventories. The drawback of the system is that most of us will be sitting at terminals instead of in 4 x 4s in front of the Bancroft Library or in the Staked Plains of Texas.

When I outline these marvels, please realize that I am describing an information retrieval system that has yet to be created because very little of the input work has begun anywhere. In all honesty, people have recognized that the system exists, that technology has reached the point of application, but no one is convinced that the absolutely essential task of entering this information commands any priority. Foundations are uninterested, or if vaguely interested, are skeptical, or worse, fearful that the information age will devour their limited resources. Meanwhile the unique bundles of evidence for the history and anthropology of the Americas are crumbling away, perhaps even to be lost before anyone admits that the priority that should have been granted should have been the highest. Ten years ago there was no fiscally responsible way to achieve preservation and dissemination; now there is. But old decisions have become like old shoes: They are comfortable—but they really won't last down the trail. Admittedly, we have new technologies for old documents, but unfortunately we still have old policies for new history. I would like to think that our counterparts in A.D. 2492 will have just as good a data base to consult as we have for this Quincentenary, and more than that, I would hope that our sense of scholarly interest and commitment will have contributed to a substantial increase in that data base. The public must realize that its future is built on its past; that cultural tradition is not oddity, but identity; that history is not data, but conscious evaluation; that archaeology is not antiquarianism beneath a trowel, but respect for the ancient, unspoken testimony of human endeavor; that anthropology is not a science that merely classifies the human species, but probes the meaning of man. Archaeology without anthropology risks lifelessness; anthropology without history risks dehumanization; and man without science and culture risks extinction. We have come 500 years in the wake of Columbus's caravels. Can we survive the next 500 without his courage and thirst for discovery?

As one of 30 federal commissioners for the celebration of the Columbian Quincentenary, my responsibilities bring before me something about 1992 on an almost daily basis. And I confess to a deeply growing concern that the short time we have left to prepare for 1992 is being filled with projects for fireworks, tall ships, parties, and esoteric publications. Some of us have pleaded that not even Columbus discovered America in a day. It took him a decade and four voyages to begin to doubt that he had reached the Indies. Why should we confine the celebration of the discovery of the Americas to a few days or a few months? Why should we spend tens of millions of dollars, private and public, on Japanese powder and Hollywood lights? Many of us insist that money to support the Quincentenary should be spent on substantive projects that will endure for centuries. And many of us feel that we should only begin to celebrate in 1992. On October 12, 1992, we should announce the inauguration of a decade of discovery. We need to go beyond, to sail again and again into the unknown as Columbus did. Our projects should reflect a renewed commitment to discovery and to the meaning of America, because America is more than a place.

America represents the freshness of human discovery and the strength of hope—while old systems bubble away in the wake of new directions. Columbus knew the world was round, but his westward thrust went straight to the heart of the Indies. And we, too, may think we are going in circles, only to discover that we, and not the world, are the mystery that craves a direct solution. In our documents and in our memories the past is with us. In our mastery of history and prehistory the future can be ours. Then and only then can the Quincentenary that we are celebrating become the Millennium—and beyond.

References

Barnes, Thomas C., Thomas H. Naylor, and Charles W. Polzer
  1981 *Northern New Spain: A Research Guide*. University of Arizona Press, Tucson.
Beals, Ralph L.
  1932 Comparative Ethnology of Northern Mexico before 1750. *Ibero-Americana*: 2. University of California Press, Berkeley.
Blackmar, Frank W.
  1891 *Spanish Institutions of the Southwest*. Johns Hopkins University Press, Baltimore, Md.
Bolton, Herbert Eugene
  1917 The Mission as a Frontier Institution in the Spanish-American Colonies. *American Historical Review* 23:42–61.
  1921 *Spanish Borderlands: A Chronicle of Old Florida and the Southwest*. Yale University Press, New Haven, Conn.
Brinckerhoff, Sidney B., and Odie B. Faulk
  1965 *Lancers for the King: A Study of the Frontier Military System of Northern New Spain, with a Translation of the Royal Regulations of 1772*. Arizona Historical Foundation, Phoenix.
Chevalier, François
  1963 *Land and Society in Colonial Mexico: The Great Hacienda*. University of California Press, Berkeley.
Deagan, Kathleen
  1987 Searching for Columbus' Lost Colony. *National Geographic*. November 172:672–675.
Di Peso, Charles
  1973 Three-Dimensional Record in Spanish and Mexican Period. *El Palacio* 4:2–13.
  1974 *Casas Grandes: A Fallen Trading Center of the Gran Chichimeca*. 3 vols. Amerind Foundation, Dragoon.
Garreau, Joel
  1981 *Nine Nations of North America*. Houghton-Mifflin, New York.
Kirchhoff, Paul
  1954 Gatherers and Farmers in the Greater Southwest: A Problem in Classification. *American Anthropologist* 56:529–560.
Lyon, Eugene
  1986 15th Century Manuscript Yields First Look at Niña. *National Geographic*. November 170:601–605.
Moorhead, Max L.
  1975 *The Presidio*. University of Oklahoma Press, Norman.

Riley, Carroll L.
   1987 *The Frontier People: The Greater Southwest in the Protohistoric Period*. University of New Mexico Press, Albuquerque.
Sauer, Carl Ortwin
   1971 *Sixteenth Century North America: The Land and the People as Seen by the Europeans*. University of California Press, Berkeley.
Thwaites, Reuben G. (editor)
   1896–1901 *Jesuit Relations and Allied Documents, 1748–1846*. 73 vol. Burrows Brothers, Cleveland.
West, Robert
   1949 The Mining Community of Northern New Spain: the Parral Mining District. *Ibero-Americana*: 30. University of California Press, Berkeley.

Part 2 ■

Texas and Northeastern Mexico

Chapter 12 ■

Thomas R. Hester

Texas and Northeastern Mexico: An Overview

The borderlands of Texas and northeastern Mexico are today usually thought of as a narrow strip along the middle and lower Rio Grande, much of it characterized as "the brush country" (or *monte*). In Spanish Colonial times, however, it was politically a much broader area, stretching from northern Mexico eastward to the pine forests of eastern Texas and western Louisiana, and along the coastline of the eastern Gulf of Mexico. The creation of this "borderlands" area reflected the concern, and sometimes the paranoia, of the Spanish about French influence and penetration into the region. Certainly LaSalle's disastrous effort to establish a colony on the Texas coast was, at the time, a major political issue to the seventeenth-century Spanish.

The area from what is now eastern Coahuila, extending eastward across the Rio Grande to the Nueces Plains of southern Texas had more grassland and less thorn-brush cover than today (Inglis 1964; Weniger 1984). Spanish accounts indicate flowing water in what are now dusty stream channels, and bison, pronghorn, and bear in areas where the only large game today is the white-tail deer. The San Antonio River (Figure 12-1) became the "river of missions," from the cluster of missions at its headwaters near present-day San Antonio down to La

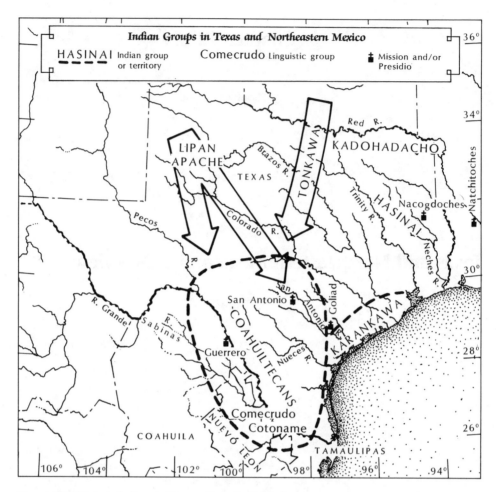

Figure 12-1. Historic Indians in Texas and northern Mexico.

Bahía (today's Goliad) on the coastal plain, running through oak-dotted prairies and plains, which are today the domain of small farms, ranches, and small towns, as well as larger towns and cities that have greatly polluted this all-important waterway of the eighteenth century.

The southern Texas-northeastern Mexico area became the focus of Spanish missions, colonies, and presidios after failed efforts in east Texas. But the Spanish always went *through* what we today call the Lower Pecos region—the canyon lands of the Pecos, Rio Grande, and Devil's rivers. They did not stop to establish missions, towns, or ranches. This was a much more hostile land, whose native Indians were probably gone by the eighteenth century and replaced by more aggressive Apache and Plains groups.

The Native American Context

As elsewhere in North America, the evidence for ancient human occupation of the Texas-Mexico Spanish Borderlands goes back at least 11,200 years, as represented by points of the Clovis complex (Hester 1980). Later Pleistocene activities are linked to the Folsom complex, especially a bison kill at Bonfire Shelter in the Lower Pecos region (Dibble and Lorrain 1968). Much of the region's prehistory, from around 6000 B.C. to the early centuries A.D. is termed the Archaic, a time of essentially modern climates, although certainly with cycles of long-term weather changes, during which hunting and gathering prevailed as a way of life among the native peoples. Indeed, hunting and gathering continued to be the major subsistence strategy in much of the Texas–Mexico borderlands right up to the time of Spanish intrusion (Hester 1980). The Archaic campsites along the coast are largely composed of shellfish accumulations (middens); in the coastal plain, there are scatters of flint debris and burned rock hearths; in the central Texas "hill country," burned rock middens represent a specialized cooking or food-processing technology; and, in the Lower Pecos, the rockshelters in the canyon walls were the preferred habitation areas (Hester 1980; Shafer 1986). In all these sites, there are large projectile points (called dart points by archaeologists), which were used to tip short spears that were thrown with a spear-thrower or atlatl (see Turner and Hester 1985). The bow and arrow as a weapons system was not introduced until after A.D. 500–700.

The advent of the bow and arrow, and several other new items of material culture, mark the Late Prehistoric period for the southern central and lower Pecos regions of the Texas–Northeast Mexico borderlands. Although there are distinctive shifts in material culture and settlement pattern, the lifeway continues to be based on hunting and gathering. A few maize cobs, found in central Texas rockshelters, suggest that limited horticulture was practiced. The latter part of this period is marked by a widespread cultural pattern known as the "Toyah phase," with an apparent emphasis on bison hunting. Other patterns of coeval date share some, but not all, of the Toyah traits (see Hester, this volume, for further discussion).

In eastern Texas, Native American development followed a different pattern. Stimulated by the culture of the lower Mississippi valley, east Texas Indian groups began to take up agriculture, make sophisticated pottery, and to live in hamlets and villages on a year-round basis. In the early centuries A.D., this cultural pattern is labeled Caddoan. Local sociopolitical units began to emerge, and there are sites with large mounds, impressive burial shaft tombs, and other distinctive features that suggest they were ceremonial or political centers. The Caddo peoples met by the early Spanish and French explorers in this region were the descendants of this earlier lifeway (Newcomb 1961).

Thus, in the eighteenth century, the Spanish found two drastically different life-styles in the borderlands area that extended from south of the Rio Grande to eastern Texas. In the east were the settled, agricultural Caddo, and in the south and west lived many nomadic hunting and gathering groups.

Hunters and Gatherers of the Borderlands

The term *hunting and gathering* often suggests to the layperson a precarious, hand-to-mouth way of life. Most commonly, however, the hunter and gatherer is supremely well adapted to the particular locale, living what some anthropologists have termed the life of the "first leisure class." Usually, they are not organized into any complex social, political, or economic units, living instead in "bands"—often family groups who work together to exploit natural resources during frequent moves through the landscape. In southern and central Texas, the plant and animal resources were relatively abundant, and seasonal plant food harvests—especially oak, pecan, and walnut in the fall, and the fruit (*tuna*) of the prickly pear in the summer—often resulted in great food surplus. The local bands gathered at those times into larger groups to take advantage of these resources. Unfortunately, we know too little about the early historic Indians of the region to assess what technologies they may have had for processing and long-term storage of, for example, the fall nut crops.

Coahuiltecan. The majority of the hunting and gathering Indians of southern Texas at the time of European contact have been lumped into the category of *Coahuiltecan*. This term was first applied in the nineteenth century to these groups, all thought to have shared a common Coahuilteco language (Campbell 1983:343; Swanton 1940). More recent research by Thomas N. Campbell (see Campbell 1988) has clearly shown that there were hundreds of small, independent Indian bands or groups across northeastern Mexico and southern Texas who shared certain traits, but probably also exhibited local or regional variation (Hester 1981) and among whom there were at least seven different languages—not just Coahuilteco. Goddard (1979) has recognized these languages as Coahuilteco, Karankawa (see below), Comecrudo, Cotoname, Solano, Tonkawa, and Aranama. In a recent review, Campbell (1983:349) has found at least 55 local Indian groups who were "probably" Coahuilteco speakers. In addition, new studies by Campbell and W. W. Newcomb, Jr. (Newcomb and Campbell ms.) have established that the Tonkawa-speakers were not native to this region, but had moved into the area (from an Oklahoma homeland) in the seventeenth century.

We know a little about many of the Coahuiltecan groups but not much about any one of them—or any one aspect of their lifeway. In the discussion that follows, the early Historic Indians of the Texas–Mexico borderlands are referred to as Coahuiltecan, with the understanding that this is a picture to be painted with a very broad brush and one that is aimed at depicting the nature of the hunter-gatherer peoples in much of this region at the time the Spanish missionization process began.

Most of Campbell's research has been oriented toward determining the specific name and geographic location of Coahuiltecan groups. Often this is all that can be done, as the Spanish recorded only meager information about the daily lives of these peoples. There have been some syntheses of these data, notably by Ruecking (1955) and Newcomb (1961), depicting a way of life drawn from widely scattered sources, both in time and space, of the early Spanish Colonial era. More recently, Salinas (1986) has prepared a major synthesis of the Indian groups of the Lower Rio Grande Valley of southern Texas and northeastern Mexico.

As a result of the impact of the Spanish and intruding Indians in the eighteenth century, none of these hunters and gatherers survived culturally or biologically to be interviewed by early anthropologists. Thus, we have to rely on the sketchy Spanish record, from explorers and missionaries, and on the singular account of Alvar Nuñez Cabeza de Vaca, who was shipwrecked on the Texas coast in 1528 (Campbell and Campbell 1981; Covey 1984) and for several years lived among the Indians of south Texas and northeastern Mexico. His accounts are our major record of these Indians before the eighteenth century missionization effort. There is also the early history of Nuevo León, compiled by Alonso de León (León et al. 1961) in the mid-seventeenth century, which provides a description of Indian life in that region (Brown 1988; Salinas 1986).

The Coahuiltecan hunter-gatherers are known to have lived in small groups, perhaps bands, to have had distinctive group names, and to have occupied specific territorial areas, which they used for hunting, plant food gathering, and fishing. The records indicate that they were mobile, camping at preferred sites a few weeks at a time. We know little about the size of their specific territories (the Payaya near San Antonio are thought to have had a "summer range" of about 30 miles; Campbell 1975: 349); or how they "shared" or overlapped territories with other Coahuiltecan (or non-Coahuiltecan) groups. Some groups consisted of about 45 persons (Weddle 1968), and reports of much higher population aggregations probably reflect the rancherías (villages comprising several Coahuiltecan groups—and sometimes other Indians) recorded by the Spanish after the disruption of the native territories had occurred in the eighteenth century. However, Cabeza de Vaca records the practice of the Coahuiltecan groups ("microbands") congregating for seasonal plant food harvests ("macrobands"), especially to collect acorns and pecans and the fruits of the prickly pear cactus.

Although it is likely that the greater part of the Coahuiltecan diet was derived from plant food collecting, as is the case, ethnographically, for most hunter-gatherers worldwide, we know that they hunted a wide range of animals. These included bison, antelope, deer, peccary, rabbits, rats, mice, and other small mammals and reptiles. Fishing was practiced by most groups, and land snails were gathered and eaten by some Coahuiltecans.

Although the terrain of southern Texas and northeastern Mexico is today a vast brushland, increasingly arid as one moves west, it was perhaps more bountiful in prehistoric times. Early historic records (see Inglis 1964; Weniger 1984) describe areas of savanna, streams that ran year-round, and in some regions, an abundance of plant and animal foods. In southern Texas, much of the hunting and gathering activities would have been concentrated on the riparian zones along major rivers and creeks (Hester 1981). High densities of plant foods as well as wildlife could be found in such locales. Certainly the faunal record left by the Late Prehistoric predecessors of the Coahuiltecans indicates the use of a diverse and extensive range of animals (Black 1986; Hester and Hill 1975). Spanish records mention the use of the bow and arrow and curved wooden sticks, perhaps rabbit-hunting clubs. They also used nets, baskets, and other food-collecting gear, and processed plant foods on stone grinding slabs or with wooden mortars and pestles.

There was minimal social and political organization among the Coahuiltecan groups–certainly no "tribes"—and those leaders designated as "chiefs" were chosen usually for specific tasks. The Spanish observed that they wore little clothing, but that they had cloaks that consisted of deer and rabbit skin. Additional details of Coahuiltecan lifeways can be found in Campbell (1983, 1988).

Karankawa. In addition to the Coahuilteco and related groups, the major population entity in this region to be affected by the Spanish were the Karankawa. Their lifeway has been summarized by Newcomb (1961, 1983), who dismisses some of the myths about these peoples—their voracious cannibalism, their great stature, and, more recently, their supposed immigration to Texas shores from the Caribbean or elsewhere in the Gulf of Mexico. Rather, they can be seen as a coastal-adapted hunting and gathering people living along the coast south of Galveston Bay to the vicinity of Corpus Christi Bay.

Karankawa subsistence activities have been reviewed by Krieger (1956). On the coastal prairies, they hunted large game including bison, deer, antelope, and, occasionally, bear, and, like the Coahuiltecans, they also trapped or collected small game, including reptiles, turtles, and the like. However, the abundant resources to be found in the Gulf, in the Laguna Madre between the barrier islands and the mainland, and in the estuaries and river mouths, were of much greater significance: shellfish (especially oysters), waterfowl, and fish of various species. The Karankawas hunted alligators not only for food, but as a source of oils used as mosquito repellent. During their subsistence activities, they moved from the mainland to the offshore barrier islands, but the timing of such movements (as well as other facets of their annual round) is unclear.

The Karankawa lived in a coastal strip that was devoid of chippable stone, and like their predecessors in Late Prehistoric and Archaic times, they often used shell as raw material for tools and utensils. Gatschet (1891:59) has recorded the manufacture of Karankawa pottery, decorated with "black paint"; this is apparently Rockport ware, a sandy-paste, thin-walled pottery that was decorated or sometimes waterproofed with asphaltum that washed up on local beaches. They obtained flint from the interior, perhaps through the kind of trade recorded by Cabeza de Vaca (Covey 1984), from which they chipped points to tip their arrows; in Historic times, sherds of bottle glass were sometimes chipped into arrow points.

We know very little about Karankawa social or political activity (see Gilmore, this volume). They, like the Coahuiltecans, lived in small groups, of 30 to 40 persons; it is said that a smoke-signal system was used to bring these groups together for ceremonies, war, or a special dance known as the *mitote* (Newcomb 1961).

Karankawa cannibalism—like that of the Coahuiltecans—was probably little more than a ritual to exact vengeance against a slain enemy. Their stature was probably comparable to that of the Coahuiltecans; the French ship captain Jean Beranger (Carroll 1983:21) measured some Karankawa in 1720, noting that they were "usually five and a half feet [tall]—though some of them [are] six feet two inches tall." Finally, no archaeological evidence of any sort exists to suggest that the Karankawa had arrived from some other area; indeed, the record indicates that their ancestors were the Late Prehistoric peoples of the coastal region.

Indians of the Lower Rio Grande Valley. The hunters and gatherers of extreme southern Texas, at the mouth of the Rio Grande, are often lumped into the Coahuiltecan grouping. Although some were doubtless Coahuilteco linguistically and culturally, there were other peoples in the region, as detailed by Salinas (1986). The Indian groups of this region were first noted by the Garay expeditions between 1519 and 1523 and later by Spanish expeditions to the area in 1686–1688. Major Spanish settlement and the establishment of missions in this region (see Figure 12-2) occurred largely in the mid-eighteenth century, as a part of the colonization of Tamaulipas by Escandón (Salinas 1986).

All 31 groups recorded by José de Escandón in his explorations of the Lower Rio Grande Valley in 1747 appear to have spoken the Comecrudo language (Goddard 1979), not Coahuiltecan. The evidence is not entirely clear (Salinas 1986:267), but Comecrudo is dominant. Later, in 1829, Jean Louis Berlandier re-

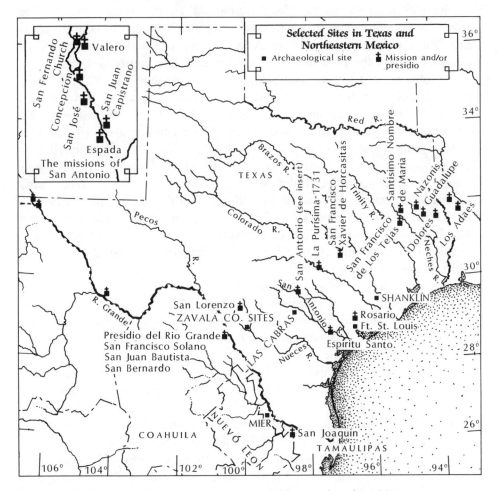

Figure 12-2. Selected Spanish missions and presidios of Texas and northern Mexico.

corded the Cotoname language (Goddard 1979) for two Indian groups in the area. Earlier linguists (e.g., Sapir 1920) have included Comecrudo and Cotoname as Coahuiltecan languages, but as I have noted previously, Ives Goddard (1979) considers them to be separate languages. Salinas (1986:263) lists Coahuilteco among several other languages spoken by certain hunter-gatherer groups in the general area.

The East Texas Agriculturalists

Caddo. The Spanish explorers and missionaries who ventured into the eastern Texas fringes of the Texas–Mexico borderlands found a wholly different Indian lifeway being followed by the peoples we know as the Caddo. These were agriculture-based, sedentary Indians, with complex social, political, and economic patterns. According to Swanton (1942:3), there were perhaps 25 tribes grouped into three or more confederacies at the time of first European contact. The largest confederacy was the Hasinai (also sometimes called the Tejas) with whom the Spanish established close links and in whose territories several missions were established (see Corbin, this volume). To the north, along the Red River, was the other major confederation, the Kadohadacho (whom Swanton terms "the Caddo proper," ibid.:7). A third group of Caddo were in western Louisiana, around the present city of Natchitoches (see Figure 12-1).

The roots of these historic peoples go back to perhaps A.D. 500 or earlier, when archaeologists detect the earliest pottery-making traditions in the region (Story's [1981] Early Ceramic). The prehistory of the Caddo themselves is divided into Early Caddoan (the Gibson Aspect), between A.D. 700–1450 and Late Caddoan (Fulton Aspect) from A.D. 1450 to 1600. A Protohistoric/early Historic Caddo episode is also recognized ca. A.D. 1600–1700. Story (1981:151) sees a decline of Caddoan cultural development from A.D. 1500 to 1700. Early ethnohistoric accounts mention sizable villages, temples, and political organization that clearly link the Historic Caddo to their prehistoric ancestors (Swanton 1942). However, we must make it clear that the term *Caddo* is used here, in relationship to Spanish impact, to refer to the southern Caddoan-speakers—the Caddo proper (Story 1981:139).

In contrast to the hunter-gatherer Indians described earlier, the Caddo relied heavily on agriculture, particularly maize, squash, and beans. Bison hunting on the Blackland Prairie to the east of Caddo territory was also important, and hunting and gathering of local game and nuts from the East Texas hardwood forests supplemented their diet.

The Caddo built substantial houses of heavy pole frameworks covered with thick grass. Houses of Caddo chiefs appear to have been larger and more elaborately equipped than those of ordinary folk. There were also temple structures, much like the houses, although larger and placed on mounds.

The extensive material culture of the Caddo included a variety of ceramics, basketry, reed mats, the bow and arrow, musical instruments, and a wide range of other artifacts (Swanton 1942). We also have a comparative abundance of data on the social organization, marriage patterns, life cycles, burial practices, belief systems, and political structure of the Caddo—this is in stark contrast to the meager information for the southern Texas–Northeast Mexico hunter-gatherers.

Although the Caddo cultural pattern was not particularly receptive to Spanish missionization efforts, their lifeway fell victim to introduced European diseases and the later, more crushing impact of Anglo-American expansion into the region. The Caddo were moved into the Indian territory in the 1850s, where they still maintain tribal identity (Newcomb 1961).

History of European Involvement

Intensive European intrusion into the Texas–Northeast Mexico borderlands begins fairly late, largely in the seventeenth and eighteenth centuries (see Eaton and Corbin, this volume). The initial Spanish contact was in 1519, with the Alvarez de Piñeda expedition, which was sent to map the coast of the Gulf of Mexico from Veracruz to Florida. The expedition camped near the mouth of the Rio Grande for 40 days (see Richardson 1958:14). But, as noted earlier, the first record of Spanish interaction with the region's Indian groups comes from Cabeza de Vaca's journal covering his eight years of captivity, most of it among the Indians of southern Texas and northeast Mexico, after his shipwreck on the Texas coast in 1528. Spanish expeditions from the southeast made initial contact with the Caddo in the mid-sixteenth century, Hernando de Soto in 1541, and Luis de Moscoso in 1542. In 1554, three Spanish galleons, loaded with treasure, sank off the coast of southern Padre Island. The Spanish sent a salvage crew, but these wrecks became the focus of intense interest first of looters and later of archaeologists in the 1960s and 1970s (Arnold and Weddle 1978).

It was not until the late seventeenth century that the Spanish once again showed any interest in the region. The Bosque-Larrios expedition traveled from Monclova (Coahuila) into the Edwards Plateau of south-central Texas in 1675, and the Domínguez de Mendoza expedition went from El Paso into west-central Texas in 1683–1684. But with reports of a French settlement established by LaSalle near Matagorda Bay in 1684, the Spanish began to take serious note of the Texas–northeast borderlands. Several expeditions set out from Nuevo León, led by Alonso de León. One succeeded in reaching Fort Saint Louis in 1689, but found it destroyed by coastal Indians. As Almaráz (1979:1) has observed, "Although De León's primary objective was exploration for the purpose of evicting French intruders from the borderlands, a significant result of that activity was the founding in 1690 of the first Franciscan missions in the piney woods of east Texas."

The turn of the eighteenth century saw in the region what Elizabeth John (1975:196) said was "a curious convergence of Spanish evangelism and French mercantilism." French traders, operating from their base at Natchitoches in what is now western Louisiana, were concerned primarily with the Caddo area of east Texas. There were initial and unsuccessful efforts at establishing Spanish missions, by Fray Massenet, in eastern Texas (San Francisco de los Tejas and

Santisimo Nombre de María) in 1690. But it was not until 1714–1716 that the Spanish again tried to found missions in that area; these were rebuilt in 1721–1722 (see Corbin, this volume).

In central and southern Texas, and on the Rio Grande of eastern Coahuila, the first major thrust came between 1699 and 1703 when missions San Juan Bautista, San Bernardo, and San Francisco de Solano, and the Presidio San Juan Bautista del Rio Grande del Norte were established near major crossings on the middle Rio Grande (see Eaton, this volume; Weddle 1968). This area soon became the "gateway" to Spanish Texas. The area of present-day San Antonio, on the San Antonio River in south-central Texas, was the next target of Spanish missionization and settlement. Six missions were established beginning in 1718 (San Francisco de Solano moved from the Rio Grande to become San Antonio de Valero—later "the Alamo"), as well as a presidio and the beginnings of a major Spanish settlement. The missions prospered, all were marked by major buildings, and some set up ranches some distance from San Antonio, such as Rancho de las Cabras, the site of recent excavations by Fox (this volume). The mission effort carried over toward the coast, with the founding of two short-lived missions, Espíritu Santo (1749) and Rosario (1754; see Gilmore, this volume), near the present city of Victoria later reestablished on the San Antonio River at Goliad (the Spanish village of La Bahía).

The missions of San Antonio and Goliad took in a myriad of hunter-gatherer groups, mostly Coahuiltecan and Karankawan, but also many groups (see Campbell and Campbell 1985) of other origins, some of whom were refugees from Spanish disruption in Nuevo León and other areas of northeastern Mexico. There was a remarkable congregation of displaced Indians in central Texas, at a locale termed the Ranchería Grande, and a series of mid-eighteenth century missionization efforts were made in that area (Bolton 1915; Gilmore 1969). Epidemic diseases and Apache attacks plagued these missions (see John 1975:284ff.), although the Apaches later allied themselves with the Spanish owing to the increased harassment from the Comanches. Attempts to provide missions and a measure of protection for the Apaches were made in the 1750s in central Texas (San Sabá; Gilmore 1967), and in the 1760s in south-central Texas (San Lorenzo; Tunnell and Newcomb 1969). Raids by Indian allies known as "Norteños" and by Comanches made these efforts short-lived.

French influence in the eastern part of the region continued through midcentury. The Norteños—the Taovaya Wichita and related groups—were particularly the focus of the French. One notable conflict between the Spanish and their Norteño foes (backed by the French) occurred in 1759 at the so-called "Spanish Fort"—a fortified Taovaya encampment on the Red River. The Spanish force led by Colonel Parilla was unable to mount a serious challenge. The competition between the Spanish and the French essentially came to an end with the Treaty of Paris in 1763 (for details on Spanish–French interaction on the Texas–Mexico borderlands, the reader should see John 1975). However, the raids of the Norteño allied groups continued to plague the Spanish and the missions deep into south-central Texas and to the La Bahía area well into the 1770s; raiding by the Comanches, sometime allies of the Wichita/Norteño groups, was also a serious problem.

What should be made clear at this juncture is that although the Spanish were having some small measure of success in the missionization of Coahuiltecan, Karankawan, and related groups, the landscape was home to many groups who were never brought into the missions or who, like the Lipan Apache, had only brief experience with that system. For example, in 1782 more than 4,000 Indians gathered on the Guadalupe River in south-central Texas; they included Lipan, Mescalero, and Natage Apaches, 600 Tonkawa, and eastern Texas and Coastal groups, including the Tejas (Caddo), Akokisas, Bidais, Cocos, and Mayeyes (John 1975:635). Weapons were traded and some Apache leaders tried, unsuccessfully, to organize a unified front to drive out the Spanish.

The Lower Rio Grande Valley was not settled by the Spanish until the middle of the eighteenth century. The adjacent Mexican state of Tamaulipas was first colonized in 1746 (Salinas 1986:27), and between 1746 and 1752, a major effort led by José de Escandón moved several thousand Spanish families from Mexico into the valley. The villages of Reynosa and Camargo on the south side of the Rio Grande, and later, Laredo, on the north side were established.

Five missions were built for the Cotoname, Comecrudo, and Coahuilteco-speaking peoples of the region. The missions were not very substantial and were notably unsuccessful; remnants of the hunter-gatherer Indians of the area persisted into the early nineteenth century. It is unclear just how many of the groups were native to the valley at the time of colonization. Some seem to have been refugees from elsewhere in northeastern Mexico, having fled the epidemics and Spanish slave traders in León.

By the 1780s and 1790s, many of the Spanish missions in the Texas–Northeast Mexico borderlands had begun to wane in importance. Only a few Indians remained in some of the missions, and Spanish settlers were petitioning for control of the mission ranch- and farmlands. Secularization orders began to be issued in 1793, but affected different missions at various times. For example, San Bernardo and San Juan Bautista were exempted, and the latter continued in operation until 1830. Moreover, Mission Refugio (see Figure 12-2) was not established at all until 1793–1795 and served a variety of coastal hunter-gatherer remnants until 1830.

History of Scholarly Research

The Texas–Northeast Mexico Spanish borderlands has a comparatively short history of archaeological research. I have already mentioned the prehistoric record and some of the key references related to its study. In terms of the Spanish Colonial era, there are many histories (e.g., the numerous volumes by Carlos Castañeda, as well as the work of Herbert E. Bolton and John Francis Bannon). Ethnohistoric research has been conducted in recent times largely by T. N. Campbell and W. W. Newcomb, Jr. Their work was preceded by the linguistic and ethnohistoric work of Albert S. Gatschet and John R. Swanton. The important works by these, and other scholars, can be found in the bibliography.

Archaeology at Spanish Colonial sites of this region appears to have begun in the 1930s. A. T. Jackson conducted excavations at Mission Espíritu Santo (see Hester, this volume) in 1933. Archaeological crews of the Works Progress Administration dug at this site later in the 1930s, directed by Roland Beard (see Reed 1938) and at Mission Rosario, also directed by Beard, in 1940–1941 (Gilmore 1974a:21). Notes and collections are curated at the Texas Archeological Research Laboratory at the University of Texas at Austin. The fieldwork was extremely poor by modern standards and caused irreparable damage to mission Indian quarters in terms of any future research. At the San Antonio missions, much restoration was carried out during the 1930s, largely under the supervision of architect Harvey P. Smith, Sr. (see Smith 1980). Trenching along the walls helped in the restoration process but damaged stratigraphic associations for later research. Nevertheless, Smith's maps and notes remain important sources today.

In 1950, a crew from the Texas Memorial Museum (Austin) conducted excavations at the presumed site of LaSalle's Fort St. Louis on the Texas coast (see Gilmore 1973). Although no publication resulted, there was a long-term museum exhibit (these materials are now at the Texas Archeological Research Laboratory). The Texas Memorial Museum also conducted excavations at Mission San Lorenzo in Real County, south-central Texas in the 1960s (Tunnell and Newcomb 1969).

The San Antonio missions were extensively excavated beginning in the 1960s, with fieldwork and publication by Mardith K. Schuetz (see 1966, 1968, 1969), then with the Witte Museum. With the establishment of a state archaeologist's position in 1966, under the State Building Commission, additional archaeological work was done in San Antonio's missions. This included Greer's study at San Antonio de Valero (the Alamo; 1967) and support and publication of Schuetz's research. The State Archeologist's Program also sponsored research at the San Sabá missions (Gilmore 1967), the San Xavier missions (Gilmore 1969), and San Augustin de Ahumada on the upper Texas coast (see Figure 12-2; Tunnell and Ambler 1967).

The 1970s saw an intensification of archaeological research at the missions and other Spanish Colonial sites, with many of these yielding data on the Indian inhabitants. These efforts included research at most of the San Antonio missions and other Spanish Colonial structures by the Center for Archaeological Research, University of Texas at San Antonio (Fox et al. 1976; Fox 1977; Eaton 1980, 1981a), and by the Texas Historical Commission (which housed the State Archeologist's office; Scurlock 1976; Scurlock et al. 1976). In part, this research had a very positive effect on the establishment of the present San Antonio Missions National Historical Park, which protects these resources.

Besides the missions, the Spanish Governor's Palace in San Antonio was partly excavated (Fox 1977), as was San Fernando Cathedral (Scurlock and Fox 1977). In the early 1980s, fieldwork began at Rancho de las Cabras (Fox, this volume), and the ranch of Mission Espada (see Ivey 1983; Ivey and Fox 1981). In addition, the Spanish materials from the 1554 shipwreck off the south coast of Padre Island were analyzed and conserved (Arnold and Weddle 1978; Hamilton 1976; Olds 1976).

In 1975–1976, the University of Texas at San Antonio conducted excavations at the missions of San Bernardo and San Juan Bautista, near present-day Guerrero, Coahuila (Eaton 1981b). The project was designed specifically not only to shed new light on these poorly known missions, but also to focus on the Indian quarters, Indian ethnohistory (see Campbell 1979), and the impact of the mission process on the Indian groups (see Eaton, this volume).

James E. Corbin (this volume) began the exploration of Spanish colonial sites in eastern Texas, especially Mission Dolores de los Ais. Miroir et al. (1975) published a study of the archaeological remains from the Nassonite post established by the French trader Bénard de La Harpe in 1719 near present-day Texarkana.

Other important studies are the research of R. King Harris (e.g., Miroir et al. 1975) into Spanish Colonial era trade beads at Texas sites, the excavations by Gilmore (1974a, 1974b) at Mission Rosario near Goliad, and Hudgins's (1986) study of materials from the Shanklin site, a historic Indian site containing artifacts typical of mission Indians, and a Spanish coin dated to 1738.

In the 1980s, much of the mission research has been conducted in San Antonio, under the general direction of Anne Fox of the University of Texas at San Antonio (this in addition to her studies at Rancho de las Cabras in nearby Wilson County). Almost all the fieldwork has been in the form of contract archaeology— looking at relatively small parts of a specific mission complex prior to its improvement and modifications (e.g., Fox 1988; Ivey n.d.). Other features of Spanish Colonial San Antonio have also been examined, especially the *acequias* (irrigation waterways) of the period (Fox 1985).

An excellent summary of the Spanish Colonial archaeology of this region is found in Daniel Fox's (1983) book and in a useful bibliographic compilation by Moore and Moore (1986; see also Scurlock and Powers 1973). In addition, Campbell and Campbell (1985) provide a detailed look at the Indians of the San Antonio missions. Gilmore (1984; and this volume) has summarized extant knowledge of the Indians of Mission Rosario; Campbell (1979) has done this for the missions at Guerrero, Coahuila; and a recent examination of the Indians encountered by Alvar Nuñez Cabeza de Vaca has been published by Campbell and Campbell (1981; see also Campbell 1988).

Chronology

A.D.

1519	Alvarez de Piñeda expedition at the mouth of the Rio Grande.
1528	Alvar Nuñez Cabeza de Vaca shipwrecked on the Texas coast; lives among coastal and interior hunter-gatherers and finally makes it back to Mexico City in 1536.
1541	Hernando de Soto makes contact with Caddo Indians.
1542	Luis de Moscoso encounters Caddo Indians on Red River.
1554	Treasure-laden Spanish ships sink off the coast of south Padre Island.
1675	Bosque-Larios expedition travels into south-central/west-central Texas.

1684	Mendoza expedition travels from El Paso into west-central Texas.
1684	LaSalle's Fort St. Louis and French Colony established near Lavaca Bay, Victoria County.
1689	Expedition by Alonso de León reaches LaSalle's colony, finding it abandoned and destroyed (later, in 1722, a Spanish presidio, Loreto, is established here).
1690	Missions San Francisco de los Tejas and Santissimo Nombre de María are established by Fray Massanet on Neches River for the Hasinai (Caddo) of east Texas.
1700	Missions San Juan Bautista and San Francisco de Solano are established near the Rio Grande at prese. t-day Guerrero, Coahuila.
1702	Mission San Bernardo is established at Guerrero.
1703	Presidio San Juan Bautista del Rio Grande del Norte is established to protect the three missions at Guerrero.
1714–1716	Six missions and two presidios are established by the Spanish in east Texas and Louisiana; they are subsequently reestablished in 1721–1722. Included is Mission Dolores de los Ais, Mission San José de los Nazonis, and, in 1721, Presidio de los Adaes, which served as the capital of Texas from 1731–1773.
1718	Fray Olivares moves San Francisco de Solano from the Rio Grande to the San Antonio River where it becomes San Antonio de Valero (the Alamo); the Villa de Bexár (later San Antonio) is established.
1719	The French trader Bénard de La Harpe establishes a post among the Nassonite Caddo on the Red River.
1720	Mission San José y San Miguel de Aguayo established on the San Antonio River.
1731	Three other missions established at San Antonio: Concepción; San Juan Capistrano; and San Francisco de la Espada.
1748–1749	Establishment of central Texas missions: San Francisco de San Xavier, San Ildefonso, and Candelaria on the San Gabriel River.
1749	Mission Espíritu Santo de Zuniga established at La Bahía (present-day Goliad) on the lower San Antonio River; Presidio La Bahía established.
1749–1755	Missions of the lower Rio Grande Valley established, as well as the towns of Camargo and Reynosa (1749) and Laredo (1755).
1750s	Rancho de las Cabras, ranch for Mission Espada, established on the San Antonio River in present-day Wilson County.
1754	Mission Nuestra Señora del Rosario established at La Bahía (Goliad) for the Karankawas.
1757	In response to Apache demands for protection, the Presidio de San Luis de las Amarillas and Mission Santa Cruz established on the San Sabá River in west central Texas.
1762	Another mission for the Apaches, San Lorenzo de la Santa Cruz, established in south-central Texas at present-day Camp Wood (Real County).
1763	Treaty of Paris; cessation of Spanish-French hostilities.
1793	Secularization of the missions begins, although some stay in operation until 1830.
1820s	Stephen F. Austin and American colonists begin to move into southeastern Texas.
1821	Mexico wins independence from Spain; the Spanish Colonial era ends.
1850s	Karankawa remnants reported exterminated in northeastern Mexico.

Bibliography

Almaráz, Felix D., Jr.
  1979 *Crossroad of Empire: The Church and State on the Rio Grande Frontier of Coahuila and Texas, 1700–1821*. Archaeology and History of the San Juan Bautista Mission Area, Coahuila and Texas. Report No. 1. Center for Archaeological Research, University of Texas at San Antonio.
  1980 *Inventory of the Rio Grande Missions: 1772. San Juan Bautista and San Bernardo*. Archaeology and History of the San Juan Bautista Mission Area, Coahuila and Texas. Report No. 2. Center for Archaeological Research, University of Texas at San Antonio.

Arnold J. Barto, III, and Robert S. Weddle
  1978 *The Nautical Archaeology of Padre Island: The Spanish Shipwrecks of 1554*. Academic Press, New York.

Bannon, John Francis
  1964 *Bolton and the Spanish Borderlands*. University of Oklahoma Press, Norman.
  1970 *The Spanish Borderlands Frontier: 1513–1821*. Holt, Rinehart and Winston, New York.

Black, Stephen L.
  1986 *The Clemente and Herminia Hinojosa Site, 41 JW 8: A Toyah Horizon Campsite in Southern Texas*. Special Report No. 18. Center for Archaeological Research, University of Texas at San Antonio.

Bolton, Herbert E.
  1915 *Texas in the Eighteenth Century*. Publications in History No. 3. University of California.

Brown, Kenneth M.
  1988 Some Annotated Excerpts from Alonso De León's History of Nuevo León. *La Tierra: Journal of the Southern Texas Archaeological Association* 15(2):5–20.

Campbell, T. N.
  1975 *The Payaya Indians of Southern Texas*. Special Publication No. 1. Southern Texas Archaeological Association.
  1977 Ethnic Identities of Extinct Coahuiltecan Populations: Case of the Juanca Indians. *The Pearce Sellards Series*, vol. 26. Texas Memorial Museum, Austin.
  1979 Ethnohistoric Notes on Indian Groups Associated with Three Spanish Missions at Guerrero, Coahuila. In *Archaeology and History of the San Juan Bautista Mission Area, Coahuila and Texas*, vol. 4. University of Texas, San Antonio.
  1983 Coahuiltecans and Their Neighbors. In *Southwest*, edited by A. Ortiz, pp. 343–358. Handbook of North American Indians, vol. 10, William C. Sturtevant, general editor. Smithsonian Institution Press, Washington, D.C.
  1988 *The Indians of Southern Texas and Northeastern Mexico. Selected Writings of Thomas N. Campbell*. Texas Archeological Research Laboratory, University of Texas at Austin.

Campbell, T. N., and T. J. Campbell
  1981 *Historic Indian Groups of Choke Canyon Reservoir and Surrounding Area*. Center for Archaeological Research Series No. 1. University of Texas at San Antonio, Choke Canyon.
  1985 *Indian Groups Associated with Spanish Missions of the San Antonio Missions National Historic Park*. Special Report No. 16. Center for Archaeological Research, University of Texas at San Antonio.

Carroll, William M. (translator)
  1983 *Beranger's Discovery of Aransas Pass*. A translation of Jean Beranger's French manuscript, edited and annotated by Frank Wanger. Occasional Papers No. 8. Friends of the Corpus Christi Museum.

Castañeda, Carlos E.
   1936–1958 *Out Catholic Heritage in Texas*, 7 vol. Von Boeckmann-Jones Co., Austin.
Chipman, D. E.
   1987 In Search of Cabeza de Vaca's Route across Texas: An Historiographical Survey. *Southwestern Historical Quarterly*, October:128–148.
Clark, John W., Jr.
   1976 The Sugar Industry at Mission San José y San Miguel de Aguayo. *Bulletin of the Texas Archeological Society* 47:245–260.
   1978 *Mission San José y San Miguel de Aguayo*: Archeological Investigation December 1974. Report No. 29. Texas Historical Commission, Austin.
   1980 Sa Reina Norteña: History and Archaeology of San José Mission. *La Tierra: Journal of the Southern Texas Archaeological Association* 7(1):3–15.
Cook, Paul J.
   1980 A Review of the History and Archaeology of Mission Concepción. *La Tierra: Journal of the Southern Texas Archaeological Association* 7(3):3–16.
   1981 A Review of the History and Archaeology of San Lorenzo, Real County, Southern Texas. *La Tierra: Journal of the Southern Texas Archaeological Association* 8(3):3–15.
Corbin, James E.
   1980 *Mission Dolores de los Ais: Archaeological Investigations at an Early Spanish Colonial Mission, San Augustine County, Texas*. Publications in Anthropology No. 2. Stephen F. Austin State University.
Covey, Cyclone (translator and editor)
   1984 *Cabeza de Vaca's Adventures in the Unknown Interior of America*. University of New Mexico Press, Albuquerque.
Cruz, Gilberto R. (editor)
   1984 *Proceedings of the Second Annual Mission Research Conference*. San Antonio Missions National Historical Park, San Antonio.
Cruz, Gilberto R., and James A. Irby
   1982 *Texas Bibliography. A Manual on History Research Materials*. Eakin Press, Austin.
Dibble, David S., and Dessamae Lorrain
   1968 *Bonfire Shelter: A Stratified Bison Kill Site, Val Verde County, Texas*. Miscellaneous Papers No. 1. Texas Memorial Museum, Austin.
Doughty, Robin W.
   1983 *Wildlife and Man in Texas. Environmental Change and Conservation*. Texas A&M University Press, College Station.
Eaton, Jack D.
   1980 *Excavations at the Alamo Shrine (San Antonio de Valero)*. Special Report No. 10. Center for Archaeological Research, University of Texas at San Antonio.
   1981a History and Archaeology of Mission San Antonio de Valero (the Alamo). *La Tierra: Journal of the Southern Texas Archaeological Association* 8(1):3–13.
   1981b *Guerrero, Coahuila, Mexico. A Guide to the Town and Missions*. Archaeology and History of the San Juan Bautista Mission Area, Coahuila and Texas. Report No. 4. Center for Archaeological Research, University of Texas at San Antonio.
Ewers, John C.
   1973 The Influence of Epidemics on the Indian Populations and Cultures of Texas. *Plains Anthropologist* 18(60):104–115.
Fox, Anne A.
   1977 *The Archaeology and History of the Spanish Governor's Palace Park*. Archaeological Survey Report No. 31. Center for Archaeological Research, University of Texas at San Antonio.
   1978 *Archaeological Investigations of Portions of the San Pedro and Alazán Acequias in San Antonio, Texas*. Archaeological Survey Report No. 49. Center for Archaeological Research, University of Texas at San Antonio.
   1981 *Test Excavations at Mission San Francisco de la Espada*. Archaeological Survey Report

No. 108. Center for Archaeological Research, University of Texas at San Antonio.

1983 The Archaeology of Spanish Sites. In *Texana I: The Frontier*, edited by LeRoy Johnson, Jr., pp. 21–24. Texas Historical Commission, Austin.

1985 *Testing for the Location of the Alamo Acequia (41BX8) at Hemisfair Plaza, San Antonio, Texas*. Archaeological Survey Report No. 142. Center for Archaeological Research, University of Texas at San Antonio.

1988 *Archaeological Investigations at Mission Concepción, Fall of 1986*. Archaeological Survey Report No. 172. Center for Archaeological Research, University of Texas at San Antonio.

Fox, Anne A., Feris A. Bass, Jr., and Thomas R. Hester

1976 *The Archaeology and History of Alamo Plaza*. Archaeological Survey Report No. 16. Center for Archaeological Research, University of Texas at San Antonio.

Fox, Anne A., and Thomas R. Hester

1976 *Archaeological Test Excavations at Mission San Francisco de la Espada*. Archaeological Survey Report No. 22. Center for Archaeological Research, University of Texas at San Antonio.

Fox, Daniel E.

1970 *Archaeological Salvage at Mission San José, December 1969, April and August 1970*. Special Report No. 3. Texas Historical Commission.

1979 *The Lithic Artifacts of Indians at the Spanish Colonial Missions, San Antonio, Texas*. Special Report No. 8. Center for Archaeological Research, University of Texas at San Antonio.

1983 *Traces of Texas History. Archaeological Evidence of the Past 450 Years*. Corona, San Antonio.

Fox, Daniel E., Dan Scurlock, and John W. Clark, Jr.

1977 *Archaeological Investigations at San Fernando Cathedral, San Antonio, Texas: A Preliminary Report*. Special Report No. 22. Texas Historical Commission, Austin.

Gatschet, A. S.

1891 *The Karankawa Indians, The Coast People of Texas*. Archaeological and Ethnological Papers of the Peabody Museum 1(2). Cambridge, Mass.

Gilmore, Kathleen

1967 *A Documentary and Archeological Investigation of Presidio San Luis de las Amarillas and Mission Santa Cruz de San Saba, Menard County, Texas*. Archeological Program Report No. 9. State Building Commission, Austin.

1969 *The San Xavier Missions: A Study in Historical Site Identification*. Archeological Program Report 16. State Building Commission, Austin.

1973 *The Keeran Site: The Probable Site of La Salle's Fort St. Louis in Texas*. Report No. 24. Texas Historical Commission, Austin.

1974a *Mission Rosario: Archeological Investigations 1973*, pt. 1. Archeological Report No. 14. Texas Parks and Wildlife Department, Austin.

1974b *Mission Rosario: Archeological Investigations 1973*, pt. 2. Archeological Report No. 14. Texas Parks and Wildlife Department, Austin.

1978 Spanish Colonial Settlements in Texas. In *Texas Archaeology, Essays Honoring R. King Harris*, edited by Kurt D. House, pp. 132–145. Southern Methodist University, Dallas.

1982 So Shall Ye Reap: The San Xavier Missions. *La Tierra: Journal of the Southern Texas Archaeological Association* 9(1):2–10.

1984 The Indians of Mission Rosario. In *The Scope of Historical Archaeology*, edited by D. G. Orr and D. G. Crozier, pp. 163–91. Laboratory of Anthropology, Temple University, Philadelphia, Pa.

1986 La Salle's Fort St. Louis in Texas. *Bulletin of the Texas Archeological Society* 55:61–72.

Goddard, Ives

1979 The Languages of South Texas and the Lower Rio Grande. In *The Languages of Native America: Historical and Comparative Assessment*, edited by Lyle Campbell and

Marianne Mithun, pp. 355–389. University of Texas Press, Austin.

Greer, John W.

1967 *A Description of the Stratigraphy, Features and Artifacts from an Archeological Excavation at the Alamo*. Archeological Program Report No. 3. State Building Commission, Austin.

1969 *Culture Change and Shifting Populations in Central Northern Mexico*. Anthropological Paper No. 13. University of Arizona, Tucson.

Gunn, Joel (editor)

1982 *Historic and Cultural Landscape Study for the San Antonio Missions*. Environmental and Cultural Services, San Antonio.

Hamilton, D. L.

1976 *Conservation of Metal Objects from Underwater Sites: A Study in Methods*. Texas Memorial Museum Miscellaneous Papers No. 4 and Texas Antiquities Committee Publication No. 1. Austin.

Henderson, Jerry, and John W. Clark, Jr.

1984 *Test Excavations at the Acequia and Other Features at Mission San José, Bexar County, Texas*. Archaeological Report No. 25. State Department of Highways and Public Transportation. Austin.

Hendricks, Frances K. (assembler)

1976 *San Antonio in the Eighteenth Century*. Clarke Printing Company, San Antonio.

Hester, Thomas R.

1977 The Lithic Technology of Mission Indians in Texas and Northeastern Mexico. *Lithic Technology* 6(1-2):9–12.

1980 *Digging into South Texas Prehistory*. Corona, San Antonio.

1981 Tradition and Diversity among the Prehistoric Hunters and Gatherers of Southern Texas. *Plains Anthropologist* 26(92):119–128.

Hester, Thomas R., and Jack D. Eaton

1983 Middle-lower Rio Grande Archaeology. In *Borderlands Sourcebook: A Guide to the Literature on Northern Mexico and the American Southwest*, edited by E. R. Stoddard, R. Nostrand, and J. West, pp. 70–74. University of Oklahoma Press, Norman.

Hester, Thomas R., and T. C. Hill, Jr.

1975 *Some Aspects of Late Prehistoric and Protohistoric Archaeology in Southern Texas*. Special Report 1. Center for Archaeological Research, University of Texas at San Antonio.

Hudgins, Joe D.

1986 A Historic Indian Site in Wharton County, Texas. *Bulletin of the Texas Archeological Society* 55:29–52.

Humphreys, Gerald, and William Singleton

1978 Historic Archaeology in Texas. In *Texas Archeology, Essays Honoring R. King Harris*, edited by Kurt D. House, pp. 69–92. Southern Methodist University Press, Dallas.

Humphreys, Sherry B.

1971 *The Skeletal Biology of Eighteenth-century Coahuiltecan Indians from San Juan Capistrano Mission, San Antonio, Texas*. Master's thesis, Southern Methodist University.

Inglis, J. M.

1964 *A History of Vegetation on the Rio Grande Plain*. Texas Parks and Wildlife Bulletin No. 45. Austin.

Ivey, James E.

1981 A Reexamination of the Site of Presidio de San Sabá. *La Tierra: Journal of the Southern Texas Archaeological Association* 8(4):3–11.

1983 *Archaeological Investigations at Rancho de las Cabras, Wilson County, Texas*. Archaeological Survey Report No. 104. Center for Archaeological Research, University of Texas at San Antonio.

n.d. *Archaeological Investigations at Mission Concepción and Mission Parkway, Part I: Excavations at Mission Concepción*. Archaeological Survey Report No. 114. Center for Archaeological Research, University of Texas at San Antonio. Submitted to the National Park Service, Santa Fe.

Ivey, James E., and Anne A. Fox
1981 *Archaeological Survey and Testing at Rancho de las Cabras, Wilson County, Texas*. Archaeological Survey Report No. 104. Center for Archaeological Research, University of Texas at San Antonio.

John, Elizabeth A. H.
1975 *Storms Brewed in Other Men's Worlds*. Texas A&M University Press, College Station.

Jones, Courtenay J., and Anne A. Fox
1983 *Archaeological Testing at Rancho de las Cabras, Wilson County, Texas, Third Season*. Archaeological Survey Report No. 123. Center for Archaeological Research, University of Texas at San Antonio.

Kirkland, Forrest, and W. W. Newcomb, Jr.
1967 *The Rock Art of Texas Indians*. University of Texas Press, Austin.

Krieger, Alex D.
1956 Food Habits of the Texas Coastal Indians in the Early Sixteenth Century. *Bulletin of the Texas Archeological Society* 27:47–58.

Kroeber, Alfred L.
1925 *Handbook of the California Indians*. Bureau of American Ethnology Bulletin No. 78. Washington, D.C.

León, Alonso de, Juan B. Chapa, and Fernando Sanchez de Zamora
1961 *Historia de Nuevo Leon, con noticias sobre Coahuila, Tamaulipas, Texas y Nuevo Mexico*. Universidad de Nuevo León, Monterrey, Mexico.

Leutennegar, Fr. Benedict (translator)
1973 *The Zacatecan Missionaries in Texas, 1716–1834*. Report No. 23. Texas Historical Survey Committee, Austin.
1977 *Inventory of the Mission San Antonio de Valero, 1772*. Special Report No. 23. Texas Historical Commission, Austin.

Martin, George C.
1972 *The Indian Tribes of the Mission Nuestra Señora del Refugio*. Bootstraps Press, Corpus Christi, Tex.

Miroir, M. P., R. King Harris, Jay C. Blaine, et al.
1975 Benard de La Harpe and the Nassonite Post. *Bulletin of the Texas Archeological Society* 44:113–168.

Moore, William, and Roger Moore
1986 *Historical Archaeology in Texas: A Bibliography*. Guidebooks in Archaeology No. 2. Center for Archaeological Research, University of Texas at San Antonio.

Moorehead, Max L.
1975 *The Presidio: Bastion of the Spanish Borderlands*. University of Oklahoma Press, Norman.

Morfi, Juan A.
1935 *History of Texas 1673–1779*. Translated by Carlos Castañeda. Quivira Society, Albuquerque.

Mounger, Maria Allen
1959 *Mission Espíritu Santo of Coastal Texas: An Example of Historic Site Archeology*. Master's thesis, University of Texas.

Newcomb, W. W., Jr.
1961 *The Indians of Texas*. University of Texas Press, Austin.
1983 The Karankawa. In *Southwest*, edited by Alfonso Ortiz, pp. 359–367. Handbook of North American Indians, vol. 10, William C. Sturtevant, general editor. Smithsonian Institution Press, Washington, D.C.

Olds, Dorris L.
1976 *Texas Legacy from the Gulf: A Report of Sixteenth Century Shipwreck Materials Recovered*

from the Texas Tidelands. Texas Memorial Museum Miscellaneous Publication No. 5; Texas Antiquities Committee Publication No. 2. Austin.

Reed, Erik K.
1938 Burials at Mission Espíritu Santo. *Central Texas Archaeologist* 4:83–95.

Richardson, Rupert N.
1958 *Texas.* Prentice-Hall, Englewood Cliffs, N.J.

Ruecking, Frederick, Jr.
1955 *The Coahuiltecan Indians of South Texas and Northeast Mexico.* Master's thesis, University of Texas.

Salinas, Martin
1986 *Historic Indian Populations of the Rio Grande Delta and Vicinity: An Approach to Definition of Basic Ethnic Units.* Master's thesis, University of Texas.

Sapir, Edward
1920 The Hokan and Coahuiltecan Languages. *International Journal of American Linguistics* 1(4):280–290.

Schaedel, Richard P.
1949 Karankawa Indians of the Texas Coast. *Southwestern Journal of Anthropology* 5:117–137.

Schuetz, Mardith K.
1966 *Historic Background of the Mission San Antonio de Valero.* Archeological Program Report No. 1. State Building Commission, Austin.
1968 *The History and Archeology of Mission San Juan Capistrano, San Antonio, Texas.* Vol. I. Archeological Program Report No. 10. State Building Commission, Austin.
1969 The History and Archeology of Mission San Juan Capistrano, San Antonio, Texas. Vol. II. Archeological Program Report No. 11. State Building Commission, Austin.
1970 *Archeological Investigations at Mission San Jose in April 1968.* Archeological Report No. 19. Texas Historical Survey Committee, Austin.
1980 *The Indians of the San Antonio Missions.* Ph.D. dissertation, University of Texas, Austin.

Scurlock, Dan
1976 *Archeological and Architectural Tests at Mission San Juan de Capistrano Church, March and April 1975.* Special Report No. 21. Texas Historical Commission, Austin.

Scurlock, Dan, Adan Benavides, Jr., Dana Isham, and John W. Clark, Jr.
1976 *An Archeological and Historical Study of the Proposed Mission Parkway, San Antonio, Texas.* Archeological Survey Report 17. Texas Historical Commission, Austin.

Scurlock, Dan, and Daniel E. Fox
1977 *An Archeological Investigation of Mission Concepción, San Antonio, Texas.* Special Report No. 2. Texas Antiquities Committee, Austin.

Scurlock, Dan, and Theodore B. Powers
1973 *Spain in North America: Selected Sources on Spanish Colonial History, Archeology, Architecture and Art.* Special Report 8. Texas Historical Commission, Austin.

Shafer, Harry J.
1986 *Ancient Texans.* Photographs by Jimmy Zintgraff. Texas Monthly Press, Austin.

Skeels, Lydia L. M.
1972 *An Ethnohistorical Survey of Texas Indians.* Archeological Report No. 22. Texas Historical Survey Committee, Austin.

Smith, Harvey P., Jr.
1980 Espada Mission: Research and Restoration. *La Tierra: Journal of the Southern Texas Archaeological Association* 7(2):3–18.

Sorrow, William M.
1972 *Archeological Salvage Excavations at the Alamo (Mission San Antonio de Valero).* Archeological Salvage Project Research Report No. 4. University of Texas at Austin.

Story, Dee Ann
1981 An Overview of the Archaeology of East Texas. *Plains Anthropologist* 26(92):139–156.

Swanton, John R.

1940 *Linguistic Material from the Tribes of Southern Texas and Northeastern Mexico*. Bureau of American Ethnology Bulletin No. 127. Washington, D.C.

1942 *Source Material on the History and Ethnology of the Caddo Indians*. Bureau of American Ethnology Bulletin No. 132. Washington, D.C.

Tate, M. L.

1986 *The Indians of Texas: An Annotated Research Bibliography*. Scarecrow Press, Metuchen, N.J.

Taylor, A. J., Anne A. Fox, and I. Wayne Cox

1985 *Archaeological Testing at Rancho de las Cabras, Wilson County, Texas, Fifth Season*. Archaeological Survey Report No. 143. Center for Archaeological Research, University of Texas at San Antonio.

Taylor, H. C., Jr.

1960 Archeological Notes on the Route of Cabeza de Vaca. *Bulletin of the Texas Archeological Society* 31:273–290.

Tunnell, Curtis D.

1966 *A Description of Enameled Earthenware from an Archeological Excavation at Mission San Antonio de Valero (the Alamo)*. Archeological Program Report No. 2. State Building Commission, Austin.

Tunnell, Curtis D., and J. Richard Ambler

1967 *Archeological Excavations at Presidio San Augustín de Ahumada, with a Historical Background by J. V. Clay*. Archeological Program Report No. 6. State Building Commission, Austin.

Tunnell, Curtis, and W. W. Newcomb, Jr.

1969 *A Lipan Apache Mission, San Lorenzo de la Santa Cruz 1762–1771*. Texas Memorial Museum Bulletin No. 14. Austin.

Turner, Ellen S., and Thomas R. Hester

1985 *A Field Guide to Stone Artifacts of Texas Indians*. Texas Monthly Press, Austin.

Weddle, Robert S.

1964 *The San Sabá Mission: Spanish Pivot in Texas*. University of Texas Press, Austin.

1968 *San Juan Bautista: Gateway to Spanish Texas*. University of Texas Press, Austin.

1973 *Wilderness Manhunt: The Spanish Search for LaSalle*. University of Texas Press, Austin.

Weniger, Del

1984 *The Explorer's Texas. The Lands and Waters*. Eakin Press, Austin.

Winfrey, D. H., and others

1971 *Indian Tribes of Texas*. Texian Press, Waco.

Chapter 13 ■

Thomas R. Hester

Perspectives on the Material Culture of the Mission Indians of the Texas–Northeastern Mexico Borderlands

The borderlands region of southern Texas and northeastern Mexico was the home of numerous bands of hunters and gatherers. The 11,000-year traditions of these lifeways were interrupted in the seventeenth and eighteenth centuries by two factors: the intrusion of Apachean groups from the north and west and the advance of the Spanish frontier from the south. Both led to the disruption of native cultural patterns, and it is likely that the hunter-gatherer peoples encountered by the Spanish missionaries in the early eighteenth century had already suffered considerably—displaced, at least in part, from their territories by the Apache and perhaps afflicted by European diseases prior to actual Spanish contact. Bolton (1916:298) has suggested that the Spanish impact spread in advance of the Spaniards themselves, with smallpox reaching into west-central Texas by the 1670s.

The Missions

Despite the situation at the beginning of the eighteenth century, the Spanish missionaries found ample Indian groups to warrant the establishment of several missions in the region. I am concerned mainly with those missions in southern Texas and northeastern Mexico for which we have considerable data, both on the Indian groups who lived within the missions and from missions at which excavations of the Indian quarters have been carried out (see Figure 12-1; Table 13-1). Additional data related to the Indian presence within the mission system and the Spanish communities in the south Texas area come from excavations at Rancho las Cabras (see Fox, this volume; Ivey 1983; Ivey and Fox 1981; Jones and Fox 1983; Taylor and Fox 1985) and in former Spanish households in what is now downtown San Antonio, Texas (e.g., Fox 1977). The mission data come from such sites as San Bernardo and San Juan Bautista, Coahuila (see Eaton, this volume); the San Antonio missions, including San Antonio de Valero (e.g., Eaton 1977; Leutenegger 1977); San Juan Capistrano (Schuetz 1968); Concepción (Scurlock and Fox 1977; Fox 1988); and San José (Schuetz 1970; Clark 1978; see

Table 13-1. Lithic Categories at Selected Sites

	Zavala County	Shanklin	Valero	Capistrano	Concepción	San José	Espíritu Santo	Rosario	Las Cabras	San Juan Bautista	San Bernardo
Arrow points											
Guerrero		x	x	x	x	x	x	x	x	x	x
Perdiz	x		x				x		x		
Scallorn	x										
Other	x	x								x	x
Dart points											
Archaic midden	x	x		x	x		x			x	x
Associated with mission tasks					x					x	x
Bifaces											
Preforms/miscellaneous tasks	x	x			x	x				x	x
Cutting tools			x	x			x		x	x	x
Chopping tools			x		x		x		x	x	x
Unifaces											
End scrapers	x	x		x	x		x	x		x	
Other	x	x	x	x	x		x	x		x	x
Perforators	x	x			x						x
Gravers		x	x		x						x
Flakes											
Modified	x	x	x	x	x		x	x	x	x	x
Debitage	x	x	x	x	x	x	x	x	x	x	x
Blades											
Modified	x			x			x			x	x
Unmodified	x			x			x	x			x
Cores											
Flake	x	x	x	x	x		x	x	x	x	x
Blade	x							x		x	x

also Campbell and Campbell 1985 for a summary of the records of Indian groups at all of the San Antonio missions); and the missions of the Goliad region, including Rosario (Gilmore, this volume; see also Gilmore 1973, 1984) and Espíritu Santo (Jackson 1933; Mounger 1959). Salinas (1986) provides glimpses of the Indian populations at missions in Nuevo León, along the Rio Grande frontier in what is now the Lower Rio Grande Valley of southern Texas. The locations of the major missions and other relevant Spanish Colonial sites are shown in Figure 12-2.

Native Peoples and Late Prehistory

The Indian groups of the region are often referred to as Coahuiltecan, although recent archaeological and linguistic research indicates considerable diversity. We can continue to refer to some of these peoples as Coahuiltecan, as many shared the Coahuilteco language and apparently a number of cultural traits (Campbell 1983). However, as Goddard (1979) has reported, as many as five or six other distinctive Indian languages were recorded in the region. There were also many groups who were refugees from northeastern Mexico and whose linguistic affiliation is unknown (T. N. Campbell, personal communication).

Archaeological research has shown differing cultural patterns across the southern Texas area in Late Prehistoric times (A.D. 1200–1700), as documented by Hester (1980) and recently summarized in Hall et al. (1986). Particularly distinctive are adaptive patterns that reflect the plant and animal resources that vary across the region (Hester 1981), and those lifeways that focused on coastal resources. It is unclear, however, that one of the most distinctive cultural entities, labeled the Toyah horizon by Black (1986), persists into the early contact period. The Toyah pattern is noted for an apparent reliance on bison hunting beginning around A.D. 1300–1400 and lasting for at least 150–200 years. Sites are characterized by extensive faunal recovery (with bison seeming to be the most significant; Black 1986), arrow points of the Perdiz type (Figure 13-1,g,h), specific tool forms such as beveled knives, end scrapers, perforators and gravers (Figure 13-1,i-k), bone tools, and bone-tempered pottery, known as *Leon Plain*. Sites of critical importance in terms of our knowledge of this Late Prehistoric phenomenon are the Hinjosa site, Jim Wells County (Black 1986), and site 41LK201, in Live Oak County (Highley 1986).

By contrast, other study areas in the interior of southern Texas would indicate that the Toyah horizon did not encompass the whole region (e.g., Hester 1981; Hester and Hill 1975; Nunley and Hester 1975). For example, in areas to the west, nearer the Rio Grande, the lithic tool kit and the subsistence patterns are clearly not of the Toyah horizon, although some traits, such as Perdiz arrow points and bone-tempered pottery, are also present (Hester and Hill 1975). We should make special note here of the presence of ceramics, as these were not recorded by the early eighteenth-century Spanish missionaries and were thought to have been introduced to Indian cultures in the region only through the mission process (Suhm et al. 1954). However, the archaeological evidence of pre-Spanish pottery making is unmistakable (Hester and Hill 1971). Even

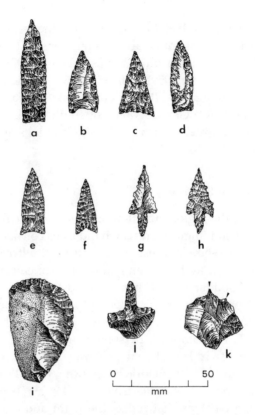

Figure 13-1. Selected chipped stone artifacts. a–f. Guerrero points from the mission era; g, h. Perdiz points (Toyah horizon); i. end scraper; j. perforator; k. graver (i–k found in both Toyah horizon and mission contexts). (Drawings by Kathy Roemer; from Turner and Hester 1985)

more important, as discussed later, is the fact that it is specifically the bone-tempered pottery tradition of Late Prehistoric times that becomes the dominant utility ware of the missions and that persists in southern Texas into the early nineteenth century.

In addition to the distinctive lithic and ceramic traits of the Late Prehistoric, there is considerable information on the technological processes of that era (see Hester 1975). Debitage analyses have shown that both flake industries and a blade technology were present in the Late Prehistoric (Hester and Shafer 1975). Blade technology may have been introduced via the Toyah horizon, where blades were used for making Perdiz points, end scrapers and other tools, but it was also present on the coast (e.g., in the Rockport complex; Hester and Shafer 1975) and in the non-Toyah patterns of southwestern Texas (Hester 1975). Again, this will become more important when we assess the nature of the lithic technologies of the missionized Indians.

The Indians at contact were also recorded as having an extensive assemblage of woven, hide, and wooden artifacts, the types of perishables that do not survive in the open campsites of the Late Prehistoric period. Basketry containers are reported, as are bows, arrows, spears, "rabbit sticks," digging sticks, wooden mortars and pestles, clothing made of rabbit skins and other animal hides, and a variety of other items. Some of these were replaced by introduced Spanish material culture, but others—especially the weapons—persisted through the Mission period.

Indians of the Missions

Although most of the missions dealt with Indians that we can term Coahuiltecan (as well as other non-Coahuiltecan refugee groups; Campbell and Campbell 1985), the Goliad missions and those in San Antonio were concerned at times with the Karankawa Indians of the central Texas coast. Mission Rosario became the focal mission for the Karankawa in the 1750s (Gilmore 1973). They were a coastal-adapted population, perhaps related to the Rockport complex of Late Prehistoric times. The Karankawas more strongly resisted the missionization process than most Coahuiltecan groups. Newcomb (1961, 1983) has described the Karankawa lifeway, and I will simply add here that they, too, took well-developed lithic and ceramic technologies into the mission context. Their practice of decorating pottery with zig-zags and other motifs using asphaltum (a natural tar that washes up on the Texas coast) is particularly notable.

Finally, with regard to the aboriginal peoples of the region, it should be pointed out that the hunting and gathering peoples known as the Tonkawa (Newcomb 1961) were also sometimes involved with the missions. Their presence in central Texas at the time of Spanish contact has led anthropologists and archaeologists to assume that they were native to the region. Indeed, some archaeologists have in the past proposed a linkage between the Historic Tonkawa and the Late Prehistoric Toyah horizon. More recently, Newcomb and Campbell (ms.) have conclusively shown, from ethnohistoric accounts, that the Tonkawa did not move into Texas (from an apparent Oklahoma homeland) until early in the seventeenth century. Thus, it is unlikely that they were responsible for the distinctive Toyah horizon cultural pattern described earlier.

The various ethnohistoric summaries of the Indians of southern Texas and northeastern Mexico, especially the work of T. N. Campbell (e.g., Campbell 1979, 1983; Campbell and Campbell 1981, 1985), have shown that we have to work with only generalized ideas about the nature of the contact period Indian cultures; details are very scarce. A recent study by Campbell and Campbell (1981) convincingly shows that the early sixteenth-century route of the shipwrecked Spaniard, Cabeza de Vaca, goes through the southern Texas area. His observations of the south Texas Indians in the 1520s and 1530s provide us with our only insight into these lifeways before they were modified by intrusive Indian groups, disease, and the mission system in the early eighteenth century.

It is from this perspective—archaeologic, linguistic and ethnohistoric—that we may examine the material culture of the southern Texas–Northeast Mexico Indian groups who went into the Spanish missions. The mission process accelerated the rate of change, and their material culture was modified in many ways.

However, it is likely that their lifeways and technologies had already undergone some change owing to the pressures from the Apache prior to the Mission era. We can see this through the accounts left behind by the missionaries and by Spaniards who inventoried the missions at various times. However, the most informative details on the artifact assemblages are derived from excavations of Indian quarters in several of the missions in the region (Table 13-1). It is largely from the results of the archaeological investigations that we can examine mission Indian material culture and obtain some general ideas as to how it was altered during the eighteenth-century mission process. Were stone tools and fragile pots immediately replaced by the metal implements of the Spanish? What Indian technologies did persist in the missions? What were these and what can we say about their continued use in light of the advent of Spanish material culture? Did any of the Indian technologies last beyond the mission era, and if so, what role did they play in early Spanish Texas?

Mission Indian Material Culture

Introduced Spanish Artifacts

As Indians were brought into the various missions, the priests dispensed various items, including crucifixes, rosaries, scissors, knives, and other artifacts of Spanish manufacture. Occasionally, there is documentation of what the Indians had in their domiciles in the way of material culture. For example, at San Antonio de Valero, an inventory made in 1772 (Leutenegger 1977) notes that the Indian families "living in the houses of said pueblo have the following utensils for their use: 11 grinding stones, 9 pots, 10 grills, 5 copper pans" (ibid.:29). A variety of farm equipment is listed for the "Indian pueblo" at San Juan Bautista also in 1772 (Almaráz 1980), but no mention is made of the household material culture. Kilns for making brick and for the firing of large earthenware vessels are noted for the Indian quarters at nearby San Bernardo (ibid.:46).

Ivey (1982:186) has appropriately reminded us that the various mission inventories of the eighteenth century were "concerned with accounting for the goods of the missions" and that there was "no interest in listing the personal possessions of the Indians." Although this makes it difficult for us to assess the range of introduced Spanish culture, or the timing of the introduction of certain goods during the Mission period, a review of Spanish materials found in the excavations of Indian quarters probably serves as a good indication of acquired Spanish items. For example, at San Juan Capistrano, Schuetz (1969) found such Spanish Colonial materials as "iron comales, stone metates and manos, copper kettles, iron spurs . . ., glass trade beads, copper jewelry, scissors, lead glazed utilitarian pottery . . . Spanish military buttons . . . and gun flints" (ibid.:43). At San Bernardo and San Juan Bautista, Spanish material culture in the Indian middens included a variety of majolica and other ceramics from Mexico, along with a few sherds of Chinese porcelain and English earthenware, scissors, needles, buttons, buckles, butcher knives, spoons, copper kettle fragments, bits of glass (such as bottle sherds), crucifixes, beads (studied by Harris and Harris ms.), finger rings, and scraps of sheet metal (Hester 1978; ms.). A similar array of materials is also known from Missions Rosario and Espíritu Santo (Gilmore 1973; Mounger 1959). It is hard to quantify the amount of Spanish goods from the mission Indian contexts. Certainly one has the impression that the metal artifacts were scarce, as there seems to have been considerable recycling of metal scraps, and for Missions San Juan Bautista and San Bernardo, I have suggested that the "material culture assemblage appears rather impoverished if one is to compare it to assemblages from the San Antonio missions" (Hester 1978:1).

Persistence of Native Technologies

The mission documents say little about the technologies of the Indians and almost nothing about any precontact crafts that might have persisted in the mission setting. There are accounts of the Indians in mission workshops—weaving, carpentry, blacksmiths, and the like (see Leutenegger 1976). However, an examination of the archaeological data makes it clear that certain prehistoric technologies continued into the mission era and perhaps beyond.

Before looking at examples from the realm of material culture, it should be noted that hunting and gathering as a subsistence technology remained important throughout the mission experience. The Spanish-introduced crops could not always be depended upon, but more important, the Indians continued hunting and gathering because it was their cultural heritage. For example, at Concepción in the 1760s, there is the following interesting passage: "Some women are in the habit of leaving the mission toward evening to eat tunas [prickly pear fruit], dewberries . . . sour berries . . . nuts, sweet potatoes . . . and other fruit and roots from the field" (Leutenegger 1976:49).

In 1749, the following related observation was recorded for Mission San Bernardo:

> Experience has taught us . . . that the motivating cause of . . . frequent desertions can be nothing else than the desire which is natural to youth; that is, from the moment of their birth upon the land they became so attached to it that they cannot forget it. . . . others came to invite them to hunt buffalo and to pick cactus pears [the tunas noted in the Leutenegger passage above] which were abundant [Almaráz 1979:21].

Salinas's (1986) study of the historic Indians of the Rio Grande Delta has provided further insights on the continued hunting and gathering activities of the region's missionized Indians. (Here it is important to recognize that none of these missions have been excavated and that historic accounts are our only data source; Salinas 1986). At Mission San Joaquín, near present-day Reynosa (Tamaulipas), Father Gomez reported in 1770 that the Indians "were still having to go to the woods for much of their food" (ibid.:283). A later report on that mission in 1785 indicated that hunting and gathering was still essential to supplement foodstuffs grown on the mission's agricultural plots (ibid.:284). Near Mier (Tamaulipas), the Garzas Indians were reported to be supporting themselves wholly by hunting and gathering as late as 1790–1818 (ibid.: 291).

Perhaps it should not be at all surprising, then, to see certain extractive and processing technologies persist in the mission Indian communities, as they clearly would have employed these in hunting, gathering, butchering, and processing wild game and plant foods.

Most notable among the native crafts seen in the archaeological record are stone tool making and pottery manufacture. Present but less common is the manufacture and use of bone implements and shell ornaments.

Stone Tools in the Missions

All of the major excavations at the missions of southern Texas and northeastern Mexico (Figure 12-2; Table 13-1) have led to the recovery of considerable quantities of lithic artifacts. These have been discussed in a monograph by Daniel E. Fox (1979) and in short papers by Hester (1977, 1982). Three sets of lithic artifacts can be recognized: (1) ancient, Archaic-age specimens picked up and brought into the missions (as at San Bernardo; Hester ms.) or representing pre-mission occupations at the locality (Mounger 1959); (2) lithics made during the mission period, including a wide range of forms described below; and (3) lithics that utilized Spanish technology, notably gunflints.

Of particular importance is what we have learned about the "recycling" of ancient, Archaic artifacts at the San Bernardo and San Juan Bautista missions. In both settings, the missions were clearly not built over a pre-mission Indian campsite. By contrast, the extensive Archaic collections at mission sites like Espíritu Santo (Mounger 1959) represent a mixing of pre-mission midden debris with later Spanish Colonial period deposits. Unfortunately, the uncontrolled excavation techniques used at sites like Espíritu Santo in the early 1930s (cf. Jackson 1933) prevent us from sorting the Archaic period materials from those of the mission Indian. At San Bernardo and San Juan Bautista (Hester ms.), Middle and Late Archaic dart point types (such as Ensor, Catan, Abasolo, Langtry, Desmuke, Tortugas, Shumla and Zavala; see Turner and Hester 1985) had surely been picked up from eroded campsites in the vicinity and brought into the mission Indian quarters for secondary use. Low-power microscopic examination of the point edges indicated to me that they had been used as knives and perforators. However, some of the small Late Archaic dart points could easily have been reused as projectile points. The Zavala type may even have been made in the mission setting since they have been found in protohistoric, seventeenth- and eighteenth-century contexts in Zavala County (south Texas), less than 50 miles east of the missions (Hester and Hill 1975).

Arrow Points. The manufacture of lithic implements during the mission period is most clearly seen in the appearance of a new projectile point form, a triangular to lanceolate series of specimens known as "mission" or Guerrero points (Turner and Hester 1985: Figure 13-2). They occur at all the missions in my sample, as well as at Rancho de las Cabras and at several historic Indian sites in southern or southeastern Texas. Because of the nature of the Indian mission deposits, it is hard to date their first appearance in this context. Certainly they

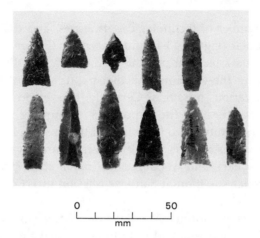

0 ⎣—⎣—⎣—⎣—⎣—⎦ 50
mm

Figure 13-2. Arrow points from Mission Espíritu Santo (41GD1). All are Guerrero points except top row middle (Perdiz) and the third from the left on the bottom row.

were present by the 1730s and continued to be made and used until the 1780s or later. I do not see any clear Late Prehistoric precedents for this form; none of the missionized groups were using this form alone as an arrow point at the time of contact. Archaeologists have sometimes lumped these points into the "Fresno" category (e.g., Mounger 1959), a Late Prehistoric grouping of triangular thin bifaces, many of which appear to me to be preforms. The Guerrero points often bear a striking resemblance to early historic East Texas arrow points, known as Talco (Turner and Hester 1985), but the Caddo who made and used those points are not present in the missions of south Texas and northeastern Mexico. Tunnell and Newcomb (1969) once suggested a link to the Lipan Apache, on the basis of their work at Mission San Lorenzo de la Santa Cruz. However, that mission was used between 1762 and 1771 and the Guerrero points show up to 30–40 years earlier in missions where the Lipan Apache were a threat, and not a part of the neophyte population! Whatever the origin, the style spread throughout the missions of the region, and was even used by groups who left the missions for hunting forays. The Shanklin site in Wharton County, southeast Texas, has yielded a number of these points, along with a Spanish coin dated 1738 (Hudgins 1984). As indicated in Table 13-1, there are occasional arrow points of other forms in the mission deposits, but they are rare and the contexts often unclear.

The only reference that I have found to the manufacture of arrows (and possibly arrow points) in the missions comes from Father Solís, who in 1767 reported that at Mission San Juan Capistrano, "old men made arrows for the warriors" (Schuetz 1976b:41). Using this brief note, we might suggest that by the middle of the mission era, the older men still had the skills to make arrows and arrow points and that possibly only this segment of the mission Indian population was responsible for making the Guerrero points. Obviously, this cannot be supported with present data. I do think it is important that the Guerrero points seem to share a number of technological attributes, and that two forms within the type, triangular (Figure 13-1) and lanceolate (Figure 13-1), are found in practically all the missions. Is it possible that only a few flintworkers were responsible for making these points and that points were traded or exchanged with Indians from various missions? Certainly, the spread of these points and their continuing use attests to the importance of hunting and to the fact that Spanish guns had not gotten into the hands of the mission Indians. Father Solís in 1768 noted that the Aranama men at Espíritu Santo were still armed with bows and arrows, spears, and wooden clubs (rabbit sticks?; Mounger 1959); he had reported a similar situation at San José Mission in 1767 (ibid.).

Other Lithic Artifacts. Nonprojectile point stone tool forms used at the missions were more variable in numbers and in technology. Flake technologies are present at the sampled missions, but blade making is found only at three (Table 13-1): San Juan Capistrano (Schuetz 1969), Espíritu Santo (Mounger 1959; personal research by the author with collections at the Texas Archeological Research Laboratory), and San Bernardo (Hester 1977).

Several important artifact categories were produced with the flakes or blades. End scrapers very much resembling their Late Prehistoric predecessors are found at some of the missions, and are especially common at Espíritu Santo. Generalized unifacial scraping tools, which we could label end scrapers and side scrapers, are found at all of the missions. Edge-modified flakes, used for casual cutting or scraping tasks appear to be equally common (or, indeed, much more frequent) but these have not been carefully sorted out in mision lithic studies. Perforators, gravers, spokeshaves are found, along with crude bifaces, some representing preforms (Archaic specimens collected from nearby sites), but occasionally bear use-wear that indicates their use as knives and choppers (Hester 1977). Cores, with facets from either flake or blade removals, are found (ibid.) and sometimes have been recycled as chopping tools. At San Juan Bautista, two choppers made of coarse chert cobbles were found with edge wear that suggests heaving cutting or chopping use, perhaps in plant processing, but more likely in the butchering of animals.

Unfortunately, the mission lithic materials are usually scattered in midden deposits and there has been little opportunity to find them in situ with associations that would perhaps reveal tool kits or at least task-specific linkages. Jack Eaton and I excavated one likely mission Indian work area on a room floor in the San Bernardo Indian quarters. A number of stone tools were found on the floor in the proximity of a hearth. They included a broken Guerrero point, 5 stemmed Archaic dart points or fragments, 4 bifaces or biface fragments, 3 edge trimmed unifaces, and 11 trimmed flakes and blades (Operation 9-C-1; Hester ms.). Some of the dart points and bifaces were soot-stained, indicating some sort of involvement with the nearby hearth or materials cooked on it. The scrapers and trimmed flakes may have been used in food processing around the hearth. And, perhaps the presence of the broken Guerrero point indicates that an arrow shaft was being refitted; the scrapers and flakes could have been used in shaping and smoothing a new arrow shaft. All of this is highly conjectural, of course; perhaps high-power microscopy might shed some light on the use of some of the artifacts in this cluster, but the lithics have to remain in Mexico and have yet to be studied in such a fashion.

Suffice it to say that the manufacture and use of stone tools was widespread and persistent in all the excavated missions of the region. This must reflect the continued importance of these tools in the pursuit of old habits, such as hunting and food gathering. It likely also reflects the fact that the area's hunting and gathering peoples were brought into the missions at different times, especially the Karankawa, who were only partly missionized at Rosario from 1758 to 1768 and who must have been making stone tools at the time. I think it is also significant that metal implements, such as knives and scissors, were not all that common or were at least hard to replace after breaking or wearing out. Metal arrow points made from metal scraps are found at most missions, but they are irregular in form and not nearly as numerous as their chert counterparts. Schuetz (1976a:12) also suggests that the "use of flint tools lasted throughout the mission period because there were never enough steel knives available on the frontier." Perhaps relevant in this regard is an observation made by Stephen F. Austin in 1821 as a result of his visit to Goliad, where the Aranamas were still residing in a mission context: "The Spaniards live poorly, have little furniture or rather none at all in their houses—*no knives*, eat with forks and spoons and their fingers" (Mounger 1959:90; emphasis mine).

There is even the possibility that flake tools were being made by Spaniards or Indians associated with or married into their households well into the early nineteenth century in southern Texas. For example, Fox's (1977) excavations in downtown San Antonio have uncovered chert flakes and debris associated with early nineteenth-century Spanish Colonial domestic trash. She offers the suggestion that "flint working activity must have continued among local residents throughout the Spanish colonial period. This may reflect the need for cutting and scraping tools during severe shortages of metal such as occurred in San Antonio during the early 1800's" (ibid.:16). She also notes that the manufacture of gunflints by non-Indians was practiced on the frontier because of the scarcity of imported British and French gunflints. Gunflints found in mission Indian deposits at San Bernardo and San Juan Bautista, as well as at some of the other missions, appear to have been the handiwork of Indian knappers and they may have filled the need for such Spanish-related items during the Mission era.

Indian Ceramic Technologies

Earlier in this chapter, I established the fact that the Indians of southern Texas and probably northeastern Mexico were manufacturing pottery prior to the time of European contact. In the Rockport complex on the southern Texas coast, sandy-paste pottery decorated with asphaltum designs was being made, perhaps by the prehistoric antecedents of the Karankawa (Campbell 1962). In the interior of southern Texas, a plain reddish-brown ware, tempered with crushed animal bone, began to be made around A.D. 1200–1300 and clearly persisted into the seventeenth or eighteenth centuries—and apparently right on into the missions. Its origins are unknown; similar pottery is found in Late Prehistoric Central Texas, where it was once thought to be linked to the Tonkawa; as I noted earlier, this linkage can no longer be considered. Although excavations and surveys across southern Texas in the past 20 years have revealed hundreds of sites producing from two to three to thousands of sherds, we are not certain of the pottery's range in northeastern Mexico. Whatever the case, the bone-tempered ware was made in quantity during the Mission period. It is found in the Goliad missions and has been called "Goliad ware"; although its basic attributes are no different from those of *Leon Plain*, some of the mission forms are more elaborate in form and decoration. As Schuetz (1969:63) has noted, it is unfortunate that the Spanish records do not mention pottery making at the missions.

Whereas bone-tempered pottery of Indian manufacture is abundant at San Juan Capistrano (Schuetz 1969), Espíritu Santo (Mounger 1959), Rosario (Gilmore 1973; note here that asphaltum designs are very common, undoubtedly linked to the Karankawa neophytes at that mission), San José (Clark 1978), and Concepción (Scurlock and Fox 1977), it is absent at Missions San Bernardo (Fox 1976) and San Juan Bautista (personal notes). Why is the bone-tempered ware so common in the Texas missions and yet wholly lacking in these two missions in Coahuila? Late prehistoric and protohistoric Indian groups just to the east of these missions were making bone-tempered ceramics (Hester and Hill 1975), and some of these groups were present in the mission populations (Campbell 1979). On the other hand, a number of the groups at these two missions had their origins in northeastern Mexico and perhaps had been beyond the range, in Late Prehistoric times, of the bone-tempered ceramic tradition. Whatever the reason, the San Bernardo and San Juan Bautista missions represent a distinctive anomaly in the otherwise widespread distribution of bone-tempered pottery in the mission Indian archaeological record.

Anne Fox has suggested (personal communication) that the abundance of Indian-made pottery in the southern Texas missions may have reflected shortages in imported Spanish ceramics from Mexico. The Indian pottery seems to have functioned largely for water storage (*ollas*) and other basic utilitarian needs. These needs, on the part of the Spanish community, apparently continued into the early nineteenth century as the bone-tempered ware is found in Spanish household debris in San Antonio (Fox 1977). Perhaps the missionized Indians made and sold pottery to the San Antonio community after the missions were secularized in the 1790s, or as Fox has suggested (personal communication), the Indian women may have married into Spanish households, bringing their pottery-making skills with them. The persistence of the mission Indian pottery tradition well into the nineteenth century is documented by John Linn (Mounger 1959:94), who reported that the Aranama women in the vicinity of Goliad "manufactured . . . water-jars used by themselves." (Although Linn's account was published in 1883, he may have been describing the Aranama Indian community known to have existed around Goliad in the 1830s.)

Concluding Comments

The purpose of this chapter has been to review some major facets of mission Indian technology of the eighteenth century in southern Texas and northeastern Mexico. The focus has been on chipped stone and ceramic technologies as these are easily documented in the archaeological record from the missions and related Spanish Colonial sites. The origins of these technologies can be traced to precontact Late Prehistoric hunting and gathering cultures of the region and then through the mission era of the eighteenth century. Some aspects of these technologies that involve the use of chert tools and pottery of mission Indian tradition apparently survived into the early nineteenth century. The persistence of these technologies, especially within the mission context gives us one measure, however imprecise, of the impact of Spanish culture on the Indian lifeway. It is clear that the Indians maintained major elements of their pre-mission material culture throughout the missionization process. In part, this may have been because of their need for such technologies to augment the hunting and food-gathering subsistence regime that continued throughout the Mission era, and it may have also been in response to the inadequate numbers of introduced Spanish material culture items such as knives and other metal goods, as well as imported pottery from Mexico. We should also consider that some of these technologies were probably preferred by the Indians over those introduced by the Spanish. Sometimes flint tools can be used in processing plant and animal materials much more effectively than metal tools used for the same tasks. When A. L. Kroeber in 1901 collected several hafted flint salmon-butchering knives from the Yurok of northwest California, he was told that these knives worked much better for this task than did the metal knives introduced by the whites (see Hester and Follett 1976; Kroeber 1925). Such a rationale might explain why the Indians at Espíritu Santo, for example, continued their use of end scrapers—but we have no record of this.

The missionization process in eighteenth-century Texas was only partly successful. Many of the mission Indians were lost to Spanish diseases (Hester 1986; Salinas 1986), many fled back to their territories and did not return to the missions (there, too, they died from diseases or from attacks by Apaches), and only a small percentage (in my opinion)—and this is difficult to quantify—were ever partly or fully acculturated. The last lived on in identifiable Indian households in the San Antonio (Schuetz 1980) and Goliad (Mounger 1959) areas for two or three decades into the nineteenth century. (Unfortunately, we do not yet have any documentary evidence as to the nature of Indian households in the Guerrero, Coahuila area after Missions San Bernardo and San Juan Bautista were secularized). Even then, it would seem from the meager evidence discussed in this chapter that certain precontact technologies had continued.

References

Almaráz, Felix, D., Jr.
  1979 *Crossroad of Empire. The Church and State on the Rio Grande Frontier of Coahuila and*

Texas, 1700–1821. Archaeology and History of the San Juan Bautista Area, Coahuila and Texas, Report No. 1. Center for Archaeological Research, University of Texas at San Antonio.

1980 *Inventory of the Rio Grande Missions: 1772. San Juan Bautista and San Bernardo.* Archaeology and History of the San Juan Bautista Area, Coahuila and Texas, Report No. 2. Center for Archaeological Research, University of Texas at San Antonio.

Black, Stephen L.

1986 *The Clemente and Herminia Hinojosa Site, 41 JW 8: A Toyah Horizon Campsite in Southern Texas.* Special Report 18. Center for Archaeological Research, University of Texas at San Antonio.

Bolton, Herbert E.

1916 *Spanish Exploration in the Southwest, 1542–1706.* New York.

Campbell, T. N.

1962 Origins of Pottery Types from the Coastal Bend Region of Texas. *Bulletin of the Texas Archeological Society* 32:331–336.

1979 *Ethnohistoric Notes on Indian Groups Associated with Three Spanish Missions at Guerrero, Coahuila.* Archaeology and History of the San Juan Bautista Area, Coahuila and Texas, Report No. 3. Center for Archaeological Research, University of Texas at San Antonio.

1983 The Coahuiltecans and Their Neighbors. In *Southwest,* edited by Alfonso Ortiz, pp. 343–358. Handbook of North American Indians, vol. 10, William C. Stuvtevant, general editor. Smithsonian Institution, Washington, D.C.

Campbell, T. N. and T. J. Campbell

1981 *Historic Indian Groups of the Choke Canyon Reservoir and Surrounding Area, Southern Texas.* Choke Canyon Series No. 1. Center for Archaeological Research, University of Texas at San Antonio.

1985 *Indian Groups Associated with Spanish Missions of the San Antonio Missions National Historical Park.* Special Report No. 19. Center for Archaeological Research, University of Texas at San Antonio.

Clark, John W., Jr.

1978 *Mission San José y San Miguel de Aguayo, Archeological Investigations, December 1974.* Office of the State Archeologist Report No. 29. Texas Historical Commission, Austin.

Eaton, Jack D.

1977 *Excavations at the Alamo Shrine (Mission San Antonio de Valero).* Special Report No. 10. Center for Archaeological Research, University of Texas at San Antonio.

Fox, Anne A.

1976 Preliminary Notes on Ceramics from Missions San Juan Bautista and San Bernardo: 1976 Season. In *The Archaeology and Ethnohistory of the Gateway Area: Middle Rio Grande of Texas,* assembled by R. E. W. Adams, pp. 16–17. Mimeographed report submitted to the National Endowment for the Humanities by University of Texas at San Antonio.

1977 *The Archaeology and History of the Spanish Governor's Palace Park.* Archaeological Survey Report No. 31. Center for Archaeological Research, University of Texas at San Antonio.

1988 *Archaeological Investigations at Mission Concepción, Fall of 1986.* Archaeological Survey Report No. 108. Center for Archaeological Research, University of Texas at San Antonio.

Fox, Daniel E.

1979 *The Lithic Artifacts of Indians at the Spanish Colonial Missions, San Antonio, Texas.* Special Report No. 8. Center for Archaeological Research, University of Texas at San Antonio.

Gilmore, Kathleen

1973 *Mission Rosario Archeological Investigations 1973.* Archeological Report No. 14, Pt. 1. Texas Parks and Wildlife Department, Austin.

1984 The Indians of Mission Rosario. In *The Scope of Historical Archaeology*, edited by D. G. Orr and D. G. Crozier, pp. 163–191. Laboratory of Anthropology, Temple University, Philadelphia, Pa.

Goddard, Ives
1979 The Languages of South Texas and the Lower Rio Grande. In *The Languages of Native America: Historical and Comparative Assessments*, edited by L. Campbell and M. Mithun, pp. 355–389. University of Texas Press, Austin.

Hall, Grant D., Thomas R. Hester, and Stephen L. Black
1986 *The Prehistoric Sites at Choke Canyon Reservoir, Southern Texas: Results of Phase II Investigations*. Choke Canyon Series No. 10. Center for Archaeological Research, University of Texas at San Antonio.

Harris, R. King, and Inus M. Harris
ms. The Study of Glass Beads, Coral Beads, and Bead Spacers From Excavations at San Juan Bautista and San Bernardo, Guerrero, Coahuila. Ms. on file with the author.

Hester, Thomas R.
1975 Chipped Stone Industries on the Rio Grande Plain, Texas: Some Preliminary Observations. *Texas Journal of Science* 26:213–22.
1977 The Lithic Technology of Mission Indians in Texas and Northeastern Mexico. *Lithic Technology* 6(1-2):9–13.
1978 The Material Culture at Missions San Juan Bautista and San Bernardo. Paper presented at the annual meeting of the Society for Historical Archaeology, January. San Antonio, Texas.
1980 *Digging into South Texas Prehistory*. Corona, San Antonio.
1981 Tradition and Diversity among the Prehistoric Hunters and Gatherers of Southern Texas. *Plains Anthropologist* 26(92):119–128.
1982 Prehistoric Continuities: Mission Indian Chipped Stone Tools. In *Historic and Cultural Landscape Survey for the San Antonio Missions*, pp. 205–210. Environmental and Cultural Services, San Antonio.
1986 Spain Meets America: The Archaeology of Spanish-Indian Relations. Paper presented at the Spanish Heritage in Texas Symposium, Texas A&M University, October, College Station, Texas.
ms. Material Culture at Missions San Juan Bautista and San Bernardo, Guerrero, Coahuila, Mexico. Ms. script on file with the author.

Hester, Thomas R., and W. I. Follett
1976 Yurok Fish Knives: A Study of Wear Patterns and Adhering Salmon Scales. *Contributions of the University of California Archaeological Research Facility* 33:3–23.

Hester, Thomas R., and T. C. Hill, Jr.
1971 An Initial Study of a Prehistoric Ceramic Tradition in Southern Texas. *Plains Anthropologist* 16(52):195–203.
1975 *Some Aspects of Late Prehistoric and Protohistoric Archaeology in Southern Texas*. Special Report No. 1. Center for Archaeological Research, University of Texas at San Antonio.

Hester, Thomas R., and Harry J. Shafer
1975 An Initial Study of Blade Technology on the Central and Southern Texas Coast. *Plains Anthropologist* 20(69):175–185.

Highley, Cheryl L.
1986 *Archaeological Investigations at 41 LK 201, Choke Canyon Reservoir, Southern Texas*. Choke Canyon Series No. 11. Center for Archaeological Research, University of Texas at San Antonio.

Hudgins, Joe D.
1984 A Historic Indian Site in Wharton County, Texas. *Bulletin of the Texas Archeological Society* 55:29–51.

Ivey, James E.
   1982 Economic History of the Missions. In *Historical and Cultural Landscape Study of the San Antonio Missions*, pp. 179–191. Environmental and Cultural Services, San Antonio.
   1983 *Archaeological Testing at Rancho de las Cabras, 41 WN 30. Wilson County, Texas, Second Season.* Archaeological Survey Report No. 121. Center for Archaeological Research, University of Texas at San Antonio.

Ivey, James E., and Anne A. Fox
   1981 *Archaeological Survey and Testing at Rancho de las Cabras, Wilson County, Texas.* Archaeological Survey Report No. 104. Center for Archaeological Research, University of Texas at San Antonio.

Jackson, A. T.
   1933 Field Notes (Espíritu Santo) Aranama Mission Mound, Goliad State Park, Goliad County, Texas. Book No. 2, 1933. On file, Texas Archeological Research Laboratory, University of Texas at Austin.

Jones, Courtenay J., and Anne A. Fox
   1983 *Archaeological Testing at Rancho de las Cabras, Wilson County, Texas, Third Season.* Archaeological Survey Report No. 123. Center for Archaeological Research, University of Texas at San Antonio.

Kroeber, Alfred L.
   1925 *Handbook of the Indians of California.* Bureau of American Ethnology Bulletin No. 78.

Leutenegger, Fr. Benedict (translator)
   1976 *Guidelines for a Texas Mission. Instructions for the Missionary of Mission Concepción in San Antonio (ca. 1760).* Old Spanish Missions Historical Research Library at San José, San Antonio, Texas.
   1977 *Management of the Missions in Texas. Fr. Jose Rafael Oliva's Views Concerning the Problem of the Temporalities in 1788.* Old Spanish Missions Historical Research Library at San José, San Antonio, Texas.

Mounger, Maria A.
   1959 *Mission Espíritu Santo of Coastal Texas: An Example of Historic Site Archeology.* Master's thesis, University of Texas, Austin.

Newcomb, W. W., Jr.
   1961 *The Indians of Texas.* University of Texas Press, Austin.
   1983 The Karankawa. In *Southwest*, edited by Alfonso Ortiz, pp. 359–367. Handbook of North American Indians, vol. 10, William C. Sturtevant, general editor. Smithsonian Institution, Washington, D.C.

Newcomb, W. W., Jr., and T. N. Campbell
   ms. The Tonkawa. Ms. submitted to the Handbook of North American Indians, Plains volume. Smithsonian Institution, Washington, D.C.

Nunley, Parker, and Thomas R. Hester
   1975 *An Assessment of Archaeological Resources in Portions of Starr County, Texas.* Archaeological Survey Report No. 7. Center for Archaeological Research, University of Texas at San Antonio.

Salinas, Martin
   1986 *Historic Indian Populations of the Rio Grande Delta and Vicinity: An Approach to Definition of Basic Ethnic Units.* Master's thesis, University of Texas at Austin.

Schuetz, Mardith K.
   1968 *The History and Archeology of Mission San Juan Capistrano, San Antonio, Texas*, vol. 1: *Historical Documentation and Description of the Structures.* Archeological Program, Report No. 10. State Building Commission, Austin.
   1969 *The History and Archeology of Mission San Juan Capistrano, San Antonio, Texas*, vol. 2: *Description of the Artifacts and Ethno-History of the Coahuiltecan Indians.* Archeological Program Report No. 11. State Building Commission, Austin.

1970 Archeological Investigations at Mission San José in April 1968. *Archeological Report* 19:1–32. Texas Historical Survey Committee, Austin.

1976a Indians of the San Antonio Area. In *San Antonio in the Eighteenth Century*, pp. 1–22. Clarke, San Antonio.

1976b The Mission Indians. In *San Antonio in the Eighteenth Century*, pp. 35–46. Clarke, San Antonio.

1980 *The Indians of the San Antonio Missions 1718–1821*. Ph.D. dissertation, University of Texas at Austin.

Scurlock, Dan, and Daniel E. Fox

1977 *An Archeological Investigation of Mission Concepción, San Antonio, Texas*. Office of the State Archeologist Report No. 28, Texas Historical Commission, Austin.

Suhm, Dee Ann, E. B. Jelks, and Alex D. Krieger

1954 An Introductory Handbook of Texas Archeology. *Bulletin of the Texas Archeological Society* 25.

Taylor, Anna J., and Anne A. Fox

1985 *Archaeological Survey and Testing at Rancho de las Cabras, 41 WN 30, Wilson County, Texas, Fifth Season*. Archaeological Survey Report No. 144. Center for Archaeological Research, University of Texas at San Antonio.

Tunnell, Curtis D., and W. W. Newcomb, Jr.

1969 *A Lipan Apache Mission, San Lorenzo de la Santa Cruz, 1762–1771*. Texas Memorial Museum, Bulletin No. 14. Austin.

Turner, Ellen S., and Thomas R. Hester

1985 *A Field Guide to the Stone Artifacts of Texas Indians*. Texas Monthly Press, Austin.

Chapter 14 ■

Kathleen Gilmore

The Indians of Mission Rosario: From the Books and from the Ground

The Indians of Mission Rosario were principally those of the Karankawan-speaking peoples. They comprised four groups, perhaps bands, named the Cujanes (for whom Mission Rosario was formed), Coapites, Cocos, and the Karankawa (see Figure 24-1). During the eighteenth century, Cujanes seemed to be the general term for these groups, who spoke a mutually intelligible language, but during the nineteenth century, Karankawa became the general term and is used here. During the eighteenth century, these peoples ranged along the central Gulf Coast of Texas between the Brazos River and Aransas Bay. Being pushed farther and farther south from their homeland by Anglo-American settlements, the Karankawa disappeared from Texas by 1858 (Campbell 1976:464).

The Karankawans practiced a seasonal-round, moving inland from the coast and the barrier islands when the cold damp winds of winter made it an unpleasant place to live. They had the reputation of being cruel, fierce, cannibalistic, and warlike and, according to Bolton (1962:282), "represented the lowest grade of native society in Texas." It is this view of the Karankawa that I attempt to refute by delineating some of their adaptive strategies and behavioral patterns from eyewitness accounts and from an analysis of their archaeological remains.

Historical Accounts

Probably the first European to make contact with the Karankawans was Cabeza de Vaca, between 1528 and 1535. Present knowledge suggests that he first lived among the Atakapans near Galveston Bay, then moved southward along the coast and lived among the Karankawa (Campbell 1976:464). Since it is not clear precisely which of Cabeza de Vaca's descriptions refer to the Karankawans, his account is not used here.

It was about 150 years later (1685) that Robert Cavelier de LaSalle encountered the Clamcoet Indians, now accepted as being Karankawans (Troike 1987:289) at Matagorda Bay. LaSalle appropriated some of their dugout canoes without permission or remuneration. Some of the natives were killed. Three years later, LaSalle's settlement was destroyed by these same Indians, only a few children being spared. Four of these children spent about three years with the Karankawans. One of them, Jean Baptiste Talon, was later interrogated about his experience and supplied a short vocabulary (Bell 1987).

He related that the women carried him and the other three on their backs away from the scene, and that they were loved by the women as if they were their own children. Nevertheless, he noted that these Indians were more cruel and barbaric than any of the other nations he had encountered. They inhabited the seashore and were continually roaming—hunting and fishing—and they had makeshift shelters, covered with buffalo skins prepared for the purpose. They had at the tip of their arrows "a sort of sharpened piece of stone, fish bones or fish teeth" (Bell 1987:230).

He said that it was easy to win their friendship and that a hatchet, a knife, a pair of scissors, a pin, a needle, a necklace or a bracelet would do so. "But also as they give voluntarily of what they have, they do not like to be refused. And while they are never aggressors, neither do they ever forget the pride of honor in their vengeance" (Bell 1987:251).

The Indians did not prevent the children from praying, but enjoyed the activity with mumbling and mimicking their prayers. They might take the prayer book or some other book they had found at the settlement and make ugly faces pretending to read, "for they are naturally clowns, buffoons, and scoffers" (Bell 1987:251). Apparently, Jean Baptiste did witness cannibalism, but the Indians told him they were cannibals toward their savage enemies only, and that they never ate Frenchmen.

Joutel (1962), of LaSalle's colony, wrote of the Indians that they were rather timid and unobtrusive. The males wore no clothing, while the females wore skins reaching from the waist to the knees. They had baskets and made some pottery for cooking.

Karankawans were encountered on Matagorda Bay in 1687 by Enrique Barroto (Weddle 1987:174), a Spaniard, who was searching for LaSalle's colony. When the Indians refused to come aboard Barroto's ship, three men took hold of one Indian to force him aboard, but, Barroto wrote, "they could not subdue him, because all these Indians are of great stature and very robust of limb."

Jean Beranger (Carroll 1983:20), exploring the coast for France in 1720, made a landfall in Aransas Bay. He found the Indians to be "tall, plump and shapely." Although he noted that most were usually about 5½ feet tall, he measured some at 6 feet 2 inches. They have a solemn look, he said, and a "handsome countenance." He noted that they ate their enemies.

Spurred by LaSalle's attempt to establish a colony and other French incursions into Spanish-claimed territory, the Spaniards in 1722 built a fort on the spot where the French village, Fort St. Louis, had been on Garcitas Creek near Matagorda Bay. A mission was built across and slightly upstream from the fort (Gilmore 1973). Some Indians appeared near the mission and the fort, and stayed at the mission until a quarrel erupted between the soldiers and the Indians that resulted in the death of Captain Ramon and the flight of the Indians.

Peña, the diarist of the Aguayo expedition of 1722, which established the fort at the site of LaSalle's colony, noted that many families came from three tribes and offered to congregate there. He wrote, "It was evident these Indians were very docile and that they would more readily than the others, devote themselves to the cultivation of the land and of their souls, because they experienced greater misery, living on fish alone and having no clothes" (Forrestal 1935:64).

In 1726, the mission was moved to the Guadalupe River where the Indians were easier to deal with, and the presidio was moved nearby shortly afterward. Pedro de Rivera made several inspections between 1728 and 1738. In his report for December 7, 1728, he observed:

> The Cocos, Carancaquases, Coapites, and Copanes, who are the Indian nations that have congregated themselves about the presidio need give no uneasiness. If the forty men left [at the presidio] exercise the vigilance which their duties require, the fort need never fear a surprise attack, both because these nations are not numerous and because they are known to lack courage, for which reason, not having the martial spirit of the others, they will be unable to start any hostilities that cannot be quickly detected by vigilance [Morfi 1935:254].

Bolton (1962:286) notes that Rivera's reports made between 1728 and 1738 indicate that Rivera regarded the four tribes as all "incapable of being reduced to mission life."

The Spaniards knew that to control the coast and protect it not only from the French, but also the English, the Indians had to be controlled. The Coahuiltecans living west of the San Antonio River and other Indian groups had entered the San Antonio River missions, but the Karankawans refused to do so, saying it was too far from their homeland.

After about 10 years of planning, Mission Rosario was established in 1754 for the Karankawans. The mission, in present Goliad County about 48 km from the coast, was not only to save the Indians' souls, but also, while these Indians occupied the coast, it could not be protected from foreign aggression, nor could settlements be made.

Father Camberos was the first missionary at Rosario. He wrote in 1758 (Gilmore 1974b) that there were 400 able to bear arms among the Cujanes, Guapites, and Coapones without counting the Carancaguases.

It has not been possible to convert the aforementioned Indians on a permanent and continued basis; [but] only for certain periods of time by sheer diligence, as well as by giving them something to eat, something has been accomplished. . . . Indians have worked in building the church, [making] clothing and the rest of the necessities, cultivating the fields, and learning to plow, and they go unwillingly to the coast when they have to retreat for lack of supplies. . . . They have never desired to do this [go to San Antonio missions], and they respond that they would rather be hungry and go naked in this, their land, than die far away . . . in no way will they go there without being forced. Let them [soldiers?] be warned that if they come for them to tie them up as has been done with others, they will flee to the sea; and they will defend themselves against the Spanish [Nunley 1975:46].

Father Solís made an inspection of the Missions in 1767 and wrote of the Rosario Indians:

They are all barbarians, given to idleness, lazy, indolent. They are gluttonous and ravenous and eat meat almost raw, roasted and dripping blood. In order to be at liberty in the wood or on the beach, they prefer to suffer hunger, nakedness and lack of shelter, which they do not suffer when they are in the mission, since the Father aids them in everything, in food and in clothing and in other necessities and comfort. . . . The Indians are very dirty, foul-smelling and pestiferous, and they throw out such a bad odor from their body that it makes one sick. . . . Although they are cowards and pusillanimous, they boast and brag of being strong and valiant, because of this they go naked in the most burning sun, they suffer and go around without covering themselves or taking refuge in the shade. In winter when it snows and freezes so that the water in the rivers is solid and the pools, lakes and marshes and creeks are covered with ice they go out from the ranch at early dawn to take a bath, breaking the ice with their body [Kress 1931:40].

Father Lopez made an inspection of the missions in 1785 (Dabbs 1940). He wrote that the Indians of the "suppressed Mission of Nuestra Senora del Santisimo Rosario" had fled in 1781 to the coast on the "persuasion of a peevish and very perverse Indian," José María. This Indian "happened to be more like a Spaniard, that is, he spoke the Spanish tongue better," and Father Lopez felt it was because of this he was able to persuade the "flexible, indiscrete and corruptible minds of the Indians" to run away. This Indian had also "committed execrable evils," causing other Indians not to return to their mission. The mission was reactivated and repaired in 1789–1790. That this was possible might be attributed to the death of José María in late 1789 (Gilmore 1984).

Father Reyes reopened Mission Rosario late in 1789 (Leutenegger 1968:592). The census he took in 1790 showed 55 Indians had returned (Gilmore 1984). The Indians told him that they "fled to the coast in 1779 because of the unreasonable and cruel punishments of the deceased Captain Cazorla and his lieutenant, Don Jose Santoja [of the nearby presidio of La Bahía] and also because the Father Ministers, now deceased, wanted to constrain and deprive the Indians of their liberty." He said the four nations—Copanes, Cojanes, Carancahuezes, and Guapites—were "better able to learn Spanish than the many I have dealt with in the interior; they learn easily what is taught them. . . . They have clear and sharp minds, are alert, docile and tractable and are highly regarded by the Spaniards" (Leutenegger 1968:592). Mission Rosario was finally abandoned in 1805, the remaining Indians going to Mission Refugio.

It was during José María's heyday that Spanish officials, especially DeMezieres, the Indian agent, believed that exterminating the Karankawans was the only safeguard against their continuing hostility (Bolton 1914:2:32).

In 1779, DeMezieres proposed exterminating or capturing and exiling the Karankawans by trickery. This proposal was the result of the murder of Louis Landrin, his son, and men, all of whom were anchored in Matagorda Bay, by a group of Karankawans led by José María. The proposed action never took place. His opinion follows:

> Although the low, cowardly, and treacherous nation of the Carancahuases is so abominable in every way—their number does not exceed one hundred and fifty men. . . . The said Carancahuases, always scattered, ever-wandering, make their residence either on the mainland, when cold and frosts drive them from the islands to seek shelter and food in the woods, or in the islands as soon as they are attracted by the abundance of fish there, of which they are extremely fond, and which they enjoy during the greater and finer part of the year. [Bolton 1914:2:298].

The Indians had complained that Mission Rosario was too far from the coast, and in 1794 another attempt was made to "tame" the Karankawans by establishing Mission Refugio, the last mission to be established in Texas. The final site was about 32 km south of Mission Rosario, where the present town of Refugio stands (Oberste 1942).

Yet the Karankawans were not tamed. They went back and forth between the two missions, returned to the woods and the seashore, and pillaged shipwrecks. Consequently, when the order to secularize the Texas missions came in 1794, it was felt that of all the missions in Texas the Indians of Rosario and Refugio were not ready to accept the responsibility of administrating the mission lands. In 1828, the order for secularization came, but it was not carried until 1830 (Walters 1951:299).

By the early 1820s, Anglo-Americans were obtaining permits from the Mexican government to settle in Texas (Wolff 1969). The Austin colony, between Galveston Bay and the LaVaca River impinged on the Karankawa territory, and the Indians retaliated by pillaging supplies along the coast (Gatschet 1891:31). Warfare resulted, with the colonists bent on exterminating the Indians. With their members decreased by warfare and disease in the nineteenth century, the survivors joined with other coastal Indians and continued to roam the coast. These groups were generally called "Kronks" by the Anglo-Americans (Campbell 1976:464).

Later descriptions of the Karankawans have also been recorded. Jean Berlandier, a botanist and naturalist, traveling in Texas about 1830 observed:

> The Cujanes were renowned for their cruelty until they were converted at the Mission of Bahia del Espiritu Santo [should be Mission Rosario]. They are excellent sailors and know every bay and inlet on the numerous islands in the Gulf. The Cujanes have an alliance with the Carancahueses, and they live in scattered

settlements along the coast from the Bay of Corpus Christi to the Bay of
Matagordo [Berlandier 1969:123].

These island people [Carancahueses], since many of them live on the Bay islands, have a reputation as the most skilled of all savages with the bow and
arrow. I have seen them attract fish in the bays and inlets by flailing the water
around their pirogues, then use their bows and arrows to shoot the fish that came
to the surface. . . . The people of all these coast tribes are extremely brave and all
are excellent swimmers. They have a musky odor about them, which the Spanish
call *amizle*, which they doubtless acquire from eating alligator. . . .

The Carancahueses are a big people, with robust, well formed, athletic bodies.
They wear their hair loose to the shoulders but cut in front to the level of the eye-
brow, like the Mexicans. . . . Their favorite weapons are the bow and dagger. This
does not mean that they underrate the gun, which they highly appreciate. It is
just that they are usually too poor to buy one [Berlandier 1969:149].

A. S. Gatschet, the ethnologist, in 1888 recorded the remembrances of Alice
Oliver about her Karankawa neighbors on the eastern side of Matagorda Bay
during the 1830s. She also remembered some words in their language.

The men were very tall, magnificently formed, with very slender hands and feet.
They were not very dark, and many of them had delicate features, and without
exception, splendid teeth. Their long, black hair was rarely combed but frequently
braided and adorned with bits of colored flannel, sometimes terminating in the
rattle of rattlesnake. . . . The women were rarely ornamented in any way, were
generally plain, short of stature, stout and usually disagreeable looking and exceedingly dirty, as were the men. . . . They were exceedingly dirty in all their
habits and had probably never known the voluntary application of water; their
continued wading in the salt water, however, kept them cleaner than might be
supposed, but the odor of the shark's oil with which they habitually anointed
their entire bodies as protection against mosquitoes, rendered them very offensive
[Gatschet 1891:17].

Mrs. Oliver also told Gatschet that

they prepared but one kind of pottery from clay, the vases having a globular bottom, so that they had to be placed into a hole in the sand. They had no handles
and measured in diameter about twelve inches. Mrs. Oliver observed their manufacture but once; then it was a man who made some pots and ornamented them
on the outside with little designs, faces, scrolls, scallops, etc., in black paint
[Gatschet 1891:59].

Remembering his personal contact with the Karankawans in the 1830s,
Smithwick wrote:

They were the most savage looking beings I ever saw. Many of the bucks were 6
feet in height, with bows and arrows in proportion. Their ugly faces were rendered hideous by the alligator grease and dirt with which they were besmeared
from head to foot as a defence against mosquitos [Smithwick 1900:13].

John J. Linn (1883), a Texas colonist, described two Karankawa chiefs in the 1830s. "Prudencia the chief was a tall well-formed man and spoke Spanish fluently. The second chief 'Antonio' I thought was the handsomest specimen of physical manhood I ever saw."

About 1843, Gatschet (1891:49) reports, 40 or 50 Karankawans applied for and were granted permission to settle south of the Rio Grande River not too far from the coast. There they continued their robberies and were soon driven to the Texas side of the river. In 1858, in a surprise attack, a Texan, Juan Cortina and others, exterminated the remainder. So ends the more than 150-year saga of a people who fought for their homeland and their way of life—their way of life, so repugnant to outsiders, being one of successful adaption to a harsh environment.

Synthesis of Accounts

Appearance. Some accounts agree that the Karankawans were tall and sturdily built. Some accounts report that they were very ugly, whereas others suggest that they were handsome individuals even by European standards. The women were short and stocky. Dyer (1917) reported that the coastal Indians smeared themselves with alligator grease to prevent sunburn while on the water and to repel insects. A coating of grease or fat would also help protect the body from the chill of icy water that the Karankawans liked to bathe in. According to Mrs. Oliver, they also used shark fat. Berlandier thought their musky odor might be from eating alligator meat.

Social Relationships. Early in the contact period (the late seventeenth century and early eighteenth century), the Karankawans appear to have been friendly but reticent. However, having "the pride of honor in their vengeance," as expressed by Jean Baptiste Talon, once their "honor" had been violated (by LaSalle, Captain Ramon, and the missionary fathers), then vengeance took over. This "pride of vengeance" may have been a motivating factor for deserting the missions and for depredations on the coast.

Father Reyes described the Karankawans in glowing terms, perhaps for several reasons: To reopen the mission he would have to show that the Indians could be missionized, and that he was the one that could do it, especially since he was in trouble with the authorities. Reyes believed that they were intelligent and had the ability to learn to speak Spanish fluently.

Both Jean Baptiste Talon and Mrs. Oliver noted that the Karankawans liked to joke and clown, although several accounts note the solemn expression on their faces. Just how the joking relationships were structured is unknown.

Social Organization. Practically nothing is known about the social organization of the Karankawans. All observers agree there was no permanent domicile; it was a hunting and gathering society with seafood being the chief procurement item. Aten (1983:68) mentions the possibility of the presence of a headman. By the late eighteenth century, the census records of Mission Rosario (Gilmore 1984) suggest that there was a hereditary "chief," perhaps for each of the groups. These records also show the family size was small, 2+ children per family, at least among those who came to the mission. There are also hints that the levirate, the practice of marrying a deceased brother's wife, was practiced, and that the extended family was the warm-season social and subsistence unit.

Reciprocity. Jean Baptiste Talon described the Karankawa as giving voluntarily of what they had, but in doing so they did not like to be refused. This implies a balanced reciprocity, an exchange of value for value, which, as stated by Aten (1983:86), "in the absence of appropriate reciprocation within a suitable period of time leads to the disruption of relations between individuals or groups." Aten (1983:80) further notes that generalized reciprocity—that is, sharing of food in a one-way flow—in a "hunting-gathering society is virtually a truism," this being an adaptive survival technique. In this view, there is no concept of ownership of property; therefore, in time of want, the Indians would take what was needed, such as the mission cattle, to the chagrin and horror of the mission padres (Gilmore 1984).

Division of Labor. The women set up and took down the portable huts when they moved, and did the cooking. The food was not well cooked, probably because wood was scarce on the coast and on the barrier islands.

It is possible the males made the pottery, since Mrs. Oliver observed one instance of pottery making by a male.

The males probably hunted animals on the mainland near the coast since their portable huts were covered with buffalo hides, prepared for this purpose, but who prepared the hides is unknown. Living on the coast, they became adept with the long bow and arrow, being able to shoot fish in the shallow waters of the bay.

Technology. According to Talon's description of the arrows of the different nations, the points were made of stone, fish bones, or fish teeth. The Karankawans probably used fish bones and teeth as well as stone tips for their arrows because of the lack of stone on the coast. The accounts of Cabeza de Vaca suggest that flint (chert) was a trade item from the interior. The technique used to prepare buffalo skins was not mentioned.

Joutel noted they had baskets and made cooking pottery. Mrs. Oliver said they made one kind of pottery with no handles and a globular bottom, that the pots were painted with black paint in small designs. Dyer (1917) noted that the Atakapans of southeastern Texas and adjoining Louisiana obtained jars from the Karankawa. These jars were fitted in cane frames and could be carried in canoes. Since the Karankawans made dugout canoes in which they traveled the coast, in all probability they also made the cane frames for the pottery vessels.

Language. Not a large vocabulary exists of the Karankawan language. Terms recorded by Jean Baptiste Talon and Jean Beranger are the earliest. Mrs. Oliver's vocabulary, recorded in 1888, consisted of those words she remembered from a contact going back more than 50 years. A few more words were recorded by Gatschet (1891) from two Tonkawa Indians who had known some Karankawan words.

Troike (1987:288), in studying these vocabularies, came to the conclusion that the Karankawan language "has no known relative." Goddard (1979:377) notes that a "consensus classification" of a group of linguists took Karankawa to be an isolate, that is, an unrelated language. Landar (1968), using in addition a vocabulary compiled by Berlandier on the Mexican border in 1828, has proposed a relationship between the Karankawan and the Carib language, and has suggested a "Karankawan invasion of Texas" about A.D. 1400. This relationship between the Karankawan and Carib languages has received no support from other linguists (see Troike 1987:290 n. 6).

Cannibalism. There is little doubt that the Karankawans practiced cannibalism, but this was a ritual cannibalism practiced on their enemies only. Ritual cannibalism is a custom not unique to the Karankawans, since many cultures around the world have practiced it.

Archaeology

Since Mission Rosario was populated (although part-time) principally by the Karankawan Indians, it can be postulated that most of the aboriginal material there was left by these Indians.

The site of the mission is 48 km from the Gulf Coast, and 4.8 km from the town of Goliad, Texas (see Figure 12-2). Large-scale excavation took place in 1940–1941, but few written records of it remain. Further excavations took place in 1973–1974 (Gilmore 1974a, 1974b). During the latter excavations, archaeologists found the presumed living quarters of the Indians along the eastern compound wall. These rooms were about 3.9m (4.3 varas) by 3.3m (3 varas). Each room had a hearth. Scattered around the rooms were bones, fish scales, mussel shells, and snail shells (Gilmore 1974b:47).

From the many bovid bones found in the excavations, it seems probable that cattle were the main item of diet at the mission, and this for people whose favorite diet was seafood. The diet probably was supplemented by sheep and goats, turkeys, and some chickens; sheep and goats also may have been utilized for their wool. Deer, pronghorn, and a small number of black bear bones were also found. That the Indians helped in the procurement of these animals seems reasonable, but living at the mission as well were Spanish soldiers and Tlaxcalan Indians who also may have been the hunters. Apparently the Karankawans were also continuing to use alligator meat or fat, as evidenced by these bones at the site.

All arrow points that have been recorded are triangular, and are similar to the "Guerrero point" (Hester 1977, and this volume), some previously being typologically classified as "Fresno." Triangular points of glass and iron were also found, indicating the use of material probably more available on the coast and barrier islands than stone, and the adaptation of an old technology to new and easily obtainable material. No recognizable points of bone were found.

The lithic material present does not indicate a specialized technology, as for example, points for shooting fish. Yet the quantity of chips and flakes suggest that tool making was taking place. In the 1973–1974 excavations, 14 stone scrapers were found, which the Karankawans may have used in hide preparation or other processing activities.

Twelve thousand aboriginal pottery sherds were found at Mission Rosario. Of these, 20 percent were either asphalt decorated or asphalt coated. Decorative motifs consist of painting of the lip, vertical squiggly lines, and some straight lines; some were coated on the interior with asphalt (Gilmore 1974b), rendering the vessel waterproof. Today natural asphalt may be found along the Texas coast, and a few pieces were found in the excavations.

The sherds with asphalt from the mission have relatively thin walls (2–5 mm thick) and are well smoothed on the exterior. The fact that they are hard implies high-temperature firing; rounded and conical bases were found.

This painted pottery, known as Rockport Black-on-Gray, has been found in Texas on the central Gulf Coast around Baffin, Corpus Christi, Aransas, Copano, San Antonio, and Matagorda bays. The distribution extends "inland as far as Goliad" and Mission Rosario (Campbell 1962; Smith 1984; Suhm and Jelks 1962:131). As with the Karankawan language, the pottery seems to have no relationship to other pottery in Texas.

Since the technique of painting pottery is known from the Huasteca area of eastern Mexico, Mason (1935:42) proposed that this technique only may have diffused from that region into Texas. Campbell (1962:332) also subscribes to this proposition. In contrast, in a study of pottery designs in the Rockport archaeological complex, Smith (1984) argued that Rockport designs and Huasteca designs have nothing in common, and proposed a Caribbean origin for the Karankawa following Landar's (1968) hypothesis based on linguistic comparisons. However, there are no archaeologic or ethnographic similarities that would support this hypothesis. Newcomb (1983:362) has commented, "That the Karankawa had a separate independent heritage is suggested by their distinct physical type. They were an exceptionally tall, long headed, robust people, physically distinct from most neighboring inland tribes." Thus their physical type, as well as their pottery and language, was unique.

Responses to Environment and Mission Life

It was the Karankawan response to a hostile environment that the missionary fathers and others of European descent were at a loss to understand. The stinking alligator grease was a necessity in a burning sun and in the presence of biting insects. Furthermore, clothes in a hot, humid climate do not cool the body. To efficiently procure the rich seafood resource that was available, it was necessary to become adept at shooting fish as the fish swam under water (thus to understand the refractive qualities of water) and to become proficient swimmers and sailors.

A balanced reciprocity, and in all probability a generalized reciprocity was practiced, providing a sharing of resources to ensure survival. After the mission was established, it became a source of food in sparse times. This food not only came from the padres, but was also taken when needed from the mission's stock of cattle. When spring came, the Indians would return to the coast, probably in extended family groups, where food was plentiful.

The asphalt-painted pottery made by the Karankawans shows evidence of a somewhat sophisticated technology: It was hard, had thin walls and round bottoms, and was painted or waterproofed with asphalt. Not only were the physical properties (such as liquifying and solidifying temperatures) of asphalt understood, but the waterproofing capabilities were recognized. Round bottoms sit securely in loose coastal sands, and waterproof jars can carry fresh water in canoes for long and frequent moves in an area where fresh water is scarce. Since this pottery is unique, one wonders if it could have been an independent development.

During the first years of contact with Europeans, the Karankawans were viewed as reticent, unwarlike, and not particularly intelligent. Yet some learned Spanish fluently, presumably at the mission, but few, if any, learned the Christian Catholic doctrine. Some may have had artistic ability, perhaps under duress. However, seeing their people being killed by Europeans, beginning with LaSalle and his men, they extended their vengeance to Europeans, retaliating in kind.

During these first phases, the Karankawans seem to have been an egalitarian, hunting-fishing-gathering society, although there may have been a "headman." Gatschet (1891:63) notes, however, that "they were ruled by two kinds of chiefs," a hereditary (male) civil chief and war chiefs probably appointed by the civil chiefs. Gatchet's authority is not cited, and Aten (1983:68 n. 2) suggests that this statement should be treated with caution. This may have been the situation at a later date, however.

The Karankawans' blood vengeance on the LaSalle colony seemed to have been satisfied and not to have carried over to the Spanish settlement 37 years later, but there was further "insult" by the Spanish soldiers and retribution was again called for. For the next 32 years, they could not be persuaded to accept mission life; then, when Mission Rosario was formed for them, they were there for intermittent periods only, and this was when food was scarce elsewhere.

For 10 years in the latter part of the eighteenth century, the Karankawans conducted active warfare along the coast by pillaging wrecked vessels and killing some of the survivors. This warfare, which took place under a strong leader, seems to have included all the mission Indians, as well as many who had never been at the mission. It also seems to have been a revitalization effort, not an economic war (cf. Schaedel 1949:135), but it was an effort to resist the "civilizing" effects of mission life and to recapture or revitalize the old way of life, as well as a vendetta against all Europeans. After the death of the leader, the effort fell apart, virtually ending the organized effort to protect their homeland and their way of life.

The leader, José María, may have been a charismatic, appointed war leader, but after his death another Indian, Manuel Alegre, probably his brother, unsuccessfully insisted to the mission fathers that he was the governor. As part of the "civilizing" methods used by the missionary father, hierarchical offices were given the Indians, but those who were given the offices were not necessarily the ones recognized by the Indians as leaders (Gilmore 1984).

Manuel Alegre married José María's widow, María del Rosario. After Alegre's death, she married Chief Andres. It is likely that Chief Prudencia was Andres's son and Chief Antonio may have been José María and María del Rosario's son (Gilmore 1984). Antonio was known as the joint chief of the Karankawans and Cocos (Kilman 1959:267). This points to a hereditary chief by this time, the early nineteenth century, which may have been stimulated by the revitalization effort and in part may have been a response to the hierarchical offices given to the Indians at the mission (see Gilmore 1984).

In sum, the Karankawans of Mission Rosario had successfully adapted to a hostile environment and resisted changing those patterns for a "civilized" mission life. This resistance became a revitalization effort linked to a blood vengeance. It appears that this effort may have stimulated a change in social organization by causing the firm status of hereditary "chief" with authority to emerge. However, the mission system may have influenced this change as well by the custom of appointing Indians to offices in a hierarchical regime.

Bolton's view that the Karankawans represented the lowest level of culture in Texas is not warranted in view of their successful adaptational strategies to a harsh and hostile environment and their achievements in technology and in mental accomplishments. Bedichek (1950; quoted in Newcomb 1961:59) wrote of the Karankawans: "In the minds of our people they are eternally damned, largely because they refused a culture we offered, resisting our proffered blessings to the last."

Acknowledgments

A different version of this chapter appeared with the title "The Indians of Mission Rosario" in *The Scope of Historical Archaeology*, edited by David G. Orr and Daniel G. Crozier, Temple University, Philadelphia, 1984.

References

Aten, Lawrence E.
  1983 *Indians of the Upper Texas Coast*. Academic Press, New York.
Bedichek, Roy
  1950 *Karankaway Country*. Doubleday, Garden City, N.Y.
Bell, Ann Linda (Translator)
  1987 Voyage to the Mississippi through the Gulf of Mexico. In *LaSalle, the Mississippi and the Gulf*, edited by R. S. Weddle, pp. 225–258. Texas A&M Press, College Station.
Berlandier, Jean Louis
  1969 *The Indians of Texas in 1830*. Smithsonian Institution Press, Washington, D.C.

Bolton, Herbert E.
1914 *Athanase de Mezieres and the Louisiana-Texas Frontier 1768–1780*. 2 vols. Arthur H. Clarke, Cleveland.
1962 *Texas in the Middle Eighteenth Century*. Reprinted. Russell & Russell, New York. Originally published 1915, University of California Publications in History, University of California Press, Berkeley.

Campbell, T. N.
1962 *Origins of Pottery Types from the Coastal Bend Region of Texas*. Texas Archeological Society Bulletin No. 32.
1976 Karankawa Indians. In *The Handbook of Texas*, vol. 3, edited by Eldon Stephen Branda. A Supplement:464–465. Austin.

Carroll, William M. (translator)
1983 *Beranger's Discovery of Aransas Pass*. Edited and annotated by Frank Wagner. Occasional Papers, vol. 8, May 1983. The Friends of the Corpus Christi Museum, Corpus Christi, Texas. Preliminary Studies of the Texas Catholic Historical Society, vol. 3, no. 6.

Dabbs, J. Autry (translator)
1940 *The Texas Missions in 1785*. Mid America, vol. 22.

Dyer, J. O.
1917 *The Lake Charles Atakapas (Cannibals) Period of 1817 to 1820*. Privately printed. Galveston, Texas.

Forrestal, Peter P. (translator)
1935 Peña's diary of the Aguayo expedition. *Preliminary Studies of the Texas Catholic Historical Society*, vol. 2, no. 7. Reprinted from *Records and Studies of the United States Catholic Historic Society*, vol. 24, 1935.

Gatschet, Albert S.
1891 *The Karankawa Indians, The Coast People of Texas*. Archaeological and Ethnological Papers of the Peabody Museum, Harvard University, vol. 1, no. 2. Cambridge, Mass.

Gilmore, Kathleen
1973 *The Keeran Site: The Probable Site of LaSalle's Fort St. Louis in Texas*. Report No. 24. Texas Historical Commission. Austin.
1974a *Mission Rosario: Archaeological Investigations 1973*. Archaeological Report No. 14, Pt. 1. Texas Parks and Wildlife Department, Parks Division, Historic Sites and Restoration Branch, Austin.
1974b *Mission Rosario: Archaeological Investigations 1974*. Archaeological Report No. 14, Pt. 2. Texas Parks and Wildlife Department, Parks Division, Historic Sites and Restoration Branch, Austin.
1984 The Indians of Mission Rosario. In *The Scope of Historical Archaeology: Essays in Honor of John L. Cotter*, edited by David G. Orr and Daniel G. Crozier, pp. 163–191. Occasional Publications of the Department of Anthropology, Temple University, Philadelphia, Pa.

Goddard, Ives
1979 The Languages of South Texas and the Lower Rio Grande. In *The Languages of Native America: Historical and Comparative Assessments*, edited by Lyle Campbell and Marianne Mithun, pp. 355–389. University of Texas Press, Austin.

Hester, Thomas R.
1977 The Lithic Technology of Mission Indians in Texas and Northeastern Mexico. *Lithic Technology* 6(1-2):9–3.

Joutel, Henri
1962 *A Journal of LaSalle's Last Voyage*. Corinth Books, New York.

Kilman, Ed
1959 *Cannibal Coast*. Naylor, San Antonio, Tex.

Kress, Margaret Kenny (translator)
1931 Diary of a Visit of Inspection of the Texas Missions Made by Fray Gasper Jose De Solis in the Year 1764–68. *Southwestern Historical Quarterly* 35:28-76.

Landar, Herbert
1968 The Karankawa Invasion of Texas. *International Journal of American Linguistics* 34:242–258.

Leutenegger, Benedict (translator)
1968 New Documents on Father Jose Mariano Reyes. *Southwestern Historical Quarterly*, 71(4):583–602.

Linn, John J.
1883 *Reminiscences of Fifty Years in Texas.* D & J Sadlier, New York.

Mason, J. Alden
1935 The Place of Texas in Pre-Columbian Relationships between the United States and Mexico. *Bulletin of Texas Archaeological and Paleontological Society* 7:29–46.

Morfi, Juan Agustin
1935 *History of Texas, 1673–1779.* Translated with biographical introduction by Carlos Eduardo Castañeda, Vol. 2 (of 2 Vols.). Quivira Society Publications, Albuquerque.

Newcomb, W. W., Jr.
1961 *The Indians of Texas.* University of Texas Press, Austin, Texas.
1983 Karankawa. In *Southwest*, edited by Alfonso Ortiz, pp. 359–367. Handbook of North American Indians, vol. 10, William C. Sturtevant, general editor. Smithsonian Institution Press, Washington, D.C.

Nunley, Carol Elaine (translator)
1975 A Translation of Spanish Documents Pertaining to Mission Nuestra Señora del Rosario. Master's thesis, unpublished manuscript on file at Texas Woman's University, Denton.

Oberste, William
1942 *History of Refugio Mission.* Timely Remarks. Refugio.

Schaedel, R. P.
1949 The Karankawa of the Texas Gulf Coast. *Southwest Journal of Anthropology* 5:1117–1137.

Smith, Herman
1984 Origins and Spatial/Temporal Distribution of the Rockport Archaeological Complex, Central and Lower Texas Coast. *Midcontinental Journal of Archaeology* 9:27–42.

Smithwick, Noah
1900 *The Evolution of a State, or Recollections of Old Texas Days.* Gammel, Austin.

Suhm, D. A., and E. B. Jelks (editors)
1962 *Handbook of Texas Archeology: Type Descriptions.* Special Publications No. 1, and Texas Memorial Museum Bulletin No. 4. Texas Archaeological Society, Austin.

Troike, Rudolph C.
1987 Karankawan Linguistic Data. In *LaSalle, the Mississippi and the Gulf*, edited by Robert S. Weddle, pp. 288–301. Texas A&M University Press, College Station.

Walters, Paul H.
1951 Secularization of the LaBahia Missions. *Southwestern Historical Quarterly* 54(3)287–300.

Weddle, Robert S. (translator)
1987 The Enriques Barroto Diary. In *LaSalle, the Mississippi and the Gulf*, edited by Robert S. Weddle, pp. 149–205. Texas A&M University Press, College Station.

Wolff, Thomas
1969 The Karankawa Indians: Their Conflict with the White Man in Texas. *Ethnohistory* 16(1):1–32.

Chapter 15 ■

Jack D. Eaton

The Gateway Missions of the Lower Rio Grande

Attempts in the late seventeenth and early eighteenth centuries to settle the northern frontier of New Spain, in the region of northern Coahuila and Texas, were slow and difficult. This part of the borderlands had little to attract settlement as the earlier explorations had found no fabled cities or mineral deposits for the Spanish to exploit. Although some mining communities did develop in south to central Coahuila in the seventeenth century, prospecting was just beginning in northern Coahuila. However, the missionaries and presidio soldiers were the ones who would pioneer settlement farther to the north; and their concerns had a very different focus—the spiritual welfare and civic instruction of the indigenous peoples.

At the start of the eighteenth century, there developed on the northern frontier a mission–presidio complex that was to have a key role in the settling of northern Coahuila and Texas. This complex, ambitiously called San Juan Bautista del Rio Grande del Norte, became the main passage into Texas from the south.

Hardly a move was made or a settlement launched on the Coahuila-Texas frontier without the direct involvement of San Juan Bautista. By 1727, there were

10 missions, 4 presidios, and 4 settlements in Texas from expeditions out of San Juan Bautista. And in time there would be more (Weddle 1968b).

What was this place called San Juan Bautista that for well over a century was the main way into Texas? Robert Weddle (1968a, 1968b) has referred to San Juan Bautista as the Gateway to Spanish Texas and Mother of Texas Missions. Felix Almaráz, Jr. (1979) refers to it as the Crossroad of Empire. Certainly it was all of this and much more.

In the early 1700s, the gateway community situated near important crossings of the Rio Grande in northern Coahuila consisted of three Franciscan missions: San Juan Bautista, San Bernardo, and San Francisco Solano (see Figure 12-2). The missions were arranged around, and in the vicinity of, Presidio San Juan Bautista del Rio Grande, which was charged with protecting the missions, and also conducting regional campaigns and escorting expeditions into Texas. In time, a Spanish civil settlement developed around the presidio. The whole community, that is, the missions, presidio, and civil settlement, was generally referred to as San Juan Bautista, which was the name of the first and most important mission to be established there (Eaton 1981; Weddle 1968b).

To better understand San Juan Bautista as the gateway to Spanish Texas, how it came to be, its role in Spanish-Indian relations, and what eventually became of this once famous place, we need to consider its history and the archaeology that has been done there. Each has an interesting story to tell.

Historical Background

Indian Conversion and Labor Management

The Spanish conquest of New Spain was far more than a remarkable military adventure and evangelistic crusade. It was also a great new experiment in social-political and economic domination and control of vast new lands inhabited by peoples whose lifeways differed greatly from European concepts of social, political, economic, and religious behavior (Hanke 1965).

The implantation of Christian Spanish civilization in New Spain would require religious conversion, workable systems of exploitation, and effective labor management to serve Spanish needs. Spain needed Indian labor. Since relatively few Spaniards were around to control the large indigenous populations in New Spain—who were expected to be the main work force for the society—a variety of institutional forms of management were tried out during the first century of occupation. Although the Spanish Crown at least attempted to apply uniform models of labor management throughout the Americas, they had to be adapted to prevailing conditions in different areas (Hanke 1965; Villamarin 1975). Labor management experiments ranged, in rough chronological order, from *slavery*, to the encomienda (labor or tribute in exchange for welfare and protection) and the repartimiento (forced labor) systems, to *free labor* (labor based upon contractual agreements). These systems, although experimental, were basically designed to exploit those Native Americans who had a degree of civilization and social order that included developed skills and crafts of use to society.

However, these systems did not work on the northern frontier, notably in the areas where the native peoples were largely hunting and gathering bands with little of what we might call the "civilized" social organization or skills needed in Spanish society. These peoples would have to be trained. Another problem was that the encomienda and repartimiento systems that developed in the Indies and advanced cultural areas of Mexico and that were meant to be benevolent, were badly abused by the Spaniards and were abolished. Thereafter, the mission program was installed for the frontier regions (Bannon 1968, 1970). Here we are only concerned with the missionizing of the borderlands region of Coahuila and Texas.

The Northern Expansion

Early Spanish advancements into Coahuila, following exploratory expeditions and military campaigns, generally were tied to the search for and exploitation of mineral deposits. By 1565, expansion had extended as far north as Parras, Saltillo, and perhaps also Monterrey in southern Coahuila (Bannon 1968; Bolton 1921). However, small prospecting expeditions probably ventured far beyond the mines. Although small parties might have reached and even crossed the middle-lower Rio Grande in the 1650s, there is no clear record of this. Northern Coahuila and south Texas had little to offer the miners, or other economic adventurers, apart from hardships. The earliest crossing of the lower Rio Grande of which there is definite record occurred in 1655 when Don Fernando de Azcué y Armendárez, the alcalde mayor of Saltillo, led a punitive campaign against the Cacaxtles, advancing well into Texas (Bannon 1968). He probably forded the river at one of the crossings on the Rio Grande that would later be the main route into Texas. In subsequent years there would be many more crossings into Texas largely for reconnaissance.

The Mission Program

The mission program was designed to gather the generally peaceful bands of Indians on the frontier into mission enclosures located in selected places. By and large, the individuals and families who came to the missions were from a variety of bands from different tribal groups, rather than whole bands (Almaráz 1979, 1980). In some areas, there was no formal presidio nearby, but a few soldiers might be assigned to the missions to help in the defense and instruction of the Indian neophytes. The purpose of the program was to convert the peoples of the region to Spanish Catholicism and to civilize them through the teaching of skills and crafts, and social organization and behavior, under a plan expected to eventually produce useful Spanish citizens (Almaráz 1979). It was deemed that the wild Apaches (and other "uncontrollable" Indians) of the region who frequently raided the missions were not worth the cost of subduing them and bringing them into the missions as neophytes, as the probable returns in labor from them were uncertain. The Spanish goal on the frontier was to missionize; the Indian reaction was generally to resist. Although some Indian groups seemed enthusiastic about entering the missions, which promised the Indians a better life and spiritual enlightenment, they soon became disillusioned after experiencing crop failures, dwindling water resources, and raids by the wild bands of the region (Weddle 1968b). Thus many fled the confines of the mission. It was then the task of the missionaries, often with the aid of presidio soldiers, to go after the fleeing neophytes and bring them back. Some neophytes never returned. The mission-presidio policy on the frontier was to control the region and its inhabitants by a peculiar combination of armed force and gentle persuasion (Almaráz 1979).

The Coahuila-Texas Frontier Missions

The missions on the Coahuila–Texas frontier were to be self-supporting institutions that would gather the Indians of the surrounding areas into enclosures designed to facilitate the control and defense of the inhabitants. The needs of these missions differed somewhat from those established at pueblos in the American Southwest, or near Indian towns of east Texas, which had long, relatively settled populations to instruct.

Put another way, the missions on the Coahuila–Texas frontier were self-contained Christian seminaries and industrial trade schools with resident (or nearby) housing provided for the neophytes (Bolton 1921). The missions were often situated near preferred Indian camps in familiar areas so as to reduce the shock of transition. The mission architectural complex consisted of the buildings required to house mission functions. The facility generally formed an inward-facing compound with restricted access to the inner courts. Some missions had a high wall enclosing the central facilities; others did not, and instead depended upon the close grouping of buildings for control and defense (Eaton 1981). The principles of defense that Spain applied were those it had learned from its experience with the Moors in defending fortified towns. As a result, the missions were sometimes better fortified than the presidios in the area.

Fundamentally, the mission complex consisted of a church, monastery (friary), granary, workshops, storerooms, and Indian housing. In organization, the church and monastery (also called the *convento*) represented the spiritual and administrative center of the mission, while the workshops and Indian housing formed the industrial and social complex (Bannon 1970). The mission also made use of the land nearby for agriculture and stock raising. Essential to the mission was an available water resource. Generally, one of the first activities in building a mission was to construct an *acequia* (water ditch) system to bring water from the nearest resource for domestic use in the mission and for field irrigation (Weddle 1968b). Although each mission on the frontier had its own distinct layout, and no two missions seemed to have been built exactly alike, the basic architectural components were much the same (Eaton 1980). This should be kept in mind when one is conducting archaeological investigations at a mission site and building function is to be determined.

Although the secular clergy generally looked after the spiritual needs of the Spaniards, the mendicant friars were given the task of instructing and converting the Native Americans. The mendicant orders represented in New Spain included the Franciscans, Jesuits, Dominicans, and Augustinians (Jones 1974). The Franciscans were given the responsibility for missionizing in Coahuila and Texas. After establishing the Franciscan Apostolic College of Santa Cruz de Queretaro in 1683, where missionaries were trained for frontier service, the friars began venturing northward (Almaráz 1979; Weddle 1968b). Since the earlier explorations produced no cities of gold or other mineral resources, Spain showed no real interest in the region of Texas. However, that attitute would soon change. Late in 1684, René-Robert Cavelier, Sieur de la Salle, sailing from France landed on the Texas coast, probably at Matagorda Bay. Although he probably intended to land at the mouth of the Mississippi River where the French had colonizing interests, La Salle decided to make the best of the situation and established his small colony, which he called Fort Saint Louis, on the Texas coast (Bolton 1921). Unfortunately, it was attacked and the colonists massacred by Indians. When Spain heard about the French colony (but not that it had been devastated) a series of military expeditions were sent out from Monterrey (and later from San Juan Bautista) to find La Salle's colony and evict the French from what Spain claimed to be its own territory (Bolton 1921; Weddle 1968b). The French fort was eventually found, but it was deserted. However, Spain wanted to install a presence in eastern Texas to demonstrate claim to that area. This was in large part what stimulated it to move northward, deeper into the frontier regions, and to establish missions there (Bolton 1921).

In 1690, an expedition was sent out from Monterrey, which included Fray Damian Massenet and assistants from the Franciscan College of Querétaro, to establish mission San Francisco de los Tejas near the Nabedache towns of the Tejas Indians on the Neches River (Yoakum 1855). However, because Indian harassment became unbearable, as the mission had been left without protection, Fray Massenet abandoned this first mission in Texas and returned to the college. For a time, the Spanish abandoned Texas as the distance to eastern Texas from southern Coahuila was too far to support any settlement on a very wild frontier. The plan was then revised: Missions were to be established in northern Coahuila, closer to the Rio Grande, a natural boundary on the northern frontier from which settlement expeditions could be launched without overextending.

The Gateway Missions

The Founding of the Gateway Missions

Late in 1699, after a short and unsuccessful attempt to operate the newly founded mission San Juan Bautista on the Rio Sabinas north of Monclova, Friars Francisco Hidalgo, Marcos de Guerrena, and Antonio Olivares moved their new mission to the north, close to the Rio Grande, where there were freshwater springs, preferred Indian camps, and suitable natural crossings. There were at least five shallow-water crossings, but the most important were at Paso de los Pacuaches, and farther downstream at Paso de las Islas and Paso de Francia. These were on the Camino Real—or "royal highway"—that would lead to east Texas.

San Juan Bautista was reestablished at the new location on New Year's Day of 1700 (Weddle 1968b). The town of Guerrero, Coahuila, now stands at this site (Eaton 1981; Hester and Eaton 1982).

Shortly after Mission San Juan Bautista del Rio Grande was established, a military contingent consisting of a small cavalry unit, under the command of Sergeant Major Diego Ramón, was assigned to protect the exposed mission. In time, the Presidio San Juan Bautista del Rio Grande was constructed near the mission. It eventually became the core of Spanish settlement in the region (Weddle 1968b).

On March 1, 1700, a second mission, San Francisco Solano, was founded to the northwest of Mission San Juan Bautista, and Fray Antonio Olivares took charge. Then in 1702 a third mission, San Bernardo, was established under the direction of Fray Alarizo Gonzalez a short distance to the north of San Juan Bautista (Weddle 1968b). Initially, these missions instructed individuals and families principally from the Chaguanes, Pachales, Mescales, and Xarames groups brought from the Rio Sabinas, and also individuals from other local bands—collectively referred to as Coahuiltecans (Campbell 1979). The three missions and the presidio formed a Spanish settlement and jumping off place for northern expansion to Spanish Texas.

In 1716, a colony expedition was organized at San Juan Bautista, and in April of that year it set out with Spanish civilians, friars, soldiers, cattle, sheep, goats, and the needed equipment to found four new missions and a presidio near the Neches and the Angelina rivers in eastern Texas, where they hoped to instruct the Tejas Indians and also present a firm Spanish presence (Bolton 1921; Weddle 1968b).

Mission to Texas

In the meantime, Mission San Francisco Solano, plagued with endless problems, barely managed to last for five years at its founding location. It began a series of moves—each of which ended in failure because of inadequate water resources, crop failures, and abandonment by the neophytes—and eventually moved back to the Rio Grande above San Juan Bautista. It was renamed San José. In April 1718, Fray Antonio Olivares, in the company of a colonizing expedition organized at San Juan Bautista, moved his San José mission north into Texas, and on the San Antonio River, and renamed it San Antonio de Valero. Eventually it came to be called the Alamo (Eaton 1980). Also established at that time, but a short distance downstream on the San Antonio River, was the Presidio de Béjar and a Spanish civil settlement that one day would become the City of San Antonio (Weddle 1968b).

The Decline of the Gateway Missions

Secularization of the missions in Coahuila and Texas, by royal decree, began in 1794, but in the San Juan Bautista area it was actually not completed until 1824, when Mexico won its independence from Spain (Almaráz 1979; Weddle 1968b).

Following secularization, the missions on the Rio Grande were eventually abandoned and fell into ruin. The usable materials, such as building stones, wooden doors and beams, and metal fittings, were stripped from them and reused in new construction in the nearby ranches. With the exception of the standing ruins of the large church at San Bernardo, begun in the 1760s but never finished, all other mission buildings were dismantled until nothing was left above ground, other than slight rises to mark their former locations (Eaton 1981; Weddle 1968b).

The military establishment at Presidio del Rio Grande continued to operate on the frontier until around 1823, when the independence movement forced many changes. When the soldiers finally moved out of the presidio, the old buildings reverted to civil use. Presidio del Rio Grande played a long and active role in the development of the borderlands (Moorhead 1975; Weddle 1968b; Weddle and Thonhoff 1976). It was the core of the San Juan Bautista gateway community where campaigns and settlement expeditions were organized that ventured across the Rio Grande and into Texas. Some of the old presidio buildings are still standing in the town square that was originally the presidio quadrangle. It had been an exposed presidio without an enclosure wall.

In 1827, the name San Juan Bautista ceased to be used when the Mexican town that grew up around the old presidio was named Villa de Guerrero, in honor of Vicente Ramón Guerrero, a revolutionary soldier (Weddle 1968b). Today, the small, quiet town of Guerrero, Coahuila, lies some 48 km downstream from the Piedras Negras–Eagle Pass crossing of the Rio Grande. There are many old buildings of the Spanish era in the town, including the remnants of the presidio. These are standing reminders of greater past glories. However, with the exception of the San Bernardo Church, nothing now remains of what was once a famous mission complex.

The Archaeology

The Need for Investigations

It became the task of archaeology to selectively excavate and document the buried mission remains in order to reestablish the ground plans and collect associated artifacts (Eaton 1977). Although there are brief descriptions of certain buildings in the inventories of the missions done in 1775, when control of the missions was transferred from the Apostolic College of Querétaro to the College of Nuestra Señora de Guadalupe de Zacatecas (Almaráz 1980), there are no plats to illustrate the actual ground plans. A large variety of artifacts and faunal remains recovered in the excavation of the mission sites relate to the actual lifeways in the missions (see Hester this volume).

A permit issued by the Mexican Office of Monumentos Históricos del Instituto Nacional de Antropología e Historia allowed the University of Texas at San Antonio, Center for Archaeological Research, to carry out excavations in 1975 and 1976 at the mission sites of San Juan Bautista and San Bernardo. No excavations were carried out at San Francisco Solano mission site (the birthplace of the Alamo), although a walkover survey was made in an attempt to identify the actual site location. But the results were not conclusive as that mission was of simple construction and was at the founding site only a short time, so that little has survived by which to recognize it.

In 1975, archaeological investigations began at the site of Mission San Bernardo, a short distance northeast of the town of Guerrero, as it was to be threatened by the development of a park and picnic area just north of the standing church (Eaton 1975). During the 1976 field season, work continued at San Bernardo and then focused on San Juan Bautista mission site, a short distance to the west of the town (Eaton 1976).

Mission San Bernardo

The standing church at San Bernardo, which faces west, was under construction in the 1760s, under the supervision of Fray Diego Jimenez, but it was never finished beyond its present state. Cruciform in plan with a dome-covered baptistry and large bell tower, it was to be a monumental structure without equal in the region.

The field investigations at San Bernardo located the wall footings of the original church, which faced south, and adjacent buildings that were constructed following the founding of the mission there in 1702. The buried remains lie to the northeast of the large standing church (Figure 15-1). The original church was much smaller and of simple linear construction. Its identification was aided by the description in the 1772 inventory that listed it as a small church with a single bell tower; it was still in use at that time.

Adjacent to the original church, the excavations uncovered wall footings of at least five more structures, in what was the monastery (*convento*) group; there may be more building remains, but no others were found during the limited and selective testing. The structure just to the east of the old church was possibly the friars' quarters and kitchen, judging by the type of debris found there. The long, linear structures extending to the north were evidently the workshops, storerooms, and granary mentioned in the 1772 inventory (Almaráz 1980). The linear structures were divided into rooms for separate functions, although the excavations were not extensive enough to identify individual rooms and their functions. However, cultural materials collected in the monastery group helped in general identification. As noted in the ground plan (which may be incomplete because of limited testing) the buildings all lie adjacent to each other in a closely organized, linear pattern with the long axis running north and south. The north end of the group seems to have been closed, possibly with an end structure. The pattern, with restricted access to the group inner court, would provide a degree of protection against hostile raids. There is no mention in the literature or the inventory of a wall enclosing and protecting the mission, and the investigators did not find any evidence of one. Evidently the buildings themselves were the only security.

The archaeological investigations subsequently shifted to the west, across the broad open space that was the mission quadrangle. There researchers uncov-

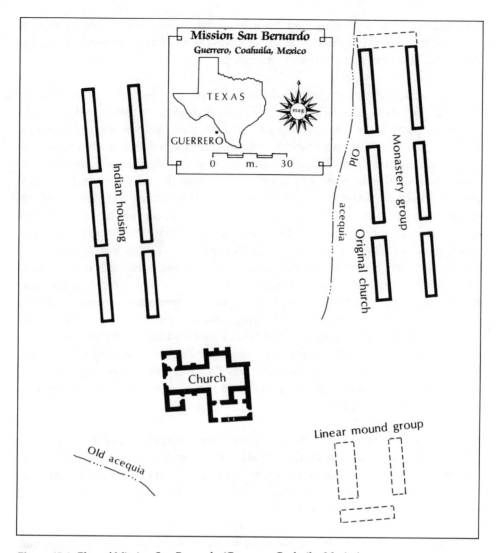

Figure 15-1. Plan of Mission San Bernardo (Guerrero, Coahuila, Mexico).

ered the wall footings of six linear structures in the same ground plan that was recorded for the monastery group. Here again we see close groupings with restricted access between buildings. Those in the east side group were built at a later date, as the 1772 inventory mentions an "Indian pueblo" being developed. It states that there were "40 houses of stone and mud already constructed. . . . [These structures] form two streets, closing off the square on one side of the church under construction" (Almaráz 1980). However, the archaeological investigations found only two rows of structures (forming one street) that line up directly north of the new church front entrance. The reference to "40 houses" certainly ties in with the many Indian apartments within the linear structures. This suggests that there may have been at least four, and possibly six, apartments within each of the linear buildings. Because all of the walls (exterior and dividing walls) and flooring had been removed, it was impossible to identify actual rooms and thus verify their size. However, trash deposits were found just outside of the structures and were sampled.

The Artifacts. The artifacts included a large variety of objects that relate to workshops as well as to domestic activity. The Indian housing trash yielded a great variety of pottery sherds representing, for example, locally made utility wares, Puebla Blue-on-White and Polychrome majolicas, fancy European wares, and even luxury wares from China (brought over on the Manila galleons). This reflects not only the diversity of pottery coming into the missions, including expensive imported wares, but also suggests that the Indians were the recipients (or scavengers) of cast-off pottery (possibly some still serviceable) from the friars' quarters or Spanish households. Notably absent from the pottery collections was Indian-made bone-tempered pottery so common at other missions in Texas.

Other artifacts from the Indian housing middens included such items as copper pot fragments, metal arrow points (made from metal scraps), glass trade beads, traditional Indian bone beads and awls, chipped stone arrow points and scrapers, and also ground stone pounding and milling implements (*manos* and *metates*). Even lost crucifixes that had been issued to the neophytes were recovered. Large scissors, metal knives, and large needles also found in the middens and building trash indicate workshop activity, and there were iron nails and other construction debris. These items, and much more, are listed in the 1772 inventory (Almaráz 1980).

The Indian Groups at San Bernardo. There were individual Indians and Indian families representing some 30 tribal groups of the region at San Bernardo, from the time of its founding to the 1772 inventory. This figure is based largely on the 1706, 1727, 1734, and 1772 censuses, and on the baptismal and burial records (Almaráz 1979, 1980; Campbell 1979).

The archaeology at Mission San Bernardo, as limited as it was, has provided us with information on the physical structure of the mission so that we may better understand how the complex was organized to house, control, and instruct the Indian neophytes. The ground plan (Figure 15-1) for Mission San Bernardo is based upon limited excavations in search of buried architectural features, and therefore probably represents a limited view of what the complex in its entirety was like in its later days and at maximum development before it was dismantled.

Mission San Juan Bautista

The original site of Mission San Juan Bautista, established in 1700, is unknown, but it is thought to have been situated near the presidio. However, if there are any remnants of it they are probably buried beneath, or incorporated into later buildings in the town. In 1740, the mission was relocated to a natural elevation about 1½ km west of town (Weddle 1968b). Here the mission developed to its ultimate complexity. However, not a single stone remained above ground to mark the place of this once famous mission. Archaeological investigations began with little more than intuitive feelings about where the church and other main mission buildings once stood. Occasional patterns of slight elevations in the ground contour were the only hint to suggest where excavations should begin.

Once the church was identified, the rest of the building remains were found and identified through knowledge of what a mission consisted of with regard to building functions and how they generally relate to each other. Slowly, the floors, walls, and doorways began to emerge until a basic ground plan was recognized (Figure 15-2). The church, which was cruciform in plan and had a single bell tower, faced west, as did the later church at San Bernardo. All structural remains were found buried much deeper than at San Bernardo, as much as a meter below the surface, and were much better preserved. Perhaps this was because it was not as close to town and therefore not as easily mined for building materials. Within the church, the excavations uncovered the broad front entrance, tower shaft (which enclosed the baptistry), transept with side altars, the main altar, and the sacristy. With the exception of the side altars, where the flooring was wood planks (some fragments remaining), all other floors were laid with locally made ceramic tiles. The 1772 inventory mentions a cemetery in front of the church, but no archaeological work was done there.

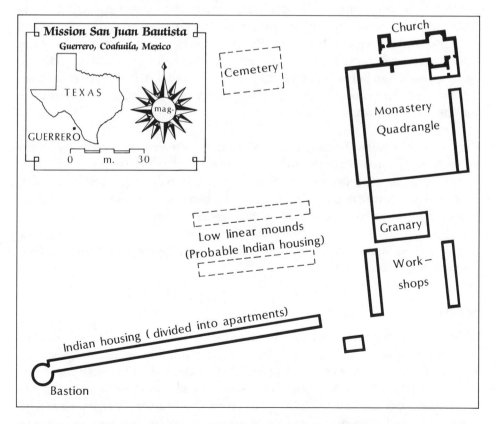

Figure 15-2. Plan of Mission San Juan Bautista (Guerrero, Coahuila, Mexico). Exact locations of doorways and dividing walls are uncertain except as shown.

Excavations continued into the monastery quadrangle, which formed an enclosed court directly south of the church. The inventory of 1772 listed 20 rooms here. South of the monastery was the granary, a relatively large structure with flagstone flooring overlying earlier tile. Some workshops were identified south of the granary, and extending west of the shops was a long, narrow structure that had been Indian apartments. The excavations uncovered the circular footing for a round bastion. This was not mentioned in the inventory or the literature. The beginning of a bastion at the end of the long structure suggests that there were plans to construct a quadrangle with a bastion on at least one, but probably two corners, of an enclosure. This indicates serious concern for permanent defense. However, the work seems to have suddenly stopped, probably when secularization occurred. Unfortunately, further testing to see if the wall continued to form an enclosure was not allowed, as the area beyond the bastion was inaccessible private property. Therefore, the ground plan for the mission remains incomplete.

At San Juan Bautista there were individuals and Indian families representing some 36 tribal groups from the region, as listed from the time of its founding in 1700 to the 1772 inventory (Campbell 1979).

The Artifacts. The artifact collections from San Juan Bautista, particularly from the Indian housing and workshop areas (where the largest collections were made) are, in types and quantities, essentially the same as those recorded at San Bernardo in the later constructions. Recovered was a broad variety of pottery types and forms, along with copper, iron, glass, shell, and stone objects like those found at San Bernardo and to be expected in the missions. However, since San Juan Bautista was relocated in 1740, materials from the two missions can only be compared for the post-1740 period.

The Faunal Remains. Large quantities of faunal remains were recovered from deposits at San Juan Bautista and San Bernardo. These include more than 50 species of creatures representing several species of fish, frogs, turtles, lizards, snakes, birds, coyote or dog, fox, raccoon, badger, skunk, domestic cat, puma, bobcat, squirrel, mice, rats, beaver, rabbits, peccary, domestic pigs, deer, sheep, goat, cow, horse, and burro. Since most of these local (and some introduced) species were found in household middens, they were probably used as food items by the mission Indians.

Summary

What have we learned about San Juan Bautista, the Gateway to Spanish Texas, from history and the archaeology? And at what point does archaeology become history? Documented history has revealed what the mission program was and why it was needed, and also how the mission, a vital feature of Spain's pioneering system, was constructed and operated on the frontier. Archaeology helps to reinforce, and even augment our understanding of the missions. An examination of the physical remains of the missions and the related artifacts, which would otherwise be lost in time, brings us much closer to understanding that remarkable institution and the humans, both Spanish and Indian, who lived there. Underlying the inevitable conflicts was a striving toward the common goal of promoting Spanish civilization in the New World. That the Indians would not become Spanish citizens, but citizens of Mexico, was perhaps in the long run irrelevant to their assimilation into organized society.

The archaeological work at San Juan Bautista and San Bernardo has demonstrated the similarities, yet differences in the missions there, notably in the organization reflected in the ground plans. These two nearby missions shared in the responsibilities of converting and instructing Indians from many different bands in the region. The Franciscan friars were truly remarkable in being able to oversee the construction of adequate facilities to control the neophytes, and to converse with and instruct the native peoples, who spoke a variety of Indian languages and dialects.

Archaeology has shown that such items as pottery vessels, described only as plates, cups, and so forth in the inventories, actually represent a variety of wares made locally and imported from as far away as central Mexico, Europe, and even China. Moreover, it has shown that the mission Indians had at least secondhand access to the luxury wares. The inventories, on the other hand, make little mention of what the Indians actually possessed or used, which was a mixed bag of mission-provided items and traditional Indian objects, some of which were brought with them to the missions, and these were items, such as marine shells, from long distances, as shown in the artifact collections.

The historical records generally refer to Indian "houses" at the missions. But the archaeology demonstrates that the houses mentioned were indeed small apartments generally within long, linear buildings that were laid out to form Indian streets, as at San Bernardo, or the long, linear structures at San Juan Bautista formed around a large quadrangle, which was also a perimeter wall designed for defense and included bastions at the corners. Evidently the plan there was to have resident-trained Indian auxiliaries defend those walls during attack.

The transition that the Indians on the frontier had experienced, from a simple hunting and gathering lifeway to a regimented and confined mission life with its complicated and demanding religious concepts, was a remarkable experiment that in the main was successful throughout the mission period. Following secularization of the missions and independence from Spain, the missionized Indians were given land to farm and stock to raise on divided mission lands, and were to a large extent assimilated into, and helped form the character of, what became Mexican society.

References

Almaráz, Felix D., Jr.
  1979 *Crossroad of Empire: The Church and State on the Rio Grande Frontier of Coahuila and Texas, 1700–1821.* Report No. 1. Center for Archaeological Research, University of Texas at San Antonio, Archaeology and History of the San Juan Bautista Mission Area, Coahuila and Texas.

Almaráz, Felix D., Jr. (translator and editor)

    1980 *Inventory of the Rio Grande Missions: 1772 San Juan Bautista and San Bernardo*. Report No. 2. Center for Archaeological Research, University of Texas at San Antonio, Archaeology and History of the San Juan Bautista Mission Area, Coahuila and Texas.

Bannon, John F.

    1968 *Bolton and the Spanish Borderlands*. University of Oklahoma Press, Norman.

    1970 *The Spanish Borderlands Frontier 1513–1821*. Holt, Rinehart & Winston, New York.

Bolton, Herbert E.

    1921 *The Spanish Borderlands. A Chronicle of Old Florida and the Southwest*. Yale University Press, New Haven, Conn.

Campbell, T. N.

    1979 *Ethnohistoric Notes on Indian Groups Associated with Three Spanish Missions at Guerrero, Coahuila*. Report No. 3. Center for Archaeological Research, University of Texas at San Antonio, Archaeology and History of the San Juan Bautista Mission Area, Coahuila and Texas.

Eaton, Jack D.

    1975 Preliminary Report on Archaeological Investigations at Mission San Bernardo. In *Archaeology and Ethnohistory of the Gateway Area, Middle Rio Grande of Texas*. Report of the 1975 investigations, submitted to the National Endowment for the Humanities by The University of Texas at San Antonio.

    1976 Archaeological Excavations at Missions San Juan Bautista and San Bernardo. In *The Archaeology and Ethnohistory of the Gateway Area, Middle Rio Grande of Texas*. Report of the 1976 investigations, submitted to the National Endowment for the Humanities by The University of Texas at San Antonio.

    1977 Archaeological Investigations at the Gateway Missions. In *The Archaeology and Ethnohistory of the Gateway Area, Middle Rio Grande of Texas*. Final report to the National Endowment for the Humanities by The University of Texas at San Antonio.

    1980 *Excavations at the Alamo Shrine (Mission San Antonio de Valero)*. Special Report No. 10. Center for Archaeological Research, University of Texas at San Antonio.

    1981 *Guerrero, Coahuila, Mexico. A Guide to the Town and Missions. Guia de la Ciudad y de las Misiones*. Report No. 4. Center for Archaeological Research, The University of Texas at San Antonio, Archaeology and History of the San Juan Bautista Mission Area, Coahuila and Texas.

Hanke, Lewis

    1965 *The Spanish Struggle for Justice in the Conquest of America*. Little, Brown, Boston.

Hester, Thomas R., and Jack D. Eaton

    1982 Middle-Lower Rio Grande Archaeology. In *Borderlands Source Book*, edited by Stoddard et al., Chapter 16. University of Oklahoma Press, Norman.

Jones, Oarah L., (editor)

    1974 *The Spanish Borderlands—A First Reader*. Lorrin L. Morrison, Los Angeles.

Moorhead, Max L.

    1975 *The Presidio. Bastion of the Spanish Borderlands*. University of Oklahoma Press. Norman.

Villamarin, Juan A., and Judith E. Villamarin

    1975 *Indian Labor in Mainland Colonial Spanish America*. Occasional Papers and Monographs No. 1. Latin American Studies Program, University of Delaware, Newark.

Weddle, Robert S.

    1968a San Juan Bautista: Mother of Texas Missions. *Southwestern Historical Quarterly* 71(4):542–563.

    1968b *San Juan Bautista: Gateway to Spanish Texas*. University of Texas Press, Austin.

Weddle, Robert S., and Robert H. Thonhoff

    1976 *Drama and Conflict: The Texas Saga of 1776*. Madrona Press, Austin.

Yoakum, Henderson

    1855 *History of Texas*. Redfield, New York.

Chapter 16 ■

Anne A. Fox

The Indians at Rancho de las Cabras

When we first began archaeological investigations at the San Antonio missions in the 1960s (Greer 1967; Schuetz 1968, 1969), persistent rumors reached us of "another mission" farther south on the San Antonio River near the town of Floresville. Subsequent inquiries in the area produced reports of a site with standing walls out in the brush, and vague stories of a mission called Las Cabras. Research into local mission history soon brought us to the realization that this must be the ranch of Mission San Francisco de la Espada, which in the records had been called the Rancho de las Cabras, or the ranch of the goats. A subsequent visit to the site revealed a sizable ruin that indeed had sections of walls 2 m high still standing in a dense mesquite thicket. It had a perimeter wall with rooms built against it and an intriguing hexagonal foundation that could be the base of a defensive tower. A flurry of concern over the proposed sale of the site in 1970 was quieted when a local rancher acquired the property as part of a larger ranch, and our attention was directed to more pressing matters in San Antonio.

However, we could never entirely forget this enticing ruin and occasionally wondered what might be done to preserve it for future research. The archaeological community was delighted to hear in 1980 that the site and about 22 ha around it had been acquired by the Texas Parks and Wildlife Department. The Center for Archaeological Research at the University of Texas at San Antonio was invited to enter into a contract to conduct a series of field seasons at Las Cabras in order to define the extent of the site, to map the ruins, and to test within them to determine the sequence of their construction. Information was also to be obtained on the people who lived there, both during mission times and afterward.

We immediately embarked upon a series of five seasons at the site, spending one month each summer in test excavations and considerable additional time in research in Spanish archives and local courthouse records. Combining all of our resources, we have been able to reconstruct the following information on the history of the site.

Historical Background

The villa of San Antonio was founded on the San Antonio River in 1718 (Habig 1968:38). At first it consisted of two establishments, Mission San Antonio de Valero, sponsored by the Franciscan college of Queretaro, and the Presidio de Bexar. The settlement was enhanced in 1720 by the establishment of Mission San José y San Miguel de Aguayo by Franciscans from the College of Zacatecas (Habig 1968:83). In 1731, a group of settlers from the Canary Islands arrived and laid out a town square next to the presidio. In the same year, three additional Quereteran missions from East Texas were moved to sites downstream from the town (Habig 1968:124). There was plenty of farmland and water for all and things went well for a while as the citizens of the town and the missions were occupied with building, planting, and harvesting. In order to feed and care for the Indians brought into their establishments, each mission acquired horses, cattle, sheep, and goats, which were pastured in the lands adjacent to the mission.

By the early 1740s, the Canary Islanders began to complain that the mission livestock was trampling their fields and damaging their crops. In order to keep the peace, each mission moved its herds and flocks to ranchland at some distance from the town (Jackson 1986:38). At first, there was so much unclaimed land that no attempt was made to issue titles. However by the 1750s, numerous local military officers and some of the more ambitious civilians began to acquire large tracts of land for ranching purposes (Jackson 1986:57), and the missions had to obtain title to the lands they had been occupying. Life at the outlying ranches was made hazardous by the constant threat of raids by hostile Lipan Apache and Comanche Indians who "killed, stole, and destroyed property with impunity" (Jackson 1986:66).

When they were first established, the San Antonio missions obtained their cattle from the Quereteran missions on the Rio Grande at San Juan Bautista (Habig 1968:202.204). Mission Espada apparently began large-scale ranching early in the 1740s (Ivey 1983:24). By June 1745, the mission had already acquired 1,150 cattle, 740 sheep, 90 goats, 31 horses, and 32 oxen (Ortiz 1745:roll 9, frame

1271). It appears from oblique references in the documents and from the artifacts found on the site that actual occupation of the mission ranch may have begun sometime in the 1750s. The actual land grant to Mission Espada for the ranch has not as yet been found, but apparently it was not issued until ca. 1765 (Ivey 1983:25).

The first official mention of Las Cabras is in 1762, when Fr. Mariano Dolores (1961:259) referred to a ranch belonging to Mission Espada with "una casa de piedra," a house or structure of stone, where the tools and equipment were kept and where the families lived who cared for the ranch. At that time, the mission owned 1,272 cattle, 4,000 sheep and goats, 156 horses, and nine burros. We have not yet been able to establish whether the term "casa de piedra" could have referred to the stone walls standing at the time of the 1772 inventory (Ivey 1983:34) or to some other structure in the vicinity that has now disappeared. Since it is clear that the stone-walled rooms now visible on the site were built against the perimeter wall and were not free standing (Taylor and Fox 1985:54), these could not have been the original building.

In 1772, the administration of the Quereteran missions in Texas was turned over to the College of Zacatecas. Before the missions were officially handed over, a detailed inventory was made of all buildings and everything within them. The inventory for Mission Espada (Sáenz de Gumiel 1772:roll 15, 4224–4425) includes the first detailed account of Rancho de las Cabras. The compound was enclosed by a stone wall one vara (0.84 m) wide and three varas (2.5 m) high, which was 158 varas (131.5 m) in circumference. The wall had two entrances, one toward the river and the other toward the plain. Inside were four jacals built of upright poles with thatched roofs, one of which was sometimes used as a church or shrine. There were corrals and pens for large livestock and horses, and a small fenced area planted in corn. The inventory also contains a detailed listing of the livestock at the ranch, which included 716 horses, mules, and burros. There were about 35 pigs, 2,700 sheep and 22 goats, and miscellaneous chickens. The ranch also had eight oxen and 1,200 cattle.   Sometime between the 1772 inventory and 1793, when the mission was secularized, the ranch probably ceased to be operated by Mission Espada. Here, again, we have so far found no documentary evidence, but it served in 1778 as headquarters for a major roundup of cattle by ranchers in the area (Pacheco 1778:roll 18, frame 7). At about this same time, Fr. Morfi (n.d.:67) noted there were 26 persons living at Las Cabras.

In summary, Rancho de las Cabras operated as the ranch for Mission Espada from about 1750 until 1790. It was inhabited by families of mission Indians who were entrusted with the care of the livestock upon which the mission depended. Except for extraordinary occasions, the ranch residents were apparently left to their own devices, as long as they tended the livestock and provided the proper number of animals weekly to the mission for slaughter (Leutenegger 1976:19). Because of their relatively unsupervised situation, we have here an opportunity to examine how mission Indians would prefer to live after a period of training and indoctrination into mission life and Spanish customs. The houses they occupied, their living habits, and the tools and implements they used would be, to a certain extent, of their own choosing.

The Mission Indians

The Indians when they first came to the missions were familiar with the use of the bow and arrow, made and used stone tools and pottery, and lived by hunting, fishing, and gathering. They lived a nomadic life and seldom had more shelter than a small temporary hut (Ruecking 1953:480–498). At the mission they were introduced to new ideas such as a formal religion, permanent houses, new types of food, metal tools and cooking utensils, and the care and use of horses and firearms. How many of these new ideas would they continue to use in the relatively free environment of the ranch? Would they continue their religious worship in this setting? In order to find the answers to these questions, we must turn to the archaeological record.

Archaeological Research

Rancho de las Cabras sits on a high point of land that overlooks the San Antonio River Valley to the north, east, and south. The rolling countryside around the site is shaped by arroyos that drain into the river to the east. The fields that surround the site have now been cleared of brush, leaving the ranch site as a prominent landmark. Sandstone block walls 1½ to 2 m high remain along the north edge of an irregularly shaped compound. The ruins of a row of stone-walled rooms stand against the north wall, preserved and protected by the collapse of thick caliche roof construction and years of windblown sandy soil. At the northwest and southeast corners are the bases of defensive towers and near the northeast corner is the outline of what appears to be a small chapel, its apse to the northwest.

Each archaeological test within and around the walls has been done for a specific purpose, and units have been kept as small as possible in order to preserve the original occupation surface of the site. Each season has addressed a small list of specific questions agreed upon by the center and the Parks and Wildlife Department archaeologists. By the end of the fifth season, most of the perimeter had been tested, and a number of questions had been answered. As usual with archaeological investigations, many more questions had arisen as work progressed than could possibly be answered in the time allotted.

After the second season, it became clear that the present outline is not the original structure (Ivey 1983). Careful examination of stonework and selective excavations revealed that there have been at least two building phases at the site (see Figure 16-1). The first compound wall, which is the one described in 1772, is an uneven hexagon built of deep red sandstone. Later additions of wall extensions, towers, and the chapel are of slightly different sandstone and the workmanship is subtly different. However, from the evidence of artifacts within these additions, the newer construction must have taken place soon after 1772, perhaps as a result of the change in administration at that time.

A large area examined near the northwest corner (Ivey 1983) revealed traces of several sequences of jacal construction that existed both before and after the 1772 inventory. The location of the footings of the northwest wall that was re-

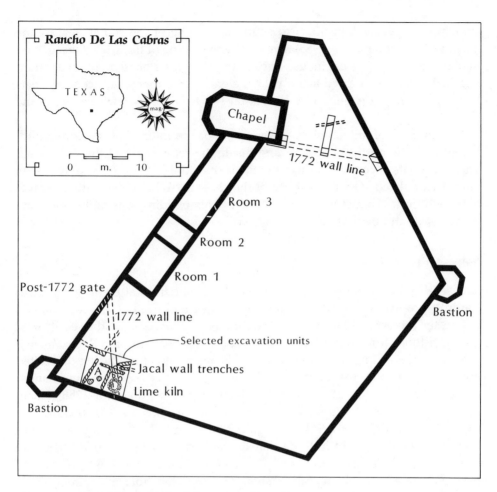

Figure 16-1. Plan of Rancho de las Cabras (near Floresville, Texas).

moved during the remodeling was also found in this unit. A kiln for making lime by burning local limestone was later built into the footing trench, probably to make lime to plaster the chapel interior, since this appears to be the only building that was plastered.

Testing at this corner also revealed the location of one of the main gates, and a complex series of trash pits outside the gate that yielded most of the material culture items from the site. The trash pits also contained a large concentration of animal bones. When the extent of this deposit was found, the excavations in this area were halted and work was concentrated on delimiting the trash disposal area, planning to return and spend a full season excavating it systematically. Unfortunately, funds for this final season are not currently available and this important investigation has not yet been done.

Testing around the south wall has indicated the presence of post holes but no further jacal structures. A careful series of trenches dug just to the original ground surface in front of the chapel (Jones and Fox 1983) revealed that there are no grave pits in this area such as are found in front of many mission churches. An excavation north to south across one of the rooms against the north wall (Taylor and Fox 1985) revealed by the dating of the artifacts recovered that the room had been in use throughout the Mission period occupation, and had been briefly used again near the end of the nineteenth century, perhaps for storage in relation to livestock-raising activities by later owners of the property.

A deep layer of animal dung covers most of the interior of the compound, except near the northwest corner and inside the rooms against the north wall. These deposits cover and protect the Spanish colonial deposits, and appear to have accumulated after the last use of the chapel. We hope that future excavations within the chapel will establish when this building was built, how long it was used, and by whom.

Indians at Las Cabras

Archaeology has demonstrated that the Indians who lived at the mission ranch continued to live in much the same way as they had lived at Mission Espada. In fact, the artifact inventories from the various field seasons could be easily mistaken for those from any mission excavation in the San Antonio River Valley.

We found evidence of a sequence of jacal construction for housing that dated both before and after the remodeling that took place after 1772. Since permanent stone Indian housing at Mission Espada was not begun until 1756 (Habig 1968:211), this sort of temporary housing would have been a logical choice for construction at the ranch. The fact that it continued to be the accepted type of housing after 1772 could indicate that the stone rooms against the north wall were inadequate for the number of people at the ranch, or it could indicate the personal preference of the inhabitants. The fact that household items were found on the floors of these jacals (Ivey 1983:Figure 1) suggests that they were not built for storage or for other ranching activities.

The living habits and food preferences of the ranch inhabitants are reflected in the artifacts that accumulated on the house floors and in the trash pits outside the gate. Sherds of bone-tempered utility wares identical to those made by the Indians before they entered the missions make up 75 percent of the ceramics. Lead-glazed and tin-glazed wares from Mexico are present in smaller amounts, along with a few sherds of oriental porcelains and French faience. The percentages and assortment do not differ perceptibly from those at the missions, with one exception. Nearly absent from the ceramic inventory are sherds of lead-glazed vessels used for the preparation of the chocolate drink enjoyed by the Franciscans and Indians on special occasions (Leutenegger 1976). Fragments of copper from various forms of cooking vessels were found, however, and some of these may represent metal versions of this type of pot.

Analysis of the faunal materials from the site indicates, as might be expected, that the Indians at the ranch relied a great deal on cattle, sheep, goats, and chickens for food. However, we also find evidence that they were hunting and fishing in the nearby vicinity, as bones of wild turkey, deer, peccary, opossum, squirrels, and cottontail rabbits are also present. Evidence of the proximity of the San Antonio River is seen in bones of alligator, turtles, and fish (McClure 1983; Steele and DeMarcay 1985).

Personal items recovered from house floors and trash pits also indicate a life-style not very different from that at the missions. To our surprise, we recovered fancy metal buckles and jewelry with faceted glass sets including rings and cru-cifixes (Ivey and Fox 1981:Table 1; Ivey 1983:Table 1). The additional recovery of a jet rosary bead (Ivey and Fox 1981:36) along with the description of one of the jacals as containing an altar and the obvious later construction of a chapel suggests that at least an outward form of religion was practiced at the site.

Other obviously Spanish items found include various fragments of bridles and other horse equipment and two branding irons (Ivey 1983:20). Spanish hardware found on the site probably came from chests or trunks used for storage.

The presence of locally made gunflints and arrow points, and numerous flakes and chips of chert possibly from their manufacture suggest that the Indians con-tinued in their knowledge and use of this basic resource throughout the Mission period. This and the continued use of Indian-made ceramics appear to be the only cultural traits that these people chose to retain from their past. This is not at all unique to the ranch population, but has also been noted in the San Antonio community (Fox 1977:14,16).

Conclusion

As a result of our investigations, we can now observe that the mission Indians who lived and worked at Rancho de las Cabras lived much as they did when at the mission. They made and used the same types of tools and ceramics, ate the same sorts of foods, and practiced at least some form of religious observa-tion. They apparently made full use of the objects and techniques provided by the Spanish, supplementing them with no more than the customary amount of their Indian ceramics and stone tools. Life at the ranch, away from direct super-vision and under the extreme stress of threat of Indian attack, might tempt Indi-ans who were a bit shakey in their indoctrination as Spanish citizens to slip back into their earlier habits. The fact that they apparently did not could be an indica-tion that only Indians of long standing and proven loyalty to the mission were chosen for this job, since it was so essential to the well-being of the mission resi-dents. It may also demonstrate the ultimate success of the missionaries' teaching in the lives of at least some of their neophytes.

References

Dolores, Fr. Mariano Francisco de los
    1961 Relación del Estado en que se hablan todas y cda una de las misiones, en el año de 1762. In *Documentos Para la Historia Eclesiástica y Civil de la Provincia de Texas o Nueva Philipinas, 1720–1779*, edited by José Purrúa Turanzas, pp. 245–275. Colección Chimalistic de Libros y Documentos Acerca de la Nueva España, vol. 12. Madrid.

Greer, John W.
1967 *A Description of the Stratigraphy, Features and Artifacts from Archeological Excavation at the Alamo.* Archeological Program Report No. 3. State Building Commission, Austin.

Fox, Anne A.
1977 *The Archaeology and History of the Spanish Governor's Palace Park.* Archaeological Survey Report No. 31. Center for Archaeological Research, University of Texas at San Antonio.

Habig, Marion A.
1968 *The Alamo Chain of Missions. A History of San Antonio's Five Old Missions.* Franciscan Herald Press, Chicago, Ill.

Ivey, James E.
1983 *Archaeological Testing at Rancho de las Cabras, 41 WN 30, Wilson County, Second Season.* Archaeological Survey Report No. 121. Center for Archaeological Research, University of Texas at San Antonio.

Ivey, James E., and Anne A. Fox
1981 *Archaeological Survey and Testing at Rancho de las Cabras, Wilson County, Texas.* Archaeological Survey Report No. 104. Center for Archaeological Research, University of Texas at San Antonio.

Jackson, Jack
1986 *Los Mesteños, Spanish Ranching in Texas, 1721–1821.* Texas A&M University Press, College Station.

Jones, Courtenay J., and Anne A. Fox
1983 *Archaeological Testing at Rancho de las Cabras, Wilson County, Texas, Third Season.* Archaeological Survey Report No. 123. Center for Archaeological Research, University of Texas at San Antonio.

Leutenegger, Fr. Benedict, O. F. M. (translator)
1976 *Guidelines for a Texas Mission. Instructions for the Missionary of a Mission Concepción in San Antonio.* Old Spanish Missions Research Library at San José Mission. San Antonio, Texas.

McClure, William
1983 Appendix. Provenience of Faunal Material. In *Archaeological Testing at Rancho de las Cabras, Wilson County, Texas, Third Season,* by Courtenay J. Jones and Anne A. Fox, pp. 54–68. Archaeological Survey Report No. 123. Center for Archaeological Research, University of Texas at San Antonio.

Morfi, Fr. Juan Augustin de
n.d. Excerpt from Viaje de Indios y Diario del Nuevo Mexico. Translated by R. E. McDonald. San Antonio Conservation Society files, San Antonio, Texas.

Ortiz, Fr. Francisco
1745 *Razón de la Visita a las Misiones de la Provincia de Texas,* vol. 1, edited by Vargas Rea, Mexico. Microfilm. Bexar Archives, Barker History Center, University of Texas at Austin.

Pacheco, Don Rafael M.
1787 Boundaries of the Roundup of 1787. Microfilm. Bexar Archives. Barker History Center, University of Texas at Austin.

Ruecking, Frederick Jr.
1953 The Economic System of the Coahuiltecan Indians of Southern Texas and Northeastern Mexico. *Texas Journal of Science* 5(4):480–497.

Sáenz de Gumiel, Juan Joseph
1772 Relación del Estado en que se hablan todas y cada una de las misiones, en el año de 1762. In *Documentos Para la Historia Eclesiástica y Civil de la Provincia de Texas o Nueva Philipinas, 1720–1779,* edited by José Purrúa Turanzas, pp. 245–275. Colección Chimalistic de Libros y Documentos Acerca de la Nueva España, vol. 12, Madrid.

Schuetz, Mardith K.

  1968 *The History and Archeology of Mission San Juan Capistrano, San Antonio, Texas*, vol. 1: *Historical Documentation and Description of Structures*. Archeological Program Report No. 11. State Building Commission, Austin.

  1969 *The History and Archeology of Mission San Juan Capistrano, San Antonio, Texas*, vol. 2: *Description of the Artifacts and Ethnohistory of the Coahuiltecan Indians*. Archeological Program Report No. 12. State Building Commission, Austin.

Steele, D. Gentry, and Gary B. DeMarcay

  1985 Appendix C. Analysis of Faunal Remains Recovered during the 1984 Excavations at Rancho de las Cabras. In *Archaeological Survey and Testing at Rancho de las Cabras, 41 WB 30, Wilson County, Texas, Fifth Season*, by Anna J. Taylor and Anne A. Fox. pp. 62–75. Archaeological Survey Report No. 144. Center for Archaeological Research, University of Texas at San Antonio.

Taylor, Anna J., and Anne A. Fox

  1985 *Archaeological Survey and Testing at Rancho de las Cabras, 41 WN 30, Wilson County, Texas, Fifth Season*. Archaeological Survey Report No. 144. Center for Archaeological Research, University of Texas at San Antonio.

Chapter 17 ■

James E. Corbin

Spanish–Indian Interaction on the Eastern Frontier of Texas

The first serious Spanish move into the eastern frontier regions of Texas came in 1690–1691 with the establishment of Missions San Francisco de los Tejas (Castañeda 1936:1:351–353) and Santisimo Nombre de Maria (Castañeda 1936:1:367-368) on the Neches River (see Figure 12-2). This move, primarily one of missionary zeal, soon failed owing to environmental hardships, an epidemic, and the recalcitrance of the local Hasinai Indians (Castañeda 1936:1:373). While there, the Spanish came to realize that the French had preceded them, and that the well-entrenched and well-adapted agricultural aboriginal population of eastern Texas could and would do pretty much as they pleased. Returning with more vigor in 1714–1716 (Castañeda 1936:2:55–60), the Spanish established a line of six missions and two presidios stretching from the Neches River to Robeline, Louisiana. In 1719, a French force moved into the eastern portion of this area, and the Spanish retreated (Castañeda 1936:2:115).

Although the basic plan was probably not well thought out, the Spanish returned again to East Texas in 1721–1722 with a larger force (Castañeda 1936:2:149), determined to stay and to keep the French out of their territory. With some minor shifts on the landscape, all of the original six missions (San

Francisco de los Tejas, Concepcíon Guadalupe, San José de los Nazonis. Dolores de los Ais, and San Miguel) and the two presidios (los Tejas and los Adaes) were reestablished (Figure 12-2; Castañeda 1936:2:148–159). The easternmost presidio, Los Adaes, and the attendant civil settlement were designated the capital of the province.

In 1729–1730, for various reasons, the Spanish abandoned Presidio de los Tejas, and the three western missions were summarily moved to the vicinity of the presidio and mission complex established at San Antonio in 1718 (Castañeda 1936:2:240). Even with the intermediate location of San Antonio, supplying the eastern outpost of Spanish Texas from home was no easy task. Faced with hunger, worn-out and broken equipment, the easterners had to fend for themselves and did not always follow the direction and rules sent out to them.

Eventually, with the cessation of French and Spanish hostilities in 1763 (Hackett 1931:1), the missions, presidio, and the civil settlement of Los Adaes were ordered abandoned. The civilian population of the capital was ordered to San Antonio, although eventually most, if not all of them, returned to their East Texas homes in 1779 under the leadership of Don Antonio Gil Y'Barbo. Denied Los Adaes and Ais as possible resettlement locations, the Adaesaños settled at Nacogdoches near the abandoned Mission Guadalupe.

During the Spanish tenure in eastern Texas, the Hasinai Caddo and their neighbors, particularly the western groups, had become very powerful, primarily as a result of their interaction with the intense horse, deer hide, and bear grease trade (Usner 1985:78) that supported French and Indian economics in Louisiana. Already well entrenched in the region, the agricultural Caddo of Spanish Texas had made a significant adaptation to the local environment. Relying on both the New World cultigens and the rich natural resources of the region, the dispersed villages of the Hasinai had little, if anything, to fear from the Spanish military, no need to trade with the Spanish, and no reason to heed the Spanish call to God. To be sure, as shown below, the Caddos had every reason to fear the proselytizing of the Spanish padres, and resisted it to the point that (as far as records show) none were Christianized during the Spanish sojourn except *in articulo mortis*.

The Documentary Evidence

One only has to look at a few of the extant contemporary documents that relate to eastern Texas to realize some aspects of the Spanish failure to adapt to certain aspects of East Texas environmental and cultural milieu. In part, some of this can be blamed on Zacatecan conservatism and possibly, the military reluctance to be there. The fact that many of those who came to the eastern frontier had come from a different environment and a confrontation with Indian societies much different from the ones they encountered may have also contributed to the malaise that was often evident to the military inspections.

In terms of the placement of the missions, one wonders how much influence the military leaders of the founding entradas had on the poor (at least from the Caddo point of view) placement of the missions within the Caddo settlements.

Of the location of Presidio de los Tejas, Peña (Forrestal 1934:59) notes that it "will occupy a good site on a hill that overlooks the surrounding country and all year round can count on water from a creek which passes close by." At Nacogdoches, Father Muñoz (Leutenegger 1980) says it is "situated on a small hill close to a creek." La Fora (Kinnard 1958:166), writing in 1767, remarks that "the mission of Los Ais is situated on a small hill near an arroyo." Muñoz, on reaching Mission San Miguel near Presidio los Adaes, describes the mission as being "situated at the peak of a small hill." Although the locations were within the dispersed villages of the local Caddo group, it seems the actual location was not one that would induce the Caddo to occupy the immediate locality.

Writing to Father Abasolo in 1749, Father Ygnacio Ciprián relates:

> When the mission [Nacogdoches] was founded in the middle of these farms, stretching from north to south for 10 leagues, the task was not so difficult for the missionary, but the Indians [after raids by the Bedai] . . . then went north and abandoned the mission, three leagues distant from the first farm and 20 leagues away through the mountains [*Ciprián* 1749:45–46].

Not only were the mission locations not enticing to the Indians, but apparently they were not conducive to Spanish subsistence as well. As early as 1727, Rivera recommended that Los Adaes be moved to a location where food could be cultivated (Magnaghi 1984:170). The Spanish, although noting the dispersed nature of the Indian rancherías, obviously (or apparently) failed to recognize the reason for the particular configuration. Tied to an agricultural experience that depended on irrigation, the Spanish, in discussing the good volume of many Texas streams, also note that their steep banks were not conducive to irrigation. Thomas Philipe de Winthuysen, interim governor of Texas from 1741 to 1744 (Magnaghi 1984:178), commented that "only at intervals are there some cleared level areas where the cultivation of corn is possible," and "the crops are seasonal as there is no source to develop irrigation." Thus Winthuysen continued the practice of his predecessors of importing corn, beans, and other foodstuff from the French at Natchitoches. "A deep creek, which never runs dry" notes Father Solís in 1767, "supplies the mission [Ais] with water but as its banks are very high it cannot be used for irrigation purposes" (Forrestal 1931:34). Interestingly, Father Solís also describes a garden "near the creek" that is "watered by hand."

That, of course, is where the Caddo fields were, and although the Caddo depended on rain as well, they planted two crops of corn (Swanton 1942:130): one at the end of April (after their fields could not be inundated) and another variety, obviously drought resistant, late. Even though this scheme generally provided the Caddos with an adequate food supply, they always maintained a two-year seed supply to safeguard against the more or less triennial drought. That the Spanish were *not* growing enough food for themselves is readily apparent. Father Muñoz (Leutenegger 1980) said that at Ais the supply of corn in the best years never exceeded three or four almudes and "due to seasonal reverses, it [farming] is a waste of work." In describing the problems of reducing the Indians, Father Ciprián reminds his superiors that they "plant their crops and reap abundantly, so much so that the presidio generally barters corn and other produce."

In 1767, a Frenchman, Pierre de Pagès (Steel 1985:4), came to Los Adaes during a trip around the world. On his first day there he traded clothes for corn, which he was able to obtain "only in very small quantities." He was assured that the settlement was absolutely destitute of corn. In describing the village environs, de Pagès said "the soil is without water and very dry, which coupled with the laziness of the inhabitants, often makes them lack food, which is limited to corn."

If the Spanish failed to provide food for their bodies, they also (from their point of view) failed to provide spiritual food for the various Caddo entities. Governor Winthuysen, as well as other governors and various inspectors, noted that "they [the Hasinai] are irreducible to political life and submitting themselves to the missions" and none of the missions "has had a single Indian reduced to the mission" (Magnaghi 1984:175). The reasons for this are twofold, as explained by Father Ciprián in 1749. First, the Indians in other areas had "been conquered as a republic by force of arms and . . . brought under civil powers" and, second, the Spanish could not "maintain them, for all of them plant their crops and reap abundantly."

Obviously, Father Ciprián understood the secular reasons for the lack of Indians at the missions, but these were only part of the problem, as Ciprián himself noted. Baptism *in articulo mortis*, that is, at the point of death, was the only way to obtain Christian souls, so that most Indian parents "generally refuse to give their consent because many are persuaded that baptism kills them." Trapped in their ideology, the priests also refrained from baptizing others for fear of apostasy.

This is not to say that there was little interaction between the Spanish and the Caddo—on the contrary, although it was not the interaction that the Spanish had envisioned. Father Solís (Forrestal 1931:34), during his visit to the Ais Mission, noted that "the Indians steal these [animals] whenever the opportunity offers. The bulls, cows, and calves are used for food, while the horses and mules are traded to the French."

At a later date, de Pagès relates:

> During my stay at the settlement [San Antonio], the Indians whose villages we had passed at San Pedro [one of the largest Caddo villages, located near the Neches River] became embroiled in a conflict with the new governor, who wanted to hinder their trade with the French at Natchitoches. They came and drove off a herd of about four hundred horses. The garrison took to arms, mounted, and followed the savages' trail for a hundred leagues without catching them; then they returned without incident to San Antonio. When they were fording the Guadalupe River, another party of the same Indians, hidden in the thickets, attacked the Spanish troops. The Spaniards defended themselves bravely for three hours, but they finally yielded to numbers, and they lost about one hundred and fifty horses and many supplies [Steele 1985:17].

Although de Pagès had noted earlier that the very industrious Caddos "raise horses for their transportation" (Steele 1985:12), it would appear that stealing horses to trade to the French was also one of their more lucrative endeavors.

The Archaeological Data

To a certain extent, Spanish expectations and inflexibility in terms of their response to the cultural and environmental situations they encountered in eastern Texas can be further demonstrated in the archaeological record. At the present time we know the location of Presidio los Adaes, and its attendant Mission San Miguel, and Missions Dolores de los Ais and San José de los Nasonis. Extensive excavations have been conducted at the presidio site (Gregory 1973, 1980) and at the site of Mission Dolores (Corbin et al. 1980). Limited excavation at the San Miguel site and controlled surface collections at San José have complemented the excavations at the other localities.

All three mission locations (Corbin et al. 1980: Figure 2; Gregory 1973: Figure 4) match the general description of locations derived from the extant Spanish documents; that is, they are all located on small hills or knolls in or adjacent to a floodplain. In each case, the location is next to a stream, usually with a smaller stream nearby; the hills or knolls are all lower extensions of more extensive upland areas. Given the topography of the locations and the placement of the mission complexes, defense rather than proselytizing seems to have been the primary concern. Although the missions were located within the area of the local dispersed Caddoan village, none of the locations are places suited to support the Indian-based community that the Spanish hoped to entice to the location. The similarity of topographic and spatial location of the mission complexes strongly suggests that the Spanish had a particular topographic model in mind that dictated the location of the complex, irrespective of the inappropriateness and/or ineffectiveness of the location. Indeed, these sites were maintained for the entire period of Spanish occupancy, in one case even after the local Caddo population had moved completely away from the mission environs.

Excavations (Corbin et al. 1980) conducted during several field seasons at the site of Mission Dolores de los Ais revealed at least two other structural mind sets that accompanied the Spanish into eastern Texas. Although approximately two-thirds of the Mission Dolores complex has been destroyed by a state highway and other construction activities in the past, the archaeological excavations eventually revealed portions of the jacal perimeter wall, portions of interior jacal structures, some large pits, and a well. These walls were constructed by first excavating a setting trench into which large posts were driven at more or less regular intervals. The spaces between the large posts were filled in with smaller poles, and the setting trench was filled in. Finally, horizontal lathes were nailed or lashed to the vertical members and the wall was then plastered with adobe mud.

Although the particular orientation of the walls (Corbin et al. 1980:Figures 17–19) was not initially considered to be particularly significant, a comparison of these wall alignments with those of other frontier missions of the same time period revealed identical orientations. At Mission Rosario (Gilmore 1974:Figure 7), 500 km to the south, and at Mission San Xavier (Gilmore 1969:Figure 6), 500 km to the west, we find the identical northeast-southwest orientation. Therefore, in three widely scattered locations with very different environmental situations, the Spanish constructed essentially the same edifices. In addition, the excavation of wells at Rosario (Gilmore 1974:Figure 6), Dolores (Corbin et al. 1980:Figure 43) and Los Adaes (H. P. Gregory, personal communication 1984) revealed that the Spanish used the same well excavation techniques in each locality. In each case, they excavated the wells as a series of stepped-down holes for the first one to two meters before sinking the main, parallel-sided shaft down to the aquifer. Although these kinds of mental templates are not in themselves surprising, they do serve to indicate that the Spanish were as rigid in dealing with the local environment as they were with the indigenous inhabitants of the area.

Nevertheless, the Spanish were not entirely inflexible in their behavior, particularly when their livelihood and physical well-being were at stake. Although there are no definite records of Indians living for any significant period, if at all, at any of the missions, most of the thousands of ceramic artifacts recovered at the site of Mission Dolores were sherds from vessels of local aboriginal manufacture. Sherds from plate rims and ring-footed flatware, but of obvious Caddoan manufacture, seem to indicate that someone was commissioning aboriginal manufacture or that local potters were creating European-style forms to enhance trade.

In addition, sherds of French faience and Chinese porcelain significantly outnumbered sherds of Mexican majolica. Only sherds from English creamware and salt-glazed vessels occurred less frequently. Obviously, the padres, as well as any other Spanish inhabitants of the mission, had to rely on sources other than those from home to supply the various utilitarian ceramic vessels needed for day-to-day living. Although trade for food was allowed with the French, most assuredly this concession did not apply to hard goods.

Conclusions

The data discussed above have provided some insight into the nature of Spanish and Indian interaction on the eastern frontier of Spanish Texas. The documents illustrate clearly some of the reasons that the Spanish were essentially unsuccessful (at least initially) in adapting to and controlling the environment of eastern Texas. In addition, the Spanish relationship with the aboriginal population was sabotaged by their rigid and conservative ideology and their worldview; this was true not only of the Hasinai, but the French as well.

We must be careful at this point to understand the nature of the documents we have used to analyze the Spanish-Indian interface in eastern Texas. For the most part, these documents deal with ecclesiastical and/or political matters. Few speak to the life and nature of the soldiers and the civilians. One suspects that something very different was going on at that social level, that in fact the Spanish were becoming Adaesaños. What speaks to that most eloquently is that most of the people living in eastern Texas in 1773 did not want to leave, and indeed, eventually returned to their homeland. That Nacogdoches went on to become an important civil settlement during the late colonial period without the hardnosed overseers of the secular and ecclesiastical hierarchies supports that view. By this later date, Hasinai- and Spanish-derived inhabitants had melded to create a new culture. One observer noted in 1804 that so many different Indian languages could be heard in Nacogdoches that one might wonder if this was not the location of the original Tower of Babel. Only the ensuing Anglo invasion and annexation of Texas would stop the process once and for all.

References

Castañeda, Carlos E.
  1936a *Our Catholic Heritage in Texas, 1519–1936*, vol. 1, *The Mission Era: The Finding of Texas, 1519–1693*. Von Boeckmann-Jones, Austin.
  1936b *Our Catholic Heritage in Texas, 1519–1936*, vol. 2: *The Mission Era: The Winning of Texas, 1693–1731*. Von Boeckmann-Jones, Austin.
Corbin, James E., Thomas C. Alex, and Arlan Kalina
  1980 *Mission Dolores de los Ais*. Papers in Anthropology No. 2. Stephen F. Austin State University, Nacogdoches.
Ciprián, Fr. Ygnacio Antonio
  1749 Letter to Fr. Juan Abasolo dated October 27, 1749; Archivo San Francisco el Grande, Mexico, vol. 5. pp. 41–47. University of Texas Archives, Austin.
Forrestal, Rev. Peter P.
  1931 *The Solís Diary of 1767*. Preliminary studies of the Texas Catholic Historical Society. Vol. I, No. 6. Austin.
  1934 *Peña's Diary of the Aguayo Expedition*. Preliminary studies of the Texas Catholic Historical Society. Vol. II, No. 7, Austin.
Gilmore, Kathleen
  1969 *The San Xavier Missions: A Study in Historical Site Identification*. Archaeological Program Report No. 16. State Building Commission, Austin.
  1974 *Mission Rosario, Archeological Investigation 1973*. Archeological Report 14, Pt. 2. Texas Parks and Wildlife Department, Parks Division, Historic Sites and Restoration Branch, Austin.
Gregory, H. F.
  1973 *Eighteenth-Century Caddoan Archeology: A Study in Models and Interpretation*. Ph.D. dissertation, unpublished manuscript on file at Southern Methodist University, Dallas.
  1980 *Presidio de Nuestra Señora de Pilar de los Adaes*. Excavations 1979. Williamson Museum, Northwestern Louisiana State University, Natchitoches.
Hackett, Charles W.
  1931 *Picardo's Treatise on the Limits of Louisiana and Texas*, vol. 1. University of Texas, Austin.
Kinnard, Lawrence (translator)
  1958 *The Frontiers of New Spain, Nicolas de LaFora's Description, 1766–1768*. Quivera Society Publications XIII, Berkeley.
Leutenegger, Benedict, O. F. M. (translator)
  1980 Letter from Fr. Pedro Muñoz and Fr. Joseph Calahora, October 31, 1727. In Corbin et al., *Mission Dolores de los Ais*. Papers in Anthropology No. 2. Stephen F. Austin State University, Nacogdoches.
Magnaghi, Russell M.
  1984 Texas as Seen by Governor Winthuysen, 1741–1744. *Southwestern Historical Quarterly* 88(2):167–180.
Steele, Corinna
  1985 A Journey through Texas in 1767. *El Companario. Texas Old Missions and Restoration Association*. 16(1):1–28.

Swanton, John R.
1942 *Source Material on the History and Ethnology of the Caddo Indians*. Bureau of American Ethnology Bulletin 132. Washington, D.C.
Usner, Daniel H., Jr.
1985 "The Deerskin Trade in French Louisiana." In *Proceedings of the Tenth Meeting of the French Colonial Society*, edited by Philip P. Boucher. University Press of America, Boston.

Chapter 18 ■

Solveig A. Turpin

The Iconography of Contact: Spanish Influences in the Rock Art of the Middle Rio Grande

The area surrounding the confluences of the Devils and Pecos rivers with the Rio Grande is included within the vast stretch of arid lands in the southwestern United States and northern Mexico variously described as a cultural sink (Newcomb 1956; Swanton 1924), an ethnographic void (Campbell 1972), and the great despoblado or uninhabited zone of Spanish Colonial times (Daniel 1955). Two historical factors produced this perception: First, early European travelers rarely traversed this area, and so most of their observations refer to the periphery rather than the core. Second, since the mid-nineteenth century, the area has been cut by an international boundary, and considerably more research has been carried out north of the Rio Grande, skewing interpretations (Thomas N. Campbell, personal communication 1988). Although the Native American presence in the region during historic times is tangentially documented in ethnohistoric sources beginning in the sixteenth century (Griffen 1969; Hammond and Rey 1966; Schroeder and Matson 1965), archaeologically it is manifested only in one rock shelter reported in the 1940s (Kirkland 1942), by scattered metal arrowpoints (Jackson n.d., Parsons 1962), and by 15 rock art panels that show evidence of European contact or display strong affinities with Plains Indian pictography.

The Spanish expeditions of the sixteenth and seventeenth centuries found little of value in the desert lands bordering the Rio Grande. Subsequent entradas were primarily retaliatory, incited by attacks on villages and ranches in Coahuila. Thus, these accounts are more often devoted to recounting Spanish political and military actions than describing the native peoples and their environment. Nevertheless, the ethnohistoric accounts are the best context for the analysis of the historic rock art during a period of massive displacement of native populations. The advent of the Plains Indians is chronicled, the expansion and retraction of Spanish influence can be traced, climatic and environmental conditions can be inferred, and a chronology of the rock art can be derived from subject matter and style.

The Lower Pecos River region is most often defined by the extent of the Archaic age Pecos River pictograph style and by the commonality of cultural materials found in dry rock shelter deposits. Now an arid rangeland cut by canyons tributary to the three major rivers, this semidesert supported a continuous human occupation for over 10,000 years. The overwhelming majority of archaeological investigations in the past 50 years concentrated on the well-preserved Archaic age material culture and art, to the neglect of the later periods. Three of the regionally defined pictograph styles, all postdating the Pecos River style, possibly reflect prehistoric episodes of cultural change, but their origins remain problematical. The historic rock art, however, is similar to that distributed over a great expanse of North America during the upheavals produced by contact with an alien culture. Thus, 15 historic rock art panels constitute a study unit defined by their geographic location within or adjacent to the Lower Pecos cultural area (Figure 18-1) rather than the art defining the region, as is the case with the Pecos River style.

The Historic Period in the Lower Pecos River Region

World and continent-wide politics undoubtedly shaped the course of history in the Lower Pecos River region, but historians and archeologists have concentrated on the more abundant sources of information generated by missions, presidios, and settled communities surrounding the despoblado. As the first detailed regional summary of contact and colonization (see also Weddle 1976), the following chronology treats only specific events of direct local effect. The differing opinions of the various chroniclers and interpreters often cannot be reconciled from the terse or obtuse accounts of Spanish diarists. Omitted are the reconstructions of Cabeza de Vaca's route from the Texas coast to western Mexico in 1535 that placed him in the area of interest, as recent interpretations suggest a more southerly passage (Campbell and Campbell 1981; Chipman 1987; Johnson 1986).

The Spanish Era

News of the effects of Spanish colonization probably reached the Lower Pecos long before any formal contact, carried by refugees from disease and oppression in northern Mexico (Griffen 1969). Slavers, who naturally left no account of their travels, may have penetrated the desert, seeking laborers for the mines and fields (John 1975:33; Schroeder and Matson 1965:7). Espejo's exploration of the pueblo country and buffalo plains in 1582–1583 crossed the northern periphery of the Lower Pecos region, recording the Jumano use of the area between La Junta and central Texas (Bolton 1908; Hammond and Rey 1966). The well-traveled Jumano would have had ample opportunity to pass information to the Lower Pecos people. Espejo's accounts of valuable ores and settled villages may well have fueled the ambitions of the first Spaniard to cross the middle Rio Grande in search of the Pecos River—Gaspar Castaño de Sosa (Hammond and Rey 1966; Schroeder and Matson 1965).

Technically, the historic period in the Lower Pecos begins in 1590 when, under pressure from the viceroy to discontinue his formerly lucrative slaving enterprises, Castaño, then lieutenant governor and captain general of Nuevo León, conceived a plan to restore his wealth by colonizing New Mexico (Hammond and Rey 1966:29–30; John 1975:33). Without permission from the Crown, Castaño left Monclova (Villa Almaden) (Figure 18-1) at the head of an expedition composed of 160 to 170 people, native interpreters, at least 10 ox carts, and herds of cattle; their goal was the Pecos Pueblo. Crossing the Rio Grande (Bravo) near present-day Del Rio (Figure 18-1), the caravan fell prey to the rugged terrain of the Lower Pecos, wandering between the Devils (Rio de las Lajas) and Pecos (Rio Salado) rivers for 26 days, searching for access to the river they thought was a highway to the Pueblos (Hammond and Rey 1966:249–256; Schroeder and Matson 1965:49).

Castaño's first mention of encounters with native groups north of the Rio Grande comes well into the journey. Near present-day Sheffield (Figure 18-1) the scouts reported coming upon people of the Tepelguan (Schroeder and Matson 1965:50–51) or Depesguan (Hammond and Rey 1966:256) nation who received them well. Both translators of the Castaño journal suggest these people may have been Jumanos (Schroeder and Matson 1965:51) or Jumano Apaches (Hammond and Rey 1966:133, 253), the same group recorded by Espejo in the general vicinity. Increasingly frequent encounters with other natives whose language was unintelligible to Castaño's interpreters also introduced the Spanish to the dog as a beast of burden. The use of the travois and the language difficulties led Schroeder and Matson (1965:56) to suggest that the caravan had met with the southern Apache. This interpretation would place the Apache here at a very early date, far sooner than actually documented by Spanish accounts.

Although Castaño's is the first recorded entrada to follow the Pecos River north from the Rio Grande, his knowledge of the route to the Rio Grande may have been gained from prior slaving expeditions (John 1975:33; Schroeder and Matson 1965:7). Thus, the absence of reference to native groups along the Rio Grande, Devils, and lower Pecos rivers could well reflect the range of Indian experience with the Spanish. If Castaño was financing his expedition by capturing slaves along the way, as alleged by the viceroy and Morlete, his pursuer (Hammond and Rey 1966:300–302; John 1975:34), he would wisely omit any mention of the crime. In addition, the sight, sound, and smell of a wagon train as large

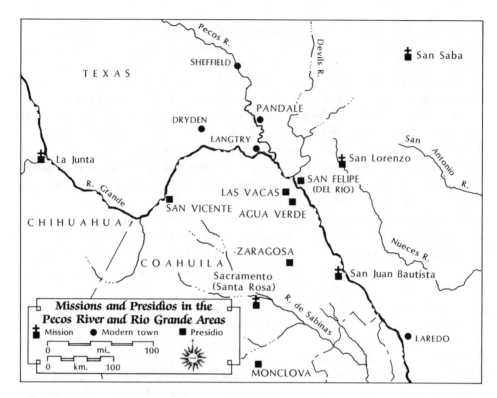

Figure 18-1. Map of the Lower Pecos River region.

as Castaño's would undoubtedly intimidate the native people, even if unfamiliar with the consequences of contact with the slavers.

Although Castaño was tracked to the Pecos pueblos, arrested, returned to Mexico, and exiled to the Philippines where he met his death, his trip illustrated to the Spanish the unsympathetic nature of the Lower Pecos. Missions established by Father Juan Larios for the natives of northern Mexico in the 1670s lasted but a few years (Steck 1932). By 1674, smallpox was already rampant among tribes listed by the missionaries as the Boboles, Guyquechales, Tiltiqui, and Mayhuam. Father Larios sent Brother Manuel de la Cruz across the Rio Grande in an attempt to locate and bring errant tribesmen fleeing from the epidemic back to the mission at Santa Rosa de Santa Maria on the Rio de las Sabinas. He found them at "a mountain range which the Indians called Dacate"; Steck (1932:10) interprets this sierra as the hills bordering the Devils River (see also Daniel 1955:82). When an estimated 180 unnamed hostiles amassed to assault Brother Manuel, the Boboles and Guyquechales united 147 warriors to protect the Spanish emissary. His account of the battle gives one of the rare descriptions of warrior dress and band size. "All came prepared for battle, well provided with arrows, with only a breechcloth of shammy skin over their privy parts and a large one of hide, over arms and chest many strips of red and yellow and white; on their head some had wreaths of mesquite leaves, others wreaths of *estofiate silvestre*, and over these wreaths some beautiful feathers." (Steck 1932:11). Once the enemy was routed, Brother Manuel led his charges, a total of 673 persons, back south of the Rio Grande, amassing others as he returned to the mission Santa Rosa.

The following year, 1675, Fernando del Bosque, accompanied by Father Larios, led an exploratory mission across the Rio Grande, heading for the "Sierra Dacate y Yacasole" (Bolton 1908:297). Bolton (1908:297) identifies Yacasole as Anacacho Mountain, southeast of modern Brackettville. Steck (1932:24) reiterates his opinion that Dacate refers to the Devils River region, assuming that Bosque eventually reached the Pecos River, which he mistook for the Rio Grande. Many of the tribes named by Bosque, such as the Bacoras, Guyquechales, Manosprietas, and Yoricas, are later found in the Guerrero (San Juan Bautista) mission records, southeast of the Lower Pecos region (Campbell 1979) (Figure 18-1).

Although Father Larios's experience with the native people was undoubtedly invaluable, Bosque omits any reference to the missions and missionaries even when his expedition passed through abandoned San Ildefonso, its grass structures still standing. However, he does describe vegetation, list the names of native groups, and describe some of their hunting practices and their population movements. The mobility of northern Mexican populations is reflected in the band compositions given by Bosque (Bolton 1908:306–307). The ratios of men to women and children are highly variable because segments of the population were often dispersed in search of food, hunting bison, or traveling for unspecified reasons.

The Great Pueblo revolts of 1680 turned the brunt of Apache force southward in search of horses to steal and communities to pillage. Mendoza's 1683–1684 expedition from El Paso del Norte to the vicinity of San Angelo in response to Jumano requests for aid against the Apache (Bolton 1908:313–343) probably touched upon the northern fringes of the Lower Pecos, his return route crossing the Pecos River in the vicinity of Sheffield, Texas (Williams 1962). LaSalle's landing on the Texas coast in 1684 and his search for the Mississippi drew Spanish attention eastward. In 1689, the most famous Jumano chief, Juan Sabeata, and his Cíbolo colleagues, reported the French presence along the Rio Grande, 67 leagues (280 km) below La Junta (Hackett 1926:257–267), which would place them in the area of modern Del Rio (Daniel 1955:89) or Langtry (Weddle 1973:166 n.). This news intensified Spanish efforts to locate and expel the intruders, leading them to seek the demented Frenchman, Jean Gery, on the fringes of the Lower Pecos at the mountain called Zacazol (Hackett 1931:143). Among the native groups assembled there were the Yorica observed by Bosque in the same area 10 years before (Bolton 1908:356).

Between 1683 and 1693, several lists of tribes living in and around the Lower Pecos region were compiled. In 1683, Juan Sabeata gave the Spanish governor in El Paso the names of 36 groups with whom he and his people traded between their home at La Junta and east Texas (Hackett 1931:136–137). Mendoza described 19 groups that accompanied him to the buffalo plains and 36 groups whom they awaited in camp (Bolton 1908:339–340). In 1693, Marin arranged his list geographically, citing 76 groups living between Durango and La Junta, including those Retana identified as going to the mouth of the Pecos for winter bison hunts; 54 groups that lived north of the Rio Grande between Texas and New Mexico; and 27 groups on the Rio Grande above La Junta and extending westward into Sonora and Sinaloa (Hackett 1926:393–396). Griffen (1969:Appendix 1) summarizes the tribes referenced in northern Mexican documents for about the same time period. All these groups are extremely difficult to fix in space, their names are often given in Spanish, and they seem to include tribes that had been eradicated by the time of reporting (Griffen 1969:Appendix 4). Their utility lies in demonstrating that the despoblado was not lightly occupied and, that by the end of the seventeenth century, the Apaches had arrived, harrying the other native groups and accelerating population movements begun by the Spanish (Hackett 1926:395).

Subsequently, the many missionary, military, and colonizing expeditions that emanated from San Juan Bautista, the gateway mission, headed east to more fertile fields for conversion and as a barrier to French expansion. The pueblo country of New Mexico was reached through La Junta (Figure 18-1), the confluence of the Mexican Rio Conchos and the Rio Grande, thus passing south and west of the Lower Pecos River region. The vast intervening area became the despoblado, or uninhabited region, unfit for Spanish colonization (Daniel 1955). By the inception of the eighteenth century, the Rio Grande between San Juan Bautista and La Junta was dominated by Apaches who raided the settlements and retreated to their bases in the wilderness. In response, the Spanish sporadically retaliated with military force in a vain attempt to pacify the region. One such expedition took place at an unspecified date early in the eighteenth century, when Don Diego Ramon, pursuing raiders of San Juan Bautista, crossed the hills called Yacatsol, reaching a wide plain and beyond to the Pecos River (Bolton 1908:297 n.; Weddle 1968:71). This is undoubtedly the same Yacasole mentioned by the Bosque expedition of 1675 (Bolton 1908:297 n.), also rendered as Sacatsol (Bolton 1908:357), and the Zacazol where the Spanish met the demented Frenchman, Jean Gery during the LaSalle turmoil (Hackett 1926:143).

In 1729, Jose de Berroterán was sent on a punitive mission to avenge victims of hostile raids across the Rio Grande. He was also to explore likely sites for a new presidio that might serve as a deterrent to the continual harassment of the colonists of northern Mexico. When warned not to harm the peaceful Cíbolos, friend of the Spanish, Berroterán replied he had never heard of such a nation (Weddle 1968:200). The Rio Grande for 50 leagues above San Juan Bautista was occupied by Apaches, Jumanos, and Pelones (Weddle 1968:200), all considered fierce and hostile. However, Berroterán's sole encounter with natives took place south of the Rio Grande when he came across friendly bison-hunting Pacuaches. Eventually defeated by the lack of water and the harsh terrain, Berroterán returned unsuccessful, having penetrated perhaps as far as modern-day Dryden (Castañeda 1936:336–345; Daniel 1955:168; Weddle 1968:196–204). His report failed to impress the authorities who sent Governor Blas de la Garza Falcon on a similar expedition in 1735 (Castañeda 1938:204–208,

Daniel 1955:174–177). His chief objective, to find a suitable location for the new presidio, was fulfilled on the San Diego River, 24 km south of Del Rio (Figure 18-1). As a corollary, the governor sent his son, Miguel, on a scouting mission to confirm Berroterán's reports of the impassable terrain north of the Rio Grande. After terrible hardship, traveling through deep snow, the younger Garza Falcon reached either the area of present-day Dryden (Castañeda 1938:206) or the Pandale crossing of the Pecos (Weddle 1968:209 n.) (Figure 18-1) where his men found a wooden cross erected atop a hill, a reminder of some prior entrada.

Although Governor Garza Falcon died a few days after his return from this expedition, his recommendations were followed and construction of the presidio of Sacramento began on the San Diego River in 1737 (Daniel 1955:178). Short-lived, prior to its completion, the site was moved 50 leagues south to the Santa Rosa valley in 1739, but it can be assumed that the area to the north was explored by soldiers stationed at Sacramento (Figure 18-1).

The futility of trekking through the rugged terrain of the Lower Pecos confirmed by Garza Falcon's reconnaissance, the next explorations for a route to the western Presidio del Norte in 1747 took a three-pronged approach. Pedro Rábago y Terán stayed south of the Rio Grande (Castañeda 1938:214–221) giving as one reason the fact that the Rio Grande had been explored as far as San Felipe and the nearby ford known as San Vicente (Weddle 1968:230, 231 n.; Figure 18-1). Until then, the landmark reference point in the Del Rio area had been Las Vacas, the waterholes near present-day Ciudad Acuña. This first mention of San Felipe suggests that the spring and creek that still bear this name were discovered by unrecorded explorations emanating from the first Presidio Sacramento.

Vidaurre, however, chose to proceed from his base in Mapimi to the Rio Grande, reaching the river about 30 km above Del Rio (Daniel 1955:199). Harried by bad weather and the rugged terrain, Vidaurre followed the south bank for three weeks until he was able to descend to the water. One week later, he came upon a ranchería of 250 Apaches who provided guides to La Junta. These Mescaleros reported that the Texas side of the Rio Grande was densely populated (Daniel 1955:201), but the ethnic affiliation of the northern groups was not given.

During the next 20 years, the Spanish attempted to establish missions for the Apache east and north of the Lower Pecos region. Within one year of its founding near San Fernando de Austria (Zaragoza) in 1754, the first, San Lorenzo, was burned by its Apache inhabitants who deserted en masse (Bolton 1962:80; Castañeda 1938:356–358). The ill-fated Mission Santa Cruz on the San Sabá River fell to the Comanche and allied bands in 1758, also within its first year of operation (Weddle 1964). Closer to the Lower Pecos River region on the headwaters of the Nueces River, the second Mission San Lorenzo [de la Cruz] survived from 1762 to 1771, absorbing the refugees from the abandonment of the San Sabá Presidio in 1768 (Tunnell and Newcomb 1969). The Apache for whom these missions were built had reversed the northerly flow of displaced populations in their continual movement south ahead of the Comanche tide (Tunnell and Newcomb 1969:176).

By 1767, when the Marquis de Rubi conducted an investigative tour of the Spanish frontier, he found it woefully inadequate to protect the royal domain. One of his conclusions was that the Sacramento presidio at Santa Rosa was too far from the Rio Grande to be effective in controlling the Apache and he recommended that it be moved to the Rio Grande, near San Felipe [Del Rio] (Castañeda 1938:209). His experiences with the hostile Indians on campaigns in 1763 and 1769 led the venerable frontier soldier, Manuel Rodriguez, to echo this proposition and call for the establishment of a string of forts along the Rio Grande, including one at Las Vacas or San Felipe (Weddle 1968:300). As a result, the presidio, renamed Aguaverde, was returned to the San Diego River in 1773 (Figure 18-1).

In the interim, raids and depredations continued. Once again, in 1773, members of the Garza Falcon and Rodriguez families rode out in retaliation for a massacre engineered by the Mescalero Apache. The joint expedition found its objective near the mouth of the Pecos, following the trail some 30 leagues north to the vicinity of Pandale (Daniel 1955:243; Weddle 1968:228). Coming across a camp undetected, the Spanish attacked, killing an untold number, capturing 16 women and children and 200 horses, and freeing 3 Spanish captives.

Two years later, a campaign to drive the Apaches north of the Rio Grande was initiated utilizing four contingents gathered from the various provinces and presidios. Coahuila's forces, under the command of then Governor Ugarte y Loyola, were to press north and west, forcing the hostiles westward into the mountains, where troops waited to annihilate them (Moorhead 1968:37–41). After three months of arduous campaigning, Ugarte's scouts encountered a hostile band along the Devils River, losing three of their ranks before relief arrived (Moorhead 1968:39; Weddle 1968:337–338, 1976:414–415). Ugarte sent a detachment up river in pursuit; they also lost one scout to the Apaches who retreated north. Eighteen days later, the Spanish party rejoined Ugarte in Presidio Aguaverde with only 10 captured horses to show for 4½ months in the field (Weddle 1968:338).

Juan Ugalde, who replaced Ugarte as governor of Coahuila, led two campaigns against the Mescalero Apache into the Lower Pecos in 1779 and 1782 (Bolton 1962:127: Castañeda 1942:8; Weddle 1968:353–354). His later successes in turning the Lipan Apaches against their kindred, the Mescalero, were to gain him some renown—the present county and city of Uvalde bear corrupted spellings of his name (Bolton 1962:127; Castañeda 1942:113–114), but his forays along the Devils and Pecos rivers did little to stem the raidings and depredations. The dispersement of the presidios along the river recommended by the Marquis de Rubi had spread the Spanish forces too thin, leaving great gaps of rugged terrain that the raiders could penetrate with ease (Thomas 1941:23).

Threatened with the collapse of the entire northern frontier, the Spanish Crown appointed Teodoro de Croix military governor, charging him to defend, stimulate, and extend the territories under his command (Thomas 1941:19). Following his inspection of the Spanish line of defense. Croix consolidated his military strength, moving the troops stationed at Aguaverde to San Fernando de Austria [Zaragoza] (Figure 18-1) in 1780 (Moorhead 1975:226; Thomas 1941:544).

Aguaverde was the closest the Spanish came to establishing a permanent base in the Lower Pecos River region (Figure 18-1). The Comanche movement southward had decimated the Apache, driving them to the Spanish for protection, but the remedy was worse than the illness.

In 1787, the Spanish at La Junta yielded to Mescalero requests for an escort of soldiers during their bison-hunting trips to the mouth of the Pecos River. Fearful of revolt, the authorities at Santa Rosa followed this precedent in November 1787 when 90 soldiers accompanied the Mescalero to the Devils River, where they were attacked by Comanche. The Spaniards subdued the Comanche, permitting them to depart in peace (Daniel 1955:282). The Comanche presence in adjacent areas had been well documented for over 30 years, so this late reference probably reflects the sporadic nature of the ethnohistoric record during this time period in the Lower Pecos region.

This encounter, however, was only a faint reflection of the future. From bases north of the Red River, the Comanche and Kiowa rode south on annual raids, passing through the despoblado en route to the settlements in Mexico (Fehrenbach 1983; Richardson 1928). The general inability of the colonial power to pacify the frontier ended in detente, disrupted by revolution and wars on both continents. Distracted by the internal throes of independence, the various Mexican governments were forced to abandon their frontiers, leaving the colonial populations undefended.

Anglo-American Domination

Although the end result of the Mexican-American war was to split the Lower Pecos region, essentially the area remained part of the *frontera*, affected by Spanish, Native American, and Anglo-American cultures. The hostilities fostered and grew, with each side of the Rio Grande accusing the other of harboring renegades and bandits (Carter 1935; Mexico Border Commission 1875). The hostile Indians were quick to recognize the advantages of an international boundary, crossing the river and political jurisdictions with impunity. The Kickapoo were to wage their declared war with Texans from their Coahuilan strongholds (Gibson 1963), while the Comanche and Kiowa continued to descend from the north, crossing the *despoblado* to strike across the Rio Grande (Fehrenbach 1983; Mexico Border Commission 1875; Richardson 1928). Any or all of these intrusive peoples may have been responsible for the pictographs painted between 1848 and 1882, but a detailed discussion of this period is beyond the scope of this chapter.

With the coming of Anglo sovereignty, a concern for linking east and west had been heightened by the economic lure of trade. The frontiersmen had long recognized the wisdom of following well-traveled Indian trails, guaranteed to be the easiest route across the rugged terrain to permanent water. Exploratory mapping expeditions (French 1850; Greer 1952; Whiting 1849, 1974) were soon followed by stage and mail routes (Austerman 1985; Duval 1871; Vestal 1942), trade caravans (Froebel 1859), freighters (Santleben 1910), cattle drives (Bell 1932), and mineral exploration teams (Woolford 1962). The journals and diaries of these early explorers, soldiers, tradesmen, and cattle drovers provide the first mention of the Spanish Colonial period pictographs at Meyers Springs (Michler in Emory 1857; Woolford 1962) and Painted Caves (Bell 1932; Duval 1871; French 1850; Froebel 1859; Santleben 1910; Vestal 1942; Whiting 1849). Post–Civil War military pressure, the eradication of the bison herds, famine, pestilence, and finally, the construction of the Southern Pacific Railroad in 1881–1882 signaled the end of the Native American presence in the Lower Pecos River region.

Internal Chronology of the Postcontact Rock Art

The Lower Pecos postcontact culture history can be subdivided into four overlapping time periods, each chronicling the sequential dominance of the region by intrusive ethnic groups. Apparently, for a short interlude, encompassing earliest Spanish contact to final eradication of the Native Americans, the region was included within the vast sea of grass that later characterized the American frontier, permitting bison to range south of the Rio Grande (Turpin 1987b). The seventeenth-century occupation may be an extension of the Infierno phase, archaeologically defined by tipi ring sites characteristically accompanied by an intrusive artifact assemblage similar to Plains bison hunting kits (Dibble 1978). Early Spanish documents refer to tribes from northern Mexico traveling to the Lower Pecos for winter bison hunts and to trade for bison products with groups from north of the Rio Grande (Griffen 1969). The Spanish interest in the region at this time was primarily exploratory. Although some northern Mexican groups were already engaged in active rebellion (Griffen 1969), the more northerly peoples were apparently retreating to the Rio Grande to avoid disease and slavery. The LaSalle incursion during this time heightened Spanish awareness of the fragility of their hold on the wilderness and perhaps enlightened the native populations about the white man's vulnerabilities (Weddle 1973). The end of this century coincides with the advent of the Apache and the expansion of the Spanish military frontier, exemplified by the founding of San Juan Bautista on the Grande south of the Lower Pecos region.

During the eighteenth century, Spanish attempts to establish a Maginot line against new and hostile native pressures met with little success. Retaliatory forays into the Lower Pecos region were rendered futile by the difficult terrain, the isolated water sources, and the mobility of the pursued raiding parties. The fortunes of the Sacramento presidio reflect the vagaries of the Spanish defenses. Established on the San Diego River in 1737, the presidio was immediately pulled back to the Sabinas, where it remained until 1773. Moved back to the San Diego and renamed Aguaverde, the presidio survived a bare seven years before the troops were removed to San Fernando de Austria. The area was largely in the hands of the Apache, the indigenous or earlier intrusive groups having been decimated or absorbed. Lasting a bare 80 years, this period ends with a whimper with the arrival of the Comanche and their Plains Indian allies, filling the vacuum left by the dissolution of Spanish empire. Archaeologically, this period remains largely undocumented except for the few early Plains pictographs.

Toward the end of the eighteenth century, the Lower Pecos became a no-man's-land separating the Comanche bases in the north from the settlements of Coahuila, a status quo that endured until the end of the Mexican-American war in 1849. The mobile lifeways of these transients from the northern Plains left few traces in the archaeological record of the Lower Pecos. Although hostilities intensified with the coming of Anglo-American sovereignty, the conflict and conquest begun at the height of Spanish Colonial might were brought to their inevitable conclusion with the eradication of all native peoples by 1882.

When placed in the context of the scant ethnohistoric sources, the postcontact rock art panels can be broadly assigned to either the early contact period of the seventeenth century or the Plains Indian dominance of the eighteenth and nineteenth centuries, overlapping the transition from Spanish to Anglo-American hegemony. The earliest panels reflect initial innocence, a curiosity about permanent architecture, domestic livestock, and clothing styles that Newcomb (Kirkland and Newcomb 1967:121) aptly described as illustrating "for the untutored what some had seen in the alien white world."

Spanish Colonial Pictographs

Two pictograph sites epitomize the apparent reaction of indigenous people to Spanish settlements. Vaquero Shelter (41VV77), now in Seminole Canyon State Historical Park, features all the elements that Newcomb (Kirkland and Newcomb 1967:107) saw as reflections of the Indian reaction to the new experience of contact. A domed church, finger-painted in bright red, is flanked by a costumed person of some importance and two vaqueros roping a longhorn cow with calf (Figure 18-2). The artist's attention to detail includes clear depictions of the cow's udder, the high pommels and cantels typical of Mexican saddlery, the Spanish official's epaulets and buttons, and his pipe, a familiar object used by both cultures. The crosses on the church are in place but incorrectly oriented, indicating that the proper alignment was not yet engrained in the artist's perceptions. Kirkland (1938:24–27) believed this was one of the few Lower Pecos pictographs that told a decipherable story, relating the Indians' first impression of the colonial Spanish and sealed with a handprint, a common signature of preliterate people.

Figure 18-2. Vaquero Shelter (41VV77) as copied by Forrest Kirkland in 1937. (Reproduced courtesy of the Texas Memorial Museum)

High on the Devils River, overlooking the permanent flow of Dolan Springs, another colonial scene is dominated by a two-towered church, a sabre-wielding horseman astride a rearing steed, and a geometric pennant design (Figure 18-3; Marmaduke and Whitsett 1975). This site, Caballero Shelter (41VV343), again visually relates the symbols of colonial power that most impressed the native mind.

A third site, Meyers Springs (41TE9), is a complex site replete with pictographs of many time periods (Jackson 1938; Kirkland and Newcomb 1967). Vignettes attributable to initial contact include four churches, crosses, and padres in habit and mitre (Figure 18-4). One church is anthropomorphized; another is apparently a conflated plan and frontal view with dashed lines indicating the aisle. Thunderbirds and sun symbols painted in the same color and style as some of the churches at Meyers Springs relate to the same painting episodes (Kirkland and Newcomb 1967).

The second series of Spanish Colonial artworks retains the concentration on Christianity, but the paintings incorporate a creeping hostility. At Missionary Shelter (41VV205), a site near the Rio Grande scoured from the wall in a massive flood in 1954 (Turpin 1987a), the central figure is an anthropomorphized church, granted human form by the addition of a head, or a priest whose body is formed by a mission, his arms the towers and his hands the crosses (Figure 18-5; Jackson 1938:Site 73b; Kirkland and Newcomb 1967: Plate 3). The missionary is pierced by a lance or arrow that penetrates his body. Newcomb felt the "figure visualizes what Lipans and Mescaleros often wanted to do and occasionally did do to missionaries" (Kirkland and Newcomb 1967:108). Stylistically, Missionary Shelter

Figure 18-3. Spanish Colonial scene at Caballero Shelter (41VV343), near Dolan Springs on the Devils River. (Copy by David G. Robinson)

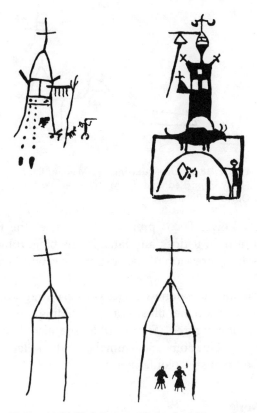

Figure 18-4. Christian motifs attributable to the Spanish Colonial period at Meyers Springs (41TE9). (Redrawn from Kirkland and Newcomb 1967 by David G. Robinson)

Figure 18-5. Composite priest-church at Missionary Shelter (41VV205). (Redrawn from Jackson 1938 by David G. Robinson)

Figure 18-6. Line drawing at Malone Ranch (41VV570). (Redrawn from Patterson 1983 by David G. Robinson)

resembles an earlier Lower Pecos prehistoric art style, the Red Monochrome (Turpin 1986b), more than it does any later Plains biographic art, so that this pictograph may be the expression of new experiences within an established tradition (Turpin 1987a).

A simple line drawing at Malone Ranch (41VV570), high on the Pecos River, also suggests hostility in a panel illustrating a building crowned by a cross, an animal, and two prone figures (Figure 18-6; see also Patterson 1983). The topics—churches, possibly domestic animals, and "killed" humans—would place this site in the Spanish Colonial period.

Plains Indian Art Works

The advent of the Plains Indians is reflected in a singular pictograph on a tributary to the Rio Grande east of the Pecos River. At Live Oak Hole (41VV169), a rectangular human figure with circular head, genitals, half-painted face, and stick limbs, is superimposed on a more ancient panel dominated by a serpentine line almost 15 m long (Figure 18-7; see also Jackson 1938; Kirkland and Newcomb 1967; Turpin and Bement, in press). A triangular-bodied bison with hooked hooves is painted in the same shade of dark red. The later figures conform to conventions typical of the Ceremonial style dated to A.D. 1000–1700 on the northern Plains (Keyser 1987). An adjacent miniature horse and rider probably indicate a span from A.D. 1625 to A.D. 1775, coincident with the Apache domination of the region.

Other scenes at Meyers Springs are executed in the Early Biographic style defined for the northern Plains (Keyser 1987). Nine hand-holding dancers are drawn with rectangular bodies, circular heads, and single-feather headdresses. This vignette holds the key to the identification of another small panel, at Bailando Shelter (41VV666) near the Rio Grande, as historic Plains Indian art (Turpin 1986a). There four dancers of similar style are flanked by shield designs, a motif that appears only in the historic art of the Lower Pecos (Figure 18-8).

The only petroglyph in this sample, Indian Map (41TE330) (Jackson 1938), is distinctly Plains in theme and style (Figure 18-9). Carved on the inside of a large boulder, apparently from a prone position, this scene shows a river valley fringed by tree-covered hills. Two types of native dwellings were erected along

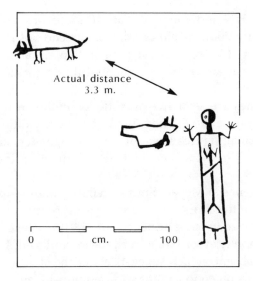

Figure 18-7. Early Plains Indian pictographs at Live Oak Hole (41VV169). (Drawn by David G. Robinson)

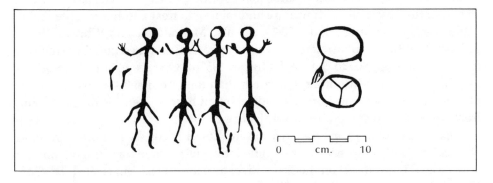

Figure 18-8. Plains-type dancing figures from Bailando Shelter (41VV666) on the Rio Grande. (Drawn by David G. Robinson)

Figure 18-9. Indian Map (41TE330), a Plains-influenced petroglyph near the Rio Grande. (Reproduced from Jackson 1938)

the bank—conical tipis and rounded huts. Dashed lines, representing foot-prints, and hoofprints indicate either trails or direction of movement. A plausible explanation for this scene is commemoration either of combat between pedestrian and equestrian forces or a successful raid for horses, both typical Plains Indian themes.

These same themes are seen at Arroyo de los Indios in northern Coahuila, some 15 km south of the Rio Grande, but in an entirely different medium and style. Thirty-eight small figures make up several vignettes, all apparently portraying conflict between horsemen and foot soldiers or the theft of horses (Turpin 1988).

Again, specific scenes at Meyers Springs reflect modes of early Plains Indian warfare. One diminutive horse, its rider wearing horns and carrying a long lance, appears to be clad in battle armor (Figure 18-10), a device abandoned once guns became common (Keyser 1987). In all the artworks attributable to this era, the gun is notably absent, which suggests either the slow acquisition of weaponry or the emphasis on coup counting in traditional Plains society.

Firearms are increasingly reported in Indian hands in accounts dating after 1770 (Daniel 1955: 231). Flintlock rifles are shown in scenes from Meyers Springs (41TE9), Prade Ranch (41RE14), and Dolan Springs (41VV485). The last site deviates from the obsession with warfare and raiding to treat another favorite Plains subject—bison hunting (Figure 18-11; see also Marmaduke and Whitsett 1975). To judge by ethnographic references, bison apparently roamed into these regions from at least the 1580s to the 1880s (Turpin 1987b). One scene at Dolan Springs may illustrate bison-hunting ritual rather than the hunt itself—a possible bison dancer, clad in robe and horns, stands erect on human feet, his tongue lolling from his mouth to symbolize death (Figure 18-11).

The final phase in Plains Indian art in the Lower Pecos sees an intensification of hostility and aggression, exemplified by vivid scenes at Ringbit Shelter (41VV339) (Figure 18-12) on the Pecos River and the Hussie Miers site (41VV327) (Figure 18-13) near the Devils River. Once again, specific panels at Meyers Springs and the now-destroyed pictographs at Painted Caves (41VV7)—described almost a century ago by Santleben (1910) as portraying the theft of horses and white captives, scalping, and war dances—probably also belong to this era of Comanche domination. These pictographs undoubtedly postdate the

Figure 18-10. Plains warriors and bison hunters at Meyers Springs (41TE9). Horse in battle-armor indicates early eighteenth century age of this pictograph. (Redrawn from Kirkland and Newcomb 1967 by David G. Robinson)

Figure 18-11. Bison hunting and ritual at Dolan Springs (41VV485).

Figure 18-12. Horse and rider "killed" by over-sized lance at Ringbit Shelter (41VV339) on the Pecos River. (Drawn by David G. Robinson)

Spanish Colonial period, but the emphasis on implacable hostility toward the white man is a natural outgrowth of the long heritage of conflict born under Spanish hegemony.

Summary: Native Reaction to Spanish Hegemony

The ethnohistoric and pictographic evidence from the Lower Pecos River region provides an indirect measure of native reaction to contact with an alien culture. Remote from the mainstream of Spanish imperialism, the local population ini-

Figure 18-13. Plains combat autobiography at the Hussie Miers site (41VV327) near the Devils River. (Drawn by David G. Robinson)

tially experienced only the ripple effect of contact as refugees moved north across the Rio Grande. The seventeenth-century Spanish accounts describe relatively peaceful encounters with northern Mexican people who apparently migrated to elude epidemic smallpox, hunt bison, and avoid impressment into Spanish servitude. Unnamed hostile groups north of the Rio Grande (Steck 1932) may well have been indigenous people crowded by the influx from Mexico. Seventeenth-century population movements are also demonstrated by the relocation of northern Mexican groups named by de la Cruz (Steck 1932), Bosque (Steck 1932), and Retana (Hackett 1926) and summarized by Griffen (1969). Additional mobility can be interpreted from the movements of the Jumanos and Cíbolas from east to west while the northern Mexican tribes formed alliances along the Rio Grande that extended from La Junta to the mouth of the Pecos River (Griffen 1969). The fate of the indigenous people, caught between Spanish, Apache, and intrusive northern Mexican groups, seems to be reflected in eighteenth-century records that list fragmentary groups drifting into south Texas and Coahuilan missions (Campbell 1979; Campbell and Campbell 1981).

The rock art evidence for these early population movements is more circum-stantial, but the impoverished missions established along the Spanish frontier were rarely able to construct permanent churches such as those shown in the rock art. The architecture of early mission churches is often unknown, the build-ings razed, and the plans unrecorded, but the various styles shown in picto-graphs from Vaquero Shelter, Caballero Shelter, Meyers Springs, Prade Ranch, Painted Caves, and Malone Ranch indicate diverse origins. A logical explanation is that refugees from northern Mexico had been exposed to permanent architec-ture, domestic animals, and Spanish clothing long before they were introduced to Texas proper.

A barrier to northerly retreat was erected when the Apache appeared on the periphery of the Lower Pecos River region at the end of the seventeenth century (Hackett 1926). A smallpox epidemic in 1706 substantially reduced the native populations, leaving a vacuum into which the Apache flowed (Weddle 1968:71–74). By 1729, they had apparently established their dominance of the Rio Grande, absorbing the Jumano into their ranks. Their enmity toward Span-ish, and later Anglo-American colonization evolved into classic Plains Indian guerrilla warfare, waged against settled communities and commerce surround-ing the Lower Pecos. The earlier intrusive peoples, decimated by disease and internecine warfare, were effectively replaced by Apaches who apparently used the rugged Lower Pecos country as a refuge when they, in turn, were pressured by the Comanche. The emergence of Plains iconography at rock art sites such as Live Oak Hole, Meyers Springs, and Bailando Shelter foreshadows the intro-duction of classic themes such as mounted warfare, coup counting, bison hunt-ing and horse theft that dominated the art of the horse cultures.

Like their predecesors, the Apache gave way in front of pressures emanating from the north. Missions established for the Apache between 1754 and 1762 on the periphery of the Lower Pecos failed largely because of Comanche pressure (Bolton 1962; Castañeda 1938; Tunnell and Newcomb 1969; Weddle 1964), but the Comanche are first mentioned locally near the mouth of the Devils River in 1787 when the Apache requested protection on their winter bison hunts. However, the Comanche and their allies the Kiowa were transients, passing through the despoblado to reach the settled communities south of the Rio Grande and forcing the Apache into strongholds in the mountains and into alli-ances first with the Spanish and later with the Kickapoo. The more mature Plains biographic art, typical of the nineteenth century, appears at Indian Map, reaching the peak of its expressive power in violent scenes at Hussie Miers and Ringbit Shelter, long after the demise of Spanish authority.

Despite its distance from centers of authority and the isolation granted by an intractable landscape, the Lower Pecos region saw a progression in the native reaction to contact that probably accurately reflects the history of peripheral areas throughout the New World. Initially, ambivalence characterized the mix between curiosity, awe, and fear. Undoubtedly, individuals reacted to these emotions in different ways, but the coping mechanism most apparent in the Lower Pecos was withdrawal of Mexican peoples north to the Rio Grande. How these in-migrations affected the indigenous people can only be presumed by comparison with later events, but plausibly they either coexisted or also migrated to unknown destinations. Growing awareness of the effect of colonization accelerated these movements until the region was ringed by more aggressive native people. As the noose drew tighter, resident populations died out, were assimilated, or drifted into mission life. The active warfare of the initial Plains period in Lower Pecos history flourished for a time until internecine conflict drove the succeeding Apache to follow their predecessors. The fluorescence of Comanche power coincided with the abdication of the Spanish and later Mexican authority. Bound by cultural and historical imperatives, the last native peoples had little alternative but to persist to their ultimate destruction by the conflict born and nurtured under Spanish hegemony.

Acknowledgments

My greatest debt is to the many Lower Pecos landowners who granted access to the historic pictograph sites: Mr. and Mrs. Burl Armstrong, Nowell and Dennis Brite, John K. Finegan, L. R. French, Gary Gerdes, Brian Hodge, Cliffton Lowry, Mrs. Florence Major, Gilbert Marshall, Mrs. Hussie Miers, Mrs. Gertrude Riedel, Mr. and Mrs. R. C. Robertson, Mr. and Mrs. J. U. Zuberbueler, Texas Tech University, and the Texas Parks and Wildlife Department. Jack Skiles and Garner Fuller supplied logistical help. Mark Parsons provided a copy of his original description and interpretation of 41VV327. Dr. T. N. Campbell was of inestimable value in locating and interpreting ethnohistoric sources. He and Dr. W. W. Newcomb, Jr., kindly commented on an earlier draft. The Texas Memorial Museum permitted reproduction of Kirkland's and other original documentation. David G. Robinson produced the line drawings and copied the Hussie Miers and Caballero Shelter panels in the field. Lee Bement was my field companion in all site visits. The project was funded by an annual grant from the Thompson Foundation of Cleveland, Ohio, and the Kleberg Foundation of San Antonio, matched by the Department of the Interior, National Register of Historic Places Survey Grant, administered by the Texas Historical Commission.

References

Austerman, Wayne R.
  1985 *Sharps Rifles and Spanish Mules, The San Antonio-El Paso Mail, 1851–1881.* Texas A&M Press, College Station.
Bell, James G.
  1932 A Log of the Texas–California Cattle Drive. Edited by J. Evetts Haley. *Southwestern Historical Quarterly* 35 (3):208–237.
Bolton, Herbert E.
  1908 *Spanish Exploration in the Southwest, 1542–1705.* Barnes and Noble, New York.
  1962 *Texas in the Middle 18th Century.* Russell and Russell, New York (reprint of original printing, 1915).
Campbell, Thomas N.
  1972 Systematized Ethnohistory and Prehistoric Cultural Sequences of Texas. *Bulletin of the Texas Archeological Society* 43:1–11.
  1979 *Ethnohistoric Notes on Indian Groups Associated with Three Spanish Missions at*

Guererro, Coahuila. Center for Archaeological Research, Archaeology and History of the San Juan Bautista Mission Area, Coahuila and Texas Report No. 3. University of Texas at San Antonio.

Campbell, Thomas N., and T. J. Campbell
1981 *Historic Indian Groups of the Choke Canyon Reservoir and Surrounding Area, Southern Texas.* Choke Canyon Series No. 1. Center for Archaeological Research, University of Texas at San Antonio.

Carter, Robert G.
1935 *On the Border with Mackenzie.* Eynon, Washington, D.C.

Casteñeda, Carlos E.
1936 *Our Catholic Heritage in Texas, 1519–1936,* vol II: *The Mission Era: The Passing of the Missions, 1762–1782.* Von Boeckmann-Jones, Austin.
1938 *Our Catholic Heritage in Texas, 1519–1936,* vol III: *The Mission Era: The Missions at Work, 1731–1761.* Von Boeckmann-Jones, Austin.
1942 *Our Catholic Heritage in Texas, 1519–1936,* vol V: *The Mission Era: The End of the Spanish Regime, 1780–1810.* Von Boeckmann-Jones, Austin.

Chipman, Donald E.
1987 In Search of Cabeza de Vaca's Route across Texas: An Historigraphical Survey. *Southwestern Historical Quarterly* 91(2):127–148.

Daniel, J. M. Jr.
1955 The Advance of the Spanish Frontier and the Despoblado. Unpublished master's thesis, University of Texas at Austin.

Dibble, David S.
1978 The Infierno Phase: Evidence for a Late Occupation in the Lower Pecos River Region, Texas. Paper presented at the 43rd Annual Meeting, Society for American Archaeology, Tucson, Arizona.

Duval, John C.
1871 *The Adventures of Bigfoot Wallace.* Claxton, Remsen and Haffelfinger, Macon, Ga.

Emory, Maj. William H.
1857 *Report on the United States and Mexican Boundary Survey.* A.O.P. Nicholson, Washington, D.C.

Fehrenbach, T. R.
1983 *Comanches, the Destruction of a People.* Alfred A. Knopf, New York.

French, Capt. S. C.
1850 *Reports of the Secretary of War with Reconnaissances of Routes from San Antonio to El Paso,* 31st Cong., 1st sess., Exec. Doc. 64, Washington, D.C.

Froebel, Julius
1859 *Seven Years Travel in Central America, Northern Mexico and the Far West of the United States.* Richard Bentley, Publisher in Ordinary to Her Majesty, London.

Gibson, A. M.
1963 *The Kickapoos: Lords of the Middle Border.* University of Oklahoma Press, Norman.

Grant, Campbell
1967 *Rock Art of the American Indian.* Promontory Press, New York.

Greer, James K.
1952 *Colonel Jack Hays: Texas Frontier Leader and California Builder.* E. P. Dutton, New York.

Griffen, William B.
1969 *Culture Change and Shifting Populations in Central Northern Mexico.* Anthropological Papers No. 13. University of Arizona, Tucson.

Hackett, C. W. (editor)
1926 *Historical Documents Relating to New Mexico, Nueva Vizcaya, and Approaches Thereto, in 1772,* vol. II. Carnegie Institution of Washington, D.C.
1931 *Pichardo's Treatise on the Limits of Louisiana and Texas,* vol. I. University of Texas Press, Austin.

Hammond, George P., and Agapito Rey
  1966 *The Rediscovery of New Mexico, 1580–1594*. University of New Mexico Press, Albuquerque.
Jackson, A. T.
  1938 *The Picture Writing of Texas Indians*. Publication No. 3809. University of Texas, Austin.
  n.d. Unpublished notes and photographs, county site files, Texas Archeological Research Laboratory, University of Texas at Austin.
John, Elizabeth A.
  1975 *Storms Brewed in Other Men's Worlds*. Texas A&M University Press, College Station.
Johnson, LeRoy, Jr.
  1986 Review of *Historic Indian Groups of the Choke Canyon Reservoir and the Surrounding Area*, by Thomas N. Campbell and T. J. Campbell. *Bulletin of the Texas Archeological Society* 54:346–355.
Keyser, James D.
  1987 A Lexicon for Historic Plains Indian Rock Art: Increasing Interpretive Potential. *Plains Anthropologist* 32(115):43–71.
Kirkland, Forrest
  1938 A Description of Texas Pictographs. *Bulletin of the Texas Archeological and Paleontological Society* 10:11–40. Abilene.
  1942 Historic Material from Fielder Canyon Cave. *Bulletin of the Texas Archeological and Paleontological Society* 14:61–71, Abilene.
Kirkland, Forrest, and W. W. Newcomb, Jr.
  1967 *The Rock Art of Texas Indians*. University of Texas Press. Austin.
Marmaduke, William S., and Hayden Whitsett
  1975 An Archeological Reconnaissance in the Devils River–Dolan Falls Area. In *Devils River, A Natural Area Survey*, Part VI of VIII, edited by Don Kennard, Natural Area Survey 4:76-109. Division of Natural Resources and Environment, University of Texas at Austin.
Mexico, Border Commission
  1875 *Reports of the Committee of Investigation*. Translated from the official edition made in Mexico (1873). Baker and Godwin, New York.
Moorhead, Max L.
  1968 *The Apache Frontier: Jacobo Ugarte and Spanish-Indian Relations in Northern New Spain, 1769–1791*. University of Oklahoma Press, Norman.
  1975 *The Presidio, Bastion of the Spanish Borderlands*. University of Oklahoma Press, Norman.
Newcomb, W. W., Jr.
  1956 A Reappraisal of the "Cultural Sink" of Texas. *Southwestern Journal of Anthropology* 12:145–153.
Parsons, Mark L.
  1962 Testing and Reconnaissance in Amistad Reservoir, Val Verde County, Texas. A report to the National Park Service on file at the Texas Archeological Research Laboratory, University of Texas at Austin.
Patterson, L. C.
  1983 An Archaeological Survey in Northwest Val Verde County. *LaTierra, Journal of the South Texas Archeological Society* 10(2):32–38.
Richardson, Rupert N.
  1928 *The Comanche Indians, 1820–1861*. Ph.D. dissertation, University of Texas at Austin.
Santleben, August
  1910 *A Texas Pioneer. Early Staging and Overland Freighting Days on the Frontiers of Texas and Mexico*. Edited by I.D. Affleck. Neale, New York.

Schroeder, Albert H., and Dan S. Matson
1965 *A Colony on the Move. Gaspar Castaño de Sosa's Journal 1590–1591*. School of American Research, Salt Lake City.

Steck, Francis B.
1932 Forerunners of Captain de Leon's Expedition to Texas, 1670–1675. *Southwestern Historical Quarterly* 36(1):1–28.

Swanton, J. R.
1924 Southern Contacts of the Indians North of the Gulf of Mexico. *Annaes XX Congreso Internacional de Americanistas*:53–59.

Thomas, Alfred B.
1941 *Teodoro de Croix and the Northern Frontier of New Spain, 1776–1783*. University of Oklahoma Press, Norman.

Tunnell, Curtis B., and W. W. Newcomb, Jr.
1969 *A Lipan Apache Mission, San Lorenzo de la Cruz, 1762–1771*. Texas Memorial Museum Bulletin No. 14. University of Texas at Austin.

Turpin, Solveig A.
1986a Bailando Shelter and Meyers Springs: Iconographic Parallels. *LaTierra, Journal of the South Texas Anthropological Association* 13(1):5–8.
1986b Pictographs in the Red Monochrome Style of the Lower Pecos River Region. *Bulletin of the Texas Archeological Society* 55:124–144 (for 1984).
1987a The Vanishing Rock Art of Texas Indians. *Heritage Magazine*. Texas Historical Foundation, Austin.
1987b Ethnohistoric Observations of Bison in the Lower Pecos River Region: Implications for Environmental Change. *Plains Anthropologist* 32(118):424–429.
1988 Arroyo de los Indios: A Historic Pictograph in Northern Coahuila, Mexico. *Plains Anthropologist* 33(120):279–284.

Turpin, S. A., and L. C. Bement
1987 The Live Oak Hole Complex: Plains Indian Art and Occupation in the Lower Pecos River Region. *Bulletin of the Texas Archeological Society*, in press.

Vestal, Stanley
1942 *Bigfoot Wallace*. Houghton Mifflin, Boston.

Weddle, Robert S.
1964 *The San Sabá Mission: Spanish Pivot in Texas*. University of Texas Press, Austin.
1968 *San Juan Bautista: Gateway to Spanish Texas*. University of Texas Press, Austin.
1973 *Wilderness Manhunt: The Spanish Search for LaSalle*. University of Texas Press, Austin.
1976 The Vanguard. In *LaHacienda*. Whitehead Memorial Museum and Val Verde County Historical Commission, Del Rio.

Whiting, William H. C.
1849 *Journal of a Reconnaissance from San Antonio de Bexar to El Paso Del Norte*, 31st Cong, 1st sess, Exec. Doc. 64, Washington, D.C.
1974 Journal of William Henry Chase Whiting, 1849. In *Exploring Southwestern Trails, 1846–1854*. Edited by Ralph P. Bieber. Porcupine Press, Philadelphia.

Williams, J. M.
1962 New Conclusions on the Route of Mendoza, 1683–1684. *West Texas Historical Association Year Book* 38:111–134, Abilene.

Woolford, Sam (editor)
1962 Notes and Documents, The Burr G. Duval Diary. *Southwestern Historical Quarterly* 65(4):487–511.

Part 3 ■

The Californias

Chapter 19 ■

Julia G. Costello and David Hornbeck

Alta California: An Overview

The European settlement of Las Californias was the last large colonial venture of Spain in the New World. Exploration of this territory took place during the 1500s, although it was not until 1697 that successful settlement began in Baja California. Jesuits eventually established 17 missions here before they were expelled in 1767. Alta California colonization came next, spurred on by the increasing presence of Russians and English on land that Spain had already claimed. After difficult beginnings, a chain of 21 Franciscan missions was established along the coast from San Diego to San Francisco between 1769 and 1823. In addition, there were four strategically located presidios to guard the missions from foreign forces and keep internal order, and three pueblos populated with colonists from Nueva España.

Political and economic conditions in Alta California changed drastically after the end of the successful Mexican War of Independence in 1821: International trade was legalized, support of the missions through the Pious Fund ended, and former mission land was gradually granted to private individuals. Between 1832 and 1836, mission buildings, property, and lands were taken from the church and placed under secular management. The native populations gradually dispersed to growing trading towns on the coast, to work on the many private ranchos, or returned to their traditional way of life. With the end of the Mexican War in 1848, the era of Hispanic California was brought to a close.

The story of Spanish colonization of the Pacific Coast of North America can be told in many ways: from the point of view of the church, which was saving souls; from that of the government, which was securing new lands for the Crown; or from that of the Native Americans, who saw the demise of their traditional cultures at the hands of foreigners. All histories are edited versions of the past; all choices of data eliminate some pieces of information and emphasize others. Most information on the Hispanic period in California has traditionally come from documents produced by literate members of European society. This summary demonstrates that information derived from the physical remains of the past has provided some new insights into these historic times.

Setting

The northern two-thirds of California is dominated by the Sierra Nevada running north and south on the east, the smaller Coast Ranges paralleling it on the west, and the large Central Valley lying between (Figure 19-1). The Transverse Ranges run east and west just above Los Angeles, and immediately south are the Peninsular Ranges, which run down Baja California. The Mojave Desert lies in the southeast part of the state. A Mediterranean climate prevails in most of California, with summer fog along the coasts. Conditions are more desertlike along the southern coast, the southern Central Valley, and southeastern quarter of the state.

In the coastal mountains, heavy winter precipitation and summer fog support needleleaf forests (redwood, pine, Douglas fir) and needleleaf-broadleaf forests as far south as the Transverse Ranges. Eastward across the Sierra Nevada, the steady increase in precipitation with higher elevation leads to an orderly succession of plant formations, from grasslands (California prairie), to mixed oak and pine woodlands and forests, to an even higher-elevation sequence of pine, pine and fir, and subalpine formations. Forests in the high mountains of Southern California are similar to this, but lower slopes are dominated by extensive sage and chaparral.

Compared with the mountainous areas, the California lowlands are relatively dry, even on the coast, and consequently support mainly treeless grasslands except along the major drainages, where there are riparian oak woodlands. Marshlands are common in the Central Valley, and scrub formations in the eastern deserts are dominated by creosote bush, saltbrush, and some Joshua tree woodlands.

The Native American Context

Before the Spanish began settling Alta California, the area lying within the boundaries of the present state was occupied by about 300,000 native peoples and had the highest population density of any area in North America (Cook

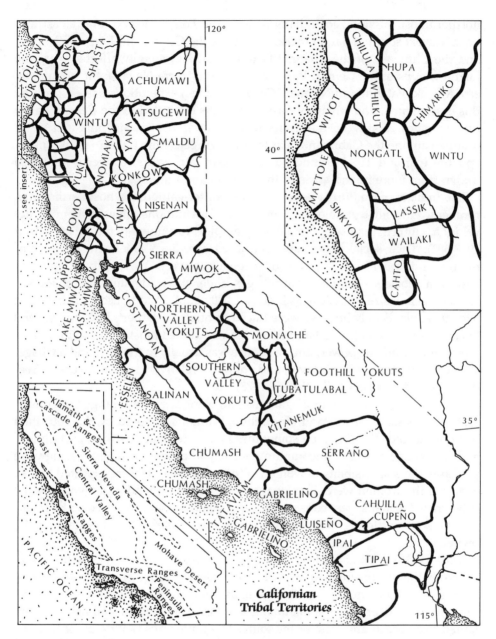

Figure 19-1. Approximate tribal territories in California. Since this map depicts the situation at the earliest periods for which evidence is available, ranges mapped for different tribes often refer to different periods. (After Heizer 1978:ix)

1976b; Kroeber 1976). The California Indians were as diverse a group as the terrain they occupied: They were associated with 4 major culture areas, 60 tribes, and 90 languages and contained both the tallest and shortest native groups in North America. Summaries of California Indian cultures are found in works by Heizer (1978a), Kroeber (1976), and Moratto (1984).

Direct Spanish contact was confined to central and southern California. The northernmost missionized Indians include the Pomo, Wappo, and Coast and Lake Miwok; south of San Francisco Bay were the Costanoan, Esselen, Salinan, and the Chumash of the Channel Islands area. Peripherally affected were the inland groups of the Central Valley and western Sierra Nevada: the Yokuts, Sierra Miwok, Patwin, and Nisenan. Several Spanish expeditions passed through this eastern area, and runaway mission Indians often fled to the Central Valley tule marshes. South of the Transverse Ranges, the coastal missions were founded among the Gabrieliño near later Los Angeles, the Luiseño to the south, and the Ipai and Tipai around San Diego. In later years, converts were also drawn from more inland areas of the Serraño and Cahuilla.

The Indians of California were complex hunter-gatherers whose fertile environment, efficient technologies, and societal institutions allowed them to develop a culture that was unusually complex for nonagriculturalists (Bean 1978:681). Their social organization included hereditary chiefs and elite, commoner, and "poor" classes, and, occasionally, slaves. Ownership of land was vested in tribelets—complexes of villages under the leadership of a chief. Villages ranged in size from 20 to as high as 1,000 people, and households included 5 to 10 people. Family lineages were traced through the father's line, and several lineages were often grouped into clans. Men controlled most of the political, religious, and economic power, and residence was usually in the husband's village. Women were respected, however, and enjoyed a relatively large measure of freedom and independence (E. Wallace 1978).

Marriages were usually monogamous and were carefully arranged in consideration of class, alliances, and kin, although unions opposed by the betrothed were not forced. Wealthy men sometimes had more than one wife, and divorce and remarriage were not uncommon. Household chores and child rearing were primarily the responsibility of women, although husbands were expected to take charge if the women were ill or unavailable. Although land was owned by the tribe, movable items were considered personal possessions; they could be inherited by sons and daughters, but were commonly interred in the grave of the owner.

Most food was obtained from gathering and collecting activities, which were primarily the responsibility of women. Food items included seeds, acorns, roots, berries, and other flora as well as shellfish and insects. Hunters, the males, brought down deer, elk, sea mammals, and birds; small game and fish were obtained from ocean and freshwater sources by both sexes. Although only a few groups in the southern part of the state practiced agriculture, California natives harvested tobacco, grapes, mesquite, and wild seeds and regularly used burning to promote the growth of seed-bearing grasses and other plants (Heizer 1978a:22).

Technologically, California Indians were skilled at working stone and hides and fashioning hunting and trapping gear. They were unsurpassed in North America in their mastery of basket making, which was entirely the women's domain. Carrying-baskets, trays, seed beaters, storage containers, winnowers and leachers, serving bowls, cradles, and watertight containers for cooking and transporting liquids were fashioned and decorated with distinctive regional techniques (Elsasser 1978). Men were adept at woodworking, and the oceangoing plank canoes constructed by the Chumash were particularly admired by the Spanish (Hudson et al. 1978).

The religious beliefs of the California Indians are poorly understood. Spiritual matters were rarely discussed with uninitiated people, and the missions drove much of the religious system underground. There was belief in the pervasiveness of spiritual power in the universe, embodied in the earth, plants, animals (including people), and celestial objects, and the possibility that this power could be acquired, lost, and manipulated through the use of proper symbols and rituals (Heizer 1978b). Rich mythologies tell of the origins of various creatures and natural features and of interactions between them. Priests were trained to mediate with spirit powers, although individuals could interact with spirits directly. Rites of passage were particularly important at puberty and death, and hallucinogenic substances were often taken to enhance communication with spirits. Priests were almost always men, but women participated in rituals to a limited extent. However, an equal number of men and women were *shaman* (doctors and healers) (E. Wallace 1978).

Music, a male activity, consisted primarily of singing accompanied by some instrumentation. It was an important part of all cultural activities, including religious rites, social events, recreation, and warfare (W. Wallace 1978). Entertainment at group gatherings was found in competitive games of athletic skill as well as team sports, guessing games, and target throwing. Gambling was pervasive and widely enjoyed by both men and women in California, bets being made on the outcome of games and competitions. Feasting and dancing were part of all social gatherings.

Trade in both necessities and luxuries established networks that tied California tribal groups together and with other parts of the west. Evidence of shell and obsidian trade with peoples east of the Sierra Nevada goes back over 8,600 years, while stone axes, cotton blankets, and pottery from the Southwest appear on some southern California sites (Heizer 1978a). Native groups within California regularly exchanged obsidian, salt, acorns, worked shells, baskets, bows and arrows, clothing, and other commodities (Davis 1973).

However, California Indians rarely traveled outside of their tribal territories, the boundaries of which were rigorously maintained (Heizer 1978b:649). Major rituals or trade feasts typically involved tribelets only within a radius of 50 to 75 miles (Bean 1978:675). Minute local variations in material culture and language attest to this provincialism. Individual groups were often at odds with their neighbors; animosities and warfare between California native groups are frequently referred to in historic accounts and are evidenced by remains found on archaeological sites (Walker et al., this volume).

In summary, the area of California missionization was inhabited by numerous native groups who lived off a land of abundant natural resources and enjoyed a benign climate. Isolated from other culture areas by the Great Basin to the east and the Pacific Ocean to the west, they were influenced only peripherally by cultures of the Northwest coast and the Southwest. Their insular existence changed dramatically after the arrival of the Spanish.

History of European Involvement

In its exploration of North America, Spain did not encounter the wealth and riches found by Cortés and Pizarro in Mexico and South America. While searching for the mythical Straits of Anián, which would provide a shortcut to Asia, sixteenth-century Spanish seafarers encountered the fog-shrouded shores of the Pacific coast. These they called California after the fabled island of amazon Queen Califia featured in a popular novel. Juan Rodríguez Cabrillo explored and made notes of his findings along the coast in 1542 (Figure 19-2). Cabrillo died on this voyage and was buried on San Miguel Island in 1543. A controversial grave marker found there in 1901 is claimed to have been left by his fellows (Heizer 1972).

In 1567, profitable and exclusive trading began between Manila in the Philippines and Acapulco in New Spain that would last until 1815. Also sailing in the "Spanish Lake" were pirates from rival European nations who plundered the returning galleons. Archaeological excavations at Indian sites around Drake's Bay north of San Francisco have identified the presence of both a sixteenth-century Manila galleon and a British privateer.

In 1595, Manila galleon captain Sebastián Rodriguez Cermeño had his ship driven ashore and lost in Drake's Bay. His cargo from Manila was apparently thrown up on the beach, as suggested by numerous waterworn pieces of Chinese porcelain that have been recovered from Miwok village sites around the perimeter of the bay. The presence of these artifacts documents the introduction of European goods into the native culture by the sixteenth century and also clearly identifies which villages were occupied at this time (Heizer 1941, 1947, 1974; Meighan 1950; Meighan and Heizer 1952). However, recent reanalysis of the porcelain fragments has provided some controversial evidence for verifying the site of the earlier historic visit of English captain Francis Drake. Differences in the decoration of the recovered sherds and their lack of water wear suggest that the English pirate traded part of his cargo to the local Indians during his one-month layover in 1579 (Von Der Porten 1972, 1984).

The final major exploration of the California coast was carried out by Spaniard Sebastián Vizcaíno, who traveled as far north as present-day Cape Mendocino in 1602–1603. The results of these early explorations of Alta California were not acted upon for over 150 years as Spain was distracted by difficulties in settling and managing other frontiers.

Establishing the Colony

European settlement began in Baja California in 1697, and by 1767 the Jesuits had established 17 missions stretching from San José del Cabo to Santa María de los Angeles (Mathes, this volume). They also established the independent Pious Fund, which provided the finances to build and maintain all the California

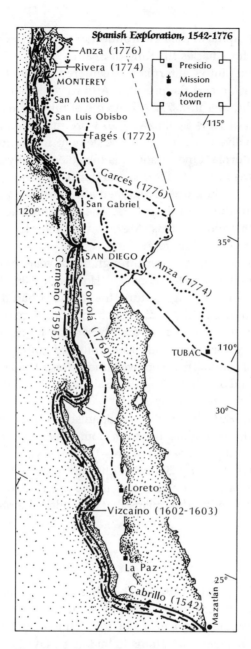

Figure 19-2. Routes of early European exploration in the Californias.

missions. In 1767, all Jesuits were expelled from Spanish lands and replaced with Franciscans and others.

Implementation of the settlement plan for Alta California was accelerated when it was rumored that Russia was planning to extend its outposts south into California (see Ferris, this volume). In 1769, a combined sea and land expedition led by Gaspar de Portolá, and accompanied by Father Junípero Serra, was dispatched to establish a settlement at San Diego and then to push north to Monterey Bay, the chosen capital of the new frontier. In June 1770, California was cere-moniously claimed for Charles III, King of Spain.

Spain's initial thrust into California was centered on two time-tested frontier institutions, the mission and the presidio. A third settlement type, the pueblo, was brought to California in 1777. All three institutions, used successfully in many frontier areas of New Spain, were to work in tandem, each performing a specific role. Initially, however, these settlement institutions, did not meet with success in California. One reason was the colony's physical isolation from the more settled areas in Baja California and northern Sonora. An early attempt to establish an overland link was abandoned after the Colorado River Yuma re-volted and drove out the Spanish in 1781. The remaining sea route, extending over 1,600 km north from San Blas, Mexico, was entirely upwind and it took over three months to reach Monterey.

The earliest missions had to suffer through initial years of minimal construc-tion, low crop production, and few converts (Hornbeck 1986). Because the native people were inexperienced in agriculture, the missions had difficulty achieving self-sufficiency. To remedy this, Spain began to send more soldiers to the Cali-fornia frontier and also expanded the supply system. By the end of 1776, three presidios and seven missions had been founded and plans for founding California's first civil community were well under way. The Hispanic population stood between 300 and 350, including 19 missionaries and 160 soldiers, and over 2,000 Indians resided at the missions.

Between 1776 and 1805, the area under Spanish control expanded considera-bly, with 19 sites strung out along the coast from San Francisco Bay to San Diego Bay (Figure 19-3). During this period of growth, the missions increased the total number of neophytes to nearly 20,000. With large and stable populations, they were able to develop agricultural and irrigation systems and simple industries, and would embark upon building plans that expanded the physical site of each mission.

Life at the Missions

Architecture and Settlement Pattern. The physical layout of all the California missions was similar (Figure 19-4). Although some drawings were made by his-toric visitors to these sites, much of our information on the configuration of rooms, use of specific areas, alterations to buildings, and locations of economic activities is derived from archaeological investigations. Many details of building construction techniques are also preserved in the archaeological record.

Central to mission life was the enclosed quadrangle, which included the church, priests' apartments, shops, storage areas, kitchens, and the *monjerio*, the sleeping area for young, unmarried women. Dwellings for Indian families usu-ally formed an adjacent complex and were first built of traditional materials, and were later replaced with rows of nearly identical adobe rooms (Hoover and Costello 1985). The soldiers' quarters, somewhat larger, were nearly always lo-cated on the opposite side of the quadrangle from the Indian dwellings.

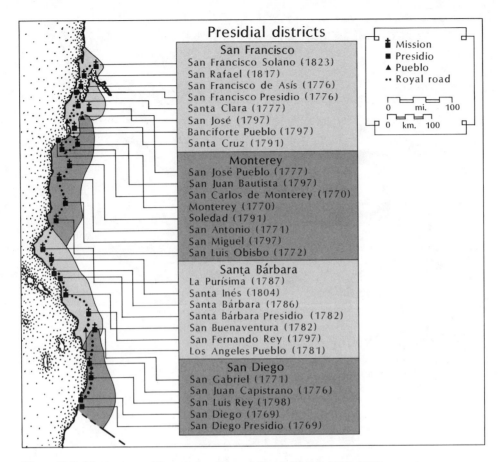

Figure 19-3. Missions, presidios, and pueblos of Alta California (1769–1832).

Many facilities located outside of the mission quadrangle have not survived. The few that have been excavated have provided important historical information. Archaeological research has recovered data on milling, tanneries (Hageman and Ewing 1980), corrals, tile kilns and tile making (Costello 1985), and lime production areas (Browne 1976; Costello 1977; Hageman and Ewing 1980; Harrington 1945). Virtually all missions had complex aqueduct systems consisting of dams, ditches, flumes, and reservoirs that brought water to agricultural fields, often extensive and decorative gardens, industrial activity areas, and mission residences. Researchers have also found filter houses that were used to purify the water, fountains for aeration, lavanderias for washing, and sometimes a system of underground clay pipes or tile-lined conduits to transport water through the quadrangle area and to individual rooms (Greenwood and Gessler 1968; Hageman and Ewing 1980; Harrington 1958; Soto 1960, 1961).

While building construction was a major mission industry in the early years of establishment, archaeological evidence indicates that building maintenance and renovation were also major ongoing activities throughout mission occupations. Room floors were commonly replaced, walls resurfaced, doors and win-

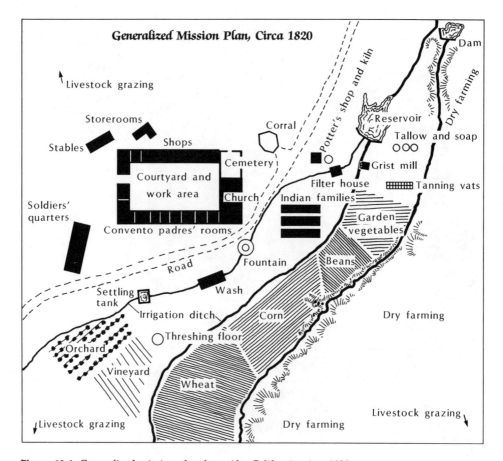

Figure 19-4. Generalized mission plan from Alta California, circa 1820.

dows relocated, rooms added, and buildings abandoned and rebuilt on new foundations (Butler 1973; Costello 1989; Felton 1985; Greenwood 1975; Marshall 1982).

Periodic damage from earthquakes is reported from virtually all missions. The original La Purísima Mission site, occupied for 25 years, was moved in 1812 following enormous destruction caused by an earthquake. Archaeological studies of both the first and second sites revealed that the builders were impressed enough with the catastrophe to redesign their new site with walls nearly twice as thick as the old. Also, no building could be over 1½ stories high, and linear rather than quadrangle formation of the buildings was favored (Costello 1975; Hageman and Ewing 1980).

In addition to buildings and structures near the mission center, there were the more remote estancias for livestock and agricultural support. At one time, Mission San Luis Rey had 20 ranches scattered over more than 100 square leagues; Mission San Gabriel owned a total of 17 ranches for raising cattle and horses, and 15 ranches for raising sheep, goats, and pigs (Burcham 1981:120). Some of these estancias were also the location of a *visita* and had a chapel (*asistencia*), which was used for occasional religious services. Although the names of many of these facilities are recorded in documents, their locations are usually unknown. Archaeological excavation of some of these sites has established specific locations and provided important information about life on these poorly documented mission stations (Chace 1966; Greenwood and Browne 1968; Hoover 1985; Schuyler 1978:72).

Indian Life. Total mission population reached its highest peak, 21,000 Indians, in 1822. Initially, missions recruited converts from local villages; once baptized, the Indians moved to the missions. This process of gathering in the local people did not occur rapidly. Archaeological investigations have demonstrated that through the early 1800s many traditional villages coexisted alongside the missions. Although records indicate that over 100 converts moved to missions from the village of Malibu between 1790 and 1810, some 130 adults were still buried in traditional fashion in the village cemetery during this time (Meighan 1987:193).

Eventually, the supply of unconverted local Indians was exhausted and the search for new souls reached out into an ever-widening circle. Dates when individual village sites were abandoned have been verified by artifacts found during excavations (King 1978:65). Except for missions such as San Diego and San José, which had access to interior populations, individual mission populations began to decline after about 1810.

Opinions vary as to how the Indians adjusted to life at the missions and whether they were willing or forced participants. The Catholic Church holds that baptism was voluntary, labor demands of the mission modest, and discontent minor in view of the enormous numbers of converts (Engelhardt 1908–1915; Guest 1979). Detractors of the system argue that there was forced recruitment, mistreatment, virtual slave labor, severe punishments, and unhealthy conditions (Castillo, this volume; Cook 1976a; Costo and Costo 1987).

There is undoubtedly some truth in both arguments: Catholicism requires conversion to be voluntary, but the Indians probably did not understand the full cultural ramifications of their baptisms; labor was modest by European standards but oppressively inflexible for traditional hunters and gatherers; punishment by the lash and incarceration were standard for all Spanish subjects, but humiliating and traumatic for native peoples. Large numbers of deaths from introduced diseases, however, are well documented on both sides. The primary killers were syphilis, tuberculosis, and dysenteries, with periodic epidemics such as the outbreak of measles in 1827–1828 (Cook 1976a:13–55).

A major obstacle to a balanced understanding of mission life is that documentary data on this period of mission history come almost entirely from the writings of the missionaries and military authorities. Although conflicts between these two groups and a well-developed Spanish bureaucracy have made these writings a rich source of information, they reflect only the Hispanic point of view. Some additional material is found in accounts of foreign travelers, but these are meager and also European in outlook.

One excellent source of information on the Native American adjustment to missionization has been found in the archaeological record. Information has also been gleaned from rare interviews with California Indians who participated in the mission system (Hudson et al. 1977, 1978; Hudson and Underhay 1978). Evidence suggests that, although some areas of traditional Native American culture changed drastically at the mission, others were more modestly affected.

Technology. Indian life was particularly affected by economic and technological innovations. Prior to the arrival of the Spanish, California Indians had virtually no experience in animal husbandry, and only in the southernmost part of the state was there pottery production and the beginning stages of agriculture. Along with religious and social instruction, the mission Indians were taught numerous European crafts and, after 1790, specialists from New Spain were hired on four-year contracts to teach more technical skills (Engelhardt 1908–1915:2:535).

Although residents adopted these new technologies well enough to build and sustain the mission system, archaeological analysis of some production sites and manufactured products suggests that often these skills were not fully mastered by the Indians. The waster-mound surrounding the brick and tile kiln at Mission San Antonio contains a large quantity of poorly made and fired wares and is enormous compared with similar kilns in Mexico and Guatemala (Costello 1985). Analysis of cement construction products also reveals that an unusually lime-rich formula was used, thought to be an attempt to compensate for problems caused by deficiencies in lime-burning and slaking (Costello 1989). It is likely that this marginal mastery of at least some Spanish technologies was paralleled by superficial adoption of other aspects of European culture.

There is considerable archaeological evidence that native practices were continued at the missions. Metal was always in short supply and stone tools and stone flakes are commonly found at all mission sites. At La Purísima Mission, bone and stone scrapers, traditional Chumash tools, were used to process cow hides (Deetz 1978:169). Baskets continued to be manufactured at the missions, often incorporating Christian or European designs; examples are preserved in several museum collections. Traditional tar (*brea*)-impregnated basket fragments were also recovered during excavations at San Buenaventura (Greenwood 1976). In the Santa Barbara Channel area, ethnographic accounts document that Chumash canoe makers and seamen also continued to practice their skills and were regularly sent out to harvest fish and sea otter pelts for trade (Hudson et al. 1978). In the southern missions where pottery-making skills were present before contact, expanded production was encouraged (Evans 1969).

Recovered artifacts also demonstrate that mission Indians used new, imported materials to reproduce or modify traditional forms: Projectile points, scrapers, and cutting tools that have been recovered are made out of bottle glass and porcelain, and ceramic forms often resemble traditional basketry shapes. Ceramics were frequently drilled and kept for use as ornaments; holes in shell beads were drilled with metal needles and pins (Greenwood 1976; Hoover and Costello 1985; King 1981).

Subsistence. Evidence has been found in the Indian houses to suggest that the manner and location of cooking continued to follow precontact traditions. Apparently cooking fires were built directly on the floor, and two hearths were generally associated with each dwelling: one located in the center of the adobe room and the other outside, in front of the door (Deetz 1978; Felton 1985; Greenwood 1976; Hoover and Costello 1985). Native American grinding implements (manos and metates) are also commonly found in Indian residence areas; they were used to grind either traditional grasses and nuts or European grains.

The diet of the Indians changed drastically with the introduction of European crops and domestic animals (Cook 1976a; Walker et al., this volume). Excavations show that beef was the primary meat consumed and that mutton was next in importance; pig was eaten only now and then, and occasionally butchered horse. Butchering was facilitated by iron knives and axes, and meat was flayed from the bone in the Spanish fashion to make *carne seca* (beef jerky) or was stewed in large pieces on the bone (Gust 1982). Wheat and corn, and secondarily barley and beans, constituted the bulk of the mission diet, supplemented by vegetables and fruits when in season.

Ethnohistoric and archaeological evidence documents the continued use of traditional Indian foods, estimated to have constituted about 10 percent of the mission diet (Cook 1976a:47). Mission records indicate that Indians were commonly excused to pursue traditional gathering activities and would often leave in great numbers for seasonal harvests (Geiger and Meighan 1976). It is animal remains, however, that are preserved in archaeological deposits and small amounts of deer, rabbit, bird, and fish bone are recovered from mission sites. Shellfish, traditionally a major food source for coastal dwelling groups, is poorly represented in excavated collections (Farnsworth 1987; Langenwalter and McKee 1985; Walker and Davidson 1989).

Another aspect of Spanish settlement that greatly affected the availability of native foods was the importation of European plants and the conversion of the countryside to rangeland (Burcham 1981). Seeds and pollen from plants preserved in adobe bricks and historical soils provide evidence of the rapid spread of introduced plant species, which overwhelmed many types of native flora (Hendry 1931; Hendry and Kelly 1925; West et al., this volume).

Religion. Ironically, religion was one of the areas of traditional Indian life apparently least affected by the Franciscan missionization of California. Shamans' whistles and crystals found in Indian residences and ethnographic accounts of religious observances testify to the continuation of traditional beliefs. Superficial Christian symbols and stories were easily adopted by the newly converted Indians who saw the pageantry and paraphernalia of Catholic services as new sources of spiritual power (Bean and Vane 1978:669–670; Hudson et al. 1977; Hudson and Underhay 1978:22).

Recent studies of interviews conducted by the early twentieth-century ethnographer J. P. Harrington provide ample evidence of the continuity of religious beliefs and practices for the Chumash of the Central California coast (Hudson et al. 1977, 1978; Hudson and Underhay 1978). As traditional beliefs permeated all aspects of Chumash life, religious practices continued in ways unnoticed by the padres. The economically important Chumash canoe society, inextricably linked with supernatural beliefs, was encouraged to continue its fishing activities during the mission period and its leaders given special consideration during legal disputes (Hudson et al. 1978). Although in some areas men's sweat lodges (*temescales*) were banned, in others the padres allowed them to be used for health reasons and therefore their religious functions could be maintained. Tobacco, universally used in California for rituals, continued to be prominent in mission life (Bean and Vane 1978).

Some religious ceremonies were also allowed to continue openly. The Blackbird Dance was performed when the last tile was put on the mission roof at San Buenaventura Mission and also to celebrate the birthday of an elder Chumash at the Indian residence at Santa Bárbara Mission (Hudson et al. 1977:84–85). Excavation of one Indian residence room at San Buenaventura revealed a concentration of steatite and finely decorated bone whistles that are associated with Chumash shaman (Greenwood 1976:170). Fired clay effigies from San Antonio Mission may have been simple toys, or may have had some religious significance to the Indian makers (Hoover and Costello 1985). A mixing of native decorative elements into paintings on the churches and other buildings may also indicate a perseverance of traditional spiritual beliefs (Lee and Neuerburg, this volume).

Burial practices were apparently more rigidly controlled by the church. Archaeological excavations of Christian burials at the cemetery at La Purísima Mission revealed that most of the bodies were laid out separately in a supine position with virtually no grave goods. This is in contrast to traditional Indian burials, in which the body was placed in a flexed position and surrounded by numerous grave offerings, and neighboring interments commonly overlapped. Two of the excavated graves, however, were exceptional in containing numerous grave goods and are thought to date to a later period when the mission was abandoned (Humphrey 1965). Although these two later burials provide testimony of the Indians' loyalty to the Catholic cemetery, the attributes of the burial demonstrate the perseverance of traditional beliefs (Hoover 1985:98).

Non-Indian Mission Populations. The Hispanic contingent of mission populations, the *gente de razón* (people of European culture) consisted of two Franciscan priests and an escolta of five to six soldiers from the district presidio. Although most of the padres and many of the presidio comandantes came from Spain, the other Hispanics were from Mexico and were virtually all of mixed Indian ancestry with some Negro and Caucasian blood. Soldiers often arrived from Mexico with their wives and children, while single men commonly married Indian women from the missions.

An analysis of artifacts recovered from excavations has enabled archaeologists to identify non-Indian occupants of specific rooms and areas. Whereas stone tools, glass and shell beads, and the floor hearths mentioned above are distinctive features of Indian dwellings, the rooms of padres and soldiers contain numerous fragments of imported ceramics and bottle glass (Costello 1989; Farnsworth 1987; Greenwood 1976; Hoover and Costello 1985). The soldiers' quarters at Mission San Antonio also contained abundant musket balls and gun flints. Unlike the Indian houses, in which ground hearths were used for cooking, the dwellings of the *gente de razón* contain the remains of elevated, counter-style *braseros* and *hornos* (Costello 1989; Hastings 1975; Kimbro 1988). A room excavated at La Purísima Mission occupied by an ex-presidio soldier and his Chumash wife contained an abundance of European, male-associated artifacts and Indian, female-associated artifacts (Deetz 1978), providing an excellent example of the cultural mixing of Californio society.

Presidios and Pueblos

Presidios, the administrative and defensive arm of Spanish settlement in California, have not endured as well as the missions on the California landscape. The only standing structures remaining are a wall in San Francisco, the chapel in Monterey, and three dwelling rooms at Santa Bárbara. Like the missions, presidios were constructed in the form of an enclosed quadrangle. The central plaza was surrounded by contiguous rooms that housed the families of the officers and soldiers, as well as barracks for single men, storehouses, and a guardhouse. A chapel usually was centrally located opposite the main gate with an adjacent residence area for the padre. The entire complex was enclosed within a perimeter defense wall.

Pueblos, civil communities, were later additions to Spain's efforts to colonize California. They were established for the purpose of supplying the military with cheaper and more reliable agricultural products than were available from government ships. Civilians were to set examples of Spanish life for the Indian to follow and act as reserve militia in times of emergency. Three pueblos were founded in California but their success was less than expected. The pueblos were never able to produce the agricultural surpluses needed to support the presidios because of low prices set by the military and lack of economic incentives (Mosk 1938).

As long as missions dominated early California settlements, the civilian and military population grew slowly, increasing from 900 in 1785 to only 3,000 in 1820. Initial contingents of soldiers totaled approximately 70 per presidio, producing a total population of about 150 people. These presidio settlements attracted civilians and retired soldiers who often remained and built homes. By 1815, all presidios except San Diego had populations of 300 to 600 persons.

Archaeological excavations at the Santa Bárbara and San Diego presidios have revealed construction techniques similar to those of the missions, and aqueducts have been found bringing water to the compound at Santa Bárbara. Each presidio had its own livestock herds, croplands, and orchards. Many of the numerous industries found at the missions, however, have not been found at presidios. The presidio communities obtained necessary goods either from government supply ships or, in later years, purchased them from the missions at cheap prices that they set themselves. As expected, artifacts from presidio excavations include fewer items associated with Native American culture. European-style bread-baking ovens were found at the San Diego Presidio along with a large barbecue and roasting pit (Ezell and Ezell 1980:87).

Graves excavated at the San Diego and Santa Bárbara presidios have provided additional information on the burial practices of these communities. Excavations showed that crypts could be simple holes or could be lined with tile or cobbles; coffins were unadorned or covered with cloth and decorated with brass tacks forming designs and initials on the lids. Children, perhaps related, were commonly added to the same coffin over the years. The racial mix of the presidio community is preserved in the skeleton of doña María Antonia Carrillo of Santa Bárbara. Analysis revealed characteristics of Caucasian, Indian, and Negro ancestry (Carrico 1973; Costello and Walker 1987; Ezell and Ezell 1980:86).

Only a thin, intermittent trickle of civilian colonists came to California. Fifty colonists arrived in 1774, followed by 240 in 1776, with only sporadic additions thereafter. By 1810, three pueblos had been founded: San José in 1777, Los Angeles in 1781, and Branciforte (present-day Santa Cruz) in 1797. The total pueblo population by 1815 was about 1800. The pueblos were poorly supported and usually did not provide the agricultural resources originally intended. No new civilian communities were founded in California after the initial three and no significant immigration took place until 1834.

In the early 1800s, Mexico's War of Independence left California isolated. Supply ships from San Blas, Nayarit, began to make fewer visits after 1798 and were discontinued altogether after 1810 (Thurman 1967). As these supply ships had been California's only regular contact with the outside world, both the military and civilian population began to depend heavily on the missions for material support. Isolated and without wages or means of support, the military extracted what they could from the missions by issuing virtually worthless script. Civilian colonists, although more independent than the military, also became indebted to the missions. By 1815, the missions were the sole supporters of Spain's program to colonize its California frontier.

Mexican Government

Legal Foreign Trade. Mexico won its independence from Spain in 1821. With independence came important changes for California: legal foreign trade and civilian access to land through direct grants.

Foreign traders had become active along the California coast, especially after 1810 when the Mexican War of Independence disrupted Spanish maritime vigilance. European manufactured items were clandestinely traded for furs, mission agricultural produce, and hides and tallow (Ogden 1941). Early, illegal contact with traders at Buenaventura Mission has been indicated by Aleut (Alaskan) Indian artifacts found during excavations (Greenwood 1975:88) and by agricultural production statistics (Costello, this volume).

When strict prohibitions against foreign trade were lifted by Mexico in 1823, missions began to legally trade hides and tallow in exchange for manufactured goods. With vast herds of cattle, the missions were able to supply large quantities of these goods, which encouraged trading houses, especially along the Atlantic seaboard, to escalate their California trade after 1826 (Dana 1840). The hides were dried at the missions, salted for travel at the seaports, and tanned in New England and Europe. This enterprise constituted the only major profitable occupation in California during the entire Spanish and Mexican rule (Burcham 1981:122).

What the missions chose to spend at least some of their newfound trading wealth on is recorded in archaeological deposits postdating the mid-1820s. English ceramic sherds predominate, accompanied by a corresponding increase in French wine and champagne bottles and English gin and whiskey bottles (Costello 1989; Farnsworth 1987). It is interesting that at the Ontiveros Adobe, a private rancho of the same period, a paucity of European goods indicates that its inhabitants participated little in this new lucrative economy (Frierman 1982).

Archaeological excavations have also revealed that some changes were made in mission facilities to support this new hide and tallow industry. The brick and tile kiln at Mission San Antonio, no longer in heavy demand for new construction, appears to have been used instead to burn bone in order to produce a fine lime for use in soaking the hides (Costello 1985; Langenwalter and McKee 1985).

Secularization and the Rise of the Ranchos. By the mid-1820s, the missions controlled vast amounts of land, large herds of livestock, and well-established agricultural production, although most institutions had experienced corresponding declines in population. These economic successes brought the missions under the scrutiny of the growing civilian population, whose only way to share in California's wealth was to obtain mission assets. Through political pressure and a liberal Mexican congress, the missions of Alta and Baja California were decreed to be secularized in August of 1833. Thus, between 1834 and 1836, almost eight million acres of land became available for civilian settlement in Alta California (Hornbeck 1979).

The terms of the decree specified that missionaries were to relinquish all control over missions but would be allowed to perform religious duties. Although provisions were made for the distribution of mission tools and land to the Indians, virtually all mission lands were granted to the civilian and military population. Where 51 land grants had been issued between 1769 and 1834, over 800 were confirmed by the Mexican government between 1840 and 1847 (Beck and Haase 1974).

Many of the mission buildings were subsequently occupied by these secular managers, and evidence of their activities, and of the general demise of mission facilities, has been revealed through archaeological excavation. At Santa Inés Mission, managers took over half of the padres' residence wing, converted one of its rooms into a kitchen by building a *brasero* along one wall, and appear to have used some of the unoccupied rooms for dumping debris (Costello 1989). A soldier and his Indian wife moved into vacant rooms at La Purísima Mission (Deetz 1978) and private dwellings appeared on mission grounds (Marshall 1982). At Mission San Antonio, the abandoned tile kiln became the site for the burial of an old, and apparently beloved, mission dog (Costello 1985; Langenwalter and McKee 1985).

Although some Indians did remain at the missions after 1833, most left. At this time, the native peoples of California virtually disappear from the documentary record. Thus, archaeological research has proven to be one of the few means of illuminating this part of their history. Evidence has been found to indicate their presence at private ranchos (Greenwood, this volume) and in some urban centers (Schulz and Barter 1985). Former neophytes are reported to have returned to the missions for visits, especially on holidays, and at Santa Inés and La Purísima at least some of the dead were brought back and interred in the mission cemetery (Costello 1989; Walker, this volume). By the time of secularization, the majority of mission Indians had been born at the missions and had no village to return to. Many did migrate to the countryside, however, and although some of their *rancherias* (villages) have been identified, none has yet been extensively excavated (Long and May 1970).

By obtaining mission lands through grants, and using available disenfranchised mission Indians for labor, private ranchos became the dominant economic force in the countryside, with an emphasis on raising cattle to build up the lucrative foreign hide and tallow trade, and later to feed the Gold Rush populations. This "Rancho" period of California history has been greatly romanticized in modern literature. Excavations at some of these sites have provided some facts to go with established fiction (Greenwood, this volume). At the Ontiveros Adobe (1815–ca. 1835), Indian-made pottery present in large numbers along with beads and stone tools provides information of a work force of Indians (Frierman 1982). At the Sepulveda rancho "Cienaga" (ca. 1820–1868), participation in the lucrative hide and tallow trade is revealed by the abundance of European goods in their imported wares (Chace 1969).

In coastal trading towns, urban centers were emerging with their own activities and social classes. These included the pueblos of Los Angeles and San José and the settlements that grew up around the former presidios of San Diego, Santa Bárbara, Monterey, and San Francisco. The influence of a growing American element in the towns produced responses from the Californios that appear to vary according to economic status. Excavations in Monterey and Sonora indicate that some successful merchant families adopted not only the material goods but the eating customs of the new Yankee culture (Felton and Schulz 1983). In contrast, comparable artifact collections recovered in San Diego at a less affluent residence show greater adherence to traditional food-related activities (Schulz et al. 1987).

Evidence of civil urban projects for these growing communities is seen in the excavated remains of extensive aqueduct systems constructed through Los Angeles, and in possible indications of efforts to clean up rotting cattle carcasses in San Diego (Schulz 1987). Excavation of the Los Angeles adobe occupied by a Scotsman and his Indian wife also provide interesting information on culturally mixed households (Wallace et al. 1959; Wallace and Wallace 1958, 1959, 1961).

History of Research

The history of archaeological research in Hispanic California begins with the local preservation and restoration movements of the early twentieth century. More systematic, large-scale reconstructions were conducted by state and local governments in the 1940s and 1950s, although archaeological excavations were still limited to providing information pertinent to physical reconstruction of the buildings. Long-term excavations by university field schools became popular in the 1960s. Also in the 1960s, in keeping with general trends in the field of archaeology, emphasis began to shift from architecture to human interactions. With the development of cultural resource management in the 1970s, archaeological efforts became diversified, with respect to both the types of sites studied and research questions posed. Recent work has focused on ethnographic and historic documentary materials with a view to enhancing interpretation of the archaeological record. Summaries of various aspects of archaeological work on Spanish and Mexican sites in California are found in Chartkoff and Chartkoff (1984), Hoover (1985), and Schuyler (1978).

After the missions were secularized in 1832, lands were divided, sold, and variously developed by private individuals. When California became a state in 1850, President Lincoln returned virtually all the central mission quadrangles to the ownership of the Catholic Church. The fate of these buildings varied greatly, depending on the amount of urban development and the nature of other events that took place in their proximity. Where there was an active parish, churches were generally preserved, and occasionally the adjoining padres' rooms, whereas other quadrangle buildings, unless reoccupied, usually crumbled back into the earth. Outlying features that were not part of the quadrangle area (such as Indian dwellings, aqueducts, mills, and kilns) have rarely survived, and only a few sites of once numerous mission ranches (*estancias*) and outlying chapels (*asistencias*) can be precisely located.

In the 1890s, public interest in the mission ruins was aroused at a time when California was actively promoting emigration. Entrepreneur Charles Lummis saw the cultural and financial opportunities in the neglected missions and spearheaded a drive to promote them as being one of the greatest financial assets of California. "A man is a poor fool," he stated, "who thinks he can do business without sentiment" (Kirker 1973:121). At the same time, the California Landmarks League worked to preserve and restore the missions, while California architects fostered Mission, and later Spanish Revival, architectural styles. Genuine historical interest colored by romantic notions of mission life, the appeal of the exotic architecture, and hopes of economic rewards inspired various movements to protect and rebuild Spanish and Mexican structures.

Reconstructions by the Catholic Church were accomplished largely through outside funding—from generous benefactors, such as William Randolph Hearst. Although conducted with great enthusiasm and widespread support, these reconstructions were often poorly researched and executed and rarely included archaeological work beforehand.

Exceptions are found at Mission San Fernando Rey (Harrington 1938, 1940, 1948) and at Mission San Luis Rey. At the latter site, resident priest Fr. Anthony Soto systematically uncovered the garden complex during nearly a decade of work (Harrington 1958; Soto 1960, 1961). Architect Harry Downie also distinguished himself by his conscientious effort to ensure that historical reconstructions were accurate at the many missions he worked on.

The two mission sites not owned by the Catholic Church are in public hands: La Purísima and Sonoma (San Francisco Solano). These are also the locations of some of the earliest archaeological investigations. The reconstruction of La Purísima Mission was a 1930 Works Progress Administration (WPA) Project under the direction of the National Park Service (Hageman and Ewing 1980). Between 1934 and 1938, excavations took place on eighteen mission buildings and features. Extensive research was also conducted on construction technologies and original fabric in order to accurately replicate the historic buildings. The scale of this project has not been equaled.

The California State Division of Beaches and Parks also conducted early excavations at Sonoma Mission under a joint agreement with the University of California (Bennyhoff and Elsasser 1954; Treganza 1956). The investigators were aware of the success of cultural reconstructions in the Southwest and were the first to formally suggest broadening the scope of California mission archaeology beyond architecture to include culture.

The first major project to incorporate this broader approach was James Deetz's study of the Indian residence at La Purísima Mission (1978). It addressed questions concerning acculturation of the Chumash by drawing on excavations previously conducted by Deetz at the nearby contact village site of Alamo Pintado. Deetz's study at La Purísima was a landmark in this turning from architectural to anthropological questions, although the discipline was to take some time in negotiating the long, wide curve of this new direction.

The 1960s also saw the beginning of long-term excavations utilizing field classes and volunteers—at the San Diego Mission (Moriarty 1969; Moriarty and Weyland 1971; Reck and Moriarty 1972) and the San Diego Presidio (Brockington and Brandes 1965; Carrico 1973; Ezell 1970, 1976; Ezell and Broadbent 1972; A Landscape of the Past 1968). Although a great deal of valuable material has been uncovered since then, comprehensive reports on these projects are still in preparation. Field schools continue to provide the means of excavation at Mission San Antonio de Padua (Hoover and Costello 1985), Mission Soledad (Farnsworth 1987), and Mission San Juan Capistrano (Magalousis and Martin 1981).

Although restoration projects continue to provide the impetus for California State Parks archaeological projects, findings now regularly include cultural as well as architectural interpretations (Felton and Schulz 1983; Schulz 1987; Schulz and Barter 1985; Schulz et al. 1987). Limited excavations have also been carried out at Hispanic sites by various private groups, archaeological societies, and individuals. Many of these published accounts are listed in the bibliography at the end of this chapter.

Excavations conducted as cultural resource management projects are making major contributions to the study of California archaeology, although few of these are published and therefore circulation of information is poor. Pertinent laws require both mandatory surveys, which have resulted in the discovery of sites previously unknown, and excavation of significant remains before they are destroyed. Investigations have also been carried out at sites that were often previously overlooked, such as aqueduct systems, butchering areas, and technological sites, and extensive archeological work has been conducted at several of the mission quadrangle areas. Excavation at San Buenaventura Mission in 1974–1976 by Roberta Greenwood (1975, 1976) provides the earliest example of these large-scale studies. Other extensive mission excavations have been carried out at San José Mission (Deitz et al., 1983) and Santa Inés Mission (Costello 1989), as well as at the field school sites mentioned above.

Our understanding of the Hispanic history of California is being increasingly enriched through the excavation of Spanish and Mexican Period sites. Many of the details of life that we are discovering in the ground are unrecorded in documents. Archaeological studies of these remains have substantially increased our understanding of this important period. Archaeological work has identified the locations and functions of unrecorded Spanish and Mexican buildings and structures and provided a more complete picture of the distribution of Hispanic culture over the landscape. Investigations into types of sites which have often been overlooked by preservationists have widened our view of the past to include technological sites such as aqueducts and kilns, and humble dwellings of *paisanos*. Unique evidence of Native American adaptations to European culture has been recovered from sites of mission, ranchos, and towns. Archaeological research has also produced information on the cultural mixing which resulted in Californio society and on how this society was affected by the arrival of the Yankees. As a result, many of our previously held assumptions about the technological, economic, social, and religious aspects of life in Alta California are now being challenged and refined.

Chronology

1535   Fortun, Ximénez, discovers Baja California.

1539   Francisco de Ulloa explores the Gulf of California.

1542   Juan Rodríguez Cabrillo explores north to the Santa Bárbara Channel Islands.

1579   Francis Drake careens *Golden Hind* in a California bay.

1595   Sebastián Rodriguez Cermeño loses his ship at Drake's Bay and returns in an open launch.

1602   Sebastián Vizcíno sails north to Monterey Bay.

1769   Portalá expedition; Mission San Diego founded; San Diego Presidio established.

1770   Mission San Carlos de Monterey founded.

1771   Missions San Antonio and San Gabriel founded.

1772   Mission San Luis Obispo founded; Pedro Fages discovers Tejon Pass.

1774   Juan Bautista de Anza brings first overland expedition to California from present-day Arizona.

1775 Second de Anza expedition to California brings 240 civilian colonists.

1776 Missions San Francisco de Asís and San Juan Capistrano founded; San Francisco Presidio established.

1777 Mission Santa Clara founded; Pueblo San José founded.

1779 Felipe de Néve issues Reglamento, first laws for California.

1781 Pueblo Los Angeles founded.

1782 Mission San Buenaventura founded; Santa Bárbara Presidio established.

1786 Mission Santa Barbara founded.

1787 Mission La Purísima Concepción founded.

1791 Missions Santa Cruz and Soledad founded.

1796 The *Otter* (Ebenezer Dorr, Captain) is first American vessel to anchor in California.

1797 Missions San José, San Juan Buatista, San Miguel, and San Fernando Rey founded; Pueblo Branciforte founded.

1798 Mission San Luis Rey founded.

1804 Mission Santa Inés founded.

1810 Hidalgo revolution in Mexico; supply ships from San Blas suspended.

1811 Kuskov begins Russian settlement at Fort Ross.

1812 Destructive earthquake in Central California, winter 1811–1812.

1817 Mission San Rafael founded.

1818 Pirate Hippolyte de Bouchard ravages coastal towns.

1821 Mexico achieves independence from Spain.

1823 Mission San Francisco Solano founded.

1823 California opened to legal foreign trade.

1834 Governor José Figueroa issues proclamation to secularize the California missions.

1846 Claiming of California for the United States.

1848 Treaty of Guadelupe-Hidalgo; discovery of gold in Sierra Nevada.

1850 California statehood.

1851 President Lincoln returns mission buildings to Catholic Church.

Bibliography

Arthur, Don, Julia Costello, and Brian Fagan
  1975 A Preliminary Account of Majolica Sherds from the Chapel Site, Royal Spanish Presidio, Santa Bárbara, California. *The Kiva* 41(2):207–214.
Avina, Rose Hollenbaugh
  1973 *Spanish and Mexican Land Grants in California*. R and E Research Associates, San Francisco.
Baer, Kurt
  1958 *Architecture of the California Missions*. University of California Press, Berkeley.
Bancroft, Herbert Howe
  1969 *The Works of Hubert Howe Bancroft*, vols. 18–24. Reprinted. Wallace Hebberd, Santa Barbara. Originally published 1886, History Co., San Francisco.
Barnes, Mark R., and Ronald V. May
  1972 *Mexican Majolica in Northern New Spain*. Occasional Paper No. 2. Pacific Coast Archaeological Society. Costa Mesa, California.

Bean, Lowell John
  1978 Social Organization. In *California*, edited by Robert F. Heizer, pp. 673–682. Handbook of North American Indians, vol. 8, William C. Sturtevant, general editor. Smithsonian Institution, Washington, D.C.
Bean, Lowell John, and Sylvia Brekke Vane
  1978 Cults and Their Transformation. In *California*, edited by Robert F. Heizer, pp. 662–672. Handbook of North American Indians, vol. 8, William C. Sturtevant, general editor. Smithsonian Institution, Washington, D.C.
Beck, Warren A., and Ynez D. Haase
  1974 *Historical Atlas of California*. University of Oklahoma Press, Norman.
Bennyhoff, James A., and Albert B. Elsasser
  1954 *Sonoma Mission: An Historical and Archaeological Study of Primary Constructions, 1823–1913*. Archaeological Survey Report No. 27. University of California, Berkeley.
Bente, Vance G.
  1980 *Test Excavation of LAn-1016ah: The Ontiveros Adobe, Sante Fe Springs, California*. Greenwood and Associates. Submitted to Redevelopment Agency, Santa Fe Springs.
Bolton, Herbert Eugene
  1917 *Font's Complete Diary: A Chronicle of the Founding of San Francisco*. University of California Press, Berkeley.
  1926 *Historical Memoirs of New California by Fray Francisco Palou, O.F.M.*, 4 vols. University of California Press, Berkeley.
  1927 *Fray Juan Crespí: Missionary Explorer on the Pacific Coast, 1769–1774*. University of California Press, Berkeley.
  1930 *Anza's California Expeditions*, 5 vols. University of California Press, Berkeley.
  1960 *The Mission as a Frontier Institution in the Spanish-American Colonies*. Texas Western College Press, El Paso.
Bowman, J. N.
  1951 Weights and Measures of Provincial California. *California Historical Society Quarterly* 30(4):315–338.
Brockington, Donald L., and Ray Brandes
  1965 The First Season's Work at the Silent City. *Journal of San Diego History* 11(4):1–29.
Browne, Robert O.
  1976 The Use of Lime at San Buenaventura. In *The Changing Faces of Main Street*, edited by Roberta S. Greenwood, pp. 199–209. Greenwood and Associates. Submitted to Redevelopment Agency, City of San Buenaventura, California.
Burcham, L. T.
  1981 *Calfornia Range Land*. Center for Archaeological Research at Davis Publication No. 7. University of California, Davis.
Butler, William B.
  1973 The Avila Adobe: The Determination of Architectural Change. *Historical Archaeology* 7:30–45.
Carrico, Richard L.
  1973 The Identification of Two Burials at the San Diego Presidio. *Journal of San Diego History* 19(4):51–55.
Carrillo, Charles
  1977 Digging at California's Roots. *Pacific Coast Archaeological Society Quarterly* 13(4):53–65.
Chace, Paul G.
  1966 A Summary Report of the Costa Mesa Estancia. *Pacific Coast Archaeological Society Quarterly* 2(3):30–37.
  1969 The Archaeology of Cieniga. *Pacific Coast Archaeological Society Quarterly* 5(3):39–70.

Chartkoff, Joseph L., and Kerry Kona Chartkoff
1984 *The Archaeology of California*. Stanford University Press, California.

Cook, Sherburne F.
1976a *The Conflict between the California Indian and White Civilization*. University of California Press, Berkeley.
1976b *The Population of the California Indians, 1769–1970*. University of California Press, Berkeley.

Cook, Sherburne F., and Woodrow Borah
1979 Mission Registers as Sources of Vital Statistics: Eight Missions of Northern California. In *Essays in Population History: Mexico and California*, vol. 3, pp. 177–311. University of California Press, Berkeley.

Costello, Julia G.
1975 Archaeological Survey of Mission Vieja de la Purísima. *Pacific Coast Archaeological Society Quarterly* 11(2):41–59.
1977 Lime Processing in Spanish California: with Special Reference to Santa Barbara. *Pacific Coast Archaeological Society Quarterly* 13(2):22–32.
1985 The Brick and Tile Kiln. In *Excavations at Mission San Antonio 1976–1978*, edited by Robert L. Hoover and Julia G. Costello, pp. 122–145. Monograph No. 26. Institute of Archaeology, University of California, Los Angeles.
1989 *Santa Inés Mission Excavations 1986–1988*. Historical Archaeology in California No. 10. Coyote Press, Salinas, California. In press.

Costello, Julia G., and Phillip L. Walker
1987 Burials from the Santa Barbara Presidio Chapel. *Historical Archaeology* 21(1):3–17.

Costo, Rupert, and Jennette Henry Costo
1987 *The Missions of California: A Legacy of Genocide*. Indian Historian Press, San Francisco.

Dana, Richard Henry
1980 *Two Years before the Mast*. Reprinted. Mayflower Books, New York. Originally published 1840.

Davis, James T.
1973 *Trade Routes and Economic Exchange Among the Indians of California*. Publications in Archaeology, Ethnology and History No. 3. Ballena Press, Ramona, Calif.

Deetz, James
1978 Archaeological Investigations at La Purisima Mission. In *Historical Archaeology: A Guide to Substantive and Theoretical Contributions*, edited by Robert L. Schuyler, pp. 160–190. Baywood, Farmingdale, N.Y.

Dietz, Stephen A., G. James West, Julia Costello, Howard L. Needles, and Vicki Cassman.
1983 *Final Report of Archaeological Investigations at Mission San José (CA-Ala-1)*. Report submitted to Mission San José, San José, Calif.

Egenhoff, Elisabeth L.
1952 *Fabricas*. Supplement to the California Journal of Mines and Geology. Division of Mines and Geology, California Department of Conservation, Sacramento.

Elsasser, Albert B.
1978 Basketry. In *California*, edited by Robert F. Heizer, pp. 626–641. Handbook of North American Indians, vol. 8, William C. Sturtevant, general editor. Smithsonian Institution, Washington, D.C.

Engelhardt, Zephyrin, O.F.M.
1908–1915 *The Missions and Missionaries of California*, 4 vols. James H. Barry, San Francisco.

Evans, William S., Jr.
1969 California's Indian Pottery: A Native Contribution to the Culture of the Ranchos. *Pacific Coast Archaeological Society Quarterly* 5(3):71–81.

Ezell, Paul H.
  1970 Chapter from the Log Book. *Journal of San Diego History* 16(4):20–24.
  1976 Excavations of the San Diego Presidio Chapel. *San Diego History News* 13(10):3.
Ezell, Paul H., and Noel D. Broadbent
  1972 Archaeological Investigations at the Casa de José Manuel Machado (The Stewart House). *Pacific Coast Archaeological Society Quarterly* 8(4):1–34.
Ezell, Paul H., and Greta S. Ezell
  1980 Bread and Barbecues at San Diego Presidio. In *Spanish Colonial Frontier Research*, compiled and edited by Henry F. Dobyns. Spanish Borderlands Research No. 1. Center for Anthropological Studies, Albuquerque.
Farnsworth, Paul
  1987 *The Economics of Acculturation in the California Missions: A Historical and Archaeological Study of Mission Nuestra Senora de la Soledad*. Ph.D. dissertation, University of California, Los Angeles.
Felton, David L.
  1985 Santa Cruz Mission State Historic Park—Architectural and Archaeological Investigations 1984–1985. Report on file, California Department of Parks and Recreation, Sacramento.
Felton, David L., and Peter D. Schulz
  1983 *The Diaz Collection: Material Culture and Social Change in Mid-Nineteenth-Century Monterey*. California Archeological Reports No. 23. California Department of Parks and Recreation, Sacramento.
Frierman, Jay D.
  1982 *The Ontiveros Adobe: Early Rancho Life in Alta California*. Greenwood and Associates. Submitted to Redevelopment Agency, Santa Fe Springs, Calif.
Geiger, Maynard, O.F.M., and Clement W. Meighan
  1976 *As the Padres Saw Them: California Indian Life and Customs as Reported by the Franciscan Missionaries 1813–1815*. Santa Bárbara Mission Archive Library, Santa Bárbara.
Greenwood, Roberta (editor)
  1975 *3500 Years on One City Block*. Greenwood and Associates. Submitted to Redevelopment Agency, City of Buenaventura, Calif.
  1976 *The Changing Faces of Main Street*. Greenwood and Associates. Submitted to Redevelopment Agency, City of Buenaventura, California.
Greenwood, Roberta S., and Robert W. Browne
  1968 The Chapel of Santa Gertrudis. *Pacific Coast Archaeological Society Quarterly* 4(4):1–59.
Greenwood, Roberta S., and N. Gessler
  1968 The Mission San Buenaventura Aqueduct with Particular Reference to the Fragments at Weldon Canyon. *Pacific Coast Archaeological Society Quarterly* 4(4):61–87.
Guest, Francis F., O.F.M.
  1979 An Examination of the Thesis of S.F. Cook on the Forced Conversion of Indians in the California Missions. *Southern California Quarterly* 61(1):1–77.
Gust, Sherri M.
  1982 Faunal Analysis and Butchering. In *The Ontiveros Adobe: Early Rancho Life in Alta California* by J. D. Frierman. pp. 101–144. Greenwood and Associates. Submitted to Redevelopment Agency, Santa Fe Springs, Calif.
Hageman, Fred C., and Russell C. Ewing
  1980 *An Archeological and Restoration Study of Mission La Purísima Concepción*. Arthur H. Clark, Glendale, Calif.
Harrington, M.R.
  1938 San Fernando Comes to Life. *Masterkey*, Vol. 12.
  1940 Real Progress at San Fernando Mission. *Masterkey* 14(3):118–119.
  1945 Shell Lime at Carmel Mission. *Masterkey* 19:70–73.

1948 The San Fernando Bells Ring Again. *Masterkey* 20(2):64–66.

1958 Digging up the Past at San Luis Rey. *Masterkey* 32(2):55–57.

Hastings, Richard B.

1975 San Buenaventura Mission, an Architectural View. In *3500 Years on One City Block*, edited by Roberta S. Greenwood. Greenwood and Associates. Submitted to the Redevelopment Agency, City of Buenaventura, Calif.

Heizer, Robert F.

1941 Archaeological Evidence of Sebastian Rodriguez Cermeño's California Visit in 1595. *California Historical Society Quarterly* 20(4).

1947 *Frances Drake and the California Indians in 1579*. University of California Press, Berkeley.

1972 *California's Oldest Historical Relic?* University of California, Lowie Museum of Anthropology. Berkeley.

1974 *Elizabethan California: A Brief and Sometimes Critical Review of Opinions on the Location of Frances Drake's Five Week's Visit with the Indians of Ships Land in 1579.* Ballena Press, Ramona, Calif.

1978a *California.* Editor. Handbook of North American Indians, vol. 8, William C. Sturtevant, general editor. Smithsonian Institution, Washington D.C.

1978b Natural Forces and Native World View. In *California*, edited by Robert F. Heizer, pp. 649–653. Handbook of North American Indians, vol. 8, William C. Sturtevant, general editor. Smithsonian Institution, Washington, D.C.

Hendry, George W.

1931 The Adobe Brick as an Historical Source. *Agricultural Hisory* 5:110–127.

Hendry, George W., and Margret P. Kelly (Bellue)

1925 The Plant Content of Adobe Bricks. *California Historical Society Quarterly* 4:361–373.

Hoover, Robert L.

1985 The Archaeology of Spanish Colonial Sites in California. In *Comparative Studies in the Archaeology of Colonialism*. BAR International Series 233, Oxford.

Hoover, Robert L., and Julia G. Costello (editors)

1985 *Excavations at Mission San Antonio 1976–1978*. Monograph No. 26. Institute of Archaeology, University of California, Los Angeles.

Hornbeck, David

1978a Land Tenure and Rancho Expansion in Alta California. *Journal of Historical Geography* (4):371–390.

1978b Mission Population of Alta California, 1810-1830. *Historical Geography* 8(1):9–12.

1979 The Patenting of California's Private Land Claims, 1851-1885. *Geographical Review* 69(4):434–448.

1982 The California Indian before European Contact. *Journal of Cultural Geography* 2(2): 23–39.

1983 *California Patterns: a Geographical and Historical Atlas*. Mayfield, Palo Alto, Calif.

1985 Early Mission Settlement. In *Some Reminiscences about Fray Junipero Serra*, edited by Francis F. Weber, pp. 27–36. Kimberly Press, Santa Barbara.

1986 California Rancheros and the Unlanded–Who Lived in Arcadia? In *Early California Reflections*. San Juan Capistrano Regional Library.

Hudson, Dee Travis, Thomas Blackburn, Rosario Curletti, and Janice Timbrook (editors)

1977 *The Eye of the Flute: Chumash Traditional History and Ritual as Told by Fernando Librado Kitsepawit to John P. Harrington*. Santa Barbara Museum of Natural History, Santa Barbara.

Hudson, Dee Travis, Janice Timbrook, and Melissa Rempe

1978 *Tomol: Th Ethnographic Notes on Chumash Watercraft by John P. Harrington*. Edited by Thomas Blackburn and Lowell Bean. Anthropological Papers No. 9. Ballena Press, Ramona, Calif.

Hudson, D. Travis, and E. Underhay.
   1978 *Crystals in the Sky: An Intellectual Odyssey Involving Chumash Astronomy, Cosmology, and Rock Art.* Ballena Press Anthropologcial Papers No. 10. Socorro, N.M.
Humphry, Richard V.
   1965 The La Purísima Mission Cemetery. *Archaeological Survey Annual Report* No. 7, pp. 179–192. University of California, Los Angeles.
Kimbro, Edna
   1988 Cocinas of Early California. Paper presented at Annual Meeting of the California Mission Studies Association, San Fernando Mission.
King, Chester D.
   1978 Protohistoric and Historic Archaeology. In *California*, edited by Robert F. Heizer, pp. 58–68. Handbook of North American Indians, vol. 8, William C. Sturtevant, general editor. Smithsonian Institution, Washington, D.C.
   1981 The Explanation of Differences and Similarities among Beads Used in Prehistoric and Early Historic California. *Ornament* 5(1).
Kirker, Harold
   1973 *California's Architectural Frontier.* Peregrine Smith, Santa Barbara.
Kroeber, Alfred L.
   1976 *Handbook of the Indians of California.* Dover Publications, New York. Originally published 1925, Bureau of American Ethnology Bulletin No. 78. Washington, D.C.
A Landscape of the Past: the Story of the Royal Presidio Excavations
   1968 *Journal of San Diego History* 14(4):5–32.
Langenwalter, Paul E., and Laurence W. McKee
   1985 Vertebrate Faunal Remains. In *Excavations at Mission San Antonio 1976–1978*, edited by Robert L. Hoover and Julia G. Costello, pp. 94–121. Monograph No. 26. Institute of Archaeology, University of California, Los Angeles.
Long, Paul V., and Ronald V. May
   1970 An Archaeological Survey of Rancho de San Felipe. *Pacific Coast Archaeological Society Quarterly* 6(4):1–54.
Magalousis, Nicholas M., and Paul M. Martin
   1981 Mission San Juan Capistrano: Preservation and Excavation of a Spanish Colonial Landmark. *Archaeology* 34(3):60–63.
Marshall, Ralph P.
   1982 An Archaeological Survey of the Ortega Vigare Adobe. *Pacific Coast Archaeological Society Quarterly*, 18(1):1–61.
Meighan, Clement W.
   1950 Excavations in Sixteenth Century Shell Mounds at Drake's Bay, Marin County. *Archaeological Survey Report* No. 9, pp. 27–32. University of California, Berkeley.
   1987 Indians and the Missions. *Southern California Quarterly* 49:187–201.
Meighan, Clement W., and Robert F. Heizer
   1952 Archaeological Exploration of Sixteenth Century Indian Mounds at Drake's Bay. *California Historical Quarterly* 31(2):99–106.
Moratto, Michael J.
   1984 *California Archaeology.* Academic Press, New York.
Moriarty, James Robert
   1969 Historic Site Archaeology at Mission San Diego de Alcalá. *Masterkey* 43(3)100–108.
Moriarty, James R., and William R. Weyland
   1971 Excavations at San Diego Mission. *Masterkey* 45(4)124–137.
Mosk, Sanford A.
   1938 Price Fixing in Spanish California. *California Historical Quarterly* 37.
Newcomb, Rexford
   1925 *The Old Mission Churches and Historic Houses of California.* J. P. Lippincott, Philadelphia.

Ogden, Adele
    1941 *The California Sea Otter Trade, 1782–1848*. University of California, Berkeley.
Polzer, Charles, S.J.
    1987 Black, Gray and White: The Founding and Fading of the California Missions. In
    Early California Reflections edited by Nicholas M. Magalousis, pp. 6-1–6-22. Orange
    County Public Library, San Juan Capistrano.
Praetzellis, Adrian
    1987 *The Archaeology of Two Features in the Casa Grande Back Lot, Sonoma, California*. Sub-
    mitted to the City of Sonoma by Thomas M. Oringer.
Reck, D. Glen, and James R. Moriarty
    1972 Primary Report on the Discovery of a U.S. Cemetery at the Mission San Diego
    de Alcalá. *Anthropological Journal of Canada* 10(2).
Schulz, Peter, D.
    1987 Archaeological Evidence for Early Bone Lime Production in Old Town San Diego.
    Pacific Coast Archaeological Society Quarterly 23(2):52–59.
Schulz, Peter D., and Eloise Richards Barter
    1985 Incised Brownware Sherds from Old Town San Diego. *Pacific Coast Archaeological
    Society Quarterly* 21(4):25–28.
Schulz, Peter D., Ronald Quinn, and Scott Fulmer
    1987 Archaeological Investigations at the Rose-Robinson Site, Old Town San Diego.
    Pacific Coast Archaeological Society Quarterly 23(2):1–51.
Schuyler, Robert L.
    1978 Indian-Euro-Americn Interaction: Archeological Evidence from Non-Indian Sites.
    In *California*, edited by Robert F. Heizer, pp. 69–79. Handbook of North American
    Indians, vol. 8. William C. Sturtevant, general editor. Smithsonian Institution,
    Washington, D.C.
Soto, Anthony
    1960 Recent Excavations at San Luis Rey Mission: The Sunken Gardens. *Provincial Annals*
    (Province of Santa Bárbara of the Order of Friars Minor) 22(4):2-5–249.
    1961 Mission San Luis Rey, California—Excavations at the Sunken Gardens. *The Kiva*
    26(4)34–43.
Thurman, Michael E.
    1967 *The Naval Department of San Blas: New Spain's Bastion for Alta California and Nootka
    1767–1798*. Arthur H. Clark, Glendale, Calif.
Treganza, Adan E.
    1956 Sonoma Mission: An Archaeological Reconstruction of the Mission San Francisco
    de Solano Quadrangle. *Kroeber Anthropological Papers* 14:1–18.
Vancouver, George
    1984 *A Voyage of Discovery to the North Pacific Ocean, and Round the World*. 3 vols. Re-
    printed. Hakluyt Society. Originally Published 1798, G. G. and J. Robinson, Lon-
    don.
Vitruvius, Marcus Pollio
    1960 *The Ten Books on Architecture*. Reprinted. Dover Publications, New York. Originally
    Published ca. 64 A.D.
Von der Porten, Edward P.
    1972 Drake and Cermeño in California: Sixteenth Century Chinese Ceramics. *Historical
    Archaeology* 6:1–22.
    1984 The Drake Puzzle Solved. *Pacific Discovery* 37(3):22–26.
Walker, Phillip L., and Katherine D. Davidson
    1989 Analysis of Faunal Remains from Santa Inés Mission. In *Santa Inés Mission Excava-
    tions, 1986–1988* by Julia G. Costello. Historical Archaeology in California. Coyote
    Press, Salinas, Calif.

Wallace, Edith
    1978 Sexual Status and Role Differences. In *California*, edited by Robert F. Heizer, pp. 683–689. Handbook of North American Indians, vol. 8, William C. Sturtevant, general editor. Smithsonian Institution, Washington, D.C.
Wallace, William J.
    1978 Music and Musical Instruments. In *California*, edited by Robert F. Heizer, pp. 642–648. Handbook of North American Indians, vol. 8, William C. Sturtevant, general editor. Smithsonian Institution, Washington, D.C.
Wallace, William J., Roger Desautels, and G. Kritzman
    1959 The House of the Scotch Paisano. *Lasca Leaves* 8(1):2–13. Los Angeles State and County Arboretum.
Wallace, William J., and Edith T. Wallace
    1958 Indian Artifacts from the Hugo Reid Adobe. *Lasca Leaves* 8(4):1–8. Los Angeles State and County Arboretum.
    1959 Archaeological Investigations in the "Patio" of the Hugo Reid Adobe. *Lasca Leaves* 9(3):55–60. Los Angeles State and County Arboretum.
    1961 Historic Objects from the Hugo Reid Adobe. *Lasca Leaves* 11(2):39–65. Los Angeles State and County Arboretum.
Waters, Willard O.
    1954 *Franciscan Missions of Upper California as Seen by Foreign Visitors and Residents*. Glen Dawson, Los Angeles.
Webb, Edith Buckland
    1982 *Indian Life at the Old Missions*. University of Nebraska Press.
Weber, Frances J., Reverend

Chapter 20 ■

G. James West

Early Historic Vegetation Change in Alta California: The Fossil Evidence

Two hundred and twenty-seven years after a short visit by the explorer Juan Cabrillo, Alta California's first permanent Spanish settlement was established in 1769. For the next five and a half decades, the Spanish extended their influence by means of missions, presidios, and pueblos along the south and central coastal margin of California (roughly one-sixth of the total area of the state; see Figure 19-3) and initiated a settlement/subsistence pattern that was to alter greatly both the cultural and natural environments.

Climate, substrate, time, topography, and biotic factors, including people, have all contributed to the evolution of California's diverse vegetation. This chapter examines the fossil evidence on the effect of the Spanish settlement on California's rangelands. Fossil evidence consists of the remains or impressions of the whole or part of formerly living plants preserved in cultural and natural contexts.

The composition of southern and central California's rangelands prior to and during Spanish settlement is not well known; but it has been postulated, on the basis of fragmentary historic records and "relict" stands, that perennial bunch grasses, mainly the needle grasses (*Stipa* spp.), were dominant (Barry 1972;

Burcham 1957, 1981). The effects of native peoples on California's rangelands is largely unknown, but they certainly burned areas of a number of plant formations (Lewis 1973; Sampson 1944). Much of the burning took place in grasslands (Belcher 1843; Clar 1957; Clyman 1926; Farnham 1850; Kroeber 1932; Maloney 1945; Pancoast 1930; Waseurtz af Sandels 1945; Wilks 1958). Undoubtedly native peoples played a role in the composition and distribution of the grassland formations, but direct physical evidence is lacking. Primarily gatherers and hunters, many California natives utilized a seasonal-round to procure resources as they became available. The burning of portions of the grasslands appears to have been part of this procurement system. With the arrival of the Spanish, this system was directly challenged. For example, in 1793 Governor Arrigilla, while in Santa Barbara, proclaimed:

> With attention to the widespread damage which results to the public from the burning of the fields, customary up to now among both Christian and Gentile Indians in this country, whose [unintelligible] has been unduly tolerated, and as a consequence of various complaints that I have had of such abuse, I see myself required to have the foresight to prohibit for the future . . . all kinds of burning, not only in the vicinity of the towns but even at the most remote distances, which might cause some detriment, whether it be by Christian Indians or by Gentiles who have some relationship or communication with our establishments and missions. Therefore I order and command all comandantes of the presidios in my charge to do their duty and watch with the greatest earnestness to take whatever measures they may consider requisite and necessary to uproot this very harmful practice of setting fire to pasture lands, . . . [and] that they exercise equal vigilance in trying to advise the Christian Indians and Gentiles of the neighboring rancherias about this proclamation and impressing upon them that those who commit such an offense will be punished, and in case some burning occurs, they are to try immediately to take the most appropriate means to stop the fire [Clar 1957:7–8].

The Spanish not only purposely disrupted the native subsistence system, they also inadvertently altered it. Ironically, Native Americans may have exploited some of the newly arrived taxa such as mustard (*Brassica* spp.) and filaree (*Erodium* spp.) (Ebeling 1986; Gayton 1948; Heizer and Hester 1973). Hispanics replaced the native land-use patterns with permanent settlements based on a pastoral way of life. Initially the Spanish settlements were subsistence operations. It was not until late in their history that they changed to a productive economy.

Spanish settlements were in or abutted 10 of California's 54 plant formations (Küchler 1977). These settlements were generally in grassland, shrub, and oak savanna since these plant formations were best suited for agriculture and stock raising. Good rangelands, water, and soils that could be tilled were of paramount importance because it was through agriculture that the native populations were to be induced into Spanish culture. Although other plant formations, such as coniferous forests, were exploited, they were far away from the primary settlements and reportedly received minimal use (Clar 1957).

The historic record of changes that the Spanish initiated in California's rangelands has been described by Aschman (1976), Biswell (1956), Burcham (1956, 1957, 1970, 1975, 1981), Frenkel (1970), Heady (1977), Parish (1920), Rossi (1979), and Wester (1975). The greatest degree of change appears to have taken place within the grasslands, in which alien species now account for 50 to 90 percent of the plant cover (Biswell 1956:21).

Changes in the flora appear to have been brought about primarily by two factors: (1) the introduction of domestic grazing animals, whose populations grew rapidly from a few hundred animals to several hundred thousand, and (2) the introduction of alien plants, mainly from the Mediterranean region, that were already adapted to severe grazing pressures. The co-occurrence of these two factors was devastating to the native flora; unrestricted grazing exterminated many of the native species, which were then replaced by more aggressive and/or less palatable species (Burcham 1956).

One would expect that fossil evidence of these radical and rapid changes would be present in both cultural and natural contexts. That evidence is the subject of this discussion.

Fossil Record

Cultural Contexts

Both macroscopic and microscopic fossil plant records derived from cultural contexts are examined in this section. These records include remains or impressions found in adobe bricks, mortar, midden, and artifacts. Plant remains from cultural contexts are notable because of the potential for close chronological control, which is lacking or is poor in many other types of deposits. Conversely, where the historical record is found wanting, plant remains may provide the only chronological control. That is to say, provided there has been no contamination, plant remains of introduced taxa that are well documented, such as eucalyptus, can provide a minimum age or *terminus post quem* (the date after which) for a deposit.

Adobe Bricks. The most productive results regarding the introduction of alien plant taxa have come from the early studies of adobe bricks by Hendry (1931), Hendry and Bellue (1936), and Hendry and Kelly (1925). By examining plant remains extracted from adobe bricks from nine historic structures in Alta California and five in Baja California, Hendry and Bellue were able to show the presence, and often the variety, at a given date, of certain agricultural commodities, weeds, and native plants (Frenkel 1970:40). Eighteen alien weed and 15 crop remains were recovered from adobe buildings dated prior to 1824 (Hendry 1931). Of the 18 alien weeds identified, Hendry (1931:126) argued that 3 species, *Rumex crispus, Erodium circutarium,* and *Sonchus asper,* penetrated Alta California prior to 1769. He reached this conclusion upon finding that the species were present in the oldest walls of several mission buildings in widely separated localities, often in the absence of other alien species, and occasionally in the total absence of cereal remains.

No further evidence to support Hendry's proposition has been found. Nevertheless, the significance of Hendry's studies on the introduction of the weedy species cannot be overestimated. For example, *Erodium circutarium*, a member of the geranium family, is found abundantly throughout California and is an important early spring forage crop. Other weedy species identified by Hendry are widespread. Like *Erodium*, they constitute a major fraction of the annual grassland that is thought to have replaced the native perennial grassland (Biswell 1956; Burcham 1957, 1975).

Since the time of Hendry's pioneering studies, additional adobe bricks have been examined for macroscopic plant remains. The results appear in unpublished reports and are not readily available. Many of the bricks analyzed were from undated features or structures. Nonetheless, the identifications are compatible with the earlier studies and a number of additional taxa have been added to the list of potential early arrivals (Galbreath n.d.; Honeysett n.d.).

The pollen content of adobe brick and mortar has been examined for a number of structures in California (Duncan n.d.; Gregory and Schoenwetter n.d.; West n.d.a, n.d.b). These studies have been primarily concerned with determining the presence of pollen, establishing when alien domesticated and weedy taxa were introduced, dating architectural features, and reconstructing earlier environments. For the most part, this type of analysis can be seen as an adjunct to, not a replacement for, macroscopic analysis.

In many instances, pollen grain identifications are not as specific as identifications based on macroscopic remains; however, pollen often is present when larger plant remains have decayed. For as yet unknown reasons, there does not appear to be any consistency in the extent of pollen preservation versus the preservation of macroscopic plant remains. Nevertheless, pollen is generally present in bricks and mortar that have been protected from weathering.

Native American Cultural Deposits. Pollen analysis of Native American cultural deposits has given conflicting results regarding the introduction of several plant taxa. In one instance, the presence of *Erodium* pollen was used with soils-geomorphic analysis to separate the historic layers from the underlying prehistoric deposits (Byrne 1986). In another study within the same area, "*Erodium*-type" pollen as well as uncharred *Erodium* seeds were reported throughout two stratigraphic sections of a single prehistoric site that may have been occupied repeatedly for 5,000 years (Spaulding 1984:987–988). Extensive bioturbation of this latter site by both Native Americans and rodents was evident (>50 percent of a late prehistoric house floor had been disturbed by rodent activity) and it is likely that the presence of "*Erodium*-type" pollen throughout the profiles is an artifact of this disturbance. *Erodium* pollen has been noted from several other prehistoric cultural contexts in California, but in all instances the deposits were probably disturbed or, less likely, the pollen grains were confused with native Geraniaceae pollen. Pollen from *Plantago lanceolata*, plantain, has been found in prehistoric archaeological deposits on the west side of the San Joaquin Valley (West n.d.c). Here, too, extensive bioturbation of the deposits was evident.

Some of the most convincing evidence to indicate that Native Americans used alien plants is presented by Heizer and Hester (1973), who found *Erodium botrys* seeds and stems in a human coprolite from Bamert Cave, a late prehistoric and early historic-age Native American site in the Sierra Nevada foothills. A corn cob and several kernels also were found in the deposits. The corn may represent a form derived from a mixture of Southwest and Mexican types, the kind that could have been introduced during the Mission era in California. Other records of macroscopic alien plant remains from Native American cultural deposits have been presented in a large number of site reports, most of which are unpublished. Discussion of these other results, some of which are of questionable value because of recognized bioturbation, is beyond the scope of this review.

Natural Contexts

Thus far, natural contexts have provided a greater variety of data on the change in Spanish period vegetation than have cultural contexts, primarily because the techniques employed and the questions addressed have covered a broader spectrum. Pollen and spore analysis, phytolith studies, sedimentary analysis, charcoal abundance, and dendrochronological fire scar studies have all provided useful information.

Phytoliths. Any discussion of historic vegetation change in California must take into account the composition of pre-Hispanic grassland formations. Opal phytoliths appear to be the most promising clue to the types of grasses that were present. Microscopic biogenic opal, formed within plant cells and cell walls, is particularly abundant in the graminoids. In the Gramineae, opal phytoliths are considered diagnostic at the subfamily and in some cases at the tribal level. There are at least three recognized types of grass silica bodies: festucoid, panicoid, and chloridoid (Twiss et al. 1969). Nearly all the important annual Mediterranean grasses that have replaced native species in California are festucoid (Bartolome et al. 1985). The two presumed native perennials, *Stipa* and *Danthonia*, contain significant amounts of panicoid opals (Barkworth 1981; DeWet 1956).

Bartolome et al. (1985, 1986) have examined opal phytoliths from two annual grassland communities—one in the Sacramento Valley, the other on the Monterey coast. At both localities, relative abundance of panicoid opal phytoliths were greater at 10-cm depths than at the surface beneath the annual grassland dominated by alien taxa. Panicoid opal phytolith abundance at a depth of 10 cm at the annual grassland site and at an adjacent relict perennial grassland site were found to be similar. These preliminary findings are the first to support with fossil data the argument that the composition of the native grassland was dominated by perennial bunch grasses.

Sediments. With the new land-use patterns and the associated vegetation change instituted by the Spanish, the sedimentation rate might be expected to change. No study has addressed directly the effect of the Spanish settlement/ subsistence system on the sedimentation rate. However, Mudie and Byrne (1980) have compared the historic rate, inclusive of the Spanish period, with the prehistoric rate for a number of coastal estuaries and a small lake. Using radiocarbon dating and the pollen of alien weeds for chronological control, they found the alien pollen age sedimentation rate was double the average pre-alien rate. None of their pollen records provided a clear indication of the effects of Spanish settlement on sedimentation rates. Yet, if their tentative date of 1820 for the appearance of *Rumex* is correct, one record from Mission Bay, San Diego, suggests a rate of about 22 cm/100 yrs before 1910. The pre-alien pollen sedimentation rate was 11.2 cm/100 yrs.

Charcoal and Fire Scars. The evidence of past fires consists of charcoal contained in sediments (Patterson et al. 1987) and dendrochronological fire scars (Stokes 1980). The presence and abundance of charcoal has been reported for a number of California sedimentary sections (Russell 1983; West 1984), but only one study has had sufficient chronological control to examine the protohistoric Native American and Spanish periods.

Byrne et al. (1977) report on variations in charcoal abundance contained in deep-sea rhythmites recovered from the Santa Barbara Basin. Preliminary results indicate that charcoal influx values are primarily a reflection of large fires occurring at a distance of less than 50 km from the sampling site. Charcoal influx values for the sixteenth and seventeenth centuries show higher interlevel variance than modern values, which are more complacent. Excluding two major fire-flood events, the average charcoal influx value is lower for the prehistoric period than for the modern period. According to Byrne et al. (1977) this indicates that large fires may have occurred "every 20–30–40 years following relatively quiet low fire periods" (ibid.:361) and that there was less net burning per unit area, per unit time in the prehistoric period.

Dendrochronological fire scars on pine trees (*Pinus lambertiana, P. ponderosa, P. Jeffreyi*) provide an important fire frequency record for the Sierra, Coast, and Transverse ranges. Forestlands were, for the most part, not directly affected by the Spanish, but the Spanish undoubtedly did have an indirect effect on forestlands through their impact on Native populations. Thus the forest fire frequency record may be a reflection of anthropogenic burning in other plant formations.

In the central Coast Ranges, Griffen and Talley (1980: 84) report that pre-Spanish fires were relatively frequent (10 years or less), whereas fire frequencies after 1809 declined. Lightning frequency is low, and only three lightning-damaged pines were noted near their study plots. They also report on a similar fire history record near the western end of the Transverse Ranges, where lightning frequencies are much higher. The one tree studied there averaged 12 years between fire scars prior to 1806.

Fire frequencies for the American pioneer period at the eastern end of the Transverse Ranges in both the ponderosa pine and Jeffrey pine forest types did not differ significantly from frequencies in the Native American period (14–19 yrs. vs. 10–14 yrs.) (McBride and Jacobs 1980:88). Neither Spanish nor Mexican period settlers used the area of the forest that McBride and Jacobs studied, but the native population that utilized the forest was reduced by as much as 50 percent during the Spanish-Mexican period. McBride and Jacobs hypothesize that sheepherders, ranchers, and lumbermen replaced the Native Americans as causal agents for wildfires beyond the natural frequency expected from lightning. Lightning has accounted for about one-third of all the forest fires during the past 20 years.

In the Sierra, away from direct Spanish influence, the tree-ring record for mean fire frequency per tree in Kings Canyon National Park was 11.4 years for the period 1775 to 1909 (Warner 1980). Warner's preliminary data suggest that fire frequency began to decline about 1880 and came to an abrupt halt in 1909. Kilgore and Taylor (1979) compared contemporary lightning-caused fire frequency with that from fire scar records and concluded that natural ignitions alone were insufficient to account for the observed fire frequency.

Pollen and Spore Records. Adam (1985) has provided the most complete listing of California pollen studies up to 1984. Only a few of the investigations that address the prehistoric/historic interface have been published.

Adam (1975) examined a pollen record from a small landslide lake south of San Francisco, identifying evidence of human influences related to logging and grazing. Decreases in *Sequoia* pollen were interpreted as marking the beginning of logging in 1853. The effects of grazing appear somewhat later, the most conspicuous change being a significant increase in Gramineae (grass) pollen in the top of the pollen profile. The only alien plant pollen noted was that of *Centaurea*, the star thistle. Because *Centaurea* pollen is present before the evidence for logging, Adam suggested that the plant may have been introduced into the area by Spanish explorers. Hendry (1931) found *Centaurea melitensis* plant remains in adobe bricks from San Fernando Rey de Espana, San Fernando (1797), and Rancho la Natividad, Salinas (1837). Also of note, but not discussed, is the discontinuous presence of small numbers of Geraniaceae pollen grains in both historic and prehistoric-age dated sediments. Adam (1967) also identified Geraniaceae pollen in one spectrum of an undated pollen profile from meadow deposits at Yosemite National Park.

Russell (1983) relied on pollen grains identified as *Rumex acetosella* and *Plantago lanceolata* to date the sediments of a small lake near Pt. Reyes in Marin County. Occasional grains of *Erodium* pollen co-occur with the *Rumex* and plantago pollen. The lake is surrounded by coastal prairie and coastal shrub formations. The ratio of grass pollen to shrub pollen grains suggests that the proportions of the grassland and shrubland before and after colonization were not constant, but that the significant increase in grass pollen values in the historic period corresponds to increased grazing. Charcoal abundance fluctuates throughout the stratigraphic section but declines greatly in the upper part of the historic age sediments.

Davis (1987) has reported finding abundant spores of the dung fungus *Sporormiella* in historic and Pleistocene-age sediments in three California localities. *Sporormiella* species are common on the dung of domestic herbivores such as cattle and horses and on the dung of megaherbivores such as deer and elk. The u-shaped frequency pattern has been interpreted by Davis as reflecting the abundance of megaherbivores during the Quaternary and the historic introduction of domestic herbivores. *Sporormiella* spores also have been observed in adobe bricks from the San Marcos Adobe near Santa Barbara (West n.d.d).

Discussion

The fossil plant record, like the historic record for California's rangelands, is uneven and in places contradictory. The uncertainty arises from incompleteness and mixing of the remains, differing levels of identification, and varying results because of differing data sets. The quantity and quality of the fossil evidence are poor because little systematic sampling has been carried out to date and there are gaps in the fossil record itself. Some taxa may have become extinct in the Spanish period, but no evidence has been found to support this contention.

The spread of alien taxa is not instantaneous, so that the first occurrence of a particular species does not imply ubiquity. Likewise, the effects on native taxa brought about by new settlement/subsistence patterns are not uniform and may be subtle (Behre 1981, 1986). Where independent chronological control is lacking or where no historical record is available, the dates of introduction or changes in the record of natural vegetation must be interpolated from other sources.

Further, owing to the common practice of rebuilding or remodeling, adobe bricks selected for analysis may not be part of the original structure. The chances that a particular taxa will be incorporated into a brick or deposit, be preserved, and be recovered during analysis also are low. Contamination of samples may occur during sampling or extraction or by bioturbation. Bioturbation, so prevalent in California archaeological sites, can be impossible to detect. Remains, particularly microscopic ones, may be moved vertically or horizontally in a deposit.

Uncertainties regarding the native verses the alien status of some taxa cannot be ignored. The incompleteness of late eighteenth and early nineteenth-century botanical records for California is well known. The limited botanical collections made at that time were not systematic and generally excluded alien or native weedy taxa (Frenkel 1970). Further, there remains the possibility, although slight, that some alien plants preceded colonization by the Spanish (Hendry 1931). Prior to permanent settlement, there were five recorded visits along the coast, which lasted from several days to a couple of months in length. Seeds also may have been transported by migrating animals.

Macroscopic plant fossils that are more or less complete generally can be identified to the specific level. Microscopic remains of plants—phytoliths, spores, pollen, and charcoal fragments—are more difficult to identify down to this level because so little is known of their morphological characteristics, as is the case of many of the pollen grains from alien taxa. As a result, various researchers have presented a number of levels of identification ranging from specific to family to newly defined taxonomic groupings. Another problem is that many alien taxa are closely related to native species and their pollen grains are not always readily distinguished under a light microscope. Nevertheless, a number of important alien taxa do appear to have pollen grains that can be reliably identified; some of these are considered below.

Alien Plant Pollen Grains

As previously mentioned, one of the pollen types often identified in historic-age contexts and occasionally in prehistoric-age deposits belongs to the geranium family (Geraniaceae). All of the Geraniaceae are insect- or self-pollinated and produce relatively small numbers of pollen grains. Three genera of Geraniaceae are present in California: *Geranium*, *Erodium*, and *Pelargonium*. There are 16 species of *Geranium*, of which 9 are aliens (Taylor 1992).

Of the native *Geranium*, two species are restricted to mountainous areas in far northern California, three to moist areas in forests above 4,000 feet, and one species (*G. bicknellii*) to the central coastal region and northwestern California. Carolina geranium (*G. Carolinianum* L.) may be naturalized from the eastern United States (Jepson 1970:589; Robbins et al. 1970:277) or may be native (Fisher et al. 1978:WI-144; Munz and Keck 1959:141; Taylor 1992). Whatever its origin, Carolina geranium is widespread in California and has been reported from the entire length of the state west of the Sierra and eastern deserts.

Only two of the eight species of *Erodium* in California are native. One, *E. texanum*, is restricted mainly to dry gravelly places in the Creosote Bush Scrub formation in the Colorado and Eastern Mojave desert regions, but occurs in a few localities in the San Joaquin Valley and its western margins (Munz and Keck 1959:144; Taylor 1992). *E. macrophyllum* has been recorded from Valley Grassland and Foothill Woodland formations in the Sacramento–San Joaquin Valley, South Coast Ranges, and Southern California, but it is relatively rare (Robbins et al. 1970:276). All of the *Pelargonium* are aliens or of horticultural origin.

Pollen grains of *Pelargonium* are diagnostically distinct but the genera *Geranium* and *Erodium* are not readily separated on the basis of pollen morphology (Bortenschlager 1967; El Oqlah 1983; Table 20-1). Three pollen types, which are based on ornamentation and sculpturing patterns, are recognized for the geraniums and erodiums found in California today (Figure 20-1). These diagnostic pollen types are not congruent with the taxonomic classifications. At the generic level, all three pollen types are evident for the *Geranium* and two types evident for the *Erodium*.

Of the species examined, native geraniums have type 1 and type 3 pollen grains (Table 20-1). Native erodiums have type 1 and type 2 pollen grains. All of the alien erodiums examined or reported, and one of the geraniums, have type 2 pollen grains. In the native erodium with type 2 pollen grains (*E. macrophyllum* Hook. & Arn.), the grain is generally larger (92–120 μ) than the pollen grains from alien Geraniaceae of the type 2 category, which range from 57 to 98 μ (El Oqlah 1983:392, Table 2; personal observation). A careful consideration of morphology and size suggests that it is possible to sort out genera, to a fair degree of confidence, of the pollen grains of the more common and widespread (weedy) native and alien Geraniaceae.

Another pollen type commonly found in historic-age deposits is *Rumex*. Between 12 and 24 species of *Rumex* (sorrels and docks) have been reported for California (Jepson 1970; Munz and Keck 1959; Robbins et al. 1970). Five alien

Table 20-1.   California Native and Alien Geraniums and Erodiums

Taxon	Origin	Type	Herbarium
Geranium carolinianum L.	?	3	UCD #51806
G. dissectum L.	Alien	3	UCD #3640
G. molle L.	Native	2	UCD #38004
G. richardsonii F. & T.	Native	1	UCD #3648
G. viscosissimum F. & M.	Native	3	UCD #27153
G. viscosissimum var. *nervosum* (Rydh.) Hitchc.	Native	?	
G. californicum J. & J.	Native	?	
G. oreganum Howell	Native	?	
G. bicknellii Britton	Native	?	
G. niuginiense	Alien	?	
G. palmatum	Alien	?	
G. pusillum Burm. f.	Alien	?	
G. pyrenaicum Burm f.	Alien	?	
G. retrorsum L'Her.	Alien	?	
G. robertianum L.	Alien	?	
G. solanderi Carolin	Alien	?	
Erodium texanum A. Gray	Native	1	UCD #11077
E. macrophyllum H. & A.	Native	2	UCD #27152
E. botrys (Cav.) Bertol.	Alien	2	UCD #21505
E. moschatum (L.) L'Her.	Alien	2	UCD #3616
E. cicutarium (L.) L'Her.	Alien	2	UCD #3583
E. malacoides (L.) Willd.	Alien	2	El Oqlah 1983:393
E. brachycarpum (Godr.) Thellung	Alien	?	
E. cygnorum Nees.	Alien	?	

Note: Type 1: Ornamentation composed of supratectal processes of variable size and shape. Type 2: Sculpturing consisting of variously arranged long and short muri. Muri forming striae, striaerugulate, or rugulate patterns. Type 3: Sculpturing consisting of baculate, echinate, or gemmate supratectal processes forming reticulate patterns.

species are weedy, as are two of the native species. Sheep sorrel (*R. acetosella* L.), like one native species, produces abundant wind-dispersed pollen. Pollen grains from sheep sorrel appear to be diagnostically distinct from grains of the three native coastal species examined by Mudie and Byrne (1980:30). However, not all sheep sorrel pollen grains can be separated with less than × 1,000 magnificaton and phase contrast from some of the other alien and native *Rumex* including yellow dock (*R. crispus*), the earliest recorded alien *Rumex* species (Bassett et al. 1978; Moore and Webb 1978; personal observation).

Conclusions

Soon after the Columbian discovery of the American continent a rapid exchange of plants between the Old World and New World began (Crosby 1972; Hendry 1934; Merrill 1954). As the Ibero-Americans extended their influence, they brought not only cultural change but also environmental change, including the introduction of many weedy taxa. They initiated alterations in California's envi-

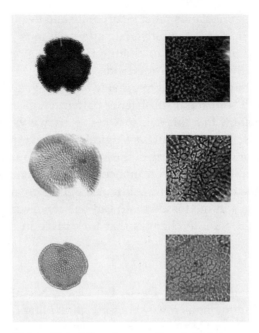

Figure 20-1. Microphotographs of Geraniaceae pollen grains. Type 1: *Geranium richardsonii* F. & T.; Type 2: *G. macrophyllum* H. & A.; Type 3: *G. carolinianum* L.

ronment that continue today, yet we have only a rudimentary knowledge of how these events came about.

In sum, evidence from the fossil record suggests that

1. The most productive historic period studies from cultural contexts are of plant remains in adobe bricks and coprolites.
2. Phytoliths mark the replacement of indigenous grasses by introduced grasses.
3. Sedimentation rates in coastal estuaries double after the appearance of pollen grains from alien plants.
4. Increases in grass pollen in historic-age sediments suggest that grazing by domesticated livestock promoted the growth of alien grasses and the displacement of native taxa.
5. Preliminary data suggest that grassland and shrubland burns in coastal southern California were more variable during prehistoric times, and that there were larger periodic fires, in contrast to the more abundant, smaller fires of modern times.
6. Fire history frequency in coniferous forests varies. In the central Coast Ranges and western Transverse Ranges there was a significant reduction in fire frequencies beginning in the early 1800s. Fire frequency did not decrease in the Sierra until the late 1800s. No evidence has been found to indicate that fire frequency in the eastern Transverse Ranges changed from the prehistoric to the historic period.

The physical record of these alterations, like the written record, is fragmentary. Although we have some insight into these changes, most of the evidence or interpretations require considerable qualification or a great deal of faith.

Differing data sets have provided nonequivalent perspectives and resolution of past conditions and events. Consequently, any effort to identify the Spanish effect on California's rangelands must incorporate and evaluate the various data sets in a systematic manner. A multivariate approach must be applied to examine the role that the Spanish had in altering California's rangelands and other plant formations of the Spanish borderlands.

In this chapter, I have attempted to provide a brief review of the physical evidence of the Spanish settlement/subsistence pattern on California's rangelands. I have also tried to show that this evidence comes from a variety of cultural and noncultural contexts. Data from archaeological sites have provided the opportunity to enhance our understanding of the invasion of alien plants and the alteration of plant formations. Data from noncultural contexts have enhanced our understanding of the cultural record. Although still poorly understood and documented, the changes in the fossil record can be seen as an example reflecting the radical and rapid cultural changes that took place in the Spanish Borderlands.

Acknowledgments

I thank Dave P. Adam, Owen K. Davis, Bill Olsen, Nick Prokopovitch, Mary S. Taylor, and two anonymous reviewers for commenting on this article. James Schoenwetter and Susan Hector provided copies of unpublished reports. Pat and Michael Smith and Will Keck commented on style. Katherine L. Keysor West, as always, helped in numerous ways and edited the draft copies. I am, of course, responsible for any errors or omissions.

References

Adam, David P.
   1967 Late Pleistocene and Recent Palynology in the Central Sierra Nevada, California. In *Quaternary Paleoecology*, edited by Edward J. Cushing and Herbert E. Wright, Jr., pp. 275–301. Yale University Press, New Haven, Conn.
   1975 A Late Holocene Pollen Record from Pearson's Pond, Weeks Creek Landslide, San Francisco Peninsula, California. *U.S. Geological Survey Journal of Research*, 3:721–731.
   1985 Quaternary Pollen Records from California. In *Pollen Records of Late-Quaternary North American Sediments*, edited by Vaughn M. Bryant, Jr. and Richard G. Hollaway, pp. 125–140. American Association of Stratigraphic Palynologists.
Aschmann, Homer
   1976 Man's impact on the Southern California Flora. In *Plant Communities of Southern California*, edited by June Latting, pp. 40–48. Special Publication No. 2. California Native Plant Society, Berkeley.
Barkworth, M. E.
   1981 Foliar Epidermes and Taxonomy of North American Stipeae (Gramineae). *Systematic Botany* 6:136–152.
Barry, W. James
   1972 *The Central Valley Prairie*, vol. 1: *California Prairie Ecosystem*. State of California, Department of Parks and Recreation, Sacramento.
Bartolome, James W., Steven E. Klukkert, and W. James Barry
   1985 Using Opal Phytoliths to Document Native Plant Community Displacement. Department of Forestry and Resource Mangement, University of California, Berkeley and State of California, Department of Parks and Recreation, Sacramento.
   1986 Opal Phytoliths as Evidence for Displacement of Native California Grassland. *Madroño* 33(3):217–222.

Bassett, John, Clifford W. Crampton, and John A. Parmelee
1978 *An Atlas of Airborne Pollen Grains and Common Fungus Spores of Canada.* Monograph No. 18. Canada Department of Agriculture, Ottawa, Ontario.

Behre, Karl-Ernst
1981 The Interpretation of Anthropogenic Indicators in Pollen Diagrams. *Pollen et Spores* 23(2):225–245.
1986 *Anthropogenic Indicators in Pollen Diagrams.* A. A. Balkema, Rotterdam.

Belcher, Edward
1843 *Narrative of a Voyage Round the World, Performed in Her Majesty's Ship* Sulphur, *during the Years 1836–1842,* vol. 1. Henry Colburn, London.

Biswell, H. H.
1956 Ecology of California Grassland. *Journal of Range Management* 9:19–24.

Bortenschlager, Sigmar
1967 Vorlaufige Mitteilungen zur Pollenmorphologie in der Familie der Geraniaceen und Ihre Systematische Bedeutung. *Grana Palynologica* 7(2-3):400–468.

Burcham, Lee T.
1956 Historical Backgrounds of Range Land Use in California. *Journal of Range Management* 9:81–86.
1957 *California Range Land.* California Division of Forestry, Sacramento.
1970 Ecological Significance of Alien Plants in California's Grasslands. *Proceedings, American Association of Geographers* 2:36–39.
1975 Climate, Structure, and History of California's Annual Grassland Ecosystem. In *The California Annual Grassland Ecosystem,* edited by R. Merton Love, pp. 7–14. Publication No. 7 Institute of Ecology, University of California, Davis.
1981 California Rangelands in Historical Perspective. *Rangelands* 3(3):95–104.

Byrne, Rodger
1986 Report on the Pollen Content of Six Samples from the 04-Tuo-1 Midden Site, New Melones Dam Area. In *Final Report New Melones Archeological Project* 6:1235–1238.

Byrne, Rodger, Joel Michaelsen, and Andrew Soutar
1977 Fossil Charcoal as a Measure of Wildfire Frequency in Southern California: A Preliminary Analysis. In *Proceedings of the Symposium on the Environmental Consequences of Fire and Fuel Management in Mediterranean Ecosystems,* pp. 361–367. General Technical Report WO-3, U.S. Department of Agriculture, Forest Service, Washington, D.C.

Clar, C. Raymond
1957 Forest Use in Spanish-Mexican California. Division of Forestry, Department of Natural Resources, State of California.

Clyman, James
1926 Diaries and Reminiscences. *California Historical Society Quarterly* 5(2):122.

Crosby, Alfred W., Jr.
1972 *The Columbian Exchange.* Contributions to American Studies No. 2. Greenwood Press, Westport, Conn.

Davis, Owen K.
1987 Spores of Dung Fungus *Sporormiella*: Increased Abundances in Historic Sediments and before Pleistocene Megafaunal Extinction. *Quaternary Research* 28:290–294.

DeWet, J. M. J.
1956 Leaf Anatomy and Phylogeny in the Tribe Danthonieae. *American Journal of Botany* 43:175–182.

Duncan, Faith L.
n.d. A Preliminary Assessment of Pollen Microfossils with Archaeological Deposits at CA-SBa-518, Mission Santa Ines, Santa Barbara County, California. Ms. on file, Laboratory of Paleoenvironmental Studies, University of Arizona, Tucson.

Ebeling, Walter
1986 *Handbook of Indian Foods and Fibers of Arid America.* University of California Press, Berkeley.

El Oqlah, A. A.
  1983 Pollen Morphology of the Genus *Erodium* L'Herit. in the Middle East. *Pollen et Spores* 25(3-4):383–394.
Farnham, Thomas J.
  1850 *"Life, Adventures and Travel in California."* Natis and Cornish, New York.
Fisher, Bill B., Arthur H. Lange, June McCaskill, Beecher Crampton, and Betsey Tabraham
  1978 *Growers' Weed Identification Handbook.* Cooperative Extension, U.S. Department of Agriculture, University of California, Berkeley.
Frenkel, Robert E.
  1970 Ruderal Vegetation along Some California Roadsides. *University of California Publications in Geography* 20:1–163.
Galbreath, Elizabeth
  n.d. Floral Analysis, In *Preliminary Archaeological Investigations at San Marcos Rancho, (SBa-109),* pp. 83–96. Archaeological field class, Spring 1978 University of California at Santa Barbara.
Gayton, Anna H.
  1948 Yokuts and Western Mono-Ethnography. *University of California Anthropological Records* 10(1-2):1–302.
Gregory, Michael M., and James Schoenwetter
  n.d. Palynology of the Aros-Serrano Adobe: Pilot study report. Department of Anthropology, Arizona State University, Tempe.
Griffen, James R., and Steven N. Talley
  1980 Fire History, Junipero Sierra Peak, Central Coastal California. In *Proceedings of the Fire History Workshop,* pp. 82–84 General Technical Report RM-81. U.S. Department of Agriculture, Forest Service, Rocky Mountain Forest and Range Experiment Station, Fort Collins, Colo.
Heady, Harold F.
  1977 Valley Grassland. In *Terrestrial Vegetation of California,* edited by Michael Barbour and Jack Major, pp. 491–514. John Wiley & Sons, New York.
Heizer, Robert F., and Thomas R. Hester
  1973 *The Archaeology of Bamert Cave, Amador County, California.* University of California Archaeology Research Facility, Berkeley.
Hendry, George W.
  1931 The Adobe Brick as a Historical Source. *Agricultural History* 5:110–127.
  1934 The Source Literature of Early Plant Introduction into Spanish America. *Agricultural History* 8(2):64–71.
Hendry, George W., and Margaret K. Bellue
  1936 An Approach to Southwestern Agricultural History through Adobe Brick Analysis. *University of New Mexico Bulletin, Anthropology Series* 5:65–72.
Hendry, George W., and Margaret P. Kelly [Bellue]
  1925 The Plant Content of Adobe Bricks. *California Historical Society Quarterly* 4:361–373.
Honeysett, Elizabeth A.
  n.d. Floral Analysis. In *The Ontiveros Adobe, Early Rancho Life in Alta California,* by J. D. Frierman, pp. 93–100. Report prepared for Redevelopment Agency, City of Santa Fe Springs, California by Greenwood and Associates, Pacific Palasaides.
Jepson, Willis L.
  1970 *A Manual of the Flowering Plants of California.* University of California Press, Berkeley.
Kilgore, Bruce M., and Dwight Taylor
  1979 Fire History of a Sequoia-mixed Conifer Forest. *Ecology* 60:129–142.
Kroeber, Alfred L.
  1932 The Patwin and Their Neighbors. *University of California Publications in American Archaeology and Ethnology* 29(4):253–423. Berkeley.

Küchler, A. Will

1977 Apendix: The Map of Natural Vegetation of California. In *Terrestrial Vegetation of California*, edited by Michael G. Barbour and Jack Major, pp. 909–938, pocket map. John Wiley & Sons, New York.

Lewis, Henry T.

1973 Patterns of Indian Burning in California: Ecology and Ethnohistory. *Ballena Press Anthropological Papers* 1:1–110. Ramona, Calif.

Maloney, Alice B. (editor)

1945 *Fur Brigade to the Bonaventura. The Journal of John Work*. California Historical Society, San Francisco.

McBride, Joe R., and Diana F. Jacobs

1980 Land Use and Fire History in the Mountains of Southern California. In *Proceedings of the Fire History Workshop*, pp. 85–88. General Technical Report, RM-81. U.S. Department of Agriculture, Forest Service, Rocky Mountain Forest and Range Experiment Station, Fort Collins, Colo.

Merrill, Elmer Drew

1954 The Botany of Cook's Voyages. *Chronica Botanica* 14(5-6):161–384.

Moore, Peter D., and Judith A. Webb

1978 *An Illustrated Guide to Pollen Analysis*. John Wiley & Sons, New York.

Mudie, Peta J., and Roger Byrne

1980 Pollen Evidence for Historic Sedimentation Rates in California Coastal Marshes. *Estuarine and Coastal Marine Science* 10:305–316.

Munz, Philip A., and David Keck

1959 *A California Flora*. University of California Press, Berkeley.

Pancoast, Charles E.

1930 *A Quaker Forty-Niner*, edited by Anna P. Hannum. University of Pennsylvania Press, Philadelphia.

Parish, Samuel B.

1920 The Immigrant Plants of Southern California. *Bulletin of the Southern California Academy of Sciences* 19(4):3–30.

Patterson, William A. III, Kevin J. Edwards, and David J. Maguire

1987 Microsopic Charcoal as a Fossil Indicator of Fire. *Quaternay Science Reviews* 6:3–23.

Robbins, W. W., Margaret K. Bellue, and Walter S. Ball 1970 *Weeds of California*. California State Department of Agriculture, Sacramento.

Rossi, Randall S.

1979 History of Cultural Influences on the Distribution and Reproduction of Oaks in California. In *Ecology, Management, and Utilization of California Oaks*, pp. 7–18. General Technical Report PSW-44. U.S. Department of Agriculture, Forest Service, Pacific Southwest Forest and Range Experiment Station.

Russell, Emily W. B.

1983 Pollen Analysis of Past Vegetation at Point Reyes National Seashore, California. *Madroño* 30(1):1–11.

Sampson, Arthur W.

1944 *Plant Succession on Burned Chaparral Lands in Northern California*. Bulletin No. 685. University of California, Berkeley.

Spaulding, W. Geoffrey

1984 Archeobotanical and Paleoecological Investigations at Archeological Sites in the New Melones Reservoir Area, Calaveras and Tuolumne Counties, California. In *Final Report of the New Melones Archeological Project* 4:3.191–3.256.

Stokes, Marvin

1980 The Dendrochronology of Fire History. *Proceedings of the Fire History Workshop*, pp. 1–3. General Technical Report, RM-81. U.S. Department of Agriculture, Forest Service, Rocky Mountain Forest and Range Experiment Station, Fort Collins, Colo.

Taylor, Mary Susan
1992 Geraniaceae. In *The Jepson Manual: Vascular Plants of California*. Jepson Herbarium, University of California, Berkeley, in press.

Twiss, P. C., E. Suess, and R. M. Smith
1969 Morphological Classification of Grass Phytoliths. *Soil Science Society of America Proceedings* 33:109–115.

Warner, Thomas E.
1980 Fire History in the Yellow Pine Forest of Kings Canyon National Park. In *Proceedings of the Fire History Workshop*, pp. 89–92. General Technical Report, RM-81. U.S. Department of Agriculture, Forest Service, Rocky Mountain Forest and Range and Experiment Station, Fort Collins, Colo.

Waseurtz af Sandels, G. M.
1945 *A Sojourn in California by the Kings' Orphan*. Grabhorn Press, San Francisco.

West, G. James
1984 A Holocene Vegetation and Climatic Sequence for California's North Coast Ranges. *American Quaternary Association Eighth Biennial Meeting, program and Abstracts*. Boulder, Colo.
n.d.a Pollen Analysis of Adobe Bricks from Mission San Jose. Report prepared for Archaeological Consulting and Research Services (ACRS), Santa Cruz, Calif.
n.d.b Pollen Analysis of Adobe from Santa Cruz Mission State Historic Park. Report prepared for State of California, Department of Parks and Recreation, Archeology Laboratory, West Sacramento.
n.d.c Pollen Analysis of Midden Samples from Mer-27. Report prepared for State of California, Department of Parks and Recreation, Sacramento.
n.d.d Preliminary Pollen Analysis of an Adobe Brick from San Marcos Rancho (SBa-109), Santa Barbara, Calif. Unpublished ms.

Wester, Lyndon L.
1975 *Changing Patterns of Vegetation on the West Side and South End of the San Joaquin Valley during Historic Time*. Unpublished Ph.D. dissertation, Department of Geography, University of California, Los Angeles.

Wilks, Charles
1958 *Columbia River to the Sacramento*. Biobooks, Oakland, Calif.

Chapter 21 ■

Phillip L. Walker, Patricia Lambert, and Michael J. DeNiro

The Effects of European Contact on the Health of Alta California Indians

The lives of California Indians were profoundly changed by the arrival of European colonists. The health consequences of contact with outsiders were particularly devastating. To comprehend the magnitude of these changes, it is essential to compare prehistoric conditions with those of the historic period. We provide this historical perspective by reviewing what is known about the changes that occurred in demography, diet, disease, and the prevalence of physical violence.

There are both strengths and weaknesses in the data that we have on the health consequences of European contact. The widespread practice of cremation biases our knowledge of prehistoric health conditions. Cremation was the preferred method of disposing of the dead in much of southern California and the Central Coast, the Central Valley, and the central Sierra Nevadas. Skeletal collections large enough to allow health assessments at the population level are only available for the Sacramento River Valley and the Santa Barbara Channel areas. In the late prehistoric period, both of these regions were inhabited by dense populations who, for the most part, practiced primary burial instead of cremation (Kroeber 1925).

Because the skeletal evidence of prehistoric health comes from areas of high population density, it gives a somewhat distorted view of the incidence of infectious disease. The large permanent villages maintained in the Central Valley and Santa Barbara Channel areas created environments conducive to the spread of infectious pathogens. Such favorable conditions for the transmission of disease were not present in less densely populated areas.

One problem with using skeletal remains to study prehistoric disease is that they only provide evidence of a limited range of conditions. Many diseases, particularly those in which people die rapidly from acute infection, do not leave osseous signs. The diseases that can be diagnosed through skeletal studies are usually those associated with chronic or degenerative conditions. Furthermore, a variety of pathogens elicit similar skeletal responses. This makes diagnosis of specific diseases difficult. Osteological studies therefore give a biased and somewhat imprecise picture of the diseases that afflicted California Indians before the arrival of Europeans.

Another problem is the dating of archaeological collections. Cemeteries often contain commingled skeletal material from the late prehistoric and protohistoric periods. This makes it difficult to differentiate prehistoric pathological conditions from those associated with European contact.

We encounter a different set of interpretive problems when historical records are used to reconstruct health conditions. Many ethnohistoric reports reflect the ethnocentric views of the early explorers and colonists. Although the mission records of births and deaths are a more objective source of information on health, they are also somewhat biased. The quality of record keeping varied from mission to mission. In addition, there were lapses in record keeping during epidemics when large numbers of neophytes were dying (Cook and Borah 1979:177–179). More important, only about 10 percent of the California Indian population ever entered the mission system (Cook 1976). We thus have few data on the changing health conditions of a large proportion of the California Indian population during the historic period.

Little skeletal evidence is available for assessing health conditions during the Mission and post-Mission periods. We were fortunate in being able to study remains from the Mission La Purísima cemetery, one of the few Mission period skeletal collections, before their reburial. Although the sample is limited, it provides an objective basis for evaluating historical reports on the health of the Indians who came to live at the missions.

Demography

Changes in population size and age-specific mortality rates are useful indices of the effects of European contact on California Indian health. These demographic variables are influenced by the incidence of disease, nutritional adequacy of the diet, and levels of interpersonal violence. They provide basic information on the quality of life.

Population densities varied significantly in prehistoric California. At one extreme were highly productive environments such as the Central Valley and the Santa Barbara Channel, where there were permanent villages with 1,000 or more inhabitants. In contrast, California's vast deserts were barely inhabited (Kroeber 1925:891).

These differences in population density had significant health consequences. Large sedentary villages create conditions favorable to the spread of infectious disease. The concentration of wastes in and around permanent villages results in sanitation problems, which, combined with frequent contacts between people living in these villages, increase the incidence of disease (Lightman 1977; Walker and Hudson 1989).

Archaeological evidence of changes in the size of California's prehistoric population comes primarily from reports on the number and size of dated cemeteries and refuse middens. Although these site-frequency data show that there was a general trend toward population increase in prehistoric California, particularly after 1000 B.C. (Breschini et al. 1986; Moratto 1984), the rate of population growth no doubt fluctuated through time and varied from area to area.

When conditions were favorable, the growth rate appears to have accelerated. For instance, data from deep-sea cores indicate that the period between 1000 B.C. and A.D. 500 was a time of high marine productivity (Pisias 1978; Walker 1986). Radiocarbon date frequencies suggest that these favorable conditions coincided with a population increase. Periods of prolonged drought or low marine productivity, on the other hand, coincided with the movement of people out of affected areas as well as increases in mortality. The period between A.D. 500 and 1100 was one of highly variable conditions that included several unusually severe droughts. Owing to these unfavorable conditions, the number of people living in marginal arid and semiarid areas of the state declined (Walker et al. 1988).

The prehistoric trend toward a population increase ended abruptly with the arrival of Europeans. Infectious diseases introduced during the sixteenth and seventeenth centuries probably resulted in at least temporary decreases in the size of some coastal tribes (Walker and Hudson 1989). In the oral history of the Chumash Indians, for instance, it is stated that just before the arrival of European colonists a series of pestilences struck people living along the coast and "people went about feeling sick until they fell backwards, dead" (Hudson et al. 1977:11).

After the establishment of the first Spanish missions, much more reliable data become available on the losses suffered by California's Indian population. Cook (1976:5) estimates that in 1770 about 135,000 Indians were living in California. This figure excludes the Modoc, Paiute, and Colorado River tribes. Calculating the losses incurred at the missions, and later losses following secularization, Cook estimates that by 1848 the population had been reduced to 88,000.

The expansion of miners and farmers into previously unoccupied areas during the 1840s and 1850s took a terrific toll on Indians living in remote areas who previously had little contact with Europeans (Harvey 1967). By the end of this period, the Indian population of California numbered no more than about 30,000 (Cook 1976:5).

The causes of the precipitous decline in the size of California's Indian population are extremely complex. They include deaths from infectious disease and increased warfare as well as a decrease in birth rate. Infectious diseases such as smallpox and measles swept through the population killing people of all ages, but especially children and the elderly. The high mortality rates were due to a lack of acquired immunity to the new diseases as well as the inability of people to care for each other because so many were seriously ill (Walker and Hudson 1989).

High child mortality rates at the missions are often cited as an important cause of the rapid decline in the Indian neophyte population (Cook 1976). The Mission La Purísima death records, for instance, show that 35 percent of the people buried in the mission cemetery were less than 20 years of age (Walker et al. 1988).

Archaeological data show that prehistoric California Indians who lived in densely populated areas, such as the Sacramento Valley and along the Santa Barbara Channel, had subadult mortality rates similar to those of the mission neophytes. In Central California cemeteries dating from the Early, Middle, and Late horizons, people under 20 years of age accounted for 23.3, 16.6, and 27.6 percent of the total deaths, respectively (Doran 1980). We have found comparable subadult mortality (31 percent) at Calleguas Creek (CA-Ven-110), a Santa Barbara Channel area site of the Middle period. Since the fragile remains of infants and children are less likely to be recovered by archaeologists than those of adults, these figures are a conservative estimate of prehistoric subadult mortality (Walker et al. 1988).

These data suggest that demographic variables other than high subadult mortality account for the decline in the size of the Mission Indian population. A low birth rate due to sterility from venereal disease has been implicated as an important cause of the decrease in the mission Indian population. As a padre at Mission Santa Barbara described it,

> The sicknesses found among these Indians are those common to all mankind, but the most pernicious and the one that has afflicted them most here for some years is syphilis. All are infected with it for they see no objection to marrying another infected with it. As a result births are few and deaths many so that the number of deaths exceed births by three to one [Geiger and Meighan 1976:74].

Diet

Europeans introduced enormous changes in the Indian diet. Under the mission system, much of the diverse array of foods on the prehistoric menu was replaced by a monotonous diet of agricultural staples such as wheat, corn, and beans. Although the Indians continued their traditional subsistence activities to some extent while they lived at the missions, the usurpation of tribal lands for agricultural activities and the ecological effects of cattle and sheep grazing gradually made these practices unfeasible. In addition, trade connections between interior tribes and coastal groups were disrupted, and an important source of supplemental resources to both areas was thus eliminated (Kelsey 1985). This disruption of prehistoric lifeways was abetted by the loss of subsistence technology that occurred when so many knowledgeable people died (Walker and Hudson 1989).

The quality, quantity, and type of food sources available to prehistoric California Indians varied greatly. The amount of animal protein in the diet depended on the local ecology. Some coastal groups, such as the Chumash of the Santa Barbara Channel, lived on a high protein diet of fish, shellfish and sea mammal meat (Walker and DeNiro 1986). Salmon were abundant in Northwestern California and the Sacramento River drainage. In arid regions of the state, sources of animal protein were meager.

These regional differences undoubtedly had some effect on health. The preference of the Santa Barbara Channel Indians for raw fish and sea mammal meat, for instance, would have exposed them to intestinal parasites that inland groups would not have encountered (Walker 1986). Although differences between coastal and interior groups in protein availability may have also affected their health, no paleopathological studies have been done to document this.

Acorns were a staple food source for many Indians, especially those living in central California. When the acorn crop failed, people relied more heavily on less desirable foods such as sage seed, buckeye, and the epos root (Baumhoff 1978). Unusually severe drought sometimes reduced the availability of these secondary (as well as primary) resources. The result was famine that sometimes lasted several years. Acute shortages were particularly likely to occur during the unproductive winter months when food stores were at their lowest. The oral history of California Indians contains accounts of terrible droughts that led to widespread starvation. One of these lasted five years: "the seeds the women had stored came to an end, and there were no acorns or islay [wild cherries]. Even the shells along the shores had only sand in them. When the men went out to get Mescal, only a few came back—the rest died of hunger" (Blackburn 1975:276).

Skeletal evidence of growth disruption provides evidence of the frequency of prehistoric food shortages. Harris lines are transverse lines of increased density seen in radiographs of long bones. These lines are laid down during the "catch-up" growth that occurs after a period of growth disruption. The frequency of Harris lines in skeletal remains from central California decreases significantly between the Early and Late periods. This has been interpreted as evidence of an increase through time in the ability of these Indians to avoid seasonal food shortages through buffering mechanisms such as storage (Dickel et al. 1984; McHenry 1968).

Studies of animal remains from Mission period villages indicate that although Indians living away from the missions incorporated domestic animals into their diet, they continued to exploit diverse faunal resources (Glenn et al. 1988; King 1982). In contrast, the faunal remains left at the missions by Indian neophytes consist mainly of bones from only two species—cattle and sheep (Lagenwalter and McKee 1985; Walker and Davidson 1989). Although poorly documented, a similar decrease in the diversity of plant foods probably occurred when the Indians moved to the missions.

There is little doubt that the diet of Indians living in the mission system was significantly different from their native diet. Using records of agricultural production, Cook (1976:47) calculated the average daily caloric intake of mission neophytes to be between 2,000 and 2,100 calories per person per day. It is difficult to determine whether this amount of food was adequate without information on such important variables as vitamin content and neophyte work load. Clearly, the diet varied significantly through time and among the various missions. We know that some of the Indians at the missions suffered crop failures and annual food shortages, particularly in the early years (Webb 1952). However, in time most of the missions were able to provide their residents with an abundant food supply. For example, after Langsdorff visited Mission Santa Barbara in 1806, he observed: "It appeared to me incomprehensible how any one could three times a day eat so large a portion of such nourishing food" [Kelsey 1984:505]. A priest at Mission San Luis Obispo described the diet there as follows:

> There are three meals a day for the Indians. In the morning they receive the atole [a mush made of grain]. At noon they have pozole, which is composed of wheat, corn, beans, or horse-beans, and rationed meat for each one. In addition they have countless kinds of wild seeds which they prepare in their private homes. At night again they have atole . . . during the year 2,000 and some odd cattle are slaughtered for food, and all that is harvested is consumed [Geiger and Meighan 1976:86–87].

Analysis of the stable isotope concentrations in human bone collagen provides an objective basis for determining the kinds of foods that contributed to the diet of prehistoric Indians as well as the Spanish settlers and Indian neophytes. The ratios of ^{15}N to ^{14}N and ^{13}C to ^{12}C tend to be higher in people who subsist predominantly on seafood than in people whose diet is composed largely of terrestrial plants and animals (Schoeninger and DeNiro 1984; Tauber 1981). The ratio of ^{13}C to ^{12}C in bone collagen also tends to increase with increased consumption of plants such as maize that use the C4 photosynthetic pathway (Tauber 1981).

Isotopic data from the Santa Barbara Channel area show a clear trend toward greater consumption of marine resources during the prehistoric period (Walker and DeNiro 1986). Analysis of stable isotopes in bone collagen from the Spanish settlers buried in the Santa Barbara Presidio Chapel (Costello and Walker 1987) and Indian neophytes from Mission La Purísima, show that marine resources and maize contributed little to the diet of people associated with the mission system (Figure 21-1). The isotopic ratios of these people indicate that they emphasized terrestrial resources in their diets. This is in marked contrast to the heavy dependence on marine resources among protohistoric coastal groups from the same area. Their values most closely resemble those of Indians who lived in interior villages during the late prehistoric period (Figure 21-1).

One way to assess changes in the nutritional adequacy of the mission diet is to compare the skeletal dimensions of prehistoric and Mission period Indians. Differences in long bone measurements provide information on the disparities in realized growth potential between groups. A comparison of the skeletal dimensions indicates that the long bones of the Mission La Purísima neophytes are significantly smaller than those of their prehistoric and protohistoric predecessors (Figure 21-2). One interpretation of these differences in body size is that

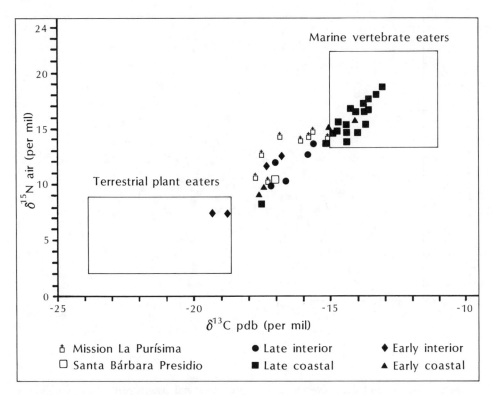

Figure 21-1. Scatter plot of nitrogen and carbon isotope ratios in human skeletal remains from prehistoric and historic period Santa Barbara Channel area sites. The prehistoric values are from Walker and DeNiro (1986): Early = early prehistoric period, Late = late prehistoric period, Interior = interior sites, Coastal = sites on the northern Channel Islands and mainland coast. The Purísima values are for people buried in the Mission La Purísima cemetery. The presidio value was obtained from the remains of Hispanic colonists buried in the chapel of the Santa Bárbara Presidio (Costello and Walker 1987). The boxes indicate the means ± 2 standard deviations of the isotope ratios for bone collagen from modern mammals with the indicated feeding preferences. (Shoeninger and DeNiro 1984; DeNiro 1985)

they reflect retarded growth, possibly attributable to the nutritional deficiency of the mission diet or the combined effects of poor nutrition and infectious disease.

Disease

European diseases had devastating consequences for California Indians, both in terms of the loss of life as well as the loss of the traditional knowledge the deceased possessed. To understand the magnitude of the effects of introduced diseases, we must view them within the context of the diseases present in California before Europeans arrived.

Paleopathological studies show that many of the pathogens that afflict modern people were present in prehistoric California. Bone lesions of the kind we now associate with streptococcal or staphylococcal infections were fairly common in some California Indian populations (see Roney 1959, 1966; Suchey et al. 1972).

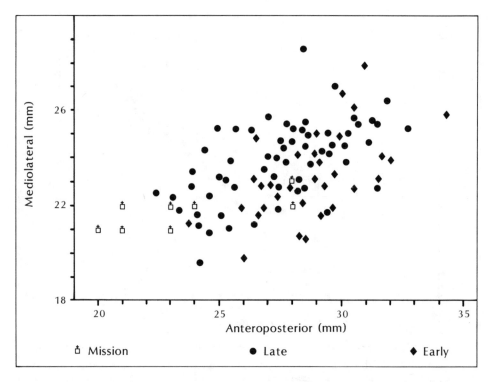

Figure 21-2. Femoral mid-shaft dimensions of the prehistoric and historic period inhabitants of the Santa Barbara Channel areas: Late = late prehistoric period; Early = early prehistoric period.

There is also paleopathological evidence that gastrointestinal infections transmitted by drinking contaminated water were prevalent in some areas (Walker 1986). The dehydration and anemia associated with these infections are a major cause of infant mortality in modern underdeveloped countries (Mata et al. 1980). Gastrointestinal infections may therefore explain the high infant mortality rates documented for some prehistoric California Indian populations.

Tuberculosis, coccidioidomycosis, and treponematosis are three additional infectious diseases reported as possibly being present in prehistoric California according to skeletal studies (Cybulski 1980; Hoffman 1987; Roney 1959).

Linear enamel hypoplasia is a health index that has been studied extensively in California skeletal collections. Hypoplasia is a condition in which grooves or bands of defective enamel pass transversely across the crowns of teeth. These enamel defects are the result of disrupted enamel matrix formation (Goodman et al. 1984:25). Hypoplasia is known to be associated with a variety of systemic disturbances including malnutrition and infections such as measles and pneumonia (McHenry and Schulz 1978:36–37).

In both Central California and the Santa Barbara Channel area, there is a tendency for the frequency of dental hypoplasia to increase between the early and late prehistoric periods (Figure 21-3). In central California, hypoplasia decreases between the Early and Middle horizons, but after that time it increases steadily into the historic period (Schulz 1981). In the Santa Barbara Channel area, the

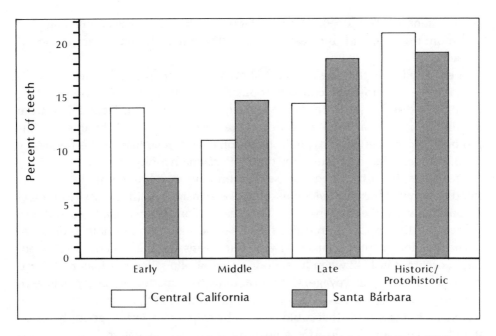

Figure 21-3. Frequency of dental hypoplasia in prehistoric and historic period Central Valley and Santa Barbara Channel areas. (Central California data are from Schultz 1981; Santa Barbara Channel data are from Walker 1988)

frequency of hypoplasia increases steadily from the Early to the Late period (Walker 1989).

This evidence of increases in the frequency of growth disruption between the early and late prehistoric periods may reflect an increase in the prevalence of infectious disease or malnutrition (Dickel et al. 1984; Walker 1989). Such an increase would be a logical outcome of the increased population densities, sedentism, and interregional economic interactions that have been documented archaeologically (see Moratto 1984).

During the late prehistoric period, a system of trade routes developed that linked people throughout California and the American southwest. The flow of people and resources within this trade network increased the chances for the transmission of disease. Groups such as the Chumash were particularly susceptible to these health hazards because their economic system emphasized the intervillage exchange of food and manufactured goods (King 1976; Walker and Hudson 1989).

Within the Santa Barbara Channel area, there was significant variation in the frequency of hypoplasia among contemporaneous late prehistoric populations. The people who lived at Saspilil, a protohistoric village on the densely populated Goleta Slough, had nearly three times the hypoplasia of their contemporaries at Skull Gulch on Santa Rosa Island (Walker 1989). The differences between these sites are probably explained by differences in population density and isolation. At Saspilil, sanitation problems and frequent contacts with visitors from other villages are likely to have increased the incidence of acute viral and bacterial infections (Walker 1989). The population of Skull Gulch was much smaller and more isolated, and thus less subject to these density-dependent causes of disease.

The limited data that are available show that the frequency of dental hypoplasia in the La Purísima neophyte population was comparable to that of some protohistoric and historic period people from the same area. Dental data from Saspilil indicate that 19.2 percent of the teeth of the inhabitants of this protohistoric village have hypoplastic lesions. This is similar to the frequency of 18.6 percent that was found for the La Purísima neophytes.

The effects that introduced diseases had on California Indians are best understood in terms of the chronology of colonial expansion. As the intensity of interactions between the Indians and European colonists increased, so did the chances for the spread of infectious disease and disruption of native lifeways.

The first documented contact between Europeans and the Indians of Alta California occurred in 1542 when Juan Rodrigues Cabrillo sailed north along the Pacific coast. During this voyage, Cabrillo and his crew made several contacts with California Indians. Cabrillo was followed by a number of Spanish explorers who were searching for ports that could be used by ships transporting goods between the Philippines and Mexico (Costello and Hornbeck, this volume).

The effects of these early contacts are unclear. It seems likely, however, that some contagious diseases were first transmitted to the native population at this time. Diseases such as venereal syphilis could have been introduced directly through contacts between sailors and coastal Indians. Infectious diseases may also have disseminated along native trade routes from sites of origin in colonial Mexico (Dobyns 1981:49–50; Walker and Hudson 1989).

The frequency of contacts between California Indians and Europeans increased dramatically after the first Spanish missions and presidios were established beginning in 1769. As the number of Indians living at the missions grew, so did the chances for the spread of disease. The aggregation of Indians within the mission compounds not only enormously increased the contact of natives with Europeans, but also created an environment highly conducive to the spread of infectious disease. During these years, wave upon wave of such virulent infections as measles, scarlet fever, smallpox, and cholera beset the Mission neophytes (Cook 1976).

Because most of the missions were located near the coast, interior tribes had less contact with the early Spanish missionaries than coastal tribes. However, there were several Spanish expeditions into the central valley beginning in the late 1700s (Hornbeck 1983). These expeditions provided opportunities for the introduction of infectious diseases to the interior. It is also likely that Indians fleeing the missions spread diseases introduced by the Europeans to nonmission Indians living inland.

In 1834, secularization of the missions forced many former Indian neophytes to take up positions as servants and hired hands for Mexican and American ranchers. This coincided with the expansion of ranching enterprises into the Sacramento River Valley, an area already occupied by a dense Indian population.

The arrival of large numbers of gold miners, ranchers, and farmers in the

1850s and 1860s had a devastating effect on interior tribes. Lethal diseases such as smallpox were spread to Indians in remote areas that had previously had little contact with outsiders. Although the loss of life was certainly great, it is difficult to accurately assess the effects of these epidemics because of the limited information we have on the fate of Indians who lived outside the mission system.

Physical Violence

The extent of physical violence California Indians endured before and after the arrival of Europeans is difficult to assess owing to differences in the types of evidence available for the two periods. Data on the intensity of prehistoric violence come mainly from skeletal studies of the frequency of wounds inflicted by clubs, spears, and arrows and from the attempts of ethnographers to reconstruct conditions in California Indian societies at the time of European contact. In contrast, our knowledge of violence during the historic period comes primarily from documentary accounts provided by European colonists and, to a lesser extent, the Indians themselves.

Ethnographic reports indicate that there was considerable intertribal variation in the prevalence of warfare and violence (Kroeber 1925; McCorkle 1978). Many of the Central California tribes practiced highly ritualized forms of combat governed by rules designed to minimize fatalities. Other groups, such as the Mojave, are well known for the highly lethal forms of warfare that their culture emphasized (Stewart 1947).

Archaeological evidence indicates that the level of physical violence in California Indian society varied significantly through time. Periods of increased violence appear to be correlated with competition over resources brought about by unstable environmental conditions. Around A.D. 500, for example, the comparatively favorable climate in California began to shift toward unstable conditions, marked by several repeated episodes of severe drought. These conditions persisted until around A.D. 1100 (Walker et al. 1988).

There is strong evidence for an increase in the level of physical violence during this period. Around A.D. 500 the bow and arrow began to replace clubs and spear throwers as weapons of warfare throughout California (Moratto 1984). Skeletal evidence suggests an increase in warfare in Central California (Moratto 1984:213–214) and in the Santa Barbara Channel area at this time. For example, at the Calleguas Creek site, which dates from about A.D. 720 to A.D. 1100, more than 10 percent of the adult population shows evidence of arrow wounds.

The level of intergroup conflict appears to have increased significantly during the late protohistoric period among tribes who came in contact with the early Spanish explorers. In the Santa Barbara Channel area explorers reported the burning of several villages as a result of warfare (Brown 1967:75–76). This apparent increase in violence may be explained in part by the social disruption caused by introduced diseases. The Indians often attributed the death and sickness from epidemics to the witchcraft of shamans in enemy villages. In April of 1801, for example, an Indian named Lihuiasu and six companions raided and burned Eljman, a small rancheria:

> He killed five persons and wounded two others solely because the Gentiles of Eljman were relatives or friends of Temiacucat, the chief of the Cuyama Rancheria belonging to Dos Pueblos on the seashore, whom they regarded as the author of the epidemic of the *dolor de costado* [pain in the side] which at the time took the lives of many Indians [Engelhardt 1932:7].

At the beginning of the Mission period, there were so few missionaries in California that physical coercion was not a viable strategy for use in subjugating the Indians. As the number of soldiers, priests, and loyal Indian neophytes under their command increased, however, the use of physical coercion became increasingly feasible as a means of controlling the Indians (see Castillo, this volume).

The arrival of large numbers of gold miners in the 1840s and 1850s greatly increased the physical violence that California Indians were subjected to. This is reflected in the following article published in 1858 in a San Francisco newspaper:

> An Indian was murdered in Santa Barbara, recently, under circumstances which call loudly for the establishment of a Vigilance Committee in that place. He was called from his house by a Sonorian [*sic*] whose name we did not learn, and who without any provocation whatever, plunged a knife in to his heart, killing him instantly. Some four or five Indians were present, witnesses to the transaction, and they pursued the murderer, caught him and carried him before a magistrate. Will it be believed that he was almost immediately released from custody, because our laws will not allow an Indian to testify against a white man? The Indians in this part of the State, in the main a harmless race, are left entirely at the mercy of every ruffian in the country, and if something is not done for their protection, the race will shortly become extinct [Heizer 1974:279].

Conclusions

Many of the ecological and demographic variables that influenced the health of prehistoric California Indians continued to be important after the arrival of Europeans. Archaeological evidence shows that the prevalence of infectious diseases increased significantly during the prehistoric period. This decline in health was no doubt a result of the health problems that people encountered when they began to aggregate in large villages. As the number and intensity of interactions among people grew, so did the opportunities for the maintenance and spread of infectious disease. These same health hazards increased dramatically during the historic period when Indians began to live at the missions. This led to the rapid spread of several highly lethal infectious diseases to which the Indians had no acquired immunity.

Although the size of California's prehistoric population fluctuated in response to variations in environmental productivity, there was a general trend toward population growth throughout the prehistoric period. Some decrease in population size may have occurred during the protohistoric period owing to contacts with early explorers. The largest decreases, however, occurred during the Mission and especially the post-Mission periods because of increasingly frequent contacts between the Indians and Europeans and an intensification of violent conflicts over land.

Although the diet of prehistoric California Indians was, in general, nutritionally adequate, there is evidence of periodic food shortages and starvation brought on by fluctuations in environmental productivity. Periods of unusually severe drought and low marine productivity greatly increased the problems that people faced in extracting an adequate food supply from their surroundings. Dietary diversity decreased dramatically when the Indians moved to the missions and adopted a diet of introduced cultigens. There is evidence that this resulted in growth retardation among mission Indians.

Acknowledgments

This research was supported by NSF Grants BNS 84-18280 and BNS 85-07836.

References

Baumhoff, Martin A.
1978 Environmental Background. In *California*, edited by Robert F. Heizer, pp. 16–24. Handbook of North American Indians, vol. 8, William C. Sturtevant, general editor. Smithsonian Institution, Washington, D.C.

Blackburn, Thomas
1975 *December's Child: A Book of Chumash Oral Narratives*. University of California Press, Berkeley.

Breschini, Gary S., Trudy Haversat, and Jon Erlandson
1986 *California Radiocarbon Dates*. 4th ed. Coyote Press, Salinas, Calif.

Brown, Alan K.
1967 The Aboriginal Population of the Santa Barbara Channel. Archaeological Survey Report No. 69. University of California Archaeological Research Facility, Department of Anthropology, Berkeley.

Cook, Sherburne F.
1976 *The Conflict between the California Indian and White Civilization*. University of California Press, Berkeley.

Cook, Sherburne F., and W. Borah
1979 *Essays in Population History: Mexico and California*, vol. 3. University of California Press, Berkeley.

Costello, Julia G., and Phillip L. Walker
1987 Burials from the Santa Barbara Presidio Chapel. *Historical Archaeology* 21:3–17.

Cybulski, J. S.
1980 Possible Pre-Columbian Treponematosis on Santa Rosa Island, California. In *Canadian Review of Physical Anthropology* 2:19–25.

DeNiro, Michael J.
1985 Postmortem Preservation and Alteration of In Vivo Bone Reconstruction. *Nature* 317:806–809.

Dickel, David N., Peter D. Schulz, and Henry M. McHenry
1984 Central California: Prehistoric Subsistence Changes and Health. In *Paleopathology at the Origins of Agriculture*, edited by M. N. Cohen and G. J. Armelagos, pp. 439–461. Academic Press, Orlando, Fla.

Dobyns, Henry F.
  1981 From Fire to Flood: Historic Human Destruction of Sonoran Desert Riverine Oases. Anthropological Papers No. 20. Ballena Press, Menlo Park, Calif.
Doran, Glenn H.
  1980 *Paleodemography of the Plains Miwok Ethnolinguistic Area, Central California.* Ph.D. dissertation, University of California, Davis.
Engelhardt, Z.
  1932 Mission Santa Ines. Mission Santa Barbara, Santa Barbara.
Geiger, Maynard, and Clement Meighan (editors)
  1976 As the Padres Saw Them. Santa Barbara Mission Archive Library, Santa Barbara, Calif.
Glenn, Brian, Phillip L. Walker, and Natalie Anakouchine
  1988 Exploitation of Faunal Resources at SBa-46. Paper presented at the 53rd annual meeting of the Society for American Archaeology.
Goodman, Alan, Debra Martin, and George J. Armelagos
  1984 Indications of Stress from Bones and Teeth. In *Paleopathology at the Origins of Agriculture*, edited by M. N. Cohen and G. J. Armelagos, pp. 439–461. Academic Press, Orlando, Fla.
Harvey, H. R.
  1967 Population of the Cahuilla Indians: Decline and Its Causes. *Eugenics Quarterly* 14:185–198.
Heizer, Robert F.
  1974 The Destruction of California Indians: A Collection of Documents from the Period 1874 to 1865 in Which Are Described Some of the Things That Happened to Some of the Indians of California. Perigrine Smith, Santa Barbara and Salt Lake City.
Hoffman, J. M.
  1987 *The Descriptive Physical Anthropology of the Cardinal Site, CA-SJO-154; A Late Middle Horizon—Early Phase I Site from Stockton, California.* Publications in Anthropology No. 12. Colorado College, Colorado Springs, Colo.
Hornbeck, David
  1983 *California Patterns: A Geographical and Historical Atlas.* Mayfield, Palo Alto.
Hudson, Travis, Thomas Blackburn, Rosario Curletti, and Janice Timbrook
  1977 The Eye of the Flute: Chumash Traditional History and Ritual as Told by Fernando Librado Kitsepawit to John P. Harrington. Santa Barbara Museum of Natural History, Santa Barbara.
Kelsey, H.
  1984 European Impact on the California Indians, 1530–1830. *The Americas* 41(4):494–511.
King, Chester (editor)
  1982 *Archaeological Investigations at Telepop (LAn-229).* Office of Public Archaeology, Social Processes Research Institute, University of California, Santa Barbara.
King, Chester
  1976 Chumash Intervillage Economic Exchange. In *Native Californians: A Theoretical Retrospective*, edited by L. J. Bean and T. C. Blackburn, pp. 288–318. Ballena Press, Socorro, N.M.
Kroeber, Alfred
  1925 *Handbook of the Indians of California.* Bulletin 78. Bureau of American Ethnology of the Smithsonian Institution, Washington, D.C.
Lagenwalter, Paul E., and L. W. McKee
  1985 Vertebrate Faunal Remains. In *Excavations at Mission San Antonio 1976–1978*, edited by Robert L. Hoover and Julia G. Costello, pp. 94–121. Monograph Institute of Archaeology, University of California, Los Angeles.
Lightman, Stafford
  1977 The Responsibilities of Intervention in Isolated Societies. In *Health and Disease in*

Tribal Societies. Ciba Foundation Symposium No. 49 (new series). Elsevier, Amsterdam.

McCorkle, Thomas
1978 Intergroup Conflict. In *California*, edited by Robert F. Heizer, pp. 694–700. Handbook of North American Indians, vol. 8, William C. Sturtevant, general editor. Smithsonian Institution, Washington, D.C.

McHenry, Henry
1968 Transverse Lines in Long Bones of Prehistoric California Indians. *American Journal of Physical Anthropology* 29:1–18.

McHenry, Henry, and Peter Schulz
1978 Harris Lines, Enamel Hypoplasia, and Subsistence Change in Prehistoric Central California. In *Selected Papers from the 14th Great Basin Anthropological Conference*, edited by D. R. Touhy, pp. 36–49. Publications in Archaeology, Ethnology and History No. 11. Ballena Press, Socorro, N. Mex.

Mata, L., R. A. Kronmal, and H. Villegas
1980 Diarrheal Diseases: A Leading World Health Problem. In *Cholera and Related Diarrheas*. 43rd Nobel Symposium. Basel:Karger.

Moratto, Michael J.
1984 *California Archaeology*. Academic Press, Orlando.

Pisias, N. G.
1978 Paleoceanography of the Santa Barbara Basin during the Last 8,000 years. *Quaternary Research* 10:366–384.

Roney, J. G.
1959 Palaeopathology of a California Archaeological Site. *Bulletin of the History of Medicine* 33(2):97–109

1966 Paleoepidemiology: An Example from California. In *Human Paleopathology*, edited by S. Jarcho, pp. 99–107. Yale University Press, New Haven.

Schoeninger, Margaret J., and Michael J. DeNiro
1984 Nitrogen and Carbon Isotopic Composition of Bone Collagen from Marine and Terrestrial Animals. *Geochim. Cosmochim. Acta* 48:625–639.

Schulz, Peter
1981 *Osteoarchaeology and Subsistence Change in Prehistoric Central California.* Unpublished Ph.D. dissertation, University of California, Davis.

Suchey, J. M., W. J. Wood, and S. Shermis
1972 *Analysis of Human Skeletal Material from Malibu, California (LAn-264).* Archaeological Survey Report. Department of Anthropology, University of California, Los Angeles.

Stewart, Kenneth M.
1947 Mojave Warfare. *Southwestern Journal of Anthropology* 3:257–278.

Tauber, H.
1981 ^{13}C Evidence for Dietary Habits of Prehistoric Man in Denmark. *Nature* 292:332–333.

Walker, Phillip L.
1986 Porotic Hyperostosis in a Marine-dependent California Indian Population. *American Journal of Physical Anthropology* 69:345–354.

1989 *Enamel Hypoplasia during 5000 years of Southern California Prehistory.* In Health and Disease in the Prehistoric Southwest II. Maxwell Museum of Anthropology Paper, in press.

Walker, Phillip L., and Katherine Davidson
1988 *Analysis of Faunal Remains from Mission Santa Ines.* Edited by J. Costello. Santa Ines Mission Excavations, 1986–1988. Historical Archaeology in California No. 1. Coyote Press, Salinas, Calif.

Walker, Phillip L., and Michael J. DeNiro
1986 Stable Nitrogen and Carbon Isotope Ratios in Bone Collagen as Indices of Prehistoric Dietary Dependence on Marine and Terrestrial Resources in Southern California. *American Journal of Physical Anthropology* 71:51–61.

Walker, Phillip L., and Travis Hudson
   1989 Chumash Healing: Changing Health and Medical Practices in an American Indian
      Society. Malki Museum Press. Banning, Calif.
Walker, Phillip L., John Johnson, and Patricia Lambert
   1988 Age and Sex Biases in the Preservation of Human Skeletal Remains. *American Journal of Physical Anthropology* 76:183–188.
Walker, Phillip L., Daniel Larson, and Joel Michaelsen
   1988 Climatic Change and Inter-regional Interaction in Prehistoric Southern California.
      Unpublished manuscript.
Webb, Edith B.
   1952 *Indian Life at the Old Missions*. Warren F. Lewis, Los Angeles.

Chapter 22 ■

John R. Johnson

The Chumash and the Missions

At the beginning of Spanish colonization in Alta California, the Chumash Indians were occupying a territory extending from the Pacific Ocean in the west to the Central Valley in the east, and from the southern Salinas Valley in the north into the Santa Monica Mountains in the south (see Figure 19-1). The estimated 18,500 Indians who inhabited this region (Cook 1978) were divided into a number of independent polities, composed of relatively large villages or groups of villages, organized around the limited authority of a hereditary chief (Geiger and Meighan 1976:125–126; Simpson 1961:57). Linguistic studies have demonstrated the existence of at least six distinct Chumashan languages, most of them named for the missions founded in their areas.

Five Spanish missions were established in Chumash territory in the late eighteenth and early nineteenth centuries. From north to south, these missions and their founding dates were San Luis Obispo (1772), La Purísima (1788), Santa Inés (1804), Santa Bárbara (1786), and San Buenaventura (1782). Two other missions, San Miguel and San Fernando, founded in 1797 in Salinan and Gabrielino territories, respectively, also recruited sizable numbers of Chumash into their folds. Over a span of 50 years, virtually all of the Chumash were incorporated into mission communities, and by the close of the Mission period their population had declined to perhaps 15 percent of its former size.

The purpose of this study is to examine some of the social, economic, and demographic processes that transformed a relatively populous aboriginal society into a remnant population residing at the missions. I focus on that part of Chumash territory that approximates the area now encompassed by Santa Barbara County and the three missions that were established therein. A total of 6,550 baptisms were recorded from villages situated in this "central" portion of the Chumash region (Johnson 1988:Chapter 4). Near the end of the Mission period in 1832, only 1,360 Indians were still living at Missions Santa Bárbara, La Purísima, and Santa Inés (Engelhardt 1923:293, 1932a:176, 1932b:129). The discussion opens with a brief explanation of why the Indians were originally drawn to the missions, then moves on to how the recruitment process progressed and what happened demographically to the Chumash population after they arrived at the missions. My primary source of information is a data file on more than 11,000 Chumash Indians compiled from mission register data (Johnson 1988:Chapter 3). I also attempt to synthesize certain conclusions from previous anthropological and historical studies of the effects of missionization on Chumash society.

Factors Influencing Migration to the Missions

The impact of missionization and the incentives for joining the missions cannot be fully understood without some knowledge of Chumash economy before colonization. Chumash territory was ecologically diverse. The Indians of the coast and islands relied primarily on the sea for their subsistence (Landberg 1965), although the type of maritime adaptation varied considerably, depending on whether mainland coastal settlements were located on the islands or on the mainland or north or south of Point Conception (Glassow and Wilcoxon 1988). Inland Chumash settlements relied primarily on a hunting and gathering subsistence base, but mountain and valley communities and pericoastal and interior areas differed with respect to the type and availability of game and of seed and acorn crops (Horne 1981; Tainter 1975). An extensive trading network linked Chumash villages situated in different ecological zones. The Chumash exchange system relied upon the use of olivella bead money produced primarily on the Channel Islands (King 1976). Also, certain villages and certain segments of the society specialized in the manufacture of implements used in economic, social, and religious life (Arnold 1987; King 1981). The most powerful chiefs, who resided in coastal villages along the Santa Barbara Channel, no doubt derived much of their wealth and authority from their ability to broker exchange between the offshore islands and inland areas (Johnson 1988:Chapter 9; King 1982:203–205).

Because Chumash society depended on economic exchange, it was vulnerable to changes introduced by European contact. For example, the Spanish capitalized on the fact that the Chumash used bead money by introducing Venetian glass beads as a medium of exchange for Chumash goods and services. When the Santa Bárbara presidio was started in 1782, the governor of California, Felipe de Neve, provided the officer in charge of construction, Lt. José Francisco Ortega, with 41 bundles of glass beads to assist him in hiring Chumash labor (Beilharz 1971:157). Ortega wrote that the Chumash were hard workers and noted if he had "enough beads to hand out to them as gifts, I feel that I shall be able to finish the presidio in a short time" (Geiger 1965:14). An early Spanish visitor to Santa Bárbara in 1792 reported that the Chumash regarded the glass beads as more valuable than the shell bead money of local manufacture (Simpson 1961:55), and archaeological studies have demonstrated that certain types of shell bead currency disappeared altogether after glass beads were introduced (King 1981a:323). The introduction of glass trade beads affected the Chumash exchange system in several ways: (1) the Spanish were considered wealthy by Chumash standards, because of their large supplies of beads, (2) because of their "wealth," the Spanish could buy Chumash goods and services using glass beads, which created new opportunities for the acquisition of wealth that had not existed previously (Martz 1984:398, 467), and (3) the indigenous bead-making economy of the Chumash islanders was undermined and replaced (King 1981:323).

Glass beads were not the only Spanish goods sought by the Chumash. Metal tools such as knives, axes, swords, and needles (the last were used to drill shell beads) were also highly valued. Blankets, clothes, and agricultural products were sought. The missionaries used the Chumash desire to acquire the European materials and to learn the new technologies to their advantage in attracting recruits to the mission communities. At Mission Santa Bárbara for example, every year a new shirt and blanket were given to all neophytes, including young children who had been baptized but who still resided with their parents or relatives away from the mission. This encouraged parents to offer their children for baptism and to keep them returning each year to the mission (Geiger 1960:28, n.d.:246). The missionaries' strategy was that "the spiritual message would be the more readily accepted if it were accompanied by economic aid" (Geiger 1960:23).

With the introduction of animal husbandry and agriculture at the missions, the Indians could count on a more stable food supply and became less subject to the seasonal vicissitudes of fishing, hunting, and gathering economies. This factor, too, provided an important economic incentive to attract Chumash to the missions. Coombs and Plog have demonstrated that the annual harvest size and the number of Chumash converted tended to covary at Mission Santa Bárbara between 1787 and 1803 (Coombs and Plog 1977; Coombs 1979). Grazing by the mission's herds and flocks also affected seed-gathering activities, which played an important role in Chumash subsistence. Not only were economically important plants eaten by the grazing animals, but the common Chumash practice of burning grasslands to encourage the growth of certain fire-following annuals was actively suppressed by the Spanish authorities because of the detrimental effects of fire on pasture areas (Timbrook et al. 1982; West, this volume).

Thus far I have emphasized some of the economic reasons for the Chumash migration to the missions, including the Spanish corner on the bead currency market, the desire for certain European-manufactured items and technologies, the greater reliability of an agricultural subsistence base, and the detrimental effects of mission herds on seed-gathering areas. There were undoubtedly non-economic motives as well: religious, psychological, social, and political. True conversion occurred in some cases (e.g., Engelhardt 1923:318–319), but some authors have speculated that other ideological motives also moved the Indians to accept the new religion. The California Indians attributed some of the advanced European technologies to supernatural power and may have joined the church in order to learn the source of this power (Hudson and Underhay 1978:17–18; White 1963:99). It is also true that hierarchical ranking and status consciousness permeated Chumash culture (Blackburn 1975:49). At the missions, a person born to a lower rank would have a greater opportunity to improve his or her social status outside the confines of traditional roles.

Political factors also may have assisted in attracting the Chumash to the missions. According to both historic and ethnographic testimonies, one of the early converts at Mission Santa Bárbara, José María Panay, was of high-ranking lineage and was instrumental in attracting many other Chumash to the mission (Johnson 1986:26–27; Kenneally 1965:18). Also, the presidio and mission of Santa Bárbara were established adjacent to the village headed by Yanonali, one of the most powerful Chumash chiefs, who was described as having authority over thirteen other villages (Brown 1967:47–48; Geiger 1965:14; Warren 1977). Yanonali's friendship was actively sought (Beilharz 1971:157; Geiger 1965:8), and in 1797 he was baptized along with a good number of his people, who were given the unique "privilege" of remaining in their village after they accepted conversion rather than having to move to the mission (Kenneally 1965:278–279). Most of those in the village, including Yanonali, accepted baptism on these terms, gaining the benefits of association with the mission and at the same time remaining in their traditional homes (Johnson 1986:28). By convincing some of the local political elite to accept baptism, the missionaries were undoubtedly planning to have more Chumash follow their leaders' examples.

Baptismal Patterns

The demographic factors involved in recruitment to the missions are reflected in the patterns of conversion revealed in the baptismal registers. The reduction of the Chumash to the missions took about half a century, from 1772 until 1822; but actually the majority from the mainland of the Central Chumash subregion entered the missions within a relatively short time span—about 20 years, from 1787 to 1806. Figure 22-1 illustrates the baptismal pattern for Chumash converts at Missions Santa Bárbara, La Purísima, and Santa Inés. Three phases of recruitment activity are discernible. The initial phase lasted 16 years, from 1787 until 1802, during which time conversion rates were relatively stable, fluctuating slightly as the missions' ability to support more neophytes gradually developed (Coombs and Plog 1977). Then in 1803 there began a sudden recruitment effort, during which virtually all remaining "gentile" Chumash in coastal and valley

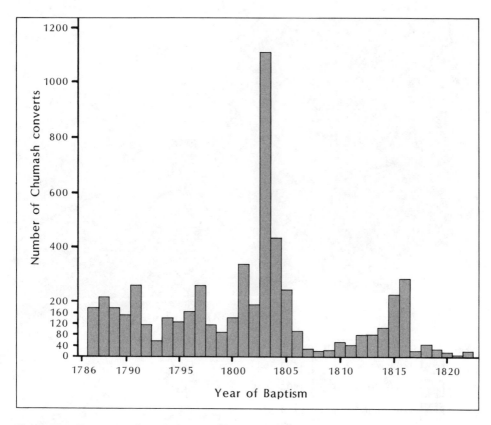

Figure 22-1. Frequency chart showing number of Chumash converts per year at missions Santa Bárbara, La Purísima, and Santa Inés.

settlements on the mainland were baptized. The immediate cause for this massive recruitment was apparently a decision by the Viceroy Iturrigaray that the California missions should continue to operate in their traditional manner by having Indian neophytes reside at the missions rather than in their native villages (Engelhardt 1930:607). Mission Santa Inés was founded in this period to effect the conversion of the remaining Chumash population in inland areas. The final phase of recruitment occurred during the second decade of the nineteenth century, when the Chumash islanders and a few *serranos* from remote interior areas arrived at the missions.

There was a definite geographic pattern to the way in which new recruits came to the missions. Those living closest to the missions were converted first, those living in the Santa Ynez Valley came next, and those living on the Channel Islands and in the furthest reaches of Chumash territory migrated last. By calculating a statistic for the mean year of baptism for the population of each Chumash village and mapping the resulting patterns, we can ascertain the rate of expansion of mission influence (see Figure 22-2). Mission La Purísima initially succeeded in recruiting over a wider territory than did Mission Santa Bárbara primarily because the region from which its converts were drawn had a lower pop-

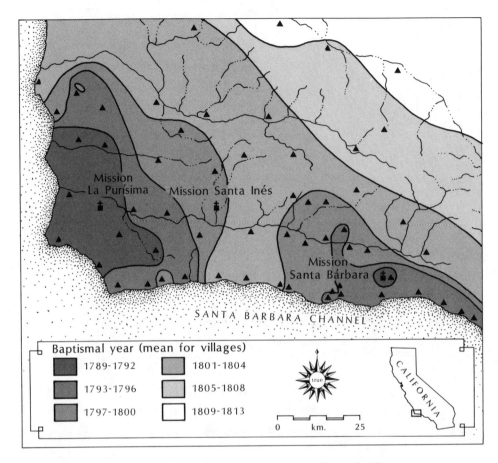

Figure 22-2. Map illustrating the rate of missionization among Chumash villages.

ulation density. At both missions there was a strong correlation between the mean year of baptism for the villages and their distance from the missions (r^2 was 0.87 for La Purísima and 0.64 for Santa Bárbara).

Several observations may be made regarding the demographic structure of the Chumash population during the early Mission period on the basis of the age and sex distribution of persons who were baptized at the missions (Johnson 1988:Table 5.1). Considering the sex ratio first, up until 24 years of age there was essentially little difference in the number of females compared to males, but in age groups 25 years and older nearly twice as many females were baptized as males. This pattern apparently reflects a higher death rate among men in Chumash society. The decline in adult males in the pre-mission population may have been the result of raids and warfare among Chumash villages, an all too frequent phenomenon that drew comment from many early Spanish observers (Brown 1967:75–76; Burrus 1967:135; Engelhardt 1932b:7; Geiger and Meighan 1976:93, 113, 139).

A second point to note is the relatively small percentage of children who were baptized at the missions: 20.5 percent of the population consisted of persons

10 years old or younger. This figure is close to the 22.5 percent documented for the Island Chumash (Johnson 1982:103), but is in marked contrast to the pattern observed among the eight missions north of the three considered here, where children made up 37.8 percent of the total number of baptisms (Cook and Borah 1979:197). Figure 22-3 presents information on the years of birth for Chumash converts baptized prior to 1810 at Missions Santa Bárbara, La Purísima, and Santa Inés. The data in Figure 22-3 would seem to suggest that the fewer numbers of young children baptized reflected either a dramatic decline in fertility and/or a greater mortality rate in younger age groups after Spanish settlement in the Chumash region. Cohorts born in native villages after 1790 were less than half the number born prior to mission times. This suggests that the more densely settled Chumash population may have been more severely affected by introduced European diseases than were the more dispersed Indian populations north of the Chumash (see also Walker et al., this volume).

Demographic Impacts at the Missions

The reduction in fertility and higher infant mortality postulated for the Chumash residing outside the mission community may be demonstrated with more certainty as having produced the drastic decline in population that occurred at the missions. In order to study the demographic processes involved, I cross-referenced baptismal and burial data for each person at the missions. Burial entries were found for 8,468 Chumash neophytes. The number of burials correlated with baptismal entries represents 90 percent of those baptized at Santa Bárbara between 1786 and 1828, at La Purísima between 1788 and 1851, and at Santa Inés between 1804 and 1844. The remaining 10 percent is made up of those living beyond the Mission period for whom no burial entry could be found, those baptized near death in their native villages whose subsequent death escaped the notice of the missionaries, those who were misidentified in the burial

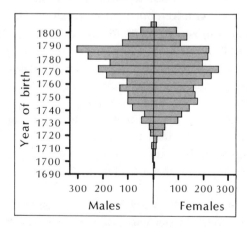

Figure 22-3. Age pyramid in five-year cohorts for Chumash converts at missions Santa Bárbara, Santa Inés, and La Purísima before 1810.

records and could not be correlated with baptismal entries, and probably a few who were fugitives from the mission system.

Several analyses were conducted on the mission register data set. First, I determined the age of death for all who were entered in the burial registers and the sex ratio for each age category (Johnson 1988:Table 5.2). Two observations were significant here: (1) children less than 5 years of age accounted for 30.3 percent of those buried in the mission cemeteries, and (2) a 1.7:1 ratio of women to men occurred for burials of persons between 15 and 24 years of age. These patterns document very high infant mortality at the missions and a high death rate for women entering their early reproductive years. The latter produced a steadily increasing sex ratio in favor of males at the missions (Cook 1976:427–432), completely reversing what had been the pre-mission condition.

A second analysis focused on the survivability of Chumash converts after they entered the mission environment (Johnson 1988:Table 5.3). The high death rates among infants were again dramatically demonstrated: 36 percent of those children less than two years of age died within their first year at the missions. Only about 38 percent in this very young age category survived until puberty. For the entire population of converts, the median number of years survived after baptism turns out to be about 12 years, which in general is a somewhat better record than was experienced by missions north of the Chumash region (Cook and Borah 1979:210–229).

Life expectancy for children born at the missions to baptized parents was also examined (Johnson 1988:Table 5.4). The most precise statistics on survivability were available for this group because age calculations were based on a known year of birth and were not dependent on missionary age estimates. Again, infant mortality was high. Fully two-thirds died before reaching five years of age, and three-quarters were deceased before puberty. This was about a 10 percent higher mortality than occurred in the populations of six missions north of the three considered here (Cook and Borah 1979:232–238).

In addition, an attempt was made to measure the birth rate at the missions by counting the number of children born at the missions each year and dividing this figure by the number of women of child-bearing age who were living in that year, that is, who were between 15 and 45 years of age. The general pattern that emerges is one of declining fertility; it reaches a low plateau during the first two decades of the nineteenth century, and then seems to rebound toward the end of the Mission period (Johnson 1988:Figure 5.4).

The demographic analyses present a bleak picture of the fate of the Chumash population at the missions. The dramatic population decline was brought about by high mortality in children less than five years of age, a decline in the number of women of child-bearing age, and a decline in fertility. The evidence derived from examining the age structure of those recruited from native villages indicates that many of these processes were occurring outside the mission environment too, but perhaps their impact was not as severe as when the population eventually became concentrated in mission communities. As is commonly known, the explanation for the demographic decline experienced by the Chumash and other California Indians during the Mission period was the introduction of diseases to which the native population possessed no natural immunity. Particularly devastating were the venereal diseases introduced by the soldiers. In 1813 the missionaries at Santa Bárbara called attention to this situation as it affected the neophytes under their jurisdiction (see quotation from Geiger and Meighan 1976:74, cited in Walker et al., this volume). Venereal diseases contributed to declining fertility and undoubtedly weakened the constitutions of infants born to infected mothers. Cook (1976:30) attributed 60 percent of the population decrease at the missions to the direct and indirect effects of syphilis.

Conclusion

In the foregoing discussion, I have identified and summarized many of the critical variables involved in the migration process and have utilized mission register evidence to document the severe demographic consequences of Spanish colonization. The archaeological and ethnohistoric evidence indicates that the reasons for Chumash migration to the missions were complex. Motivating factors included economic, ideological, social, political, and demographic pressures. It appears that the Chumash were not forced to convert, although once having committed themselves by undergoing the rite of baptism, neophytes were not allowed to leave the mission communities except for monthly visits to relatives in their native villages. Those who attempted to escape from the mission system were sought and punished if found (Guest 1979).

Once the recruitment process began, it perpetuated itself. As the population in the villages declined because of emigration to the missions and because of fewer children owing to the effects of introduced diseases, the social and economic balance of native society was upset, and those remaining in the villages were more likely to follow the example of friends and relatives who had already joined the mission communities. A feedback situation was thereby created: The more who left for the missions, the fewer were around to participate in the social and economic life of the villages, making it more likely that even more would depart. Unfortunately, the relatively greater economic and social security that the missions offered was offset by the disastrous effects of diseases introduced by the Europeans. The unintentional but tragic result of missionization was that only a remnant population had survived when the Mission period came to a close.

References

Arnold, Jeanne E.
  1987 *Craft Specialization in the Prehistoric Channel Islands, California*. University of California Publications in Anthropology, vol. 18. Berkeley.
Beilharz, Edwin A.
  1971 *Felipe de Neve: First Governor of California*. California Historical Society, San Francisco.
Blackburn, Thomas C.
  1975 *December's Child: A Book of Chumash Oral Narratives*. University of California Press, Berkeley.

Brown, Alan K.
1967 *The Aboriginal Population of the Santa Barbara Channel*. Reports of the University of California Archaeological Survey No. 69. Berkeley.

Burrus, Ernest J.
1967 *Diario del Capitán Comandante Fernando de Rivera y Moncada. Colleción Chimalistac de Libros y Documentos Acerca de la Nueva España*, vols. 24 and 25. Ediciones José Turanzas, Madrid.

Cook, Sherburne F.
1976 *The Conflict between the California Indian and White Civilization*. University of California Press, Berkeley.
1978 Historical Demography. In *California*, edited by R. F. Heizer, pp. 91–98. Handbook of North American Indians, vol. 8, William C. Sturtevant, general editor. Smithsonian Institution, Washington, D.C.

Cook, Sherburne F., and Woodrow Borah
1979 *Essays in Population History: Mexico and California*, vol. 3. University of California Press, Berkeley.

Coombs, Gary
1979 Opportunities, Information Networks and the Migration-Distance Relationship. *Social Networks* 1: 257–276.

Coombs, Gary, and Fred Plog
1977 The Conversion of the Chumash Indians: An Ecological Interpretation. *Human Ecology* 5(4):309–328.

Engelhardt, Zephyrin
1923 *Santa Barbara Mission*. James H. Barry, San Francisco.
1930 *The Missions and Missionaries of California*, vol. II, rev. ed. Mission Santa Barbara, Santa Barbara.
1932a *Mission La Purísima Concepción de María Santísima*. Mission Santa Barbara, Santa Barbara.
1932b *Mission Santa Inés: Virgen y Martir*. Mission Santa Barbara, Santa Barbara.

Geiger, Maynard
1960 *The Indians of Mission Santa Barbara*. Mission Santa Barbara, Santa Barbara.
1965 *Mission Santa Barbara, 1782–1965*. Franciscan Fathers of California, Santa Barbara.
n.d. *History of Mission Santa Barbara*, vol. 1, *The Spanish and Mexican Periods (1786–1846)*. Unpublished manuscript. Santa Barbara Mission Archive Library.

Geiger, Maynard, and Clement W. Meighan
1976 *As the Padres Saw Them: California Indian Life and Customs as Reported by the Franciscan Missionaries, 1813–1815*. Santa Barbara Mission Archive Library, Santa Barbara.

Glassow, Michael A., and Larry R. Wilcoxon
1988 Coastal Adaptations near Point Conception, California, with Particular Regard to Shellfish Exploitation. *American Antiquity* 53:36–51.

Guest, Francis F.
1979 An Examination of the Thesis of S. F. Cook on the Forced Conversion of the Indians in the California Missions. *Southern California Quarterly* 61(1):1–77.

Horne, Stephen
1981 *The Inland Chumash: Ethnography, Ethnohistory, and Archeology*. Ph.D. dissertation, University of California, Santa Barbara.

Hudson, Travis, and Ernest Underhay
1978 *Crystals in the Sky: An Intellectual Odyssey Involving Chumash Astronomy, Cosmology and Rock Art*. Ballena Press, Socorro, N.Mex.

Johnson, John R.
1982 *An Ethnohistoric Study of the Island Chumash*. M.A. thesis. University of California, Santa Barbara.
1986 The Chumash History of Mission Creek. *Noticias: Quarterly Bulletin of the Santa Barbara Historical Society* 32(2):21–37.

1988 *Chumash Social Organization: An Ethnohistoric Perspective.* Ph.D. dissertation, University of California, Santa Barbara.

Kenneally, Finbar
1965 *Writings of Fermín Francisco de Lasuén.* Academy of American Franciscan History, Washington, D.C.

King, Chester D.
1976 Chumash Intervillage Economic Exchange. In *Native Californians: A Theoretical Retrospective*, edited by Lowell J. Bean and Thomas Blackburn, pp. 289–318. Ballena Press, Socorro, N.Mex.

1981 *The Evolution of Chumash Society: A Comparative Study of Artifacts Used in Social System Maintenance in the Santa Barbara Channel Region before A.D. 1804.* Ph.D. dissertation, University of California, Davis.

King, Linda B.
1982 *Medea Creek Cemetery: Late Inland Chumash Patterns of Social Organization, Exchange and Warfare.* Ph.D. dissertation, University of California, Los Angeles.

Landberg, Leif C. W.
1965 *The Chumash Indians of Southern California.* Southwest Museum, Los Angeles.

Martz, Patricia C.
1984 *Social Dimensions of Chumash Mortuary Populations in the Santa Monica Mountains Region.* Ph.D. dissertation, University of California, Riverside.

Simpson, Lesley Byrd
1961 *Journal of José Longinos Martínez 1791–1792.* John Howell Books, San Francisco.

Tainter, Joseph A.
1975 Hunter-Gatherer Territorial Organization in the Santa Ynez Valley. *Pacific Coast Archaeological Society Quarterly* 11(2):27–40.

Timbrook, Jan, John R. Johnson, and David D. Earle
1982 Vegetation Burning by the Chumash. *Journal of California and Great Basin Anthropology* 4:163–186.

Warren, Claude N.
1977 The Many Wives of Pedro Yanonali. *Journal of California Anthropology* 4:242–248.

White, Raymond C.
1963 Luiseño Social Organization. *University of California Publications in American Archaeology and Ethnology* 48:91–194.

Chapter 23 ▓

Ed. D. Castillo

The Native Response to the Colonization of Alta California

With the approach of the Columbian Quincentennial and recent efforts to canonize Junípero Serra, considerable attention has been focused on the many accomplishments of the Spanish in Alta California. What frightens many people is the thought that Hispanic boosterism and religious conviction stirred up by these twin events may again attempt to mask the not so flattering realities of the Spanish Colonial empire. What many apologists for the Spanish mission system have in common is an extremely low and disparaging attitude toward the Indians of California. Their reasoning appears to suggest that whatever befell the native peoples of Alta California during the mission era, it was preferable to their native culture, and in fact, somehow uplifting. Despite legal and Christian moral arguments put forward by Franciscan historians and others, the Spanish Crown/Franciscan empire benefited only a handful of natives. The vast majority of California mission Indians were simply laborers in a larger quest for worldwide domination by that eighteenth-century empire. It seems important to the majority of the descendants of these mission Indians that a voice be raised in their defense concerning the alleged benefits Indians received under the Spanish empire. It is equally important to document and analyze native resistance and adaptation to that empire's institutions. Without such efforts, I am afraid that we may find our recollection of this period to be represented only by the dashing Hispanic soldier/explorers, pious padres, romantic dons, and, of course, the "docile" mission Indian.

Spain's plans for the extension of its church/crown empire into Alta California were prompted by fears of rival European encroachment of its northwestern frontier. The instruments of conquest were time-tested and reliable. First, Spanish soldiers and Franciscan priests would occupy strategic places along the coast. The soldiers would establish military forts or presidios, while the Franciscans established missions. The missions, however, had power and functions far beyond simple religious conversion. They were to be the economic backbone of the colony. Once Indians were baptized, they were no longer free to leave the missions. These institutions eventually developed into huge feudal estates, on lands stolen by Franciscan and military authorities, and grew rich from the efforts of a mass of unpaid forced laborers. Over two hundred years of experience in this sort of activity guided the priest Junípero Serra. The final step in this process was the importation of civilian colonists (sometimes criminals recruited from frontier prisons) to establish pueblos. Supposedly after 10 years under Franciscan authority, the Indians were to be granted pueblo lands and were to take their place as peons in colonial society. However, over the years the Franciscans found one excuse after another to extend their authority over the Indians. Reluctant to give up this rich empire, Franciscans blamed Indians themselves for the delay. Neophytes were finally wrenched from the grip of the Franciscan order after almost 70 years of feudal domination (Bolton 1964:187–211). Secularization laws that followed provided extremely limited opportunities for ex-neophytes to claim lands. No systematic effort was made by church or secular authorities to inform these survivors of their "rights" under Mexican Laws.

Mission Conditions

The beneficiaries of the Crown and Franciscan plan of empire rapidly discovered the hard reality of colonial exploitation. In the beginning, most California Indians were lured into the missions with gifts and other clever inducements. Almost at once, assaults on female neophytes commenced. This unleashed an epidemic of venereal diseases among the Indians. But that was only the beginof humiliating and degrading treatment suffered by the neophytes and gentiles (non-Christians) alike. The colonists' livestock began to devastate native food. Indian lands were seized for colonial institutions. Their game was hunted without permission, and forced labor was introduced. Whole villages were uprooted and forced to relocate at the mission site. Young unmarried neophytes of both sexes were locked up in crowded barracks at night. All native religious behavior was forbidden. Native culture was to be abandoned in exchange for a life of coercive paternal domination (Cook 1976:1–161).

The rigid discipline required by the Franciscans was enforced through religious propaganda, threats, and intimidation. Squads of soliders with their technologically superior weapons and horses were stationed at each mission. These soldiers were reinforced by royal presidio troops stationed at four points along the Camino Real. The priests also orchestrated a system of informants, with some natives acting as majordomos, and kept the neophytes in line with liberal doses of the whip. Examples and analysis of these conditions can be found in the writings of Spanish church and military authorities, foreign visitors, and historians and anthropologists (Bancroft 1886–1887:Volumes I and II; Cook 1976; Costo 1988; Geiger and Meighan 1976).

Catastrophic attacks of virulent European diseases took a heavy toll of native lives. Spanish medical practices being ineffective, the priests could only watch as thousands of their laborers suffered and died. The death rates for these epidemics ranged as high as 60 percent of the total population (Cook 1976:3–34). This unfortunate situation fueled the Franciscan demand for more laborers. Thus missionary-inspired paramilitary expeditions began to recruit reluctant tribes for conversion as early as 1797 (Cook 1976:75).

As a result of missionization and the military occupation of their country, the unfortunate natives suffered a rapid and steep population decline (see Walker and others in this volume). In some cases, the process became irreversible and whole tribes eventually disappeared (Cook 1976:399–446).

Internal Resistance

Not surprisingly, the Indians began to react negatively to this threatening situation. Resistance to the colonial "new order" emerged almost at once. This study reviews native passive and active resistance to the missions, missionaries, and soldiers on this remote rim of Christendom.

Undoubtedly passive resistance to the new order was the most widespread negative response to the classic mission environment. Several factors made this so. The nearly total absence of experience in organizing and carrying out warfare hampered native military organizational efforts. Traditional political authority seldom went beyond the village level. The neophytes were targets of a well-established church–military plan featuring an elaborate system of native informants, majordomos, and coopted local captains. These factors, combined with the cultural shock of removal from their native villages and the conglomeration of other native groups thrown together and withering under virulent catastrophic epidemics, provided ample cause for internal resistance.

Infanticide and Abortions

One of the most disturbing trends in passive resistance was infanticide and a-bortions practiced by native women. A contemporary sympathetic observer married to a San Gabriel neophyte informs us, "They necessarily became accustomed to these things [being raped by Spanish Soldiers], but their disgust and abhorrence never left them till many years later. In fact every white child born among them for a long period was secretly strangled and buried" (Heizer 1968:70).

The priests went to extremes to prevent such practices. Lorenzo Asisara, a

Santa Cruz neophyte, tells us about Padre Ramon Olbés's attempt to stamp out this practice:

> He (Olbés) saw that two of the [neophyte women] were scratched in their faces because they had been fighting out of jealousy. He separated them to ascertain why they had scratched [each other]. One was sterile and the other had children. When the father became aware of the cause of the quarrel, he asked the sterile one why she didn't bear children. He sent for the husband, and he asked him why his wife hadn't borne children. The Indian pointed to the sky (he didn't know how to speak Spanish) to signify that only God knew the cause. They brought an interpreter. This [one] repeated the question of the father to the Indian, who answered that he should ask God. The Fr. asked through the interpreter if he slept with his wife, to which the Indian said yes. Then the father had them placed in a room together so that they would perform coitus in his presence. The Indian refused, but they forced him to show them his penis in order to affirm that he had it in good order.
>
> The father next brought the wife and placed her in the room. The husband he sent to the guard house with a pair of shackels. The interpreter, on orders from the father, asked her how it was that the face was scratched. She replied that another woman had done it out of jealousy. The father then asked if her husband had been going with the other woman; she said yes. Then, he asked her again why she didn't bear children like the rest of the women.
>
> Fr. Olbés asked her if her husband slept with her, and she answered that, yes. The Fr. repeated his question "why don't you bear children?" "Who knows!" answered the Indian woman. He had her enter another room in order to examine her reproductive parts. She resisted him and grabbed the father's cord. There was a strong and long struggle between the two that were alone in the room. She tried to bury her teeth in his arm, but only grabbed his habit.
>
> Fr. Olbés cried out and the interpreter and the alcalde entered to help him. Then Olbés ordered that they take her and give her fifty lashes. After the fifty lashes he ordered that she be shackled and locked in the nunnery. Finishing this, Fr. Olbés ordered that a wooden doll be made, like a recently born child; he took the doll to the whipped woman and ordered her to take that doll for her child, and to carry it in front of all the people for nine days. He obligated her to present herself in front of the temple with that [doll] as if it were her child, for nine days.
>
> With all these things the women who were sterile became very alarmed. The vicious father made the husband of that woman wear cattle horns affixed with leather. At the same time he had him shackled. In this way they brought him daily to mass from the jail. And the other Indians jeered at him and teased him. Returning to the jail, they would take the horns off him [Asisara 1877].

This brutal reaction seems to suggest that the Franciscans suspected all infertile women of practicing abortions. The public beatings and humiliations were aimed at preventing such behavior.

Cook concluded that negative environmental factors, such as unsatisfactory diet, diseases, and the oppressive restrictions on native physical and cultural expression contributed to the elaboration of an occasional sporadic cultural phenomenon (abortion and infanticide) into a serious attempt to check population growth (Cook 1976:112).

Another form of passive resistance among long-term neophytes was slow and poorly accomplished work. Reid informs us about the mental state of the neophytes: "At first surprise and astonishment filled their minds; a strange lethargy and inaction predominated afterwards" (Heizer 1968:76). This holds no surprises for scholars of forced labor and slavery. Few, if any, who are compelled to work do so with enthusiasm, skill, or accuracy.

Religious Resistance

Although the priests had physical control of the converts, the Franciscans could not control the neophytes' minds. It was impossible to prevent the Indians within the mission system from respecting the shaman and secretly carrying out native religious practices. Neither priests nor soldiers could prevent Indian parents from passing on traditional knowledge and beliefs. Considerable documentation exists that attests to the widespread and surreptitious native religious practices in the mission (Cook 1976:148–153; Geiger and Meighan 1976). This form of passive resistance is linked to several Indian uprisings like the 1785 Toypurina Revolt at San Gabriel, and the 1801 Chupu Cult unrest that developed among the Chumash Indians (Cook 1976:150). Some evidence suggests that the 1824 Chumash uprising may have been triggered by neophyte allegiance to tradition (Sandos 1985). Near the end of the mission era, Father Boscana was forced to conclude, "Superstitions of a ridiculous and most extravagant nature were found associated with these Indians, and even now in almost every town or hamlet the child is first taught to believe in their authenticity" (Boscana 1933:61).

Fugitivism

A transitional step between passive and active resistance was fugitivism. This was by far the most widespread form of active resistance. There can be no doubt about the longing on the part of the neophytes to return to their homes and old way of life. Lieutenant Otto Von Kotzebue visiting California in 1816 was moved to record this melancholy event in the lives of Santa Clara neophytes:

> Twice in the year they receive permission to return to their native homes. This short time is the happiest period of their existence; and I myself have seen them going home in crowds, with loud rejoicings. The sick, who cannot undertake the journey, at least accompany their happy countrymen to the shore where they embark and sit there for days together mournfully gazing on the distant summits of the mountains which surround their homes; they often sit in this situation for several days, without taking any food, so much does the sight of their lost home affect these new Christians. Every time some of those who have the permission run away, and they would probably all do it, were they not deterred by their fears of the soldiers [Quoted in Cook 1976:81].

Fugitivism was the most immediate route to freedom from Spanish authority. Official Spanish reports of this phenomenon began to appear in 1781 and became increasingly acute until the missions were dismantled by the Mexican Republic in 1834–1836. Yet these *cimmarones* (runaways) had considerable difficulty in maintaining themselves once free. Spanish domestic animals destroyed much of the native economy. Neophytes in whose territory missions were established were forced to flee into other tribal territories. The unhappy consequence of this was that neighboring gentile villages became infected with Spanish diseases and church-sponsored military expeditions were brought to their rancherías. These expeditions, whose purported mission was to return runaway neophytes, frequently seized gentile women and children and took them to the missions. Later, when the missions began to militarily recruit distant tribes to bolster the dying populations, fugitivism became epidemic. Although fugitivism was not easily maintained, a significant number of Indians found it preferable to the authoritarianism of Franciscan rule (Cook 1976:56–64).

Indians usually escaped from church/military authority individually or in small groups. However, massive defections began to occur as early as 1795. In September of that year, 200 Costanoan neophytes abandoned Mission Delores to escape the cruelty of Padre Danti (Bancroft 1886–1887:I:709). In the last years of the mission system, massive escapes increased steadily. Of the total 81,586 neophytes who were baptized, thousands escaped temporarily but 3,400 escaped permanently (Cook 1976:59). Most central and northern mission neophytes fled into the central valley of California, which Padre Payeras called "a republic of hell and diabolical union of Apostates" (Bancroft 1886–1887:II:331). The ones who escaped were only those young enough and healthy enough to flee. Too often the very young, the old, and the multitude of the infirmed were unable to escape their oppressors.

Fugitivism occurred because of the neophyte dissatisfaction with mission life. But the Franciscans were not about to allow their forced laborers to simply walk away. Once within the missions, neophytes were not free to leave. If they fled, they were hunted down by soldiers, priests, Indian allies, and sometimes Hispanic civilians. Pagan villages that harbored runaways were punished. Village captains were either flogged or killed (if they resisted), and a number of unlucky pagans were required to join the captives and march back to the missions, where further beating awaited them (Cook 1960). Russian otter hunter Vasilli Petrovitch Tarakanoff witnessed this chilling episode of brutality to captured runaways:

> They were all bound with rawhide ropes and some bleeding from wounds and some children were tied to their mothers. The next day we saw some terrible things. Some of the run-away men were tied on sticks and beaten with straps. One chief was taken out to the open field and a young calf which had just died was skinned and the chief was sewed into the skin while it was yet warm. He was kept tied to a stake all day, but he died soon and they kept his corpse tied up [Rawls 1984:38].

Such treatment is not easily forgotton. Twentieth-century descendants of mission Indians kept oral histories of Spanish oppression. One of John P. Harrington's Chumash informants says this of her grandmother's attempts at running away, "[She] had run away many, many times and had been recaptured and whipped till her buttocks crawled with maggots" (Laird 1975:18). Other similar stories continue to be passed on from generation to generation (Costo 1988:131–156).

As the years of Spanish mission activities progressed, the cycle of brutality increased steadily. Force and threats were used to keep Indians working in the Franciscan plantation-like missions. Military forays to recapture the thousands of runaways confirmed for the interior Indians the tales of a Franciscan "reign of terror" told to them by the runaways. Soon both fugitives and gentile rancherías bordering on areas of Franciscan occupation began to offer armed resistance to the church/military expeditions looking for the fugitives. However, in contrast to earlier experiences, these interior groups began to acquire Spanish horses and arms, and, perhaps most important, they began to understand the threat that Spanish colonization posed to their families, homes, economy, culture, and ultimately their lives.

Individual Assassination

A particularly native reaction to the missionary violence and oppression was for servants to poison the Franciscans. In aboriginal society, powerful witches were sometimes poisoned by their clients or rivals (Kroeber 1976:851–879). Many Indians viewed the priests as powerful witches. From a native point of view, this made sense. It was easy to see the soldiers and civilians were men like themselves. But the padres' religious, political, and military power wreaked havoc upon Indian families, land, natural resources, and their culture (Shipek 1986:13–14). Several assassination attempts, some using poisons, occurred.

In 1801, three neophytes poisoned both priests at Mission San Miguel. While those two were recovering, a third priest (Father Pujol), sent to replace them, was himself poisoned by the neophytes and died within a month. Three neophytes were eventually arrested, but escaped because of a drunken sentinel, only to be recaptured later (Bancroft 1886–1887:II:147–150). For trying to kill a padre with a stone in 1805, the military flogged a San Miguel neophyte 25 lashes on nine successive feast days and 35–40 lashes on nine successive Sundays, while different groups of neophytes were compelled to watch (Bancroft 1886–1887:II:163–164). Also in 1801, Ipai neophytes killed a particularly sadistic majordomo (a thug employed by the padres to enforce discipline) at Mission San Diego (Cook 1976:129). At the same mission three years later, Padre Panto was given a lethal dose of poison by his personal cook Nazario. The terrified neophyte admitted killing the priest to escape the padre's intolerable beatings. Just before the assassination he had received in succession 50, 25, 24, and 25 lashes with a whip (Bancroft 1886–1887:II:345).

In October of 1812, Padre Quintana of Santa Cruz Mission had made for him a wire-tipped whip (which cut the buttocks deeply) and used it on nine luckless neophytes. When this new instrument of torture was introduced and the priest nearly beat two Indians to death, a number of them decided to kill the sadistic padre. On the night of October 11, Quintana was lured outside the mission compound and strangled. The conspirators placed the padre's body in his bed to suggest that he had died of natural causes. And indeed the ruse worked. The priest was buried two days later. However, about two years later the assassination was uncovered as the result of an argument between two neophytes over the priest's stolen booty. Fourteen neophytes were arrested and imprisoned. Eventually eight were convicted and sentenced to 200 lashes each and to presidio labor for 10 years in chains. Evidence exists to suggest that only one of the condemned survived his sentence (Bancroft 1886–1887:II:388).

Armed Resistance

Violent group hostilities during the Spanish occupation gradually evolved as Indians watched the Spanish replace traditional village-based leaders with those groomed for leadership by the Spanish priests. The Ipai and Tipai Indians, whose territory was the site of the old Mission San Diego, were the first Indians to offer widespread armed resistance. This was a classic example of resistance orchestrated by traditional village-based leaders. The trouble began within a month of the founding of the Mission San Diego (June 1769). The Ipai showed no fear of the Spanish but expected gifts from them for the use of their territory and resources. Seeing the scurvy-ridden garrison, the Indians refused all offers of food, but asked for cloth. When Spanish gifts failed to satisfy the natives, they attempted to pillage the supply ship anchored in the bay. The Spanish responded with persuasion, threats, and even the noise of firearms. These demonstrations were met with ridicule.

On August 15, the local Indians entered the Spanish compound to seize the clothing and gifts they expected. When met with resistance, they killed one of the colonists and wounded a priest and three others. Junípero Serra witnessed this attack, cowering in a hut, and had a colonist drop dead at his feet. The Spanish responded with a volley of musket balls, which killed three Indians and wounded several. The attackers fled, and an uneasy peace ensued. The Ipai remained both skeptical and hostile to Spanish intentions, failing to provide even one convert for nearly two years (Bancroft 1886–1887:I:137–139).

Spanish presence in Ipai territory resulted in a soon to become familiar pattern. Padre Luis Jayme wrote prophetically to his superiors,

> At one of these Indian villages near this mission of San Diego, which said village is very large, and which is on the road to Monterey, the gentiles, therein many times have been on the point of coming here to kill us all, and the reason for this is that some soldiers went there and raped their women, and other soldiers who were carrying the mail to Monterey turned their animals into their fields and there ate up their crops. Three other Indian villages have reported the same thing to me, several times [Geiger 1970a].

He further presented evidence of three additional gang rapes, one of which describes a blind Indian woman being beaten and carried screaming into the woods to be ravaged. Father President of the Missions, Junípero Serra failed to address this issue of sexual abuse of his charges in any of his reports to his superiors. Tragically, the pattern persisted throughout the Spanish empire in Alta California (Cook 1976:24–25).

Perhaps inspired by this and other offensive behavior on the part of the colo-

Figure 23-1. Costanoans fighting Spanish soldier by T. Suría, ca. 1791. (Courtesy of the Bancroft Library, University of California)

nists, two traditional leaders—Francisco of Cuyamac and Zegotay of Matamo—began to call upon all the villages for miles around to rise up and kill the Spaniards. Eventually nine villages joined together to form an army of at least eight hundred warriors. They devised a plan to simultaneously attack the presidio and the new mission site several miles away. On November 4, 1775, about half of the group surrounded the mission, neutralized the neophytes, and prematurely attacked the Spaniards there. First torching the tule roofs of the compound, the Ipai killed a blacksmith, a carpenter, and Padre Jayme. In the confusion of smoke from the burning buildings, the rest of the colonists, several of whom were wounded, sought shelter in a tiny adobe structure and managed to hold out until dawn, at which time the attackers withdrew.

In the meantime, the second group of natives, on their way to attack the presidio, feared that the fires, smoke, and gunshots at the mission under siege would alert the soldiers and abandoned their plans (Bancroft 1886–1877:I:249–255).

The outcome of this episode clearly demonstrates the Spaniards' determination to militarily enforce Franciscan domination in and around San Diego, and the Ipai intentions in seeking to destroy the mission. One leader, captured and questioned after the inevitable punitive military campaigns, clearly stated the native viewpoint. They wanted to kill the priests and soldiers "in order to live as they did before" (Cook 1976:66).

In fact, the Ipai proved to be the most troublesome challengers of Spanish authority. Two years after the destruction of mission San Diego, the local Indians killed a Spanish soldier just north of San Diego. Several months later, the Ipai of Pamó Ranchería rounded up three neighboring bands to drive the Spaniards out of their territory. They sent a message challenging the soldiers to fight. Presidio soldiers surprised the Ipai at Pamó, killing two and burning several others. Most of the rest surrendered. The four village captains were convicted by a military court of trying to "kill the Christians." The sentence was death, despite the fact that the presidio court had no legal authority to execute Indians. The leaders—Aachil, Aalcuirin, Aaaran, and Taguagui—were executed by firing squad with the blessings of Padre Lasuen on March 11, 1778. This was the first public execution in California (Bancroft 1886–1887:I:315–316).

The Ipai's violent group resistance to Spanish colonization bears witness to their recognition of the threat that the Spanish presented to their freedom, culture, land, and natural resources. Neither Spanish soldiers nor priests could compel these Indians to relocate permanently at the mission site. Cook summarized their response to missionization this way: "Being endowed not only with considerable energy and drive . . . They were never tractable as laborers. Beyond the distance on one day's march they remained unconquered and predominantly unconverted throughout mission history" (Cook 1976:66).

The most successful native rebellion against Spanish colonization was organized and executed by a Quechan *Kʷaxót* (civil leader), whom the Spanish called Salvador Palma. The territory of the Quechan peoples included lower Colorado River drainage. Spanish explorers pioneered a route linking Sonora and the new province of Alta California through the heart of Quechan territory between 1774 and 1776. Spanish authorities soon recognized that this route was the only possible overland communications and supply line between New Spain and Alta California. It therefore became essential to establish friendly relations with the numerous and powerful Quechan nation (Bowman and Heizer 1967). Despite a shower of gifts to Palma and other leaders, the Spanish found the Quechan difficult to control. On their side, the Quechan found the colonists who began to arrive in 1780 to be without the promised gifts and to be generally lazy and obnoxious.

The Spanish monarch had declared that no Quechan lands would be given to Spanish colonists (Bolton 1930:V:399–401). Despite this official policy, by January of 1781, 160 Spanish colonists, soldiers, and four priests had established two pueblos within Quechan territory. This group began flogging the Indians and expropriated their farmlands. At this point, an additional 140 *gente de razón* (Hispanicized colonists), under Capt. Fernando Rivera Y Moncada, and 257 head of hungry stock animals arrived at the new pueblo Concepción. This last group also arrived without the promised gifts and their stock promptly devoured already tightly stretched Quechan resources. These actions triggered a plan to violently eject the Spanish from their territory.

On a hot July 17, 1781, the Quechan attacked both pueblos with war clubs and arrows. In two days of fighting, 55 Spaniards were killed, including 4 Franciscan priests, 31 soldiers, and 20 settlers; 67 civilians and 5 soldiers were captured (Forbes 1965:204). Three major punitive expeditions were organized over the next year that accomplished little more than the negotiated release of the captives and the sacking of a few Quechan villages. Spanish plans to execute Palma and three other leaders of the revolt failed. Furthermore, they were never again able to establish themselves among the Quechan and thus lost the only over-land route between Alta California and New Spain. Significantly, this was the first time that the Spanish had faced Indians of California who were mounted on horseback and using some Spanish weapons, including firearms. This omnious trend was to continue and expand in later Indian and Spanish military conflicts (Forbes 1965:207).

Four years later, a plot to kill the priests and soldiers at Mission San Gabriel was organized by a 24-year-old female shaman named Toypurina. She was sister to the captain of *Japchivit* village. Allied with her was the neighboring traditional *Tumi* (chief or captain) called Nicholas Jose of *Sibapet* village. The conspirators were trapped and disarmed by alerted sentries. Although her plan to be rid of the colonists failed, she was able to express her contempt for them at her trial. She warned Christian Indians not to believe in the priests: "I hate the padres and all of you [referring to soldiers present at her interrogation] for living here on my native soil—for trespassing upon the lands of my forefathers and despoil-ing our tribal domains" (Temple 1958:148). Toypurina was exiled while Nicholas Jose and two other village captains were sentenced to terms of labor at the pre-sidio.

The San Diego, Colorado River, and San Gabriel uprisings were organized and led by leaders whose authority sprang chiefly from tribal societies threat-ened by Spanish colonial activities. Later resistance leaders tended to be more talented and charismatic neophytes with no claim to traditional leadership sta-tus. Indeed, they arose from the chaos and breakdown of traditional societies within the mission system.

A kind of guerrilla warfare emerged as the Spanish military grip tightened about areas of Hispanic occupation. Disenchanted neophytes often fled their re-spective missions and joined like-minded bands of refugees. Typical of the type of leadership to evolve was a Coast Miwok named Lupugeyun, called Pomponio by the Spanish. This daring and resourceful ex-neophyte led a band of followers who pillaged and raided missions and rancho estates from Soledad to Sonoma. Despite numerous military campaigns organized to capture this renegade, he remained active for five years. After being captured and killing a soldier during his escape, he and a trusted lieutenant fled north toward his ancestral home in Marin County. There he was pursued by soldiers and Hispanic civilians to a can-yon near Novato. After a hard fight, Pomponio and his wounded companion were captured in the fall of 1823. He was shackled and imprisoned at Mission Carmel. A military court ordered Pomponio to be executed by firing squad. That sentence was carried out on February 6, 1824. That the authorities viewed this renegade's career as a real threat to Hispanic control can be established by the extraordinary contemporary correspondence that refers to Pomponio as an in-surgent (Brown 1975)! Later renegades, like Laquisamne Santa Clara Alcalde (called Yozcolo), followed a similar strategy of guerrilla resistance established by Pomponio (Holterman 1970a).

After 1800, a large-scale stock-raiding complex emerged along the fringes of the occupied territories. Oftentimes escaping neophytes would seize mission stock as they fled into the pagan interior. Once free, many allied themselves with interior groups in order to raid the mission's horse herds to maintain themselves (Holterman 1970b; Waitman 1970). A brisk horse trade with interior tribes developed as a result (Broadbent 1974). These activities stimulated a 40-year cycle of military campaigns, which became increasingly violent. Near the end of the Mexican era in California history, these interior groups threatened to expel the colonists from all interior settlements (Cook 1960, 1962).

Armed uprisings among Indian neophytes in whose territory long-established colonial institutions existed were much more difficult to carry out successfully than those cited earlier. Shortly following California's hesitant allegiance to the newly independent Mexican Republic, a widespread armed rebellion broke out among California neophytes at the Santa Inés, La Purísima, and Santa Bárbara missions. These three missions occupied Chumash Indian territory.

The Chumash originally numbered approximately 18,000 persons. Their subsistence economy was based on widely diverse ecological resources extending from the arid interior mountains to the Channel Islands off the coast of south-central California. These numerous, intelligent, and friendly native peoples won praise from the normally disparaging priests. Inexorably, the yolk of Hispanic oppression engendered widespread disenchantment with colonial life (Heizer 1978:506). This disenchantment was in fact present throughout all zones of colonial occupation. However, circumstances unique to the Chumash set in motion a series of events that led directly to armed rebellion, pitched battles with soldiers, and eventually wholesale abandonment of the Mission Santa Bárbara.

We know that the Chumash as well as most neophytes within the mission system continued to practice many of their traditional religious cults, despite the priest's energetic attempts to destroy Indian religion. Many returned to one such cult following a devastating epidemic in 1801 (Heizer 1941). To combat this trend, a number of local Franciscans developed *confesionarios* (confessional aids). These were bilingual guides, in the native dialect and Spanish, to aid priests in confessing the neophytes. Especially effective was Padre Señán whose *confesionarios* became increasingly used to determine the number of followers of the ?Antap Cult and the extent to which the neophytes had retained pagan sexual practices that they were supposed to have abandoned. Although neophytes might be physically and psychologically coerced into accepting serflike conditions, many found solace in familiar Native traditions. This was especially true as withering waves of murderous diseases flowed over the terrified Chumash neophytes. According to a recent study of this subject, "The significant revelation of the *confesionarios* is that Chumash culture remained vital but came increasingly under Franciscan scrutiny and attack, especially after 1820!" (Sandos 1985:118).

Considerable military experience was acquired by Chumash neophytes owing to the appearance of an Argentine privateer off the coast of Alta California in 1818. Priests at Santa Bárbara and La Purísima organized their neophytes into military units. At Santa Bárbara the 180-man force was organized into archers, infantry, and cavalry lancers. They were allowed to choose their own corporals and sergeants. The padres reported the neophytes engaged in these activities with *enthusiasm*. Although the expected invasion failed to provide combat experience, the lessons of European tactics, mass drill, and collective action were not lost on the Chumash.

Then a significant omen suddenly appeared in the form of a large comet in the December skies of 1823. It eventually developed two tails and persisted until March 1824. According to Chumash traditions, such conditions foretold of a sudden change and a new beginning (Hudson and Underhay 1978). As the approaching pre-Easter confessions of 1824 promised to be another threatening Franciscan probe of indigenous culture, the pressure on the Chumash soon reached a flash point. Only a spark was needed to ignite the hostility that had built up toward Franciscan and military colonial authority.

The routine beating of a La Purísima neophyte visiting a relative imprisoned at Mission Santa Inés inaugurated armed resistance. Neophytes from both La Purísima and Santa Inés attacked the mission guards with arrows the Saturday afternoon of February 21, 1824. A building was set on fire and two Indians were killed attacking the priests and soldiers. The Hispanics were trapped in a barricaded building until soldiers arrived the next day, by which time the rebellious neophytes had fled to the Mission La Purísima.

The neophytes there had risen up on the same day under the leadership of the charismatic and gifted La Purísima neophyte, Pacomio. They drove the priests and soliders and their families into a storeroom. Four *gente de razón* travelers who had stopped at the missions during the siege were killed by the neophytes. Seven neophytes were killed before this brief but violent skirmish ended. In exchange for their surrender, the soldiers agreed to abandon the mission and flee to Santa Inés. The local priest insisted on staying but could do little to stop the rebellion. The bewildered priests witnessed an astounding display of military preparation to defend this fortress of the rebellion. Neophytes erected palisade fortifications, cut weapon slits in the church and other buildings, and positioned two swivelguns. It was apparent that they expected an attack and were preparing to fight a pitched battle with Hispanic authorities (Bancroft 1886–1887:II:530).

On the opening day of hostilities, the Santa Inés neophytes sent a call to arms to the trusted alcalde Andrés Sagiomomatsse of mission Santa Bárbara. Fearing for the lives of his fellow neophytes, Andrés demanded that the priest order the mission *escolta* (guards) to withdraw and return to the Santa Bárbara Presidio. The local priest rode to the presidio to deliver the demand. He successfully secured the written order of the commandant for the withdrawal of the mission guard. When the priest returned, he found Andrés had broken into the armory and supplied his followers with bows, arrows, and machetes. Following receipt of their commandant's orders to withdraw, the Indians disarmed the escolta, two of whom resisted and were hacked with machetes. The soldiers were then allowed to retreat. Immediately the commandant ordered his troops to march on the mission. There they found a considerable force of Indians, several of whom were now carrying firearms. A fierce engagement erupted throughout the mission compound. Four soldiers suffered arrow wounds, and withdrew, leaving the Indians in control of the mission. Andrés's followers counted three dead and two wounded. Following this skirmish, the neophytes looted the priest's quarters and seized church valuables. All fled into the nearby San Marcos Mountains. After the neophytes withdrew, soldiers pillaged and looted the quarters of both neophytes and priest and managed to kill the five neophytes too old or sick to join their kinsmen.

Unable to secure sufficient nonmission Indian support in a planned assault on Santa Bárbara, Andrés and his followers withdrew deeper into the interior. At the same time, the Channel Island neophytes seized the mission's two *tomols* (oceangoing Chumash canoes) and with fifty men, women, and children fled Santa Cruz Island (Hudson and Underhay 1978).

For several weeks Pacomio's La Purísima rebels refused to surrender the mission, nor would Andrés and his followers return to the abandoned Santa Bárbara mission. The expected counterattack on the La Purísima neophytes came in mid-March when 109 cavalry, infantry, and artillery troops surrounded the 400 defiant pagans and neophytes under Pacomio. As the soldiers came within range, they were met with a volley of musket shot, the blast of the neophytes' cannons, and a shower of arrows. The soldiers' four-pounder cannon, benefiting from an experienced crew, was able to shatter the warriors' defenses. When the Indians tried to break out of their encirclement and flee, they were stopped by the cavalry. Finding no other option, they used the priest who remained in their midst to negotiate a surrender. The rebels suffered 16 dead and many wounded, whereas only one soldier died and two others suffered wounds (Stickel and Cooper 1969).

Following a military tribunal, seven Indians were executed, and four of the leaders of the revolt, including Pacomino, were sentenced to 10 years of presidio labor and perpetual exile. Eight others were sentenced to 8-year terms of presidio labor (Bancroft 1886–1887:II:153).

Andrés and his followers celebrated their endeavors deep in the pagan lower San Joaquin Valley. At last free of Hispanic colonial authority, the Indians abandoned their thin veneer of Hispanic Catholicism and reveled in their newfound freedom (Cook 1962:153–154). Native determination to establish their new-won independence was expressed in this manner by the defiant neophytes, who refused to return to colonial society: "We shall maintain ourselves with what God will provide us in the open country. Moreover we are soldiers, stonemasons, carpenters, etc. and we will provide for ourselves by *our* work" (Geiger 1970b:352).

The first attempt by Mexican military authorities to recapture the fugitives ended after the execution of a bound prisoner. A second military expedition departed from Santa Bárbara on June 2. Meeting another column of soldiers in the interior, the expedition now totaled 130 soldiers and a four-pounder cannon. Accompanied by two priests, the expedition was under orders from the governor to recapture the Santa Bárbara neophytes by offering them a pardon.

As scattered groups of the rebel neophytes were contacted, a difficult decision had to be made. These native people were forced to choose between a life of exile far from the many sacred places of their former domain and a life under the totalitarian regime of the mission. Eventually, with the aid of a neophyte named Jaime, a number of the fugitives made the difficult decision to return to Franciscan authority. Although many rebellious neophytes eventually drifted back to their ancestral homes, a significant number refused to return and fled even deeper into the interior (Cook 1976:60). The soldiers apparently were satisfied with their efforts and returned to the coast.

About 10 years later, an Anglo trapping party headed by Joseph Reddeford Walker working the rivers of northeastern Kern County, stumbled upon the rebel Chumash sanctuary. Now numbering between 700 and 800 persons, the community was prosperous, with fields of corn, pumpkins, melons, and other crops and a lively horse trade. The mounted tribesmen apparently had successfully adopted some beneficial European practices and integrated them into their native culture. However, Walker's party, or others like it, introduced a malaria epidemic in the Central Valley of California that wiped out nearly three-quarters of the Indian population of California (Cook 1955:303–326). Apparently the defiant Chumash who refused to submit to mission authority shared this melancholy fate.

Conclusions

A critical examination of the relationship between the Spanish colonists and Indian societies they penetrated reveals a clear and well-defined pattern of both military and mendicant coercion. Despite the "good intentions" and Christian legal and moral arguments put forward by advocates of Serra's canonization, the Spanish colonization scheme for Alta California rested upon a total contempt for culture and human and property rights of the Indians. This view was shared by both the military and Franciscan authorities. The Franciscan contempt for Indians is well documented by Lausen, Boscana, and others. It is likewise true that no credible evidence exists to suggest the Indians loved Serra, nor other Franciscans. In fact, contrary evidence exists. An early eyewitness at the Mission San Gabriel observed, "The Indians with some few exceptions, refused to eat hogs alleging the whole family to be transformed to Spaniards" (Heizer 1968:86). The colonizers themselves argued over who was more cruel to the Indians, the Franciscans or the military. At least one Franciscan priest, Padre Antonio de La Concepción Horra, had the moral strength to complain to his college about the abuses his order inflicted upon the neophytes. For this "disloyalty" he was beaten, declared insane, and exiled from California (Bancroft 1886–1887:I:593). It is especially important to compare regular crimes like theft and murder to those that can be classified as "political crimes" against colonial military and church authorities. These "political crimes" included "all forms of fugitivism, apostasy, refusal to complete set tasks, conspiracies to overthrow the existing regime, theft or destruction of army or mission property and finally armed opposition to missionaries, soldiers, or even civilians" (Cook 1976:114). Cook's analysis of Spanish punishment reveals this disturbing conclusion: 90 percent of the "crimes" committed by the neophytes were directed against the colonial authorities and their military, mendicant empire (Cook 1976:122). The feudalistic conditions within Spanish-occupied California are well documented by both contemporary foreign visitors as well as church and military authorities. The overwhelming reliance on propaganda, and fear to maintain their control of the Indians in this remote corner of the empire is familiar to all objective historians and anthropologists (Heizer et al. 1975).

Resistance to the Spanish occupation of Alta California seems to have taken three forms: internal resistance, flight, and fight. Resistance within the mission system took the form of infanticide, abortions, slow or poor work performance, and surreptitious practice of native religious ceremonies. In addition individual priests were assassinated. Whether they were escaping Hispanic authority temporarily (as did Estanislao and his Miwok followers; see Holterman 1970b) or permanently (as did Santa Inés Chumash), alcalde neophytes represent the flight complex. Those who chose to stand and fight—as did Coast Miwok Pomponio, the Chumash Pacomio, and the Ipai leader Francisco of Cuyanac—represent the third type of response to Hispanic colonial rule.

Leadership in the armed resistance of California Indians also underwent a gradual evolution from tribally based leadership, like that of Francisco of Cuyamac or Salvadore Palma of the Quechan, to the charismatic neophytes with little or no claim to tribal leadership authority, like the Chumash Pacomino and the coast Miwok rebel Pomponio.

An important development in these armed rebellions and the increasingly stiff resistance offered to Spanish authority, was the gradual adoption of Spanish arms, horses, and military tactics. As early as the Colorado River Uprising of 1781, the rebellious Quechan who had killed Spanish soldiers used their captured firearms and horses to resist the military expeditions sent to punish them. In 1812, Tachi Yokuts had dug pits from which they discharged arrows and crippled horses to protect their villages from Spanish forays "seeking" converts (Bancroft II:338). The astounding military display of the La Purísima uprising has already been discussed. The stock-raiding Indians of the interior of California had adopted horses from the beginning of their exploits in the 1790s. Some resistance leaders like Estanislao fortified their interior villages with elaborate horse trenches and palisade fortifications (Holterman 1970b).

Careful examination of this little-known and poorly understood period of Indian–white conflict clearly demonstrates a widespread dissatisfaction with mission life and colonial authority. No reasonable person can argue that the California Indians in any way benefited from a colonization scheme that confiscated their land and resources; uprooted entire villages; forced them to migrate to the feudalistic mendicant estates on the coast; subjected them to daily floggings, forced labor, and wholesale sexual assaults on their wives and daughters; and resulted in the deaths of thousands of innocent men, women, and children. To do so would require an act of faith that could not be altered by the facts. Perhaps that is what the whole controversy concerning Serra's canonization and the true nature of the California missions is about.

References

Asisara, Lorenzo
1877 Memorias de la Histora de California. Jose Maria Amador's interview. Bancroft Library, University of California, Berkeley.

Bancroft, H. H.
1886–1887 *History Of California*, 7 vols. The History Company, San Francisco.

Bolton, H. E. (editor)
1930 *Anza's California Expeditions*, 5 vols. University of California Press, Berkeley.
1964 The Mission as a Frontier Institution in the Spanish Borderlands. In *Bolton and the Spanish Borderlands*, Edited by John Francis Bannon. University of Oklahoma Press, Norman.

Boscana, G.
1933 *Chiningchinich: A Revised and Annotated Version of Alfred Robinson's Translation of Father Geronimo Boscana's Historical Account of the Belief, Usages, Customs and Extravagencies of the Indians of This Mission of San Juan Capistrano Called Acagchemsm Tribe [1846]*. Edited by P. T. Hanna. Fine Arts Press, Santa Ana, Calif.

Bowman, J. N., and R. F. Heizer
1967 *Anza and the Northwest Frontier of New Spain*. Southwest Museum Papers No. 21. Highland Park, Calif.

Broadbent, S.
1974 Conflict at Monterey: Indian Horse Riding 1820–1850. *Journal of California Anthropology* 1:86–101. Malki Museum, Banning.

Brown, A. K.
1975 Pomponio's World. *The Argonaut* No. 6 (May). San Francisco.

Cook, S. F.
1955 The Epidemic of 1830–1833 in California and Oregon. University of California Publications in American Archaeology and Ethnology, vol. 43. Berkeley.
1960 Colonial Expeditions to the Interior of California: Central Valley, 1800–1820. Anthropological Records 16:239–292. University of California, Berkeley.
1962 Expeditions to the Interior of California: Central Valley, 1820–1840. Anthropological Records 20:151–214. University of California, Berkeley.
1976 *The Conflict between California Indians and White Civilization*. University of California Press, Berkeley.

Costo, Rupert, and Jeanette (editors)
1988 *The Missions of California: A Legacy of Genocide*. The Indian Historian Press, San Francisco.

Forbes, Jack
1965 *Warriors of the Colorado:The Yumas of the Quechan Nation and Their Neighbors*. University of Oklahoma Press, Norman

Geiger, M. (editor)
1970a *The Letters Of Luis Jayme O.F.M.* Dawson Book Shop, Los Angeles.
1970b Fray Antonio Ripoli's Description of the Chumash Revolt at Santa Barbara in 1824. *Southern California Quarterly* 52:345–364.

Geiger, M., and C. Meighan
1976 *As the Padres Saw Them: California Indian Life and Customs as Reported by the Missionaries, 1813–1815*. Mission Archive Library, Santa Barbara.

Heizer, R. F.
1941 A California Messianic Movement of 1801 Among the Chumash. *American Anthropologists* 43:128–129.
1968 *The Indians of Los Angeles County: Hugo Reid's Letters of 1852*. Southwest Museum, Los Angeles.

Heizer, Robert F. (editor)

1978 *California*. Handbook of North American Indians, vol. 8, William C. Sturtevant, general editor. Smithsonian Institution, Washington, D.C.

Heizer, Robert F., Karen M. Nissen, and Edward D. Castillo

1975 *California Indian History: A Classified and Annotated Guide to Source Materials*. Publications in Archaeology, Ethnology and History 4. Ballena Press, Romona, Calif.

Holterman, T.

1970a The Revolt of Yozcolo: Indian Warrior and the Fight for Freedom. *The Indian Historian* 3(2):19–25.

1970b The Revolt of Estanislao. *The Indian Historian* 3(1):43–55.

Hudson, Travis, and Ernest Underhay

1978 *Crystals in the Sky: An Intellectual Odyssey Involving Chumash Astronomy, Cosmology and Rock Art*. Anthropological Papers No. 10. Ballena Press and Santa Barbara Museum of Natural History, Socorro and Santa Barbara.

Kroeber, A. L.

1976 *Handbook of the Indians Of California*. Dover, New York.

Laird, Carobeth

1975 *Encounter with an Angry God*. Malki Press, Banning, Calif.

Rawls, J. J.

1984 *Indians of California: The Changing Image*. University of Oklahoma Press, Norman.

Sandos, J. A.

1985 Levantamiento: The Chumash Uprising Reconsidered. *Southern California Quarterly*, Summer:109–133, Los Angeles.

Shipek, F.

1986 *The Impact of Europeans upon the Kumeyaay*. Cabrillo Historical Association, San Diego, Calif.

Stickel, E. G., and A. E. Cooper

1969 The Chumash Revolt of 1824: A Case for Acheological Application of Feedback Theory. *University of California at Los Angeles Archeological Survey—Annual Report* 11:5–22.

Temple, T. W.

1958 Toypurina the Witch of the Uprising at San Gabriel. *Master Key* 32(5):136–154.

Waitman, L. B.

1970 Raids and Raiders of the San Bernardino Valley. *Quarterly of the San Bernardino County Museum Association* 18(1):1–16.

Chapter 24 ■

Robert L. Hoover

Spanish–Native Interaction and Acculturation in the Alta California Missions

Introduction

Among the historically known instances of directed culture change, the enculturation of Native Americans into the European lifeway is probably the most significant in terms of its implications for global development. Of all the major colonial empires that were involved in the transformation of Amerindian lifeways, none was more geographically widespread or more systematic in its methods than Spain. It not only dominated the initial phase of European colonial expansion in the Western Hemisphere, but it continued to be a major colonial power until 1820, after which it lost possession of its mainland American territories. In the interim, Spain undertook the single largest and longest program of enculturation ever attempted. The nature and results of this program are still not completely understood. They varied in terms of time, space, method, and effect. A complex combination of religious establishments, military posts, and civil settlements were utilized variously on the different frontiers of the Spanish New World to achieve the Hispanization of the land. Of all the regions of the Spanish empire that developed by this process, California has been one of the best studied by archaeologists, historians, and ethnographers. However, controversy surrounds some of the conclusions of this research.

The processes of culture change are a particularly complex area of contemporary ethnohistorical research (Social Sciences Research Council 1954). Studies of culture change based on patterns left in the archaeological and historical records provide an understanding of the processes responsible for dynamic interrelationships both within and outside cultural systems. As archaeologist Stanley South has observed, "As we delineate change and dynamics between systems, we can begin to understand something about cultural evolution"(South 1977:327).

It has been difficult to reach a clear understanding of cultural processes in California owing to a century-old controversy over the role of the Spanish Franciscan missions and their effect on the native population of California. The beginnings of this controversy can be traced to the popular work of Helen Hunt Jackson (1963) and the histories of Herbert Howe Bancroft (1884). Both were highly critical of Hispanic institutions in general and Franciscan missionary activity in particular. This view generated considerable criticism, particularly from Zephyrin Englehardt (1912), who devoted much of his life to discovering documentary evidence of an economically successful and productive mission system in California. Another major figure to emerge in this debate was Herbert Eugene Bolton, who generally portrayed the California missions in a favorable light. Beyond this, he proposed a wider perspective to the question of the success or failure of the missions. In his most famous essay, Bolton (1917) focused on the primary role played by missionaries in the Spanish colonial system.

The general public is still confused by modern views on the subject, which portray California missions as either bucolic paradises on earth or as early concentration camps containing vast numbers of unwilling neophyte natives. Much of the literature focuses on the mission system as an intrusive force that was a truncating factor in the development of native cultures rather than examining the nature of culture change resulting from contact. Care must be taken to treat documentary sources with caution and to evaluate native oral traditions that have changed greatly over time in accordance with the needs and outlook of each generation. Being based on the evidence of material culture, archaeology can do much to overcome the biases of the oral and documentary history of the missions. At the same time, recent models from the social sciences, such as world systems theory, are useful devices for a functional understanding of the role of missionaries and Indians in a larger framework (Wallerstein 1974, 1980).

Acculturation

Conversions

The discussion of mission acculturation logically begins with the process of conversion. Under the Spanish, the process followed a consistent overall pattern throughout the eighteenth century. On initial contact, a meeting was arranged with native leaders. They were given gifts and an explanation of why it was necessary for them to obey the power of the Spanish Crown, as well as a guarantee of protection in exchange for peaceful cooperation. Missionaries took this opportunity to describe the basics of Christianity, the rite of baptism, and the principles of Christian life (Griffen 1969:1–5, 1979: 108–110). The missionaries completely misunderstood the time required and processes involved in transforming the native population into Spanish citizens. They failed to recognize the elaborate political and religious aspects of the local cultures and the differences between cultures. Rather, the missionaries believed that they were creating *gente de razón*—people of reason—out of a people living in natural chaos with no social organization. The native was viewed as a cultural tabula rasa on which could be inscribed the characteristics of "rational" beings—urban, agricultural, Christian, and Spanish-speaking. This view was heavily colored by national chauvinism and cultural ethnocentrism.

The question—and it is a complex one—is, what initially attracted a native population that had evolved and adapted over thousands of years to a radically different ideology (Chartkoff and Chartkoff 1984)? Undoubtedly, the fantastic technology of the Europeans, with their objects of metal, glass, and ceramics must have impressed them and may even have been interpreted as a sign of great spiritual power. Even the native ritual leaders, while viewing the Spanish padres as competitors, must have been awed by the latters' access to apparently unlimited supernatural power and material goods. This initial fascination with European goods gradually paled as the Indians became more familiar with them.

Some groups may also have gone to the missions to secure more abundant food during times of scarcity, to escape from traditional enemies, or to appease victorious Spaniards after suffering a military defeat. To the average Indian in a stratified chiefdom society, the mission represented an opportunity to improve one's social position, which involved accepting a new religion and its accompanying technology. Blocked from advancement in a rigid society of ascribed statuses, native commoners readily accepted the new order in an attempt to invert traditional roles. The traditional hereditary elite was replaced in the mission by a more fluid hierarchy in which anyone could advance who had the ability and was willing to cooperate with the Spanish regime. The old ritual elite found themselves increasingly isolated and, as a last resort, often initiated abortive resistance movements (Heizer 1941:128–129; Stickel and Cooper 1969). Thus, there were many complex reasons for the initial Indian conversions.

The question of whether physical force was used in these conversions has been raised by a number of researchers, mostly Anglo scholars familiar with a different tradition of native-European relationships. However, Spanish law was quite clear on this matter:

> No governor, lieutenant, or *alcalde ordinario* can or may send armed parties against the Indians with the purpose of reducing them into missions, or forcing them to work in mines, or for any other pretext. The penalty for violation of this law is loss of office and payment of 2,000 pesos. But if some Indians should cause harm to Spaniards, or to peaceful Indians, whether in their persons or in their property, then we certainly allow [these same officials] to send armed parties, within three months [of the perpetration of the crime], to punish them or to take them prisoner [Archivo General de Indias n.d.].

Military force was theoretically reserved for those who assaulted Spaniards or missionized Indians, rebelled against Spanish authority, stole horses and other livestock, or harbored mission neophyte fugitives. As these situations became more common after 1810, the frequency of military activity increased. Even then, there was no question of herding masses of natives to the missions for purposes of conversion (Guest 1979).

The animistic tribal religions of the California Indians were very amenable to syncretization. Guest (1938:26) points out that native culture served as a screen through which some religious innovation was received. Aspects of Christianity that were compatible with the native culture were accepted; the remainder were ignored. The resulting ideology of the neophytes consisted of fragments of Christian and pre-Christian elements. Of course, there was the mandatory imposition on the natives of some Hispanic customs, especially in the moral and religious areas. However, native beliefs were often accommodated in unconscious ways. For example, Indian dances were often incorporated into Christian rituals or were performed at fiestas (Hudson and Underhay 1978:23–24). Although these picturesque dances appeared to be harmless recreation to the missionaries, they preserved traditional knowledge in the minds of the natives.

Thus, conversion did not simply mean that one set of religious beliefs was being replaced by another. Nor did this blending process confine itself to supernatural ideologies. In the eighteenth century, Spanish missionary activity was intimately connected with the concept of *españolismo*—Spanishness—and the mission was considered an instrument of the state. Although Spanish policy was relatively protective of native populations, it promoted *hispanidad* (Hispanity) in an attempt to transform native groups into Spanish citizens. Religion, language, clothing, social organization, technology, and work habits were all affected by this policy. California missions were dynamic centers for planned culture change. The missions harbored a minimum of disruptive outsiders, allowing the missionaries to manipulate to some degree the processes of acculturation in a planned and systematic manner. The Franciscans provided material objects of immediate and obvious value. In return, the new religion required changes in the area of personal discipline—a new ideology, different work habits, universal monogamy, a sedentary life, and changes in dress. Craft instructors from Spain were sent to the California frontier at state expense in the 1790s to train the neophytes in a number of specialized occupations (Archibald 1978:146–152).

Under the missionaries' policy of *reducción*, converted California natives were concentrated at each mission, where they lived a communal life. The result was a nucleated settlement that differed greatly in size and function from the dispersed settlements of prehistoric times. This policy allowed closer supervision, and thus more effective religious instruction and economic production. In addition, the policy removed the population from the surrounding countryside, freeing it for agriculture and grazing and forever altering the natural environment (see West, this volume). However, all neophytes were not confined to the missions throughout the year. Some were granted leaves of up to two months, during which they visited and recruited relatives. During that time, they foraged in the traditional manner and relieved the pressure on mission food stores (Coombs and Plog 1974). Mission San Luis Rey was a notable exception to the policy of concentration. The padres preferred to establish chapels near diffuse Indian villages and visit them periodically. Thus, only a small proportion of its native converts lived at the mission at any one time, and much of the native culture was preserved.

Mortality

One tragic and certainly unintended result of the policy of concentration was the well-known decimation of the missionized Indians by communicable European diseases for which they had no immunity (Cook 1976). This problem was first encountered in the West Indies in the late fifteenth century. With no knowledge of microorganisms or modern immunization techniques, the Spaniards were at a loss for a solution and could only think that epidemics were manifestations of divine wrath. The densely concentrated nature of the typical mission created ideal conditions for the spread of disease, although the relatively isolated nature of the California frontier shielded the missions from the worst epidemics until 1828. The ineffectiveness of common remedies for diseases such as smallpox made some padres reluctant to attempt a cure, for if the patient died, as was usually the case, all of his relatives would blame the Spaniards (Guest 1983:6). Many natives fled the missions in fear and spread contagion further outside Spanish territory, nearly depopulating the San Joaquin Valley during the Mexican period (1821–1846).

The Spanish government was genuinely concerned about this high death rate, both for humanitarian and economic reasons. A royal *cédula*, or decree, was issued dealing with the treatment of smallpox victims. Its contents were transmitted to Governor Pedro Fages in 1786. Reflecting the most advanced medical thinking of the day, the decree directed that victims be isolated to prevent the spread of infection (California State Archives 1786). In 1797, Viceroy Branciforte circulated more detailed instructions that specified strict quarantine and decontamination procedures (Soler 1798a) and described the process of immunization by means of variolation (Soler 1798a; 1798b). This was the same year that Edward Jenner discovered the safer method of true smallpox inoculation in England. Within the limits of contemporary medical knowledge, the Spanish officials and padres of the eighteenth century demonstrated remarkable concern for the health of their native population. Nearly all of the missions had dispensaries, medical supplies, and medical books.

Diet, Work Routine, and Discipline

One factor influencing neophyte mortality was the nutrition of the Indians at the missions. The most detailed study of this topic to date has been presented by Stodder (1986), who compares Costanoan diet and nutrition in prehistoric times with that of the mission period. The shift from foraging to agriculture took several thousand years in the Neolithic Near East and Mexico. In California, it occurred virtually overnight. Stodder indicates that mission agriculture eventually provided great food surpluses that were less sensitive to seasonal and annual fluctuations than aboriginal resources. However, this was achieved at the expense of greatly reduced variety and nutritional balance. The standard diet of beans, peas, lentils, and cereals was deficient in high-quality proteins, Vitamins A and C, and Riboflavin. These nutritional deficiencies made the neophytes, particularly women and infants, more susceptible to disease. The following passage describes Mission Santa Cruz in 1819:

> The Indians at the Mission of Santa Cruz, after prayers in the morning at church, received their orders as to their labors at the church door; they then went to breakfast, and had their meal together of boiled barley, which was served out to them from two large cauldrons by means of a copper ladle. . . . At 11 o'clock the bell was rung to call them together . . . the dinner consisted of a mixture of cooked horse beans and peas. At the end of the hour the bell was rung again, and all went to work again until about sunset when each received his ration of boiled corn. Indians who had families were given meat also [Heizer 1974:80].

Thus, the mission provided three meals a day, but of a very high carbohydrate content. Most missions also distributed meat on saints' days, which were frequent in the eighteenth century. Excavations behind the dormitory for married Indians at Mission San Antonio revealed a tremendous number of butchered cattle (Hoover and Costello 1985). These had clearly been used partly for food, as evidenced by butcher marks on the bones. Since meat could not be effectively transported without refrigeration and since the neophytes were virtually the only local residents, they must have had ample access to beef.

The native response to the mission diet was to supplement it with wild foods whenever possible. At Mission Santa Bárbara in 1812,

> The meals of the Indians [Chumash] can not be counted, because it may be said that for them the day is one continuous meal. Even during the night, should they awaken from sleep, they are want to reach out for something to eat. The meals at the mission consist of meat, corn, beans, peas, etc. Of these, an abundance is given to each neophyte by the missionary fathers, and they prepare it as suits them best. Besides what the mission gives them, they are very fond of what they lived on in paganism, as the meat of deer, rabbits, squirrels, or any little animal they can catch, while those on the shore have a craving for whatever the ocean produces [Webb 1952:40].

The wild foods available as nutritional supplements varied from one mission to another and also depended on the duties of the individual neophytes. The Chumash of the Santa Barbara Channel lived in an area of richer marine and terrestrial resources than their northern neighbors (see Walker et al. this volume). Field workers and herders would have greater opportunity to hunt and gather in the traditional manner than craft specialists at the mission. Stodder

(1986:33) believes that, as agricultural production became more efficient, neo-phytes were permitted to do less hunting and gathering. In addition, as Choris (1913:4) noted in 1816 at Mission Dolores, "In their free time, the Indians work in gardens that are given to them; raise therein onions, garlic, cantaloupe, wa-termelons, pumpkins, and fruit trees. The products belong to them and they can dispose of them as they see fit."

The shift from food collecting to food production experienced by the mission neophytes also directly affected their daily work routine. Recent comparative studies of living societies have indicated that the amount of work in person-hours varies greatly with the mode of subsistence. Foragers generally require more land and accumulate smaller food surpluses, but require only a modest input of person-hours to obtain sufficient food. Food producers, particularly ag-riculturalists, use smaller amounts of land more intensively to yield larger sur-pluses, but they pay a tremendous price in increased person-hours spent in food production (Harris 1971:204). Also, as we have seen, the abundance of agricul-tural foods may be based on relatively few species and may not provide a nutri-tionally balanced diet. The frequent Spanish references to native reluctance to work were a reflection of their own ethnocentric European agricultural experi-ence rather than the amount of time that the natives knew was necessary for traditional subsistence. Many neophytes probably saw no need or sense in la-boring from dawn to dusk for food that they could obtain easily in another man-ner.

As the missions shifted from being centers of subsistence to being commercial institutions in the early nineteenth century (see Costello and Hornbeck, this vol-ume), the work load became more onerous, particularly because of the demands of the civilian and military population and foreign traders. As a result of popula-tion decline, there were fewer neophytes in the work force. Even though the work might be less intensive, it was clear that individuals were working harder.

When examining the question of mission discipline, the modern reader must confront his or her own twentieth-century biases rather than those of the eight-eenth century. It is very difficult for us to reconcile the fact that neophytes who were delinquent in their duties and responsibilities certainly received corporal punishment with the padres' numerous statements indicating that they loved the neophytes. This was actually a paternalistic love, as most Spaniards viewed the natives as "children of nature" who were gradually being transformed into fully civilized Europeans. The padres were not only eighteenth-century Europe-ans, but also Spanish Catholics. In Spain at that time, it was customary to pun-ish children with shouts, imprisonment, and whippings when they misbehaved or failed to learn their lessons. Clerics and laymen alike would publicly flagel-late themselves with knotted cords at penitential services. In general, it appears that most missionaries thought the neophytes were less responsible for their mis-behavior than European children. Therefore, punishments were usually milder. "In an average school, a person would receive more punishments for not know-ing his lesson than he would receive here [at the mission] for living in concubi-nage" (Guest 1974:201).

Fugitivism

A number of native neophytes, once they had been converted and settled at the missions, decided to return to their original life-style. This, of course, was in opposition to Spanish missionary policy. The individuals were treated as fugitives to be returned to their mission of origin. Fugitivism was largely the result of the three factors already discussed: the daily work schedule, to which the neophytes were unaccustomed; diseases, from which so many died; and the corporal punishment imposed for infractions of mission routine. However, after the initial founding of each mission, prospective converts became well aware of disease, workshifts, and punishments both from firsthand observation and from the reports of Indian neophytes who were sent out to recruit them. Although these three factors were certainly important, the natives' advance knowledge of mission living conditions points to other factors that might have encouraged the neophytes to become fugitives.

Such factors may include the rather perfunctory instruction given the neophytes before baptism, the common practice of housing hostile native groups at the same mission, and the language and culture differences between Spaniards and various native groups. Guest (1983:37) has pointed out, for example, that competing native factions often fought and murders were even committed at Mission San José in 1817.

Sometimes the soldiers at the missions were a source of irritation and abuse, especially in the Mexican period. Each mission had a guard—escolta—of about five soldiers whose primary duty was to protect the mission community from hostile raids. These soldiers often married local Indian neophytes and became craft instructors. However, friction between some soldiers and Indians increased in the northern missions as a result of growing fugitivism and raiding.

Even in the worst of times, when fugitive neophytes were organizing the Sierra Miwok and Yokuts in raids on Mexican settlements, they formed a distinct minority of the mission population. Many neophytes served as military auxiliaries in campaigns against the raiders. They were usually armed with bows and arrows and fought on foot. Neophyte infantry were often more effective than mounted soldiers in dealing with hostile groups in mountainous areas where missile support was essential. It was unusual for a punitive expedition to set out without such auxiliaries (Hoover 1982:312–314; Phillips 1975:41).

Acculturative Studies and Archaeology

As a mission became more involved with the world economy, the degree of integration of the neophytes into this system was reflected in the increasing appearance of imported goods. Archaeologists measure this process of acculturation through changes in the material culture of the neophytes. Several different approaches to material culture studies have been employed to measure the types and direction of acculturation that occurred in California missions. James Deetz (1963) pioneered one approach during his excavations at La Purísima Mission in 1962 and 1963. Dividing the artifact assemblage into traditional classes, such as chipped stone, iron, copper, and so on, he compared quantitative differences between the neophyte dormitory and a nearby historic village midden. The results suggested that there was greater acculturation among neophyte males than among females.

In retrospect, there are several problems with this comparison. First, two unlike sites—a midden and dormitory floors—were being compared. Second, the volume excavated to obtain each sample was different. Therefore, absolute numbers of artifacts could be misleading. Finally, artifacts related to various functions were split into different groups obscuring the complexity of acculturation. The differing ethnicity of the dormitory residents also affected the results.

A second method, employed initially at Mission San Antonio (Hoover and Costello 1985), utilized a modified classification system devised by Quimby and Spoehr (1951) for the Great Lakes region. This system has recently been expanded to include 10 groups of artifacts:

a. imported objects that represent new elements of the culture (e.g., wine bottles)
b. imported objects that directly replace prehistoric forms (e.g., glass for shell beads)
c. imported forms made of local materials (e.g., tiles)
d. imported forms, locally made, using local and imported materials (e.g., clothing with metal buttons)
e. imported forms, locally made, using imported materials and techniques (e.g., iron tools)
f. local forms modified by the substitution of imported materials (e.g., porcelain and glass projectile points)
g. local forms modified by the substitution of imported materials and involving a different technological principal to achieve the same end (e.g., ceramic bowls for steatite bowls)
h. local forms with new elements that change the meaning of the artifact (e.g., baskets with Spanish coats-of-arms woven into the design)
i. local forms of the same appearance and meaning, but using an imported technique (e.g., shell beads drilled with iron wire)
j. prehistoric forms that continue unchanged (e.g., mortars and pestles).

This qualitative system can be easily quantified, but it also is not without its drawbacks. In measuring the degree and rate of acculturation, how does one weight the various categories? Is an imported artifact indicative of greater acculturation than a native form, however modified?

While excavating at nearby Mission Soledad, Paul Farnsworth (1986) recently developed a third system of comparison based on a modified version of South's (1977) artifact pattern analysis. First used on colonial sites of the Southeast, this system deals with entire assemblages and the functional groups within them. A final group of "other activities" allows the researcher to add artifacts pertaining to additional activities, each as a separate class.

Farnsworth's comparisons of San Antonio, Soledad, and La Purísima show great similarities in artifact patterning. This patterning differs greatly from that at Spanish St. Augustine. This is not surprising, as the St. Augustine Indians were ceramic-using horticulturalists, and most residents were Spanish soldiers, government officials, and supporting specialists who practiced mestizaje—intermarriage—with local Indians on a grand scale (Deagan 1983). The neophytes at Mission San Antonio appear to have had greater access to, or preference for, imported and locally made pottery and glass bottles than those at La Purísima. A pottery manufacturing industry established at San Antonio in the 1790s supplied wares to other missions.

Summary

The process of native acculturation in the missions of California was extremely complex. Different cultural elements were more susceptible or resistant to cultural change. This process also varied among the various missions and among the various aboriginal groups. Traditional native cultural patterns and values served to screen, filter, and even define what was accepted and absorbed from the Spanish. Accepted traits may have had entirely different meanings from the context of native cultures.

The processes of cultural change affected mainly the native population owing to the unequal power relationship between Indians and Spaniards. However, acculturation was not entirely unidirectional. Evidence of floral remains from the soldiers' barracks at Mission San Antonio suggests that the Indian wives of the soldiers were collecting and serving native foods in traditional ways.

Most important, both historical and archaeological data indicate that the Indians were not simply passive recipients of whatever new traits the Spanish chose to introduce. They creatively adopted those traits that were useful or advantageous and ignored many others. Far from being helpless pawns, mission neophytes attempted to manipulate changing conditions to their own advantage insofar as was permitted. The cultural instability of the times provided opportunities for many individuals, both as supporters or resisters of the Spanish regime.

References

Archibald, Robert
    1978 *The Economic Aspects of the California Missions*. Academy of American Franciscan History, Washington, D.C.
Archivo General de Indias
    n.d. Recopilación de leyes de los reinos de las Indias, vo.X, titula IV, libro III, Seville.
Bancroft, Hubert Howe
    1884 *History of California*, vol. I. History Co., San Francisco.
Bolton, Herbert Eugene
    1917 The Mission as a Frontier Institution in the Spanish American Colonies. *American Historical Review* 23:42–61.
California State Archives
    1786 Letter to Pedro Fages. California Archives Provincial State Papers 6:80–83.
Chartkoff, Joseph L., and Kerry Kona
    1984 *The Archaeology of California*. Stanford University Press.
Choris, Louis
    1913 *San Francisco One Hundred Years Ago*. A. N. Robertson, San Francisco.
Cook, Sherburne F.
    1976 *The Population of the California Indians, 1769–1970*. University of California, Berkeley and Los Angeles.

Coombs, Gary, and Fred Plog
  1974 Chumash Baptism: An Ecological Perspective. In *Antap: California Indian Political and Economic Organization*, edited by L. J. Bean and T. F. King, pp. 137–154. Anthropological Papers No. 2, Ballena Press, Ramona, Calif.

Deagan, Kathleen A.
  1983 *Spanish St. Augustine: The Archaeology of a Colonial Creole Community.* Academic Press, New York.

Deetz, James J. F.
  1963 Archaeological Investigations at La Purisima Mission. *Archaeological Survey Annual Report* 5:163–208. University of California, Los Angeles.

Englehardt, Zephyrin
  1912 *Missions and Missionaries of California.* Old Mission, Santa Barbara.

Farnsworth, Paul
  1986 Spanish California: The Final Frontier. *Journal of New World Archaeology* 6:4:35–46. University of California, Los Angeles.

Griffen, William B.
  1969 *Culture Change and Shifting Populations in Central Northern Mexico.* Anthropological Papers No. 13. University of Arizona, Tucson.
  1979 *Indian Assimilation in the Franciscan Area of Nueva Vizcaya.* Anthropological Papers No. 33. University of Arizona, Tucson.

Guest, Francis F.
  1974 *Fermin Francisco de Lasuén (1736–1803): A Biography.* Academy of American Franciscan History, Washington, D.C.
  1979 An Examination of the Thesis of S. F. Cook on the Forced Conversion of Indians in the California Missions. *Southern California Quarterly* LXI:1:1–77. Historical Society of Southern California, Los Angeles.
  1983 Cultural Perspectives on California Mission Life. *Southern California Quarterly* LXV:1:1–66. Historical Society of Southern California, Los Angeles.

Harris, Marvin
  1971 *Culture, Man and Nature.* Crowell, New York.

Heizer, Robert F.
  1941 A Californian Messianic Movement of 1801 among the Chumash. *American Anthropologist* 43:128–129.

Heizer, Robert F. (editor)
  1974 *The Costanoan Indians.* Local History Studies, vol. 18. California History Center, Cupertino.

Hoover, Robert L.
  1982 The Death of Yóscolo. *Pacific Historical Review* LI:3:312–314. University of California, Berkeley.

Hoover, Robert L., and Julia Costello (editors)
  1985 *Excavations at Mission San Antonio, 1976–1978,* Institute of Archaeology Monograph No. 26. University of California, Los Angeles.

Hudson, Dee Travis, and Ernest Underhay
  1978 *Crystals in the Sky: An Intellectual Odyssey Involving Chumash Astronomy, Cosmology, and Rock Art.* Anthropological Papers No. 10. Ballena Press, Socorro.

Jackson, Helen Hunt
  1963 *A Century of Dishonor.* Harper and Row, New York.

Phillips, George Harwood
  1975 *Chiefs and Challengers: Indian Resistance and Cooperation in Southern California.* University of California, Berkeley and Los Angeles.

Quimby, George I., and Alexander Spoehr
  1951 Acculturation and Material Culture. *Fieldiana: Anthropology* 3:6:107–147.

Social Sciences Research Council
  1954 Acculturation: An Exploratory Formulation. *American Anthropology* 56:973–1002.

Soler, Pablo

1798a Documents, Mission San Antonio C-C31, folder 7. Ms. in Bancroft Library, University of California, Berkeley.

1798b Documents, Mission San Antonio C-C31, folder 9. Ms. in Bancroft Library, University of California, Berkeley.

South, Stanley

1977 *Method and Theory in Historical Archaeology.* Academic Press, New York.

Stickel, E. Gary, and Alice E. Cooper

1969 *The Chumash Revolt of 1824: A Case for an Archaeological Application of Feedback Theory.* Archaeological Survey Annual Report for 1969. University of California, Los Angeles.

Stodder, Ann Lucy W.

1986 *Mechanisms and Trends in the Decline of the Costanoan Indian Population of Central California.* Archives of California Prehistory No. 4. Coyote Press, Salinas.

Wallerstein, Immanuel

1974 *The Modern World System I: Capitalist Agriculture and the Origins of the European World-Economy in the 16th Century.* Academic Press, New York.

1980 *The Modern World System II: Mercantilism and the Consolidation of the European World-Economy, 1600–1750.* Academic Press, New York.

Webb, Edith B.

1952 *Indian Life at the Old Missions.* Warren F. Lewis, Los Angeles.

Chapter 25 ■

W. Michael Mathes

Baja California: A Special Area of Contact and Colonization, 1535–1697

The Natural Environment

The peninsula of Baja California is perhaps a unique ethnographic area of North America. The peninsula is some 1,700 km long, averages 75 km in breadth, and rises from sea level to average altitudes in excess of 1,400 m. It is bounded on the west by the Pacific Ocean and on the east by the Gulf of California (Figure 25-1). The climate of the northern half of the area is similar to that of the continental Pacific coast, with a dry season between the months of May and November and cold, constant rains during the remainder of the year. In contrast, the southern half is regulated by the tropical pattern of western Mexico and thus has a dry season during the months of October to June and tropical cyclonic storms occurring in the remaining months, particularly August and September. Average rainfall throughout the area is approximately 100 to 160 mm per annum, and temperatures range from 0° C in December-January to 45° C in July-August. With the exception of the Desierto de Sebastián Vizcaíno about midpeninsula, the level coastal plain rarely exceeds 5 km in breadth on either coast, thus creating a narrow, rocky, mountainous region with deeply eroded washes rapidly descending their respective watersheds. Except at the highest

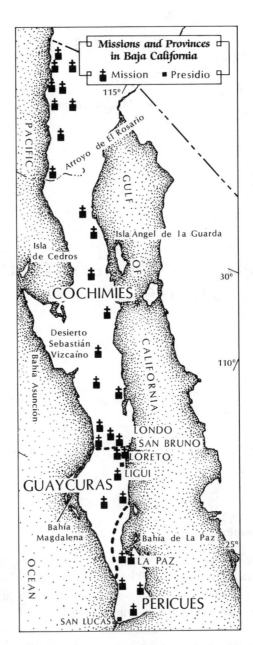

Figure 25-1. Historic ethnological distributions and missions in Baja California.

elevations, the flora is typical of lower Sonoran zones, with chaparral, sage, and cactus interspersed among low thorn trees and bushes; the fauna consists primarily of desert rodents, rabbits and hares, coyote, reptiles, occasional antelope, deer, and desert sheep, and a wide variety of birds.

At a point on the Pacific coast some 300 km south of the modern international border, the Arroyo de El Rosario delineates the ecological, meteorological, and geographical beginning of peninsular California. This point also marks the boundary of the truly peninsular ethnological groups that populated the remaining 1,400 km from north to south: the Cochimí, Guaycura, and Pericú. These peoples, now extinct, were differentiated primarily on the basis of language; their material culture—marginal paleolithic and adapted to subsistence in an extremely arid, barren, and rugged environment—was virtually identical (Massey 1949). These three groups had a maximum combined aboriginal population of less than 25,000 (Mathes 1984) and were composed of small extended families that rarely exceeded 20 persons. Occasionally these families joined to form a larger temporary ranchería when an abundant harvest or hunt occurred in a certain area, or to participate in some important event in their life cycle.

Unlike most areas of the Western Hemisphere, reports of the existence of the peninsula of Baja California attracted European attention prior to its actual discovery through the description of "California," a fabulous island rich in gold and pearls "to the left hand of the Indies," ruled by queen Calafia, in the popular early sixteenth-century novel, *Las Sergas de Esplandián*. Its striking similarity to "Cihuatlán" (Land of Women) reported to Fernando Cortés on the west coast of New Spain in 1523 made it a major goal of exploration and established it as a region that might produce great wealth. Also unlike other areas, Baja California was not permanently occupied by Europeans immediately after its discovery. Its Spanish discoverers found it unattractive for settlement because of its geographical isolation, apparent lack of great and immediate wealth, harsh climate, and limited arable land. Thus its native peoples experienced only periodic contact prior to definitive occupation. Between November 1533, when it was first sighted, and October 25, 1697, when permanently settled, Baja California was visited by 19 documented expeditions, which, over the intervening 164 years spent approximately 2,535 days or 6.95 years within areas populated by the Cochimí, Guaycura, and Pericú.

Although this contact was generally brief, extremely irregular, and usually limited to the immediate coastal areas, during the period before permanent settlement the native groups of Baja California had become familiar with, and in some cases acculturated to, various aspects of Spanish customs, language, religion, ships, weapons and materiel, and livestock, which modified their culture so that it conformed in varying degrees to Spanish ideals. Although most of the earlier expeditions confined their efforts to geographical discovery and charting, later voyagers occasionally provided valuable ethnographic descriptions in their obligatory diaries and reports, thus diffusing knowledge of the peninsular peoples among governmental officials, other interested explorers and navigators, and prospective colonists and missionaries.

Earliest Contact and Exchange

The initial discovery of California in November 1533 by the mutineer Fortún Ximénez led to a violent confrontation between the Spanish and Pericúes. In an attempt to take pearls from the Indians, Ximénez and his party were killed, and but for the few crewmen who remained aboard the *Concepción*, subsequent contact might have been delayed indefinitely. However, the initiator of the 1533 exploration, Fernando Cortés, personally determined to occupy the region, and in May 1535 arrived at the Bahía de La Paz with a fleet of three ships carrying calves, sheep, hogs, and a large number of horses. The men were armed with harquebuses, lances, shields, swords, and daggers, and many were mounted. Although the extant documents of the expedition do not record the reaction of the Pericúes who observed their arrival, there can be no doubt that these strange men and their accoutrements became a familiar sight before the Spanish abandoned their colony of Santa Cruz in the spring of 1536 (Mathes 1981:45).

Later expeditions in the sixteenth and seventeenth centuries were equipped in a similar manner. In 1596, Sebastián Vizcaíno carried horses, cattle, and mastiffs to Cabo San Lucas and La Paz, and in 1615 Nicolás de Cardona used the fighting dogs to repel an attack by Guaycura on the coast north of Bahía de La Paz. In 1633 and 1636, Francisco de Ortega recorded the carrying of chickens and lambs to La Paz, and in all probability the expedition also carried some horses. Knives, hatchets, axes, pieces of forged iron, mirrors, and glass beads were exchanged for pearls among the Pericú and Guaycura by Vizcaíno in 1596 and 1602, by Cardona in 1615, Ortega in 1632–1634 and 1636, and by Francisco de Lucenilla in 1668. As required by Royal Order, attempts were made to evangelize and attract natives to the faith, ranging from the public celebration of mass during the Vizcaíno, Cardona, and Lucenilla voyages to actual baptism by Father Diego de la Nava during the Ortega expedition of 1633–1634. In 1636 Ortega reported that broken Spanish was spoken by some Pericúes in La Paz, and a similar report was made in 1644 by Alonso González Barriga among the Pericú at Cabo San Lucas, some of whom were found to have blondish hair. This was the first documentation to suggest the beginnings of mestizaje on the peninsula, although there was earlier mention of the disappearance of crew members of the Vizcaíno and Ortega expeditions for short periods among the Pericú. Although such clandestine relationships are infrequently documented, it is difficult to believe that during a century or more of contact with soldiers and mariners, they did not exist (Mathes 1981:45).

Earliest Ethnographic Descriptions

Unfortunately, no ethnographic descriptions survive from the Cortés expedition of 1535. However, his lieutenant, Francisco de Ulloa, who explored the Gulf of California from Cabo San Lucas to the region of Isla Angel de la Guarda and the Pacific coast northward to Isla de Cedros between August 31, 1539, and April 5, 1540, provides a brief description of the Cochimí in the area of Bahía San Luis Gonzaga:

> We saw on shore an old man and another young man with three or four boys. Seeing us approaching them, the young man demanded of one of the boys his bows and some arrows which he had left at a little distance . . . they arose and the old man came toward us . . . the rest began to flee up a high hill and presently the old man started after them. We seized him to . . . find out if he could

understand the Indian we brought from . . . Santa Cruz. He spoke another language. The rest were naked people without any clothing, garments or covering. Their hair was cut two or three fingers long.

They had a little enclosure of woven grass without any cover over the top, where they lodged, ten or twelve paces from the sea. We found inside no sort of bread nor anything resembling it, nor any other food except fish, of which they had some which they had killed with well-twisted cords which they had and with some thick hooks made of tortoise shell bent in fire, and with others, smaller, made of thorns. They kept their drinking water in certain skin pouches which we thought must be the stomachs of seals. They had a little raft which they must have used in fishing. It was made of canes tied in three bundles, each part separately, and then all tied together, the middle section being larger than the laterals. They rowed it with a slender oar, little more than half a fathom long, and two small badly made paddles, one at each end. We judged the people to be nomads, possessed of little intelligence [Wagner 1929:22; Hakluyt 1904:219–220].

In the area of Bahía de Cedros, Ulloa noted that the Cochimí

kept their drinking water in the stomachs of fish. We found a bowl like the small one found among the people of . . . Santa Cruz and this led us to conclude that this land and people are all one.

. . . they began to shout in a language which the Indian we brought from . . . Santa Cruz did not understand nor did they understand him.

He and the others . . . we saw on the rafts and on land, eight or ten men, were naked people of good appearance. Their hair was trimmed two or three fingers long. Altogether they had two or three bows with arrows. The rafts of canes on which they came out were larger than the first I described above, but of the same make and style. They rowed with the same sort of sticks and paddles [Wagner 1929:24–25; Hakluyt 1904:IX:221–222].

After returning southward and rounding Cabo San Lucas, at Bahía Magdalena, Ulloa came into conflict with the Guaycura:

These Indians approached so crouched and hidden, one from the other, that our sentries did not see them. . . . They attacked us with such marvellous spirit and ferocity and with such a rain of arrows, javelins and stones, that they did not permit us to show a face from under our bucklers. . . .

The people who came and waged war on us this day were naked people of medium appearance. Some had long black hair and all the rest wore theirs cut two to three fingers long. Many of them wore hanging about their necks shining shells of the kind in which pearls grow. In their ears they wore pieces of wood two inches thick. Their arms were slender bows, taller than they, arrows of cane or wood with flint points and some lances. . . .

. . . they again came out to the rock in the water and again placed another shell there and a few little skeins of strings, like those the Indians of . . . Santa Cruz wear on their heads . . . they again came . . . and hung . . . a diadem, such as some of them wear on their heads, made of woven thread, very thick, all covered with fine red feathers, well tied and fastened in, in such manner that it looked more like thread with little black feathers standing up along the edges. It was as much as five fingers or more wide in the middle, the ends pointed [Wagner 1929:30–34; Hakluyt 1904:IX:247–250].

Arriving at Isla de Cedros, Ulloa again encountered the Cochimí:

> Five rafts came out from the island . . . which carried one and two and three
> and four and five men inside. They went out to sea . . . and . . . fished. . . .
> The Indians, seeing that we were going to land, armed themselves with many
> stones and great clubs which they employed with both hands, and with much
> spirit and determination prepared to prevent our landing. . . .
> . . . it appeared that they brought their drinking water from a distance in the
> paunches of seals. . . . we found nothing except some seal-skins in which they
> slept and protected themselves from the cold, some seals' paunches in which they
> had water, fishing lines and hooks made of thorns of certain cactuses. . . .
> . . . the Indians of this island . . . are naked people with holes in their ears. In
> their habitations we found some hollow pipes, as much as a palm long, made of
> baked clay, and in them a certain burnt herb which they must use like tobacco
> [Wagner 1929:38–45; Hakluyt 1904:IX:257–274].

Unfortunately, Ulloa's observations were not repeated for over a half century.
The surviving documentation of the expedition of Juan Rodríguez Cabrillo,
which visited the Pacific coast of the peninsula from July 3 to September 23,
1542, and March 18 to April 10, 1543, contains no ethnographic information although contact was made on various occasions (Wagner 1929:79–93), and the
exhausted voyagers Francisco Gali in 1584 and Pedro de Unamuno in 1587, having crossed the Pacific from Manila, were of no mind to delay their arrival in
Acapulco. Similarly, the English corsair Thomas Cavendish, awaiting the Manila
galleon at Cabo San Lucas from October 24 to November 29, 1587, and his victim, the *Santa Ana* under Tomás de Alzola, who, with his survivors, remained
at the cape from November 14, 1587, to January 2, 1588, were far too concerned
with other matters to bother with descriptions of the Pericú. This was also the
case with Sebastián Rodríguez Cermeño and his crew, who sailed the Pacific
coast from December 15, 1595, to January 4, 1596, hoping to make New Spain
after the wreck of the *San Agustín* at Drakes Bay. Nevertheless, all of these navigators and their men had contact with Baja California natives, occasionally for
periods of several weeks (Mathes 1968).

Initial Attempts at Colonization

Under more favorable circumstances, while attempting to establish a permanent
settlement on the peninsula between September 3 and December 1, 1596,
Sebastián Vizcaíno provided valuable information about the Pericúes at Cabo
San Lucas:

> I saw a number of undressed Indians, naked without any form of cover or
> clothing, notably large of body and well built, with bows and arrows and fire-
> hardened shafts the points of which are like a dart. . . .
> The people are so bestial and barbaric that standing or sitting or any way at all
> that they desire they attend to the necessities of nature without any form of con-
> cern nor respect, and their language is so barbaric that it sounds more like the
> bleating of sheep than the speech of people. . . .

That day the Indians brought me some presents of fruits of the land which were pitahaya and some small, round fruit of the texture and size of white plums of Castile with a rough skin like a peach and of a good flavor, the seeds of which had a center of the same flavor as Castilian walnuts. . . . They also gave me dead lizards and snakes, a food which must be highly esteemed among them . . . and they brought other triangular fruit the size of garbanzos and of the same flavor as chestnuts, and other black ones of a hard skin and the size and flavor of pine nuts, and some thick white roots.

While exploring to the north of his colony of La Paz, on the coast near Ligüí, Vizcaíno encountered the Cochimí:

Five canoes which were like rafts made of reeds, very well constructed and strong, came out, and in each of them were three or four Indians with their bows and arrows, somewhat smaller in body and more agile than the first, but naked like them . . . they gave us some more fish . . . but . . being suspicious of them I ordered . . . our return . . . to the anchorage . . . and turning to look back we saw almost 100 Indians who approached firing arrows [Mathes 1965:Doc. 29].

Returning to the peninsula to explore and map the Pacific coast between June 11 and October 30, 1602, and February 3 and 14, 1603, Vizcaíno described the Guaycura of Bahía Magdalena:

A large number of Indians came out from different places with their bows and arrows and fire-hardened darts, although in peace. . . . They are well-formed people of good physique, although naked and living in rancherías; their ordinary food is fish and aloe root . . . they fish with weirs, and also have many clams and mussel; there are many whales which at times go aground on the beach of this bay, for we found many of their bones.

Continuing up the coast, in August Vizcaíno encountered a Cochimí settlement at Bahía Asunción: "Some Indian rancherías were found and in their little huts they had sea lion skins from which they made sandals" (Mathes 1965:Doc. 57).

The search for an inside passage to the north, up the Gulf of California, and Spanish hopes to settle the austere peninsula through private investors lured by possible wealth in pearls, led to a concentration of voyages under viceregal license into the gulf in the seventeenth century. In 1615, Nicolás de Cardona, nephew of a Sevilla entrepreneur, made the first of these voyages. At La Paz he noted that the Pericú

are peaceful, easy to convert to the Holy Gospel. The have never known idolatry or any other religion.

The information which these Indians have given about the land and its people is that they are governed by a king and chieftans, and that these are inland, distant from this port, pointing to the north. They are all naked; the women wear from the waist down some strips of twisted cotton and bird feathers. Their arms are bows and arrows and fire-hardened shafts. Their boats are of three bundles of thin cane, two on the sides and one in the middle, very well tied, so that in each one of these two persons travel. They also have another type of boat which are of three branches nailed in the same way. In each one an Indian goes out to fish. They row with both hands, with an oar with two paddles. They have harpoons made of branches, fishooks of burned tortoise shell, and cactus fiber cording. They are great swimmers and divers. They wear their hair long and tied; use many feathers of different colors and worked oyster shells. They enjoy running and wrestling; they are corpulent, strong, long-limbed, and healthy. They have no considerable goods, property or fields because they are fishing and lazy people who move from one place to another as the schools of fish and oyster beds move [Mathes 1970:Doc. 32].

Voyages of Exploitation and Alliance

Cardona suffered numerous setbacks in his attempts to settle the peninsula, and his failure to comply with the terms of his license gave rise to a legal struggle. After lengthy hearings, the rights to explore and colonize were transferred to Francisco de Ortega who, after 17 years of Spanish absence, reestablished Spanish contact with the Pericú. In 1632 at Cabo San Lucas, pilot Esteban Carbonel de Valenzuela described the arrival of the expedition:

The Indians when they saw us lined up on some sand hills, more than 300 of them with darts like lances, and a chieftan walked along the beach speaking in their language, and we made signs to them that they should come out, and the chieftan, launching a raft of five branches into the water, with an oar and two paddles arrived at the frigate, remaining a little distant . . . he went back to land talking to his people who left their arms and all came aboard on rafts . . . they took us to a freshwater lake to fill our jugs because the water they drink is kept in fish stomachs like bladders and smells of seafood. They brought many roasted and raw sardines, and some split grains of pearls damaged by fire because to eat the meat they roast the oysters first . . . sending a soldier to explore the Pacific coast . . . from a hill from which he descended perspiring . . . an old Indian woman came out to him with water from her ranchería, another Indian woman gave him a half of a roast fish, and an Indian man made him a roll of dried grass to sit on, and having seated him, cleaned the sweat from his face with his hand. This aforesaid soldier one night stayed to sleep in the ranchería, and they gave him a bed made of heart of palm fiber and a blanket of very soft deerskin and a pillow of pelican skin filled with feathers. Two Indians guarded him all night and each time he got up they got up with him and put him back to bed, and he noted that all night an Indian man or woman was singing in the language, and on tiring another sang. . . . One Indian was there who would be some 50 years old, of very fine body over two meters in height with well formed feet and legs. . . . On their rafts which they use to go out and fish they carry five or six darts and some harpoons, and seeing fish which we seamen call jumping fish . . . they impale them with those darts, and if they do not die with one they keep throwing others since the shafts are of light branches, although the point is of heavy, hard wood, they will not carry the fish to the bottom [Mathes 1970:Doc. 37].

Father Diego de la Nava, chaplain of the expedition, also provided an excellent description of the Pericú at Cabo San Lucas similar to that of Carbonel, but stated that the beds were "a form of palm mat which they use with skins with the hair removed with which they cover themselves," and that at La Paz

the Indians made us understand that others, their enemies, were coming to the
attack and that we should favor them . . . we fired the artillery . . . and the Indians became calm and were thankful . . . they are very well disposed people, and
of good build, and are naked, and the women, even the youngest, with great
chastity wear worked hides and a form of skirt which seems made of cactus fiber
[Mathes 1970:Doc. 34].

Ortega himself seconded the report of Carbonel, relating the incident of the
tired soldier and noting that the Pericú were "well disposed, robust, and agile
for anything." He also seconded Nava's report of the conflict at La Paz and of
the chastity of the women. On his return to La Paz in October 1633, Ortega witnessed a major event documenting the constant demographic pressure that occurred on the restricted peninsula and the funerary customs of the Pericú:

The king of the Indians, Bacarí, with all of his captains came to beg us to remain . . . they were very content with being protected by us since these Indians
are at war with others who inhabit the coast to the west and are called Guaycuras
. . . the Indians on seeing that we had built a fort, came to live next to us due to
the fear they had of the Guaycuras. The wars these Indians have are over some
fisheries and a place where much tobacco and camote, a root like sweet potatoes
of Spain, are gathered. On the 2nd of December the prince Conichí, son of Bacarí,
king of this land who was named Don Juan in Holy Baptism, left this camp, and
having taken with him over 200 Indians to the said fishing and shellfish site, after
eight days, while he and his companions were sleeping, the king of the
Guaycuras surprised and attacked them. The said Conichí, his wife, and a son of
two years who was baptized were killed, along with over 30 persons including
women and children. They brought to this camp, where the Spanish were located,
the dead prince and his wife and son and took them to the place where the father
was settled, and after preparing them and placing them on platforms, Bacarí noti-
fied all the nearest settlements and rancherías, and a very large number of Indians having gathered, they cried night and day, and the crying and wailing was
heard for over a league. Having been on the platforms for three days, Bacarí
called Captain Francisco de Ortega and all of his men and two priests to be present at the burial of his son, which was done with great solemnity. . . . Bacarí
asked the captain for six axes to cut wood, and with them he ordered his Indians
to cut the trees where his son was accustomed to sit in the shade, and they closed
and cut off the trail which Conichí was accustomed to take to the settlement. During those ten or twelve days following the burial many Indians from all the islands and the mainland gathered . . . and all together, wailing and exclaiming for
the dead prince, these Indians cut all of their hair which they customarily wear
hanging to the waist . . . they made a fire and burned the said hair and all
painted themselves black.
    The nature of these Indians is very affable and there has been no sign of idola-
try among them, and they do not have more than one wife. They place their love
in their children and food. They bury in our manner, they are very well formed
and of very good body and very light. . . . In the summer they are always at sea
in some rafts which they have and which they take out four and six leagues, for
from it they take their sustenance. . . .
    On 22 February of this year of 1634, Captain Francisco de Ortega, wintering in
this port . . . proposed an entry to the interior . . . for us to become friends of the
king of the Guaycuras and negotiate peace with our Indian friends of the port of
La Paz. On the 28th of said month, Captain Francisco de Ortega left this said

port, taking in his company 20 soldiers and the vicar Diego de la Nava . . . and having marched for two days toward the west . . . Bacarí Don Pedro arrived with 200 Indian friends, thinking we were going to fight with the Guaycuras, and although we made many attempts to have him return, he did not want to, and marching another day . . . making noise so that the Guaycuras would go away . . . at noon, arriving at a waterhole, Bacarí Don Pedro . . . found a ranchería of Guaycuras, and surrounded them, and being unable to stop them . . . they killed some Indians . . . they had a great feast for the victory which they gained over the Guaycuras. The method and custom of fighting of these Guaycura Indians is with a dart and arrow, and by surprise when their opposite is sleeping they attack in the early morning at dawn, and after the skirmish they retire to the bush and to the west coast [Mathes 1970:Doc. 46].

The wreck of Ortega's ship south of La Paz in 1636 forced him to abandon his enterprise in the Californias, and, as was the case with Cardona, hearings were held and the license was transferred to Pedro Porter y Casanate, a professional navigator and mariner, educated at the University of Zaragoza in Spain. Confronted with delays, as were his predecessors, Porter was involved in fundraising when his captain, Alonso González Barriga, was ordered to sail to Cabo San Lucas to alert the Manila galleon to the presence of corsairs on the coast north of Acapulco. Arriving at the cape on January 27, 1644, González and his men went ashore, where they were received by the Pericú:

On disembarking on land an old chieftain came leading a large number of Indians . . . in signs of peace and love the Indians received them with happiness, throwing sand into the air and offering bows and arrows by placing them on the ground. . . . They were decorated and painted on their bodies in various colors, they wore much featherwork on their heads, and hanging around their necks they wore mother-of-pearl shells with many holes in them; and anything that was given to them, they put on their heads or in their top-knots.

The men are more corpulent, stronger and well-built than those of New Spain. Their hair is somewhat blond and they wear it long. They are naked. The women are good looking and are dressed from the waist down. The Indians are very docile and peaceful. . . .

. . . They are more afraid of the dogs than of the harquebuses. . . .

A whale washed up on the coast and in five days the Indians cut it to pieces with their axes which are of stone. The Indians to the interior, with whom they wage war and are called Guaycuras, wished to come to the whale, but the coastal Indians made it understood that they needed the help of the Spaniards. . . .

. . . no form of idolatry was found among these Indians, they are not thieves nor liars, nor do they become drunk or use beverages; they smoke tobacco and have it in abundance, and like us they give it a name.

. . . the Indians are all divers, and they showed where the pearl oyster beds were, offering through signs to go and bring them out.

They were . . . in this port until 21 February [Mathes 1970:Doc. 105].

Although not as specific as González, Porter, in a report following his voyage to the peninsula between October 23, 1648, and January 4, 1649, reiterated much of the description of the Pericúes, adding:

> In the ports where I anchored they always received me in peace and regaled
> me with fish and other foods. . . . I made a dictionary of their language . . . they
> paint themselves various colors and styles, and with curious clips and feathers
> adorn their heads and the long hair which they use. . . .
> . . . some groups pierce their noses and ears and put shells and tubes of to-
> bacco in them, and decorate their bodies with brand spots in different places
> [Mathes 1970:Doc. 102].

Bankruptcy and ill health forced Porter's retirement, and with the universal poor fortune of the seventeenth-century voyagers, interest in acquisition of the license waned. In 1664 Bernardo Bernal de Piñadero obtained the permit, and after a month of navigation in the Gulf of California returned to the mainland, narrowly escaping a full mutiny by disgruntled seamen. Four years later, he was followed by Francisco de Lucenilla, who sailed the coast of the peninsula from La Paz northward between May 20 and July 2, 1668. This voyage also failed owing to discontent among the crew, whose expectations of sharing in a great wealth of pearls were not met. By virtue of the character of their leaders and constant problems, neither Bernal nor Lucenilla produced ethnographic information, although the former left two mutineers abandoned on Isla San José, their fate being unknown (Mathes 1970:II).

First Mission Attempt at La Paz

The constant failure to colonize the peninsula by royally and privately financed civil enterprises led Spain to change its policy regarding the Californias. The Society of Jesus had, in 1671, become the recipient of a major bequest by Alonso Fernández de la Torre for the establishment of missions in the north, and after extensive hearings it was adjudged that a part of the funds could be applied to California. Nevertheless, the isolation of the region and the higher cost of evangelization on the peninsula led to the formation of a joint expedition that would seek the foundation of a mission at La Paz as well as permit the exploitation of pearl oyster beds. Led by Admiral Isidro de Atondo y Antillón, accompanied by Jesuit Fathers Eusebio Francisco Kino, Matías Goñi, and Juan Bautista Copart, and following a difficult crossing of the gulf, the expedition reached La Paz on April 1, 1683, and began to construct some temporary buildings. The struggle between the Pericúes and Guaycuras was reaching a crescendo, and within a short time Atondo and his men became involved:

> On 17 May a mulatto seaman was carried off or went to live with the Indians
> and I asked several times offering them gifts for bringing him until I found out
> from other good Indians we called "serranos" that they later killed him and for
> this I apprehended one of their captains, holding him hostage. . . . On 6 June two
> captains with 150 Indians came to attack . . . they began to surround us and I
> went out to encounter the captain we called Pablo . . . and reprehended him . . .
> and to not suffer discredit . . . from these Guaycuras . . . I determined . . . to give
> them a spraying of shot before they could advance on us . . . the others remained
> in ambush in the bush . . . and I ordered a small cannon and some harquebuses

to be fired and ten fell . . . and at the same time they fired some arrows which fell in our trench, and after this, all that was desired was to arrive at the ship with the supplies and the horses [Mathes 1974:Doc. 25].

Father Kino in a report of August 10, 1683, clarified the problem:

Almost all of these have wives and some, although few, more than one, and many children, and this is understood to mean the Guaycuras closest to this port of La Paz who are the most belicose people, but the "Curos" who are more tame and very friendly to the Spanish nation are of a very large number of people and souls: In the port of San Bernabé or Cabo San Lucas [Mathes 1974:Doc. 25].

Second Mission Attempt at San Bruno

Following the abandonment of La Paz, Atondo and Kino sailed the gulf coast in search of an adequate mission site. On October 5, 1683, well within the territory of the Cochimí, the arroyo of San Bruno was discovered and there the mission of the same name was founded. Not having been subject to conflict with Europeans or other indigenous groups and having undergone relatively little contact, the Cochimíes of San Bruno, called Didíos or Didíus by Kino, were receptive of Spanish settlement and exploration. The mission, although constantly short of supplies, maintained a small population and permitted the founding of a small visiting station named San Isidro at the Cochimí site of Londó. Several of the soldiers guarding the site observed what they construed as idolatrous practices among the peoples of the area, and Atondo sent a squad to investigate. They reported

that on Monday, 6 November of the present year of 1684, at about 12:00 noon . . . they saw that the Indian Captain of the Didiu group, whom we call Leopoldo (although he is not baptized), went up to the top of a hill dressed in a thread net, intertwined with locks of hair which covered him from his shoulders to his feet like a Turk; and on his head he wore a net like a hood or cowl made from feathers of various colors which fell over his shoulders. In his right hand he carried a white paddle with two square holes, 80 centimeters in length, and in his left hand, his bow and arrows. Having gone up on a rock which is on the peak of said hill, he gave great shouts and made many gestures, and having been on the said rock for a time, he came down with such violence that he caused the witnesses great surprise. Whereupon, many persons came out to receive him, and within an hour other pagan Indians, about 14 in number dressed in the same manner, went up with said captain and, passing under said rock without stopping, they went down to the ranchería.
. . . the following day . . . they saw a great procession go out of the ranchería led by the said Captain Leopoldo with one of his women following him, and then followed an Indian man and women. In this manner men and women went out intermingled with some canes in their hands and bunches of feathers on their heads, dancing and making reverences to a bust the size of a newborn child with its face painted black, its hair long, and three bunches of white feathers on its head, those in the middle standing out and the others hanging down, and with some type of clothing which the witnesses could not distinguish. This bust was

carried by the last Indian in the procession who walked bending over with it and, having arrived at a place where they had nailed up a branch of pitahaya and next to it a forked pole lower than said pitahaya on the points of which were placed some circles of sticks from a tree they call copal over which were woven branches of the said tree, and above which were flags of branches painted red, blue and white. Said bust was placed under said cover of branches a little above the ground at the foot of a great pile of seeds which they call medesé [mesquite seed]. When they placed it there, the dancing stopped for a while and then later it again continued for two days and nights in the following manner: Some went out after others, men and women intermingled, and formed a great line, and the captain on arriving at the end of it, with all of his people, stopped next to the said bust and all began to talk and at the same time bent down in an act of humiliation to it. Afterwards they rested for about a quarter of an hour and again formed the same line with the same ceremonies, and the last day of the dance, in the early dawn, they gave such a great shout that they caused the infantry to take up their arms, thinking that the Indians were advancing upon them. At the same time they heard a great wailing among the women and, in a short while they began to sing, continuing throughout the day with sporadic shouts and dances. At sunset they sat in a circle in several places and began to pass out the said medesé seed which they had piled up in front of said bust . . . it seemed that there were 2,500 Indians. . . . This same day Captain Leopoldo arrived at . . . San Isidro . . . and asked permission . . . to bathe himself where the horses drink. Having received permission . . . he brought other pagan Indians, one of whom was so ill-treated . . . he could barely move. They put him in said waterhole and, after bathing himself, they brought him before the said captain who began to look at him very attentively and then lowered his head and began to cry. Together they all returned to the ranchería, they divided the leftover provisions among everyone, and afterwards they went to their lands [Mathes 1974:Doc. 29].

Owing to a shortage of funds and problems of sending supplies across the gulf from the recently established Jesuit missions in Sinaloa, San Bruno was abandoned on May 8, 1685. Twelve years transpired before contact was again established between Spaniards and the peoples of Baja California. However, on that occasion, through the efforts of Jesuit Fathers Juan María Salvatierra, Francisco María Píccolo, and Juan de Ugarte, the occupation of Nuestra Señora de Loreto in 1697 was definitive. The establishment of 11 additional missions extending from Cabo San Lucas to San Ignacio within the following three decades brought all indigenous groups and subgroups directly into contact with Europeans, and the majority of their population was in the process of becoming at least partly acculturated to their way of life. The selective acceptance or rejection of European culture, or its temporary adoption, were no longer alternatives, and other radical changes among the Pericú, Guaycura, and Cochimí were occurring.

Results of Transitory Contact

Although some European disease was undoubtedly introduced during the transitory contact period, there is no evidence that it had a major impact upon native cultures. Agriculture and animal husbandry had increased the nutritional level of Baja California groups, but the concentration of indigenous populations in missions made them more susceptible to infection, and the permanent presence of Europeans in a region lacking natural resistance to smallpox, measles, and venereal disease elevated the extent of contagion, frequently to epidemic level, thus initiating the process that eventually led to the extinction of native Baja Californians within a century and a half (Mathes 1984).

It is also evident that events occurring during the period of transitory contact altered ethnological patterns prior to permanent European occupation. Apart from the obvious modifications of material culture accruing through the acquisition of iron implements, manufactured cloth and ornaments, and domestic plants and livestock, an awareness of the methods and wishes of the Spanish, which allowed indigenous peoples to accept that which was perceived as beneficial and reject or feign acceptance of that which was seen as not, was acquired. In this respect the ethnological observations of highly educated European Jesuits such as Salvatierra (1971), Píccolo (1962), Johann Jakob Baegert (1942), Segismundo Taraval (1931), Miguel del Barco (1973), and the informants of Miguel Venegas (1979) were often distinct from those of earlier explorers.

Two problems in particular are related to religion and territorial occupation. Although transitory and mission sources agree that the worship of images or idolatry was absent among the natives of Baja California, there can be little doubt as to the accuracy of the Atondo report of what clearly was a funerary ceremony. The presence of some form of image, probably that of the deceased, was unmistakeable and was known to Atondo's men only through stealth. Spaniards made their religious zeal known, and on multiple occasions native peoples participated in Christian ritual to please them; they certainly would have avoided displeasure by openly practicing their native ceremonies (Mathes 1974b).

Of far greater significance, the demographic pressure within the peninsula evidenced by the displacement of the Pericú from the shores of the Bahía de La Paz and their being forced to the south by the Guaycura between 1684 and 1720, shows two distinct concepts of the peoples of that region (León-Portilla 1976; Mathes 1975; Reygadas and Velázquez 1985). Whereas missionaries found the inhabitants of La Paz to be bellicose (Bravo 1970), their predecessors universally found them to be friendly and peaceful (Mathes 1975). Had the Jesuits perceived the long-standing pressures upon the Pericú, it is possible that the disastrous Pericú revolt of 1734–1737—brought about because that group was further confined to a highly limited geographic area, their pre-mission customs were greatly curtailed, and they were subjected to an enforced peace with a traditional enemy, the Guaycura—could have been averted. If such were the case, the deaths of two Jesuits, the spread of smallpox and syphilis by Spanish and Yaqui troops, and the virtual annihilation of a unique native group could have been prevented (Taraval 1931).

Permanent Occupation

By the time of the expulsion of the Society of Jesus from Spanish domains in 1767, Jesuit missions in Baja California had spread virtually throughout the areas occupied by Cochimíes, Guaycuras, and Pericúes, and Jesuit exploration had established contact further to the north among the Yuman groups. Having failed to colonize the peninsula after 150 years, the Spanish found the ultimate answer in the Jesuit mission system. On the peninsula, however, this system was distinct from the majority of contemporary mission provinces and from those established later in the Californias by Franciscans and Dominicans. In addition to the benefits of prior geographical and ethnological knowledge of large areas of Baja California, the Society of Jesus was granted, and maintained, almost absolute control over the admission of Europeans to the region, and, until the mid-eighteenth century, prohibited secular settlement. The European population that occupied the peninsula, primarily soldiers and their immediate families, was directly in the service of the missions and thus rigidly conformed to the policies and standards set by the Jesuit superior. The Jesuit missionaries themselves were multinational by birth (Spanish, Spanish-American, Alsatian, Croatian, Italian, Bohemian, Austrian, Scottish) and were university educated and usually from families of means. Subsequent missionary activity in the Californias would be restricted to native subjects of the Spanish Crown of lesser intellectual stature and thus more easily subjected to civil jurisdiction.

When viewed in the perspective of European expansion in the Western Hemisphere, the form of contact and colonization in Baja California was as unusual as the region itself. Discovered within five decades of the first Columbian voyage and contemporarily with the conquest of Peru, it was well known to Western navigators, cartographers, chroniclers, and adventurers for over two centuries before it was opened to them.

References

Baegert, Juan Jacobo
  1942 *Noticias de la Península Americana de California*. José Porrúa, México.
Barco, Miguel del
  1973 *Historia Natural y Crónica de la Antigua California*. Edited by Miguel León-Portilla. Universidad Nacional Autónoma de México, México.
Bravo, Jaime
  1970 *Testimonios Sudcalifornianos*. Edited by Miguel León-Portilla. Universidad Nacional Autónoma de México, México.
Hakluyt, Richard
  1904 *The Principal Voyages, Traffiques, and Discoveries of the English Nation*, vol. IX. James MacLehose and Sons, Glasgow.
León-Portilla, Miguel
  1976 Sobre la Lengua pericú de la Baja California. *Anales de Antropología* 13:87–101.
Massey, William C.
  1949 Tribes and Languages of Baja California. *Southwestern Journal of Anthropology* 5:272–307.
Mathes, W. Michael
  1965 *Californiana I: Documentos para la Historia de la Demarcación Comercial de California, 1583–1632*. José Porrúa Turanzas, Madrid.
  1968 *Sebastián Vizcaíno and Spanish Expansion in the Pacific Ocean, 1580–1630*. California Historical Society, San Francisco.
  1970 *Californiana II; Documentos para la Historia de la Explotación Comercial de California, 1611–1679*. José Porrúa Turnazas, Madrid.

1974a *Californiana III: Documentos para la Historia de la Transformación Colonizadora de California, 1679–1686.* José Porrúa Turanzas, Madrid.

1974b A Case of Idolatry among the Cochimí. *The Masterkey* 48:98–107.

1975 Some New Observations Relative to the Indigenous Inhabitants of La Paz, Baja California Sur. *Journal of California Anthropology* 2:180–182.

1981 Problems of Ethnohistorical Research in Baja California. *Journal of California and Great Basin Anthropology* 3:44–48.

1984 Población Indigena de California. In *Memoria VI, VII y VIII Semanas de Información Histórica de Baja California Sur*, pp. 29–34. Gobierno de Baja California Sur, La Paz.

Píccolo, Francisco María

1962 *Informe del Estado de la Nueva Cristiandad de California, 1702.* Edited by Ernest J. Burrus. José Porrúa Turanzas, Madrid.

Reygadas, Fermín, and Guillermo Velázquez Ramírez

1985 Investigación arqueológica reciente en los municipios de La Paz y Los Cabos. In *Memoria VI, VII y VIII Semanas de Información Histórica de Baja California Sur*, pp. 97–118. Gobierno de Baja California Sur, La Paz.

Salvatierra, Juan María de

1971 *Juan María de Salvatierra, S. J.: Selected Letters about Lower California.* Edited by Ernest J. Burrus. Dawson's Book Shop, Los Angeles.

Taraval, Sigismundo

1931 *The Indian Uprising in Lower California.* Translated by Marguerite E. Wilbur. Quivira Society, Los Angeles.

Venegas, Miguel

1979 Obras Californianas del Padre Miguel Venegas, S. J. 5 vols. Edited by W. Michael Mathes, Vivian C. Fisher, and E. Moisés Coronado. Universidad Autónoma de Baja California Sur, La Paz.

Wagner, Henry R.

1929 *Spanish Voyages to the Northwest Coast of America in the Sixteenth Century.* California Historical Society, San Francisco.

Chapter 26 ■

David Hornbeck

Economic Growth and Change at the Missions of Alta California, 1769–1846

For more than a century, the California missions have received considerable attention in both popular and scholarly books and in journals. Much of this literature is based on romantic and rather exaggerated notions of mission society that have created numerous stereotypes and misconceptions about the California missions. The most common are the following two contrasting stereotypes: (a) missions were ruthless institutions constructed and maintained for the express purpose of enslaving the Indians, and (b) missions were benevolent institutions in which the Indian and padre lived in harmony, tranquility, and peace. Probably the most widely held misconception that has found its way into both grammar school books and college texts is that the missions were deliberately located one day's journey apart to assist travelers moving up and down the California coast. In truth, missions were located in areas containing large numbers of Indians, particularly in close proximity to water, building materials, and potentially irrigable land.

Scholarly attention, however, has focused on more concrete aspects of mission growth and decline, particularly social and cultural concerns, and only a few scholars have considered the economic structure of missions (see Archibald

1978; Francis 1976). In the absence of accurate details from specific economic studies, the popular view of the mission economy has become, to a large extent, the accepted view. This view usually pictures benevolent missionaries and Indians living an arcadian existence in splendid isolation with few economic pressures, all of which changed abruptly when land-hungry ex-soldiers despoiled the missions and grabbed mission-Indian property (Hornbeck 1986).

Most scholars look at the economic base of the missions in terms of the prescribed legal and social role of the Indians, rather than seeing the overall mission as a dynamic institution. The mission system of the 1830s was a completely different social and economic system than it was during the 1780s. Through time its function on the frontier had changed as had its relationships with the Indian, civilian, and military populations. The specific functional changes are difficult to identify because we seldom focus our attention on change within the system; rather, we tend to confine our analysis to the specifics of one mission, treating our findings as unique to that mission. We tend not to generalize in our attempts to understand the California missions and their socioeconomic relationships. Thus, we have no conceptual framework or general overview upon which to drape our detailed analysis; as academics, we provide our readers with long lists of facts about specific missions, leaving popular views to guide our reader's interpretations. This essay provides a framework for future research in this direction by suggesting four elements that formed the basis of economic change in the mission, proposing a graphic synthesis of mission economic growth and change, and identifying a major reason for the changes in the economic structure of the California missions.

The Basis of Economic Change

Figure 26-1 depicts a simplified view of economic development and change. Four elements are said to affect mission development: population characteristics, cultural attributes, technology, and resources. A simple flowchart using directional arrows shows the cause and effect links. Population characteristics are intimately tied to mission growth in that the changing composition of the population and

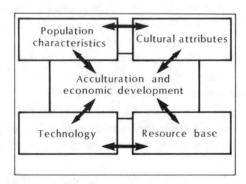

Figure 26-1. The major factors affecting mission growth in Alta California.

the rate of demographic growth determine the course of development of the mission and its growth pattern. Linked with population characteristics by a two-way arrow are cultural attributes. The effects on mission growth here, though not often emphasized, are profound, especially during early settlement. Cultural attributes include the social, cultural, political, and economic organization of both Indian and Spanish societies. The contact and conflict between the two contrasting value systems and the resolution of differences between the two can either facilitate or hinder development.

At the bottom of Figure 26-1 are technology and resources, which form an integral part of mission development. Technology, its application, and use dictate how and what resources will be exploited for growth. Resources, on the other hand, are not constant from place to place and are defined according to the level of technology available. Resources can be both physical and human.

In sum, the economic development of and change in the mission system can be viewed as a complex network of causes and effects through time. Indeed, the elements identified here are interlinked in such a complex fashion that it is difficult to place them in specific categories or combinations without a better understanding of how the mission system worked internally. If we cannot fully understand how the missions functioned, at least we know that the elements discussed here are highly interrelated, that each mission had particular combinations of investments in each element, and that these established the conditions for development. As acculturation institutions, the missions emphasized growth and development through mediating cultural attributes and population. As economic institutions, the missions necessarily emphasized technology and the exploitation of resources, which included the Indians themselves.

A Synthesis of Mission Economic Growth and Change

At the outset of Spanish settlement in California, missions were not considered economic entities. Rather, they were viewed as acculturation institutions supported by the church and government. Missions were founded to convert, protect, and civilize the California Indians, aiming to produce loyal Spanish subjects who would populate the California frontier (Engelhardt 1930). Thus, the missions were frontier institutions organized to resettle Indians into compact units that were to be forged into a community organization based on religion and supervised by Franciscan missionaries. Directed cultural change through demonstration, persuasion, and force (if necessary) was the primary objective of each mission (Cook 1976a; Guest 1979).

In the Spanish government's strategy to colonize California, the missions were given two important economic assets: free access to as much land as was necessary to support the mission Indian, and the free use of mission Indians as laborers. These two assets formed the basis of the mission economy and enabled the mission to produce surplus (agricultural and manufactured) products for use beyond its basic subsistence requirements. The production of surpluses became an integral part of a mission's success in its acculturation efforts; surplus allowed it to increase the number of neophytes. With careful planning, plentiful resources, and free labor, mission production increased rapidly to the point that the surplus could not be consumed entirely within the mission system and the missionaries began to seek outside markets. Eventually the missions came to dominate all aspects of California's economy—something they were never intended to do.

Figure 26-2 presents a bell-shaped curve that describes change in the mission system between 1769 and 1836. The graph can be read at different levels: It shows three stages of growth and change, as well as individual social, economic, and geographical elements that changed through time. The left side can be described as a period of growth in which the mission system underwent three significant changes. At the outset there were a few missions struggling for survival, attempting to establish an organized and permanent foundation. During the first 20 years, the missions were able to establish an agricultural base, acquire technical skills, develop the ability to work within environmental constraints, and understand the diversity of the California Indian culture. In overcoming many of the difficult problems associated with initial settlement, the missions entered upon a rapid growth phase, in which the mission system was able to increase both the number of converts and agricultural output and rapidly expand along the California coast. Each phase of the growth and development side of the curve represents a different emphasis on population, cultural attributes, technology, or resources, which in turn affects a mission's organization, operation, and production. It might be said that much of the emphasis during growth and development was on population and cultural attributes. The left side of the curve, then, portrays the mission as a rapidly expanding system, focusing on managing population and mediating cultural attributes as it moved toward its goal, which was to acculturate the California Indian.

The middle part of the curve reflects a slower rate of growth. As growth slowed, the missions underwent a subtle transition—they began to shift their emphasis from acculturating Indians to producing surpluses for use outside the mission. Most important in this transition was the decline in the rate of conver-

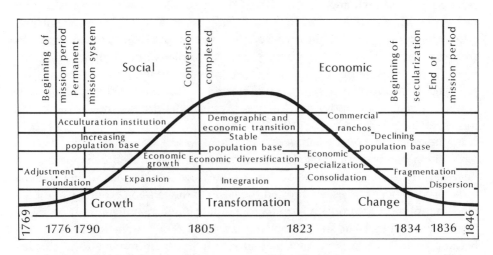

Figure 26-2. How mission economic development changed through time.

sion and the continuing high death rate. Thus the missions were left with a constant population based on internal births rather than external converts. That the overall mission population continued to grow slowly until the early 1820s was due to the number of missions added to the system in the later years. The increasing demands made on the missions from the civilian and military population for both agricultural and manufactured products meant that they had to devote a significant part of their labor force to producing for outside demand. Thus, the mission system underwent both a demographic and an economic transition at the same time, as more and more emphasis was placed on the use of technology and the identification of new resources, rather than on recruiting Indians or expanding the mission system into other areas.

The right side of the curve represents a decline in population followed by secularization and an attempt to preserve mission life into the 1840s in some areas. Emphasis shifted to the use of technology and resources. With commercial opportunities from the hide and tallow trade on the rise, the missions began to allocate more and more of their labor force to satisfy commercial livestock opportunities. During the 1820s, the missions completed their transition from social to commercial institutions. Social and economic roles among the neophytes and between neophytes and mission administrators necessarily changed. Those missions with access to resources (both physical and human) were able to maintain themselves. Because of the variations in mission resources, there was differential regional growth, and thus wealth became concentrated in a few missions. During these years few new expansion projects were initiated and labor was allocated to maintain existing facilities. Thus, the mission system was able to persist during a period of declining population because it no longer needed a large labor force either to maintain itself or to engage in commercial livestock production.

This situation began to change in 1834. Commercial success and the civilian population's growing demand for access to land and resources led to the secularization and eventual collapse of the mission system. With the loss of land and labor, the social infrastructure so carefully nurtured by the missionaries floundered. Indians, the primary mission resource, scattered. After 1836, there were attempts to continue the missions with civilian administrators, who attempted to carry on using Indian labor. A few Indians did remain at each mission, attempting to preserve the only way of life they knew.

During the early years of Spanish settlement in Alta California, 1766–1775, the missions experienced great difficulty in establishing a firm agricultural base (Hornbeck 1985). Without fully understanding California's environment, especially its climate, the Spanish founded missions at locations inappropriate for agriculture. As a result, initial harvests were poor and few Indian converts were attracted to the missions. Agriculture was a tenuous year-to-year gamble, and without government aid the missions would have failed. The missions had their first successful harvest in 1774, but it was not until 1776 that they began to overcome some of the early environmental difficulties and that harvests were sufficient to carry any of them through at least one year.

The main problem facing the missionaries between 1776 and 1790 was how to generate enough agricultural surplus to encourage new Indians to come into and remain at the missions, and thereby increase the mission's labor force. The missionaries realized that agriculture depended upon available labor and that available labor depended upon agricultural surpluses. Therefore, throughout the 1770s and well into the 1780s, the missionaries' main concern was to balance labor and agriculture. Available surpluses were allocated to establishing a firm agricultural base; by 1785–1790 mission crops had been expanded and yields had increased sufficiently so that labor could be diverted to other mission tasks.

In 1790, at the insistence of the missionaries, the government sent skilled artisans to California to teach the mission Indians various trades. Between 1790 and 1805, the missions, with skilled and newly trained labor at hand, were able to make substantial gains in constructing mission buildings, increasing agricultural production, and producing basic manufactured goods. A small trade had developed with Mexico by the mid-1780s, with missions sending agricultural produce in return for manufactured goods, luxury items, and religious items (Archibald 1978). High transportation costs and high prices in Mexico made the trade unprofitable for the missions. To compensate, the missions began to trade some of their surplus to the military. The military found mission products cheaper than those shipped from Mexico. Through a complicated arrangement, missions exchanged goods for military warrants that were redeemable in Mexico or bartered for goods at the presidial store. After 1790, the military became the missions' major trading partner. Through trade with the missions, the military was relieved from purchasing food supplies in Mexico and having them shipped to California. The items that the military had shipped to California were typically those most frequently in demand by the missions. In trading with the military, the missions found themselves at a disadvantage: they had to sell low through military warrants and to buy high in Mexico, or they had to barter their products with the military directly at low prices, in return for high-priced goods (Mosk 1938). However, labor was free and in ample supply, so the actual loss to the missions was marginal.

Trade outside the Spanish empire was forbidden, but in isolated California, trade regulations were difficult to enforce. Missions with surpluses found it easy to supply an occasional passing ship in return for needed manufactured goods. Although the opportunities for this sort of smuggling were not numerous during this period, they were available, and the missionaries were not deterred by conviction of law.

Between 1790 and 1805, the missions were thus able to dispose of their surplus production through a number of outlets in exchange for items that would improve agriculture and expand basic manufacturing. As a result, irrigation systems were started and completed, new crops introduced, better agricultural equipment purchased, new buildings added, and more tools and equipment purchased for manufacturing enterprises. For most of the missions, economic expansion was accompanied by an increase in the number of Indian workers (Hornbeck 1983:46–49).

Between 1805 and 1823, the mission economy involuntarily entered a new phase in its development. The Mexican revolution was in progress and all trade and government support for California was cut off. The now isolated civilian and military population turned almost exclusively to the missions for support, and within a few years all of Hispanic California was dependent upon mission surpluses. The military continued to purchase items from the missions and pay in warrants that were never to be collected. The civilian population also came to depend on mission manufactured products and Indian labor. By 1815, the missions were the sole support of Spain's scheme to colonize its northern frontier.

The new economic pressures forced upon the missions led to an increase in mission smuggling and, to some degree, specialization in manufactured goods. Mission surpluses began to find their way aboard an increasing number of foreign vessels in exchange for cash or for goods that were used either at the missions or traded to the military. As the demand increased, many of the missions began taking advantage of local resources and unique mission Indian skills by specializing their production: some in grain crops, others in leather goods, blankets, or garments. By the end of Spanish rule in 1822, the California missions were playing the dual role of acculturating the Indians and satisfying the economic needs of frontier California. Out of necessity, missionaries had become farmers, manufacturers, and traders. The economic success of the missions and, in turn, the success of Spanish colonization of California, thus came to rest entirely on the use of neophyte Indian labor to produce surpluses.

California fared much better under the more liberal economic policies of Mexico, at least until 1834. Beginning in 1823, the authorities opened California to legitimate foreign trade and encouraged new colonization by making land available to individual settlers. Although a less isolated and less restrictive atmosphere prevailed in California after 1822, the missions continued to dominate economic affairs, but only for a short time. The basic ingredients of mission economic success had been free labor and access to land; after 1821 the missions began to lose population rapidly and their claim to vast areas of land was challenged by an increasing civilian population.

The first step the missions took that would begin their economic decline was, surprisingly enough, to engage in open commercial trade. In 1823, when the missions were allowed to trade freely, they contracted with a trading company to take all of their hides and tallow in exchange for manufactured goods. What has come to be known as the hide and tallow trade brought to California a wide assortment of luxury and manufactured goods that ranged from pots and pans to lace curtains. With their vast herds of cattle, the missionaries were able to supply large quantities of hides and tallow, thus encouraging trading houses in England and the United States to engage in the California trade. By 1830, much of the missions' surplus production was allocated to increasing their livestock herds for the hide and tallow trade instead of attempting to stem the decline of the neophyte population. Missions were rapidly shifting from agrarian self-sufficient communities to commercial farms that were land extensive and labor short. To satisfy the economic needs of California after 1810, the missions had expanded their ability to produce surplus but had not expanded their labor base. Participation in commercial trade provided the needed manufactured goods, but at the same time required fewer labor inputs. Thus, the missions, with a declining labor base, continued to produce surpluses, which, in turn, were reinvested in the form of livestock, which required less labor inputs than the production of surplus agriculture.

The commercial success of the missions brought them under the scrutiny of the growing civilian population. The missions held vast areas of land in trust for the neophytes, making Mexico's liberal land tenure laws almost meaningless in California. Without land to graze cattle, most civilians were removed from participating in the lucrative hide and tallow trade. Removal of the missions was the only way the civilian population could share in California's newfound wealth. As a result of political pressure on the liberal Mexican congress, the missions were secularized between 1834 and 1836, and almost six million acres of prime agricultural and grazing land along the California coast were released. After secularization, the missions were quickly replaced by civilian ranchos granted by Mexico. The rancho, the last Hispanic frontier institution in California, like the mission, came to dominate the California landscape by controlling large grants of land and by using ex-neophyte Indians as free labor.

Between 1836 and 1846, the mission system underwent a significant change. Because the missions were the major prop to California's economy, the government could not allow them to completely disintegrate. At the outset of secularization, missions were placed under administrators whose duty it was to maintain mission production and to encourage Indians to remain as wage laborers. The administrator system did not fare well because mission land, livestock, and labor were quickly appropriated by the civilian population. Next, the government attempted to lease the missions, but this scheme also failed. By 1842, the economy had improved and the California government, always in need of money, sold to the highest bidders the few missions that had yet to be fragmented into ranchos. A few Indians remained at only a few missions, notably those in Southern California, eking out a subsistence.

Surplus Labor

Figure 26-2 is a heuristic device for understanding mission growth, development, and change; it provides a graphic view of economic growth and change in the California missions, but does not identify how the missions were able to move from a social to an economic institution. If the change identified in Figure 26-2 is measured by the amount of Indian labor allocated to various mission tasks, then Figure 26-3 provides a view of how missions were able to change without significantly altering their structure.

Figure 26-3 illustrates in a general way how surpluses were allocated through time and their overall impact on the mission system. Without more detailed analyses of the mission economy, it is impossible to attempt a more complete synthesis of mission Indian labor. Thus, Figure 26-3 is an exploratory survey and is presented as a working hypothesis of how the basic mission economy operated. The hypothesis is based on an economic variable common to all mis-

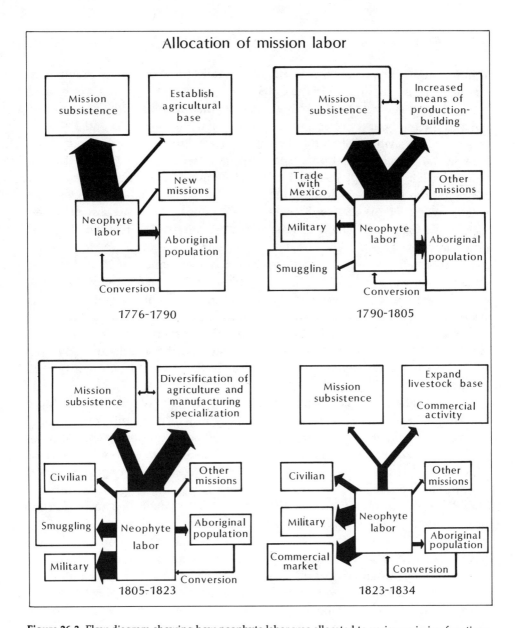

Figure 26-3. Flow diagram showing how neophyte labor was allocated to various mission functions.

sions and one that was instrumental in shaping mission economic policies: surpluses arising from Indian labor. Initially these surpluses were allocated to the task of encouraging more Indians to come into the missions, but later they were allocated to economic endeavors that supported the mission as a commercial enterprise. The allocation of surpluses was an important factor that led to economic growth and prosperity and also gave rise to the conditions that eventually led to secularization.

Conclusion

Although romantic images are colorful, they reflect few of the conditions that stimulated economic change in the California missions. The diagrams presented in this chapter allow us to differentiate distinct time periods in the mission system and thus to treat it not as a continuous system between 1769 and 1846, but rather as an evolving system that began as an acculturation institution and developed into a commercial one. The mission system was able to persist and maintain itself long after its social role had diminished by shifting to another role using the same labor, capital inputs, and social foundation. The left side of the curve in Figure 26-3 is the side we study most often and associate with missions in California. The mission system, as we normally read about it, extends only from 1769 to 1805, possibly as late as 1815. Although we have considerable information about the California missions throughout their history, we usually associate them, and the data we gather, with the early years. The early and middle phases have received the bulk of mission analysis, but little effort has been devoted to assessing the mission as it evolved from an acculturation institution into a commercial institution, the right side of the curve. We need to view the mission not as the entity that played that romantic or early role, but as one that underwent considerable change throughout its 65-year term in California.

This overview of the California mission economy is only a beginning. More detailed analysis is needed to unravel the way in which the mission economy functioned. The first step toward this goal would be to investigate the socioeconomic organization of the mission, because much of the economic success achieved by the missions was dependent upon the nature, organization, and use of Indian labor. Thus, we need to know many more things about mission labor: What was the daily work regime and how was it established and enforced? Was there an extensive division of labor, and, if so, how did it work? Did the missionaries view Indian labor as a social or economic function of the mission? How much labor was necessary to operate the mission and how much was diverted to other, nonmission projects? How much Indian labor was exploited? Answers to these questions will lead to a better understanding of the origin, value, and use of surplus labor and of how the missions were able to use Indian labor to dominate California's economic development for more than 50 years.

In addition to questions relating to labor, there are a host of basic economic questions to be posed and answered. Perhaps the most significant of these is, How were the missions able to make the transition from an acculturation institution to a commercial livestock system without undergoing significant reorganization? How did access to regional and local resources affect economic development? To what extent did management skills and technology affect economic growth?

This chapter has offered some ideas on how the mission economy worked, but what is written here should be considered only a small part of the total picture. It is important that other, more detailed studies be conducted on the overall mission economy in order to reduce our dependency on stereotypes and popular impressions.

Acknowledgments

I would like to thank Virginia Oliver and Victor Konrad for their assistance in reading an earlier version of this chapter, and Dennis Coady for his cartography.

References

Archibald, Robert
    1978 *The Economic Aspects of the California Missions.* Academy of American Franciscan History, Washington, D.C.

Bannon, John Francis
    1979 The Mission as a Frontier Institution: Sixty Years of Interest and Research. *Western Historical Quarterly* 10 (3).

Cook, Sherburne F.
    1962 Expeditions to the Interior of California's Central Valley, 1820–1840. *University of California Anthropological Records*, Berkeley 2 (5).
    1976a *The Conflict between the California Indians and White Civilization.* University of California Press, Berkeley.
    1976b *The Population of the California Indians, 1769–1970.* University of California Press, Berkeley.

Cook, Sherburne F., and Woodrow Borah
    1979 Mission Registers as Sources of Vital Statistics: Eight Missions of Northern California. In *Essays in Population History: Mexico and California*, vol. 3. University of California Press, Berkeley.

Engelhardt, Zephyrin
    1930 *Missions and Missionaries of California*, vols I and II. 2nd ed., Santa Barbara.

Francis, Jessie Davis
    1976 *An Economic and Social History of Mexican California.* Arno Press, New York.

Guest, Francis F.O.F.M.
    1979 An Examination of the Thesis of S. F. Cook on the Forced Conversion of Indians in the California Missions. *Southern California Quarterly* 61(1).

Hornbeck, David
    1978 Land Tenure and Rancho Expansion in Alta California. *Journal of Historical Geography.* December.
    1983 *California Patterns: A Geographical and Historical Atlas.* Mayfield, Palo Alto.
    1985 Early Mission Settlement. In *Some Reminiscences about Fray Junipero Serra*, edited by Francis F. Weber, Kimberly Press, Santa Barbara.
    1986 California Rancheros and the Unlanded—Who Lived in Arcadia? In *Early California Reflections.* San Juan Capistrano Regional Library.

Meighan, Clement
    1987 Indians and California Missions. *Southern California Quarterly* 49.

Mosk, Sanford A.
    1938 Price Fixing in Spanish California. *California Historical Quarterly* 37.

Servin, Manual P.
    1965 The Secularization of the California Missions: A Reappraisal. *Southern California Quarterly* 47.

Chapter 27 ■

Julia G. Costello

Variability among the Alta California Missions: The Economics of Agricultural Production

Between 1769 and 1823, 21 Franciscan missions were established along the coast of Alta California. The first few missions were spread out over the littoral and gradually others filled in areas between them. Four presidios were interspersed to provide military support and to enforce the laws of Spain. Three pueblos were also established to encourage civilian emigration, although these institutions were never very successful.

The chain of missions, physically remote from New Spain is traditionally treated as one cohesive political and economic entity. External influences such as changes in colonial policies, government, and international trading conditions were uniformly felt throughout Alta California. The mission system also underwent changes as it developed into a mature colonial institution (Hornbeck, this volume). These changes have been observed in rates of conversion (baptism), births, and deaths and livestock and crop production (Cook 1979; Johnson, this volume). The character of California mission life as a whole has therefore changed over time as a result of external factors and systemwide development (Table 27-1).

Much of the archaeological research on mission sites has been concerned with

Table 27-1. Phases of Mission Development in Alta California

Adjustment (1769–1776)
The earliest missions were not supplied with regular economic support beyond their initial founding, so that times were difficult for the six early missions.

Foundation (1776–1790)
Policies were readjusted and regular support was established for the missions; they began to produce reliable food supplies and to attract converts. Five new missions were established.

Expansion (1790–1805)
Nearly all the physical and geographic development of the missions was completed: All the missions but two were founded; most major building programs were completed; all major industries and technologies were established; and mission populations steadily increased.

Integration (1805–1823)
Spanish support and control were diverted by the Mexican War of Independence, and Alta California operated as an independent and self-sufficient entity. Most missions attained their largest populations and greatest production in this period. The final two missions were founded in 1817 and 1823.

Specialization (1823–1834)
The new Mexican government lifted restrictive Spanish trade regulations; foreign commercial ships increased their visits, and hides and tallow were traded for manufactured goods. Indian populations declined.

Fragmentation (1834–1836)
Missions were secularized and their lands leased to private managers; the cohesiveness of the California mission system was destroyed. Allocation of ranchos to the growing Hispanic population increased.

Dispersion (1836–1846)
Mission lands were rapidly sold as private ranchos. Indians dispersed to work as laborers on ranchos or in pueblos, or returned to native areas in the interior. The Hispanic period ended when the new U.S. government took control.

interactions between different social groups, cultural continuity and adaptation, economic activities, technological adaptations, and living conditions at the mission. Because of the external changes and internal development that affected the missions, answers to these questions will vary according to which phase of the mission system is being addressed.

It is also likely that internal, local variables at individual missions influenced their social, cultural, and economic responses within these historical phases. In order to bring the reality of the past into sharper focus and to improve the interpretation of data at specific sites, it is important to determine how individual missions compare with each other in their adherence to, or deviation from, general patterns.

Measuring Variability

This study is a modest attempt to test the waters of this inquiry: How variable were conditions between individual missions? What was the range of mission response to major external changes that affected Alta California?

The data chosen for analysis are livestock and crop production statistics from the annual reports that each mission was required to submit between 1783 and 1831 (Engelhardt 1915:535) and population records as derived from mission baptismal registers. The agricultural statistics reflect the quantity of food produced at the missions, and the population figures indicate the numbers of people involved in production and consumption. By comparing the two, we can obtain an indication of the relative economic success of individual missions as well as some measure of the quality of life as reflected in the abundance of food resources.

Admittedly, there are some problems with these statistics. The harvest sizes and numbers of livestock reported by the Franciscans may have been misrepresented. In addition, some clerics apparently enumerated livestock down to single animals, whereas others rounded herds off to the nearest ten, hundred, or thousand. Reports of the number of range animals, particularly in the case of cattle and sheep, which grew to enormous holdings at each mission, must certainly be an approximation.

It is also known that mission agricultural production was supplemented by traditional food gathering activities of the Indians. The amount contributed to the mission larders through these practices was not recorded, but is thought to have been about 10 percent of the mission diet (Cook 1976:47). Archaeological investigations have revealed the presence of some native plants and animals from mission contexts, although only in small quantities (Walker et al., this volume).

Even with these reservations, an analysis of agricultural and population statistics should provide significant comparative information on agricultural production at missions. Problems with possible falsification of production reports or inaccuracies in livestock enumeration were likely prevalent to the same degree at all missions and should not greatly affect relative statistics. It is also significant that the missions experienced no economic repercussions from reporting either larger or smaller production, which might have led some to alter their annual reports. The degree to which mission food resources were supplemented by traditional gathering and hunting appears to be minor and certainly would have varied over the life of an individual mission and according to periodic shortages.

Original records of agricultural and population statistics have survived in various repositories in California, although they are not readily accessible, except for the copies made by Fr. Zephyrin Engelhardt, O.F.M., for his series of books on 16 of the 21 California missions. These published statistics were used in the present analysis (see Engelhardt 1920, 1921, 1922, 1923, 1924, 1927, 1929a, 1929b, 1929c, 1930, 1931, 1932a, 1932b, 1963, 1973a, 1973b). Although some clerical errors have been noted in Engelhardt's figures (Hornbeck, personal communication) they are relatively minor and should not appreciably affect results of the present analysis.

This study of variability in agricultural production between the California missions is organized around the presidio districts. Each mission in California was associated with one of four presidio districts (see Figure 19-3), which defined geographic, economic, military, and political subsystems within the colony. The districts are spread along the north-south Pacific coast and are therefore also convenient groupings from which to compare the effect of variations in California's climate on agricultural production. Three presidio districts—San Diego, Santa Bárbara, and Monterey—are compared (the northernmost district, San Francisco, is not examined as statistics were only available for one of its missions). The Santa Bárbara district is then examined closely in an effort to identify the economic patterns of its five missions.

Methods of Analysis

Measuring Agricultural Production

To normalize production statistics for each mission, I divided total annual volume of crops harvested and total annual livestock numbers by the size of each mission's population. The resulting figures represent annual per capita production and indicate the relative abundance of food resources and therefore the ability of the missions to feed its inhabitants or trade in surplus foodstuffs.

Annual crop production per capita (Table 27-2) is based on the total number of fanegas (1 fanega = 1.57 bushels) reported for the major crops of wheat and corn plus the minor crops of barley, beans, and peas. Annual livestock production per capita figures (Table 27-3) reflect total mission animal holdings dominated by sheep and cattle with horses, goats, mules, and pigs in decreasing quantities. These two annual production figures reveal how much food was theoretically available to each person at a specific mission.

Crop statistics are further analyzed by comparing the reported annual amount harvested to that sown. Whereas the annual crop production per capita ratio measures how much food was actually produced per inhabitant, the harvest-to-sown ratio indicates how successful farming efforts were each year (Table 27-4). Another useful agricultural statistic is the quantity sown each year divided by the current population to give per capita sown (Table 27-5). Although harvests

Table 27-2. Average Annual Mission Production of Crops Per Capita (in fanegas)

Years averaged	Presidio district			District mission average
	San Diego	Santa Bárbara	Monterey	
1784–1790	2.4	3.1	2.4	2.5
1791–1800	3.6	3.3	2.5	3.1
1801–1805	3.7	3.7	3.2	3.5
1806–1811	3.8	3.3	2.9	3.3
1812–1817	3.5	4.8	2.7	3.7
1818–1823	3.7	4.2	3.8	3.9
1824–1827	2.1	3.0	3.4	2.8
1828–1832	2.1	2.4	2.1	2.2
Average	3.1	3.5	2.9	3.1

Note: 1 fanega = 1.57 bushels.

Table 27-3. Average Annual Mission Livestock Per Capita

Years averaged	Presidio district			District mission average
	San Diego	Santa Bárbara	Monterey	
1784–1790	6	3	4	4
1791–1800	12	7	8	9
1801–1805	15	10	10	12
1806–1811	16	14	17	16
1812–1817	14	19	22	18
1818–1823	18	21	25	21
1824–1827	15	15	22	17
1828–1832	20	20	24	21
Average	15	14	17	15

Table 27-4. Average Annual Mission Harvested-to-Sown Ratio

Years averaged	Presidio district			District mission average
	San Diego	Santa Bárbara	Monterey	
1784–1790	29	32	23	28
1791–1800	27	27	13	22
1801–1805	21	25	19	22
1806–1811	22	22	15	20
1812–1817	20	29	15	21
1818–1823	40	19	17	25
1824–1827	10	13	13	12
1828–1832	12	14	9	12
Average	23	23	16	20

Table 27-5. Average Annual Per Capita Sown per Mission

Years averaged	Presidio district			District mission average
	San Diego	Santa Bárbara	Monterey	
1784–1790	.10	.13	.11	.12
1791–1800	.14	.14	.19	.18
1801–1805	.18	.14	.18	.18
1806–1811	.18	.17	.21	.20
1812–1817	.20	.18	.19	.20
1818–1823	.17	.24	.24	.23
1824–1827	.23	.22	.29	.27
1828–1832	.20	.19	.25	.23
Average	.17	.18	.21	.19

depend on numerous factors throughout the growing season, the per capita sown ratio reveals how much the mission *intended* to increase or decrease its agricultural production each year. Because numerous factors influence harvests, crop production values tend to fluctuate much more than livestock statistics, which are not as greatly affected by annual vicissitudes of climate, pestilence, or other critical factors.

Variables of Change

A basic premise in analyzing variability within the California missions is that they were uniformly affected by external factors. For this analysis, the external forces of change are described in identified phases of California mission history (see Table 27-1) and consist of political, economic, demographic, and geographic factors that affected the entire colony (see Hornbeck, this volume).

Differences in mission response to these external factors can be attributed to the influence of internal, local variables. General categories of these internal variables and their potential influence are discussed below.

Ecological. A number of ecological variables may affect livestock and crop production: quality of arable land, quality of available pasture, availability of water, rainfall, and length of the growing season. The first three of these were generally controlled for in the establishment of the missions. That is, sites were chosen for their proximity to agricultural land and year-round water sources, and all missions constructed complex and efficient aqueduct systems to maximize surface-water collection.

Some differences exist in the climate along the coast and should be reflected in mission production statistics. Missions north of the Transverse Ranges (north of Los Angeles) have warm Mediterranean summer climates, and rainfall increases from 14 to 20 inches annually from south to north. Below the Transverse Ranges, the San Diego Presidio district has a semiarid steppe climate with annual rainfall of about 9 inches and the smallest annual surface water runoff (Kahrl 1978). The length of the growing season decreases from south to north, which may reduce the northern missions' advantage of greater rainfall.

Episodic weather conditions such as droughts or abundant rainfall certainly affected mission production. These regional variations should influence production statistics over a larger geographic area and thus should be distinguishable from individual mission performances.

Geographical. Geographical variables such as proximity to roads, coastal ports, and other missions are not likely to account for differences in mission production. All the missions in California were linked by El Camino Real, and by the end of the eighteenth century had neighboring institutions. All missions also had a coastal port within their jurisdiction, although some of these ports were more accessible than others.

Some significant effects may result from the proximity of individual missions to presidios and pueblos. Although proximity of governmental support may have been an asset during the early phases, in later years civil populations increasingly drew on mission livestock, crops, labor, and land. By 1815, after the termination of supply ships from New Spain, missions provided for the entire economic support of presidios and pueblos.

Relocation of mission sites, commonly done for economic reasons, may be associated with increases in agricultural production.

Local Historical. Agricultural production may also have been affected by certain aspects of local history at each mission, such as time of founding, characteristics of the Indian groups missionized, leadership of the padres, participation in the hide and tallow trade, and the granting of ranchos.

The rate of initial economic success of each mission is expected to be affected by the relation of its founding date to overall California mission development (Hornbeck 1983:46–47). Relatively slow initial periods of growth and low agricultural and livestock production ratios are expected for the earliest missions, while those founded later should have benefited from the overall strength of the system.

The extent to which each mission chose to participate in the lucrative hide and tallow trade (1823–1834) was presumably a decision of the resident padres. Increased participation should be reflected by a sudden drop in livestock statistics. It is expected that those with the largest herds, and largest per capita ratios, would be the most enthusiastic participants.

The rate at which mission lands were parceled off into private ranchos may be correlated with a drop in agricultural production. Eighteen private ranchos were established under Spanish rule and Mexico granted thirteen more between 1822 and 1831 (Avina 1973; Beck and Haase 1974).

Although there was certainly some variation among tribal groups in Spanish California, measurable variables that might have affected the economic success of missions they resided at were not identified. Similarly, the personal leadership and administrative qualities of Franciscan fathers would certainly have influenced their mission economies. This factor, which is difficult to quantify, also was not addressed.

General Agricultural Production Trends

Throughout Alta California, crop production for missions founded prior to 1776 had the worst per capita crop production rates of the entire Mission period, certainly a result of the lack of governmental support and problems inherent in starting farming enterprises in a new geographic area. Missions founded after 1776 began with much higher per capita crop production rates, because agricultural techniques were being refined, Spanish ships provided needed supplies and help was available from already established missions. By 1790, per capita crop production reached stable values, which continued to rise gently until about 1823 (Table 27-2). The period from 1823 to 1834 saw a drop in per capita crop production throughout California; the largest number of single worst years for individual missions occurred in this time period.

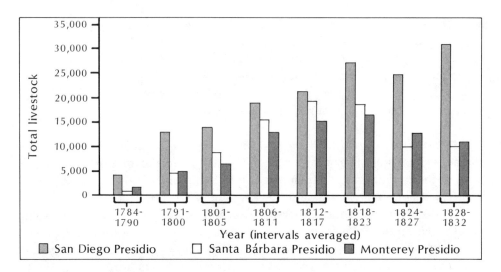

Figure 27-1. Total mission livestock averaged by Alta California presidio district.

This major drop in crop production is also reflected in the harvest-to-sown ratios, which drop markedly after 1823 (see Table 27-4), breaking a pattern of relative stability that had prevailed since at least 1784. The drop is particularly significant as the quantity sown during this same period increased markedly (see Table 27-5). Since this pattern seems to prevail throughout the colony, it may be due to some major climactic change. Alternatively, the drop in crop production could be associated with the introduction of new economic opportunities in exporting cattle hides and tallow and a corresponding shift in the allocation of mission labor away from tending planted crops.

Livestock holdings and per capita livestock ratios showed steady increases from the earliest years of the California missions until 1823 (see Table 27-3). Unlike per capita crop production, which began high at missions later founded, initial per capita livestock figures begin low for each mission; livestock holdings apparently had to be built up at each institution from similar, small herds. After 1823, when Alta California was opened to legal, foreign trade, total average numbers of livestock drop significantly. This probably reflects the liquidation of cattle for the production of hides and tallow. The per capita livestock ratio dropped slightly at the beginning of this period, although declining populations at the missions mitigated the depletion of herds and ratios rose by 1832.

Comparisons between Presidio Districts

Santa Bárbara and San Diego districts sowed and harvested about the same amount of crops per person, while agricultural production was lowest in the Monterey district (see Tables 27-4 and 27-5). In Monterey, a very low harvest-sown ratio required larger amounts to be sown per person. Differences in local climate may be responsible for these production variations, the shorter Monterey growing season affecting crop raising there. Poorer growing conditions required larger per capita plantings.

Some production fluctuations on a district-wide basis appear to have been caused by short-term climate variations. The San Diego district had record harvests between 1818 and 1823 that enabled them to substantially lower the amount sown each year, and the Santa Bárbara district had an excellent series of seasons between 1812 and 1817. Livestock holdings generally increased at all presidio districts from the early years to about 1823 (Figure 27-1).

The most dramatic changes in district agricultural production occurred after 1823. As already mentioned, two major changes in agricultural production correspond with the change to a Mexican government in 1821 and the legalizing of trade in hide and tallow in 1823: (1) a dramatic decline in total numbers of livestock and (2) a decline in both crop and livestock per capita ratios. The phase from 1823 to 1834 is therefore characterized by a shift toward ranching and away from agriculture; less crop resources are available per capita at the missions, although livestock per capita holdings show only a small decline in the early part of this phase.

For individual districts, there was considerable variation in this pattern (Figure 27-1). At the San Diego and Monterey districts, livestock declined an average of 2,700 and 3,200 head per mission between 1823 and 1827, respectively. For San Diego, with total herds nearly double the size of the other mission districts, this represented only a modest 9 percent loss in livestock per mission, while the Monterey district lost about 20 percent of each mission's total herds.

If these declines in livestock can be correlated with entrance into the hide and tallow trade, the Santa Bárbara Presidio district appears to have entered the new mercantile venture with remarkable enthusiasm. Not only does total livestock decline by an average of 45 percent per mission after 1823 (over 8,500 head at each mission), but there is also a small but surprising drop in livestock numbers between 1818 and 1823, which suggests early, illegal trading.

Toward the end of the this phase, between 1828 and 1832, the San Diego district is unique in showing large gains in total livestock; these gains suggest that the missions were accumulating rather than selling surpluses. Santa Bárbara district livestock numbers remained relatively stable, whereas Monterey's continued to decline. The rise in per capita livestock holdings during this time period (Table 27-3) reflects district populations that are declining faster than the livestock. In all districts, crop harvests remain poor and per capita production stabilizes only in San Diego.

Summary

The presidio districts all seem to have responded in much the same way to influences in the various historic phases until the opportunity for participation in an international hide and tallow trade was presented. Apparently the Santa Bárbara district then entered the market early and illegally, and later became the most active participant in the legal foreign trade economy. In contrast, the San Diego district's enormous livestock holdings were apparently only modestly tapped during the early years of the legal hide and tallow trade, and hardly at all in later years. The Monterey district suffered from poor crop production, probably because of its cooler climate; however, it had the largest per capita livestock holdings of any district and was a respectable participant in the legal foreign trade.

Like generalizations about the entire California mission system, this overview of activities by presidio districts will certainly be refined when their constituent missions are individually studied. That is indeed what happens when the Santa Bárbara district is scrutinized in the following section.

Missions of the Santa Bárbara Presidio District

Foundings and Populations

Prior to 1782, no missions had been established in this district; the Santa Bárbara area missed the trying times and struggles of the early years in California. Three missions were founded between 1782 and 1787: San Buenaventura, Santa Bárbara, and La Purísima. The last two missions in the district were San Fernando Rey (1797) and Santa Inés (1804). La Purísima and Santa Bárbara missions were the most populous and reached their peak populations about 1803, with 1,520 and 1,792 Indians, respectively. The other three missions reached their maximum levels between 1811 and 1816: San Fernando Rey with 1,081, San Buenaventura with 1,328, and Santa Inés with 768.

Observations on Agricultural Production

In the preceding analysis of presidio districts, the Santa Bárbara district had the highest per capita crop production average (Table 27-2). This is almost entirely accounted for by Missions Santa Inés and San Buenaventura, which had the highest crop production rankings of all the California missions (Table 27-6). The

Table 27-6. Santa Bárbara Presidio District, Average Annual Crops Per Capita

Years averaged	Missions					
	San Buenaventura	Santa Bárbara	La Purísima	San Fernando	Santa Inés	Average
1784–1790	4.3	1.7	2.9			3.0
1791–1800	4.9	2.2	2.3	4.8		3.5
1801–1805	5.0	2.7	3.0	4.3	4.8	4.0
1806–1811	3.7	2.8	2.7	3.9	3.6	3.3
1812–1817	5.2	4.2	5.0	4.0	5.8	4.8
1818–1823	4.9	2.9	4.2	3.6	5.4	4.2
1824–1827	2.3	3.3	3.4	1.6	4.4	3.0
1828–1832	3.4	1.7	3.1	1.0	3.3	2.5
Average	4.2	2.7	3.3	3.3	4.5	3.6

reasons for this high productivity cannot be due simply to geography or climate, but must be related to yet unidentified local variables.

A districtwide drop in crop production between 1806 and 1811 is due to poor harvests, which were probably a result of local climate or pestilence problems. After 1817, all missions show a major drop in their harvest-to-sown statistics. Throughout the district, missions that sowed the greatest amount of grain per person had the lowest harvested-to-sown ratios, resulting in similar production levels for all the missions.

Most of the missions evidenced regular growth in herds between 1784 and 1823 (Figure 27-2). However, San Buenaventura, distinguished for having nearly twice as many livestock as any other district mission, began losing large numbers of animals between 1818 and 1822. After 1823, all missions dropped in total numbers: San Buenaventura, San Fernando Rey, and Santa Bárbara most markedly; Santa Inés and La Purísima less so. This drop in livestock is discussed in more detail in the next section.

Santa Bárbara consistently had the lowest per capita agricultural and livestock ratios of any mission in the district. Although Santa Bárbara had average numbers of livestock, it had the highest population in the district and therefore the lowest per capita production (Figure 27-2). It is tempting to relate these poor production records to its geographical proximity to the Santa Bárbara Presidio community, which may have taxed the mission's resources. However, similar situations at other districts would have to be studied before this generalization could be justified.

The rate of crop production was excellent at Mission San Fernando Rey prior to 1823, after which it dropped to the district's lowest recorded per capita production figures (Table 27-6). The mission's per capita livestock ratio, like Santa

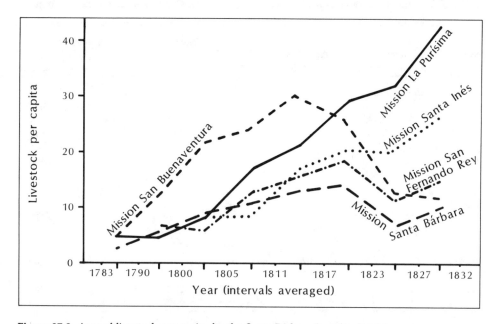

Figure 27-2. Annual livestock per capita for the Santa Bárbara Presidio district.

Bárbara's, always remained low. The answer to this livestock production may be found in the early removal of mission land for ranchos (Avina 1973). Prior to 1834, five land grants totaling over 237,000 acres had been made in the Santa Bárbara Presidio district. Four of these grants, totaling nearly 211,000 acres, were made between 1795 and 1804 and consisted of lands within the San Fernando Rey jurisdiction. The fifth grant was for over 26,000 acres in the Santa Bárbara Mission area. This removal of probably some of the best agricultural lands may have severely affected San Fernando Rey's livestock economy.

Another local historical event may account for a significant jump in production at La Purísima Mission after 1812 (Table 27-6). The mission was relocated to a new site about 5 km away from the original, which may have had both better water resources and access to agricultural lands.

Impacts of the Hide and Tallow Trade

As already mentioned, the Santa Bárbara district may have been dabbling early and illegally in the hide and tallow trade before trade restrictions were lifted in 1823. However, the district's individual mission statistics make it clear that the only early participant is Mission San Buenaventura, which shows a drop of nearly 9,000 head of livestock (24 percent of its herds) between 1818 and 1823; 80 percent of these were cattle (Figure 27-2, Table 27-7). San Buenaventura apparently decided to illegally capitalize on this new trading opportunity, although why it was unique among the Santa Bárbara district missions in making this decision is unknown.

Table 27-7. Santa Bárbara Presidio District, Average Annual Changes in Livestock Holdings

Years averaged	Total change in livestock	Percentage of herds	Change in Livestock Categories			
			Cattle	Sheep	Horses	Miscellaneous
San Buenaventura Mission						
1818–1823	−8,726	−24	−7,572	+627	−1,324	−457
1824–1827	−17,448	−62	−10,166	−5,150	−2,406	+274
1828–1832	−2,108	−20	−8	−2,050	−47	+10
Santa Bárbara Mission						
1824–1827	−8,716	−62	−1,533	−5,250	−340	−1,593
1828–1832	+1,067	+20	+508	+467	+59	+33
La Purísima Mission						
1824–1827	−5,586	−25	−967	−4,595	−87	+63
1828–1832	+48	t	+484	−88	−192	−156
San Fernando Rey Mission						
1824–1827	−8,700	−50	−6,100	−2,512	−35	−53
1828–1832	+2,240	+25	+2,467	+683	−175	−735
Santa Inés Mission						
1824–1827	−2,478	−21	−183	−2,117	−14	−164
1828–1832	+1,003	+11	+1,003	+25	−294	+269

Note: t = less than 0.5 percent.

Although there is a similar drop in total livestock for all the missions in the district after 1823, a closer look at the categories of animals reduced reveals some surprising differences (Table 27-7). San Buenaventura continues its enthusiastic production of hides and tallow by cutting cattle herds by an enormous 10,000 head. Sheep were also cut by over 5,000 head and nearly 2,500 horses were eliminated from this mission's livestock holdings.

The second most active trading mission in the district is San Fernando Rey, which depleted livestock herds by 50 percent between 1823 and 1827. Seventy percent of this is cattle, over 6,000 head, while the balance is largely seen in the sheep flocks.

Although Santa Bárbara appears as though it would join this pattern with a drop of 62 percent of livestock after 1823, only 18 percent of this decline consists of cattle. Over 5,200 head of sheep account for the generous share of this depletion.

A similar situation is found at La Purísima Mission. The comparatively modest 25 percent drop in total livestock here is caused by the removal of nearly 4,600 sheep from mission assets; cattle herds drop by less than 1,000 head. Santa Inés experienced the smallest drop in total livestock (21 percent), of which sheep account for virtually the entire amount.

Therefore, it appears that although San Buenaventura and San Fernando Rey were apparently holding *matanzas* (large slaughters of cattle) and making contracts with foreign traders, Santa Bárbara and La Purísima were only modestly involved in the new economy and the participation of Santa Inés was negligible. However, the three northern missions were making major reductions in their sheep holdings. The reasons for this are unknown, although it may reflect a more prudent, long-term strategy to free more of their grazing lands for cattle. Reduction of sheep would also reduce labor requirements of the more demanding flocks in the face of both declining populations and demands for wool products.

After the initial drop in livestock after 1823, herds at most missions increase slightly in numbers of both cattle and sheep through the end of the mission tenure (Figure 27-2; Table 27-7). Exceptions are found at San Buenaventura, where cattle herds remain virtually the same size and the sheep are cut by another 2,000 head; and at La Purísima, where the livestock size remains stable. Declining populations at Santa Inés and La Purísima resulted in dramatic increases in per capita livestock holdings at these missions.

Summary

Missions within the Santa Bárbara district varied considerably in their per capita production of crops and livestock. San Buenaventura and Santa Inés ranked the highest in California, whereas Santa Bárbara and San Fernando Rey were among the lowest. However, most showed general increases in production until 1823. San Buenaventura appears to have begun early and illegal trading in hides and tallow after 1818. With the legalization of foreign trade in 1823, all missions experienced major reductions in total livestock. At the district level, this drop consisted of equal numbers of cattle and sheep although at individual missions the ratio varied enormously.

The economic situation at individual missions can be summarized as follows:

San Buenaventura was initially the best overall provisioner in the district. This mission was one of the first to become active in the hide and tallow trade, although it did so illegally, and it continued as the largest volume trader in cattle products in the district.

Santa Bárbara was the most populous and consistently poorest economic producer of all the missions in the district. This mission began modest trading in hides and tallow when trade restrictions were lifted in 1823, but made substantially larger reductions in sheep. By 1832, cattle herds were increasing, so that apparently not all surplus was being sold.

La Purísima Mission was a respectable producer of both crops and livestock and, like Santa Bárbara, participated comparatively modestly in the hide and tallow trade but made major reductions in sheep holdings. La Purísima began to show some increase in cattle herds by the end of the Mission period.

San Fernando Rey had good crop production prior to 1823, after which it fell to the lowest rates in the district. In contrast to the trends in most other missions, per capita livestock statistics never improved much over time. This poor livestock production may have been due to the early loss of mission lands to private ranchos. San Fernando Rey was an early participant in the hide and tallow trade, second only to San Buenaventura, although it later began to accumulate cattle surpluses.

Santa Inés Mission was an excellent agricultural producer and had livestock herds of a respectable size. Although it was like Santa Bárbara and La Purísima in making large reductions in sheep herds at the inception of legal trade, cattle herds were minimally affected. Toward the end of the Mission period its cattle herds increased again. The agricultural economy of the Santa Inés Mission appears to have remained successful and stable through secularization.

Conclusions

General patterns of economic development have previously been observed for the California missions. These patterns are valuable for assessing colony-wide responses to external changes. The present analysis focuses more closely on the constituent missions and demonstrates significant variation in economic responses between presidio districts, particularly between individual missions.

The variation in production was caused by some ecological variables, particularly between presidio districts. Some geographical factors may have been important for individual missions, although local historical factors appear to have been the most influential. Poor agricultural production at San Fernando Rey may be attributed to the removal of large parcels of mission land for private ranchos. The extent of mission participation in the hide and tallow trade between 1823 and 1832 varied enormously within the Santa Bárbara presidio district.

The above findings suggest that it is important to identify specific economic patterns at individual missions when reconstructing the particulars of mission life. The economy of individual missions is likely to affect conclusions about legal and illegal trade relations, access to imported material goods, diversion of mission resources to hide and tallow production, labor demands on Indian populations, quantity and quality of food supplied, and even relationships between Hispanic and native populations.

Acknowledgments

I greatly appreciate the assistance of Philip Walker, David Hornbeck, and Michael Glassow in developing this essay as well as the comments of Glenn Farris and two anonymous reviewers on an earlier draft.

References

Avina, Rose Hollenbaugh
  1973 *Spanish and Mexican Land Grants in California*. R & E Research Associates, San Francisco.
Beck, Warren A., and Ynez D. Haase
  1974 *Historical Atlas of California*. University of Oklahoma Press, Norman.
Cook, Sherburne F.
  1976 *The Conflict between the California Indian and White Civilization*. University of California Press, Berkeley.
  1979 Mission Registers as Sources of Vital Statistics: Eight Missions of Northern California. In *Essays in Population History: Mexico and California*, vol. 3, pp. 177–311. University of California Press, Berkeley.
Engelhardt, Zephyrin, O.F.M.
  1915 *The Mission and Missionaries of California*, vol. 4. James H. Barry, San Francisco.
  1920 *San Diego Mission*. James H. Barry, San Francisco.
  1921 *San Luis Rey Mission*. James H. Barry, San Francisco.
  1922 *San Juan Capistrano*. The Standard Printing Company, Los Angeles.
  1923 *Santa Bárbara Mission*. James H. Barry, San Francisco.
  1924 *San Francisco or Mission Dolores*. Franciscan Herald Press, Chicago.
  1927 *San Gabriel Mission and the Beginnings of Los Angeles*. Mission San Gabriel, San Gabriel.
  1929a *San Antonio de Padua: The Mission in the Sierras*. Mission Santa Bárbara, Santa Bárbara.
  1929b *Mission Nuestra Sonora de la Soledad*. Santa Bárbara Mission, Santa Bárbara.
  1929c *San Miguel, Archangel: The Mission on the Highway*. Mission Santa Bárbara, Santa Bárbara.
  1930 *San Buenaventura: The Mission by the Sea*. Mission Santa Bárbara, Santa Bárbara.
  1931 *Mission San Juan Bautista: A School of Church Music*. Mission Santa Bárbara, Santa Bárbara.
  1932a *Mission Santa Inés: Virgen Y Mártir and Its Ecclesiastical Seminary*. Mission Santa Bárbara, Santa Bárbara.
  1932b *Mission La Concepciön Purísima de Maria Santísima*. Mission Santa Bárbara, Santa Bárbara.
  1963 *Mission San Luis Obispo in the Valley of the Bears*. W. T. Genns, Santa Bárbara.
  1973a *San Fernando Rey: The Mission of the Valley*. Ballena Press, Ramona, Calif.
  1973b *Mission San Carlos Borromeo (Carmelo): The Father of the Missions*. Ballena Press, Ramona, Calif.
Hornbeck, David
  1983 *California Patterns: A Geographical and Historical Atlas*. Mayfield Publishing, Mayfield, Calif.
Kahrl, William L.
  1978 *The California Water Atlas*. State of California, Department of General Services.

Chapter 28 ■

Roberta S. Greenwood

The California Ranchero: Fact and Fancy

Through the processes of fiction, legend, art, and film, an archetypal figure of the Californian ranchero has emerged that reflects an idealized image, which is accurate—at most—for only a few individuals, and during a limited period of time. Historical documents and the growing body of archaeological data reveal instead that Spanish colonization was slow to spread beyond the presidios and pueblos, that land grants proliferated in the Mexican period after secularization of the missions, reached a peak in 1844, and that a variety of factors prompted a rapid decline in ranchero holdings, power, and culture after 1850.

Even the mission itself as a center of colonization and acculturation was not a Californian innovation; the Mexican states of Sonora, Sinaloa, and Baja California Sur had been missionized between 1590 and 1769, and some of the native congregations in Sonora and Sinaloa had already been turned over to Indian management before the settlement of Alta California had begun (Mason 1986:9). The typical nineteenth-century colonists were soldiers, and 50 to 66 percent of the settlers were stationed at one of the presidios, missions, or pueblos. The first two civil settlements were the pueblos of San José (1776) and Los Angeles (1791), which Governor Felipe de Neve sponsored to obtain grain and meat for the presidios when Father Serra objected to this use of mission supplies. In 1790, when the population (other than California Indians) reached 100, about 70 percent were born in the three northern Mexican states, half of these of European ancestry although born in Mexico, and the remainder of mixed racial descent, mestizos or mulatos (Mason 1986:5). In the 1793 census, only 30 individuals, or about 3 percent, were European Spaniards (Ríos-Bustamente 1986:27).

Early Spanish Settlement

The actual granting of lands outside the mission system was authorized as early as 1773. The first concession was 140 square varas (1.4 ha) near Carmel Mission, awarded to Manuel Butron (var.: Buitron) and his Indian wife in 1775 (Cowan 1977:112). Neve had established the mechanisms for gradual extension of the pueblos by granting additional lots and fields, as had been done at San José in 1777. Governor Fages was authorized to grant tracts up to three leagues (5,266.8 ha)[1] in size, as long as they did not encroach on a pueblo or harm any mission or Indian ranchería (Bancroft 1888:257). The next three grants, all large tracts in southern California, were to set the pattern for further distributions. In 1784, Fages awarded approximately 300,000 acres (121,410 ha) to Manuel Nieto, about 75,000 acres (30,352.5 ha) to Juan José Domínguez, and some 36,000 acres (14,569.2 ha) to José María Verdugo. All were prime lands along the Pacific coast and San Gabriel and Santa Ana rivers; that they were well chosen in terms of the local economic base, population centers, trade, and transportation corridors is demonstrated by the major cities that have since developed within their boundaries.

By 1800, there were 18 missions in California, the four presidios that were intended to become pueblos in time, three towns with about 100 heads of families, and about 20 or 30 ranchos occupied under provisional permits but without legal title to the land (Bancroft 1888:258). From the very beginning, the rancheros and the townsmen of the pueblos relied on Indian labor to tend the fields and herds in exchange for food, cloth, hardware, beads, and wine or brandy. Such contact was opposed by the missions, although facilitated and regulated by the *comisionado*, a political office created by Governor Fages in 1786 (Mason 1986:12).

The culture transplanted to Alta California and further shaped by political, economic, and environmental factors was only superficially "Spanish." The language incorporated many Indian words, the Catholic religion was colored by both Indian syncretism and Mexican ambience—for example, the Virgin of Guadalupe and the influence of Spain on the settlers who arrived from North Mexico had long since become generalized and attenuated during the similar process of missionization in the previous century (Ríos-Bustamente 1986:27). The imported mestizo culture was thus a hybrid. The cultivation of corn, beans, chiles, and squash; use of a four-legged, shaped metate for milling; architecture based on adobe rather than plastered stone masonry; diet staples of tortillas and frijoles; and even the poncho-styled serapes and broad-brimmed sombreros were all traits of mestizo, not Iberian, life (Chartkoff and Chartkoff 1984:269).

Much of the early civilian settlement outside of the organized pueblos followed the general pattern of the mission system along the California littoral, often occupying lands first cleared, used, or irrigated by the missions, or filling in between them. In Los Angeles County, for example, the area known as Mission Viejo, first developed and grazed as the original site of Mission San Gabriel, was the scene of such a struggle for control between the padres and newcomers.

> The proximity of the settlers, especially from the class that could be induced to exchange Mexico for California, was sure to prove troublesome to the Mission. Large tracts of land never tilled before had been rendered productive by the Indian converts under the supervision of the Franciscan friars. . . . The colonists . . . preferred to possess themselves of land already cultivated. . . . [They] endeavored to obtain from governors, under one pretext or another, grants of the lands which they coveted, notwithstanding that such areas were owned and had been cultivated or used as pastures by Mission Indians for the benefit of the neophyte community [Engelhardt 1927:62–63].

The history of this particular vicinity is typical of many of the small, early claims. An unsuccessful application was filed by the soldier José Francisco Ortega in 1791; one portion was granted later to Dona María Soto, who was already in residence; the governor granted the mission's irrigation facilities to another claimant; an Indian obtained a grant that was never patented; and there ensued a succession of unrecorded grants, conflicting claims, appeals, boundary disputes, litigation, bankruptcies, and problems sufficient to delay some of the patents into the 1880s (Greenwood et al. 1988a:17–25).

Only about 25 ranchos were granted during the entire Spanish period from 1769 to 1821 (Sánchez 1986:16), in contrast to the rapid proliferation that was to follow under Mexican hegemony. The typical dwelling was a small, dirt-floored adobe sited on an open hillside. Introductions into the material culture were largely products that were imported from or through Mexico, for example, metal tools, Majolica and Chinese ceramics, domestic animals, imported cultigens, and certain food staples, or the results of crafts taught at the missions, such as hide tanning, brick and tile making, carpentry, and local pottery. The typical archaeological assemblage of the first ranchos would thus illustrate a social order that synthesized a North Mexican adaptation to isolation in Alta California, incorporating an Iberian base much diffused by centuries in the New World, and also reflecting the presence of the acculturated Indians on whose labor the system relied.

Prior to the Mexican revolution, the closed Spanish mercantile system constituted an impediment to the growth and prosperity of the first ranchos. The Spanish Crown required its citizens to sell their produce and livestock to army quartermasters at set prices, and to purchase all supplies from the same source. In addition to the trade monopoly and price-fixing, the rancheros were further impoverished by the closure of ports to foreign trade and competition with the missions (Sánchez 1986:18–19).

Expansion under Mexico

The pace of settlement and economic development began to accelerate after Mexico finally achieved independence from Spain in 1822. The new republic gradually transformed the Spanish colonies into a nearly self-sufficient state with an economy based on cattle ranching and expanded trade (Chartkoff and Chartkoff 1984:270–271). Immigration, which had been so slowed during the political struggles that the settlers numbered only 3,220 persons in 1821 (Ríos-Bustamente 1986:25–28), resumed and the relaxations on shipping resulted in rapid growth of the hide and tallow industry. The immediate effect was the demand for more land to raise stock; the expansion of pastoralism spread Mexican settlement farther than the Spanish influence had ever penetrated, and directly affected a greater number of Indian groups as well (Figure 28-1). About 26 grants were awarded between 1822 and secularization in 1834, just about doubling the total made in the previous 38 years under Spain (Lavender 1972:106).

The only marketable products were hides and tallow, but currency had little value in California, since little could be acquired there through cash purchase. Foreign commerce was essential not only for the importation of manufactured goods but for the generation of tariffs which, along with tithes, constituted the sole territorial revenue. Together they barely supported the garrisons. Writing in 1828, José Bandini deplored the designation of Monterey as the sole legal port of entry for foreign goods, pointing out that tallow packed in *botas* could not withstand so long and hot a journey; that exploiting the natural resources of California would require a much larger population; and that unless impediments

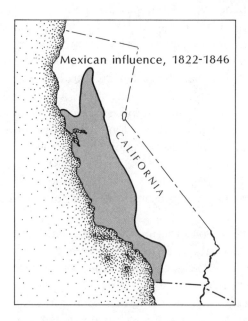

Figure 28-1. Areas of Mexican influence, 1822–1846. (After Chartkoff and Chartkoff 1984: Map 47)

to trade and immigration were overcome, "Even the natives will seek a more favorable environment" (Bandini 1951:20).

One of the few secular adobes of the Mexican period for which dates of construction and abandonment have been established with fair certainty is the *casa de campo* of Patricio Ontiveros, in Los Angeles County. It was occupied from ca. 1815, when this retired soldier was appointed majordomo of Mission San Juan Capistrano, until 1835. Built in mission style almost certainly by neophyte workers, it had massive stone foundations outlining three lineal rooms of unequal size, mud-plastered adobe walls, and a frequently renewed earthen floor. Ontiveros did not own the land; the adobe was built on the Nieto rancho, and it was the conflict between Missions San Gabriel and San Juan Capistrano over grazing rights and legal problems over the Nieto title that prompted Ontiveros to abandon the adobe and seek his own rancho soon after secularization facilitated the partition of mission rangelands.

Excavation has revealed the effects of grazing and occupation on the natural environment, the scarcity of consumer goods such as glass or metal objects, self-sufficiency in food, and new data about stockraising practices (Frierman 1982). The range was originally covered by perennial bunch grasses and forbs of the valley grassland plant community, but these became reduced by grazing and the native cover was replaced by exotic forage plants such as bur clover, sour clover, pigweed, wild oats, red-stem filaree, and mustard. Pollen data demonstrate that the original floral community recovered after abandonment until row crops and orchards were planted by subsequent owners in the 1870s. Foods produced by the rancho included wheat, barley for *atole*, and corn, which was processed into *nixtamal* and *masa* for tortillas with lime burned on the site. Cultigens included red and pink beans, tomatoes, peppers, watermelons, and peaches. Certain weeds introduced from Mediterranean Europe—still common on the site—would have provided greens in the winter and spring: cheeseweed, pigweed, wild radish, and mustard. The primary meat consumed was beef, slaughtered and dismembered in the Mexican tradition, but the diet was supplemented or varied with sheep, pigs, chickens, turkeys, geese, ducks, and a little fish, all of which left their evidence in prepared refuse pits originally used for the burning of lime.

Some food storage vessels were imported from Mexico, but most of the cooking was done in utilitarian brown ware pottery made at the adobe. The identity of the local clay has been confirmed by neutron activation (NAA) and X-ray fluorescence spectroscopy (XRF) analyses. Other evidence of the Indian presence includes polished soapstone, flaked chert, and beads of shell and glass, although no ranchería was mentioned in historical accounts or depicted on old maps.

Such an occupation was probably typical of the Mexican period prior to secularization. Production was not much above the level of bare subsistence; remains in the refuse pits suggest that cattle were being killed for domestic consumption, and not in any great numbers for their hides or tallow. The rather casual attitude toward grazing rights and claim boundaries, between the two missions and also between Nieto and Ontiveros, emphasizes the early Californio's regard for the land—which was considered to be almost valueless aside from its function of growing cattle (Lavender 1972:107). It seemed limitless in the empty landscape, and he counted his wealth in animals instead.

During the late mission years and increasingly after the British trade monopoly was dissolved in 1828, the rancheros struggled to make their subsistence economy competitive with the missions in the production of hides and tallow. For this they depended on mestizos, laborers from the pueblos, and Indians from the missions and rancherías, and they sought to enlarge their holdings. There was greater access to goods. For example, in 1833, Juan (John) Forster, who did not yet own land, purchased a cargo recently arrived in La Paz for $50,000 and sold the shipment in San Diego and Los Angeles (Tanner and Lothrop 1970:200–201). Yet despite the shift from a subsistence life-style to participation in the growing market economy, the ranchos could not compete with the missions. The ecclesiastical forces maintained economic and political power through their vast herds, extensive lands under cultivation, access to Indian labor, and cooperative organization structure (Sánchez 1986:19).

Colonization had been encouraged by such acts as the decree of 1825, which provided that newly settled lands would be tax-free for the five years after publication, and by the selling of shares for $100 in colonizing companies. The company of Don José María Híjar comprised 19 farmers; 11 painters; 12 seamstresses; 8 carpenters; 8 tailors; 5 each of shoemakers, tinners, and silversmiths; 6 teachers, 2 each of hatters, physicians, barbers, saddlers, and blacksmiths; plus a mathematician, machinist, gardener, surgeon, ribbon maker, *rebozo* maker, midwife, distiller, candymaker, vermicelli maker, navigator, founder, porkman, musician, vintner, apothecary, boatman, and carriage maker, all bound for Los Angeles (Tanner and Lothrop 1970:201, 221). The roster suggests the skills and trades that were needed. Yet at the time of secularization in 1834, there were still only 51 land grants in California, most of them awarded to officers and men of the occupying forces (Gates 1967:3). The population was stretched thin along the 500-mile coastline, numbering only some 300 in the capital at Monterey. A colony twice-removed, since Mexico (or New Spain) was itself a Spanish colony, the province remained an essentially clerical society until factional disputes within Mexico eventually brought an end to the power of the padres (Chartkoff and Chartkoff 1984:272–274; Pitt 1971:2–4).

Effects of Secularization

A new group of leaders espoused *liberalismo* and anticlericalism. Mariano Vallejo, Juan Àlvarado, and José Castro were joined by the Carrillos in Santa Barbara, Juan Bandini in San Diego, Pio and Andrés Pico in Los Angeles in a reflection of the unrest going on in all of Latin America (Pitt 1971:3). Although the Spanish government had already begun planning to secularize the missions prior to the Mexican Revolution, agitation for secularization increased in the 1820s, and the act finally passed on August 17, 1833, was to exert a more immediate and profound effect on California than the change from Spanish to Mexican rule.

The immediate result was a shift in wealth and power, and a flood of land claims, as the vast mission lands were dispersed and their herds slaughtered for quick profit. Between 1834 and 1842 alone, more than 300 ranchos were granted, most of them ex-mission lands (Robinson 1979:31). There were 453 claims in 1841–1846, and 277 in 1844–1846 alone (Gates 1967:7). The peak year was 1844, when 120 claims were filed. Within modern county boundaries, there were 88 ranchos in Monterey, 68 in Los Angeles, 55 in Santa Clara, 46 in Santa Barbara, 42 in San Luis Obispo, and 40 in San Diego (Cowan 1977:135–141). Ultimately more than 800 private land grant cases would come before the U.S. Land Commission after statehood, and about 600 would be confirmed (ibid.:10).

The period between secularization and 1848 was the zenith of ranchero life and the hide and tallow trade. Some of the richest lands in the state were suddenly available for private use; Mission San Fernando, for example, had possessed 350 square miles (90,650 ha) of fine agricultural and range land (Sánchez 1986:19). If there ever was a time when the life-style of the rancheros approached the sterotype, it was within these few years. The display of wealth was facilitated by the new, skilled colonists, and a cash economy supported by the growing pueblos supplanted the barter system. Yet it must be said that despite the vast size of many of the land grants, only about 25 Californio families really attained the status of landed gentry, and very few of them were Iberians (ibid.:25). The culture remained that of "the pastoral Californio variant of Norteño Mexican regional culture" (Ríos-Bustamente 1986:28) as the population gradually grew from both a rapid rate of natural increase and a steady immigration from Baja California and Sonora. The newcomers represented both friends or relations of the Californios already resident and members of the colonizing groups. Still an essentially pastoral people, they maintained cultural continuity through language, oral traditions, religion, and the cohesiveness of the extended patriarchal family.

Under both Spanish and Mexican rule, status was based on wealth (first in animals, later in land), ethnicity, and family. Stratification became more marked after secularization with the greater disparity in land ownership and the transfer of political and economic power from the clergy to a small group of rancheros and prominent individuals. The larger ranchos replaced the missions as centers of economic production in the pastoral tradition, while the pueblos would gradually become the focus of population growth, social life, and mercantile activity (Camarillo 1979a:102–103). There was also a gradual admixture of other cultures, exemplified at one end of the economic scale by the Yankee traders and others arriving in increasing numbers from the eastern United States, and at the other by colonists from New Mexico, who were invited to settle in exchange for protecting the rancheros against Indian raids.

It was the rancheros who benefited from secularization, not the Indians. In the stratified society that had changed only in the identity of those at the top, wealth and political power were controlled by the largest landowners and the provincial administrators—who were most often related. Typically of mestizo origin, although frequently claiming Spanish descent, they rarely made up more than 20 percent of the non-Indian population and 10–20 percent of the pueblo residents. Larger in numbers and lower in status were the 60–80 percent of the pueblo population, small-scale farmers, skilled and unskilled laborers. Descendants of the original settlers plus later colonists, the typical pobladores were the mestizo-mulatto-Indio people of the north Mexico borderlands. At the bottom of the social structure were the ex-neophyte and nonmission Indians whose identity was further reduced by intermarriage and assimilation (Camarillo 1979a:103–104).

Some of the late ranchos were vast in scale. The Yorba family was able to acquire claims to 213,331 acres (86,335 ha) along the Santa Ana River in Los Angeles and San Bernardino counties, in addition to the Arroyo Seco grant of 48,857 acres (19,772.4 ha) in the Sacramento Valley. Bernardo Yorba, the patriarch, ruled his domain from a 50-room adobe maintained by 26 domestic servants, more than 100 workers to tend the livestock, 4 wool combers, 2 tanners, a dairyman, harness maker, 2 shoemakers, a carpenter, plasterer, wine maker, and even a household jester (Greenwood et al. 1988b). Mariano Vallejo employed 600 vaqueros and other workers; John Sutter, probably even more. Land ownership was concentrated among the few, as exemplified by the Pico family, whose total claims exceeded 700,000 acres (283,290 ha) (Gates 1967:7–9).

Archaeological Insights

Of the many propositions regarding economic and social change, interaction between the Indians who constituted the basic labor force and the new wave of Euro-American settlers, settlement patterns within the huge ranchos, degree of self-sufficiency, and other questions, few have yet been tested archaeologically. Many of the same localities first occupied by the Indians, subsequently by the missions, and later by the rancheros have, for all the same reasons, been developed into modern communities or routes of travel, obliterating the remains of early years. Many of the smaller adobes that would illuminate the lives of the less illustrious have simply melted away without leaving surface evidence, since they would not have seemed attractive to the early preservationists. The grander establishments that still survive as monuments to the past have often been restored, well or badly, without benefit of scientific study and are not currently accessible to investigation.

Wherever tested, archaeological methods have been fruitful. One significant conclusion is that subsurface remains do persist, whether the surface has been cultivated, inundated, or subject to oil production or urban development. The site of the Aros-Serrano Adobe, for example, was relocated from approximation of historical records.[2] Although there were no surface indications in an area that had been deliberately cleared, then overgrown with woodlands and seasonally inundated, stone foundations, features such as paved paths, activity areas, and a well, trash deposits, and even fallen adobe walls were found. The remains were sufficiently intact to illuminate the life of the Serrano family, who did not own either the land they used or the home they occupied (Greenwood et al. 1987). This study, which helps to balance the glorified image of the wealthy ranchero, also provides insight into architectural evolution.

It has been stated as a generalizing principle that early secular adobes of modest scale were typically two or three rooms arranged in lineal order, while the more prosperous built two-story homes around courtyards. Stone foundations were expected. However, recent tests at Rancho Los Cerritos, built in 1844 by Jonathan Temple, revealed that the adobe bricks of this otherwise typical two-story, three-wing structure were laid directly into the subsoil. Other adobes, both earlier and later, that lack stone foundations include the De La Osa Adobe at Los Encinos and the Robinson Adobe in San Diego. Adjacent and contemporary adobes in San Diego, including the Casa de Pedrorena, were built with stone footings. Other variants include a Mormon adaptation utilizing very thin walls and 9-inch adobe bricks (Greenwood and Foster 1987:29) and a chronologically diagnostic example with a cement-mortared stone foundation at the Yucaipa Adobe (Lester Ross, personal communication 1988). There is not yet a demonstrable correlation between the presence of a foundation and the nationality of the builder, use of Indian labor, availability of stone, chronology, or geographic location.

The Aros-Serrano Adobe, built ca. 1870 by Mexican-born Antonio Aros, was traditional in its use of stone foundations, plastered and whitewashed adobe walls, broad porches, lack of chimney or fireplace, and limited fenestration. Its floorplan, on the other hand, illustrates a transition to Euro-American architecture that may prove to be a timemarker. The configuration is almost square with four rooms, two on either side of a central hallway. It most resembles the Rodriguez Adobe in Orange County, "considered quite modern in its day"; the later, built ca. 1860, had an interior stairway leading to a sleeping loft, which was probably true of the Aros-Serrano Adobe as well (Greenwood et al. 1987). Although living on the fringes of Yorba property and the new town of Rincon, the family endeavors in diversified agriculture, dairy enterprises, and a small roadside business were probably far more typical of most of the population. Their material possessions illustrated participation in the market economy of both food and fashion, yet the family cohesiveness that brought the Serranos to live in the adobe of their relation, Aros, illustrates the traditional traits of kinship obligation and pastoral enterprise. Despite their growing indebtedness and pressures from the increasing population growth and local economic competition, the family stayed together at the adobe, guarded their privacy, remained staunchly religious, and extended hospitality to kinfolk. Sra. Serrano spoke only Spanish for her 90 years; her daughters stayed at home and never married. This cultural isolation and involution has been identified as a characteristic of California's Mexican population from 1848 to the 1880s (Ríos-Bustamente 1986:30).

Generalizations derived from historical documentation—for example, that British ceramics began to replace Mexican imports after the Spanish regime—are certainly possible and often testable. However, the archival base is itself biased against those who did not achieve title to land or other avenues to prominence and thus fails to explicate, much less explain, particularistic situations. It is necessary to approach covariation to assess the differential persistence of ethnic/national traits, or to gain an understanding of cultural processes as they responded to the scarcity of manufactured goods in Alta California. Although the data clearly demonstrate the shift from Mexican to European ceramics from the occupation of the Ontiveros Adobe in 1815–1835 to one of the Sepulveda adobes with estimated dates of 1836–1868 (Table 28-1), additional linkages are likely. As mission majordomo, Ontiveros had access to both Indian labor and Mexican imports through San Juan Capistrano, while Sepulveda held political offices and was one of the wealthiest men in southern California (Sleeper 1969). At the Ontiveros household, nearly 80 percent of the ceramics were made by Indians of clays available on site; a generation or more later, as much as 10 percent of the ceramic inventory was still locally made, despite a broad variety of English, Scottish, French, and American products. The presence and survival of the Indian pottery could not be predicted from historical records. The acquisition of Euro-American goods may have constituted an addition, or even a replacement, within the Indian household, whereas reliance on local pottery constituted a transformation or loss of status for Ontiveros.

How the Indian population perceived the newcomers and the degree to which the imported crafts, tools, and products represented additions *or* replacements in their culture are questions that have not been adequately investigated. Postmission contact sites would tend to be ephemeral, short-lived, seasonal, or functional (i.e., sheep camps); it is not likely that many could be recognized from surface indications. Further, the tendency to categorize sites within some of the larger study projects as either prehistoric or historical may mean that those falling between the cracks or overlapping this arbitrary distinction will be overlooked.

Indians in the Rancho Period

Many of the Indian residential clusters called rancherías by the Spanish represent the modified survival of prehistoric occupations into historical times— particularly those in which population density prior to contact was one factor in the location of a specific mission. Some rancherías are depicted on diseños

Table 28-1. Origin of Ranchero Ceramics
(percent)

Ceramic Type	Ontiveros Adobe 1815–1835 (Frierman 1982)	Sepulveda Adobe 1836–1868 (Chace 1969)
Majolica (Puebla types)	11	—
Brown Ware (locally made)	79	10
Lead Glazed and Bruñido (from North Mexico)	5	5
Chinese Export	5	4
European	7	78
United States	<0.01	2
	n = 3549	n = 751

or other historical maps, but they may not have left surficial remains. The most abundant evidence of the Indian presence at such sites as the Olivos, Los Cerritos, Bandini-Cota, or Aros-Serrano adobes, for example, has been the brown ware pottery made from local clays; from context and associations, it appears that the craft persisted well into the 1880s. New Indian settlements co-occurred with the late ranchos since Indians were required to attach themselves to a rancho and be gainfully employed, at least seasonally (William Mason, personal communication 1986). In effect, the *padrino* system resulted in the substitution of the land baron for the padre. As the system was described in 1856,

> It will be seen that, by this law, the overseer of a large rancho has but to be a "Justice of the Peace" and he is enabled to buy and keep Indian servants as he may want them, and to punish them at his discretion. . . . Each of the large cattle ranches near Los Angeles and San Bernardino has from fifteen to thirty Indians permanently occupied [Ord 1978:21].

Don Bernardo Yorba's more than 200 Indians employed in farming, herding, and domestic labor had one or more rancherías and their own cemetery (Greenwood et al. 1988b). Isaac Williams ruled "almost as a feudal baron" at Chino with 75 Indians living "in huts near his home" (Black 1975:2). At the Yorba-Slaughter Adobe, Indians were employed well into the 1880s; they were paid in silver dollars, but the account books record deductions made for advances against tobacco, shoes, flour, and clothing (Greenwood et al. 1988b:17–20). The Indians were identified only by their given names (e.g., Vinturo Indian) and there were runaways.

The events precipitating the war with Mexico in 1846 and the effects of the Gold Rush in 1849 are matters of historical record. The factors that had the most immediate effect on the rancho system were the explosive gain in population and great diversity in its origins. The non-Indian population of California rose from 15,000 in 1848 to 224,435 in 1852, whereas the Indian population fell from 100,000 to 50,000 in the same period, and would fall to 17,738 by 1860 (Cook 1976:56; Lavender 1972:165).

Decline of the Ranchos

The leisurely life-style and the very lands of the rancheros gave way under the pressure for rapidly expanded food production, raw materials for construction, and new infrastructures to provide administrative, financial, and distributive services. Urbanism and large-scale agriculture combined to replace the once dominant Mexican culture with that of the ever more numerous Anglo-Americans. Even as they lost their lands, the pobladores faced competition at the low end of the unskilled labor market with new minorities such as the Chinese and the more recent immigrants from Mexico.

Natural catastrophes in southern California (the floods and drought of the 1860s), the Civil War, completion of the railroad, replacement of ranching by agriculture—all contributed to the land boom of the 1880s and the end of the ranchos, many of which were still locked in protracted and costly litigation over patents to the land. By 1880, the Mexicans had generally been dispossessed of their ranches or farms, and the racial and class divisions that had evolved in 1860–1880 now pervaded the urban occupational structure. Although still a minority in actual numbers, those with Anglo surnames had become the dominant landowners and urban merchants by 1870 (Camarillo 1979b:61–65). The change was rapid; in Los Angeles, Mexicans made up more than 75 percent of the population in 1850, but only about 47 percent by 1860. The Spanish-speaking population of Los Angeles fell to 19 percent in 1880, and to about 6 percent at the turn of the century, which was probably the low point of population share, political representation, and economic power (Ríos-Bustamente 1986:31–33). The causes and results of discrimination and isolation, "barrioization," have been examined by Camarillo (1979a, 1979b) and tested archaeologically at the Ortega Adobe in Ventura (Greenwood and Foster 1984).

The studies of historical architecture have implications for regional settlement patterns, as well as revealing the arrangement of structures and configuration of individual buildings at any given site. Best known are the locations of the principal dwellings (usually the last) of the most prominent rancheros and of those monuments that have been preserved. However, each of the more prosperous citizens, such as Yorba or Sepulveda, built many houses for a variety of reasons: to provide for their many children, to establish claims and occupation on new lands, to handle seasonal activities, and to symbolize enhanced status as their wealth increased. Most of these remain to be discovered, along with the modest dwellings of the less affluent and the rancherias of the Indians who served them. This is particularly true of those who did not own the land that they occupied.

Archaeology has been productive in controverting local legends, as well as demonstrating unanticipated survivals and the research potential of subsurface deposits where the superstructure may be gone. At the site of the Monterey-style Olivas Adobe in Ventura, the small, one-story adobe at the rear of the courtyard had been interpreted as the first, temporary home used while the family was building the more imposing residence. However, excavation determined that the smaller structure not only postdated the main dwelling, but was the successor to an even smaller adobe built earlier on the same spot. The diseño and other documents suggest that there were additional adobes along the creek bank that can perhaps be relocated (Greenwood and Foster 1986). Clues from General Land Office field notes, old maps, court records, assessments, and other documents, combined with aggressive testing in the field, have begun to fill many of the gaps in the physical and social landscape to provide a more accurate picture of population density, factors that favored settlement, transportation and irrigation systems, uses of the land, and activity areas.

It remains to be demonstrated whether any single trait or assemblage of cultural materials of the later years can be identified archaeologically as Indian. Because the Native Americans adopted farming, domestic animals, and metal tools and other products of commerce with such rapidity, there are few remains of aboriginal lifeways or crafts to be excavated. Although some female tools and subsistence practices persisted in the mission context, dispersion, increasing contacts, and urbanism after secularization accelerated the pace of acculturation. Some of the last Indian skills to remain would be basketmaking and ceramics. Further, from the days of the missions forward, the new culture was more than a composite of Spanish, Indian, and African traditions, and it was uniquely Mexican. The so-called Spanish heritage of California is derived largely from "descendants of Indian peoples from the western coast of Mexico, who had themselves undergone a similar process of colonization and missionization only a century or so before" (Ríos-Bustamente 1986:27). From limited studies of urban sites, it appears that nationality or ethnicity will be much harder to demonstrate for second- or third-generation Indian and Chicano families than, for example, for the Chinese (Greenwood and Foster 1984:99).

Culture Contact and Change

Many of the questions that remain beyond the reach of historical documentation can be addressed by archaeology. For example, the replacement of Mexican and Chinese ceramics by European and, ultimately, American products can be predicted from the literature. However, the persistence of locally made Indian pottery well into the 1880s, or the differential in distribution between the ranchos, presidios, and pueblos is not a matter of record. Architectural practices and evolution are another example showing that meaningful data accrue from excavation. To understand settlement patterns and land use, it is necessary to locate and study early or unimposing sites no longer visible on the surface, if the myths of the colorful ranchero are not to be perpetuated on the basis of structures that have been preserved as landmarks. Scientific technologies such as XRF and NAA applications to ceramics; palynological studies of soils, adobe, and mortar; scanning electron microscopy of plaster (Greenwood et al. 1987); remote sensing; faunal analysis; and other analytical approaches have helped to replace subjective judgments.

The broad problem of culture contact will be a continuing concern for future studies, to the extent that human behaviors are reflected in the archaeological record. Comparisons are needed to define the life of the Indians under the mission system and their experience on the ranchos and in the pueblos. Questions about which aspects of the imposed culture were additions, as opposed to replacements, need to be investigated at contact sites and historical rancherías. The same kinds of questions apply to the early Mexican pobladores and later waves of immigrants, and to the ranchero families of declining fortunes. Not as individuals, of course, but as a culture, the Californio became extinct within a generation of the Gold Rush (Pitt 1971; Wollenberg 1970:55).

The California rancheros did not live on a frontier as usually defined: They produced a single commodity dependent on a foreign market, they needed to import or impress a labor force, and they were part of a stratified society. The rancho system was not even an innovation in Alta California since both the social and physical attributes derived from the missions: the choices of place, irrigation, routes of travel, production for trade, organization of the labor force, and elements of the architecture. It remains a challenge to archaeology to demonstrate the discontinuities in Spanish-speaking California in the physical aspects of culture apart from the cohesiveness sustained by sentiment, language, and kinship. Such investigations must not be limited to testing postulates drawn from historical sources lest the results constitute a self-fulfilling prophecy, nor should they be based on assumptions about continuity and regularity in human behaviors.

Notes

1. Vara and league are historical units of measure; both were used interchangeably as linear and areal (square) measures, and both differed slightly at different times and in different parts of the southwest. For purposes of conversion into metric equivalents, the vara is understood here as 33 inches, and the league, as used in Alta California for the early grants under Mexican law, as 4388 acres, or 1755.61 ha. For fuller discussion, see Bowman 1947.

2. Locations of adobes in text: Aros-Serrano Adobe (northwest of Corona, San Bernardino County); Bandini-Cota Adobe (northwest of Corona, Riverside County); Olivos Adobe (city of Ventura, Ventura County); Ontiveros Adobe (city of Sante Fe Springs, Los Angeles County); Ortega Adobe (city of Ventura, Ventura County); Rancho Los Cerritos (city of Long Beach, Los Angeles County); Sepulveda Hacienda (Irvine Ranch, Orange County); Yorba Hacienda (southeast of Yorba Linda, Orange County); Yorba-Slaughter Adobe (northwest of Corona, San Bernardino County).

References

Bancroft, Hubert Howe
  1888 *The Works of Hubert Howe Bancroft*, vol. 34. *California Pastoral 1769–1848*. History Co., San Francisco.
Bandini, José
  1951 *A Description of California in 1828*, translated by Doris Marion Wright. Friends of the Bancroft Library, Berkeley.
Black, E. B.
  1975 *Rancho Cucamonga and Dona Merced*. San Bernardino County Museum Association, Redlands.
Bowman, J. N.
  1947 Weights and Measures of Provincial California. *California Historical Society Quarterly* 30[4]:315–338.
Camarillo, Albert
  1979a *Chicanos in a Changing Society*. Harvard University, Cambridge.
  1979b Historical Patterns in the Development of Chicano Urban Society: Southern California, 1848–1930. In *The American Southwest Image and Reality*, pp. 31–119. William Andrews Clark Library, Los Angeles.
Chace, Paul G.
  1969 The Archaeology of "Cienaga," [sic] The Oldest Historic Structure on the Irvine Ranch. *Pacific Coast Archaeological Society Quarterly* 5[3]:39–55.
Chartkoff, Joseph L., and Kerry Kona Chartkoff
  1984 *The Archaeology of California*. Stanford University, Stanford.
Cook, Sherburne F.
  1976 *The Population of the California Indians 1769–1970*. University of California, Berkeley.
Cowan, Robert G.
  1977 *Ranchos of California*. Historical Society of Southern California, Los Angeles.
Engelhardt, Fr. Zephyrin, O.F.M.

1927 *San Gabriel Mission and the Beginnings of Los Angeles*. Mission San Gabriel, San Gabriel.

Frierman, Jay D.
1982 *The Ontiveros Adobe: Early Rancho Life in Alta California*. Greenwood and Associates. Prepared for the Redevelopment Agency, City of Santa Fe Springs.

Gates, Paul W.
1967 *California Ranchos and Farms 1846–1862*. State Historical Society of Wisconsin, Madison.

Greenwood, Roberta S.
1976 *The Changing Faces of Main Street*. Redevelopment Agency, City of San Buenaventura.

Greenwood, Roberta S., and John M. Foster
1984 *The Ortega Adobe, West Main Street*. Greenwood and Associates. Prepared for the Redevelopment Agency, City of San Buenaventura.
1986 Archaeological Investigation of the Olivas Small Adobe. *Architectural and Archaeological Investigation of the Olivas Small Adobe*, part 2. Gilbert Arnold Sanchez and Greenwood and Associates. Prepared for Department of Parks and Recreation, City of San Buenaventura.
1987 Archaeological Investigation of Los Cerritos Adobe. *Historic Structure Report*, part 3. Gilbert Arnold Sanchez. Prepared for the City of Long Beach, Calif.

Greenwood, Roberta S., John M. Foster, and Anne Q. Duffield
1987 *Historical and Archaeological Investigation at the Aros-Serrano Adobe*. Greenwood and Associates. Prepared for the U.S. Army Corps of Engineers, Los Angeles District.
1988a *The First Historical Settlement in Los Angeles County: Investigations at Whittier Narrows*. Infotec Research Inc. and Greenwood and Associates. Prepared for the U. S. Army Corps of Engineers, Los Angeles District.
1988b *Historical and Archaeological Study of the Yorba-Slaughter Adobe, San Bernardino County*. Infotec Research Inc. and Greenwood and Associates. Prepared for the U.S. Army Corps of Engineers, Los Angeles District.

Lavender, David
1972 *California: Land of New Beginnings*. Harper and Row, New York.

Mason, William M.
1986 Alta California during the Mission Period, 1769–1835. *Masterkey* 60[2-3]:4–14.

Ord, E. O. C.
1978 *The City of the Angels and the City of the Saints, Or a Trip to Los Angeles and San Bernardino in 1856*, edited by Neal Harlow. Huntington Library, San Marino.

Pitt, Leonard
1971 *The Decline of the Californios*. University of California, Berkeley, Los Angeles, London.

Ríos-Bustamente, Antonio
1986 The Barrioization of Nineteenth-Century Mexican Californians: From Landowners to Laborers. *Masterkey* 60[2-3]:26–35.

Robinson, W. W.
1979 *Land in California*. University of California, Berkeley, Los Angeles, London.

Sánchez, Federico A.
1986 Rancho Life in Alta California. *Masterkey* 60[2-3]:15–25.

Sleeper, Jim
1969 The Many Mansions of José-Sepulveda. *Pacific Coast Archaeological Society Quarterly* 5[3]:1–38.

Tanner, John D., Jr., and Gloria R. Lothrop (editors)
1970 Don Juan Forster Southern California Ranchero. *Southern California Quarterly* 52[3]:195–230.

Wollenberg, Charles (editor)
1970 *Ethnic Conflict in California History*. Tinnon-Brown, Los Angeles.

Chapter 29 ▇

Georgia Lee and Norman Neuerburg

The Alta California Indians as Artists before and after Contact

Body painting, basketry, pottery, small-scale sculpture, shell inlay, sand painting, and rock art are the principal figurative arts practiced by precontact native Californians that are known to us from actual examples or representations. Many of these are ephemeral, and our knowledge of them has come from early accounts and sketches. The bulk of our evidence comes from rock painting sites, some of which are extraordinary examples of the art. Other decorated items such as painted mortuary poles and burial slabs are also mentioned in early descriptions; no actual examples of the former have survived. However, a few painted slabs are extant; most were recovered from burial contexts (Lee 1978). The designs on these are usually geometric, although some lizard-like figures and a fish motif painted on sandstone slabs were recovered from San Nicolas Island (Bryan 1970).

Presumably, most of the aboriginal figurative arts continued with only minimal or gradual change among the tribes that were not contacted until the American period. However, what happened to these arts and crafts among the missionized Indians? How much disappeared, how much did, in fact, survive—even in modified form—and how did these become a part of the new forms required by the invading culture? These are questions that we can attempt to investigate.

The Artists

Although we know little of the status of the artist in precontact society in California, it appears likely that shamans were those who executed rock paintings (Driver 1937:126; Hedges 1982:1; Hudson and Underhay 1978:147; Vastokas and Vastokas 1973:55–130). Most shamans were male, and although an occasional reference mentions women as shamans, they seem to have been in the minority (Gayton 1976:210; Handelman 1976:396). It is thus assumed that the majority of rock paintings were the result of male-oriented activities.

As specialists in the sacred, shamans were considered powerful and potentially dangerous and were treated with awe, respect, and caution. As artists, their creativity was interpreted as a personal gift from the spirits, a kind of divine inspiration that enabled them to render visible the great spirits that only they could see and control. However, when gathered into the mission system, "wizards" (as the priests called them) were targeted as threatening troublemakers and were singled out for punishment and/or elimination (Heizer 1968:87). It is thus questionable that former shamans were offered the opportunity to work as artists under the missionaries; probably other, naturally talented, individuals were given these opportunities, and it is perhaps not too bold to assert that their position in the Franciscan missions was also a privileged one, just as those who learned Spanish well would have merited special treatment.

Body Painting

In precontact times, paint was used lavishly on clothing and bodies; the designs had precise meaning, identifying the tribelet as well as symbolizing status and position of the individual (Hudson and Blackburn 1985:316; Simpson 1961:56). For example, body paint identified women of marriageable age (Hudson and Blackburn 1985:316–317). Boscana (1978:156) also described tattoo patterns. Body painting—at least for ceremonials—survived into the second decade of the nineteenth century without change, to judge from drawings of native dances made at the northern missions by European visitors (Kroeber et al. 1977:Figures 88, 100, 102). The missionaries seem to have made little effort to suppress the dances as they probably were unaware of the meaning of both the designs and the dances.

Basketry

Basket making, a female activity, was an art in precontact societies. Most examples were made with meticulous detail and often there is a distinct design relationship between bowls of wood, stone, and basketry (Hudson 1977a). Some design elements that appear on baskets are also found on other forms of portable art as well as in rock paintings (Lee 1981:45).

Figure 29-1. Basket from the San Diego area with stylized mission motifs. (Southwest Museum)

Basket making continued because of its usefulness, and only rarely were new designs introduced, such as the Spanish coat-of-arms on three baskets from Mission San Buenaventura (Smith 1982:Figures 1, 2, 5) and the stylized short-hand for a mission found on some trays said to be from the San Diego area (Figure 29-1); (see Neuerburg 1987:Figure 1). New forms such as a Spanish hat collected by Vancouver (Kroeber 1973:Figure P) and lidded baskets had little or no impact on the craft so that traditional forms and designs continued into this century, although some motifs such as animals and flowers were added in the American period. To the Spanish, basket making was a utilitarian craft only and was not even considered a minor art form.

Pottery

Some pottery with painted designs had been produced in the desert regions, but none seems to have been made at the missions. However, floor tiles were made by Indian labor; a few of them, found at Missions La Purísima, Santa Bárbara, and San Antonio, have typical Indian designs made by impressing a design into the soft clay before firing (Figure 29-2). Examples of these are said also to be both at the presidio and at Fort Guijarros in San Diego (Paul Ezell, personal communication 1980; Ron May, personal communication 1986); undoubtedly many more are hidden in construction.

Tiny clay figures were made at some sites, such as Mission San Antonio, and some may have been of Christian subjects (Ferguson and Hoover 1983:Figures 1, 2). Others were of animals, and again we may assume that they did not come to the attention of the padres or, if they saw them at all, they would have considered them toys.

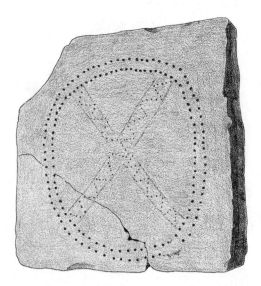

Figure 29-2. Floor tile made by Indians at Mission La Purísima showing typical Chumash Indian design motifs; approximately 25 cm².

Small Sculpture

Small sculptural pieces from the Gabrielino and Chumash areas were sacred talismans, and probably represented dream or spirit helpers (Hudson 1978; Hudson and Blackburn 1986:171; Lee 1981:45–55). The majority of stone effigies are in the form of animals or birds; others are so abstract that their intent is unclear, and still others may be composite creatures. Many are highly finished and extremely attractive with a pleasant tactile quality. These artifacts, as well as nearly everything else made by Native Americans, had supernatural dimensions in the form of a spirit either inherent in the object or imparted to it by the artisan (Hudson and Blackburn 1982:24).

Although the so-called pelican effigies found in Chumash and Gabrielino territory closely correlate with a carefully executed painting in black and grey on an exterior wall at San Juan Capistrano (Neuerburg 1987:53), evidence for a survival into historic times of small-scale sculptures is scanty; however, a little limestone plaque at Mission Santa Bárbara (Figure 29-3) appears to be native work. It shows a schematic figure of a saint in a niche, possibly copied from a detail of the canvas altarpiece in the mission church (Figure 29-4). A statue of the patron that is still above the altar also served as the model for a stone figure that once occupied the center of the gable of the church facade until the 1925 earthquake (Neuerburg 1977b:Figures 1, 2). It was accompanied by three other stone figures of Faith, Hope, and Charity, also based on imported, although not yet identified, models. These were all probably the work of a neophyte called Paisano (Hudson 1977b:16) who also carved the animal water spouts on the lavanderia next to the fountain. The forepart of a stone horse on the filter house at San Buenaventura Mission was apparently the work of two neophytes there. Animal heads in stone served as water spouts at San Gabriel, while human

Figure 29-3. Limestone plaque with figure of a saint in a niche (Mission Santa Bárbara).

masks served that purpose in the lavanderia in the garden in front of Mission San Luis Rey.

At Santa Bárbara a plaster relief of a cross flanked by triangular flags above a native geometric motif was once inside the right-hand bell tower (Neuerburg 1980:151). Its placement suggests astronomical implications.

Wooden sculpture is more problematical, although the figure of Saint Anthony made for the chapel at the Asistencia of Pala (in San Diego County) and a plaque of the Lamb of God from the front of the altar and a relief of a soul in purgatory, both at Carmel, suggest that wood carving may have been extensively practiced (Neuerburg 1987:15,21). Certainly much of the ornamental work on furniture could have been done by the neophytes. Leather carving is another area as yet unexplored, although it would have no precontact precedents.

Shell Inlay

Shell inlay was used extensively along the coast, with some of the finest pieces coming from the Chumash, who were noted for their fine craftsmanship and workmanship. They also had kinship-based guilds or brotherhoods that provided hereditary access to the supernatural power necessary to excel in their craft (Hudson and Blackburn 1982:24).

Figure 29-4. Detail of painted altarpiece at Mission Santa Bárbara, sent in 1806.

The shells used for inlay ranged from abalone to tiny disks made of Olivella; with asphaltum for an adhesive, beads were set in decorative patterns on bowls, pipes, and stone pendants. Bone objects often had disk beads applied as an overlay on the surface (Lee 1981:36).

The Chumash technique of inlaying with mother-of-pearl survives in a rare example on the old tabernacle at Mission Santa Bárbara, where it is combined with a mother-of-pearl cross from the Holy Land (Neuerburg 1987:58). The technique is similar, and another technique of inlaying paintings with that material had been used earlier in Mexico (Dujovne 1984).

Sand painting

Sand painting has been recorded from the Gabrielino and Luiseño areas; among the Luiseño it was associated with elaborate initiation rites that also included ordeals and hallucinogenic substances (Moratto 1984:116). Simple drawings were also made in the ground with sticks (Boscana 1978:156). This most transitory media is represented only by a few sketches.

Rock Painting

Some of the most interesting examples of California Indian paintings are found in cave shelters from northern Baja to about the middle of the state. However, those that show cross-cultural interaction are along the central coast near established missions. The rock art of the Chumash Indians is particularly outstanding. The complex and colorful paintings that likely depict mythological beings, cosmology, vision, and dream (Lee 1977) seemingly were made in the course of working magic to achieve control over natural forces and man-made crises (Lee 1981:20).

Designs that are found at both rock art sites and at the missions are checkerboard motifs, zigzags and diamond chains, dentates, sun-wheels, mandalas, and simple circles. Such abstracted geometric designs, which appear to be (to us) simple motifs, probably represented significant objects or important spirit beings, commemorated events, had magical significance, or symbolized prayers and offerings. In many aboriginal cultures, the most sacred concepts are not represented in the art at all, or if they are, they are hidden in geometric motifs that only bear symbolic relationships to the meaning behind them (Chipp 1971:161). Geometric designs may also have been inspired by drugs ingested in the various coming-of-age rites that were common throughout the tribes of California (Blackburn 1977:93; Latta 1977:589).

It appears certain that increased ceremonial activity occurred after the arrival of the Spanish, when people were dying from introduced diseases and the society was under extreme stress. Thus, ceremonies—including the execution of rock paintings—were an effort to bring supernatural power to avert death and drive the intruders out of their area (Hudson and Underhay 1978:72).

We have evidence of mission pigment being utilized in rock paintings at two Chumash sites. One is the San Emigdio site (in the southwest San Joaquin Valley) in eastern Chumash territory and the other is near Santa Bárbara. The San Emigdio site has been described (Lee 1979) as having unusual colors in the paintings—colors that were common in mission usage but unknown to the natives prehistorically (Grant 1965:Plates 27, 28 and Frontispiece). These are green, blue-green and a true bright orange. All are somewhat opaque, which in itself is an unusual characteristic in Chumash rock painting. The opaque quality of the pigments at the San Emigdio site and the colors at both sites are atypical enough to warrant consideration.

Pigments available to native Californians were hematite (red ochre) or cinnabar for the color red; white, usually obtained from diatomaceous earth; and black, which might be obtained from charcoal, hydrous manganese oxide, burned graphite, or asphaltum. Although yellow ochre (limonite) is quite common in a natural state, it was rarely used in rock painting. All are fairly transparent in appearance. This contrasts with the pigments at San Emigdio, which appear to have been mixed with a white substance, making them light-reflective and therefore more vivid. No other known site in Chumash territory has this opaque quality in the pigment. However, Indian neophytes who were painting mission walls would have been familiar with the art of mixing pigments in order to obtain particular colors, as in the mission "instruction" for painters; mixing gypsum or lime with the powdered pigment (Hageman and Ewing 1979:165–166) would result in a characteristic opacity. Webb (1945:149) also states that diatomaceous earth, when mixed with pigment, gives the requisite colors. Mission records show requests and receipts for malachite and azurite to be sent from Mexico for pigments to decorate the missions (Webb 1952:233). This might well be the source of these unusual colors found at the San Emigdio site. It appears that the motifs painted in this cave shelter were made, at least in part, with mission pigments and perhaps were intended to activate supernatural forces against the Spanish, and give new power to their old cosmic themes.

The Santa Bárbara site has a mandala-like motif consisting of wedge-shaped rays that radiate out from a center, quite typical for the Chumash style; however, the colors are pink and green and have an exact match in the still extant church paintings at Mission San Miguel (cf. Neuerburg 1987:Figure p. 45). One might assume that these same colors were common at Santa Bárbara and Santa Inés missions also. It is of interest that the site is located near the pass that leads between these two missions.

We have no precise information as to instruction in the arts at the missions. As early as 1771, Mission San Gabriel requested a book on "how to paint without a teacher—or something similar" (Neuerburg 1987:7), but it has not survived. None of the artisans sent from Mexico to teach crafts to the neophytes specifically taught figurative arts, although many of them had artistic talents, as did some of the soldiers and at least one of the friars. The neophytes would have acted as assistants and eventually might teach others. Spanish documents are silent on all of this.

Once incorporated into the mission system, native talents used in sand painting and rock art were transfered to more European outlets such as decorating walls and painting on canvas. Of the latter, only the 14 paintings of the Stations of the Cross made at San Fernando and now at San Gabriel Mission and a single canvas representing the Archangel Raphael at Mission Santa Inés have come down to us (Neuerburg 1977a:Figures 1, 2; 1987:40, 41). All are surely based on prints or other paintings as opposed to being original compositions, but in the one case in which a precise comparison has been found, the Indian artist has modified his model, intensifying its religious impact while applying a native interpretation to one certain detail (Neuerburg and Engstrand 1986:Figures 15, 16). The artist achieved a significant change in emphasis by manipulating the placement of the figures; and Jesus' mother, the Virgin Mary, is transformed into a girl since the concept of a mature woman as a virgin may have seemed a contradiction to a native. It must be the work of an artist who wholeheartedly attempted to accept Christianity, and he gave himself a prominent position as a supporter of the condemned Christ (Figures 29-5, 29-6). Although these paintings are traditionally attributed to a single artist, Juan Antonio, one can find evidence of several hands, even within the same canvas. The painting of the Archangel is chiefly notable for the strong Indian cast of the facial features.

Recent research has demonstrated the extent of the use of wall painting at the missions and much of this, though not all, was surely executed by Indians

Figure 29-5. Fourth Station of the Cross, painted by Indians at Mission San Fernando, now at Mission San Gabriel.

Figure 29-6. Mexican engraving (reversed) of Fourth Station of the Cross. (Private collection)

both under the close supervision of artisans from Mexico or more or less on their own.

Only at San Buenaventura is there any contemporary written record of the work having been done by the Indians, although none is named (Neuerburg 1987:55). John Harrington's informant, Fernando Librado, identified the artist as Juan Pacifico and said that he also decorated the church at Santa Bárbara (Hudson 1977:8). However, he probably only worked as an apprentice there, to judge by the difference in execution between the two sites. The designs are totally European in origin and must come from a pattern book. In fact, the only detail that has even vague Indian parallels is the stepped terrace frieze on top of the dado (Neuerburg 1987:23). The parallels come principally from Arizona and New Mexico, although one unique petroglyph (Figure 29-7) on a hilltop near Chatsworth at the northern end of the San Fernando Valley has a similar motif (Neuerburg and Engstrand 1986:Figure S).

It should be emphasized at this point that almost all motifs used in mission wall decoration can be shown to have European origin. If, as is frequently the case, certain motifs can be paralleled in native motifs, they were not seen as such by the missionaries any more than the pagans of ancient Rome recognized the meaning of symbols used by the early Christians. Certainly by the eighteenth century the Catholic Church had little need for hidden symbols and except for a few motifs such as the cross, practically all decorative motifs were essentially

Figure 29-7. Petroglyph on top of a conical hill near Chatsworth (San Fernando Valley, California).

seen as no more than decoration. If the neophytes chose to recognize meanings of their own in these designs, they kept them to themselves, and the missionaries probably felt they had little reason to be suspicious.

The Asistencia of Pala, in contrast to Mission San Buenaventura, appears on the surface to have little European character, yet only one or possibly two motifs cannot be shown to have European parallels, and everything else would have been seen as perfectly acceptable by Father Peyri, who seemingly gave his local charges a free hand (Neuerburg 1987:71, 72). Their loyalty is shown in the Christian cross, which is the most used motif; there are perhaps as many as a hundred or more. In no other church in California was it used so extensively.

At San Fernando, several clearly native motifs were placed above doors in the father's dwelling, and a figure of an Indian with a bow was painted next to a door in the *sala* (Neuerburg 1987:66–69). Other designs are European in origin, including the vintage scene over a door, one of the rare narrative scenes painted on a mission wall, although a deer hunting scene over an exterior door is a narrative version of a purely Indian subject (Neuerburg 1977a:Figure 9, 1987:7).

These examples were all probably authorized or accepted, if not necessarily encouraged, by the missionaries, but other designs painted or incised on mission walls could more properly be called "abusive" in intent and certainly were not done for the missionaries. Examples must have been ubiquitous, but extensive groups can now only be seen at San Juan Capistrano and San Miguel, and these have been noted only recently. Elsewhere little original plaster surface survives.

At San Miguel designs are all incised and are within the church itself (Neuerburg 1987:3, 8). They seem to be limited to the body of the church, outside the altar railing, and are not found higher than the top border of the dado. They consist of lunar-like tallies, cross-hatching, mandala or sun-signs, human figures, and other clearly native designs. The only non-Indian motif is a ship, one that is known also from rock art sites (Lee 1975:118–120). Their location in the church can be explained by the fact that they would have to have been done while the neophytes were seated or kneeling on the floor during services.

At San Juan Capistrano, they appear on exterior walls only and are both painted and incised (Neuerburg 1982; 1987:8, 53, 54). Most of these appear to have been done while the neophytes were standing as they are at eye level and would have been meant to be seen. They are on the first or second layer of whitewash and are easily distinguished from later graffiti, which are always names or dates. When painted, the colors are mostly black or a copper green, although there is a small amount of red.

Some of these designs are paralleled in rock art. A stick figure with a skirt may be a representation of the Tobet mentioned in *Chinigchinich*, the unique account of native religion at this mission written by Father Boscana, but most are either of uncertain interpretation or simply undecipherable because of their condition. Among the graffiti, lunar tallies abound; there is a particularly fine example on the door frame of the sacristy of the Stone Church at San Juan Capistrano. One tiny incised design next to the door of the *sala* appears to represent an acorn granary. One might hypothesize that the designs began to be placed on the walls after the earthquake of 1812 as sympathetic magic. Father Boscana, be-cause of his interest in native beliefs, may have even encouraged this form of what should normally have been a forbidden artistic expression. But then he may also have seen these as nothing but childish doodles, as did the other mis-sionaries.

Incised designs are also found in California Indian arts; these markings on small stone tablets (Lee 1981:40–44) have been recovered from sites throughout the state. Their function is unknown and they date from early as well as late time periods (Lathrap and Hoover 1975:98–99). They also have a parallel at rock painting sites in the form of tallies and cross-hatching; these may be either painted or incised (Lee 1975:119).

Conclusion

We can only surmise that since the goal of the mission system was to bring the new converts into the mainstream of European culture as good Christians and taxpaying subjects of the Spanish Crown, the more the Indian's work resembled the imported model the better. If the result seemed a bit naive or crude to the Father, he was likely to be indulgent, but he certainly would not have encour-aged the use of native motifs. If the Indian artist chose to keep to himself his own interpretation of what he executed that fact was ignored by the missionar-ies. In time, these secondary meanings probably came to be forgotten, especially among those who were born and raised in a mission community and had little or no contact with the dying culture.

A small painting of Our Lady of Refuge, now at Mission Santa Clara, was painted in the late 1840s or early 1850s by an ex-mission Indian named Eulalio for Maria de Las Nieves Castro (Spearman 1950–1951). It differs in no way from other typical Mexican representations of the subject, and only the documenta-tion links it to an Indian. However, an embroidered panel done by Indian girls at the school of the first nuns in Santa Barbara is a curious combination of Euro-pean design with urns of flowers, a figure of Saint Joseph, a pair of parrots, and a group of native California animals and birds certainly chosen by the Indians rather than the sisters. Old ideas die hard.

References

Blackburn, Thomas
    1977 Biopsychological Aspects of Chumash Rock Art. *Journal of California* Anthropology 4(1):88–94.
Boscana, Fr. Geronimo
    1978 *Chinigchinich*. Malki Museum Press, Banning, Calif.
Bryan, Bruce
    1970 *Archaeological Explorations on San Nicolas Island*. Paper No. 22. Southwest Museum, Los Angeles.
Chipp, Herschel
    1971 Formal and Symbolic Factors in the Art Styles of Primitive Cultures. In *Art and Aesthetics in Primitive Societies*, edited by Carol F. Jopling, pp. 147–170. E. P. Dutton, New York.

Driver, Harold E.
  1937 Culture Element Distribution VI: Southern Sierra Nevada. *University of California Anthropological Records*, 1(2):53–154. Berkeley.
Dujovne, Marta
  1984 *Las pinturas con incrustaciones de nacar*. Universidad Nacional Autonoma de Mexico, Mexico.
Ferguson, Catherine C., and Robert L. Hoover.
  1983 Ceramic Effigies from Mission San Antonio. *Masterkey* 57(1):28–33.
Gayton, Anna H.
  1976 Yokuts-Mono Chiefs and Shamans. In *Native Californians: A Theoretical Retrospective*, edited by Lowell John Bean and Thomas C. Blackburn, pp. 175–223. Ballena Press.
Grant, Campbell
  1965 *The Rock Paintings of the Chumash*. University of California Press, Berkeley.
Hageman, Fred C. and Russell C. Ewing
  1979 *An Archaeological and Restoration Study of Mission La Purísima Concepción*, edited by Richard S. Whitehead. Santa Barbara Trust for Historical Preservation. Santa Barbara, Calif.
Handelman, Don
  1976 The Development of a Washo Shaman. In *Native Californians: A Theoretical Retrospective*, edited by Lowell John Bean and Thomas C. Blackburn, pp. 379–405. Ballena Press.
Hedges, Ken
  1982 Phosphenes in the Context of Native American Rock Art. *American Indian Rock Art*, VII & VIII:1–10.
Heizer, Robert
  1968 *The Indians of Los Angeles County: Hugo Reid's Letters of 1852*. Paper No. 21. Southwest Museum, Los Angeles.
Hudson, Travis
  1977a *Chumash Wooden Bowls, Trays, and Boxes*. Paper No. 13. San Diego Museum, San Diego.
  1977b Some John P. Harrington Notes regarding Chumash Masons at Missions Santa Barbara and San Buenaventura. *Pacific Coast Archaeological Society Quarterly* 13(3):15–21.
  1978 An Unusual Stone Effigy from San Clemente Island, California. *Journal of California Anthropology* 5(2):262–266.
  1979 *Breath of the Sun: Life in Early California as Told by a Chumash Indian, Fernando Librado to John P. Harrington*. Malki Museum Press, Banning, Calif.
Hudson, Travis, and Thomas C. Blackburn
  1982 *The Material Culture of the Chumash Interaction Sphere, Vol. 1: Food Procurement and Transportation*. Anthropological Papers No. 25. Ballena Press.
  1985 *The Material Culture of the Chumash Interaction Sphere*, vol. III: *Clothing, Ornamentation, and Grooming*. Anthropological Papers No. 28. Ballena Press.
  1986 *The Material Culture of the Chumash Interaction Sphere*, vol. IV: *Ceremonial Paraphernalia, Games, and Amusements*. Anthropological Papers No. 30, Ballena Press.
Hudson, Travis, and Ernest Underhay
  1978 *Crystals in the Sky: An Intellectual Odyssey involving Chumash Astronomy, Cosmology and Rock Art*. Ballena Press and Santa Barbara Museum of Natural History.
Kroeber, A. L.
  1973 *Basket Designs of the Mission Indians of California*. Ballena Press, Ramona, Calif.
Kroeber, Theodora, Albert B. Elsasser, and Robert F. Heizer
  1977 *Drawn from Life: California Indians in Pen and Brush*. Ballena Press, Socorro, N. Mex.
Lathrap, Donald W., and Robert L. Hoover.
  1975 *Excavations at Shilimaqshtush: SBa-205*. Occasional Paper No. 10. San Luis Obispo County Archaeological Society.

Latta, Frank
  1977 *Handbook of Yokuts Indians*. Rev. Bear State Books, Santa Cruz, Calif.
Lee, Georgia
  1975 An Historical Rock Art Site Northwest of Jalama. In *Excavations at Shilimaqshtush: SBa-205*, pp. 118–120. Occasional Paper No. 10. San Luis Obispo County Archaeological Society.
  1977 Chumash Mythology in Paint and Stone. *Pacific Coast Archaeological Society Quarterly*, 13(3):1–14.
  1978 Decorated Burial Markers and Portable Art of the Indians of the Santa Barbara Coast. *American Indian Rock Art* 4:177–186. American Rock Art Research Association.
  1979 The San Emigdio Site. *Journal of California and Great Basin Anthropology*, 1(2):295–305.
  1981 *The Portable Cosmos: Effigies, Ornaments and Incised Stone from the Chumash Area*. Anthropological Papers 21. Ballena Press.
Moratto, Michael
  1984 *California Archaeology*. Academic Press, New York.
Neuerburg, Norman
  1977a Painting in the California Missions. *American Art Review* 4(1):72–88.
  1977b Indian Carved Statues at Mission Santa Barbara. *Masterkey* 51(4):147–151.
  1980 More Indian Sculpture at Mission Santa Barbara. *Masterkey* 54(4):150–153.
  1982 Indian Pictographs at Mission San Juan Capistrano. *Masterkey* 56(2):55–58.
  1987 *The Decoration of the California Missions*. Bellerophon Books, Santa Barbara.
Neuerburg, Norman, and Iris H. W. Engstrand
  1986 Early California Reflections. An Exhibit presented at the San Juan Capistrano Regional Branch of Orange County Public Library, August 30 through October 11.
Simpson, Lesley (editor)
  1961 *Journal of Jose Longinos Martinez*. John Howell Books, San Francisco.
Smith, Lillian
  1982 Three Inscribed Chumash Baskets with Designs from Spanish Colonial Coins. *American Indian Art Magazine* 7(3):62–68.
Spearman, A. D.
  1950–1951 Our Lady of Refuge Patroness of California. *Academy Scrapbook* 1:234–238.
Vastokas, Joan M., and R. K. Vastokas
  1973 *Sacred Art of the Algonkians: A Study of the Peterborough Petroglyphs*. Mansard Press, Ontario.
Webb, Edith
  1945 Pigments Used by the Mission Indians of California. *The Americas*, vol. II(2). Washington D.C.
  1952 *Indian Life at the Old Missions*. Warren F. Lewis, Los Angeles.

Chapter 30 ■

Glenn J. Farris

The Russian Imprint on the Colonization of California

Russian Entry into the North Pacific

The second arrival of Vitus Bering in the North Pacific in 1741 was not immediately known to the Spanish colonial world. His exploration was the natural outgrowth of several centuries of eastward expansion carried out by Russia's own brand of Cossack "mountain men" and fur traders who rapidly infiltrated the huge land of Siberia (see Chevigny 1965:28–30; Dmytryshyn et al. 1988).

Bering died in the course of this exploration, but word of the discovery of Alaska was brought back to European Russia. Along with reports on the northern reaches of America, the survivors brought valuable furs, and by 1743 fur companies were making their way to the new world. Initially their activity was concentrated in the Aleutian Islands and at the island of Kodiak, and just barely touched mainland Alaska. The most valuable fur was that of the sea otter (*Enhydra lutris*), which brought great sums in the Chinese market. The problem was that this animal was difficult to hunt. Only the Aleuts, with their skin-covered *baidarkas*, or kayaks, were capable of catching them in any numbers. Most Russians were never truly skilled at this type of hunting, so they pressed the Aleuts into doing the work for them. This was mainly accomplished by taking hostages in the village and thus compelling the men to perform this hunting.

Word got to the outside world, and soon the European nations were sending exploring expeditions of their own to this new area of the North Pacific. One of the best known of these was that of Captain James Cook (1778). The Spanish were very interested in these developments and from at least the early 1760s there was a lively correspondence and reportage on what the Russians were doing. They were particularly concerned with Russian forays into the *Mar del Sur* (South Pacific?) (see Hilton 1981: 197–224).

Although the Spanish had touched on Alta (Upper) California's coast on several occasions (Rodríguez Cabrillo in 1542; Unamuno in 1587; Cermeño in 1595; Vizcaino in 1602 [Mathes 1968]), the first real effort at occupation did not come until 1769, with the arrival of a military expedition accompanied by Franciscan priests. This was preceded by the convening of a junta in the west Mexican port city of San Blas on May 16, 1768. At this meeting a royal order dated January 23, 1768, was read to the assembled group "imparting definite knowledge of the attempts which the Russians have made to facilitate their communication with this America, warned his Excellency [the Marqués of Grimaldi] to dispatch instructions and orders to the Governor of California to observe from there the designs of that nation and to frustrate them as far as possible" (Watson and Temple 1934:20).

Furthermore, they were to undertake a land and sea expedition to locate the harbor of Monterey and there establish a "presidio and settlement at that place which is truly the most advantageous for protecting the entire west coast of California and the other coasts of the southern part of this continent, against any attempts by the Russians or any northern nation" (Watson and Temple 1934: 22).

This stimulus to the colonization of Alta California came on the heels of another dramatic event: the expulsion of the Jesuits from Baja California (and all Spanish domains) in 1767. The Franciscan priests were thus relative newcomers, almost directly from the Old World and full of missionary zeal, which was put to work in the founding and developing of 19 missions and 4 presidios before the dreaded Russians even set foot in California.

The Russian fur-hunting enterprise, although only modestly sponsored by the government, had a good deal of government involvement in terms of permission, representation, reports, and oversight) during the first 60 or 70 years (Dmytryshyn et al. 1988:xl–xlvi). The endeavor was basically supported by private enterprise, with some 42 Russian companies participating in the years 1743–1797 (Gibson 1976:3). By 1799, one company prevailed. It was known as the Russian-American Company (often indicated by the Cyrillic letters *PAK*). Having received a charter from Tsar Paul I, it was granted a monopoly on all hunting, trading, and mining on the northwest coast of America above the fifty-fifth parallel for a period of 20 years (Tikhmenev 1978:53–55). This consolidation allowed the company to concentrate on expansion, and the governorship of the area was placed in the energetic hands of Alexander Baranov. Unfortunately, he was not strongly backed by the directors of the company (in part because of the distance from the home office) and was thus forced to effect his own discipline in the colonies. The truly incredible problems of resupply from European Russia forced the company to rely on the various foreign ships that made their way to Kodiak, and later to the second capital at New Archangel (Sitka). One of the enterprising traders to make this journey was an American named Joseph O'Cain who, in 1803, entered into a joint venture with Baranov. O'Cain took a number of Aleut hunters and their *baidarkas* on a hunting trip down the coast of California. The results of this trip were very rewarding, not only because they took a good number of pelts but also because they did not lose a single man (Chevigny 1965:102). The success of this expedition, combined with the decimation of sea otters in the northern waters, started Baranov thinking about expanding southward.

However, he could really do nothing until he could obtain some ships. In 1804 there had not been a Russian ship to arrive from the Siberian port (Okhotsk) for five years. When it finally came, it was carrying a councillor to the tsar, Nikolai Rezanov, who was also the son-in-law of the founder of the Russian-American Company, Shelikov, and a major stockholder. Rezanov came at a time when the Alaskan colony was close to desperation. The food supplies, particularly grain and vegetables, were virtually exhausted. Rezanov soon decided that the only recourse was to sail to Spanish California and purchase supplies. He did so in 1806, and despite official antagonism, managed to win over the commandant of the San Francisco presidio, José Argüello, and his daughter, Concepción, and to return with supplies to New Archangel.

Additional expeditions were sent, one to the Oregon Country in 1808 with the ill-fated ship, the *Sviatoi Nikolai*. When this ended in disaster, plans for Oregon were scrapped in favor of a move directly on California (Owens and Donnelly 1985:3–5). The second group came in the ship *Kodiak* led by Ivan Kuskov, Baranov's chief deputy, to reconnoitre the coast and even to slip into San Francisco Bay in search of sea otters. When they returned with over 2,000 sea otter pelts, the decision was made to concentrate on California (Khlebnikov 1976:107).

The initial expeditions had been so promising that plans were made to establish a firmer base. The Russians first concentrated on the port of Rumiantsov (Bodega Bay) in 1811. This lay conveniently beyond the area actually occupied by the Spanish. The Russian leader of the expedition, Ivan Kuskov, soon decided that this base was a little too exposed, both by sea and land. He then searched the coast to the north until he found a place that had an acceptable cove and timber for building and that offered protection from land attack in the form of steep coastal mountains rising to some 1,500 feet. Kuskov set about making friends with the local Kashaya Pomo people and quickly put his men to work erecting a stockade and buildings. By the fall of 1812 *Krepost'* (Fort) Ross had come into being.

The Spanish military quickly sent emissaries to protest the establishment of the settlement, but also to make observations about its strength. The early accounts are quite fascinating in that the frontier Spanish soldiers found themselves confronted with an architecture and customs that stretched their ability to describe. Coming from a place with only adobe brick buildings never more than one story high, they were overwhelmed to find structures of two stories built of timbers (Argüello 1814).

Relations with the Spanish and Mexicans

In a proclamation to the Californian people delivered in 1812, Russian-American Company officials in Saint Petersburg called upon the good relations of Russia and Spain as allies in the then ongoing Napoleonic Wars to look favorably upon trade between the Russian settlements in Alaska and the Spanish in California. The message was said to be delivered to the commandant, Manuel Ruiz, in San Vicente (Baja California) and forwarded to Governor Goycoechea. However, the reply was that no decision could be made until Madrid had been consulted (Bancroft 1886a:294–296).

Russian-American Company representatives had to tread the fine line between seeking the cooperation of the Spanish (after 1821, Mexican) authorities and rejecting the Spaniards' frequent demands that they leave. In some ways it was easier during the Spanish period because (1) the seat of power was so far removed from their settlement; (2) the joint interests of two Christian monarchies provided common ground, particularly in Russian dealings with the then powerful missions; and (3) the Spanish had not really moved north of San Francisco Bay until 1817, with the establishment of Mission San Rafael.

The concern of the Spanish had the happy result of producing the majority of the useful detailed observations on the Russian settlements. Both officers and priests were pressed into this sort of intelligence gathering (e.g., Argüello 1814; Estudillo 1816; Payeras 1822; Vallejo 1833). In 1817, a more direct approach was taken in which the Spanish Foreign Minister, Zea Bermúdez, via the Russian Ambassador to Spain, D. P. Tatishchev, demanded of his Russian counterpart, K. V. Nesselrode, information on this southerly incursion of the Russian-American Company. A description and detailed map of the Ross settlement were duly provided in August 1817 and form one of the most valuable documents on the fort (Figure 30-1; see also Fedorova 1973:358–360). Although we generally date this map to 1817, it must have been prepared before this time, because the Spanish letter of request had only been sent in April 1817 and there would not have been enough time to send it to Fort Ross and receive a reply in the intervening four months. The quality of this map is quite excellent as was found when it was placed on a mylar sheet and superimposed on a modern aerial photograph of the area surrounding the fort.

During the first 10 years or so of the existence of the settlement, the main emphasis was on the hunting of sea otter and fur seals. This took the Aleut hunters into a wide variety of the coastal areas reachable from Fort Ross, ranging from Trinidad Bay (Khlebnikov 1976:108–109), north of Eureka, to forays right into San Francisco Bay. This latter area was reached by carrying the light skin boats over the neck of Marin County and putting in probably at San Pablo Bay. Normally these expeditions were successful because the Spanish did not have adequate ships to patrol the area, not to speak of being unable to catch the swift

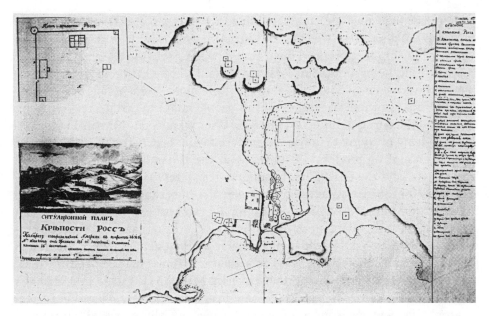

Figure 30-1. Map of Fort Ross in 1817. (Courtesy of Prof. Nicholas I. Rokitiansky and the California Department of Parks and Recreation)

baidarkas. However, the Aleuts were forced to land from time to time to obtain fresh water and were open to capture. There are a number of accounts in the records of captive Aleuts (or Kodiaks) held by the Spanish. On his formal visit in 1816, the round-the-world explorer, Otto von Kotzebue, undertook to ransom some of the captured Aleuts and their Russian overseers. In other cases, these people were kept, sometimes willingly, by the Spanish and often integrated into the community. A man identified as a native of Petropavlosk on the peninsula of Kamchatka, named Bolcoff, arrived in California ca. 1815 aboard some Russian ship and settled in. As a trained shoemaker, he was a welcome addition. He took the Hispanicized name José, had his Russian Orthodox baptism regularized, married into a Californian family, and rose to be an alcalde in Santa Cruz (Bancroft 1886a:723).

Under various sea captains, hunting was also undertaken surreptitiously at many spots on the coast further south from San Francisco. In some cases, the Kodiaks would simply be dumped off on some offshore island for an extended period and picked up later. The main such base was at the Farallon Islands, where a regular contingent was maintained over the years. These people were not seaborne, in fact did not have a boat at their disposal, but were periodically resupplied from Port Rumiantsov (Corney 1965:170–171).

Another more dramatic and tragic case was that of contingent of 25 Russians and Kodiaks left on San Nicolas Island off the coast of Southern California in 1825 (Heizer and Elsasser [1973:16] suggest they were dropped off by the Brig *Baikal*). They eventually killed the male Indian inhabitants except for one old man and took over their women (Phelps 1983:172–173). After about a year, the women had their revenge and slaughtered the Russian and Kodiak men. It is uncertain whether these Kodiaks and Russians were meant to stay so long, or whether the ship that brought them simply was unable to return.

Apart from the hunting, Fort Ross was meant to be a major agricultural supplier to the Alaskan colonies. Great efforts were made to encourage animal husbandry, the growing of grain, and the cultivation of fruit trees (Gibson 1976:112–140). An agricultural expert, E. L. Chernykh, spent 10 years in the California settlement trying to introduce modern methods (Chernykh 1967), but the limited amount of good land coupled with the generally inexperienced farm labor, pests, and the coastal fog in summer conspired to keep production low.

Despite the official antagonism between the Mexican government and the Russians (the tsar refused to recognize republican Mexico), there was a certain amount of friendly intercourse. The artisans at Fort Ross are said to have provided much material for the new mission at Sonoma in 1823, which was founded, in part, to block the Russian settlement from moving inland. In 1833, the new commandant for the northern district, Mariano G. Vallejo, reported visiting Fort Ross in order to purchase "200 rifles, 150 cutlasses, 200 saddles, etc." to supply his new garrison at Sonoma (Archives of California 1833). Two years later, Vallejo concluded a truce with the chief of a tribe against which he had fought, Succara of the Satiyomi (a Southern Pomo tribelet), and the treaty contained the following telling statements:

> Article 4—As a guarantee of the good faith of the Satiyomi nation, the Great Chief Succara will send to reside in Sonoma his brother, Cali-vengo (*Loma brava*) and his sons, Ipuy Succara and Calpela Succara who will be housed in the house of the Commandant General, during which time if they comport themselves well will be treated as if they were *Russian officials*.

> Article 9—The chiefs of the Satiyomi promise by the end of a month to deliver in the valley of Sonoma *or in the Fort Ross* all the children of Caynamero and Suisún tribes who have fallen prisoner in the course of the last three years.

> Article 10—The Commandant General M. G. Vallejo gives the order to his majordomo of the estate of Petaluma that for each prisoner who is delivered by Succara or his subordinates in the post of Sonoma or *at Fort Ross* will be given to the disposition of Succara an unbroken horse (*un caballo de falsa rienda*) [Vallejo n.d.: 299ff., emphasis supplied].

These provisions seem to suggest not only a close relationship between the Russians and the neighboring Indian peoples, but also a remarkable level of accommodation between the Mexicans and the Russians. It must be remembered that at this time the Mexican position was still very weak in the area and it may have been an act of *realpolitik* on the part of Vallejo. Later, he was more adamant in his objections to the Russian presence. The "Lausanne Incident" of 1840 is a case in point. The U.S. ship *Lausanne* coming south from the Oregon Country chose to land at the Russian port of Bodega rather than one of the Mexican ports where they would have to pay heavy duties. Vallejo sent Ensign Lázaro Piña to take charge of the port, but the Russian manager, Alexander Rotchev, appeared and refused his orders. This led to a period of even more strained relations until smoothed over through the intercession of Russian Chief Administrator Kuprianov (Bancroft 1886b:171-177).

Interaction with Other European Powers in the Pacific

For the most part, the other European powers had little impact on the Russian settlement in the Pacific. The Hudson's Bay Company (HBC), under the protection of Great Britain, was a major competitor in the area, but seemed to accept that California was outside its sphere of influence. At the same time, the HBC pursued a policy of exterminating the beaver in the area south of its western headquarters at Fort Vancouver. Fur brigades armed with steel traps were sent annually down to the Bonaventura (the Sacramento) River to trap beaver and other animals. By and large they did not intrude on the sea otter trade; their ultimate mission was to trap out the Sacramento River area and thus discourage other fur companies (principally American) from encroaching on their territory in the northwest. In at least one incident, however, a combined brigade under the command of John Work was sent to check the north coast of California for beaver. This required that they pass by Fort Ross. The Russian manager at the fort, Peter Kostromitinov, initially objected to the passing, especially because of the size of the group (163 men, women, and children), but Work insisted that there was no other way to proceed. Kostromitinov ultimately gave permission, but insisted that they continue on by and not camp near the fort (Maloney 1944:23–24). This passing of such a large group, with some 400–450 horses and mules, made quite an impact on the native Kashaya people and two of the best descriptions of this event were passed down in Kashaya folk history (Oswalt 1964:246–249, 250–253; Farris 1989b).

The Hudson's Bay Company had several skirmishes with the Russians in the Alaska–Canada area. The so-called Stikine Affair brought things to a head and resulted in an agreement between the HBC and the RAC in 1839 to respect each other's territories. Part of the agreement stipulated that the HBC would become the main supplier to the RAC in terms of foodstuffs and manufactured goods (Gibson 1989).

The fledgling United States also weighed in by invoking the Monroe Doctrine of 1824 to warn the Russian government against any imperial ambitions in the area. However, the United States made no real effort to eject the Russians from California. On March 13, 1833, the American fur trapper Ewing Young came to the fort with seven men and put 199 beaver pelts into the safekeeping of the Russians for transfer to the American Monterey merchant, John B. R. Cooper (National Archives n.d.). In 1837, William A. Slacum (1912:205–298) visited Fort Ross and reported back to Secretary of State John Forsythe on the situation and conditions there.

Various other countries showed interest in the Russian settlement, particularly the French. Several of their round-the-world expeditions visited Fort Ross over the course of the Russian occupation and have left us with valuable descriptions. In 1828, Auguste Bernard Duhaut-Cilly completed a marvelous drawing of the fort (see Duhaut-Cilly 1929). In 1839, another captain heading a worldwide scientific expedition, Cyrille LaPlace, spent the month of August at Fort Ross (LaPlace 1854). Finally, in 1841, came the French foreign service officer, Eugène DuFlot de Mofras, who was fully aware of the imminent departure of the Russians and sent dispatches home suggesting that France consider taking over the Russian holdings there (DuFlot de Mofras 1842; Wilbur 1937:248).

Relations with the Indians

The Russians' involvement with the Kashaya Pomo Indians living around Fort Ross and the Coast Miwok people around Bodega Bay has often been extolled as exemplary, particularly when compared with the treatment they received from the Spanish and Americans (e.g., Spencer-Hancock and Pritchard 1981:311). However, the reality was not quite as benign as has been suggested, although there were several good reasons why the Russian-American Company authorities would have treated these people with more consideration. It must be remembered that the experience of the company in Alaska had been very bloody, with numerous killings on both sides. In dealings with the Aleuts, Kodiaks, and the Tlingit, the Russians suffered through ambushes, massacres, and even pitched battles. After the *Kolosh* (Tlingit and their allies) attack on the redoubt at Sitka in 1802, the Tlingit stronghold was finally retaken in 1804 in a major assault by Russian forces under Baranov on its defenders, led by Kot-le-an (Katlian) (Chevigny 1942:217–221).

Things were different with the California Indians. For one thing, the Russians did not need to press them into service (at least not initially) to do the hunting, since they had brought their own skilled Aleuts. For another, the California Indians were far less warlike than were the Tlingits. They were also concerned enough over the movement north of the Spaniards that they welcomed a powerful ally. For their part, the Russians always referred to this part of California as New Albion, the name given it by Sir Francis Drake following his claim to the land in 1579. Thus the question of Spanish title was considered to be in doubt, and it became reasonable to deal with the local Indian peoples. On September 22, 1817, a formal agreement was concluded between the representatives of the Russian-American Company, including the visiting dignitary Leontii Hagemeister, and several local Indian chiefs including Tchu-Gu-An, Aman-Tan, and Gem-Le-Le, as well as several unnamed others. As part of the agreement, the Indians donated the land locally called Mad-Zhi-Ni (Metini) and expressed their readiness to render assistance to the Russians, while the Russians indicated that they would protect the Indians from attack (Spencer-Hancock and Pritchard 1981:308–309). The Indians were given some gifts including a medal decorated with the Russian Imperial emblem and the inscription, "Allies of Russia," on the reverse. Interestingly, the chief was strongly admonished that "it was not adviseable for him to come to the Fort without it [the medal]. It also obliged Indians to be loyal and render help to the Russians should the occasion arise" (Spencer-Hancock and Pritchard 1981:309).

A second reason why the Russians got on well with the Indians was the fact that they were not actively trying to proselytize. The Indians were permitted, even encouraged to remain in their own villages, rather than be drawn into the settlement. The exception, of course, was the intermarriage between the Russian and Aleut workers at Fort Ross and Bodega Bay (Port Rumiantsov) in which local women became wives of the settlers (see Jackson 1983:240–241).

That this practice was prevalent is indicated in the census for Fort Ross of 1820 prepared by Ivan Kuskov. In it, there were listed 273 people in the colony: 148 men, 71 women, and 54 small children. The full list with relations is worth considering:

> The men were as follows: 23 Russian, 3 Iakuts [from Siberia], 5 Creoles, and 116 Kadiak Eskimos, Aleuts and Alaska Indians (only 7 Kadiak Eskimos were considered "in the service of the Company").

> From among the 12 women who were either cohabiting or married to Russian men, the breakdown was as follows: 4 Creole, 2 Kadiak Eskimo, and 4 Indian women "from the region of Ross," one "Bodegin" [probably Coast Miwok] Indian woman, and one without indication of nationality referred to by the name of Anisia.

> From among the women who lived with the Creole men there were 3 Kadiak Eskimos, one Creole, one Aleut from the Fox Islands and one Indian woman "from the region of Ross."

> Among the 50 women cohabiting with them [i.e., the male Alaskan natives], one counts 17 "common law wives from the region of Ross [Kashaya]," 10 "from the river Slavianka [the Russian River, and thus also Pomo], 9 "Bodegin" [Coast Miwok], 8 "Kadiak," one Creole; the nationality of the others is not indicated [Fedorova 1975:12].

From this we can see that at least 42 of the 71 women who had become part of the Fort Ross settlement were California Indians. It is important to consider what a small portion of the overall settlement was actually ethnic Russian. At that time, it amounted to only about 8 percent. Unfortunately, relatively little remains of the experience and recollections of the Alaska natives who came to Fort Ross. One delightful exception is provided by Peter Kalifornsky, descendant of one of the initial contingent to arrive at Fort Ross (Kari 1983).

As mentioned above, there were eventually some antagonisms and exploitation of the California Indians on the part of the Russians. The most blatant was reported by the governor of Russian America, Ferdinand von Wrangell, following an inspection tour in 1833. Von Wrangell related that the common practice at harvest time was to forcibly gather "up to 150 [Indians], who for 1½ months are occupied with Company field work, and without their assistance it would not be at all possible to reap and haul the wheat from the plowland to the threshing floors" (Gibson 1969:210). He goes on to tell how the Indians are allotted "only flour for gruel as food: from this meager food and with the strenuous work the Indians toward the end are in extreme exhaustion. However, complaints and requests were received by me not from these people but from *promyshlenniks* on salary" (Gibson 1969:211). In an additional comment he says:

> I have authorized providing the Indians and the Aleuts the best food, as against
> formerly, and especially paying the Indians somewhat more generously for work.
> Not only humanity but also wisdom demand that the Indians be encouraged
> more: from the bad food and the negligible pay the Indians have stopped coming
> to the settlement for work, from which the Factory found itself forced to seek
> them in the tundra, attack by surprise, tie their hands, and drive them to the set-
> tlement like cattle to work: such a party of 75 men, wives and children was
> brought to the settlement during my presence from a distance of about 65 *verstas*
> (43 miles) from here, where they had to leave their belongings without any atten-
> tion for two months. It goes without saying what consequences there must be in
> due course from such actions with the Indians, and will we make them our
> friends? I hope that the Factory, having received permission from me to provide
> the Indians decent food and satisfactory pay, will soon see a change in their dis-
> position toward us [Gibson 1969:211].

Other Russians, including Von Wrangell (1839), Kostromitinov (1839), and the naturalist and early ethnographer, Il'ya Voznesensky (Bates 1983; Blomkvist 1972; Okladnikova 1983) showed continued interest in the native peoples around Fort Ross and Bodega Bay. Evidently, with such high-placed concern, relations overall did remain good with the Russians, as is shown by some comments by the Swedish traveler, G. M. Waseurtz af Sandels, who visited the abandoned Fort Ross in 1843. He tells of encountering Indians while on his way to the fort who took him for a Russian. As it happened, he not only spoke the language, but also knew some of the former Russians at the fort. These were ethnic Finns who came to occupy a larger proportion of the population toward the end of the Russian occupation. These Indians not only spoke Russian (Oswalt 1958), but vowed that they would not work for the Mexicans, so great was their linger-ing distrust for the latter (Van Sicklen 1945:80).

This distrust seemed to be justified in a violent manner a few years later, in August 1845, when there was a raid on the Indian village at Fort Ross. Mexican rancheros from the neighboring area had come to attempt to capture Indians for forced labor. Most of the Indians managed to escape, but the rancheros caught two old men and beat them in an effort to find out where the others were. They also found two young Indian women hiding in the loft of the house occu-pied by the European manager of the property, William Benitz. These women were gang-raped and then taken off to the ranches (Archives of California 1845; Farris 1984).

Archaeological Finds on Russian Sites in California

Real archaeological work on Russian sites has been limited to Fort Ross and to the Farallon Islands. The excavation project on the Farallones at sites designated CA-SFr-1 and CA-SFr-24 was undertaken in 1949 by Francis Riddell, Ynez Haase, Arnold Pilling, and Franklin Fenenga (Riddell 1955). There was a small *artel* (an outlying camp or substation) there for about 30 years. These sites pro-duced the main collection of artifacts found in California that are most probably of Kodiak or possibly northwest coast origin. To date, no excavation has been made at the site of the large Aleut village at Fort Ross.

Artifacts of aboriginal manufacture along with numerous pieces of ceramics of the early nineteenth century as well as fragments of distinctive "Russian" brick (5½ to 6 inches wide) indicate the acculturated life-style of these people (Pilling n.d.; Riddell 1955:9–10).

By far the major archaeological work done in the study of Russian California has been centered on the site at Fort Ross. Unfortunately, the other major site, Bodega Bay, has been largely destroyed through municipal development over the years and no archaeological reports are available from the site. Fort Ross has been fortunate in being more remote and long occupied by the Call family, which established a ranch there in 1873 and held the property until it was turned over to the state parks system. Over the years, unofficial archaeology was done in the park by various rangers, notably former curator, John McKenzie, who has compiled an invaluable body of notes and observations about the fort. Scholars also became intrigued with Fort Ross and wrote several master's theses (see Haase 1952; Hatch 1922; Smith 1974) and a dissertation (Kennedy 1955) on the Russian settlement and its effect on the local Indian people. The first major excavation project resulting in a published report was not accomplished until 1953, when Adan E. Treganza (1954) tested the area of the stockade walls during a time of reconstruction of the east and west walls. The main focus of the excavation was clearly to answer architectural questions and as such it provided an important foundation for future studies and salvaged critical information on the construction of the stockade walls that would otherwise have been lost in the reconstruction effort.

Little additional archaeological work was done until the 1970s. Interest in archaeological work was renewed when a tragic accidental fire consumed the Russian chapel in October 1970. Before it was reconstructed, William E. Pritchard carried out an archaeological excavation of the building site (see Spencer-Hancock and Pritchard 1982). Further work was done in response to a decision to enclose the stockade. For nearly a century, the main coast road (California Route 1) had passed directly through the middle of the old stockade area, so that the Department of Parks and Recreation found it difficult to develop fully, much less protect, the park. It was decided to realign the road to bypass the fort and permit the north and south stockade walls to be reconstructed. Excavations in advance of the construction of the bypass road were carried out in 1971 and 1972. With the removal of the road through the fort, plans could go forward for the reconstruction of two of the important buildings within the stockade, the Kuskov House and the Officials' Quarters. A series of excavations took place in various parts of the interior area of the stockade, principally in the years 1972–1977, by Sonoma State University (Officials' Quarters) and Cabrillo College (Fur Warehouse) and by archaeological teams working directly for the Department of Parks and Recreation. An overview of the combined historical information and the archaeological work was prepared by Bryn Thomas in 1976 and again was primarily concerned with questions about the architecture of the fort (Thomas 1976).

In 1981 the present author undertook an excavation of the site of the Old Warehouse or Fur Warehouse (Farris 1981; 1989a). While doing preliminary historical research, I came upon a major error in the translation of a number of invaluable inventory documents that gave the dimensions of virtually all of the buildings, not only at Fort Ross, but also at the outlying bases of Bodega and the Russian ranchos. This error had to do with a too literal translation of French and Spanish terms for the equivalent of "fathom." The result was a recomputation of these inventory descriptions, which increased the dimensions by some 16 percent (Farris 1983).

There is a certain level of frustration and disappointment when excavating on a "Russian" site in California. It stems from the dearth of clearly Russian artifacts. For the most part, the Russian-American Company relied on the importation of goods through American and British merchants who plied the west coast of America. Ceramics, glass, gunflints, and, of course, many perishable goods such as cloth, all came from the same suppliers who visited the other ports of the Pacific coast. In all the excavations and accidental finds at Fort Ross, for example, there are only about two or three pieces of ceramic that are definitely of Russian manufacture (see O'Connor 1984:70). One of these, a small fragment of white earthenware with the partial impressed mark of "-tnikova" (in English transliteration) is believed to associate with the Gzhel potter, E. M. Gusyatinikov who was active in the late eighteenth and early nineteenth centuries (Popov 1957:126). An intriguing association is that there was a Nikolai Mikhailovich Gusyatnikov who was a stockholder, possibly even a director, in the Russian-American Company in the period 1807–1818 (Fedorova, personal communication 1984). However, we are also aware of the presence of a variety of artisans and craftsmen at the Russian settlements who made everything from bricks to ships. The making of fired bricks was a particular undertaking at Fort Ross up until 1832 and subsequently at Bodega Bay, according to Von Wrangell (Gibson 1969:207). These bricks were quite distinctive in their size, being significantly larger than the standard English or American bricks of the time. The making and hauling of these bricks required the labor of a number of California Indians (Gibson 1969:211). A nascent shipbuilding industry failed when four vessels constructed there became unseaworthy after only a few years owing to poor-quality (or perhaps not sufficiently cured) oak.

Another artifact type found at Fort Ross indicated the acculturation of the Kashaya people: projectile points made of flaked bottle glass. The importance of this material to a people used to working in obsidian is made obvious by the fact that they adopted the Russian word for bottle to refer to broken glass while they borrowed the Spanish word *botella* to refer to the vessel itself (Oswalt 1971). The development of the Mexican mission and settlement at Sonoma no doubt interrupted the once-thriving obsidian trade from the inland sources (Annadel and Napa Glass Mountain), making the use of bottle glass more desirable. It seems likely that the relative paucity of remains of broken bottles from the Russian site itself at Fort Ross may be due to recycling by the Indians.

Departure of the Russians in 1842

By 1839 the Russians were ready and willing to sell out their holdings in California. A combination of political pressure, economic failure of the settlement, and the assurance of supplies through the treaty with the Hudson's Bay Company made such a move desirable. The question became, to whom should they sell? They first turned to the HBC, which toyed with the idea but ultimately decided to reject it. Next they approached Mariano Vallejo (Vallejo 1841). But politically Vallejo saw no point in paying for the property since he argued that the Russians did not own the real estate and they would probably have to abandon the improvements, which could thus be taken for free. Commandant Rotchev had another idea: sell the property to the founder of the new settlement on the confluence of the Sacramento and American rivers, John Sutter. The ambitious Swiss offered to pay $30,000 and the deal was struck in late 1841 (Sutter Papers). Sutter set about removing the livestock and dismantling the buildings for transport up to New Helvetia, and the era of imperial Russia in California came to an end.

Conclusion

Russian movement into the North Pacific Basin in the first half of the eighteenth century excited a Spanish reaction to protect their *Mare Nostra*. The long coastal area of Alta California needed to be explored, settled, and defended. The combined ecclesiastic and military force that ventured forth to San Diego and points north in 1769 was meant to secure this frontier. In the end, the actuality of the Russian presence was fairly innocuous, but the colonization effort was hardly in vain considering the subsequent expansion of the British and Americans into the northwest Pacific. Had this Spanish presence not developed when it did, the whole cultural history of Alta California would certainly have been very different. The Russian approach to colonization in California formed a notable counterpoint to that of the Spanish, but in both cases they relied heavily on the presence and participation of the native peoples as an integral part of their new community, albeit as second-class citizens. The actual Russian presence in California lasted only about 30 years, but its net effect from potential threat to political retreat was an important stimulus to the real colonization of California.

Acknowledgments

I would like to thank the following people for their help in reviewing earlier drafts of this chapter: Mrs. E.A.P. Crownhart-Vaughan of the Oregon Historical Society, Professor James R. Gibson of York University, Downsview, Ontario, and Professor W. Michael Mathes of the University of San Francisco.

References

Archives of California
  1833 Letter from Figueroa to Vallejo, dated April 11, 1833. Department of State Papers, Benecia Military, vol. 79:33–35. Ms. on file, Bancroft Library, Berkeley.
  1845 Sonoma—Proceso contra Antonio Castro y socios acusados de haber extraido a mano armada una porcion de indios gentiles. Ms. on file, Archives of California, Departmental State Papers, Benicia, Tomo V, vol. 39, pp. 390ff.

Argüello, Luis
    1814 *Sobre el presidio ruso de Ross. San Francisco 1814*. Archives of California. Provincial State Papers, vol. 19:365–368. Ms. at Bancroft Library, Berkeley.
Bancroft, Hubert Howe
    1886a *The Works of Hubert Howe Bancroft, Vol. XIX. History of California, Vol II, 1801–1824*. The History Company, San Francisco.
    1886b *The Works of Hubert Howe Bancroft, Vol. XXI. History of California, Vol. IV, 1840–1845*. History Co., San Francisco.
Bates, Craig D.
    1983 The California Collection of I. G. Voznesensky. *American Indian Art Magazine*. Summer:36–41, 79.
Blomkvist, E. E.
    1972 A Russian Scientific Expedition to California and Alaska, 1839–1849: The Drawings of I. G. Voznesenskii. Translated by Basil Dmytryshyn and E. A. P. Crownhart-Vaughan. *Oregon Historical Quarterly* 73(2):101–170.
Chernykh, E. L.
    1967 Agriculture of Upper California: A Long Lost Account of Farming in California as Recorded by a Russian Observer at Fort Ross in 1841. *Pacific Historian* 11(1):10–28.
Chevigny, Hector
    1942 *Lord of Alaska: The Story of Baranov and the Russian Adventure*. Binfords and Mort, Portland, Oreg.
    1965 *Russian America: The Great Alaskan Adventure, 1741–1867*. Viking Press, New York.
Corney, Peter
    1965 *Early Voyages in the North Pacific, 1813–1818*. Galleon Press, Fairfield, Wash.
Dmytryshyn, Basil, E. A. P. Crownhart-Vaughan, and Thomas Vaughan (editors)
    1988 *Russia's Penetration of the North Pacific Ocean, 1700–1799: A Documentary Record. Vol 2: To Siberia and Russian America: Three Centuries of Russian Eastward Expansion, 1558–1867*. North Pacific Studies Series, vol. 10. Oregon Historical Society.
DuFlot de Mofras, Eugène
    1842 Mélanges par M. de Mofras—Manuscrits, vol. 2, no. 3. Ms. at Bancroft Library, Berkeley.
Duhaut-Cilly, Auguste Bernard
    1929 Duhaut-Cilly's Account of California in the Years 1827–1828. Translated by Charles Franklin Carter. *California Historical Society Quarterly* 8(4):306–336.
Estudillo, José Maria
    1816 Establicimiento puesto por los rusos al sur de cabo Mendocino . . . San Francisco, 27 Octubre, 1816. Photostat in the Bancroft Library, Berkeley. (Original in the National Archives, Washington, D.C.)
Farris, Glenn J.
    1981 Preliminary Report of the 1981 Excavations of the Fort Ross Fur Warehouse. Ms. on file, California Department of Parks and Recreation, Resource Protection Division, Sacramento.
    1983 Fathoming Fort Ross. *Historical Archaeology* 17(2):93–99.
    1984 An Account of a Raid for Indian Slaves at Fort Ross in 1845. Ms. on file, California Department of Parks and Recreation, Resource Protection Division, Sacramento.
    1989a Archaeology of the Old *Magasin* at Ross Counter, California. In *Proceedings of the Second International Conference on Russian America* (Sitka, Alaska, August 22, 1987), in press.
    1989b Recognizing Indian Folk History as Real History: A Fort Ross Example. *American Indian Quarterly*, in press.
Fedorova, Svetlana G.
    1973 *The Russian Population in Alaska and California, Late 18th Century–1867*. Translated and edited by Richard A. Pierce and Alton S. Donnelly. Limestone Press, Kingston, Ontario.

1975 *Ethnic Processes in Russian America*. Translated by Antoinette Shalkop. Occasional Paper No. 1. Anchorage Historical and Fine Arts Museum.

Gibson, James R.

1969 Russia in California, 1833: Report of Governor Wrangel. *Pacific Northwest Quarterly* 60(4): 205–215.

1976 *Imperial Russia in Frontier America: The Changing Geography of Supply of Russian America, 1784–1867*. Oxford University Press, New York.

1989 The "Russian Contract": The Agreement of 1839 between the Hudson's Bay and Russian-American Companies. *Proceedings of the Second International Conference on Russian America* (Sitka, Alaska, August 20, 1987), in press.

Haase, Ynez

1952 *The Russian American Company in California*. Unpublished Master's thesis, University of California, Berkeley.

Hatch, Flora Faith

1922 *The Russian Advance into California*. Unpublished Master's thesis, University of California, Berkeley.

Heizer, Robert F., and Albert Elsasser (editors)

1973 *Original Accounts of the Lone Woman of San Nicolas Island*. Ballena Press, Ramona, Calif.

Hilton, Sylvia Lyn

1981 *Descripcion de las Costas de California* por Iñigo Abbad y LaSierra. Coleccion Tierra Nueva e Cielo Nuevo III. Instituto "Gonzalo Fernandez de Oviedo", Madrid.

Jackson, Robert H.

1983 Intermarriage at Fort Ross: Evidence from the San Rafael Mission Baptismal Register. *Journal of California and Great Basin Anthropology* 5(1&2):240–241.

Kari, James

1983 Kalifornsky, the Californian from Cook Inlet. *Alaska in Perspective* 5(1):1–10.

Kennedy, Mary Jean

1955 *Culture Contact and Acculturation of the Southwestern Pomo*. Unpublished Ph.D. dissertation, University of California, Berkeley.

Khlebnikov, Kyrill

1976 *Colonial Russian America: Kyrill T. Khlebnikov's Reports, 1817–1832*. Translated with introduction and notes by Basil Dmytryshyn and E. A. P. Crownhart-Vaughan. Oregon Historical Society, Portland, Oreg.

Kostromitinov, Peter

1839 Bemerkungen über die Indianer in Ober-Kalifornien. In *Beitrage zur Kenntniss des Russischen Reiches und der Angranzenden Lander Asiens*, edited by K. E. v. Baer and Gr. v. Helmersen, pp. 80–96. St. Petersburg, Russia.

LaPlace, Cyrille

1854 *Campagne de Circumnavigation de la Frégate l'Artémise pendant les années 1837, 1838, 1839, et 1840 sous le commandement de M. LaPlace, capitaine de vaisseau*, vol. 6. Firmin Didot Frères, Paris.

Maloney, Alice B.

1944 Fur Brigade to the Bonaventura (Part 3). *California Historical Quarterly* 23(2):19–40.

Mathes, W. Michael

1968 *Vizcaino and the Spanish Expansion in the Pacific Ocean, 1580–1630*. California Historical Society, San Francisco.

National Archives

n.d. Report of Governor Wrangell to Head Office, No. 197, dated April 28/May 9, 1834. Records of the Russian-American Company, microfilm roll 36. Washington, D.C.

O'Connor, Denise Maureen

1984 *Trade and Tableware: A Historical and Distributional Analysis of the Ceramics from Fort Ross, California*. Unpublished Master's thesis, Department of Anthropology, California State University, Sacramento.

Okladnikova, E. A.
   1983 The California Collection of I. G. Voznesensky and the Problems of Ancient Cultural Connections between Asia and America. *Journal of California and Great Basin Anthropology* 5(1&2):224–239.
Oswalt, Robert L.
   1958 Russian Loanwords in Southwestern Pomo. *International Journal of American Linguistics* 24(3):245–247.
   1964 Kashaya Texts. *University of California Publications in Linguistics*, vol. 36. Berkeley.
   1971 The Case of the Broken Bottle. *International Journal of American Linguistics* 37(1):48–49.
Owens, Kenneth N., and Alton S. Donnelly
   1985 *The Wreck of the Sv. Nikolai: Two Narratives of the First Russian Expedition to the Oregon Country, 1808–1810.* Western Imprints, Portland, Oreg.
Payeras, Mariano
   1822 Diario de su caminata con el Comisario del Imperio, Noticias sobre Ross. 1822. Ms. copy on file, Bancroft Library, Berkeley.
Phelps, William Dane
   1983 *Alta California 1840–1842: The Journal and Observations of William Dane Phelps, Master of the Ship Alert.* Arthur H. Clark Company, Glendale, Calif.
Pilling, Arnold R.
   n.d. Glazed Ceramic Relationships in California. Ms. 213 on file, University of California Archaeological Survey. (Currently, University of California Archaeological Research Center.)
Popov, O. S.
   1957 *Rysskaya Narodnaya Keramika.* Moscow.
Riddell, Francis A.
   1955 *Archaeological Excavations on the Farallon Islands, California.* Papers on California Archaeology, No. 34. Archaeological Survey Report No. 32. University of California, Berkeley.
Slacum, William A.
   1912 Document, Slacum's Report on Oregon, 1836–1837. *Oregon Historical Society Quarterly* 13(2):175–224.
Smith, Janice Christina
   1974 Pomo and *Promyshlenniki:* Time and Trade Goods at Fort Ross. Unpublished Master's thesis, University of California, Los Angeles.
Spencer-Hancock, Diane, and William E. Pritchard
   1981 Notes on the 1817 Treaty between the Russian American Company and the Kashaya Pomo Indians. *California History* 59(4):306–313.
   1982 The Chapel at Fort Ross, Its History and Reconstruction. *California History* 61(1):2–17.
Sutter Papers
   1841 Inventaire des Biens meubles et immeubles qui se trouvent au port de Bodego [sic], à l'établissement de Ross et aux Ranchos de la Compagnie Russe-Américaine. Ms. at Bancroft Library, Berkeley.
Thomas, Bryn
   1976 Historic Sites Researches at Fort Ross, California: A Presentation of Data Derived from Historical and Archeological Methods Applied to the Site with Emphasis on the Officials' Quarters. Ms. on file, California Department of Parks and Recreation, Resource Protection Division, Sacramento.
Tikhmenev, P.A.
   1978 *A History of the Russian-American Company.* Translated and edited by Richard A. Pierce and Alton S. Donnelly. University of Washington Press, Seattle.
Treganza, Adan E.
   1954 *Fort Ross: A Study in Historical Archaeology.* Archaeological Survey Report No. 23. University of California, Berkeley.

Vallejo, Mariano G.

 1833 Informe Reservado sobre Ross. Archives of California, Department of State Papers, vol. ii: 68ff. Bancroft Library, Berkeley.

 n.d. Historia de California, vol. 3, pp. 299ff. Ms. on file at the Bancroft Library, Berkeley.

Van Sicklen, Helen Putnam

 1945 *A Sojourn in California by the King's Orphan. The Travels and Sketches of G. M. Waseurtz af Sandels, a Swedish Gentleman Who Visited California in 1842–43.* Grabhorn Press, San Francisco.

Von Wrangell, Ferdinand

 1839 Statische und etnographische Nachrichten über die Russischen Besitzungen an der Nordwestkuste von Amerika. In *Beitrage zur Kenntniss des Russischen Reiches und der angranzenden Lander Asiens,* edited by K. E. Baer and Gr. v. Helmersen, pp. 66–79. St. Petersburg, Russia.

Watson, Douglas S., and Thomas Workman Temple, II

 1934 *The Spanish Occupation of California: Plan for the Establishment of a Government. Junta or Council Held at San Blas, May 16, 1768. Diario of the Expeditions Made to California.* Grabhorn Press, San Francisco.

Wilbur, Marguerite E.

 1937 *Duflot de Mofras' Travels on the Pacific Coast,* vol. 2. Translated and annotated by Marguerite Eyer Wilbur. Fine Arts Press, Santa Ana, Calif.

Contributors

E. Charles Adams is associate curator of archaeology at the Arizona State Museum (University of Arizona) and director of the Homolovi Research Program. Specializing in late prehistoric, protohistoric, and historic Pueblo culture in the U.S. Southwest, he has conducted excavations at the historic Hopi village of Walpi and is at present involved in the development of a state park focusing on several fourteenth-century ancestral Hopi pueblos. A long-standing research interest has been the origin and development of the Pueblo katsina cult and its relation to aggregation during the late prehistoric period in the Pueblo Southwest.

Ed D. Castillo is an independent scholar and a Southern California Indian of the Cahuilla tribe. He has studied U.S. frontier history and American social and cultural anthropology, specializing in California Indian history. His research has been supported by the National Endowment for the Humanities, the Ford Foundation, and the California State Office of Planning and Research. He is currently a curriculum specialist at the Mendocino County Office of Planning and Research.

James E. Corbin is associate professor of anthropology in the Department of Sociology at Stephen F. Austin State University (Nacogdoches, Texas), with research interests in Caddoan and Spanish Colonial ethnohistory and archaeology. He has conducted archaeological research in various areas of Texas and on the North Slope of Alaska. He served two terms as editor of the *Bulletin of the Texas Archeological Society* and is currently editor of *La Tinaja*, a newsletter for the study of archaeological ceramics.

Linda S. Cordell, formerly professor of anthropology at the University of New Mexico, is at present Irvine Curator and Chairperson of the Anthropology Department at the California Academy of Sciences (San Francisco). She specializes in prehistoric Pueblo Indian archaeology and has conducted excavations and surveys at sites in the Rio Grande and Upper Pecos valleys of New Mexico. She is author of the book, *Prehistory of the Southwest*, and is coeditor and contributor to the Smithsonian Press volume *Dynamics of Southwest Prehistory*, in addition to numerous articles in scholarly journals.

Julia G. Costello lives in the Sierra Nevada foothills of California where she teaches at Columbia and San Joaquin Delta Colleges and has a consulting firm. She has conducted research at Missions La Purísima Vieja, San Antonio de Padua, Santa Iñes, and at the Santa Bárbara Presidio. In addition to her work on California Spanish colonial sites, she has published on Gold Rush history and archaeology, Asian ceramics, and the evolution of gold mining communities.

Michael J. DeNiro is a professor of geology at the University of California, Santa Barbara. He is a specialist in the reconstruction of prehistoric diet and environmental conditions through the analysis of stable isotope ratios in plant and animal remains.

David E. Doyel, former director of Museum and Archaeology Programs for the Navajo Tribe, is currently the director of Pueblo Grande Museum and archaeologist for the City of Phoenix (Arizona). He has conducted extensive archaeological research in the southwestern United States. His long-term research interests include the evolution of agricultural societies and exchange systems in aboriginal North America.

Jack D. Eaton is acting director of the Center for Archaeological Research, the University of Texas at San Antonio. His primary specialization is in Maya studies, and he has conducted extensive fieldwork in Yucatan, Belize, and Guatemala. He has also carried out excavations at Spanish Colonial mission sites on the borderlands in northern Coahuila and in Texas, and he is administrator and principal investigator for cultural resource management contracts dealing with prehistoric and historic site investigations in south Texas.

Glenn J. Farris is a State Parks archaeologist in California. Specializing in historic archaeology and ethnohistory in California, he has worked on numerous archaeological and archival projects, including the early nineteenth-century Russian settlement of Fort Ross on the Sonoma Coast, as well as Spanish and Mexican sites throughout the state. A particular interest is cultural interaction of Euro-American (Spanish, Russians, Anglos) and Native Americans. His earliest fieldwork was in Israel (Wailing Wall and the Dead Sea) and Norway (Tonsberg and Oslo), but since 1976 he has concentrated on California.

Anne A. Fox is the director of the Laboratory at the Center for Archaeological Research, University of Texas at San Antonio. She specializes in historical archaeology, with special emphasis on San Antonio and south Texas in the Spanish and Mexican periods. Her particular interests include early Texas architecture and eighteenth- and nineteenth-century ceramics.

Kathleen Gilmore is adjunct professor and research archaeologist at the Institute of Applied Sciences, University of North Texas at Denton. She has specialized in historical archaeology, with an emphasis on Spanish and French colonial settlements in and near the Spanish Borderlands. She has conducted collections research and excavations at sites in Texas, Louisiana, and North Carolina.

Roberta S. Greenwood is a research associate in archaeology at the Natural History Museum of Los Angeles, and president of the cultural resource management firm of Greenwood and Associates. She has directed archaeological excavation, documentary research, and collections analysis for many sites representing the mission, secular adobe, and rancho occupations of California. Her research and publications have received awards from the National Endowment for the Humanities, American Association for State and Local History, and the Annual Conference of California Historical Societies.

Thomas R. Hester is professor of anthropology and director, Texas Archeological Research Laboratory, at the University of Texas at Austin. A specialist in Texas archaeology, he has also done extensive research in the Maya area and in Mesoamerican lithic technology; other fieldwork has been carried out in California, Montana, Mexico, and Egypt. Research interests include various aspects of prehistoric technology, craft specialization, and processes of change in material culture.

David Hornbeck is professor of historical geography at California State University, Northridge. He is past president of the Western Social Science Association and the Borderlands Scholars. His research interests include the economic development of Spain's northern frontier during the eighteenth and nineteenth centuries.

Robert L. Hoover is professor of anthropology at California Polytechnic State University in San Luis Obispo, where he served as chairman for seven years. He is a member and former chair of the State Historical Resources Commission. His fieldwork has focused on the prehistoric Chumash and Salinan cultures and on the archaeology of Hispanic California. He has also published on the archaeology of Africa, Southeast Asia, and the Southwest. His long-term research interests include technology, ethnobotany, protohistoric acculturation, and the historic archaeology of Brazil.

John R. Johnson is curator of anthropology at the Santa Barbara Museum of Natural History (California). He has specialized in the archaeology and ethnohistory of the South Central California Region. He has recently completed his doctoral dissertation on Chumash social organization based on archival sources.

John L. Kessell is associate professor of history at the University of New Mexico. The author of several well-received books, he has focused his research and writing on the American Southwest in the Spanish colonial period. He is currently editor of *The Journals of don Diego de Vargas*, a multivolume, bilingual edition of the principal archives of New Mexico's late seventeenth-century governor and recolonizer.

Patricia Lambert is a graduate student in anthropology at the University of California, Santa Barbara. She is currently doing research on faunal collections and human skeletal remains from Southern California.

Georgia Lee is a research associate of the Institute of Archaeology, University of California (Los Angeles); the Santa Barbara Museum of Natural History; and the Instituto de Estudios, Universidad de Chile, Isla de Pascua. She specializes in the study of rock carvings and paintings and her long-term research interests include documentation of the rock art of Easter Island as well as intensive study of the art of Chumash Indians of California. She is editor and publisher of *Rapa Nui Journal*, a periodical that is concerned with the archaeology and anthropology of Easter Island.

Hartman H. Lomawaima is assistant to the director of the R. H. Lowie Museum of Anthropology, University of California at Berkeley. He is a *Honwungwa* (Bear Clan member) from the Hopi village of Sipaulovi on Second Mesa.

Mark Lycett is a doctoral student in anthropology at the University of New Mexico. He has extensive archaeological experience in the American Southwest, and has also excavated in India. His major research interest is studying the impact of European colonization on native land-use practices.

Randall H. McGuire is an assistant professor of anthropology at the State University of New York, Binghamton. A specialist in the archaeology of the southwestern United States and northwestern Mexico, he has conducted research in southern Arizona and northern Sonora. He has also done historical archaeology using nineteenth-century materials from Arizona and upstate New York. He and Elisa Villalpando are currently conducting archaeological research in the Altar Valley of Sonora.

W. Michael Mathes, professor emeritus of history at the University of San Francisco, is a member of the Academia Mexicana de la Historia and Orden Mexicana del Aguila Azteca. He is active in research and publication relative to Western Mexico and Baja California, and has published extensively in the field in the United States, Mexico, and Spain.

Charles F. Merbs is professor of anthropology at Arizona State University. A physical anthropologist with research interests in North and South America and northeast Africa, he specializes in the study of human osteology, disease ecology, and medical genetics.

Norman Neuerburg is professor emeritus of art history at California State University, Dominguez Hills. As a scholar in the field of the art and architecture of the California missions he not only works with original documents but carries out above-ground archaeology on mission buildings. He has uncovered notable remains of painted wall decorations of the Spanish and Mexican period at a number of the missions.

Charles W. Polzer, S.J. directs the Documentary Relations of the Southwest Project at the Arizona State Museum. As curator of ethnohistory at the museum, he specializes in contact period studies that rely heavily on Spanish Colonial archives. Since the early 1970s, he has pioneered innovative approaches to documentary finding aids and the application of electronic scanning for the optical-digital storage of document images. He has appointed and serves as a member of the Christopher Columbus Quincentenary Jubilee Commission.

Lori Stephens Reed is a graduate student in the Department of Sociology and Anthropology at New Mexico State University. Her research interests include northern Rio Grande ceramic production and exchange, and prehistoric Southwestern political organizations. She is the author of several scholarly papers on southwestern archaeology.

Katherine A. Spielmann is assistant professor in the Department of Anthropology at Arizona State University. Her long-term research interests include interdependence among nonstratified societies, prehistoric diet, and zooarchaeology. Specializing on relations between Southwestern and Plains populations, she has conducted excavations on the High Plains of Texas and at Gran Quivira Pueblo, New Mexico.

David Hurst Thomas is curator of anthropology at the American Museum of Natural History (New York). A specialist in North American prehistory, he has conducted extensive research in the Great Basin and the American Southeast, including the discovery and long-term excavation of sixteenth- and seventeenth-century *Mission Santa Catalina de Guale* (St. Catherines Islands, Georgia). He has published three archaeology textbooks, written several dozen monographs and scientific articles dealing with archaeological method and theory, and served as general editor for the 21-volume work *The North American Indian*.

Solveig A. Turpin is currently associate director of the Texas Archeological Research Laboratory at the University of Texas at Austin. Her major research interests are hunter-forager adaptations to arid lands with an emphasis on the rock art of the Lower Pecos River region. Recent publications address mortuary practices, settlement patterns, rock art, and material culture of southwest Texas and northern Mexico.

Steadman Upham is associate dean of the Graduate School at New Mexico State University, where he also serves as associate professor in the Department of Sociology and Anthropology. He has conducted fieldwork throughout the American Southwest and is a specialist in the archaeology of the late prehistoric and protohistoric periods. His long-term research interests include the evolution of political and economic systems, and his work has been published in a variety of books, monographs, and scholarly journals.

María Elisa Villalpando is an archaeologist with the Centro Regional del Noroeste de INAH in Hermosillo, Sonora. Her research has focused primarily on aboriginal cultures of the Sonoran coast. She has undertaken archaeological field research on the island of San Esteban, in the Altar Valley, and at other locations in Sonora. At present she is completing her Ph.D. in Mexican history at the Colegio de México.

Phillip L. Walker is a professor of anthropology at the University of California, Santa Barbara. His research interests include osteology, faunal analysis, and paleoanthropology. He is currently doing research on prehistoric human biological and cultural adaptation to the Santa Barbara Channel Island environment.

G. James West is regional archaeologist for the Bureau of Reclamation, Sacramento, and a research associate at the Department of Anthropology, University of California, Davis. His specialization is Quaternary palynology, and research interests include the study of human interaction with the environment and the reconstruction of past vegetation and climate. Current research is directed toward the late Pleistocene and Holocene vegetation and climate history of northwestern California.